Safe FIREFIGHTING
Levels I & II

D1736446

Steve Kidd

John Czajkowski

Garry Briese

 **McGraw-Hill**
Higher Education

Boston   Burr Ridge, IL   Dubuque, IA   New York   San Francisco   St. Louis
Bangkok   Bogotá   Caracas   Kuala Lumpur   Lisbon   London   Madrid   Mexico City
Milan   Montreal   New Delhi   Santiago   Seoul   Singapore   Sydney   Taipei   Toronto

The McGraw-Hill Companies

McGraw-Hill
Higher Education

SAFE FIREFIGHTING: LEVELS I AND II

Some ancillaries, including electronic and print components, may not be available to customers outside the United States.

The Fire Service is constantly evolving, with firefighting techniques changing almost daily. Firefighters must face the challenge of this ever-changing, dynamic work environment throughout their careers. The authors and the publisher of this work have checked with sources believed to be reliable in their efforts to provide information that is complete and generally in accord with the standards accepted at the time of publication. However, in view of the possibility of human error or changes in firefighting technology and practices, neither the authors nor the publisher nor any other party who has been involved in the preparation or publication of this work warrants that the information contained herein is in every respect accurate or complete, and they are not responsible for any errors or omissions or for the results obtained from use of such information. Readers are encouraged to confirm the information contained herein with other resources.

✹ This book is printed on recycled, acid-free paper containing 10% postconsumer waste.

1 2 3 4 5 6 7 8 9 0 QPV/QPV 0 9 8 7

ISBN 978–0–07–338284–5
MHID 0–07–338284–1

Publisher: *David T. Culverwell*
Senior Sponsoring Editor: *Claire Merrick*
Outside Developmental Services: *Julie Scardiglia*
Editorial Coordinator: *Michelle L. Zeal*
Marketing Manager: *Kelly Curran*
Senior Project Manager: *Kay J. Brimeyer*
Senior Production Supervisor: *Laura Fuller*
Cover/Interior Designer: *Laurie B. Janssen*
(USE) Cover Image: *Steve Kidd, Delve Productions Inc.*
Senior Photo Research Coordinator: *John C. Leland*
Compositor: *Carlisle Publishing Services*
Typeface: *10/12 Melior*
Printer: *Quebecor World Versailles, KY*

All photos are © McGraw-Hill Higher Education, Inc./Photography by Delve Productions.

We dedicate every word in this book to your safety.

We hope you do the same.

Steve Kidd
John Czajkowski
Garry Briese

About the Authors

Steve Kidd worked for 28 years with Orange County Fire Rescue Division, Florida, where he retired as a Company Officer. Along with John Czajkowski, he coauthored a 25-part Fire Service video training series and drill guide as well as the popular vehicle rescue video training series, *Carbusters!* Steve is a Technical Editor for *FireRescue Magazine* and has written numerous articles and a regular monthly column on fire and rescue-related topics over the past 20 years.

John Czajkowski worked for 31 years with Orange County Fire Rescue Division, Florida, where he retired as a Company Officer. He was a Charter Member of the Transportation Emergency Rescue Committee of the IAFC (International Association of Fire Chiefs) and lectured on vehicle rescue at many events, both in the United States and abroad. With Steve Kidd, he coauthored a 25-part Fire Service video training series as well as the popular vehicle rescue video training series, *Carbusters!* He has written many articles on Fire Service and rescue topics for several national fire publications.

Garry Briese is the Executive Director of the International Association of Fire Chiefs, having come to that position after serving in a similar post with the Florida College of Emergency Physicians. He has served with volunteer, combination, and career fire departments, is an original member of the *Carbusters!* extrication team, and has coauthored two textbooks for First Responders. He is a well-known speaker and instructor and is considered to be one of the thought leaders for today's fire and emergency services.

Brief Contents—*Safe Firefighting: Levels I and II*

Contents

CHAPTER 4

Preconnected Attack Lines   79

CHAPTER 5

Response Safety and Vehicle Crashes   107

CHAPTER 6

Extinguishing Small Fires   131

CHAPTER 7

Ground Cover Fires   149

CHAPTER 8

Passenger Vehicle Fires   165

CHAPTER 9

Supply Hose Lines 185

CHAPTER 10

Large Attack Lines 217

CHAPTER 11

Single-Family-Dwelling Fires 241

CHAPTER 17

Building Construction 393

CHAPTER 18

Ventilation and Fire Behavior 415

CHAPTER 19

Safety and Survival for Interior Firefighters 445

CHAPTER 20

Residential Structure Fires 489

CHAPTER 26

Flammable Gas Firefighting   621

CHAPTER 27

Rescue Awareness   641

CHAPTER 28

Post-Fire Activities   673

Foreword

A book about *safe* firefighting . . . wow. I thought to myself, they'll bombard the bookstores when that one comes out . . . *not.* But then I realized that we are deep within some major changes in the Fire Service.

We are in the middle of some very positive changes in our business. And the primary change or renaissance we are experiencing is the fact that "we" are actually looking at—and taking action on—injury and death on the job. The Fire Service suffers almost one hundred and a dozen dead firefighters annually: about half from medical causes and the other half from driving too fast, not using seat belts, blowing stop signs and red lights, falling out (or off) of the apparatus, and experiencing building collapses, flashovers, burns, trauma, and other tragic events. We also suffer up to 100,000 serious injuries each year. *We have a problem. But who is really impacted by this "problem"?*

So often we accept out deaths as part of the job. Sometimes they are, but that is rare. You know and I know that it is a *rare* event when we are attempting to save a life and one or more of us die. Much more often than not, we die when we drive dumb, when we don't belt up, when we don't think about risk/benefit when going in, and when we are unhealthy. Heroes? Yes. All firefighters are heroes due to the very nature of the job. But heroic deaths? They are few and far between. We just don't talk about that, and as honorable a profession—career or volunteer—as this is, we do honor *all* firefighters who go before us, as we should. But we all know the real facts. And finally, we are starting to deal with it.

So what is the answer? *Training.* That's the *answer* and it is just that simple. And that is the *challenge*—not so simple.

There is a clear line between stupidity and bravery. There are many firefighters who have gone before us who have died horribly tragic but heroic deaths while attempting to save a life. Sometimes that is what must happen. But it is rare—*very rare.* The great majority of American firefighter line-of-duty deaths are clearly avoidable and can be avoided without any negative impact on the services you, as a firefighter, Officer, or Chief, provide. *Safe Firefighting: First Things First* will not negatively impact your love for

the job, your ability to provide service, or your "feeling" like a firefighter. What it will do is allow you to continue to *enjoy* being a *live* firefighter instead of having your spouse, kids, parents, and whoever else loves you watch you get fed through an IV for the rest of your life—or visit your grave. After all, once we are dead, we are dead. It's our family members—with a hard focus on our children, spouse, parents, and siblings—who suffer long after we are buried. And they spend the rest of their lives wondering if "that" death was "worth it" or not . . . and so often they know the truth as we know it.

Firefighter training. That's the answer and one of the most exciting tools we now have. A critical part of that solution is this book, *Safe Firefighting.* It's the "non-sexy" name of this series *and* it is the culture we are starting to become—slowly. But we are getting there.

Why this book? Because this book *is* different. It helps us focus on what really matters—and what is just not *that* important. Make no mistake about it—this book was written 100% outside the box.

This is what matters: Identifying the fire "problem" on the scene, getting water on the fire, venting, staffing, protecting ourselves first, arriving in one piece, having applicable building construction info, understanding and applying "go in/don't go in," and having competent command officers. What doesn't matter: How a smoke detector works and what the inside of a hydrant looks like. This can be important info and may be worthwhile to know, but this info won't save your life as a firefighter. *Identifying the fire problem on the scene, getting water on a fire, knowing when to and when not to go in, and properly venting a structure <u>will</u>.*

There are heroes in our business. Some are recognized for risks that mattered and some are the ones who do work behind the scenes so that we can all come home safely. The writers of *Safe Firefighting*—Steve Kidd, John Czajkowski, and Garry Briese—fall into the second category. Steve, John, and Garry have decades of dirty, hands-on fire and rescue experience. And they have already impacted our business. But they decided to do more. They understood the need for a "new approach" in training firefighters—one way off the "traditional" scale—and they did something about it.

Safe Firefighting is not for all firefighters. Some will kick, scream, and whine about this approach and will refuse to consider changing. That's good. It will help the rest of us identify who gets it—and who doesn't.

Does this book suggest you can't go inside anymore? Not at all. Does it imply you will no longer be able to save life and property? Of course not. Does it stop us from performing as an effective and aggressive department or company? Absolutely not. This book takes all that and puts it in perspective to ensure that the right components exist so that we can do the job, based upon our ability to survive more often—much more often than we have in our past.

Billy Goldfetter
Deputy Fire Chief
Loveland-Symmes Fire Department
City of Loveland and Symmes Township, Ohio

Preface

Welcome to the Fire Service! This training program has been developed to help your instructors train you to be a competent, safe firefighter.

Firefighting is rewarding work and will give you great satisfaction in helping your community in times of emergency. Your community relies on and, indeed, expects the best possible work from you in any emergency. They really have no one else to turn to. When a fire or rescue emergency occurs, the Fire Service must answer the call, with the goal being that all of our members survive without injury or death and all of the victims are given the best possible chance for survival.

Firefighting is dangerous work and it is probably more dangerous than it has to be. There is a long tradition of regarding firefighters as heroes. There are instances in which firefighters are heroes, and we will not diminish those who have made sacrifices for their community. However, we must train and work so that any firefighter death or injury is one too many. We can never accept that it just happens or that firefighters sometimes die because they are heroes doing heroic things. Remember, you have a family that depends upon you and needs you just as much as your community does.

Firefighting is important work. It requires training and preparation. Experienced firefighters are hard to replace. You are needed alive, healthy, and working. Death and injuries to firefighters have devastating effects on both the community and the Fire Department. Your goal should be to do the very best job at all times. Returning alive and well and ready to answer the next call is important to us all.

At the end of the day, we want a thinking firefighter—one who is ready to adapt to changes, and willing to use new and safer techniques. Just as important, we want a firefighter who will also carry on a tradition of quality and dedication that will make his or her community and, indeed, our nation, a much safer place to live and work.

Program Description

Our curriculum is divided into three main levels of training, each progressively building upon the previous one as you proceed. The outcome we all want is

a competent firefighter—a firefighter who will safely and efficiently perform the best possible job.

This program contains the most up-to-date and innovative information available today and is a unique learning system that provides skills training and review through the DVD that accompanies each part.

Safe Firefighting, Part 1: First Things First

The first part of this training material covers Exterior Operations level firefighting and is provided in a separate manual and DVD; it is also included as the first part of this book. It is the initial orientation and training for firefighters who will not be going inside to fight a structural fire. It empowers the new firefighter to assist with most exterior firefighting and emergency rescue operations. At this level, firefighters need close supervision and have only the capabilities to assist the next two levels of firefighters trained in this program. By providing condensed training to the newest firefighter, the fire department can get personnel safely involved in some Fire Department emergency operations sooner, while the firefighter completes more advanced training. This approach is a great help for fire departments that are in dire need of personnel, particularly volunteer departments.

Throughout the entire three-part volume, you will be taught what you need to know in context. You will quickly find out that we are basing our information on scenarios, which will allow us to branch off to specific skills that will also be needed on other fire emergencies. By doing this, we hope to make the training interesting and pertinent to the job.

Your department may have more requirements after you start working with them. In fact, they probably will have more training for you, including learning how to do things "their way." Our goal is to get the most effective and important training to the firefighter at each level of training with the unnecessary "fluff" removed.

Safe Firefighting, Part 2: Inside Operations

Inside Operations is the second part of this series and is provided in this book and DVD. This intermediate level of training prepares you to be qualified to fight an interior structural fire as part of a team. You will still be expected to be under direct supervision during firefighting operations.

With the information provided at this level, you will also get in-depth training in responding to and handling more types of fire and vehicle crash emergencies. At the end of *Safe Firefighting, Part 2,* our goal is to have a firefighter who works well with the firefighting crew, uses safe and effective techniques, is able to recognize dangerous situations, and responds in a manner that is safe for him- or herself and the public.

Safe Firefighting, Part 3: Leading the Team

With the information provided at this level, firefighters will become capable of leading a firefighting crew during a fire scene operation. They will be able to identify the type of emergency at hand, select the best method to deal with the fire, and supervise a firefighting crew.

Firefighters at this level of training will be indirectly supervised by the Incident Commander, but, by and large, will be able to make their own decisions for handling their part of the emergency. These personnel will also learn how to handle more types of fire and emergency situations through added scenario-based training.

By learning from the printed matter, DVD, and CD, as well as through a lot of skills practice with your instructors, we want to give you the best and most interesting training possible today. Our goal is that our program will get the firefighter through each level quickly and effectively with the desired result. Safety will never be compromised and will always be stressed in all training and demonstrations.

Steve Kidd
John Czajkowski
Garry Briese

Guided Tour

Features to Help You Study and Learn

What You Will Learn in This Chapter Each chapter opens with an overview of the topics covered in the chapter.

What You Will Be Able to Do This chapter-opening feature lists the skills the reader will have after reading the chapter and practicing the skills.

Reality! These brief readings present a combination of real-life situations and motivational introductions by the authors that set the stage for the training in the chapter, stressing the reasons firefighters need to learn the materials.

Passenger Vehicle Fires

What You Will Learn in This Chapter

In this chapter we will introduce you to vehicle fire operations, starting with personal protective equipment (PPE) and proper safety zones at vehicle fires. Then we will discuss vehicle design and burn characteristics. We will conclude the chapter with extinguishment techniques for vehicle fires.

We should also mention what you will *not* learn in this chapter. Fighting fires that involve a single automobile or light truck is much different from fighting fires in cargo-type vehicles or large, over-the-road equipment. Large vehicles often carry dangerous cargo and, at the very least, large amounts of flam-

What You Will Be Able to Do

After reading this chapter and participating in the practical skills sessions, you will be able to

1. Participate as a team member in setting up a typical safety zone and the traffic control needed at the scene of a vehicle fire.
2. Demonstrate how to check the wheels and remove the keys of a vehicle involved in a fire.
3. Explain the safety risks of a vehicle fire and the importance of wearing full PPE and SCBA at a vehicle fire.
4. Describe the burn characteristics of the passenger vehicle fire

165

Reality!

Safety Lesson: A NIOSH Report

Wear Your Gear, Even on Small Fires!

On August 1, 2002, a firefighter in South Dakota was severely burned while fighting a fire that was consuming a wheat field. He had responded directly to the fire in his personal vehicle (POV) where he met up with another firefighter whose POV, a pickup truck, was equipped with a 75-gallon water tank and a gasoline-driven pump. According to the NIOSH report, although numerous firefighters responded to the scene, there was no Incident Command System established. The firefighters on the scene dispersed on their own as they arrived on the scene. The victim and the firefighter with the pickup truck talked on the scene and agreed that the victim would spray water from the bed of the truck while the other firefighter drove.

The two firefighters proceeded through a gate and into the field near the encroaching head of the fire. While fighting the fire, the victim was wearing tennis shoes, denim jeans, a T-shirt, and a baseball cap. A sudden gust of wind blew fire and smoke over the truck. The driver immediately pulled the truck forward and to the right. It is unknown if the victim fell from the truck as a result of being overcome by the fire and smoke or from the sudden forward movement of the truck. He ran about 200 yards, where he encountered a barbed wire fence and became entangled in the barbed wire. Other firefighters rushed to his aid, and the victim was evacuated by a medical helicopter to the burn center, where he died 5 days later from his injuries.

Follow-Up

NIOSH Report #F2002-37

After this incident was reviewed and evaluated, the NIOSH investigative report recommended that the following practices be implemented:

- Ensure that firefighters follow established procedures for combating ground cover fires.
- Develop and implement an Incident Command System.
- Provide firefighters with personal protective equipment (PPE) that is appropriate for wildland fires and is also NFPA 1977 compliant.
- Provide firefighters with appropriate wildland firefighter training.

Small Ground Cover Fires

Firefighters are called upon to perform many different jobs, including extinguishing **ground cover fires**. Ground cover fires occur in grassy vacant lots, rural wooded areas, parks, and even in the median areas on roadways (Figure 7-1). These fires are quite different from building fires. Ground cover fires are more like large Class A trash fires in that the fuel is spread out over a wider area. The tactics that firefighters use to extinguish these fires must take into consideration such elements as weather conditions, the humidity level, the type and arrangement of foliage, natural and manmade **firebreaks**, and the direction the fire travels as it burns.

In the United States, urban and suburban areas have been encroaching more and more on the wildland areas surrounding them. This spread is referred to as the **wildland/urban interface**. In this interface there is little or no separation between homes and even commercial buildings and the heavily wooded areas they are near. Property loss can result when large wildfires occur and outstrip local firefighting capabilities.

At this point in your training, we are going to limit our discussion to small ground cover fires. Even though we see and hear about the massive fires that occur in vast wildland areas, most ground cover fires are less

FIGURE 7-1 Ground cover fires are very common, even in urban areas. Most are small enough to be extinguished with a small hose line.

150   Chapter 7   Ground Cover Fires

Safety Lesson: A NIOSH Report   Provided as appropriate to the text chapters, this feature details true, documented events reported to NIOSH about injuries and fatalities to firefighters on the job. This feature also includes recommendations to prevent similar tragic events.

View It!   This icon indicates the chapter skills presented on the DVD located in the back of the book.

Practice It!   This feature provides step-by-step instructions and photographs that detail many of the day-to-day individual skills firefighters will use.

Evolution   Here the reader will find step-by-step instructions and photographs that detail an essential firefighting process. The steps and photos work together to depict an evolution of tasks.

---

is similar to a task you may be doing on the emergency scene, you will probably need to take similar safety preparations before doing the task. For example, if you wear eye protection when using a saw on the emergency scene, you should do the same while using a saw in the fire station.

Use safe practices when handling tools and equipment. If you are not sure how to safely use a tool, don't use it. Ask for help and let someone show you the safe way to operate it. Consult user manuals and be sure to read, understand, and follow all safety precautions.

If routine station maintenance duties require you to work above the floor level—for example, from a ladder—then you should have someone with you as a safety person and you should use the proper equipment for the job (Figure 1-20). Most ladders carried on a fire truck are designed to be used on soft ground—not on slick hard floors—so don't go for the easy-to-grab ladder on the truck instead of taking the

NIOSH Reports

The National Institute for Occupational Safety and Health (NIOSH) conducts a program that is designed to determine the factors that cause or contribute to firefighter deaths and serious injuries suffered in the line of duty. This organization's intent is to help researchers and safety specialists develop strategies for preventing similar future incidents. Throughout this book, you will find examples of the lessons learned from some of these reports. It is our hope that you will take the time to read each lesson seriously, with the understanding that one or more firefighters have died in the reported incidents. We hope that you will learn something that can prevent you from suffering a similar fate. You can access the NIOSH reports on the Internet at http://www.cdc.gov/niosh/firehome.html or call 1-800-36NIOSH.

View It!

Go to the DVD, navigate to Chapter 3, and select *SCBA: Donning the Facemask.*

Practice It!

Donning the Facemask

Donning the facemask is the final step you take before you begin breathing from the system. Use the following steps when donning a facemask:

1. It makes no difference whether you don the mask by placing your chin in first and dragging the straps over your head or whether you use the ball-cap method (Figure 3-38). In the ball-cap method, you hold the straps on the back of your head and drag the mask down over your face (Figure 3-39). The main thing to remember is to have nothing between the rubberized face piece and your skin. The straps should be adjusted so that the mask fits snugly against your face. You should cover all remaining exposed skin once the mask is in place.

FIGURE 3-38

FIGURE 3-39

2. Start with your protecti... around your neck and y... Center the harness on ... any hair that may be be... mask. Starting with the ... them two at a time unti... (Figure 3-40).

3. Check the seal by cove... mask and inhaling gent... should not feel any leak... your face (Figure 3-41).

Evolution 11-1

Maneuvering a Small Attack Line During an Exterior Attack

This drill has been developed to practice the skills necessary to establish a water supply and to apply water from the exterior to a simulated single-family-dwelling fire, using a small attack line. The firefighters will be working either to establish the water supply or to deploy, set up, and apply a fire stream to the simulated building fire (Figure 11-61). The drill should be repeated, switching firefighter positions so that each person can practice the training drill in both positions.

Training Area: Open area; level ground free of trip hazards

Equipment: Equipped pumper

Training burn building or other acquired building

Sustained water supply source, or static or water main system with hydrant

PPE: Full protective clothing and scba, on and ready for use

1. A fully equipped pumper with a crew consisting of a driver, a Company Officer, and two firefighters is positioned away from the water supply and simulated dwelling fire. All individuals are appropriately protected in PPE with their seatbelts on and ready to respond. A signal is given and the pumper responds to the simulated fire.

2. The pumper positions at the water supply source. A firefighter dismounts safely and removes any equipment necessary to establish a connection to the water supply, including supply hose lines. The firefighter signals for the pumper to proceed with a layout of supply hose while approaching and positioning at the simulated fire.

3. When the pumper positions at the fire, the second firefighter safely dismounts and receives orders from the Company Officer to deploy a small attack line and prepare to flow water onto the building from a safe area.

4. After establishing a connection to the water source, the first firefighter walks next to the supply hose line, straightening it out as he or she approaches the fire scene. This firefighter then arrives at the fire scene, locates the Company Officer, and receives orders to assist the second firefighter on the small attack line.

5. While the two firefighters are flowing water from the small attack line, they are directed to reposition it several times. They will also be directed to change the flow pattern of the stream.

FIGURE 11-61 Using a small attack line, firefighters will establish a water supply or apply water to a simulated building fire from the outside.

6. When the drill has been completed, the crew will properly relieve pressure, disconnect, drain, and reload all the supply and attack hose. They should trade positions and repeat the drill.

View It!

Go to the DVD, navigate to Chapter 11, and select *Exterior Attack, Large Attack Line.*

Safety Tips!   This feature provides information firefighters should use to keep themselves safe while performing their varied duties.

Tips!   Here the reader will find information to perform his or her duties more effectively.

Boxed Information   These boxes feature additional, specialized information for firefighters.

Key Words   Key words are bolded in the text and also appear with their definitions in boxes following their first mention so that readers can learn the terminology specific to firefighting. These terms, along with their definitions, are also provided alphabetically in the glossary at the back of the book.

Safety Tips!

Observe the following safety rules when responding to emergencies:

- Never disconnect your seatbelt while the vehicle is in motion, even to put on additional gear such as air packs.
- Never stand while riding on a fire apparatus. If you arrive too late to sit in an approved seat, then dismount and get on the next apparatus ready to respond.
- Wear hearing protection or communication devices while responding (Figure 5-22).
- Responding to an emergency is not a time for any "horseplay." Not behaving professionally will cause undue distraction for the Company Officer and the driver.
- Never dismount the apparatus without checking with your Company Officer.
- When dismounting from the apparatus, always check in all directions. Look for traffic and obstructions or hazards on the ground below (Figure 5-23). Carefully step off the apparatus, using the handholds provided to

FIGURE 5-23   Always look in all directions before dismounting from the apparatus. Look for traffic and obstructions or hazards on the ground below. Carefully step off the apparatus, using the handholds provided.

Tip!

Some departments have found it helpful to place a heavy tarp on the ground to help protect the bottom of the portable tank from sharp objects. This added layer of protection is a good idea if there is any reason to expect that damage can occur.

Portable Fire Pumps

Portable pumps are carried on some fire apparatus and deployed at the water source. They come in two basic styles: land-based and floating. These pumps are usually used to refill tenders or to supply a fire apparatus at a fire scene. If the portable pump is land-based, then a drafting operation is set up using hard suction hose to draw water from a static source into the portable pump. A supply line is then hooked into the portable pump. If the portable pump is a floating type, then it floats on the surface of the water source and supplies water through a supply line to where it is needed.

Portable pumps do not provide a great deal of water but are adequate for filling booster tanks and attacking small fires. The main difference between a land-based portable pump and a float pump is that the float pump has no hard suction hose attached. It simply draws the water from beneath it as it floats on the surface.

than an acre in size and are controlled by a small crew of firefighters. These smaller fires occur everywhere—in big cities and in small, rural communities.

KEY WORDS

Firebreak   An area, either manmade or natural, that provides no fuel for a spreading ground cover fire. Firebreaks are used to halt the spread of and assist in controlling ground cover fires.

Ground cover fire   A category of brush fire that is smaller than a wildfire—usually less than an acre in size and handled by one firefighting crew. The majority of brush fires in the United States fit this description.

Wildland/urban interface   The situation in which urban and suburban growth has intruded into open wildland areas, increasing the exposure of wildfires to homes and businesses in the area.

Wildfires

Firefighters who work routinely on **wildfires** in wildland areas receive additional training specific to these very different and much larger fire incidents. The operations for wildfires involve an extensive Incident Management System (IMS) and different firefighting apparatus, such as air **tankers** and fire-line tractors. These fires are major events and require some prequalification training in order to understand their scope and to understand and participate in tactical operations (Figure 7-2). This special training can result in certification and becoming a "red-card" status **wildland firefighter**. Though structural firefighters like you will respond to and assist in these events, you will be assigned duties within your scope of training and your capabilities, as established by your agency.

FIGURE 7-2   Large brush fires require extensive training and are coordinated through a very formal Incident Management System

KEY WORDS

Tanker   An airplane equipped to deliver large amounts of water or other extinguishing agents to a ground cover fire via an air drop.

Wildfire   A large ground cover fire that involves many acres of open wildland.

Wildland firefighter   A firefighter trained for fighting fires in open wildland areas.

Fire Movement and Behavior

Ground cover fires involve natural plant growth fuels burning in an open area. These fuels can be grass, brush, and even trees, as well as combinations of these items. These fires are usually handled by one or two firefighting crews.

Depending on wind direction, the topography of the landscape, and the dryness and arrangement of the ground cover growth involved, the fire tends to spread outward. As it burns, it moves in the direction of the wind. In hilly or mountainous areas, the fire tends to burn up a slope toward the unburned area until it is affected by winds at the top of the hill or mountain (Figure 7-3).

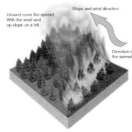
FIGURE 7-3   Fire tends to move downwind and uphill. A fire burning up the side of a hill will move until it is affected by winds at the top of the hill.

Wildfires   151

Do It! This feature summarizes the key information covered in the chapter, focusing on what the firefighter recruit should do after reading the chapter.

Prove It This assessment section includes knowledge and skills assessments.

Knowledge Assessment This documentation tear-out sheet is a multiple-choice quiz the firefighter recruit can take and submit to his or her Instructor or Company Officer. Each quiz allows the reader to ensure that he or she has mastered the information before moving on to the next chapter.

Skills Assessment This documentation tear-out sheet allows the firefighter recruit to demonstrate to his or her Instructor or Company Officer the skills acquired after reading the text and practicing the skills.

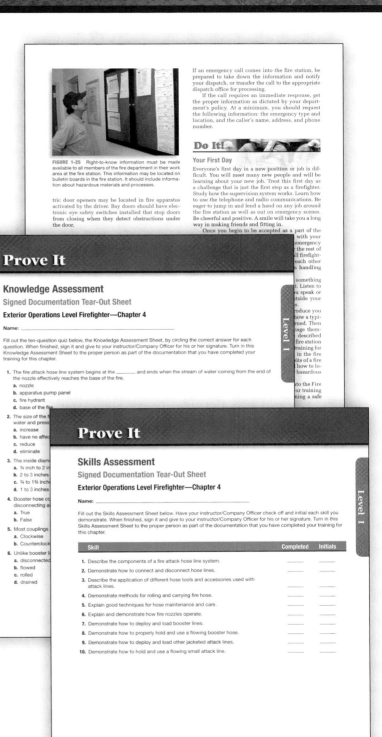

FIGURE 1-25 Right-to-know information must be made available to all members of the fire department in their work area at the fire station. This information may be located on bulletin boards in the fire station. It should include information about hazardous materials and processes.

tric door openers may be located in fire apparatus activated by the driver. Bay doors should have electronic eye safety switches installed that stop doors from closing when they detect obstructions under the door.

If an emergency call comes into the fire station, be prepared to take down the information and notify your dispatch, or transfer the call to the appropriate dispatch office for processing.

If the call requires an immediate response, get the proper information as dictated by your department's policy. At a minimum, you should request the following information: the emergency type and location, and the caller's name, address, and phone number.

Do It!

Your First Day

Everyone's first day in a new position or job is difficult. You will meet many new people and will be learning about your new job. Treat this first day as a challenge that is just the first step as a firefighter. Study how the supervision system works. Learn how to use the telephone and radio communications. Be eager to jump in and lend a hand on any job around the fire station as well as out on emergency scenes. Be cheerful and positive. A smile will take you a long way in making friends and fitting in.

Once you begin to be accepted as a part of the

Prove It

Knowledge Assessment

Signed Documentation Tear-Out Sheet

Exterior Operations Level Firefighter—Chapter 4

Name: _____

Fill out the ten-question quiz below, the Knowledge Assessment Sheet, by circling the correct answer for each question. When finished, sign it and give to your instructor/Company Officer for his or her signature. Turn in this Knowledge Assessment Sheet to the proper person as part of the documentation that you have completed your training for this chapter.

1. The fire attack hose line system begins at the _____ and ends when the stream of water coming from the end of the nozzle effectively reaches the base of the fire.
   a. nozzle
   b. apparatus pump panel
   c. fire hydrant
   d. base of the fire

2. The size of the f___
   water and press___
   a. increase
   b. have no affec___
   c. reduce
   d. eliminate

3. The inside diam___
   a. ¾ inch to 2 in___
   b. 2 to 3 inches
   c. ¾ to 1¾ inch___
   d. 1 to 3 inches

4. Booster hose co___
   disconnecting a___
   a. True
   b. False

5. Most couplings
   a. Clockwise
   b. Counterclock___

6. Unlike booster l___
   a. disconnected
   b. flowed
   c. rolled
   d. drained

Level 1

Prove It

Skills Assessment

Signed Documentation Tear-Out Sheet

Exterior Operations Level Firefighter—Chapter 4

Name: _____

Fill out the Skills Assessment Sheet below. Have your instructor/Company Officer check off and initial each skill you demonstrate. When finished, sign it and give to your instructor/Company Officer for his or her signature. Turn in this Skills Assessment Sheet to the proper person as part of the documentation that you have completed your training for this chapter.

Skill	Completed	Initials
1. Describe the components of a fire attack hose line system.	___	___
2. Demonstrate how to connect and disconnect hose lines.	___	___
3. Describe the application of different hose tools and accessories used with attack lines.	___	___
4. Demonstrate methods for rolling and carrying fire hose.	___	___
5. Explain good techniques for hose maintenance and care.	___	___
6. Explain and demonstrate how fire nozzles operate.	___	___
7. Demonstrate how to deploy and load booster lines.	___	___
8. Demonstrate how to properly hold and use a flowing booster hose.	___	___
9. Demonstrate how to deploy and load other jacketed attack lines.	___	___
10. Demonstrate how to hold and use a flowing small attack line.	___	___

Level 1

Student Signature and Date _____   Instructor/Company Officer Signature and Date _____

105

Supplements

For the Student
Student DVD

- DVD of firefighting skills packaged in the back of the text
  - More than 100 essential skills demonstrated by video
- Includes Digital Flashcards
  - 280 flashcard for self-study

For the Instructor
Instructor DVD

- PowerPoint Slides with videos embedded
  - More than 500 PowerPoint Slides

Instructor CD

- PowerPoint Slides
  - More than 500 PowerPoint Slides
- Lesson Plans (Instructor's Manual)
  - Full-color lesson plans in PDF format
- Instructor's Computerized Test Bank
  - Test bank is computerized and also provided in Word files

Acknowledgements

The authors and publisher wish to thank the following individuals and organizations for their assistance with this project:

Glen Ellman, *photographer*
Alex Menendez, *videographer and photographer*
George Mullins, *technical advisor*
Casselberry Fire Department, Florida
Central Florida Fire Academy
Ocoee Fire Department, Florida
Orange County Fire/Rescue Department, Florida
Seminole County Fire Division, Florida
Granbury Fire Department, Granbury, Texas

Reviewers

Brian J. Ball
Richland Community College
Decatur, IL

Tom Bentley
John Wood Community College
Quincy, IL

Oren Bersagel-Briese
Castle Rock Fire and Rescue Dept.
Castle Rock, CO

Tracy G. Braley
Brevard Community College
Cocoa, FL

Chief Will Chapleau EMT-P, RN, TNS
Chicago Heights Fire Dept.
Chicago Heights, IL

John Deckers
Avon Volunteer Fire Department
Avon, CT

David K. Donohue, MA, EMT-P
West Virginia RESA VIII
United States Capitol Police HMRT
Shepardstown, WV

Bob Downs
Kirkwood Community College
Cedar Rapids, IA

Todd R. Gilgren
Arvada Fire Protection District
Arvada, CO

Glenn Garwood
Paramedic I/C, Program Manager
Sterling Heights Fire Dept.
Oakland Community College
Auburn Hills, MI

Darryl J. Haefner
College of DuPage
Glenn Ellyn, IL

Mark Hammond
Kentucky Fire Commission State Fire Rescue Training
Ashland, KY

Mark Johnson
Hinsdale Fire Department
Hinsdale, IL

Michael Klauer
Asbury Fire Department
Asbury, IA

Captain Bob Lynch
Cookeville Fire Department
Cookeville, TN

Stephen S. Malley
Weatherford College Fire Academy
Weatherford, TX

Al Martinez
Fire Science Coordinator, Prairie State College
Fire Chief, Steger Fire Department
Chicago Heights, IL

George P. Melendrez
Professor Emeritus
Columbia College, Fire Technology
Sonora, CA

Louis N. Molino, Sr. CET
Fire and Safety Specialists, Inc.
College Station, TX

Kevin P. O'Brien
Albuquerque Fire Department
University of New Mexico EMS Academy
Eastern New Mexico-Roswell
Albuquerque, NM

Bruce Palmer
North Georgia Technical College
Clarkesville, GA

John Shirey
Triangle Tech
Pittsburgh, PA

Mark B. Silverman
Brevard Community College
Fire Training Academy
Cocoa, FL

Lori Thompson
North Georgia Technical College
Clarkesville, GA

Lt. Mike Wheeler
Prairie State College
Chicago Heights, IL

Safe Firefighting Part 1

Level 1
FIRST THINGS FIRST

1

Welcome to the Fire Service

What You Will Learn in This Chapter

This chapter will introduce you to the Fire Service. You will learn how a typical fire department is organized and governed. You will also take a look at how we organize our operations at a fire or other type of emergency. The chapter ends with a look at your safety while at the fire station and suggestions for your first day as a firefighter.

What You Will Be Able to Do

After reading this chapter, you will be asked to tour the fire station so you will know where to find things that are important to your safety. After reading the chapter and taking the tour, you will be able to

1. Properly notify the Station Officer that you are in the station.
2. Locate all emergency exits.
3. Secure the station.

4. Locate and use important information about any hazardous materials that are found in the fire station.
5. Receive and transfer incoming phone calls to the fire station.

Reality!

Beginning Your Career

It is important that you are successful while you are introduced to the inner workings, organization, and safety considerations of the Fire Department. As you will read in this chapter, the Fire Department maintains a rank structure that is utilized in both emergency and nonemergency operations. It is important for you to understand how this structure operates and where you will fit into it.

There are courtesy considerations and fire station manners that, if followed, will help you make a good first impression. Be a good listener when you first start out. There is so much you need to learn, even after you have completed all of your recruit training.

You also need to understand that safety is just as important around the fire station as it is at your own home or business. Perhaps there is an even more important reason for being safe at the fire station: It is the property of your community, built with everyone's money.

Remember, everyone wants you to succeed. Your instructor, your new supervisor, and your fellow firefighters will all contribute a serious investment of time and effort to ensure that you will be successful while you are in the fire service.

Unique North American Fire Service Terminology

Apparatus usually refers to Fire Service firefighting vehicles, like engine company units, truck company units, and rescue company units. You will see these terms used further in the text as *fire apparatus* (meaning any rolling piece of equipment), *fire engine* (a conventional pumper truck), *truck, ladder,* or *aerial apparatus* (meaning aerial or ladder truck), and *rescue apparatus* (meaning rescue truck). We use these terms frequently and you will undoubtedly hear them in your training sessions.

Organization of the Fire Department

Your fire department is no different from any other organized group of individuals with a common goal. Everyone has a job to do, and all must work within the Fire Department organization and management system. It is important for you to become familiar with the basic workings of your fire department's organization. All Fire departments share some similarities.

Some fire departments are staffed by full-time, paid firefighters (paid department), while others may be fully staffed by volunteers (volunteer department) who respond when there is a call for help. Some departments are a combination of paid and volunteer staff (combination department) in which a paid staff is available for the initial response to an alarm that is augmented with volunteers. A varia-

tion to these types of departments includes firefighters who are paid a small stipend to remain available in an area during designated hours so that they can respond quickly to an emergency. This type of department is referred to as a paid-on-call department.

Basic Work Groups: The "Company"

The basic work groups of most fire departments are composed of the first level of work teams, which are known as the *company*. The crew of each company consists of the team assigned to the apparatus or job task. The firefighters on a crew are usually managed by a first-line supervisor who may hold the rank of Senior Firefighter, Sergeant, Lieutenant, or Captain, depending on the organization and tradition of your department. Regardless of what rank your fire department designates for this lead role, the person in charge of the company is the Company Officer.

Companies are usually designated according to the type of their apparatus and the job they generally perform on the emergency scene. Traditionally, the crews are divided into engine companies, ladder or truck companies, and rescue or squad companies. There are also many specialized work groups such as **hazardous materials** (hazmat) units and technical rescue companies, and other specialized companies (Figures 1-1, 1-2, and 1-3). The list can go on and on. It is important for you to become familiar with the various company-level work groups in your fire department. You will need to understand how they are staffed and the specific functions each one has at the emergency scene.

KEY WORD

hazardous materials (hazmat) Materials and processes that present a hazard to human health through poisoning, chemical and thermal burns, radioactivity, explosiveness, chemical reactivity, or carcinogenic exposure.

Engine Companies

Engine companies are the most common type of Fire Service company and have the general fire and rescue task responsibilities; however, they may also be utilized for rescue or truck operations if the need arises (Figure 1-4). These units usually carry a supply of water, a hose to connect to a sustained water supply, and a pump to push the water supply through hose lines to the nozzles for fire extinguishment

FIGURE 1-1 A hazardous materials unit.

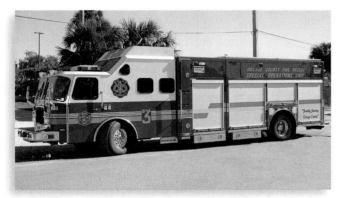

FIGURE 1-2 A technical rescue company.

FIGURE 1-3 An aerial ladder unit (truck company).

FIGURE 1-4 Engine companies have their own pump and carry water, manpower, equipment, and hose to the fire emergency.

FIGURE 1-5 An engine company firefighting crew and Company Officer.

(Figure 1-5). The firefighting crew is usually led by the Company Officer.

In many areas of the United States, the engine company is cross-trained to handle many of the jobs encountered on the emergency scene. The jobs that are handled on the emergency scene are based on the needs and capabilities of each community served by each fire department. Smaller departments are often required to have engine companies deliver many varied types of service to their community. The larger the fire department, the more likely it is that the companies will be more specialized into engines, rescues, and trucks.

Truck Companies

Compared to engine companies, truck companies have a more specialized function of additional fire and rescue task responsibilities. They also have elevated fire attack capabilities (Figure 1-6). They may or may not be equipped with their own **water supply.** They also have special training to deliver advanced **ventilation** and **forcible entry** techniques when needed on the emergency scene. Truck companies can provide fire **overhaul** and **salvage** capabilities and add personnel to assist in the overall firefighting effort.

water supply The water used for extinguishing fires that is carried to the fire by apparatus; pumped from static sources like ponds, rivers, and lakes; or obtained from pressurized water delivery systems through water mains and fire hydrant access points.

ventilation Techniques applied to building fires that allow smoke and hot gases to escape from a building involved in a fire. These techniques may also be utilized for atmospheres hazardous to health and life (such as a hazardous gas release inside a building).

forcible entry Methods of gaining access into a locked or obstructed building or vehicle by applying tools to physically dislodge and open a gate, doorway, or window.

overhaul The techniques and methods applied on an emergency fire scene that lessen the progress of the fire damage. The fire scene is checked for fire extension and hidden fires that are then extinguished. These techniques and methods include measures that help make buildings safe after a fire.

salvage Measures taken by firefighting personnel that help reduce property damage to rooms and content during and after a fire.

Rescue Companies

Rescue companies usually do not have a pump, water, or hose. Their primary function is to perform rescue at a fire as well as to assist in other firefighting activities. They may be called upon to rescue citizens as well as Fire Service personnel on the emergency scene. In some fire departments, these units are staffed by firefighters trained as **Emergency Medical Technicians (EMTs)** and **Paramedics,** which greatly enhances the emergency rescue and medical care capabilities of the department.

Technical rescue operations, like those situations that involve the rescue of victims trapped in unusual or special circumstances, are primarily handled by a rescue or truck company with specially trained personnel and with assistance from engine companies (Figure 1-7).

KEY WORDS

Emergency Medical Technician (EMT) A person trained in emergency prehospital care at a level above basic and advanced first aid.

Paramedic A prehospital emergency care provider who is trained at a level above Emergency Medical Technician.

technical rescue Any rescue discipline requiring specialized knowledge, skills, and tools. Technical rescue includes water, vehicle, rope, building collapse, trench, and confined space rescue.

Company Officers

The Team Leader or Company Officer in charge of the unit may be predesignated for each company, or the team for each unit may be assembled as firefighters arrive on the emergency scene. This latter scenario is more common in a volunteer fire department than in a fully paid or combination-type department. As a new

FIGURE 1-6 Truck companies perform many tasks, including forcible entry, ventilation, and overhaul and salvage capabilities. They also provide an elevated fire attack capability.

FIGURE 1-7 Some fire departments have Special Rescue units that provide technical rescue capability for the community.

firefighter, it is very important for you to learn who is in charge of these companies. It most likely will be your Company Officer on the emergency scene and therefore will be the people who will directly supervise your actions (Figure 1-8).

Chain of Command

The operations are organized by an established **chain of command.** This chain of command is the management plan for any emergency operation (Figure 1-9).

▓▓▓ KEY WORD ▓▓▓

chain of command The organization of supervisory levels within a fire department, generally utilized for both emergency and nonemergency operations.

FIGURE 1-8 The Company Officer will most likely be your immediate supervisor. He or she will be the engine company team leader.

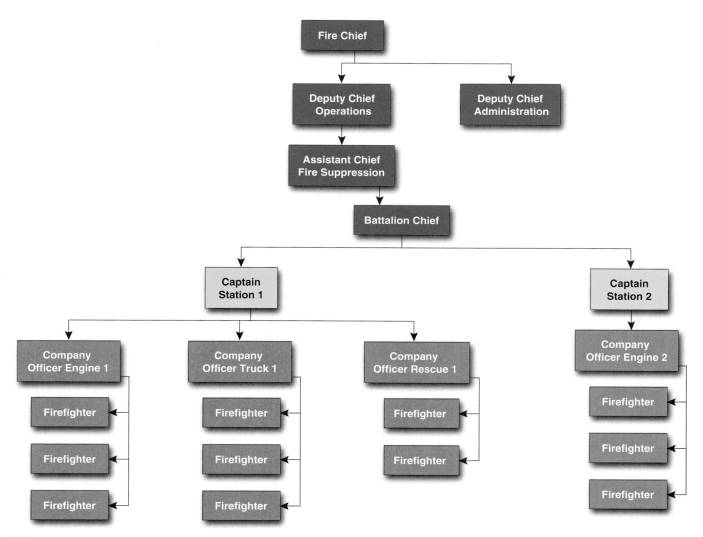

FIGURE 1-9 A typical chain of command. This chain of command details the structure of the Fire Department as it works at a typical emergency operation.

Mid-Management

The individual companies are supervised as a group by the next layer of supervision in the fire department. These ranks have many names, but they are mid-management personnel and may be designated as Captains, Battalion Chief, District Chief, or, in some instances, Assistant Chief. This all depends on the organizational makeup of your department.

In most cases, midlevel supervisors manage two or more Company Officers and serve as the commanders of emergency incidents involving two or more companies.

Upper Management

There is a lot more to a fire department than the basic companies. Many organizations are divided into divisions or bureaus that cover emergency and nonemergency operations. There can also be an Emergency Medical Division that handles the delivery of **Emergency Medical Services (EMS)** by the department, if provided. Either an Assistant Chief or a Deputy Chief, who answers directly to the Fire Chief, manages most divisions. An Assistant or Deputy Chief usually manages large incidents that involve several companies working on the scene.

▇▇▇ KEY WORD ▇▇▇

Emergency Medical Services (EMS) A group of organizations that provide emergency medical prehospital care to the community.

Department Divisions

A larger fire department may be further divided into divisions that serve under the command of a division head. For now, let's concentrate on the typical divisions you may encounter.

Administration Division Besides emergency operations, fire departments also have nonemergency work groups under their administration. Larger departments may have an Administration Division that coordinates nonemergency operations like supply and facility maintenance.

Fire Prevention Division A good fire prevention program is an excellent approach to increasing firefighter safety. A Fire Prevention Division performs fire inspections and assists in building code enforcement. They may also handle arson investigations of suspicious fires and the delivery of public fire education programs. Fire prevention is a very important job of the fire service for its community. In recent years, more emphasis has been placed on the delivery of good fire prevention programs for the public.

Training Division A Training Division provides recruit training and ongoing training programs for firefighters. These programs include weekly drill training for volunteer departments and daily training programs for paid firefighters. The Training Division also provides assistance for Company Officers so that they can provide training to their work groups.

Communications Division Probably one of the most important divisions within any emergency agency is the Communications Division. The main role of the Communications Division is to operate the alarm office. In this office, call takers receive the initial call for help, process the information, and dispatch the appropriate units to handle the situation (Figure 1-10). Fire departments today communicate through many more ways than a simple telephone and two-way radio. Pagers, e-mail, and cell telephones are very common in most fire departments. All of these communications channels are coordinated by the Communications Division.

The Fire Chief

Almost all fire departments are led by a Chief Officer, Fire Commissioner, Fire Chief, or Fire Administrator. This individual is the top person in the chain of command as well as the manager of the fire department. There might be staff personnel who work with this individual to administer the department. This person may have many other jobs to perform, depending on the size and scope of the individual fire department he or she manages.

In volunteer fire departments, the Chief can be an elected position, for a specific length of time, such as one or two years. Some departments use a governing board to appoint their Chief.

FIGURE 1-10 The Communications Division receives emergency calls, processes the information, and dispatches the appropriate fire units to the scene. This division is vital to Fire Department operations.

In some paid or volunteer fire departments, the Chief may be hired or appointed by the local government. Regardless of how the individual is placed in the position, this person is the chief executive of the organization. You should make it a point to identify the Chief of your department.

Governing Bodies

Fire departments are often under the control of local government (Figure 1-11). This governing body can be a city or county council with elected representatives serving on a board. Some fire departments may be part of another organization such as a private industry—for example, an **Industrial Fire Brigade.** Some other fire departments may be part of a government entity, such as a military fire service or federal forestry service. There may be a board of fire commissioners that approves budgets and defines policy. In volunteer fire departments, the governing board may be called a Board of Directors.

Today, more and more is being required of fire departments by the communities they serve. Most fire departments deliver some level of Emergency Medical Services to their community. In addition, responsibility for hazardous material incident mitigation is often given to the local fire department.

The Fire Service is usually the first emergency agency to arrive and begin initial steps to handle disasters, both natural and manmade. On the national level, fire departments are also an integral part of the United States' Homeland Defense response strategy.

▇▇ KEY WORD ▇▇

Industrial Fire Brigade An organization similar to a fire department that protects a single business or business complex. This organization is generally privately funded and operated.

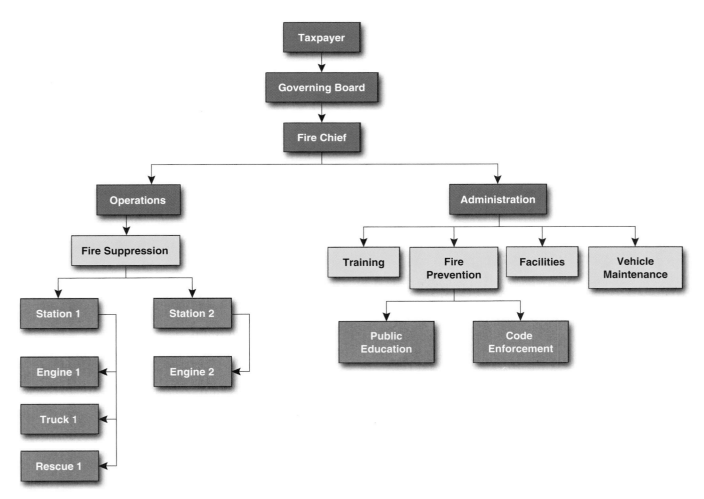

FIGURE 1-11   A typical organizational chart. The Fire Department organization begins with the taxpayer and ends with the newest firefighters, covering all branches of the organization.

Introduction to Incident Command

At first glance, the fireground or emergency scene may seem to be in total chaos (Figure 1-12). Watching firefighters working inside a burning structure while others outside work furiously to break windows, stretch hose lines, and control the scene may make you wonder how they know what to do and when to do it. As chaotic as it may seem, the emergency operations at a fire or rescue event are usually well coordinated through the use of an **Incident Command System (ICS).** When you become familiar with the basic framework of a typical Incident Command System, fireground operations will make a lot more sense to you.

When you arrive at the scene of an emergency, you operate under the command of your Company Officer. The Company Officer is responsible for your safety as much as you are; therefore, the Company Officer wants to keep in close contact with you at all times. The first rule of any emergency operation is that there is absolutely *no* room for **freelancing** of any type. Do not wander away from your team for any reason, even if you are not working at the moment. After you complete the Exterior Operations level portion of your training, you will be assigned tasks that can be completed in a safe area outside the burning building. If, for some reason, you are assigned to a Company Officer who is not familiar with you, be sure the officer knows your level of training so that you are not assigned duties that are beyond the scope of your training (Figure 1-13).

FIGURE 1-13 It is important that you make sure your Company Officer knows your level of training so that you are not assigned duties beyond your capabilities.

▨ KEY WORDS ▨

Incident Command System (ICS) An organization of supervision at an emergency that designates supervisory levels and responsibility.

freelancing Working independently of the Incident Command System, without the knowledge of the Incident Commander. *Freelancing* is seen as a negative term and is usually associated with an unsafe activity.

The Incident Commander

If the situation requires more than one company to handle the problem, an Incident Command System is established. Under the Incident Command System, a single officer, the **Incident Commander,** coordinates the different companies operating on the scene. This coordination enhances everyone's safety, reduces any redundant actions on the scene, and, most of all, coordinates the radio communications, keeping the radio chatter to an efficient minimum. To accomplish this, all of the on-scene radio communications are directed between operating companies and the Incident Commander (Figure 1-14). Only the Incident Commander talks directly to the communication center.

The first arriving person, most often the officer on the first arriving unit, should establish the Incident Command System. On the radio, the arrival report may sound something like this: "*Engine 1 on the scene, heavy fire showing from the first floor of a single-story, wood-frame house. Engine 1 establishing command.*" Now everyone who is responding can develop a mental picture of what is burning and knows exactly who is in charge. As more companies arrive, the command and control of the event is passed to

FIGURE 1-12 Initially, watching the Fire Department working at an emergency may seem chaotic. However, after you become more familiar with the Incident Command System, it will make more sense to you.

FIGURE 1-14 At a typical emergency scene with an Incident Command System established, all radio communications are made through the Incident Commander and not directly with the dispatchers.

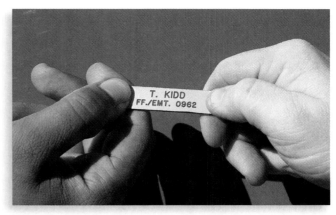

FIGURE 1-15 PAS tags allow the Incident Command System to track firefighters at an emergency scene. Immediately after you arrive at the scene, your Company Officer hands these tags to the Incident Commander.

higher-ranking officers so that the Company Officer can keep his or her crew intact.

KEY WORD

Incident Commander (IC) The person in charge of an emergency operation command structure and consequently in charge of the emergency incident at hand.

Personnel Accountability System

The Incident Commander uses a **personnel accountability system** to track each individual who is operating on the scene. Personnel accountability systems allow the Incident Commander to group individuals by crews and track them by job assignments. A firefighter gives a tag that indicates his or her name to the Company Officer (Figures 1-15 and 1-16). The Company Officer groups the tags for everyone on the crew and hands them to the Incident Commander or the Commander's designee so that everyone operating on an emergency scene is accounted for at all times.

KEY WORD

personnel accountability system An identification system used to track fire department units as well as personnel on the emergency scene.

Working Groups

If the emergency situation is particularly large and includes several companies operating simultaneously,

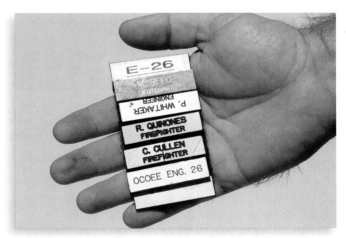

FIGURE 1-16 The PAS tag indicates your name and is grouped with other members of your firefighting team. A team is usually identified by the company designation for the fire unit.

the Incident Commander will probably divide the operating crews into separate groups that are each led by a group supervisor. Depending on local practices, these groups are called *sectors, branches, divisions,* or *work groups.* On the radio, a typical order may sound something like this: "*Command to Engine 1, report to the Fire Attack Branch for outside ventilation duties*" (Figure 1-17).

In order to establish uniform terminology, many agencies have decided to recognize the National Incident Management System (NIMS), which prefers the terms *division, branch,* and *group.* However, many departments still use the term *sector* to describe the smaller divisions of responsibility at an emergency. It is important that you become completely familiar with the terminology used by your department and other departments in your area.

FIGURE 1-17 Several individual teams of firefighters may be assigned to a subdivided area of the emergency scene called a *branch*, and the branch is supervised by a Fire Officer.

Codes and Standards

There are many codes and standards that your fire department utilizes as guidelines in almost every aspect in which it operates. Is it vital that an Exterior Operations level firefighter like yourself be thoroughly knowledgeable about these many standards and rules? Not really, but you do need to know that they exist and that many times your fire department operates a certain way because of these standards and rules.

National Fire Protection Association (NFPA)

Probably the main source for Fire Service standards comes from the **National Fire Protection Association (NFPA).** This organization writes standards that cover everything from the boots you wear to the types of hose and nozzles you use. The training program you are taking now is covering areas of knowledge identified by NFPA Standards.

KEY WORD

National Fire Protection Association (NFPA) An organization that sets fire codes and standards recognized by most fire department organizations in the United States.

Occupational Safety and Health Administration (OSHA)

The rules of the federal **Occupational Safety and Health Administration (OSHA)** also greatly affect the fire service. They mainly deal with safety issues in emergency as well as nonemergency operations.

KEY WORD

Occupational Safety and Health Administration (OSHA) A federal governmental agency that establishes regulations that apply to many aspects of employee safety at the workplace.

National Institute for Occupational Safety and Health (NIOSH)

The **National Institute for Occupational Safety and Health (NIOSH)** is another safety regulator used in the Fire Service. This federal agency sets standards for tools and techniques and also investigates many line-of-duty Fire Service injuries and deaths. (See "Safety Lesson: A NIOSH Report" later in this chapter.)

We will point out national standards and codes where necessary. For now you need to know that they exist and that they govern many of the procedures and kinds of equipment used by the fire service.

KEY WORD

National Institute for Occupational Safety and Health (NIOSH) A federal agency concerned with improving employee safety in the workplace.

Fire Department Rules and Regulations

Every organization has a set of rules and regulations that guide how that organization operates. Your department may have rules and regulations, standard operating guidelines or procedures, or organizational bylaws that both govern how things are done and provide guidance.

For you as an Exterior Operations level firefighter, it is probably important that you identify these guidelines and start to learn them as they apply to you. They include things such as how you are to respond to an emergency call, the protective equipment to be used at each type of call, and the Incident Command System procedures.

Routine, day-to-day activities such as training, equipment checkout procedures, and station duty assignments are also included in the rules and regulations. Every fire department has its routine, or nonemergency, operations that are scheduled daily. They also have their emergency operations, which can happen at any time. You will spend much more time at the fire station in routine operations than you will on actual emergencies.

FIGURE 1-19 Fire stations house vehicles and can contain offices, living areas, storage areas, and public meeting areas.

Fire Stations

Fire stations are unique buildings in the community. They contain the fire and rescue units and equipment used to respond to emergencies (Figure 1-18). The firefighters who respond on those units may be working in the stations, as in a full-time paid department, or they may respond to the station facilities to answer emergency calls, as in volunteer fire departments. In every community, fire stations are a source of pride and honor.

Fire stations, in fact, are owned by the citizens of the community, and the public feels at ease going into their fire station for help. In times of public emergencies and disasters, fire stations may be the only functioning public buildings in the community. People tend to go to their local fire station for help and information during these times.

These buildings usually have vehicle bays that house the various fire and rescue apparatus, a workshop area for tool and equipment maintenance, and a living area for firefighters and the public (Figure 1-19).

FIGURE 1-18 Fire stations are spaced throughout the community and are an integral part of any neighborhood.

The living area (day room or ready room) usually has some sort of kitchen and dining area, a training or lounge area (sometimes called a ready room), and offices. In fire stations that are staffed around the clock, dorm facilities for on-duty crews may be provided. Additional meeting and activity rooms, government offices, and fire emergency communications facilities may be attached, depending on the design and needs of the community.

Be sure to ask someone to show you around the fire station and get to know the building and facilities. Take note of exit locations, emergency notification procedures, and fire extinguisher locations. Find out who is normally in charge of the facility and introduce yourself to that person.

Station Safety

We are going to discuss fire station safety by covering three areas: (1) station safety for firefighters, (2) right-to-know requirements, and (3) station safety for visitors.

Station Safety for Firefighters

As you continue your training, you will learn a great deal about safety on the emergency scene. You'll become familiar with when to put on your safety gear and how to safely extinguish various types of fires. Your safety at the fire station is just as important as scene safety. Unfortunately, many individuals assume that safe practices can be sidestepped in the nonemergency circumstances of the station. However, many injuries and even deaths occur during nonemergency routines at the fire station.

To begin with, we must all keep the following rule in mind: *If the action you are taking at the fire station* is similar to a task you may be doing on the emergency scene, you will probably need to take similar safety preparations before doing the task. For example, if you wear eye protection when using a saw on the emergency scene, you should do the same while using a saw in the fire station.

Use safe practices when handling tools and equipment. If you are not sure how to safely use a tool, don't use it. Ask for help and let someone show you the safe way to operate it. Consult user manuals and be sure to read, understand, and follow all safety precautions.

If routine station maintenance duties require you to work above the floor level—for example, from a ladder—then you should have someone with you as a safety person and you should use the proper equipment for the job (Figure 1-20). Most ladders carried on a fire truck are designed to be used on soft ground—not on slick hard floors—so don't go for the easy-to-grab ladder on the truck instead of taking the time to use a proper stepladder. Don't be tempted to use the fire truck as a work platform by climbing up on the hose bed to do something as simple as changing a light bulb. It is too easy to walk off the side of the truck or fall as you are climbing up or down. Bottom line: *Use the proper tool for the job.*

Next, if there is a safety hazard that might be pointed out to the public at a fire inspection, the same rules apply at the fire station. A frayed wire on an extension cord is dangerous whether in a business, home, or fire station—the rules don't change.

FIGURE 1-20 If you need to reach elevated areas in a fire station, use the proper ladder. Ladders on a fire truck may not be appropriate. Make sure to use the proper tools and equipment for the job at hand.

NIOSH Reports

The National Institute for Occupational Safety and Health (NIOSH) conducts a program that is designed to determine the factors that cause or contribute to firefighter deaths and serious injuries suffered in the line of duty. This organization's intent is to help researchers and safety specialists develop strategies for preventing similar future incidents. Throughout this book, you will find examples of the lessons learned from some of these reports. It is our hope that you will take the time to read each lesson seriously, with the understanding that one or more firefighters have died in the reported incidents. We hope that you will learn something that can prevent you from suffering a similar fate. You can access the NIOSH reports on the Internet at http://www.cdc.gov/niosh/firehome.html or call 1-800-35NIOSH.

 ## Safety Lesson

A NIOSH Report

An In-Station Accident

Accidents and injuries can happen to almost anyone, almost anywhere. The sad truth is that most accidents could have been prevented if everyone involved had been aware of the hazard associated with their actions as well as the proper safety steps one should take to prevent harm from those hazards. Fire and EMS departments are in the business of taking care of the victims of accidents; however, it is often the firefighter or EMS worker who is the injured person needing help.

On January 16, 2000, a 53-year-old male volunteer firefighter died after an extension ladder slipped out from under him while he was conducting routine maintenance work on the garage door at the firehouse. The victim and another firefighter had used a 14-foot fire service extension ladder to climb to the top of a rescue truck. They had used the rescue truck as a platform to work from as they assisted a civilian in changing the garage door opener. The victim had removed the existing door opener and was in the process of going to assist in readying the new door opener when the ladder slipped out from under him. The victim fell headfirst to the concrete floor.

When the victim fell to the floor, the second firefighter was left on top of the rescue truck with no way down but to jump. The civilian called 911 and attempted to render aid to the victim as the second firefighter jumped to the floor and ran next door to inform the victim's wife. Help arrived within minutes and the victim was transported to the local hospital via helicopter. He died the next day.

Follow-Up

NIOSH Report #F2000-07

The NIOSH investigative report concluded that three simple recommendations could have prevented this accident:

- Fire departments should ensure that ladders are used in accordance with existing safety standards.
- Fire departments should designate an individual as the fire station Safety Officer for all in-house maintenance to identify potential hazards and ensure that those hazards are eliminated.
- Fire departments should consider the use of mobile scaffolding, personal lifts, scissor lifts, or boom lifts instead of the top surface of a fire truck.

 Safety Tip!

Here are some safety tips for working in the fire station:

1. **Learn the layout of the station.**
   - Know how to exit the building and identify the exits.
   - Locate all the fire extinguishers and building fire systems.
2. **Practice good housekeeping.**
   - Keep all walkways and floors clear of clutter, spills, and trip hazards.
   - Keep the fire station and apparatus clean at all times.
   - Empty the trash often.
   - Keep all flammable materials in proper containers and cabinets.
3. **Keep the fire station secure.**
   - Keep unescorted visitors out of the vehicle bays.
   - Secure the station when no one is there.
   - Know how to report an emergency from the fire station.
4. **Maintain a safe attitude.**
   - Use care and proper protective gear when utilizing tools and equipment.
   - Always be careful working around apparatus in the vehicle bays.
   - There is no place for "horseplay" at the fire station.

Right-to-Know Requirements

As much as firefighters would like them to be, fire stations are no different from any other public access building in the community. Employers are required by law (OSHA) to inform their employees, including volunteers, about any hazardous materials operations or hazardous materials located at their workplace.

Fire stations post a public notice of right-to-know information for employees. They also should have files, kept on the property, that identify all hazardous chemicals, materials, and processes on site.

Regularly check the bulletin board for safety notices and information. Make it a point to become aware of any right-to-know information within the fire station. This information is posted in an area accessible to all employees. The person in charge of the station can tell you where this information is located.

Station Safety for Visitors

When the public comes into a fire station, they should be kept safe at all times. It is very important that they be greeted properly and asked if they can be assisted. A firefighter should stay with visitors until they have completed their business or have found the individual they are looking for.

Visitors should never be allowed to wander through the station by themselves. This likely leads only to trouble and may expose them to injury. By far the most dangerous place for the public is in the vehicle bays. Equipment may be out on the floors and vehicles may be entering or leaving the facility. An emergency call may come in and the vehicles will have to be used to respond quickly. Escort visitors to the vehicle bay area and lead them back into the office area of the fire station (Figure 1-21). Never leave visitors alone in the vehicle bay.

FIGURE 1-21 All visitors to a fire station should be escorted, especially in the vehicle bays.

Your Fire Station

Fire stations are multipurpose buildings that serve many functions in the community. When you visit a fire station for the first time, it is important that you introduce yourself to the person in charge and explain why you are there. As a new member, whether a volunteer or paid firefighter, you should then be shown the station.

Fire stations usually have a public access area that contains the entrance area or foyer, with offices used for things like communications and dispatch, staff functions like fire prevention and training, administrative offices for Chiefs, and offices for station crew supervisors.

Locate All Emergency Exits

While touring the station, look for all exits from the building (Figure 1-22). Just like any other building, fire stations can experience an emergency and a quick exit may be required. Assess the exit doorway. Does it have a lock or a latch? Will an alarm sound when you open it? Where does the exit door lead—to another interior space and then outside, or directly out of the station?

Find the Fire Extinguisher Locations

Fire extinguishers will probably be located near the office area, the kitchen and lounge areas, the vehicle bays, and the sleeping and meeting room areas.

FIGURE 1-23 Learn the locations of the fire extinguishers in your station.

Check the types of extinguishers in each location (Figure 1-23).

Learn How to Secure the Station

During your station tour, be sure to ask about securing the fire station. You need to know how to properly lock as well as unlock the facility (Figure 1-24). Some stations issue keys to all personnel. Others may have lockbox devices with a combination lock or electronic cardkey access.

You should also ask about and learn the procedures for opening and closing vehicle bay doors. Elec-

FIGURE 1-22 During your initial station tour, notice the locations of the exit doors.

FIGURE 1-24 It is important to know how to secure the fire station.

FIGURE 1-25 Right-to-know information must be made available to all members of the fire department in their work area at the fire station. This information may be located on bulletin boards in the fire station. It should include information about hazardous materials and processes.

tric door openers may be located in fire apparatus activated by the driver. Bay doors should have electronic eye safety switches installed that stop doors from closing when they detect obstructions under the door.

Locate Important Information About Any Hazardous Materials Found in the Fire Station

You should ask about any right-to-know information posted in the fire station. Find this location and note the processes and materials listed (Figure 1-25). Ask the person who is showing you around where these notices are located and how they are stored. Remember to read this information regularly so that you become familiar with it.

Learn How to Answer an Incoming Phone Call to the Fire Station

During your orientation visit to the fire station, it is important that you learn how to take a phone call. These calls are usually for fire department business, but occasionally they can be an emergency call for help. It is important to answer the phone in a professional, polite, and serious manner. Doing so conveys professionalism and reflects the respect you have for your community. A typical phone call reception should be, "*Hello, _____ Fire Department, (Your Name) speaking. How can I help you?*"

Always be ready to take a message or transfer the call to the appropriate person. Never hang up on a caller—always be prepared to give assistance.

If an emergency call comes into the fire station, be prepared to take down the information and notify your dispatch, or transfer the call to the appropriate dispatch office for processing.

If the call requires an immediate response, get the proper information as dictated by your department's policy. At a minimum, you should request the following information: the emergency type and location, and the caller's name, address, and phone number.

Do It!

Your First Day

Everyone's first day in a new position or job is difficult. You will meet many new people and will be learning about your new job. Treat this first day as a challenge that is just the first step as a firefighter. Study how the supervision system works. Learn how to use the telephone and radio communications. Be eager to jump in and lend a hand on any job around the fire station as well as out on emergency scenes. Be cheerful and positive. A smile will take you a long way in making friends and fitting in.

Once you begin to be accepted as a part of the department, you will then begin to bond with your coworkers as you face the challenges of emergency work. This bonding will stay with you for the rest of your life—it is the invisible tie that binds all firefighters together. You have to depend upon each other to survive as well as to be successful in handling emergencies.

Always be the student. Set out to learn something every day you work at the fire department. Listen to others and be observant. Think before you speak or do anything. Most of all, never work outside your training and capability. Be safe at all times.

Our first chapter was intended to introduce you to the Fire Service. First we talked about how a typical fire department is organized and governed. Then we explained how fire departments manage themselves at emergency scenes. Finally, we described the makeup of a fire station and discussed fire station safety. You were also provided with skills training for notifying the Station Officer that you are in the fire station, how to locate all the emergency exits of a fire station, how to secure the fire station, and how to locate and use important information on any hazardous materials or processes in the fire station.

We hope that this first introduction into the Fire Service has inspired you to go on with your training and that you will be successful in becoming a safe firefighter for your community.

Prove It

Knowledge Assessment

Signed Documentation Tear-Out Sheet

Exterior Operations Level Firefighter—Chapter 1

Name: _____

Fill out the ten-question quiz below, the Knowledge Assessment Sheet, by circling the correct answer for each question. When finished, sign it and give to your instructor/Company Officer for his or her signature. Turn in this Knowledge Assessment Sheet to the proper person as part of the documentation that you have completed your training for this chapter.

1. NIOSH routinely investigates line-of-duty firefighter injuries and deaths.
   a. True
   b. False

2. The person who is in charge of an engine or truck company is commonly referred to as a
   1. Chief Officer.
   b. Division Chief.
   c. Company Officer.
   d. Firefighter.

3. Which of the following divisions conducts building inspections and enforces fire codes?
   a. Training
   b. Fire Prevention
   c. Supply
   d. Maintenance

4. Fire departments are often under the jurisdiction of
   a. local governments.
   b. state governments.
   c. the federal government.
   d. national agencies.

5. Complex fireground operations are usually controlled by
   a. a senior firefighter.
   b. an Incident Establishment System.
   c. an Incident Command System.
   d. a national standard.

6. Emergency personnel working at emergency scenes are usually tracked by some sort of
   a. personnel warning system.
   b. personnel accountability system.
   c. special transponders.
   d. radio frequencies.

Level I

7. In the Incident Command System, subdivisions of the command system are commonly referred to as
   a. sides.
   b. parts.
   c. sectors.
   d. divisions.

8. It is acceptable to allow visitors to the fire station to roam freely throughout the building.
   a. True
   b. False

9. A fire truck hose bed makes a great platform for working on lights at the ceiling of the fire station vehicle bay.
   a. True
   b. False

10. Any hazardous materials stored or used on the station property will be listed on the _____ kept in the fire station.
   a. right-to-know notice
   b. Internet listing
   c. rules and regulations
   d. Company Officer's desk

Prove It

Skills Assessment
Signed Documentation Tear-Out Sheet
Exterior Operations Level Firefighter—Chapter 1

Name: _____

Fill out the Skills Assessment Sheet below. Have your instructor/Company Officer check off and initial each skill you demonstrate. When finished, sign it and give to your instructor/Company Officer for his or her signature. Turn in this Skills Assessment Sheet to the proper person as part of the documentation that you have completed your training for this chapter.

Skill	Completed	Initials
1. Give the name of the person in charge of the station.	_____	_____
2. Describe the general layout of the fire station.	_____	_____
3. Describe the types and numbers of units in the vehicle bay areas.	_____	_____
4. State how many exits there are from the building.	_____	_____
5. Describe the locations of the exits.	_____	_____
6. Demonstrate how to answer a phone call and make an outgoing business call.	_____	_____
7. Demonstrate how firefighters can enter the locked fire station.	_____	_____
8. Demonstrate how to properly secure the fire station.	_____	_____
9. Demonstrate how to safely open and close the bay doors.	_____	_____
10. Show the location of the station bulletin board and the right-to-know information.	_____	_____

Student Signature and Date _____   Instructor/Company Officer Signature and Date _____

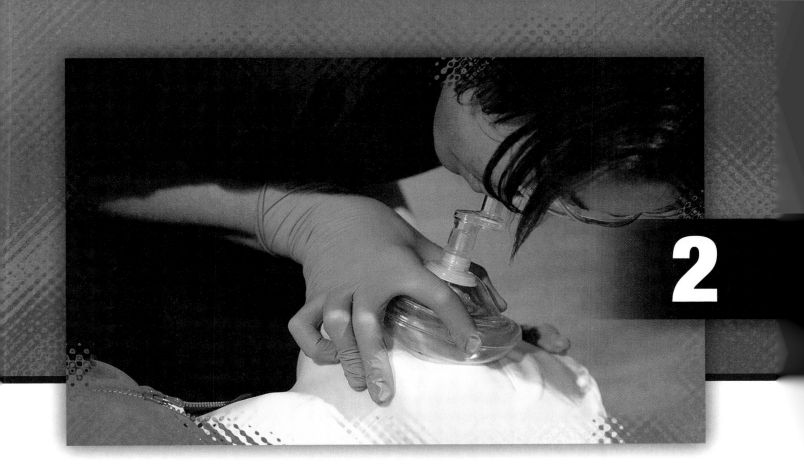

2

Basic First Aid and CPR

What You Will Learn in This Chapter

This chapter will introduce you to some fundamental first aid practices, which include a safe approach to the scene, the legal implications of your actions, and several steps you can take prior to the arrival of the Emergency Medical Services.

What You Will Be Able to Do

After reading this chapter and practicing the skills in a classroom setting, you will be able to

1. Describe some of the steps you can take in allowing a safe approach to a scene in which someone has been injured.
2. Describe the principles of the standard of care, consent, and abandonment.
3. Demonstrate the steps for ensuring infection control and body substance isolation.
4. Describe the ABCs of first aid.
5. Demonstrate the head tilt–chin lift and jaw-thrust maneuvers for opening a person's airway.
6. Demonstrate abdominal thrusts.
7. Demonstrate assessing a patient's carotid pulse.
8. Demonstrate rescue breathing.
9. Demonstrate proper chest compressions for a pulseless person.
10. Demonstrate the proper use of an automatic external defibrillator (AED).
11. Demonstrate the methods for applying direct pressure and a pressure dressing to control external bleeding.
12. Describe the signs and symptoms of shock and demonstrate the steps for managing a patient who is in shock.
13. Demonstrate the application of a cold compress.
14. Describe the severity of burns.
15. Demonstrate the treatment of a burn injury.

Basic Emergency Care

Firefighters must respond to and handle all kinds of emergency situations. There are times when someone is injured and that person needs emergency first aid care on the scene. For this reason, it is important for all firefighters to have a basic knowledge of first aid, cardiopulmonary resuscitation (CPR), and infection and body substance isolation (BSI) techniques.

Safety Lesson

A NIOSH Report

An On-Scene Collapse

On November 2, 2001, a 62-year-old male volunteer firefighter collapsed at the scene of a vehicle fire as he was bringing a tool to the Chief. Despite immediate CPR at the scene and subsequent advanced life support both in the ambulance and at the hospital emergency department, the firefighter died.

Follow-Up

The NIOSH Investigative Report (Report #F2002-24) concluded with several recommendations, including that the fire department "Consider including an automatic external defibrillator as part of the basic life support equipment for fire department vehicles."

You will learn about automatic external defibrillators and CPR in this chapter.

First Aid Training

There are several levels of emergency medical certification that you can obtain, including the classifications **Emergency Medical Responder (EMR)**, Emergency Medical Technician (EMT), Advanced Emergency Medical Technician (AEMT), and Paramedic. In addition, fundamental lifesaving certifications are available in **cardiopulmonary resuscitation (CPR)** and automatic external defibrillator (AED) training. To what level you can expect to be trained during the next few years usually depends upon the level of emergency medical care your department provides. Because this text and the accompanying DVD provide training for the External Operations

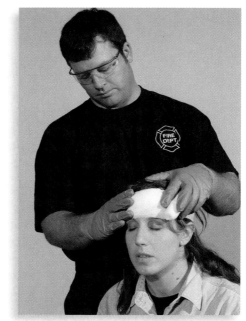

FIGURE 2-1 First aid is the care given to a patient prior to the arrival of higher trained and equipped prehospital emergency medical providers.

level of firefighting, we will concentrate on first aid, CPR, and the use of AEDs.

First aid is the care that a person, while acting alone or as part of a team, can reasonably give prior to the arrival of higher trained and equipped prehospital emergency medical providers (Figure 2-1). Assisting a person who is not breathing, controlling bleeding, providing initial treatment for burns, and assisting a person who is in shock are the fundamentals of first aid.

Knowing first aid is important in everyday life. Most people do not think about providing initial treatment until an injury occurs. With a little training, more lives can be saved. It is important that the actions we take fall within the standard of care that is associated with our level of training.

KEY WORDS

Emergency Medical Responder (EMR) A designation for an emergency professional trained in very basic first aid and rescue skills.

cardiopulmonary resuscitation (CPR) The process of providing breathing and blood circulation to someone who has stopped breathing and whose heart is not beating effectively.

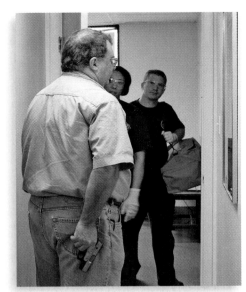

FIGURE 2-2 In order to protect yourself, be sure look for any hazardous conditions that may be present at the scene. You do not want to become a patient yourself.

Initial Approach

In providing first aid, your first responsibility is to yourself. Never rush in blindly to render aid without first assessing the scene (Figure 2-2). To be effective in your first aid efforts, you must first be aware of what caused the problem so that you can maintain a safe attitude in everything you do—otherwise, you can fall victim to the same fate. A good example is when a person is electrocuted. Although the victim may be severely burned and possibly not breathing, it is vital to your own safety that you take the first step of ensuring that the victim and his or her immediate area are not energized with electrical power before you begin to render aid. This may involve waiting for the power company to arrive to control the power. The same rules apply when any other danger is present.

Automobile crashes are particularly dangerous after the fact, due to traffic hazards. Therefore, your first step in rendering first aid at the scene of a traffic accident must be to make yourself visible by donning a reflective vest and controlling the traffic before you begin patient care. It is essential to the victim that you survive so you can render first aid—so, yes, ensuring your personal safety is the first step to rendering care.

It is always preferable that you make the scene safe when practical rather than move an injured pa-tient to a safer location. Moving a traumatized victim can cause further harm. However, there are times when moving the patient to a safe location is the only practical action to take—for example, when the patient is in danger of smoke inhalation or burns from an uncontrolled fire, or the patient is in water and is in danger of drowning. If you must move a trauma patient to a safer location, try your best to move the patient's spine as little as possible, keeping his head and neck in line with his body and in a neutral position as you go.

Gain Consent

When people are injured, those around them often panic. Being trained in first aid and providing a calm, reassuring presence goes a long way toward calming all those involved. Unfortunately, there will be times when not everyone who needs your help will want it. This is often the case when someone is injured during a violent act or while under the influence of alcohol or illicit drugs. Law enforcement personnel should stabilize any potentially violent scene before you approach the area. Even when there is no act of violence or personal hazard present, some people simply do not want to be helped. Your next step is to establish a "connection" with the patient and gain her **consent** for the treatment you are about to render. Just speaking in a calm, respectful tone is usually all it takes. Introduce yourself to the patient and ask her name. Explain what you are about to do and ask the person if it is all right with her to do it.

In most cases, you should take the time to seek the patient's permission before you touch the patient. If the person is a minor and his or her parent or guardian is not present to give their consent, then it is implied that you have permission to treat the child. If the patient is unconscious, heavily intoxicated, or otherwise unable to make an informed decision, then he is unable to give his informed consent for treatment. In this case, it is implied that you have permission to help the patient. However, if the person is conscious and unruly, you should try to keep the patient calm to prevent him from doing more harm. In this case, you should wait for law enforcement and/or more highly trained medical providers to arrive to assist you, except in the following situations: (1) when the injury is life-threatening, or (2) if more harm will come by delaying treatment for the time it would take for other emergency care providers to arrive.

consent   Permission granted to a rescuer by an injured or ill patient that allows the rescuer to provide first aid to that patient.

Do No Harm

Having consent to treat a person does not allow you to do more than a careful person with your level of training should do at a given emergency. You should have a good reason for every action you take, and you can take those actions as long as they do no harm. For example, you are about to receive training about how to use direct pressure with a pressure dressing to control bleeding from an arm laceration. You should not take this process a step further by improvising a tourniquet, which could potentially starve the limb of oxygen and blood, causing the patient to ultimately lose the arm. Stay within the limits of your training.

Call for Additional Help

The second action you should take on nearly all emergencies is the following: *Call for additional help!* At this point in your training, any wound that requires more than a Bandaid® to control the bleeding should be assessed by someone with more medical training than you. After you are sure of your personal safety, activate EMS by calling for help. When you reach a dispatcher, be prepared to stay on the line for further instructions. Even though you will have some initial first aid training by the end of this chapter, many dispatch centers have certified Emergency Medical Dispatchers on duty who can give you more in-depth instructions for the situation.

Once you have begun treatment, it is your responsibility to stay with the patient until you are relieved by another medical provider with an equal or higher level of training. To do otherwise could be interpreted as **abandonment,** for which you can be held liable unless leaving the patient is the only way you can activate EMS.

abandonment   Failing to stay with a patient and/or to continue delivering care until relieved by another medical provider with the appropriate level of training.

FIGURE 2-3   Practicing basic body substance isolation is not only required of emergency responders, it is also plain common sense.

Infection Control and Body Substance Isolation

Before we discuss bleeding control and CPR, we should spend a little more time on your personal safety and health (Figure 2-3). Since the 1980s, the fire and rescue community has been aware of the spread of AIDS (acquired immune deficiency syndrome) and HIV (human immunodeficiency virus) in the general population. There is probably a greater threat of infection by tuberculosis, hepatitis, and many other diseases. For example, **hepatitis C** can live within a dried clot of blood for as long as seven days. In addition, **tuberculosis** can be transmitted with a simple cough. These biological threats have resulted in regulations requiring proper awareness, isolation control, and protective measures. For this reason, all emergency responders are required to have training in **body substance isolation (BSI)** practices.

The most effective, and therefore the most important, step you can take to protect yourself from communicable disease is proper **handwashing;** this step also helps to prevent spreading germs. Washing your hands before and after contact with any patient, even if you are wearing gloves, and frequent hand-washing throughout the day are vital habits to have. Properly washing your hands involves removing all jewelry, vigorously rubbing your hands together under warm water with soap, and taking care to wash the palms and backs of your hands, between your fingers, and your wrists. After washing, rinse your hands with your fingers pointing downward so that the germs flow off and away with the soap. Take care to avoid touching any part of the sink area with your clean hands, using a paper towel to turn off the faucet if necessary.

▨▨▨ KEY WORDS ▨▨▨

acquired immune deficiency syndrome (AIDS) A viral disease that attacks the body's immune system. HIV, the virus that causes AIDS, is commonly spread by direct contact with the body fluids of the infected person.

human immunodeficiency virus (HIV) An immune deficiency disease that often is followed by AIDS.

body substance isolation (BSI) Procedures and practices used by rescue and fire personnel to protect themselves from exposure to diseases spread by direct contact with body substances.

Level I

Review It!

Go to the DVD, navigate to Chapter 2, and select *Handwashing*.

Practice It!

Proper Handwashing

Take a few minutes to practice the steps for properly washing your hands:

1. Remove all your jewelry (Figure 2-4).

FIGURE 2-4

2. Wash your palms, the backs of your hands, between your fingers, and your wrists with warm water and soap for at least a minute. Rub them vigorously (Figure 2-5).

FIGURE 2-5

3. Dry your hands and use a paper towel to shut off the faucet, taking care not to touch any part of the sink with your bare hands (Figure 2-6).

FIGURE 2-6

Infection Control Programs

When you respond as a firefighter, even if you are not trained as an emergency medical provider, you will eventually encounter the body fluids and airborne pathogens that contribute to the spread of infectious disease. You should be aware of the threats these diseases pose to you, how to protect yourself from them by using proper isolation protection, and how to effectively clean clothing that may have been in contact with body substances.

Your department should have an ongoing infection control program to address these issues. Requirements for an infection control program are defined in NFPA 1500, the Standard on Occupational Safety and Health, and are required by the Code of Federal Regulations (29 CFR 1910.1030). These requirements cover the following topics:

- Utilization of personal protective equipment
- Procedures and guidelines for infection control on the job
- Proper methods for disposing of contaminated items and medical waste materials
- How to clean and decontaminate exposures to yourself as well as to your equipment and clothing
- What to do if you have been exposed to infectious agents
- Medical considerations
- Immunization requirements

An awareness program addresses the many diseases, apart from the ones already mentioned, that can be spread by and contracted from contaminated biological exposure. It provides instruction in how to use universal precautions and the decontamination facilities in the fire station, as well as the proper notification practices to document your exposure.

Body Substance Isolation

Several types of contaminated materials provide avenues of disease exposure, including:

- Blood
- Airborne secretions (cough and sneeze)
- Body substances
- Human feces
- Body fluids
- Food
- Direct contact
- Used needles

Personal protective equipment (PPE) for infectious disease isolation includes items found in a

TABLE 2-1 Contents of a Typical Body Substance Isolation (BSI) Kit

- Splash-resistant eyewear
- Face protection devices
- Fluid-resistant garments
- Patient isolation garments, bags
- Sleeve protectors, shoe covers
- Emergency medical gloves
- Sharps container
- Contaminated wastes container

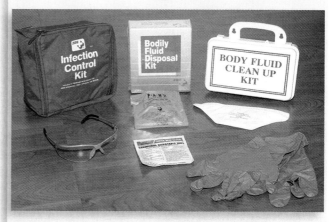

FIGURE 2-7

typical body substance isolation kit (Table 2-1 and Figure 2-7).

KEY WORD

personal protective equipment (PPE), *medical* Specially designed clothing and protective equipment that provides overall body protection. It includes head, eye, hand, foot, and respiratory protection. PPE is approved for the hazard that a firefighter or rescuer can expect to encounter in a particular working environment.

Universal Precautions

When you are dealing with or are exposed to body substances, it may be difficult to determine which material can be a potential risk to you. For this reason, we take **universal precautions** when potentially exposed to body substances. These precautions include wearing eye protection (splash-resistant eyewear), hand protection, (approved, nonlatex, disposable

FIGURE 2-8 Always place disposable medical garments and gloves as well as any medical and biological waste in an approved biological waste container.

medical gloves), and other body protection (such as a splash-resistant gown) as needed.

After dealing with an emergency involving a potential infectious exposure, it is very important to properly dispose of protective gloves and garments. These items, along with any disposable medical waste (such as used dressings and bandages), should be placed in approved biological waste containers and bags for proper disposal. The containers are marked with a biological waste emblem. The waste bags are red with a **biological waste emblem** (Figure 2-8).

Nondisposable items should be properly cleaned and disinfected at a cleaning and disinfecting wash area approved by the fire station. This area has approved cleaning gloves, detergent disinfecting soap, and an antiviral solution. All items must be thoroughly washed and dried before placing them back into service.

When clothes and fire gear are exposed to bloodborne pathogens, they should be washed as soon as possible. This should be done by the fire department.

Safety Tip!

It is not recommended that firefighters take their exposed clothing and gear home to wash it in their home washing machines because home washing machines do not reach the high temperature necessary to do the job.

If you believe you have been directly exposed to an infectious disease, your department has a procedure to report and document the exposure. This procedure includes the proper way to document the exposure, who to direct your report to, and additional actions to be taken.

There are also several immunizations that can be taken to help reduce risks of infectious disease. Check the immunization requirements of your department. You may have already been immunized as part of your qualification for recruitment by the department.

■■■ KEY WORD ■■■

universal precautions Infection control practices, such as using eye and face protection, disposable gloves, and disposable outer garments, that can protect individuals from diseases that may be transmitted through blood and other body fluids.

The ABCs of First Aid

Life-threatening injuries or conditions almost always involve a person's airway, breathing, and/or blood circulation. We refer to this as the ABCs of emergency care: **A**irway, **B**reathing, and **C**irculation. Assessing a patient's ABCs allows you to know if there is an immediate danger to life. If the patient is talking, then you can properly assume that the patient has an open airway and is breathing and his blood is circulating. If you see obvious bleeding, then the patient's circulation will eventually become compromised, so that would be your first priority of care.

Airway Management Techniques

If you approach a patient who is sitting upright, is unable to speak, and is obviously not breathing, then you could surmise that the patient is probably not able to breathe because his airway is obstructed—possibly by a foreign body, which is often the case with a patient who is choking. In this case, your obvious priority is to open the patient's airway by using **abdominal thrusts.**

■■■ KEY WORD ■■■

abdominal thrusts An emergency maneuver used to clear an obstructed airway.

Review It!

Go to the DVD, navigate to Chapter 2, and select *Abdominal Thrusts.*

Practice It!

Abdominal Thrusts

Use the following steps when performing abdominal thrusts:

1. Take proper BSI precautions and activate EMS.
2. Determine if the patient is choking and, if possible, obtain consent to treat him or her (Figure 2-9).

FIGURE 2-9

3. Stand behind the patient, wrapping your arms around the patient's waist while making a fist with one hand (Figure 2-10).

FIGURE 2-10

4. Grasp your fist with your other hand and place it into the patient's abdomen above the navel while avoiding the bottom of the patient's breastbone (Figure 2-11).

FIGURE 2-11

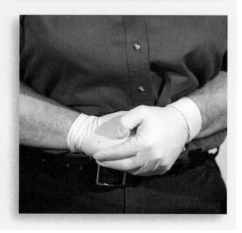

5. Thrust your fist inward and upward quickly and as many times as needed to expel the foreign body from the patient's airway (Figure 2-12).

FIGURE 2-12

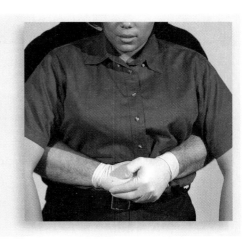

Upper Airway Management

Probably the object that most commonly occludes an unconscious person's airway is the tongue. When a person becomes unconscious, the muscles relax and the tongue can fall backward into the throat, occluding the airway (Figure 2-13).

If the patient is unconscious, check for the presence of spontaneous breathing by watching the patient's chest for movement and by listening closely for sounds of air passing through his nose and mouth. If the patient is not breathing, reposition his airway using either a head tilt–chin lift or a jaw-thrust maneuver. The head tilt–chin lift maneuver is very simple to accomplish; however, it involves manipulating the patient's head and neck a bit (Figure 2-14). Therefore, this maneuver is not recommended if the patient has been injured. It should also not be used if the patient has fallen in such a way as to potentially cause a neck injury or if there is trauma to the oral area. In these cases, a jaw-thrust maneuver should be used.

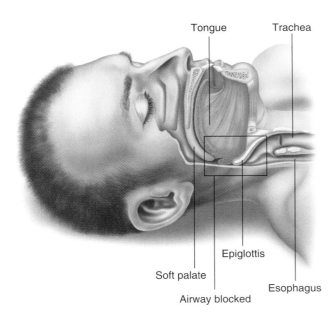

FIGURE 2-13 Airway blocked by tongue.

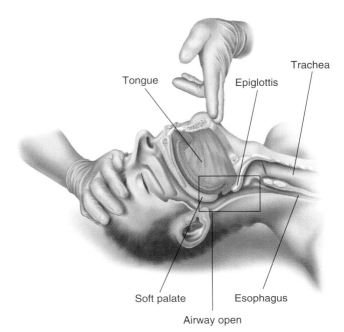

FIGURE 2-14 Head tilt-chin lift maneuver opens the patient's airway.

Review It!

Go to the DVD, navigate to Chapter 2, and select *Head Tilt–Chin Lift Maneuver.*

Practice It!

Head Tilt–Chin Lift Maneuver

Use the following steps when performing the head tilt–chin lift maneuver:

1. Take proper BSI precautions and activate EMS (Figure 2-15).

FIGURE 2-15

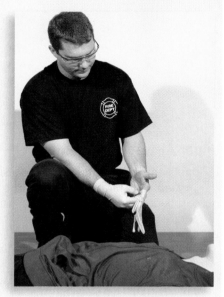

2. Place the patient on his back and kneel beside his head (Figure 2-16).

FIGURE 2-16

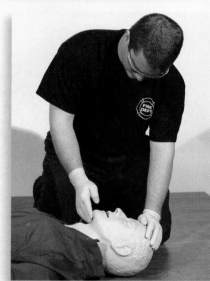

3. Place one hand on the patient's forehead and the other below the patient's chin. Now gently lift the chin and tilt the patient's head back (Figure 2-17).

FIGURE 2-17

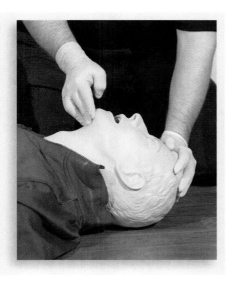

 **Review It!**

Go to the DVD, navigate to Chapter 2, and select *Jaw-Thrust Maneuver.*

Practice It!

Jaw-Thrust Maneuver

Use the following steps when performing the jaw-thrust maneuver:

1. Take proper BSI precautions and activate EMS (Figure 2-18).

FIGURE 2-18

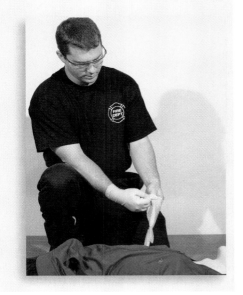

—Continued

2. Place the patient on his back and kneel above the patient's head (Figure 2-19).

FIGURE 2-19

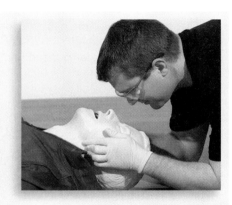

3. Place a hand on either side of the patient's head, with your thumb resting on the patient's cheekbones and your fingers underneath the patient's lower jaw. Your fourth and little finger of each hand should be behind the angled part of the patient's lower jaw, with the rest of your hand above the angle of the jaw (Figure 2-20).

FIGURE 2-20

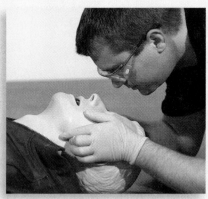

4. Thrust the patient's lower jaw forward with your fingers while using your thumbs for leverage (Figure 2-21).

FIGURE 2-21

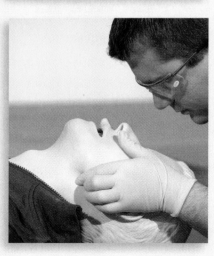

Once you have ensured that the patient's airway is open, you should check to see if he has started breathing on his own. Then assess the patient's pulse. If the patient is breathing and has a pulse, and he is not a victim of a traumatic injury, place him on his left side so that secretions can drain naturally from his mouth, thus helping to avoid further choking. This position is called the **recovery position.**

KEY WORD

recovery position Positioning a patient on his left side so that secretions can drain naturally from his mouth, thus helping to avoid further choking.

Go to the DVD, navigate to Chapter 2, and select *Pulse Check.*

➡ **Practice It!**

Pulse Check

Use the following steps when performing a pulse check:

1. Place two fingers on the patient's "Adam's apple" and slide them downward to find your landmark. Do not use your thumb (Figure 2-22).

FIGURE 2-22

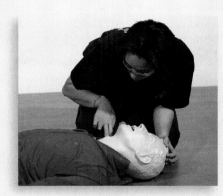

2. Apply gentle pressure until you feel the patient's pulse (Figure 2-23). Do not press too hard as this can occlude the pulse.

FIGURE 2-23

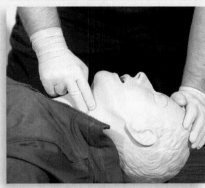

CPR

Cardiopulmonary resuscitation (CPR) is the foundation of emergency lifesaving skills. Virtually everyone should have some sort of CPR training. Opening the patient's airway (**A**irway), providing rescue breathing (**B**reathing), and applying chest compressions to force the patient's blood to circulate (**C**irculate) are vital for a cardiac arrest victim's chance of survival. CPR is a skill that requires certification, and the guidelines for CPR are updated frequently; therefore, detailed CPR guidelines are not provided in this text.

Airway

The fundamentals of providing adult CPR include the following: opening the airway, activating EMS, assessing for breathing, providing rescue breaths, checking a pulse, and providing chest compressions. We have already discussed the first steps: checking the patient's airway, assessing for breathing, and taking a pulse. Next we will practice the sequence by adding rescue breathing and chest compressions to the cycle. If your fire department does not provide CPR certification classes, you can contact the

American Heart Association or the American Red Cross for information on where you can obtain this certification.

KEY WORDS

American Heart Association An organization that provides certification and training for heart-related prehospital care such as CPR.

American Red Cross An organization that develops and provides certification of various levels of first aid training and CPR.

FIGURE 2-24 Pocket masks allow you to use the air in your own lungs to perform rescue breathing for the patient while providing protection for you.

Breathing

A pocket mask should be part of your first aid kit. Pocket masks come in two basic styles—the full face mask, which is rigid, and the smaller, folding mask that can fit in a small pouch on your keychain. Either type provides a barrier against body fluids, and mouth-to-mask ventilation is a better avenue for providing breaths than mouth-to-mouth breathing. While it isn't absolutely essential that you have a pocket mask for rescue breathing, the risks make it an essential element of a well-stocked BSI kit. If you do supply breaths mouth-to-mouth, you will need to follow appropriate exposure notifications, as previously discussed in this chapter.

When you first encounter an unconscious patient, you should perform three quick steps during the initial moments: (1) assess for scene safety, (2) don your BSI equipment (gloves and protective eyewear), and (3) activate EMS by instructing someone to call 911. The next steps you take involve establishing unresponsiveness in the patient, assessing the patient's need for CPR, and providing the necessary care. Before we put it into a full sequence, let's talk a little about rescue breathing and chest compressions.

Rescue breathing occurs when you literally provide air to the patient by blowing into the patient's mouth to fill the lungs. Equipped EMRs, EMTs, AEMTs, and Paramedics have very specific tools to do just this. However, if you are alone when you encounter the patient, you will only have a pocket mask,

so you will have to rely on the air in your lungs to provide the rescue breaths. Seal the patient's nose and mouth with the pocket mask (Figure 2-24). If you are using the folding type, pinch off the patient's nose as you open the airway with either the head tilt–chin lift or jaw-thrust method. Seal the mask's breathing tube with your mouth and deliver slow, purposeful breaths, watching for the patient's chest to rise. If it doesn't rise, reposition the patient's airway and try again.

Circulation

Chest compressions circulate the blood when you push down on the patient's breastbone (called the *sternum*), thus compressing the heart and lungs. The key to proper chest compressions is proper hand placement on the patient's chest. Place the heel of one hand squarely on the center of the patient's breastbone, about an inch or so above the bottom of the sternum. The object is to avoid pressing down on the lower tip of the breastbone as this can injure the patient and will also diminish the effectiveness of your compressions. Each compression should be 1½ to 2 inches deep on an average-size adult. Compressions should occur at a rate of approximately 100 per minute, stopping every 30 compressions to deliver 2 rescue breaths.

 Review It!

Go to the DVD, navigate to Chapter 2, and select *CPR Fundamentals.*

Practice It!

CPR Fundamentals

The following steps should be used when performing the fundamentals of CPR:

1. Assess the scene, take proper BSI precautions, and activate EMS (Figure 2-25).

FIGURE 2-25

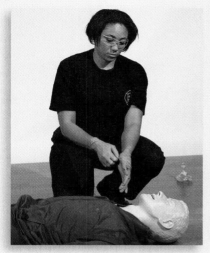

2. Open the airway (Figure 2-26).

FIGURE 2-26

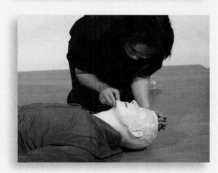

3. Assess breathing—look, listen, and feel (Figure 2-27).

FIGURE 2-27

4. If the patient is breathing, place him in the recovery position (Figure 2-28).

FIGURE 2-28

—Continued

Level I

The ABCs of First Aid   **35**

5. If the patient is not breathing, give 2 rescue breaths at 1 second per breath (Figure 2-29).

FIGURE 2-29

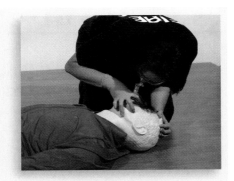

6. Assess for a pulse, taking no more than 10 seconds (Figure 2-30).

FIGURE 2-30

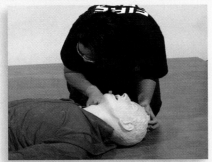

7. If there is no pulse, give 30 chest compressions (Figure 2-31).

FIGURE 2-31

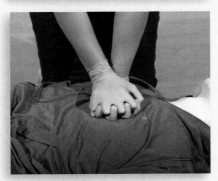

8. Open the patient's airway and give 2 rescue breaths (Figure 2-32). Repeat this cycle of breaths and compressions.

FIGURE 2-32

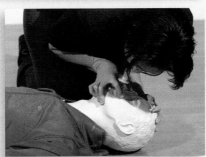

9. Assess for a pulse and breathing (Figure 2-33). Repeat the cycles until you are relieved by another rescuer, or an AED or EMS arrives.

FIGURE 2-33

10. If the patient recovers, place him in the recovery position (Figure 2-34).

FIGURE 2-34

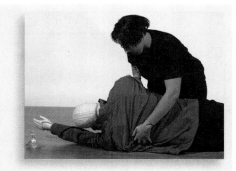

11. If the patient's circulation is present but the patient is not breathing, continue rescue breathing, delivering 1 breath every 5 to 6 seconds, and reassess the circulation every 2 minutes (Figure 2-35).

FIGURE 2-35

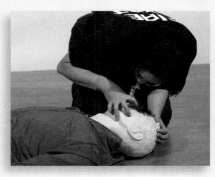

Automatic External Defibrillators (AEDs)

In addition to CPR, early defibrillation is recommended as a vital part of the initial treatment for a person in cardiac arrest. **Automatic external defibrillators (AEDs)** are becoming commonplace in government buildings, in shopping malls, and on passenger aircraft, and they are carried by many Emergency Medical Responders. AEDs are easy to learn and simple to use. They should be a part of your CPR certification training (Figure 2-36).

Automatic external defibrillators are just that—automatic. They are designed to give verbal instructions about their use, assess the patient's electrical heart activity, and automatically deliver a cardiac shock (defibrillation) only when necessary. An AED will not deliver a shock to someone who shouldn't be shocked. Early defibrillation is now viewed as being just as important as early CPR to the patient's chance of survival.

The key to using an AED is to properly place the sticky pads on the patient's chest and then ensure that no one is touching the patient when you have the machine assess the patient and deliver the shock. When you apply the pads, align them as indicated in the drawings on the pad's wrapper. Take the time to press them firmly against the patient's skin, making sure that the gel inside the pad makes good contact with the skin. AEDs that you will encounter in the field will have printed placement directions somewhere on the inside cover and will also provide additional verbal instructions with use.

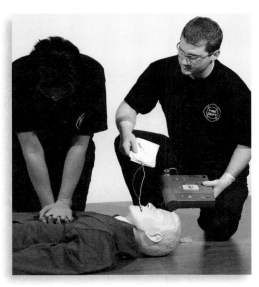

FIGURE 2-36 Automatic external defibrillators (AEDs) are becoming more common in public buildings. Your CPR training should include AED application.

▰▰▰ KEY WORD ▰▰▰

automatic external defibrillators (AEDs) Devices that are located in many types of public access areas and provide defibrillation (cardiac shock) in case of sudden heart attack with a loss of breathing and pulse.

Review It!

Go to the DVD, navigate to Chapter 2, and select *Automatic External Defibrillation*.

Practice It!

Automatic External Defibrillation

The steps below should be used to perform automatic external defibrillations. *Note:* This sequence begins with BSI in place.

1. Continue CPR while you turn on the AED and attach the AED pads (Figure 2-37).

FIGURE 2-37

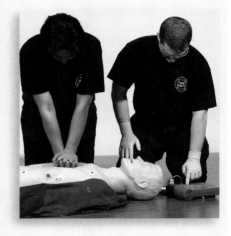

2. Direct the rescuer to stop CPR and ensure that everyone is clear of the patient (Figure 2-38).

FIGURE 2-38

3. Initiate analysis of the patient by pushing the *analyze* button (Figure 2-39). If the AED does not detect a shockable rhythm, resume CPR for 5 cycles and check again. Continue until ALS providers take over or the victim starts to move.

FIGURE 2-39

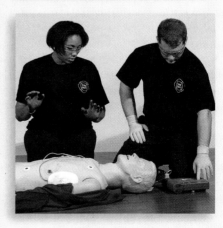

4. Deliver a shock (push the *shock* button) as indicated by the machine (Figure 2-40).

FIGURE 2-40

5. Assess for a pulse and direct the resumption of CPR if necessary (Figure 2-41).

FIGURE 2-41

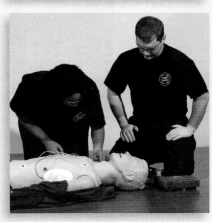

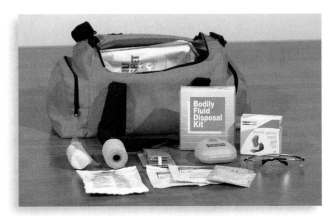

FIGURE 2-42   A simple first aid kit.

First Aid Supplies

An essential part of first aid is having the necessary supplies. A simple first aid kit should contain the following items (Figure 2-42):

- BSI kit
- Reflective traffic safety vest
- Pocket mask
- Sterile dressings
- Conforming gauze
- Adhesive tape
- Flashlight
- Scissors
- Disposable blankets

Controlling Bleeding

A person can tolerate a minimal amount of blood loss without suffering any significant consequences. However, even a small wound can cause a person to lose a dangerous amount of blood, so small wounds should not be taken lightly. Also, remember to take BSI precautions before you encounter any blood.

Most open bleeding can be controlled with direct pressure. A pressure dressing consists of a sterile dressing and a bandage to hold it in place. Take note of the size and depth of the wound before applying bandages so that you can relay this information to the appropriate medical personnel. To control the bleeding, cover the wound with one or several sterile dressings and apply direct pressure with your gloved hand. These steps should slow or stop the bleeding. Leave the pressure dressing in place once the bleeding has been controlled and wrap it with a gauze bandage. It is important that you don't pull the bandage away from the wound because doing so can pull away any clots that may have formed on the wound, starting the bleeding process again.

Once the pressure dressing is applied, if possible, elevate the wound to help slow the bleeding further. If you need more dressings because blood is soaking through them, apply the new dressings on top of the bandage and add another gauze bandage to hold it in place. Even though the bleeding may have been stopped by the pressure dressing, the patient should seek further medical attention.

Review It!

Go to the DVD, navigate to Chapter 2, and select *Applying a Pressure Dressing.*

Practice It!

Applying a Pressure Dressing

Use the following steps when applying a pressure dressing:

1. Take BSI precautions and activate EMS (Figure 2-43).

FIGURE 2-43

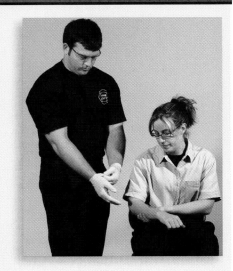

2. Inspect the wound for any loose debris and remove any debris from the surface of the skin (Figure 2-44).

FIGURE 2-44

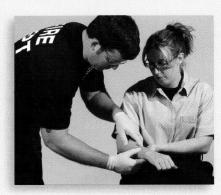

3. Cover the wound with a dry, sterile dressing and apply direct pressure with your hand (Figure 2-45).

FIGURE 2-45

4. Once the bleeding has slowed, wrap the dressing with a stretch gauze bandage (Figure 2-46).

FIGURE 2-46

Review It!

Go to the DVD, navigate to Chapter 2, and select *Bandaging an Impaled Object.*

Practice It!

Bandaging an Impaled Object

Use the following steps when bandaging an impaled object:

1. You may encounter a patient who has an object impaled through his skin (Figure 2-47). This object may be as simple as a nail or as complex as a piece of steel passing through the length of his body. In any case, *DO NOT REMOVE THE IMPALED OBJECT.*

FIGURE 2-47

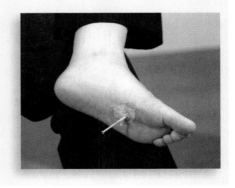

—Continued

2. Take BSI precautions and activate EMS (Figure 2-48).

FIGURE 2-48

3. Take manual control of the impaled object (Figure 2-49). Inspect the wound for any loose debris and remove any debris from the surface of the skin. *DO NOT REMOVE THE IMPALED OBJECT*.

FIGURE 2-49

4. Place sterile dressings around the object and wrap a stretch gauze bandage around the object in a crisscross manner (Figure 2-50). You should secure the foreign object in place while applying pressure to the wound.

FIGURE 2-50

Bruises

Not all bleeding is external. Blunt trauma usually leaves a bruise, as do broken bones and sprains. The treatment for a simple bruise is the application of a cold compress. Chemical cold packs are the most common tool for treating bruises; however, something as simple as a bag of frozen vegetables from the kitchen will work well. Avoid placing the cold compress directly on the skin. A washcloth or sterile gauze dressing provides enough insulation to allow the cold to penetrate while preventing skin irritation from direct skin contact with extreme cold.

Shock Management

Shock occurs when the patient's circulation is compromised. It can be due to a heart condition, blood loss, internal bleeding, a head injury, or other medical causes. Shock requires advanced medical intervention. However, you can take some steps to help the patient between the time that you activate EMS and the arrival of advanced medical care.

You need to recognize the signs of shock. Some of the signs of shock include

- Pale, cool, clammy skin
- A rapid, weak pulse
- A hollow or sunken appearance to the eyes
- Shallow breathing
- Nausea, vomiting
- Dizziness and/or a diminished level of consciousness
- Unexplained or excessive thirst

Review It!

Go to the DVD, navigate to Chapter 2, and select *Shock Position.*

Practice It!

The Shock Position

Use the following steps to place patients in the shock position:

1. The best position for most shock victims is on their back. If the cause of a patient's injury could include a possible injury to the neck, it is important that you keep the patient's head and neck in position.

2. Ensure the ABCs and elevate the patient's feet about a foot off the ground if possible (Figure 2-51). Obviously, if the patient has a hip or lower leg injury, you should not elevate the patient's feet.

FIGURE 2-51

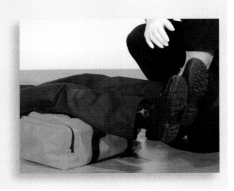

Review It!

Go to the DVD, navigate to Chapter 2, and select *Recovery Position.*

Practice It!

The Recovery Position

If the patient is vomiting or is about to vomit, the best position is on her side so that no vomit falls back into the airway, causing her to choke. Use the following steps to place patients in the recovery position:

1. Place the patient on her left side if possible to help prevent vomiting. This is called the recovery position (Figure 2-52).

FIGURE 2-52

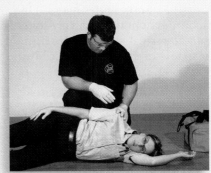

2. Maintain the patient's body temperature as much as possible until help arrives (Figure 2-53). Do not give the patient anything to eat or drink.

FIGURE 2-53

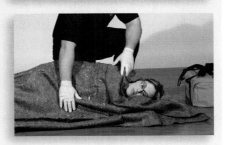

Level I

Burns

When you are on an emergency scene in which someone has a burn injury, you will hear various terminology. This terminology relates to the cause or type of burn, the extent or size of the burn area, and the severity of the burn damage to the skin.

Types of Burns

People can be burned in many different ways (Figure 2-54). They can be exposed to open flame, hot objects, or radiant heat from the sun or fire. These cause thermal burns. Examples of thermal burns include severe sunburn, burns to extremities from a flash fire, and burns to the hands from touching a hot object like a stovetop burner.

People can also receive burn damage to their respiratory tract from inhaling hot smoke or even chemical fumes. This is a serious condition, and patients with respiratory burns need to be transported rapidly to an emergency medical trauma care facility.

Individuals exposed to acid- or alkaline-based substances can sustain a chemical burn. An example of this type burn is a worker in a chemical processing plant who accidentally gets an acid product on his skin.

People can also receive burn injuries from electrical shock. Examples include an electrical utility company worker who touches a high-voltage electrical line and an individual who is struck by lightning. Smaller-voltage exposures can also cause minor burns to hands and fingers. One problem you may encounter when assessing someone who is burned from electrical shock is the difficulty in determining the extent of the burn. These burns might cause only a

small damaged area on the skin but extensive damage to internal tissues and organs.

The Extent and Severity of Burns

The size of the burn is one of the determining factors for the extent of the burn injury. The larger the area of the body and the more skin damaged, the more severe the injury. The severity of burn injuries is also measured by the depth of the damage. Generally speaking, the deeper the burn damage, the higher the degree of injury.

Superficial burns are sunburn-like injuries. The damage is only to top layers of skin and will usually heal after a week (Figure 2-55).

Partial-thickness burns are accompanied by blistering of the burn area. These burns are deeper injuries of the skin and may take a few weeks to heal (Figure 2-56).

Full-thickness burns extend deeply into the skin and create damage to tissues below the skin. These burns require extended care. In many cases, full-thickness burns that cover a large percentage of the body can eventually result in the patient's death (Figure 2-57).

First Aid for Burns

Burn injuries present their own peculiar set of circumstances and treatments. The best first aid treatment is

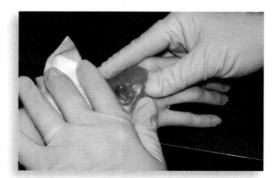

FIGURE 2-54 People can be burned in many different ways, including from thermal, chemical, and electrical sources.

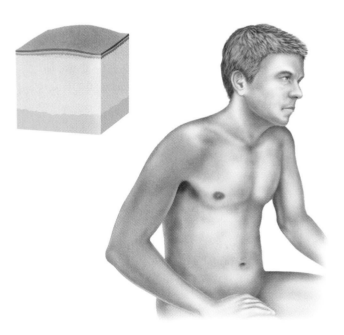

FIGURE 2-55 A superficial burn.

44   Chapter 2   Basic First Aid and CPR

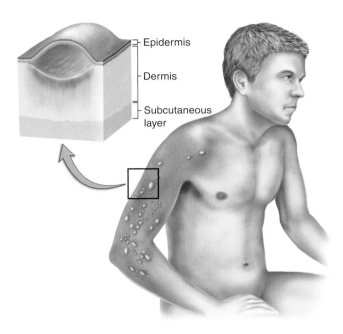

FIGURE 2-56 A partial-thickness burn.

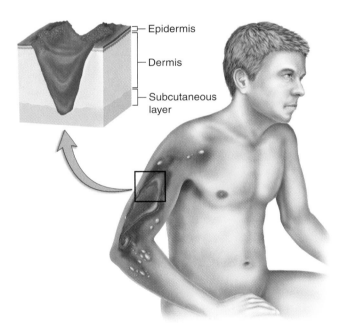

FIGURE 2-57 A full-thickness burn.

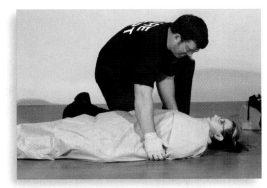

FIGURE 2-58 Burn blankets provide the best patient cover for burn patients.

simply cooling the area with water and covering the burn site with a dry, clean dressing with little or no bandaging. You should also keep the patient warm with a light, clean blanket (burn blankets provide the best patient cover) (Figure 2-58).

Care should be taken not to break any blisters. Also, never apply ointments or fluids except water to a burn injury.

Burn patients should be treated for shock and transported to an emergency trauma care facility.

Do It!

Advancing Your First Aid Skills

In this chapter, "Basic First Aid and CPR," you have learned many skills and techniques for rendering effective first aid. In your career as a firefighter, you can participate in much more in-depth training for all of the topics presented here. Providing some level of prehospital care is becoming more common for fire services in the United States, especially as they increase their responsiveness to their communities. We strongly suggest that you continue your education and training in EMS through advanced study.

Prove It

Knowledge Assessment

Signed Documentation Tear-Out Sheet

Exterior Operations Level Firefighter—Chapter 2

Name: _____

Fill out the ten-question quiz below, the Knowledge Assessment Sheet, by circling the correct answer for each question. When finished, sign it and give to your instructor/Company Officer for his or her signature. Turn in this Knowledge Assessment Sheet to the proper person as part of the documentation that you have completed your training for this chapter.

1. Your first responsibility when approaching an injured person on an emergency scene is
   a. patient safety.
   b. your safety.
   c. controlling any bleeding.
   d. obtaining consent.

2. Which of the following terms applies to an injured minor whose parent or guardian is not present?
   a. *Nonconsenting*
   b. *Ineligible*
   c. *Implied consent*
   d. *Too risky*

3. Wearing splash-resistant eyewear, approved disposable medical gloves, and additional body protection when needed is an example of
   a. universal precautions.
   b. advanced first aid preparation.
   c. hazardous materials protection.
   d. excessive protection.

4. The *C* in the *ABCs of first aid* stands for
   a. cover.
   b. cancer.
   c. circulation.
   d. caution.

5. When performing abdominal thrusts, the breastbone is compressed by the fist.
   a. True
   b. False

6. If a person has fallen off a ladder and is not breathing, which maneuver should be used to open the airway?
   a. Head tilt
   b. Nose thrust
   c. Chin lift
   d. Jaw thrust

7. To control bleeding, place sterile dressings over the wound and
  a. call for help.
  b. apply direct pressure with your hand.
  c. loosely tape them in place.
  d. go for help.

8. Excessive bleeding can cause a person to go into shock.
  a. True
  b. False

9. When positioning a person in shock, if she is about to vomit, the patient should be placed _____.
  a. on her left side
  b. on her back
  c. on her stomach
  d. sitting upright in a chair

10. A burn patient with blistering over the burn site would have which of the following types of burn?
  a. Superficial
  b. Full thickness
  c. Partial thickness
  d. Shallow

Student Signature and Date _____   Instructor/Company Officer Signature and Date _____

Prove It

Skills Assessment
Signed Documentation Tear-Out Sheet
Exterior Operations Level Firefighter—Chapter 2

Name: _____

Fill out the Skills Assessment Sheet below. Have your instructor/Company Officer check off and initial each skill you demonstrate. When finished, sign it and give to your instructor/Company Officer for his or her signature. Turn in this Skills Assessment Sheet to the proper person as part of the documentation that you have completed your training for this chapter.

Skill	Completed	Initials
1. Demonstrate proper adherence to universal precautions, donning body substance isolation protection, and handwashing.	———	———
2. Describe the procedure for reporting body substance exposure.	———	———
3. Demonstrate abdominal thrusts to a standing patient.	———	———
4. Demonstrate the head–lift maneuver.	———	———
5. Demonstrate the jaw-thrust maneuver.	———	———
6. Demonstrate CPR.	———	———
7. Demonstrate AED operation.	———	———
8. Demonstrate how to control bleeding with a pressure dressing.	———	———
9. Demonstrate how to hold a dressing in place when applying a bandage to the arms and legs.	———	———
10. Demonstrate how to dress and bandage a head laceration.	———	———
11. Demonstrate how to dress and bandage a neck laceration.	———	———
12. Demonstrate how to apply a dressing and bandage to a wound involving an impaled object.	———	———
13. Demonstrate how to move a person with a leg wound into the shock position.	———	———
14. Demonstrate how to treat a burn injury to an extremity.	———	———

Student Signature and Date _____   Instructor/Company Officer Signature and Date _____

3

Protective Equipment

What You Will Learn in This Chapter

In this chapter you will learn how to use and care for the most important gear you will use—your personal protective equipment. This equipment includes protective clothing, a self-contained breathing apparatus, and a personal alert device that electronically signals to others that you are in trouble. You will also learn more about an important safety component of incident management that was introduced in Chapter 1: the personnel accountability system.

What You Will Be Able to Do

After reading this chapter and practicing the skills in a classroom setting, you will be able to

1. Describe the components of personal protective clothing used for structural firefighting.
2. Describe the components of an entire personal protective equipment ensemble used for structural firefighting.
3. Properly don and wear all of your personal protective clothing.
4. Describe the procedures for the care and cleaning of your personal protective clothing.
5. Describe the components of a self-contained breathing apparatus (SCBA).
6. Demonstrate the proper way to check and assemble an SCBA.
7. Properly don an SCBA from the seat-rack position.
8. Properly don an SCBA from the ground using the coat method.
9. Properly don an SCBA from the ground using the over-the-head method.
10. Properly check and employ a personal alert safety system (PASS) in both automatic mode and manual mode.
11. Report to your immediate supervisor or the Personnel Accountability Officer when responding to an emergency.

Safety Lesson: A NIOSH Report

Personal Protective Clothing Is Essential!

On August 8, 1999, three volunteer firefighters were burned, one critically, while trying to control a fire involving a recreational vehicle (RV) that was parked next to a single-family dwelling. Two volunteer fire departments responded with two engines and a total of five personnel. Engine 1 arrived first, with a driver/operator and no other firefighters on board. The driver/operator deployed a booster line to protect the exposed side of the house and then turned his stream to the burning RV in an attempt to control the fire. Engine 2 arrived with three personnel, and a fourth volunteer arrived in his personal vehicle.

As the firefighters of Engine 2 were pulling hose from their truck, the RV's 50-gallon gasoline tank ruptured and its burning fuel spilled down the inclined driveway toward the firefighters of Engine 2. The intense fire lasted only about 15 seconds; however, it engulfed the firefighters as it ran down the sloped driveway toward them. Although at least two of the firefighters had placed their protective clothing in the truck prior to their response, none of the firefighters on the scene were wearing their personal protective clothing or breathing apparatus during the incident. Of the three who were burned, the critically injured firefighter died 8 days later from the full-thickness burns he received over 96% of his body—he had been totally engulfed in fire. The driver/operator of Engine 2 saw the flames coming toward the engine and was forced to flee. He received partial-thickness burns on his back. The other firefighter from Engine 2 received partial-thickness burns to his arms and legs as he attempted to outrun the flames.

Follow-Up

NIOSH Report #F99-34

Among other recommendations, the NIOSH investigative report concluded the following:

- Fire departments should develop and implement standard operating procedures (SOPs) that
  - Consider the available firefighting equipment, staffing, and resources within a community;
  - Outline how an incident management system will be best implemented within the specific community, given the anticipated staffing and equipment response levels;
  - Outline the proper positioning of fire apparatus on the fire scene; and
  - Outline the proper selection and use of hose line(s) for mounting an attack to control a fire.
- Fire departments should develop and implement a policy requiring the use of personal protective equipment and protective clothing.
- States and municipalities should provide adequate financial support and administrative leadership for fire departments, thus ensuring that adequate training and equipment are provided for firefighters.

Personal Protective Clothing

One of the first signs to a new firefighter recruit that he or she is really getting into the fire service is getting your firefighting gear. Images of firefighters working at a big fire, with all the excitement that goes along with it, are conjured up as each item is fitted and assigned. It is vitally important that you understand how **personal protective clothing (PPC)** protects you, how to use it properly, and the care you will be required to give it. Although at this point in your training you won't be going inside a burning building, the previous case study should impress upon you the importance of wearing your full protective gear at any hazardous incident.

KEY WORD

personal protective clothing (PPC) Protective clothing worn by firefighters during emergency fire control operations. This ensemble includes protection for the eyes, head, hands, feet, and body.

Types of Protective Clothing

Many types of firefighting protective clothing are available today. Many of these are designed for specific uses. You will probably be issued a standard set of protective clothing for structural firefighting and perhaps another set for wildland firefighting (Figures 3-1 and 3-2). Other specialized sets of gear are required for emergency operations, such as hazardous materials operation (Figure 3-3). In this chapter, we are going to talk about structural firefighting only. You will be trained in the other types of protective clothing as you become qualified by your department to perform other types of emergency operations.

FIGURE 3-1 Protective clothing for structural firefighting.

FIGURE 3-3 Protective clothing for a hazardous materials incident.

FIGURE 3-2 Protective clothing for wildland firefighting.

FIGURE 3-4 A firefighter in typical full personal protective clothing (PPC).

Components of Protective Clothing

Your protective clothing is a combination of several items, each of which must be in place with all the others before maximum protection is established (Figure 3-4). For example, if you do not have your gloves on at a fire, you are not fully protected and you are exposing yourself to injury.

The full set of protective clothing includes the following:

- Firefighter coat and pants
- Boots to protect your feet
- Gloves to protect your hands
- A hood to protect your head from heat
- A firefighter helmet for head protection
- A pull-down protective visor and goggles for eye protection

All of this clothing must pass rigorous tests and certifications. The clothing is very expensive, so it is important that you take care of it.

Protective gear must be comfortable to wear and as easy as possible to work in. Try to use care when being fitted for your gear. Properly fitting gear will significantly increase your protection in high-heat situations.

Coat and Pants

A firefighter's coat and pants are made up of three layers of protection. The first layer, the outer shell, is somewhat flame-retardant. It is not, by any means, flameproof. However, in a flash-fire type incident, it may give you a few seconds to get out of the heat and survive. An important component of the outer shell is the reflective trim, which makes you more visible to others when working in dark conditions.

The second and third layers of protection are in the inner liner, which is a combination of a thermal barrier and a moisture barrier (Figure 3-5). These barriers help protect you from excessive heat and water from the outside. They are also designed to allow your body to release some of the heat that builds up from exertion at the fire. For this reason, it is important that

you keep all the components of your coat and pants together; don't remove the liners.

Boots

Your boots are made of either rubber composite materials or leather. Their soles are resistant to puncture. Nails, the sharp edges of steel, and glass can wreak havoc on unprotected shoes and boots. These boots also have steel toes for added foot protection. The boots are heat resistant as well, and they do not let water in.

Gloves

Your gloves are designed to go with the coat. If your coat has built-in wristlets with a thumbhole, then your gloves do not need wristlets built into them (Figure 3-6). If your coat has no wristlets, then you need gloves that have that protection sewn into the glove (Figure 3-7). This type of glove is specially designed to protect against both heat and puncture while pro-

FIGURE 3-6 Gloves and coat with wristlets for structural firefighting.

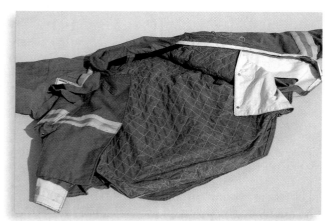

FIGURE 3-5 The inner liner is a combination of a thermal barrier and a moisture barrier that help protect the wearer from excessive heat.

FIGURE 3-7 Gloves and coat without wristlets for structural firefighting.

viding as much dexterity as possible to the hands and fingers.

Hood and Helmet

Your fire hood provides protection to your exposed head and neck (Figure 3-8). It is somewhat flame-resistant.

A firefighter's helmet is uniquely designed. It is impact-resistant to protect the firefighter from falling objects, shield from water, and provide protection from heat. The suspension inside is provided to give you some impact resistance. More importantly, it provides ventilation for heat release from the top of your head. Reflective trim for visibility is a very important part of a firefighter's helmet.

The helmet also features a small, partial hood that is connected to the inner lining of the helmet. It is important that you always pull down this hood when you wear the helmet at a fire emergency to protect your ears and neck.

Your helmet also has a pull-down eye shield. This shield provides superficial eye protection for

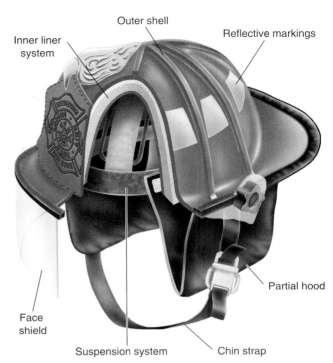

FIGURE 3-10   The components of a structural firefighting helmet.

Labels: Outer shell; Inner liner system; Reflective markings; Partial hood; Face shield; Suspension system; Chin strap

instances in which you are in a hurry, or you are not wearing goggles or the face piece of your **self-contained breathing apparatus (SCBA).** Your eyes can still be exposed to objects flying up from underneath the pull-down eye shield. **The addition of safety-approved goggles or your SCBA face piece greatly enhances the eye protection you receive from the pull-down eye shield on your helmet (Figure 3-9).**

A helmet has an inner liner, a suspension system, a partial hood, a chin strap, and eye shields. It is important that all of these components are in good working order and are used at all structural fires (Figure 3-10).

▩ KEY WORD ▩

self-contained breathing apparatus (SCBA) Personal protective equipment worn by firefighters to provide respiratory protection in an atmosphere that is hazardous to life.

Other Protective Gear

Other protective gear, such as an SCBA and a personal alarm system, are additional devices that allow a firefighter to be completely protected. This additional gear is referred to as complete personal protective equipment and will be discussed in more detail later in this chapter.

FIGURE 3-8   The firefighter's hood provides protection to the head and neck.

FIGURE 3-9   A typical structural firefighting helmet.

Donning Protective Clothing

Personal protective clothing is your lifeline at any emergency. Your fire department and Company Officer have standard guidelines for you to follow that advise you when to don the protective clothing and how much protective clothing will be necessary. At times, full protection is needed; at other times, you can dress down. Your Company Officer, the Incident Commander, or a designee will determine when to remove your gear. *When in doubt, keep your gear on.*

Review It!

Go to the DVD, navigate to Chapter 3, and select *Methods of Donning Personal Protective Clothing.*

Practice It!

Methods of Donning Protective Clothing

Most protective clothing for structural firefighting is easy to don and doff (that is, put on and take off). You will quickly become so accustomed to donning and doffing that they will become second nature to you. It is important to develop the correct habits for donning protective clothing so that they become automatic.

1. With the pants folded down around the boots, step into the boots and pull the pants up and into position with the suspenders. Close the front flap and adjust the waist as needed (Figure 3-11).

FIGURE 3-11

2. Put on the hood, pulling it down around your neck (Figure 3-12).

FIGURE 3-12

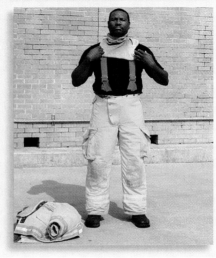

3. Now don the fire coat, fastening the front (Figure 3-13).

FIGURE 3-13

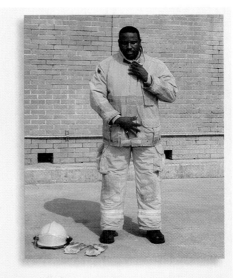

4. Next, pull up the hood so that it covers any exposed skin and place the fire helmet on your head, making sure that the partial hood on the helmet is in position. Attach the chinstrap (Figure 3-14).

FIGURE 3-14

5. Pull down the face shield or put on protective goggles (Figure 3-15).

FIGURE 3-15

—Continued

Level I

6. Pull on the gloves (Figure 3-16).

FIGURE 3-16

The Care and Maintenance of Protective Clothing

Because your protective clothing is so important to your safety and survival, you must know how to care for and maintain your gear. Your department has specific policies regarding this care and maintenance, but there are a few general rules.

Storing Personal Protective Clothing

Store your gear in a dry place that is easy to access yet protects the gear from the weather. Do not store your gear in the apparatus bay where it can collect diesel particulates.

Cleaning Personal Protective Clothing

Fire Service protective clothing should be cleaned a minimum of every 6 months. It is recommended that this cleaning be done professionally or at least in **professional-grade washers** operated by the fire department. Dirt and products of combustion will start to degrade the fire-resistance capabilities of the materials. It is important to wash this gear after every structural fire. Fire gear contaminated with petroleum products should be removed from service immediately and sent for professional cleaning.

This clothing should never be cleaned using chlorine bleach, which degrades the fire-protective qualities of the clothing materials. To prevent cross-contamination after washing the clothes, be sure to operate the washer several times, empty of clothes, to rinse it clean after washing the fire gear.

If the structural-fire clothing has been contaminated with **body substances,** follow recognized cleaning procedures to decontaminate the clothing. If the clothing is contaminated with biological or chemical contaminants, your department may have to dispose of the gear if it cannot be properly decontaminated.

Inspecting Personal Protective Clothing

Inspect all of your protective clothing, including boots, gloves, and helmet, for cleanliness and damage. Your coat and pants should be intact, with no rips, tears, or raveled threads. Reflective trim is very susceptible to tears, burns, and unraveled seams. Do not simply tear off the damaged portion of trim—the trim is an essential part of your safety. Go through the proper channels within your department to have your gear repaired using an approved repair method.

Boots should be watertight and not leaking water. If they leak, they should be repaired or replaced.

Helmets should have an operating chinstrap, be cleaned of debris, and be checked for scrapes and wear. Exposed fiberglass fibers, or exposed wire supports or unraveled threads on a leather helmet, are indicators that the helmet needs to be replaced. Extreme heat damage is indicated by severe color change or even deformation of the face shield or the helmet itself. In all cases, the helmet should be considered for replacement when any of these changes occur.

All of your safety gear is designed to give you maximum use and protection. Proper care and maintenance will ensure that you receive the most protection from your gear. Always follow the manufacturer's recommendations as well as your fire department's guidelines for caring for your protective fire gear.

Self-Contained Breathing Apparatus (SCBA)

Your personal protective clothing is designed to protect your skin. However, to complete your ensemble of **personal protective equipment (PPE),** you must also protect your respiratory system. A self-contained breathing apparatus (SCBA) completes your protective gear. While every component of your PPE is essential, the SCBA is probably the most critical component of the ensemble when you are exposed to toxic smoke, hazardous gasses, and steam.

KEY WORD

personal protective equipment (PPE), *firefighting* The protective equipment firefighters wear when fighting fires, especially in a hazardous atmosphere. This gear includes a complete set of personal protective clothing with the addition of a self-contained breathing apparatus (SCBA) for respiratory protection.

SCBA Systems

An SCBA is the heaviest component of your PPE. The most common type of SCBA used for firefighting is the positive-pressure, open-circuit system. The **open-circuit system** provides clean, dry air from a compressed air cylinder at a pressure that is slightly above that of the surrounding air. The positive pressure of the air inside your mask helps reduce the incidence of toxins entering the facemask area—the pressure is constantly pushing out a small amount of air through any gaps between the mask and your skin, and this prevents toxins from pushing into the mask through those gaps. As you breathe, your exhaled air is exhausted through an exhalation valve on the face piece, which is necessary to prevent you from breathing the carbon dioxide that is present in your exhaled breaths. Because the exhaled air is expelled to the atmosphere and is not contained within the mask, this type of breathing system is called an *open-circuit* system. The system is "open" because the air in the cylinder is consumed or "used up" as you breathe.

KEY WORD

open-circuit system A type of SCBA system that provides clean, dry air from a compressed air cylinder, through a regulator, at a pressure slightly above that of the outside atmosphere. Exhaled air is exhausted through a valve on the face piece.

Who Can Wear an SCBA

Before you don and use an SCBA, you need to take some important steps. First, you must be physically capable of bearing the weight of the gear. **You must pass a physical examination by a physician.** Next, you should undergo a "fit test" in which different sizes of air masks are fitted on your face and checked for leaks by a certified SCBA technician or industrial hygienist. It is recommended that your face be clean shaven because excess facial hair can cause leaks. Finally, you must undergo extensive training on the use of your SCBA before you enter any hazardous atmosphere.

SCBA System Components

The components of an SCBA system are featured in Figure 3-17.

FIGURE 3-17 The components of a self-contained breathing apparatus (SCBA) system.

Cylinders

The air cylinders firefighters use come in different sizes and pressures, depending on the manufacturer and the type of systems purchased by your department. In general, the cylinders are referred to as *30-minute, 45-minute,* and *60-minute* cylinders. Do not let this unofficial rating deceive you into thinking that you can get a full 30 minutes of use out of a "30-minute" cylinder. In reality, a 30-minute cylinder may provide 20 minutes of air, but 15 minutes is the average. The rate at which you use the air in a cylinder depends on several factors, including your physical condition and size, the amount of physical activity you are performing, and the temperature in which you are working.

It is important to note that while a 60-minute cylinder won't provide a full 60 minutes of air, it *will* provide twice as much "working time" as a 30-minute cylinder. The air cylinder has a pressure gauge that indicates the amount of air pressure inside. A remote pressure gauge allows the wearer to check the cylinder pressure while wearing the SCBA. Newer units have a "heads-up display" inside the mask that gives you constant information on the amount of air remaining in the cylinder.

Although the added air supply will allow you to remain in a contaminated atmosphere longer, the extra air capacity that a 45- or 60-minute air cylinder provides should be considered "safety" air. It is not intended to allow you to work longer than you should before stopping to rest in a safe location. Because of the heat buildup and physical toll that firefighting presents, most agencies do not allow firefighters to work much more than 35 minutes in full protective clothing before they rest.

Alarms

An audible, low-air alarm will let you know when you are nearing the end of your available air. Many manufacturers now offer a vibrating and a visual alarm. Just as you might expect, the amount of breathing time you will get out of the system once the low-air alarm sounds depends on the same factors that come into play when determining the work time you will get from a cylinder. Without exception, the most important thing to remember is that when your low-pressure alarm sounds, it is time to leave the hazardous scene. . . . immediately!

 **Safety Tip!**

Proper air management is a must for firefighter safety. Maintain a constant awareness of the remaining air levels in the SCBA, keeping in mind the amount of time it will take you to reach a safe atmosphere. Waiting until a low-pressure alarm activates may be too late.

Regulators

The air contained in the compressed air cylinder is stored at a high pressure. The high-pressure air flows through a high-pressure hose to the regulator, where it is reduced to a usable pressure. On some SCBAs, the regulator connects directly to your facemask. On others, the regulator is on your waist belt and a low-pressure tube delivers the air at the regulated pressure to your facemask. Most regulators have an emergency bypass valve, which is red. As its name indicates, the emergency bypass valve allows high-pressure air to bypass the regulator in case of a failure. By slightly cracking open the emergency bypass valve, you will receive the remaining air in the cylinder at a fairly fast rate. If you ever encounter a reason to use this valve, do so to escape the hazardous area and immediately report the SCBA failure to an officer. You should take steps to ensure that the SCBA is not used again before a qualified technician repairs it.

Straps

The cylinder, high-pressure hose, low-air alarm, and regulator are connected to the backpack, which is fitted with harness straps. The harness has shoulder straps and a waist strap. Whenever you wear an SCBA, it is essential that all of the straps are properly fastened and adjusted.

Checking and Assembling an SCBA

Most fire departments carry their breathing apparatus already assembled and in racks, ready to use, on the fire truck. However, you should be familiar with the simple steps for connecting the air cylinder to the backpack and checking the SCBA to ensure its readiness for use. This check should be performed daily as well as before and after each use.

Go to the DVD, navigate to Chapter 3, and select *SCBA Visual Inspection.*

Practice It!

Visual Inspection of an SCBA

Use the following directions to visually inspect the various components of an SCBA:

1. *Face piece.* Check for cracks or tears in the rubber seal. Look for any debris that may be in the exhalation valve. Look for any loose clamps. Put the mask on and check the exhalation valve by exhaling gently while blocking the breathing tube with your hand (Figure 3-18).

FIGURE 3-18

2. *Regulator.* Check for cleanliness and any signs of external damage. Operate the main-line valve and emergency bypass valve to check for smooth operation (Figure 3-19).

FIGURE 3-19

3. *High-pressure hose.* Look for external damage and check the O-ring on the coupling for damage or deformity (Figure 3-20).

FIGURE 3-20

—Continued

Level I

4. *Harness straps.* Look for excessive wear to the straps and check all stitching for any obvious damage. Make sure that all hardware on the straps is clean and operable (Figure 3-21).

FIGURE 3-21

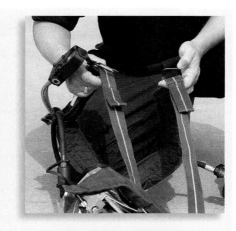

5. *Audible alarm.* Look for any obvious external damage (Figure 3-22).

FIGURE 3-22

6 *Cylinder.* Look for any signs of damage, any gouges, or any abraded areas. Any deformity should be brought to the attention of the Company Officer. Check the pressure gauge and make sure that the cylinder is filled to the appropriate level. To check for accuracy, compare the cylinder gauge to the regulator gauge (Figure 3-23).

FIGURE 3-23

Donning and Doffing an SCBA

There are several acceptable methods for donning and doffing an SCBA, and none is better than any other in most cases. Your main concern should be to put the apparatus on safely and rapidly. The end result should be a properly adjusted and fastened harness assembly.

Review It!

Go to the DVD, navigate to Chapter 3, and select *SCBA: Seat-Rack Donning.*

Practice It!

Seat-Rack Donning of an SCBA

This method of putting on an SCBA requires that you start with it in the seat rack.

1. **Do not take off your seat belt.** Place your arms through the shoulder straps, leaving the straps loose for the moment (Figure 3-24).

FIGURE 3-24

2. Fasten the waist belt, taking care to keep it separate from your seat belt, which should remain fastened any time the truck is in motion (Figure 3-25).

FIGURE 3-25

3. After the truck has come to a full stop and just before exiting the truck, unfasten your seat belt and adjust the shoulder straps to a good fit (Figure 3-26).

FIGURE 3-26

Level I

Go to the DVD, navigate to Chapter 3, and select *SCBA: Coat Method Donning.*

Practice It!

Coat Method Donning of an SCBA

This method of putting on an SCBA requires that you start with it on the ground.

1. Kneel behind the SCBA. Check the SCBA cylinder pressure to make sure the cylinder is full. Make sure that the main line valve and the emergency bypass valves on the regulator are closed. Open the main cylinder valve fully (Figure 3-27). Listen for the low-pressure alarm to sound briefly as the system is charged.

FIGURE 3-27

2. Check both the cylinder pressure gauge and the remote air pressure gauge. Make sure they are within 100 psi of each other. If they are not, do not use the SCBA (Figure 3-28).

FIGURE 3-28

3. Grasp the shoulder strap that is on the same side as the air regulator and lift the pack off the ground, slinging it over your shoulder (Figure 3-29).

FIGURE 3-29

4. Place your other arm through the offside strap. Allow both of your hands to travel down the straps to the adjustment buckles, pulling the backpack snuggly to a comfortable position (Figure 3-30).

FIGURE 3-30

5. Clip the waist strap and adjust it to a snug, comfortable fit (Figure 3-31). At this point, most of the weight of the SCBA should be carried on the waist strap.

FIGURE 3-31

Review It!

Go to the DVD, navigate to Chapter 3, and select *SCBA: Over-the-Head Method.*

Practice It!

Over-the-Head Donning of an SCBA

This method of putting on an SCBA requires that you start with it on the ground.

1. Kneel behind the SCBA. Check the cylinder pressure of the SCBA to make sure it is full. Make sure that the main line valve and the emergency bypass valves are closed on the regulator. Open the main cylinder valve fully (Figure 3-32). Listen for the low-pressure alarm to sound briefly as the system is charged.

FIGURE 3-32

2. Check both the cylinder pressure gauge and the remote air pressure gauge. Make sure they are within 100 psi of each other. If they are not, do not use the SCBA (Figure 3-33).

FIGURE 3-33

—Continued

Level I

3. Reach between the shoulder straps and the backpack, grasping the backpack on each side (Figure 3-34).

FIGURE 3-34

4. Lift the assembly over your head, allowing the SCBA to slide down your back with the shoulder straps falling into place (Figure 3-35). Allow both hands to travel down the straps to the adjustment buckles, pulling the backpack snuggly to a comfortable position (Figure 3-36).

FIGURE 3-35

FIGURE 3-36

5. Clip the waist strap and adjust it to a snug, comfortable fit (Figure 3-37). At this point, most of the weight of the SCBA should be carried on the waist strap.

FIGURE 3-37

Review It!

Go to the DVD, navigate to Chapter 3, and select *SCBA: Donning the Facemask.*

Practice It!

Donning the Facemask

Putting the facemask on is the final step you take before you begin breathing from the system. Use the following steps:

1. It makes no difference whether you put the mask on by placing your chin in first and dragging the straps over your head or whether you use the ball-cap method (Figure 3-38). In the ball-cap method, you hold the straps on the back of your head and drag the mask down over your face (Figure 3-39). The main thing to remember is to have nothing between the rubberized face piece and your skin. The straps should be adjusted so that the mask fits snugly against your face. You should cover all remaining exposed skin once the mask is in place.

FIGURE 3-38

FIGURE 3-39

2. Start with your protective hood pulled down around your neck and your coat collar pulled up. Center the harness on your head and clear away any hair that may be between your head and the mask. Starting with the bottom straps, tighten them two at a time until you create a snug fit (Figure 3-40).

FIGURE 3-40

3. Check the seal by covering the opening in the mask and inhaling gently for 10 seconds. You should not feel any leaks as the mask squeezes to your face (Figure 3-41).

FIGURE 3-41

—Continued

4. Now check the exhalation valve by exhaling gently (Figure 3-42). Don't exhale too hard or you can damage your eardrums.

FIGURE 3-42

5. Now connect to your air supply and inhale to start the airflow (Figure 3-43).

FIGURE 3-43

6. Pull your protective hood up and over the straps to cover any exposed skin (Figure 3-44). Make sure that the hood doesn't cover any part of the lens or the exhalation valve.

FIGURE 3-44

7. Now put your helmet on with the earflaps down and fasten the chinstrap snugly under your chin, taking care that it doesn't pass over the top of the low-pressure hose (if your SCBA is equipped with one) (Figure 3-45).

FIGURE 3-45

8. Now fasten your collar for a final bit of protection (Figure 3-46).

FIGURE 3-46

Practice It!

Breathing Compressed Air

You may feel a bit claustrophobic when you put an SCBA on the first time. Your entire PPE provides you with a protective environment that is new to you. It is not unusual for an inexperienced person to go through an entire 30-minute SCBA cylinder of air in less than 15 minutes.

1. Be aware of your breathing rate while working. You will get more than enough air from a properly functioning SCBA with each breath. However, excitement will cause you to breathe rapidly, thus cutting down your "working time" from the air supply.

2. Practice as often as you can with the SCBA so that you will remain comfortable in your "new environment" (Figure 3-47).

FIGURE 3-47

Returning an SCBA to "Ready-to-Use" Status

Remember: Most emergency equipment is only as good as the last person who used it. In other words, you should return the equipment to a "ready-to-use" status before you put it away. This is especially important with SCBAs. Returning an SCBA to ready-to-use status starts with the way you remove the mask when you are through using the apparatus. Simply grabbing the mask and dragging it over your head will eventually stretch the straps, diminishing their service life. Instead, loosen all the straps before gently removing the mask (Figure 3-48).

Once you have taken off the mask, loosen all the straps fully and clean the mask, following the man-

ufacturer's recommendations for sanitizing it. Make sure to thoroughly dry the mask before placing it back in service. Take care not to get water into a low-pressure air hose. If some water gets into the hose inadvertently, allow the hose to dry thoroughly before you use it again.

Loosen all the straps on the backpack and clean them with mild soap and water, and then allow them to dry. Inspect the straps and place a fresh air cylinder in the backpack. Perform an operational check of the entire SCBA and place it back into service (Figure 3-49).

Do not attempt to fill a compressed air cylinder unless you have received specific training from your

FIGURE 3-48 Make sure to loosen all straps and gently remove the mask to avoid stretching the straps.

FIGURE 3-49 Loosen the harness straps before cleaning the mask with mild soap and water.

Self-Contained Breathing Apparatus (SCBA)   **69**

Level 1

agency in following the fill-station manufacturer's instructions. Compressed air cylinders must be inspected on a regular basis by a technician who is certified to do so. Although it is a very rare event, the failure of a compressed air cylinder usually has catastrophic results and can be deadly, so make sure to follow the manufacturer's guidelines *exactly*.

Personal Alert Safety System (PASS)

It is very easy to become disoriented when working in a smoke-filled environment. A **personal alert safety system (PASS)** is a small electronic device that is designed to detect your movement or your lack of movement. It sounds a very loud alarm if it determines that you have remained stationary for a predetermined length of time. The purpose of this device is to signal to other firefighters that you need help and to give them an audible signal that helps them in locating you. All PASS devices feature two modes of operation: (1) a manual activation mode in which you can activate the alarm when you need help, and (2) an automatic activation mode, which will sound a pre-alert in the form of a short, lower-volume signal to let you know that the PASS device has sensed you aren't moving. The pre-alert signal is designed to help prevent false alarms. The PASS will go into a full alarm mode within seconds of sounding the pre-alert.

There are many different brands and types of PASS devices available. However, the two main differences are in the way you turn on the device. An ordinary PASS must be switched on before you enter a hazardous atmosphere (Figure 3-50). An *integrated* PASS is built into your SCBA and is automatically turned on when you open the air cylinder to use the breathing apparatus (Figure 3-51). Because it is very important to use every safety device available to you when you enter a hazardous atmosphere, it is important to ensure that the PASS is on and working whenever you use an SCBA, regardless of the way it is turned on.

FIGURE 3-50 An ordinary PASS must be switched on before you enter a hazardous atmosphere.

FIGURE 3-51 An integrated PASS is automatically turned on when the air cylinder on the SCBA is opened for use.

 **Review It!**

Go to the DVD, navigate to Chapter 3, and select *Personal Alert Safety System.*

Inspecting a Personal Alert Safety System

Note: The following steps are the general operating procedure for a PASS. Follow all of the manufacturer's directions for operating your particular device.

1. Inspect the outside of the unit for any deformities and for cleanliness (Figure 3-52).

FIGURE 3-52

2. Turn on the device and listen for a signal that indicates that it is armed (Figure 3-53).

FIGURE 3-53

3. Shake the device when you hear the pre-alert to make sure that it returns to a ready state (Figure 3-54).
4. Leave the device motionless. It should sound a pre-alert within 30 seconds.
5. Allow the device to remain motionless until it again sounds a pre-alert signal and then allow it to go into a full alarm mode.

FIGURE 3-54

6. Reset the alarm to a ready state (Figure 3-55). Now check the alarm's manual alert switch for operation.
7. Turn the device off.

FIGURE 3-55

It is extremely important that you turn off the PASS when you are not in a hazardous atmosphere. It is also important for you to control the PASS when training with your SCBA. False alarms can desensitize other firefighters into assuming that someone simply forgot to turn off his or her PASS.

Level I

Reporting to Command

Another item that is essential to every firefighter's safety is a personnel accountability system. In this system, the Incident Commander or a designee accounts for every person as they enter and exit a hazardous area or environment. To keep track of everyone, the Accountability Officer will use some form of a tracking system in which each firefighter reports to his or her Company Officer, who then reports to the Accountability Officer.

Safety Tip!

One of the most important components of the personnel accountability system—and probably the most important to *your* safety—is that you never work alone in a hazardous area. Anyone wearing an SCBA must work as part of a team of at least two people. While it is important that you learn how to "self-rescue," there is often nothing more important to your safety than a partner. SCBA masks limit your visibility, and the protective seal provided by your PPE isolates many of your senses. Therefore, working within a group means that everyone looks out for each other's safety. NEVER WORK ALONE WHEN WEARING AN SCBA!

Practice It!

Personnel Accountability System

The following steps are components of the personnel accountability system:

1. To make this procedure easy to use on the emergency scene, most fire departments assign each firefighter some type of accountability tag (Figure 3-56).

FIGURE 3-56

2. Each individual firefighter's tag is grouped with the rest of the tags from that company to form a "passport" for that company.

3. The passport is then given to the Accountability Officer, who keeps track of the entire company as a group or as individuals, according to their assignments at the emergency scene (Figure 3-57).

FIGURE 3-57

Safety Tip!

While personnel accountability is a very important function of command, the accountability system is only as good as the individual firefighter on the scene. It is your responsibility to give your accountability tag to your Company Officer before you board the fire apparatus in responding to an emergency. If you are a volunteer who arrives on the scene in your personal vehicle, then you should report to the command post, give your accountability tag to the Accountability Officer, and wait for a job assignment. *DO NOT FREE-LANCE!* Even the most seasoned fire veteran must work within the Command system.

Do It!

Be Safe!

In this chapter you learned how to use and care for the most important gear you will use, your personal protective equipment. This gear includes protective clothing, an SCBA, and a personal alert device (the PASS), that electronically signals others when you are in trouble. You also learned an important safety component of incident management, the personnel accountability system. This information is important. Hopefully you have gained important skills in using this protective gear and understand its importance to your overall safety on the fire emergency scene.

Level I

Knowledge Assessment

Signed Documentation Tear-Out Sheet

Exterior Operations Level Firefighter—Chapter 3

Name: _____

Fill out the ten-question quiz below, the Knowledge Assessment Sheet, by circling the correct answer for each question. When finished, sign it and give to your instructor/Company Officer for his or her signature. Turn in this Knowledge Assessment Sheet to the proper person as part of the documentation that you have completed your training for this chapter.

1. A firefighter's protective clothing is made up of several pieces, all of which must be in place for maximum protection.
   a. True
   b. False

2. How many layers of protection are provided in a set of structural firefighting coat and pants?
   a. Two
   b. Four
   c. Three
   d. Five

3. Maximum eye protection is provided by the pull-down face shield on a fire helmet.
   a. True
   b. False

4. At a minimum, how often should your fire service protective clothing be cleaned?
   a. Every 6 months
   b. Every 6 weeks
   c. Every 4 months
   d. Every 5 months

5. A complete ensemble of personal protective equipment is not complete without
   a. a uniform shirt.
   b. a self-contained breathing apparatus.
   c. flameproof socks.
   d. a personal accountability tag.

6. Which of the following is *not* a contributing factor to your rate of air use when breathing from the air bottle of your SCBA?
   a. Your physical condition
   b. The amount of physical activity you are performing
   c. The temperature in which you are working
   d. The PASS timer

7. The _____ knob opens the emergency bypass valve on your self-contained breathing apparatus.
   a. green
   b. red
   c. blue
   d. yellow

8. Which of the following is the final step of putting on your SCBA before breathing from the system?
   a. Putting on your gloves
   b. Putting on your helmet
   c. Putting on your facemask
   d. Putting on your hood

9. A personal alert safety system (PASS) has an audible alarm that detects your movement and
   a. the SCBA air tank level.
   b. your radio signal.
   c. your lack of movement.
   d. the atmospheric pressure.

10. Which of the following phrases best describes what the personnel accountability system provides to firefighters and crews working on an emergency scene?
    a. A tracking system
    b. An alarm system
    c. A strategy system
    d. An alert device

Student Signature/Date _____   Instructor/Company Officer Signature/Date _____

Skills Assessment

Signed Documentation Tear-Out Sheet

Exterior Operations Level Firefighter—Chapter 3

Name: _____

Fill out the Skills Assessment Sheet below. Have your instructor/Company Officer check off and initial each skill you demonstrate. When finished, sign it and give to your instructor/Company Officer for his or her signature. Turn in this Skills Assessment Sheet to the proper person as part of the documentation that you have completed your training for this chapter.

Skill	Completed	Initials
1. Describe the components of personal protective clothing used for structural firefighting.	_____	_____
2. Describe the components of an entire ensemble of personal protective equipment used for structural firefighting.	_____	_____
3. Properly put on and wear all of your personal protective clothing.	_____	_____
4. Describe the procedures for the care and cleaning of your personal protective clothing.	_____	_____
5. Describe the components of a self-contained breathing apparatus (SCBA).	_____	_____
6. Demonstrate the proper way to check and assemble an SCBA.	_____	_____
7. Properly put on an SCBA from the seat-rack position.	_____	_____
8. Properly put on an SCBA from the ground.	_____	_____
9. Properly put on an SCBA from the ground using the over-the-head method.	_____	_____
10. Properly check and employ a personal alert safety system (PASS) in both automatic mode and manual mode.	_____	_____
11. Describe what you need to do when you use the personal accountability tag • When you ride the apparatus • When you drive your personal vehicle to the scene	_____	_____

Student Signature/Date _____   Instructor/Company Officer Signature/Date _____

Preconnected Attack Lines

4

What You Will Learn in This Chapter

This chapter will introduce you to various small hoses, nozzles, and equipment. It will also show you how fire hose is loaded and pulled off the fire apparatus. You will learn how to hold and flow a small fire attack hose under full operating pressure.

What You Will Be Able to Do

After reading this chapter and practicing the skills in a classroom setting, you will be able to

1. Describe the components of a fire hose system.
2. Demonstrate how to connect and disconnect hose couplings.
3. Describe the application of different hose tools and accessories that are used with fire hose.
4. Demonstrate the methods for rolling and carrying fire hose.
5. Explain good hose maintenance and care techniques.

6. Explain and demonstrate how fire nozzles operate.
7. Demonstrate how to deploy and load booster hose.
8. Demonstrate how to properly hold and utilize a flowing booster line.
9. Demonstrate how to deploy and load a preconnected attack line.
10. Demonstrate how to hold and utilize a flowing small attack line.

Reality!

Fire Hose

This chapter provides our first discussion about hose. The subject of fire hose is broken down into two categories: *attack* and *supply*. The **attack line** is used to carry the water from the pump to the fire. The **supply line** is used to move water from its source—for example, a fire hydrant, tanker truck (also known as a tender), or pond—to the pump. In this chapter,

79

we will discuss the fire hose that is used to attack and extinguish most fires, the preconnected attack line.

The preconnected attack line is your primary fire-extinguishing tool as well as your main lifeline. It protects you by allowing you to put a water barrier between you and the fire. Additional protection is provided in that you can follow the fire attack line out of an unsafe area to the pumper or to a safe area. In this way, it automatically marks your trail for a safe retreat—in most cases.

For these reasons, you must understand the importance of becoming familiar with, and well trained in, the applications and use of fire attack lines. They are the primary tool you will use to extinguish most fires and they are your lifeline for safe firefighting.

KEY WORDS

attack line   The hose that is used to carry the water from the pump to the fire.

supply line   The hose that is used to move water from its source—for example, a fire hydrant, tanker truck (also known as a tender), or pond—to the pump.

Fire Service Terminology

It is important that you understand the terminology you will hear when you are working with fire hose:

- *Hose* refers to a section of hose. This term may also indicate multiple sections of hose.
- *Fire hose* refers to a section of hose used for firefighting purposes in the fire service. It can also refer to multiple sections of fire hose.
- *Hose line* refers to one or more sections of hose being utilized for any of the following reasons:
  - To deliver a water supply to the fire **apparatus** pump
  - To deliver water from the pump to the nozzle, which converts the water into a fire stream that flows toward the seat of the fire
  - To protect any exposures to a fire
- *Attack line* refers to a hose line used to deliver a fire-extinguishing stream to the seat of the fire. It includes the nozzle at the end of the hose line.
- *Small attack line* refers to a fire attack hose line that is ¾ inch to 2 inches in diameter.
- *Large attack line* refers to a fire attack hose line that is 2½ inches or more in diameter.

- *Supply line* indicates a hose line used to deliver a supply of water from a water supply source to the fire apparatus pump.

KEY WORD

apparatus   Rolling equipment (such as an engine, a truck, or a rescue unit) that is used in the Fire Service.

Attack Lines

When we speak about attack lines, we are really talking about a hose system. It is a system because it is made up of several pieces of equipment, sections of hose, and a nozzle used by firefighters to apply water to the desired location. This system ultimately functions to extinguish the fire. With a proficient knowledge of the system, its components, and how they work together, as a firefighter, you will work safely and effectively.

An attack line begins at the pump on the fire *apparatus* and ends at the stream of water that comes from the end of the nozzle (Figure 4-1). It results in a **fire stream** that effectively reaches the base of the fire. The pump on the apparatus is designed to deliver enough water through the system to provide an effective stream of water to the fire. The pump panel is where the flow of water through the attack lines is regulated both for volume (how much water) and pressure (how fast it moves) (Figure 4-2). The volume is expressed in gallons per minute (gpm) and the pressure is expressed in pounds per square inch (psi). These two forces help determine the amount of water and the reach of the fire stream coming from the nozzle.

KEY WORD

fire stream   The flow of water from the open end of a fire nozzle that reaches the desired location (that is, the fire).

Safety Tip!

When handling fire hose, always wear at least head, eye, hand, and foot protection. Full bunker gear is preferable.

FIGURE 4-1 A fire attack line system starts at the pump and ends at the nozzle tip.

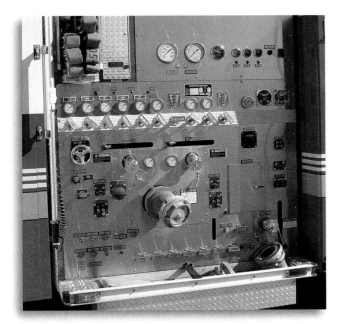

FIGURE 4-2 The pump panel on the fire apparatus is where the water supply coming into the pump and the water flow going into the fire attack lines is controlled.

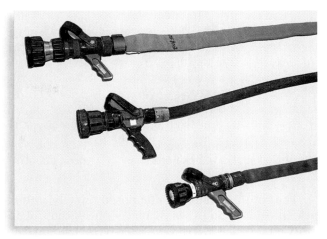

FIGURE 4-3 A 1-inch booster hose line and a 1¾-inch attack line. Small attack lines are ¾ to 2 inches in diameter and are usually carried in a preconnected configuration on the fire truck.

FIGURE 4-4 The most commonly used preconnected fire attack lines are small attack lines. These lines are 1½, 1¾, to 2 inches in diameter.

As you can see, there is a great deal to learn about hose and water and how we use them to put out fires. There will be much more detailed training provided in later parts of this text as well as in the other parts of this training curriculum that you can use as your training advances.

Small Attack Lines

Small attack lines have a diameter of ¾ inch to 2 inches, which is measured on the inside diameter of the hose. They are usually categorized as booster lines, which are on a reel and are seldom removed from the truck, and preconnected attack lines. Technically, both fall under the category of preconnected lines because they are carried on the truck already connected to the pump with the nozzle attached and arranged in a way so that they can be quickly deployed for use (Figure 4-3).

Preconnected Attack Lines

The most common type of fire attack hose lines you will use for fighting fires are 1½ inches, 1¾ inches, and 2 inches in diameter (Figure 4-4). These attack hose lines primarily come in lengths of 50 feet and are usually made of multilayered, jacketed hose material. They can also be made of lightweight, synthetic, rubberized materials (Figure 4-5).

FIGURE 4-5 Construction of a typical 1¾-inch fire attack hose line.

FIGURE 4-6 Typical threaded male hose coupling.

FIGURE 4-7 Typical threaded female hose coupling.

The couplings are male (exposed threads) and female (threads inside a swivel end)—one of each, at opposite ends of the hose (Figures 4-6 and 4-7). The male coupling is one piece—a sleeve with threads on the outside of the end. The female coupling has two parts—a sleeve and a swivel on the sleeve that contains the hose gasket. The threads are on the inside of the swivel end. The design of the threads is standard throughout most of the Fire Service in the United States and is referred to as **national standard threads (NST).**

Rocker lugs or rocker pins on the couplings provide a grip point for a spanner wrench. Spanner wrenches (or "spanners") are used to grip the rocker lugs of overtightened couplings to break them free. Standard couplings are designed to screw together in a clockwise direction. Conversely, they are loosened by being turned counterclockwise. Resist the temptation to overtighten couplings with spanners, as doing so compresses the gasket and can cause leaks rather than prevent them. Couplings should be hand-tight.

One lug on each of the couplings is usually marked with a Higbee indicator, which is a small notch cut into one of the lugs (Figure 4-8). The Higbee indicator helps you align the threads for proper tightening. Align the Higbee indicators across from each other and the couplings should tighten smoothly without cross-threading.

There are other types of hose couplings available. These couplings provide quick-connect features that allow rapid connecting of hose lines (Figure 4-9). Check with your department about connecting and disconnecting techniques if your department uses this type of fire hose.

Attack lines can be found in a few basic configurations on the fire apparatus. They can be loaded in specific hose bed areas and preconnected together and to the fire apparatus pump via a discharge port. They may also be preconnected into a bundle for use as a high-rise pack. This bundle makes it easier to carry fire attack hose up to higher floor levels of a multistory building when fighting a fire. Spare sections of hose may also be carried rolled and stored in a disconnected configuration and used to extend existing preconnected attack lines.

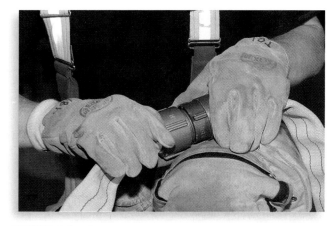

FIGURE 4-8 On threaded hose couplings, align the Higbee cuts on each coupling before you screw them together.

FIGURE 4-9 Quick-connect couplings, shown here on large-diameter supply hose.

■ KEY WORD ■

national standard threads (NST) A nationally recognized Fire Service specification that established the number and size of threads used in fire hose couplings. This specification is recognized throughout most of the United States.

Review It!

Go to the DVD, navigate to Chapter 4, and select *Small Attack Line Stretch.*

Practice It!

Stretching Small Attack Lines

Small attack lines are usually preconnected in lengths of 100 to 200 feet and are loaded in hose bed areas of the fire apparatus. Because small attack lines are loaded in many different configurations, you need to learn about and practice with the methods your fire department uses to pull the load and deploy the lines.

The following techniques can be used to pull and stretch any preconnected, small attack line:

1. Pull the correct hose load, grasping the loops that extend beyond the hose bed in which the hose is loaded (Figure 4-10). Then either back away from the apparatus until the hose clears the hose bed and then turn and walk toward the fire, or walk away from the apparatus with the line feeding off your shoulder. The method used depends upon the type of hose load.

FIGURE 4-10

2. Hold the loops firmly as you walk away from the apparatus, letting go of the loops as you feel a tug from the apparatus (Figure 4-11). Keep as much slack as you can; you need this slack to maneuver the hose at the fire. When you reach your preliminary position outside the hazardous area, drop the excess hose and arrange it in long loops. It is best to get as much into position as possible before the attack line is charged with water. The attack line is more difficult to move after it is charged.

FIGURE 4-11

—Continued

Level I

3. Signal the driver when you are ready for water to fill the hose. Slowly open the nozzle to let out excess air and to adjust the nozzle to the desired pattern and flow (Figure 4-12). Then close the nozzle before advancing the line.

FIGURE 4-12

4. A second firefighter or the pump operator should walk the deployed attack line, straightening any kinks in the line (Figure 4-13).

FIGURE 4-13

5. Maneuver the charged attack line into position and open the nozzle slowly, directing the water to the desired point on the fire (Figure 4-14).

FIGURE 4-14

6. Larger attack lines flow much more water than smaller lines. Therefore, they are handled differently and require more strength and skill to maneuver into position. Many times they require two firefighters for best operation and positioning. Much more **nozzle reaction** is present with these lines, which is a reaction to the volume and pressure of the water flowing from the nozzle. Anticipate this force and brace your body against the hose line at your hip and knee. Lean into the hose line with your body (Figure 4-15).

FIGURE 4-15

 Review It!

Go to the DVD, navigate to Chapter 4, and select *Loading Small Attack Lines.*

 Practice It!

Loading Small Attack Lines

Small preconnected attack lines can be loaded in a "ready-for-use" manner using several different styles of loads. Because different methods of loading attack lines are used by different fire departments, we will cover only the main steps for working as a team member while loading an attack line. The various types of hose loads are described in the next level of this curriculum. For now we will concentrate on general methods you can follow to assist with the process.

Use the following guidelines when loading small attack lines:

1. Confirm that the water has been shut off at the apparatus pump. Open the nozzle to allow any water pressure to be released. Then take the nozzle off the hose line (Figure 4-16).

FIGURE 4-16

2. Disconnect the sections of hose and drain each section of hose. If the hose is to be loaded on the scene, stretch the lines out and reconnect them after they have been drained. Assist in loading the hose into its storage location and reattach the nozzle (Figure 4-17). *Note:* If the hose is to be replaced at the fire station, drain and roll it for secure storage on the apparatus. When you return to the fire station you may be required to clean it before loading the hose.

FIGURE 4-17

Booster Attack Lines

Most booster attack hose is made of multiple layers of hard, synthetic rubber materials. These lines generally come in 100-foot lengths and are stored on the apparatus prewound on hose reels. These hose reels can be located in several places on fire apparatus, including inside compartments, or near the hose bed or behind the cab of the fire apparatus (Figure 4-18). Lightweight booster lines have a rubber liner and a cloth jacket for reinforcement. They also have a helix-coiled wire that gives the hose its permanent round shape.

Booster attack lines are attached together with male and female couplings (Figure 4-19). The female coupling is made of a sleeve and a swivel with a gasket located inside the swivel. Make sure these gaskets are in place when connecting the sections of any fire hose. The male coupling is constructed of one piece and has exposed threads. These threads need to be protected from damage. Never drag exposed male couplings across the ground, as doing so will damage the threads.

Booster hose line couplings usually have small grip points that are recessed. They require a special type of spanner wrench called a Barway spanner for disconnecting and connecting (Figure 4-20).

 **Safety Tip!**

Booster lines do not provide sufficient water flow for interior fire attack, dumpsters, or to extinguish a well-involved car fire. Booster lines should be used only for small to medium exterior fires, such as trash fires or field fires that involve grass or very low brush. Think of a booster line as a utility line, not an attack line.

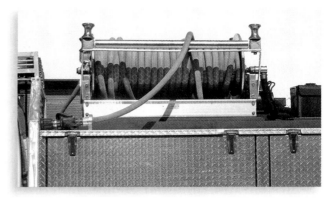

FIGURE 4-18 Booster line hose reels can be located in several different places on fire trucks.

FIGURE 4-19 Booster line couplings, with the male and female connected.

FIGURE 4-20 Barway spanner wrenches are specially designed for booster line hose couplings.

Go to the DVD, navigate to Chapter 4, and select Booster Attack Line Stretch.

Practice It!

Stretching Booster Attack Lines

Use the following steps to stretch a booster hose:

1. Grasp the nozzle and step down from the apparatus, and then turn toward the fire. Stop a short distance from the apparatus and grab some slack line to take with you. If someone else is advancing with the nozzle, grab the hose about 25 feet behind him or her and help pull the line (Figure 4-21).

FIGURE 4-21

2. When you are near the fire but in a safe area, stop and point the nozzle at the ground and slowly open it (Figure 4-22). Doing so bleeds trapped air from the hose and ensures that you have water and the desired stream pattern at the nozzle before approaching the fire.

FIGURE 4-22

3. Shut off the nozzle and hold the line under your arm and the nozzle at a comfortable level, keeping a hand on the operating valve as you approach the fire (Figure 4-23).

FIGURE 4-23

—Continued

Level I

4. Now flow water onto the base of the fire to extinguish it (Figure 4-24). Make sure to hold the flow of water until the fire is completely extinguished.

FIGURE 4-24

Review It!

Go to the DVD, navigate to Chapter 4, and select *Loading Booster Attack Lines.*

Practice It!

Loading Booster Attack Lines

In loading a booster attack line, always wear gloves when handling the line to protect your hands from any glass or other sharp edges that may have become embedded in the hose. You will also need to have a rag handy to remove any dirt from the hose as you load it.

Use the following steps to load a booster attack line:

1. Bring the nozzle end back to the apparatus at the hose reel. Load the booster line by operating the hose reel rewind button and rolling the hose back onto the reel. Try to keep the roll as neat as possible—and never allow the nozzle to scrape along the ground, as doing so can damage the nozzle (Figure 4-25).

FIGURE 4-25

2. Allow the line to pass through a rag held by your gloved hand to wipe away dirt and grime (Figure 4-26). Inspect the hose for any obvious cuts or other damage as it passes through your hand.

FIGURE 4-26

3. Make sure the nozzle is secure and that its valve is in the *off* position.

One-Inch Jacketed Attack Lines   Your fire apparatus may be equipped with a jacketed attack line that is 1 inch in diameter. Many departments have started using this small-diameter hose instead of booster lines for trash fires and small grass fires. Consequently, 1-inch jacketed hose is commonly referred to as a *trash line*. These lines can be located in a special hose bed area or in a compartment on the fire apparatus. They may or may not be already preconnected to the apparatus pump. Their design features a single, synthetic jacket, with a male coupling at one end and a female coupling at the other. These lines come in 50- to 100-foot lengths. One-inch jacketed hose lines lie flat when empty and are generally preconnected with the nozzle attached, or rolled up and stored in a compartment on the apparatus (Figure 4-27).

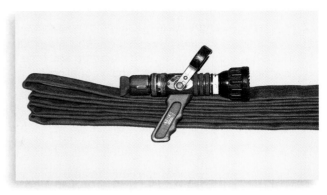

FIGURE 4-27 One-inch, single-jacketed hose lines lie flat when loaded and are preconnected with the nozzle attached. They are also referred to as *trash lines*.

Good flow

No kinks, adequate flow of water through attack line

Good fire stream

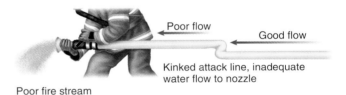

Poor flow

Good flow

Kinked attack line, inadequate water flow to nozzle

Poor fire stream

FIGURE 4-28 The effects of a kinked hose line.

Hose-Handling Techniques and Hose Tools

General Hose-Handling Techniques

There are a few general hose-handling tasks that are common to most types and configurations of fire hose. These techniques will help you safely and efficiently handle a fire hose as you work with it both at the actual fire emergency and during routine maintenance and handling operations.

Because small attack lines are flat when empty, they are prone to severe water flow restrictions when the hose is kinked under pressure (Figure 4-28). *Never walk by a kink in any hose line without straightening it.* Every kink is a danger to the crew on the nozzle and will greatly reduce the effectiveness of the fire stream.

Review It!

Go to the DVD, navigate to Chapter 4, and select *Connecting Hose Sections.*

Practice It!

Connecting Hose Sections

Use the following procedure to connect two sections of fire hose to each other by yourself:

1. Check the female end for the gasket and insert the male end, lining up the Higbee indicators. Rotate the female coupling clockwise while holding the male coupling in your other hand (Figure 4-29).

FIGURE 4-29

—Continued

2. If you are having trouble holding the male end as you connect the sections, simply step just behind the male end, which will turn it upward and hold it in place as you tighten the female coupling (Figure 4-30).

FIGURE 4-30

3. Tighten the hose couplings until they are hand-tight. Move on to the next section to be joined.

Use the following method if you have someone to help you connect the hose sections:

1. One person grasps the male end and holds it stationary at waist level.

2. The second person checks for a gasket, attaches the female coupling to the male coupling, and then turns the swivel, screwing the two sections together hand-tight (Figure 4-31). *Tip:* The person holding the male coupling should look away while the person holding the female side does the work. Doing so will prevent the two people from moving the couplings independently, which will cause the couplings to misalign.

FIGURE 4-31

Hose Tools

There are many types and styles of hose tools available today. These devices are specialized tools that are used for various purposes with fire hose and include spanner wrenches, hose straps, and hose clamps. Each has its purpose and use.

Spanner Wrenches

Spanner wrenches are used to tighten and loosen hose couplings. On most hose fittings, there is a flange or lug on the outside of the couplings. The spanner has an indented grip to grasp the pin or lug for turning the coupling end (Figure 4-32). Firefighters should always grab two wrenches because they will need to grasp both hose couplings with the tools to tighten or loosen them.

Do not use spanners to overtighten couplings—doing so will only damage the gasket and make it hard to uncouple the hose later.

FIGURE 4-32 Always be ready with two spanner wrenches to tighten and loosen couplings—one for each hose coupling. Do not overtighten the couplings.

Review It!

Go to the DVD, navigate to Chapter 4, and select *Using Spanner Wrenches*.

Practice It!

Using Spanner Wrenches

Use the following procedure when tightening or loosening hose couplings with spanner wrenches:

1. Place one spanner wrench so that it fits the lug and will turn the coupling in the desired direction.

FIGURE 4-33

2. Place the second spanner wrench so that it holds the opposite coupling in place as you turn the coupling (Figure 4-33).

3. Loosen the couplings as shown (Figure 4-34).

FIGURE 4-34

4. If tightening couplings, always remember that they will eventually need to be uncoupled, so only tighten them hand-tight.

Hose Straps

Hose straps are tools that provide firefighters with a handhold on a hose line. They are also excellent for securing hose lines to railings or ladders when needed. Hose straps consist of a metal handle attached to a heavy, webbed strap material. On one end, an open-clasp hook, designed to attach back onto the strap itself, allows the tool to be attached quickly (Figure 4-35).

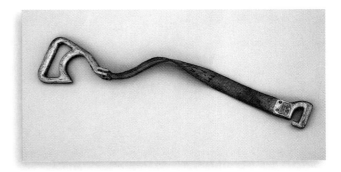

FIGURE 4-35 Hose strap.

Level I

Review It!

Go to the DVD, navigate to Chapter 4, and select *Using Hose Straps.*

Practice It!

Using Hose Straps

The following method outlines the steps for and benefits of using hose straps:

1. Wrap the hose with the webbing of the strap and hook it back onto itself as shown in Figure 4-36.

FIGURE 4-36

2. The firefighter can now handle the charged hose effectively, using the handle of the strap as a good grip (Figure 4-37).

FIGURE 4-37

3. In addition, the strap can be used to hook the charged hose to a ladder rung or railing. Doing so is a quick method of securing the charged hose to these areas (Figure 4-38).

FIGURE 4-38

Hose Appliances

Any device through which water passes that is not a handheld nozzle is considered a hose appliance. These appliances include master stream devices, hose coupling adapters, reducers, and devices to connect three or more hoses together.

Coupling Adapters

Coupling adapters are appliances used to connect male to male or female to female. Coupling adapters come in two main configurations: double male and double female adapters (Figure 4-39). The double male adapter consists of one sleeve with threads on the outside of each end. The double female adapter is made up of one sleeve with a threaded swivel at each end. Adapters are used to change the end of a hose section to a male or female end.

Reducers

Reducers are specialized hose coupling adapters that change the size of the end coupling. They are usually constructed of one piece. They feature a female end that is the size of the male end of the hose and a male end that is the smaller size of the hose or nozzle the coupling is hooked into (Figure 4-40).

Gate Valves

Gate valves are hose appliances that are hooked into the supply- and attack-line water systems to control the flow of water through those systems. For small attack lines, they are made up of the valve body and various configurations of gates. These valves can take an incoming water stream and divide it into two or more water streams, each with its own gate.

Two examples of gates used with small attack lines are the gated wye and the water thief. The gated wye usually takes in water from a larger supply, like a 2½-inch or 3-inch supply, and then divides it into two 1½-inch or 1¾-inch lines, each with its own gate valve (Figure 4-41). The water thief has a similar configuration except that the larger supply stream travels through the main gated valve assembly and discharges the same size stream. There are small attack-line gates on either side of the main gate valve assembly.

FIGURE 4-39   Double male and double female coupling adapters.

FIGURE 4-40   Reducer coupling on an attack line.

FIGURE 4-41   Gated wye valve.

FIGURE 4-42 Siamese device.

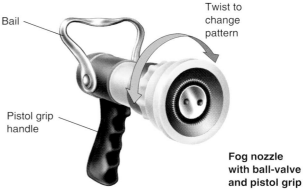

Twist to change pattern

Bail

Pistol grip handle

(a) Gated nozzle

Fog nozzle with ball-valve and pistol grip

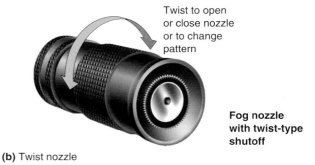

Twist to open or close nozzle or to change pattern

(b) Twist nozzle

Fog nozzle with twist-type shutoff

FIGURE 4-43 Fog nozzles: (a) gated nozzle and (b) twist nozzle.

Siamese Devices

Siamese devices take two or more supply lines and join them into one supply line (Figure 4-42). These devices typically have a flapper valve inside each intake opening that shuts off if only one line connected to the device is flowing water. A Siamese allows two lines to be combined with one line to increase pressure and flow.

Nozzles

General Nozzle Operations

Handheld fire nozzles will open in one of two ways: (1) with an operating valve handle (often called the bale or gate valve) on top of the nozzle body or (2) by twisting on the nozzle (Figure 4-43). In addition, handheld fire nozzles may or may not have a grip handle on the bottom.

Fire nozzles should always be opened and closed slowly to prevent a **water hammer** (Figure 4-44). A water hammer is a reaction to the sudden starting or stopping of water flow through hoses and pipes. This hammer effect can cause damage to the hose, pipes, and fittings.

▰▰▰ KEY WORD ▰▰▰

water hammer A reaction to the sudden starting or stopping of water flow through hoses and pipes that momentarily increases the pressure to sometimes dangerous levels in all directions on the line and pump.

FIGURE 4-44 Open and close the fire nozzle slowly to prevent a water hammer effect.

Types of Nozzles

There are two general types of nozzle designs: fog and solid bore (Figure 4-45). Fog nozzles allow the water pattern to be adjusted, usually by turning the tip end of the nozzle. The pattern of spray can be adjusted from a wide to a narrow pattern, depending on the effect desired from the stream coming from the nozzle.

FIGURE 4-45 A comparison of fog and solid bore nozzle streams.

FIGURE 4-46 Some fog nozzles have adjustment rings that the firefighter can use to change the flow of water from the nozzle.

A solid bore nozzle has a gate valve for turning the water on and off. It also features an opening through which the water exits the nozzle, with no adjustment ring. Solid bore nozzles are good for providing a longer or more solid stream of water from the nozzle than is usually accomplished with a fog nozzle.

Adjusting Nozzles

Nozzles come in various designs and capabilities. Some nozzles will allow an adjustment to the pattern of the water stream coming from the tip of the nozzle, as in fog nozzles. Some also have an additional adjustment ring that allows the firefighter to adjust the flow of water (measured in gpm). This additional adjustment ring lets the firefighter change the flow to suit his or her needs (Figure 4-46). Additionally, you can reduce the flow coming out of the nozzle by slightly closing the gate valve. This is an easy way to adjust

FIGURE 4-47 Proper hand grip and positioning with a small attack line.

the gpm flow if there is no regular adjustment ring on the nozzle.

Holding Nozzles

Hold the nozzle waist-high at your side, with the hose under your arm and one hand either on the body of the nozzle (for nozzles without a pistol grip) or on the pistol grip; your other hand should be on the gate valve control (the bale) or the twist valve, depending on the style nozzle you are using (Figure 4-47). The hose should trail out behind you. Be ready to shut off the nozzle, especially if you trip and fall. Make sure the nozzle is closed before you pass the hose to another person or lay it down.

Safety Tip!

Hose lines can burst while under pressure, a coupling can fail, or a nozzle is left in an open position and then the line is charged. Each of these can result in an out-of-control hose line, often called a "wild line." An out-of-control hose line is a lethal weapon. The only safe way to control a wild line is to shut it off at the pump panel.

Hose Rolls

When a fire hose is going to be stored for later use or transported to another location, it is best to roll the hose into a small bundle. We are going to describe three methods to roll fire hoses: (1) the straight roll, (2) the donut roll, and (3) the double donut roll.

Go to the DVD, navigate to Chapter 4, and select *Straight Roll.*

Practice It!

The Straight Roll

The most common method of rolling a fire hose is the straight roll. The straight roll is an easy method to roll up fire hose as well as protect the male threaded end of the hose.

Use the following technique to roll a fire hose in a straight roll:

1. Stretch the hose sections out flat. Then start at the male end, folding the male end into the hose and rolling it away from you as you proceed (Figure 4-48).

FIGURE 4-48

2. Continue rolling the hose until it is completely rolled up (Figure 4-49).

FIGURE 4-49

3. Grasp the hose at the top of the roll or tuck it under your arm to carry it (Figure 4-50).

FIGURE 4-50

Go to DVD, navigate to Chapter 4, and select *Donut Roll*.

Practice It!

The Donut Roll

The donut roll technique provides a single roll with both the female and male ends of the hose on the outside of the finished roll. This roll allows the firefighter to access both ends of the hose at the same time.

Use the following technique to perform a donut roll:

1. Lay the hose out flat, bringing the two couplings evenly alongside of each other (Figure 4-51).

FIGURE 4-51

2. Return to the fold in the hose, straightening the hose as you go. With one foot at the fold, kneel and at the point where your knee touches the ground, grasp the part of the hose with the male coupling and begin to roll the hose. The hose will feed itself into one roll as you go along (Figure 4-52).

FIGURE 4-52

3. Finish by straightening the roll. The male end will be protected by the overlap of the female side of the hose (Figure 4-53).

FIGURE 4-53

—Continued

Level I

Review It!

Go to the DVD, navigate to Chapter 4, and select *Double Donut Roll.*

Practice It!

The Double Donut Roll

A good way to roll a hose and provide a smaller profile with a rolled hose is the double donut roll. This roll is easy to do and results in both ends of the hose on the outside of the roll.

Use the following technique to create a double donut roll:

1. Lay the hose out flat, bringing the two couplings evenly alongside of each other (Figure 4-54).

FIGURE 4-54

2. Return to the folded end of the two sides and fold the middle, rolling two rolls at the same time (Figure 4-55). Continue rolling the hose over a loop of webbing or rope that can serve as a hand grip later.

FIGURE 4-55

3. Finish rolling the hose and you will have a lower-profile, twin donut roll that is easy to roll out and provides both ends of the hose to the firefighter (Figure 4-56).

FIGURE 4-56

—Continued

A second method, the self-locking double donut roll, is accomplished with the following steps:

1. Lay the hose out flat, bringing the two couplings evenly alongside of each other, with two loops folded at the beginning of the roll (Figure 4-57).

FIGURE 4-57

2. After the hose is rolled up, pass one loop into the other to create a convenient carry loop (Figure 4-58).

FIGURE 4-58

Hose Carry

The usual method for quickly and safely gathering an uncharged (unfilled) fire hose and moving it into the fire scene is the shoulder carry. Dragging couplings across the ground will cause undue wear and will likely cause damage to the couplings. Don't do it.

 Review It!

Go to the DVD, navigate to Chapter 4, and select *Hose Carry Technique.*

 Practice It!

Hose Carry Technique

Use the following method to quickly gather and carry a fire hose:

1. Begin at one coupling of a section of fire hose, placing a loop of the hose over your shoulder with the coupling in front (Figure 4-59).

FIGURE 4-59

2. Continue looping the hose until all sections of it are draped over your shoulder and the end coupling is off the ground.

3. You are now ready to move the hose to the desired location (Figure 4-60).

FIGURE 4-60

—Continued

An alternative method to carry empty hose is accomplished with the following steps:

1. Place the hose on its edge on the ground (Figure 4-61).

FIGURE 4-61

2. Bunch the hose together in the middle of the loops (Figure 4-62).

FIGURE 4-62

3. Lift and place the hose on your hip or shoulder and carry it to the desired location (Figure 4-63).

FIGURE 4-63

General Care of Fire Hose

The first step in picking up or putting away fire hose is to bleed the water pressure from the hose after the line has been shut off at the fire apparatus. Next, disconnect the nozzle. Then disconnect the hose sections. Finally, walk along the hose, placing it over your shoulder or raising it to your waist, helping the water drain as you walk the line.

Depending upon the practices of your department, the hose is then either placed back on the unit as a hose load, or rolled and returned to the station for storage or cleaning prior to being loaded on the apparatus. Follow the manufacturer's directions and department procedures for washing the fire hose.

After the hose is cleaned and rinsed, it can be placed on its side and allowed to dry. Some facilities may have hose-drying towers or hose-drying machines on which to place wet hose for drying. Make sure to check the hose and couplings for any obvious damage as you wash and maintain it. Look for frayed jacket material and other damage like burns and holes in the jacket of the hose. Check couplings for damaged threads, deformed or damaged sleeves and swivels, and missing gaskets.

 Safety Tips!

Follow these safety tips when working with a charged and flowing fire attack line:

- It is safest to shut off the flow of water before repositioning a line. However, if you must move and flow water at the same time, be ready to shut down the line quickly at the nozzle if you fall or direct the flow into other firefighters. Keep your hand on the bale.
- Hoses flow a large volume of water at high pressures. Directing this flow at fellow firefighters can cause serious injuries, especially from straight streams of water flowing from the nozzle.
- It is preferable to have a second firefighter backing up and assisting the firefighter on the nozzle.
- When you shut down your attack line, be sure to notify your supervisor that you have done so. Your supervisor will notify the driver of the apparatus.

Do It!

Hose Work

Hose work is a fundamental part of firefighting. Although you won't be advancing a line for an interior attack at this point in your training, you may be asked to deploy a line to the edge of the safe zone while the interior firefighters prepare for entry. You may also be ordered to operate an exterior hose stream. Like most fundamentals in the Fire Service, there are a few hose fundamentals that must be followed to ensure the safety and welfare of everyone involved. First, never pass a kink in a hose without straightening it. Second, when on the nozzle, keep your hand on the shutoff bale and be ready to immediately close or open the flow when asked. Third, open and close all valves slowly and deliberately to avoid water hammers.

Prove It

Knowledge Assessment

Signed Documentation Tear-Out Sheet

Exterior Operations Level Firefighter—Chapter 4

Name: _____

Fill out the ten-question quiz below, the Knowledge Assessment Sheet, by circling the correct answer for each question. When finished, sign it and give to your instructor/Company Officer for his or her signature. Turn in this Knowledge Assessment Sheet to the proper person as part of the documentation that you have completed your training for this chapter.

1. The fire attack hose line system begins at the _____ and ends when the stream of water coming from the end of the nozzle effectively reaches the base of the fire.
   a. nozzle
   b. apparatus pump panel
   c. fire hydrant
   d. base of the fire

2. The size of the fittings, couplings, and hose appliances that water passes through can _____ the volume of water and pressure of the stream as it flows out of the nozzle.
   a. increase
   b. have no affect on
   c. reduce
   d. eliminate

3. The inside diameter of small attack lines is _____ .
   a. ¾ inch to 2 inches
   b. 2 to 3 inches
   c. ¾ to 1¾ inches
   d. 1 to 3 inches

4. Booster hose couplings usually require a special type of spanner wrench called a Barway spanner wrench for disconnecting and connecting the couplings.
   a. True
   b. False

5. Most couplings are designed to screw together in a _____ direction. They should be tightened hand-tight.
   a. Clockwise
   b. Counterclockwise

6. Unlike booster lines, the 1-inch jacketed line needs to be _____ before it is loaded.
   a. disconnected
   b. flowed
   c. rolled
   d. drained

7. _____ are used to tighten and loosen hose couplings.
   a. Hose adapters
   b. Water thieves
   c. Spanner wrenches
   d. Gate valves

8. The _____ usually takes in water from a larger supply, like a 2½-inch or 3-inch supply, and then divides it into two smaller hose lines.
   a. gated nozzle
   b. hose adapter
   c. gated wye
   d. hose divider

9. Nozzles should be held waist-high at one's side, under the arm, with one hand either on the body of the nozzle (for nozzles without a hand grip) or on the hand grip; the other hand should be on the valve.
   a. True
   b. False

10. The first step in putting away fire hose is to _____ .
    a. disconnect the nozzle
    b. disconnect the hose sections
    c. bleed off excess water pressure
    d. drain the hose

Student Signature and Date _____   Instructor/Company Officer Signature and Date _____

Skills Assessment

Signed Documentation Tear-Out Sheet

Exterior Operations Level Firefighter—Chapter 4

Name: _____

Fill out the Skills Assessment Sheet below. Have your instructor/Company Officer check off and initial each skill you demonstrate. When finished, sign it and give to your instructor/Company Officer for his or her signature. Turn in this Skills Assessment Sheet to the proper person as part of the documentation that you have completed your training for this chapter.

Skill	Completed	Initials
1. Describe the components of a fire attack hose line system.	_____	_____
2. Demonstrate how to connect and disconnect hose lines.	_____	_____
3. Describe the application of different hose tools and accessories used with attack lines.	_____	_____
4. Demonstrate methods for rolling and carrying fire hose.	_____	_____
5. Explain good techniques for hose maintenance and care.	_____	_____
6. Explain and demonstrate how fire nozzles operate.	_____	_____
7. Demonstrate how to deploy and load booster lines.	_____	_____
8. Demonstrate how to properly hold and use a flowing booster hose.	_____	_____
9. Demonstrate how to deploy and load other jacketed attack lines.	_____	_____
10. Demonstrate how to hold and use a flowing small attack line.	_____	_____

Level I

Student Signature and Date _____   Instructor/Company Officer Signature and Date _____

Response Safety and Vehicle Crashes

What You Will Learn in This Chapter

In this chapter you will learn actions you can take to help you remain safe while on the roadway, both as a driver and while working at the scene of an emergency. You will learn your responsibilities for responding to the fire station, riding in an emergency vehicle, and safely setting up a proper traffic safety system. We will also cover some of the primary elements of an Emergency Vehicle Operator's Course (EVOC).

What You Will Be Able to Do

After reading this chapter and practicing the skills in a classroom setting, you will be able to

1. Respond safely to the fire station in your personally owned vehicle (POV).

2. Demonstrate how to safely get on the fire apparatus and the use of seatbelts.

3. Demonstrate safely getting off the fire apparatus and awaiting instructions from the Company Officer.

4. Demonstrate proper personal protective clothing for daytime and nighttime traffic control operations.

5. Demonstrate how to safely deploy traffic cones to establish traffic safety lanes for the fire apparatus and emergency workers.

6. Describe the different benchmarks to be encountered on a typical vehicle crash scene in which there is no entrapment.

7. Assist in identifying and handling hazards typically present on a vehicle crash scene.

8. Identify hot, warm, and cold zones of operation on a vehicle crash scene.

Reality!

Wear Your Seatbelt!

Firefighter safety and health is the cornerstone of everything we do. If you are to continue assisting people at the myriad of emergencies that you will encounter, you must maintain a safe and healthy attitude for every alarm.

Safety Lesson

A NIOSH Report

On January 21, 2002, a 26-year-old firefighter was fatally ejected from his personal vehicle, which he crashed while responding to a house fire. The 8-year veteran firefighter served in a volunteer fire department with 22 firefighters serving a population of approximately 5000 in an area of about 35 square miles.

According to the state police report, the firefighter was ejected through the sunroof of his SUV during one of three complete rollovers. The police report indicates that the victim was not wearing his seatbelt at the time of the crash and that an "unsafe speed" was a contributing factor to his death.

Follow-Up

The NIOSH Investigative Report (#F2002-04) recommended: "The fire department shall develop standard operating procedures for safely driving fire department vehicles during nonemergency travel and emergency response and shall include specific criteria for vehicle speed, crossing intersections, traversing railroad grade crossings, and the use of emergency warning devices. Such procedures for emergency response shall emphasize that the safe arrival of fire department vehicle at the emergency is the first priority." The report went on to recommend that fire departments ensure that all personnel responding in privately owned vehicles follow the same practices.

Driving Safety

After heart-related fatalities, vehicle accidents involving firefighters are the second leading cause of firefighter deaths. Vehicle crashes in both personally owned vehicles (POVs) and emergency appa-

FIGURE 5-1 Whether driving to the fire station to work or responding to an emergency call, always drive responsibly and safely.

ratus happen far too often and must be reduced through proper driver training for members of the Fire Department.

Responding to an Emergency Call in Your Privately Owned Vehicle

As a firefighter, perhaps one of the most dangerous things you will do on a regular basis is to drive to the emergency. In many jurisdictions, especially in volunteer fire departments, firefighters respond in their POVs to the fire station in order to take emergency apparatus to an emergency. They may be required to respond directly to the emergency scene in their private vehicles (Figure 5-1). Even if you are going to and from the station, you still need to be careful. Whatever your destination, you need to be aware of the potential dangers and how to minimize those dangers.

Defensive Driving

We recommend all new recruits attend a **defensive driving** course and eventually an **Emergency Vehicle Operator's Course (EVOC)** before driving any fire or rescue apparatus. A defensive driving course, which also instructs course attendees about departmental, local, and state-level laws and regulations related to private vehicle response, should be given to new firefighters as soon as possible. The basic rules of the road and the laws of physics apply to POVs as well as to fire apparatus. Later in this chapter we'll discuss these components while explaining an EVOC training program.

KEY WORDS

defensive driving   A method of driving that emphasizes paying close attention to other drivers on the roadway and anticipating and avoiding driving dangers.

Emergency Vehicle Operator's Course (EVOC)   A driving course for operators of emergency vehicles that teaches students how to safely operate and control fire and rescue emergency vehicles.

Defining a True Emergency

Before talking about the causes of many fatal vehicle crashes for firefighters, we need to talk briefly about what defines a true emergency. Many emergency driving rules and regulations assume that the responder is responding to a true emergency. Unfortunately, many firefighters respond to the fire station for incidents that are not true emergencies and, in the process, expose themselves and the public to unnecessary risks.

The Emergency Vehicle Operator's Course developed by the U.S. Department of Transportation (DOT) defines a true emergency as *a situation in which there is a high probability of death or serious injury to an individual or significant property loss, and action by an emergency vehicle operator may reduce the seriousness of the situation.* The majority of fire department call-outs are not true emergencies, and firefighters who drive to the fire station or the emergency scene in their POVs usually do not need to drive as if it were a true emergency.

In today's world, many firefighters are liable for and are charged with negligence if they are involved in a vehicle crash. In simple terms, negligence is either the act of doing something that a reasonable or prudent person would not do, or not doing something that such a person would do in a given situation. The bottom line is that driving to an emergency does not make you immune from being prosecuted if you fail to follow traffic laws.

Causes of Fatal Vehicle Crashes

Statistics show that the main causes of fatal vehicle crashes in which firefighters use their private vehicles are driving too fast, not using seatbelts, rollover crashes, crashes at intersections, the use of alcohol, and head-on crashes (Figure 5-2).

Excessive Speed

Almost every crash studied involved some level of speeding. Firefighters should not exceed the speed

FIGURE 5-2   Firefighter deaths in crashes are caused mainly by driving too fast, not using seatbelts, rollovers, crashes at intersections, the use of alcohol, and head-on collisions.

limit when responding in their private vehicles. Time can be gained by using safe, efficient routes and practicing safe driving habits. Speedy, careless driving risks lives and should always be avoided.

Lack of Seatbelt Use

Not using a seatbelt has contributed to many fatalities. Firefighters should set an example for the community by following the law and wearing their seatbelts at all times (Figure 5-3). It is a proven fact that seatbelt use reduces injury and death in traffic crashes, and basically eliminates the chance of ejection from a vehicle.

Rollover Crashes

Firefighters must maintain control of their vehicles. No one driving any type of vehicle should drive at speeds that cause the vehicle to overturn. Because they are tall, many types of fire apparatus are top-heavy and tend to tip over if driven too fast through a curve. This is especially true of tanker/tenders. In addition, because all kinds of fire apparatus are heavy, a contributing factor to many rollover crashes is simply running off the pavement onto a soft shoulder of the road, where the tires dig in and make the truck flip, or the driver overcorrects and causes the vehicle to roll over.

Crashes at Intersections

Many crashes occur at intersections. During a response, firefighters must recognize the dangers of passing through an intersection. When driving with

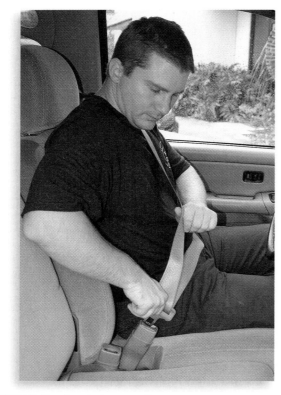

FIGURE 5-3   Seatbelts save lives—always use them!

FIGURE 5-4   Taking a right-of-way that is not yours can result in head-on collisions that have deadly results.

your sirens and lights flashing, you are merely asking the public to allow you to proceed. However, if they do not yield to you, you do not have the right to claim the right-of-way. Before entering the intersection, you must stop with the signal, whether it is a yield sign, a stop sign, or a stop light. This driving rule must be followed with no exceptions, whether you are in a POV or a fire apparatus with lights and sirens in use. Always follow local, state, and fire department regulations when driving your POV to the fire station or the emergency scene. *No* emergency is worth the death of or injury to firefighters or innocent civilians in the community. Also use extreme care at railroad crossings. Remember: Trains don't stop on a dime and they can't yield to you.

Alcohol Use

Firefighters are not available for service if they have consumed any alcohol within eight hours prior to an alarm. Any violation of this rule is a clear and serious act of negligence.

Head-On Crashes

Head-on crashes between vehicles can occur when firefighters take a right-of-way that is not theirs (Figure 5-4). Again, firefighters must wait for the public to yield the right-of-way. Driving into oncoming traffic

is extremely dangerous to firefighters and the public and is not allowable under any circumstances.

Private Vehicle Use

Firefighters who receive alarms off duty and have family members with them in their private vehicle are not available to respond to the calls. Family members have been injured in crashes involving firefighters responding to the fire station or the emergency scene with family members in their POVs.

Your fire department will have an established policy regarding private vehicle use. This standard guideline includes information about when and how to respond safely. The policy also includes response requirements under different conditions and techniques. These requirements include speed limits, proper intersection clearance, the use of warning devices and safety devices, seatbelts, and driving practices in bad weather or limited visibility. If safe driving guidelines are not followed, the department should impose severe consequences.

Safe Driving Attitude

A safe driving attitude is an important part of driving safely. It is also crucial to prospective firefighters. Firefighters who are good drivers have the following qualities:

- They respect the danger involved in driving any vehicle.
- They respect other drivers on the roadway and follow all traffic laws, including speed limits, road sign directions, and signals.
- They always have all safety equipment and seatbelts in use while driving.
- They follow fire department rules and regulations regarding driving.

Driver Training

As a firefighter applicant, your driving record will be a factor in your membership in the Fire Department. Many younger drivers have not been driving long enough to gain good experience and respect for the road. This lack of experience can be compensated for with proper and extensive driver training, including an Emergency Vehicle Operator's Course and Collision Avoidance Training.

Emergency Vehicle Operator's Course (EVOC)

One of the first things you will want to do after you have completed your recruit training is to drive and operate various fire department apparatus (Figure 5-5). It is the nature of the business, the need to bring staffing and equipment to the emergency scene, that dictates that driving apparatus is such a high priority. Before driving any fire apparatus, you should receive training in defensive driving and you should also take a course in emergency vehicle operations. You must be certified not only to drive emergency vehicles, but to be physically and mentally ready to operate them.

Fire and rescue apparatus are bigger, heavier, and much more complex than regular automobiles, SUVs, or pickup trucks. Because of their weight, they take much more time and effort to stop. Most modern fire apparatus have antilock braking systems that help you maintain control of the truck during emergency braking.

Using a safe following distance is a key driving safety technique. There are two methods for calculating a safe following distance. The first method is the 3-second rule. This rule requires that you pick a marker—perhaps a tree or a post on the side of the roadway—and begin a count of three ("1001, 1002, 1003") when the vehicle in front of you passes the marker; you should not pass the marker before having reached the third count. If you are responding to an emergency, this distance (the traveling time) should be increased to allow you more reaction time. The second method is to estimate apparatus lengths. Estimate one apparatus length between your vehicle and the vehicle in front of you for every 10 miles per hour that you are traveling.

Fire apparatus need regular maintenance and inspection (Figure 5-6). Their fuel levels must be maintained at the ready, which means approximately three-quarters full or more at all times. EVOC training will also teach you how to perform a routine safety check of the fire apparatus, including inspection pro-

FIGURE 5-5 Driving any fire apparatus requires training and physical and mental ability.

FIGURE 5-6 An EVOC course will teach you vehicle safety inspection as well as safe driving skills.

cedures for things such as mirrors, windshield wipers, emergency brakes, signaling devices, and specific machinery and equipment. Vehicle problems must be repaired as soon as possible and should always be reported to the appropriate officer as soon as they are discovered. You must document any vehicle problems quickly and accurately.

Never operate a Fire Department vehicle unless you have received the proper training and have had sufficient time to become familiar with driving that vehicle. You should be certified by your department as having passed all required training and orientation before driving any vehicles.

Classroom Training

EVOC training includes a classroom portion in which students learn about many aspects of driving that they had perhaps never thought of previously. Students learn about the attitudes and experience necessary to operate an emergency vehicle. Driving skills that are adequate with a POV are not sufficient with fire apparatus. You need to be much more careful and learn to anticipate potential road dangers while responding. Your number one priority is your safety and the safety of the crew on the apparatus. You are also responsible for the safety of the general public. The driver of the fire apparatus is the person ultimately responsible for its safe operation.

Legal Requirements

Operators of emergency vehicles are subject to all traffic laws unless they are specially exempted from certain laws while responding to an emergency (Figure 5-7). Even with those exemptions, they are still accountable for their driving decisions and actions. As noted earlier, a red light and a siren only "ask" others to allow you to go against traffic signals. They do not give you the right-of-way or permission to break traffic rules such as speed limits.

Operators need to comply with state, local, and Fire Department requirements for training and licensing. These requirements can include defensive driver and EVOC training, a valid driver's license, minimum age requirements, and a good driving record.

Physical Forces

Many forces act upon an emergency vehicle as it speeds down the roadway to the emergency scene. How these various physical forces affect the apparatus are addressed in the EVOC classroom. These forces include velocity, friction, inertia and momentum, and centrifugal force.

Velocity   Velocity is the speed of an apparatus. The faster a unit travels, the more force is needed to slow it down and stop it. The total **stopping distance** of an apparatus is the reaction time plus the braking distance (Figure 5-8).

▓▓▓ KEY WORD ▓▓▓

stopping distance   The total distance needed to stop a vehicle. This distance is calculated by adding the reaction time plus the braking distance.

Friction   The term *friction* applies to the brakes used to stop the apparatus and the grip of the wheels to the surface of the roadway. Fire truck brake components are much more substantial than those of regular ve-

FIGURE 5-7   When driving to an emergency, even though you may be exempt from certain driving regulations, you are still accountable for your driving decisions and actions.

Reaction Time + Braking Distance =

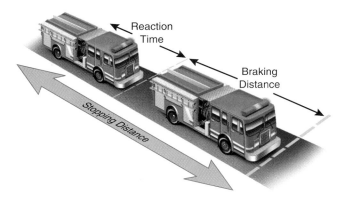

FIGURE 5-8   Reaction time is the time it takes to put your foot on the brake. Braking distance is the time it takes the brakes to stop the truck. The total of the two is the stopping distance for a vehicle.

FIGURE 5-9 Fire apparatus tires and wheels are big. Their large size provides more surface contact with the roadway than the tires and wheels of smaller vehicles.

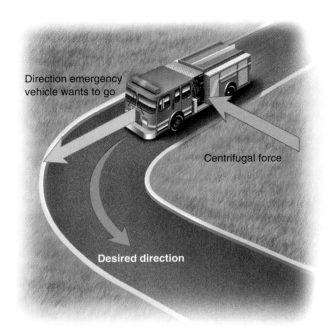

FIGURE 5-10 You must slow down when driving in a curve so that centrifugal force doesn't "push" the vehicle you're driving off the roadway.

hicles. Their tires and wheels are also bigger in order to provide more surface contact with the roadway (Figure 5-9).

Momentum and Inertia Momentum is to the force that builds in an object in motion that tends to keep it in motion. This law applies to moving vehicles such as fire apparatus. The term **inertia** refers to how a moving fire apparatus tends to keep moving when started and to stay still when stopped. Fire apparatus have more momentum than lighter and smaller vehicles. It takes more force to stop them, and they hit with more force than smaller vehicles when involved in a collision.

KEY WORDS

momentum The law of nature that describes the force that builds in an object in motion that keeps it moving. The more velocity an object has, the more momentum it has and thus the more force it will take to slow down that object and stop it.

inertia The law of nature that states that objects set into motion tend to remain in motion and objects that are stationary tend to remain stationary unless acted upon by another object.

Centrifugal Force Centrifugal force the force that affects an object traveling in an arc or circle, such as a vehicle driving on a curve in the roadway. As the vehicle goes around the curve, centrifugal force acting on the vehicle tends to make the vehicle move outside the edge of the curve (Figure 5-10).

KEY WORD

centrifugal force The force that acts upon an object traveling in an arc or circle that pushes the object away from the center of the arc or circle.

Practical Driver Training

Practical driver training includes driving a road course and being tested on the operation of equipment specific to the fire apparatus (Figure 5-11).

Safety rules that you must follow when driving any fire apparatus on a practice driving course include the following:

- When on the driving course, you should always have someone with you.
- A common signal term like *stop* or *halt,* agreed to beforehand, should be used to stop the driving operation if a safety concern develops.

FIGURE 5-11 Driver training includes practical driving as well as the operation of the equipment on that specific apparatus.

FIGURE 5-12 When backing up the apparatus, always have a second person at the rear of the apparatus to watch for hazards and safety concerns.

- When backing up the apparatus, always have a second person at the rear of the apparatus to watch for hazards and safety concerns (Figure 5-12).
- Practice when road surface conditions are good, never speed, and follow the manufacturer's recommendations for driving the particular fire apparatus.

You will need to complete a timed and graded driving test that includes the following exercises and maneuvers:

- A serpentine exercise
- An alley dock maneuver
- The opposite alley exercise
- A diminishing clearance exercise
- A straight line exercise
- A turnaround maneuver
- A lane change exercise

Other driving exercises may be added to the driving course, depending on the requirements of your fire department and the specific fire apparatus for which you are being trained.

Collision Avoidance Training (CAT)

Another driver training course that you may be required to take is **Collision Avoidance Training (CAT).** This course teaches you how to react when you lose control of your vehicle. It also teaches safe driving habits, especially under inclement roadway conditions such as ice and rain. This course is taught mainly to law enforcement officers, but your department may require you to attend such a course.

KEY WORD

Collision Avoidance Training (CAT) Driver training that specializes in gaining control of vehicles under different adverse situations and roadway conditions.

Riding Safety

Responding to emergency calls is one of the most common things you will do as a firefighter (Figure 5-13). When the alarm is received and the firefighting crew assembles around the apparatus, many things happen simultaneously.

The driver quickly scans the apparatus as he approaches it. He looks for any obstructions near the vehicle, checking that all auxiliary plugs and hoses are detached and the wheel chocks have been pulled out of place. He also checks for people in and around the vehicle, as well as for any equipment that is out of place and compartment doors that are open.

The Company Officer checks to see if the crew is getting ready and listens for additional information on the call. She begins formulating the response route and a plan of action to handle the potential emergency situation.

The firefighters don their PPE and prepare to board the apparatus. It is important that you don your basic protective clothing *before* you board the truck, with two exceptions: (1) you are the driver, or (2) the bulky clothing will impede the proper wearing of your seatbelt. In these cases, don the equipment immediately after arriving on the scene.

FIGURE 5-13   Safely responding to emergencies on the fire apparatus is one of the fun points of being a firefighter.

FIGURE 5-14   PPE for vehicle crash incidents should start with protection similar to the gear used for structural firefighting. This gear includes head, eye, hand, body, and foot protection.

View It!

Go to the DVD, navigate to Chapter 5, and select *Working Around Large Vehicles Safely.*

Personal Protective Equipment and Clothing

The level of protective clothing will be dictated by the type of the incident. In general, PPE for vehicle crash incidents should start with protection similar to the gear used for structural firefighting. This gear includes head, eye, hand, body, and foot protection. It is also important to maintain body protection. Many agencies allow the use of full-length, long-sleeve jumpsuits with some degree of fire resistance. If the situation is more hazardous, firefighters may need full PPE for structural firefighting, including an SCBA. Remember that you should wear a bright, reflective traffic vest whenever you are working near traffic (Figure 5-14).

Hearing Protection

A component of your PPE that is specific to responding is hearing protection. Hearing loss is a very common risk in loud work environments. Most modern fire apparatus have an intercom system that provides a protective headset. This headset allows you to hear radio traffic as well as talk among the members in the cab of the truck while responding. The headset eliminates the extra noise associated with sirens and loud horns. Make sure to put on the headset as soon as your seatbelt is buckled.

Working Around Large Vehicles Safely

Fire apparatus present several blind spots to the driver that aren't always obvious to individuals working near them. It is important that you respect these blind spots. Never turn your back on a moving vehicle, especially when it is moving in a tight area, such as when backing into a firehouse (Figure 5-15). You will notice that most fire trucks have a backup alarm that sounds whenever the truck is in reverse. While this signal is a clear warning of potential danger, many firefighters become complacent and are subsequently injured.

Never try to grab or get on or get off of a moving fire truck (Figure 5-16). This may sound obvious, but several firefighters have been injured or even killed while trying to board a truck as it was rolling out of the station.

Never ride on the tailboard or running boards of a fire truck. Although it is no longer a common practice to ride on the tailboard, it is often tempting to step up on it when the truck is backing up a long way or moving a short distance on the scene. *DON'T DO IT!*

A common type of accident involving fire trucks occurs while the truck is being backed up. Most departments require a backup spotter to help avoid these incidents. If you are the spotter, it is important that you remain visible and in a safe position while directing the driver. Wear your Class III reflective

FIGURE 5-15 Fire apparatus have blind spots to the driver that aren't always obvious to individuals working near them. It is important that you respect these blind spots. Never turn your back on a moving vehicle, especially when it is moving in a tight area.

FIGURE 5-17 While directing the driver, you must remain visible and in a safe position. You must wear your Class III reflective traffic vest and a helmet, and you should stand so that you can see the driver in the outside rearview mirror.

FIGURE 5-16 Never try to grab or get on a moving fire truck. Several firefighters have been injured or even killed while trying to board the truck as it is rolling out of the station.

FIGURE 5-18 Wear hearing protection if you are going to be working near a pumping truck for an extended period of time.

the other side. When possible, use a portable radio for better communication with the driver.

When the fire truck is in the pumping mode, the engine runs at high revolutions, causing a lot of noise. Make sure to wear hearing protection if you are going to be working near the truck for an extended period of time (Figure 5-18).

Response Safety

Response safety involves many factors. As a firefighter, you will need to know how to work safely when responding to calls as well as when assisting at vehicle crash scenes.

traffic vest and a helmet and stand so that you can see the driver in the outside rearview mirror (Figure 5-17). Never cross behind a moving truck. If you must cross over to the other side of the vehicle to check clearance, signal the driver to stop and then walk to

Responding to Calls Safely

As a firefighter, you need to check your side of the apparatus as you quickly put on your protective clothing. Follow these steps to respond safely to calls:

1. Before you leave for the call, close any open compartments and check for any obstructions under and near the unit (Figure 5-19).

FIGURE 5-19

2. Prior to leaving, make sure any onlookers stand clear of the apparatus.

3. The extent and type of protective clothing you need depends on the type of emergency and the policy of your Company Officer and your department.

4. Safely climb onto the apparatus and sit down in your designated position. You will have a personal accountability system (PAS) tag. Hand this tag to your Company Officer as soon as you get onto the fire apparatus (Figure 5-20).

FIGURE 5-20

5. Put on your seatbelt and check the area around you for any loose tools or unsecured equipment (Figure 5-21).

FIGURE 5-21

6. Signal to the driver and the Company Officer up front that you are belted in and ready to go. The apparatus will leave the station. It is extremely important that you remain seated and with your seatbelt in place during the entire response.

Follow these safety rules when responding to emergencies:

- Never disconnect your seatbelt while the vehicle is in motion, even to put on additional gear such as air packs.
- Never stand while riding on a fire apparatus. If you arrive too late to sit in an approved seat, then dismount and get on the next apparatus ready to respond.
- Wear hearing protection or communication devices while responding (Figure 5-22).
- Responding to an emergency is not a time for "horseplay." Not behaving professionally will cause undue distraction for the Company Officer and the driver.
- Never dismount the apparatus without checking with your Company Officer.
- When dismounting from the apparatus, always check in all directions. Look for traffic and obstructions or hazards on the ground below (Figure 5-23). Carefully step off the apparatus, using the handholds provided to steady yourself.

Assisting at Vehicle Crash Scenes

One of the most hazardous areas in which an emergency worker can work is on or near a roadway. Working around a vehicle crash scene is dangerous, regardless of the size of the incident. Moving traffic always poses a threat to emergency workers working in the roadway. The crashed vehicles present several threats to your

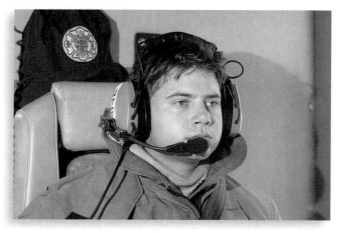

FIGURE 5-22 When responding to an emergency, wear hearing protection or communication devices.

FIGURE 5-23 Always look in all directions before dismounting from the apparatus. Look for traffic and obstructions or hazards on the ground below. Carefully step off the apparatus, using the handholds provided.

FIGURE 5-24 Many firefighters and rescue workers are injured or killed by being struck by other vehicles while they are off the apparatus and working in the streets.

safety, including the unstable vehicles themselves, dangerous fluids on the ground, and many other hazards. To organize the activities around the crash scene, we generally establish two types of work zones: the traffic control zone and the work safety zone.

Traffic Control

An important reality of firefighting is that you will probably respond to more incidents involving motor vehicle crashes and roadway emergencies than you will to structure fires. Annually, many firefighters and rescue workers are injured or killed by vehicles while they are off the apparatus and working in the streets (Figure 5-24).

FIGURE 5-25 The apparatus should be parked so that it serves as a shield to protect everyone from flowing traffic.

The driver of the fire apparatus and your Company Officer will already know how to properly position the apparatus in a **fend-off position** (Figure 5-25). This position is used to protect the emergency scene on the roadway. A good driver will park the unit safely, always applying the emergency brake and using proper emergency lights as a warning to all directions of traffic.

KEY WORD

fend-off position The positioning of emergency apparatus on a roadway in order to protect the temporary work area in the street by blocking it with apparatus.

The most dangerous aspect of a traffic crash scene is that traffic is still flowing around the general area. Night operations compound this situation immensely. It is essential to everyone's safety that the firefighters take immediate steps to establish a traffic control zone around the entire crash area. The first step is to park the apparatus in a fend-off position. The traffic control zone can then be established by identifying and marking it with reflective traffic cones, road flares, or other traffic control devices. It is always preferable to turn traffic control over to law enforcement as soon as possible (Figure 5-26). Doing so allows a better-qualified person to direct traffic and allows rescue team members to assist with the rescue.

FIGURE 5-26 Turning traffic control over to law enforcement as soon as possible allows a better-qualified person to direct traffic. It also releases rescue team members to assist with the rescue.

 **View It!**

Go to the DVD, navigate to Chapter 5, and select *Traffic Control Safety.*

 **Safety Tips!**

Traffic Control Safety When working in traffic, you should wear the appropriate protective clothing and a reflective vest.

- You should wear full protective clothing and/or a Class III vest when working near traffic. Your department will have established guidelines for you to follow that describe the minimum personal protective clothing required (Figure 5-27).
- To be seen at night, use flashlights and light the scene with portable lighting (Figure 5-28).
- Road flares can be used only when there are no flammable materials or vapors present. Do not strike a road flare without full protective clothing and eye protection in place. Make sure to get permission from your Company Officer.

FIGURE 5-28 To be seen at night, use flashlights and light the scene with portable lighting.

FIGURE 5-27 You should wear appropriate protective clothing and a Class III vest when working near traffic.

Practice It!

Traffic Control Safety

Whenever possible, traffic control should be performed by law enforcement officers. However, in their absence, this job usually falls to firefighters. After making sure that you are wearing the appropriate protective clothing, assist in setting up traffic cones. Place them toward the traffic approaching the rear of the fire apparatus in the fend-off (blocking) position. Cones with reflective collars are recommended for night use.

1. Work in pairs where possible, especially if traffic from one direction must be stopped to allow traffic from the other direction to pass through (Figure 5-29). Communicate with your partner, preferably visually as well as by radio. Be prepared to warn the other firefighter directing traffic if a vehicle unexpectedly continues against the oncoming traffic.

FIGURE 5-29

—Continued

2. Place a tapering pattern of 5 cones in a stretch of roadway at a distance of about 75 feet from the rear of the apparatus. This placement provides a transition for traffic from the present pattern to the new lane pattern established by your apparatus placement and the placement of cones (Figures 5-30 and 5-31). As an added precaution, the NFPA suggests that a DOT-approved reflective sign stating "Emergency Scene" be used for additional warning.

FIGURE 5-30

3. For multilane, large-volume traffic and limited-access freeways, place the cones farther apart, perhaps doubling the distance to 150 feet from the rear of the apparatus to the tapered end of the pattern. This placement of cones will allow motorists time to react to the lane changes and the slower speeds near the crash emergency scene (Figure 5-32).

FIGURE 5-31

4. If conditions permit, road flares may be placed next to cones to gain motorists' attention as they approach. Road flares can help create a temporary, safe control zone in which to respond to the emergency.

FIGURE 5-32

5. Make sure that oncoming traffic is completely stopped before allowing the other direction of traffic to proceed.

 Safety Tips!

Use the following precautions when placing cones and controlling traffic:

- Never assume that the driver of a vehicle sees you or understands the traffic pattern requirements. Remember that many drivers are distracted, perhaps under the influence, or just don't understand the situation.
- Never stand in the traffic lanes, and be ready at all times to step out of the way of traffic.
- Keep your eye on the traffic and never turn your back on it. Face traffic when placing cones and be ready to warn others if a vehicle breaks through your blocking cones and heads for the fire apparatus (Figure 5-33).
- When walking around the corner of a unit near traffic lanes, always stop and carefully lean and look around the corner of the unit for oncoming traffic (Figure 5-34).
- Your fire department will most likely have standard guidelines for working and controlling traffic. Make sure to go over these guidelines as soon as possible when you report for you first duty.

FIGURE 5-33 Face traffic when placing cones.

FIGURE 5-34 When walking around the corner of a unit near traffic lanes, always stop and carefully lean and look around the corner of the unit for oncoming traffic.

FIGURE 5-35 After safely responding to the emergency call, arriving on the scene, and setting up traffic control, the next step will be to set up a safety zone around the crash scene.

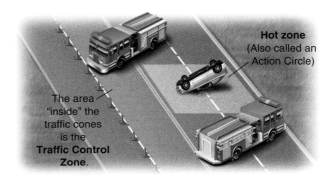

FIGURE 5-36 Safety zones include the hot zone, which immediately surrounds the crash, and the traffic control zone, which covers the area protected by traffic control devices.

Safety Zones

After safely responding to the emergency call, arriving on the scene, and setting up traffic control, you must attend to the actual vehicle crash (Figure 5-35). Your next step will be to set up a safety zone around the crash scene. At this stage in your training, we will discuss a crash emergency with injuries and no entrapment.

Establish a safe area that extends completely around the vehicles and the hazards involved. This safe area is divided into **safety zones** designated as *hot, warm,* and *cool* zones, which extend out in all directions (Figure 5-36). The extent of each zone depends on the hazards presented. Generally, the **hot zone** includes those areas immediately inside and adjacent to the involved vehicles and wreckage. The **warm zone** extends 10 to 15 feet from the vehicles and wreckage, and is commonly referred to as the **action circle.** The **cool zone** extends out from the warm zone as needed for crowd and traffic control. This zone is where tools, equipment, and extra personnel are staged until needed in the hot and warm zones.

▓ KEY WORDS ▓

safety zones Areas established on any emergency scene that designate the areas of operation and the level of hazard or control required. Examples of safety control zones include traffic control zones as well as *hot, warm,* and *cool* zones.

hot zone The area immediately adjacent to the patient or hazard on a crash scene.

warm zone The work area that extends 10 to 15 feet away from the crashed vehicle(s).

action circle The area encompassed by the warm zone and including the hot zone where the actual rescue activities take place.

cool zone The area beyond the warm zone on a crash scene (beyond 10 to 15 feet). Tools, equipment, and extra personnel are staged in this zone until they are needed in the hot and warm zones.

With an emphasis on personal safety, in your firefighter training you will get the skills needed to establish and maintain safety zones. These skills include scene assessment, hazard control, stabilizing heavy objects, accessing the patient, creating a path of egress for the patient, treating and removing the patient, and securing the scene afterward.

 **Tips!**

Crash Scene Benchmarks

Crash scenes can be better understood by viewing them in stages or benchmarks:

1. *Scene size-up.* The main goal is to look for immediate hazards and the number and severity of injured patients (Figure 5-37).

FIGURE 5-37

2. *Traffic control.* A traffic control zone is used to detour traffic away from the crash scene. Tools should be staged inside the protected traffic control zone (Figure 5-38).

FIGURE 5-38

3. *Work zones.* Work zones usually include hot, warm, and cool zones and often are marked with yellow caution tape. All firefighters who enter the hot or warm safety zones must wear appropriate PPE and must evacuate all bystanders from this area (Figure 5-39).

4. *Task assignments.* The Company Officer will establish a quick plan of action, advising the firefighters of his or her plan and giving work assignments.

FIGURE 5-39

—Continued

5. *Hazard control.* Hazards are controlled as they are encountered. Vehicles carry flammable fuel and oils, and hot radiator fluids, and can also have damaged batteries that release battery acids. In addition, undeployed air bags may discharge unexpectedly (Figure 5-40). Many scene hazards, such as destabilized heavy vehicles or objects or downed power lines, can pose a serious threat to firefighters (Figure 5-41). Firefighters must therefore be aware of scene elements at all times.

FIGURE 5-40

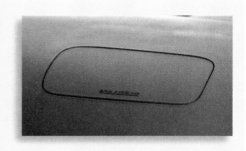

FIGURE 5-41

FIGURE 5-42

6. *Gaining access and delivering patient care.* Firefighters will gain access and provide first aid to injured individuals as soon as they can (Figure 5-42). Your job will probably involve assisting firefighters with more advanced emergency medical training or other medical personnel with packaging and removing the patients. Remember to use proper body positioning when helping to move patients, especially those who are on backboards (Figure 5-43).

FIGURE 5-43

7. *Securing the scene.* Once patients have been transported to emergency facilities, secure all tools and equipment. Traffic control equipment will be returned to the fire apparatus *after* the scene is turned over to law enforcement.

Safety Tip!

Depending on the extent of the crash and the units necessary to manage it, personnel accountability systems may be used at vehicle crash scenes to keep track of firefighters (Figure 5-44).

FIGURE 5-44 Personnel accountability systems are used for tracking firefighters on larger or more complicated incidents.

Do It!

Driving Safety

After actual firefighting activities, driving is the next most dangerous thing you will do as a firefighter. For this reason, we stress the importance of good driving habits. You must respond to the station or emergency in a safe manner and, above all, protect yourself, your fellow firefighters, and the community. Additional resources that are sent out to take care of a firefighter involved in a collision while responding to a call detracts from the initial emergency at hand.

Think about the importance of returning home to your family. Slow down! Stop at all signals! Wear your seatbelt! If you cannot drive safely and responsibly, then do not become a firefighter.

Prove It

Knowledge Assessment

Signed Documentation Tear-Out Sheet

Exterior Operations Level Firefighter—Chapter 5

Name: _____

Fill out the ten-question quiz below, the Knowledge Assessment Sheet, by circling the correct answer for each question. When finished, sign it and give to your instructor/Company Officer for his or her signature. Turn in the Knowledge Assessment Sheet to the proper person as part of the documentation that you have completed your training for this chapter.

1. A defensive driving course for firefighters covers the state and local requirements and regulations for POV responses.
   a. True
   b. False

2. The U.S. DOT defines a _____ as a situation in which there is a high probability of death or serious injury to an individual or significant property loss, and action by an emergency vehicle operator may reduce the seriousness of the situation.
   a. fire emergency
   b. true emergency
   c. rescue incident
   d. true rescue scene

3. _____ is the omission of doing something that a reasonable, prudent person would ordinarily do, or doing something that such a person would not do.
   a. A true emergency
   b. Diligence
   c. Negativity
   d. Negligence

4. Lack of _____ has contributed to many fatalities.
   a. intelligence
   b. seatbelt use
   c. a rear view mirror
   d. speed

5. The extent and type of protective clothing you need depends on the _____ as well as the policy of your Company Officer and your department.
   a. type of fire apparatus
   b. type of weather
   c. type of emergency
   d. response route

6. When getting off the apparatus, always check _____.
   a. for your gloves
   b. in all directions for traffic and hazards
   c. the rear of the apparatus only
   d. the front of the apparatus only

7. When placing traffic cones on a typical two-lane roadway, how many, at a minimum, should you place within 75 feet of the rear of the fire apparatus?
   a. 10
   b. 6
   c. 12
   d. 5

8. The safety rule to use when placing traffic cones is to _____.
   a. always walk toward traffic
   b. always turn your back to traffic
   c. never turn your back to traffic
   d. always walk away from traffic

9. The _____ is the reaction time plus the braking distance.
   a. total stopping distance
   b. total braking distance
   c. total inertia distance
   d. total velocity distance

10. The two methods for determining a safe following distance when operating a fire apparatus are the _____ rule and estimating _____.
   a. 3-minute; one apparatus length
   b. 3-second; one apparatus length
   c. 1-second; two apparatus lengths
   d. 5-second; one apparatus length

Prove It

Skills Assessment

Signed Documentation Tear-Out Sheet

Exterior Operations Level Firefighter—Chapter 5

Name: _____

Fill out the Skills Assessment Sheet below. Have your instructor/Company Officer check off and initial each skill you demonstrate. When finished, sign it and give to your instructor/Company Officer for his or her signature. Turn in this Skills Assessment Sheet to the proper person as part of the documentation that you have completed your training for this chapter.

Skill	Completed	Initials
1. Provide proof of completion of an approved defensive driving course.	_____	_____
2. Demonstrate safe mounting of the fire apparatus, handing over the PAS tag, applying hearing-protection headsets, and the use of seatbelts.	_____	_____
3. Demonstrate safe dismounting of the fire apparatus and waiting for instructions from the Company Officer.	_____	_____
4. Demonstrate proper personal protective clothing for daylight traffic control.	_____	_____
5. Demonstrate proper personal protective clothing for nighttime traffic control.	_____	_____
6. Safely deploy traffic cones in a transition area behind a fire apparatus on a simulated two-lane roadway.	_____	_____
7. Safely deploy traffic cones in a transition area behind a fire apparatus on a simulated multilane, high-speed, limited-access highway.	_____	_____
8. Demonstrate how to direct traffic in two directions with only one lane open.	_____	_____
9. Participating as a team member, demonstrate how to safely assess a vehicle crash scene.	_____	_____

Student Signature and Date _____ Instructor/Company Officer Signature and Date _____

Extinguishing Small Fires

What You Will Learn in This Chapter

In this chapter we will discuss what makes a fire burn and how the material that is burning affects the way we extinguish the fire. You will learn how to select the proper fire extinguisher for different types of fires and how to use it on a small fire. Finally, you will learn how to use two of the small fire attack hose lines on your engine to extinguish slightly larger fires.

What You Will Be Able to Do

After reading this chapter and participating in the practical skill sessions, you will be able to

1. Explain the three phases of an unconfined fire.
2. Explain how heat from a fire causes the fire to spread to other combustible materials.
3. Explain the fire classification system and how it affects the selection of a fire extinguisher.
4. Employ the proper fire extinguisher to extinguish a small fire.
5. Describe the elements of the fire tetrahedron.

Reality!

Small Fires Are Dangerous!

It is very easy to become complacent when working around small fires. At first glance, a small trash fire burning in a vacant lot doesn't look much different from a campfire. A small fire in a cooking pot on top of a stove can easily be extinguished by simply placing the lid back on the pot. A fire burning in a steel refuse dumpster located away from any exposures looks simple enough to extinguish. However, it is not the size of the fire that is of concern—it is the content of the fire that can make it dangerous.

Consider a trash fire. Burning lawn waste and household papers produce smoke that is irritating to the eyes, but as long as you remain upwind it doesn't pose a problem for you. But what happens when that simple trash fire contains an aerosol can, such as a hairspray or spray paint can? Both will rupture from the heat of the fire, often producing a large fireball that can engulf someone standing nearby. The can of spray paint may also contain a steel agitator ball that immediately becomes a flying projectile that can be lethal. The potential for injury at a trash fire is compounded at a dumpster fire because most dumpsters are unsecured and can contain almost any hazardous material dumped by unauthorized individuals.

Because of these issues, practice the following safety recommendations when working around small fires:

- Wear your protective clothing, including using your helmet and visor, whenever you are working near a fire of any size.
- Use your SCBA whenever working near a dumpster fire.
- If possible, know what is burning and use the appropriate extinguisher or extinguishing agent for the type of fire.

Fire Characteristics and Classifications

Have you ever seen a fire? Of course you have. Fires are common. However, starting with this chapter you will look at fire in a different way for the rest of your life. We won't be delving into the intricacies of fire chemistry and behavior, but we will study what makes a fire burn, what makes it spread, and how fires are classified by what is burning. These few simple concepts lay the foundation for every fire-extinguishing method we use.

What Makes a Fire Burn

An open flame is evidence that the process of combustion is occurring (Figure 6-1). Four things need to come together for combustion to occur: fuel, heat, oxygen, and the chemical reaction that keeps the flame burning. These four elements of combustion are often depicted as the **fire tetrahedron** (Figure 6-2). Take away any of the four elements of the fire tetrahedron and fire is not possible. For example, if a piece of paper is burning and you spray it with water, you are rapidly cooling the fuel to below the temperature at which paper burns and are therefore taking away the element of heat. If you place a heavy blanket over the burning piece of paper instead of spraying it with water, you smother the fire, which means you remove the element of oxygen. The same result is achieved, whichever element of combustion is removed.

▰▰ KEY WORD ▰▰▰▰▰▰

fire tetrahedron A depiction of the four elements required for combustion to occur: fuel, heat, oxygen,

FIGURE 6-1 Evidence that the combustion process is happening? A flame.

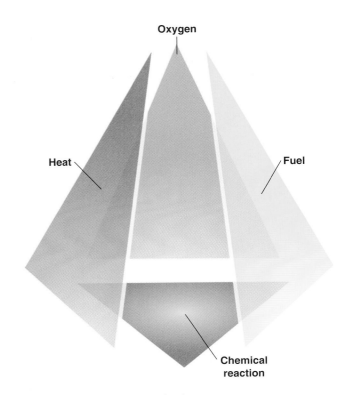

FIGURE 6-2 The fire tetrahedron.

and the chemical chain reaction that keeps the flame burning.

Why Fires Grow

A normal fire in an unconfined area goes through three phases after it is ignited: (1) the growth phase, (2) the fully developed phase, in which all of the material is involved in the fire, and (3) the decay phase, in which the amount of available fuel is reduced as the fire consumes the material. This is true for most fires that burn in an outdoor area that is free of any confinement.

Because the smoke and flammable gasses that are generated by the burning process are confined, fires that start in a confined area, such as a building, go through an additional phase called *flashover.* During flashover, the smoke and heated gasses combine with the right amount of heat and oxygen to ignite suddenly. This is the reason the best course of action for anyone who is inexperienced and ill-equipped to fight an interior fire is to evacuate the area immediately. Interior firefighting is for firefighters who have been trained to Level 1 and above.

Fires grow based on the amount of fuel available to burn. Flames can easily spread to other combustible materials near the original fire through heat transfer; therefore, knowing how flames spread can help you contain a fire. Heat transfers by three primary means: (1) **conduction,** (2) **convection,** and (3) **radiation.**

An example of conducted heat occurs when a fire is on one side of a steel wall. The fire is consuming the fuel, yet the heat penetrates the steel wall, which in turn heats up. Through conduction, the steel wall ignites any combustible material that is touching the other side of the wall (Figure 6-3).

Convection occurs when the fire heats the air near it. When fire is within a building, hot air rises and dissipates if it isn't confined, for example, by the ceiling. Therefore, in most circumstances, any combustible materials that are above a fire are at the most risk of burning due to convection (Figure 6-4).

When we talk about radiation, we aren't referring to nuclear reactive materials. Radiation is the means by which we receive our heat from the sun. Radiation related to fire involves heat transfer from normal, combustible materials that are burning. Open flames emit heat from the light of the flames by the process of radiation. Radiant heat transfer doesn't depend on air currents or direct contact with the flame to spread a fire. For example, a large fire burning outside a building can ignite the curtains inside the building when some of the energy of the original fire radiates through a glass window (Figure 6-5).

▰ KEY WORDS ▰

conduction   A type of heat transfer in which the hot flame or fire-heated object is in direct contact with another, cooler object and heats it up.

convection   A type of heat transfer that occurs when the fire heats the air near it, causing the heated air to rise.

radiation   A transfer of heat through light waves. We receive our heat from the sun through radiation.

Fire burns in a metal dumpster, heating the sidewall.

Branches from the tree rest against the hot sidewall of the dumpster.

The tree branches catch fire.

FIGURE 6-3   Conducted heat transfer.

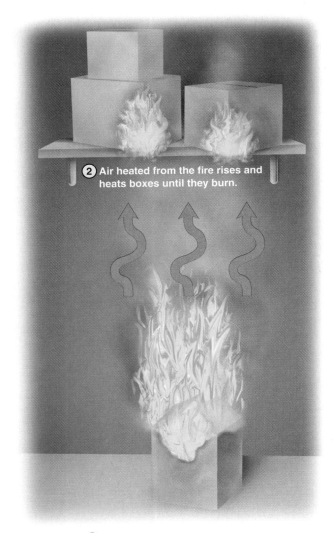

② Air heated from the fire rises and heats boxes until they burn.

① Fire burns below a shelf with boxes.

FIGURE 6-4 Convection heat transfer.

① Fire burns in a car next to a house.

② Heat radiates to the house, igniting it.

FIGURE 6-5 Radiant heat transfer.

The Fire Classification System

Generally speaking, there are five classes of materials that burn (Figure 6-6). This classification was established to help fire departments and the community select the proper fire extinguishers to use in putting out fires. Table 6-1 shows this classification.

Portable fire extinguishers have labels indicating the types of fires they are designed to extinguish. An extinguisher containing only water is usually effective only for a Class A fire (Figure 6-7). An extinguisher containing a basic dry chemical usually extinguishes Class B fires, so it is referred to as a Class B extinguisher (Figure 6-8). If the extinguisher contains an extinguishing agent that is dry and nonconductive, then it might be useful in extinguishing both Class B and Class C types of fires, so it is referred to as a Class BC extinguisher. Most dry chemical extinguishers contain a multipurpose chemical that is effective against the first three types of fires, so these are referred to as Class ABC extinguishers.

Class D fires, which involve flammable metals, require a fuel-specific extinguishing agent, so specialized dry powder extinguishers rated for Class D fires are used. Because burning metal is a rare event and is thought of as a hazardous materials type of fire, we will not be discussing Class D fires in detail at this point in your training.

FIGURE 6-6

TABLE 6-1 The Fire Classification System
Class A: Normal, ordinary combustibles in their solid form, such as wood, paper, and cloth
Class B: Flammable liquids, such as oil, gasoline, and kerosene
Class C: Any fire involving energized electricity
Class D: Flammable metal fires
Class K: Cooking oils and fats

FIGURE 6-7   Water pressure fire extinguisher.

FIGURE 6-8   Dry chemical fire extinguisher.

Only recently has the Fire Service started looking at cooking oils and fats as a separate class of fire. Most problems encountered with Class K fires are handled on a small scale with a Class B extinguishing agent. Class K agents are usually found in large cooking facilities with automatic extinguishing systems and not in small, portable fire extinguishers.

Fire Classification and the Fire Tetrahedron

The fire classification system is directly related to the fire tetrahedron. A Class A fire is usually extinguished

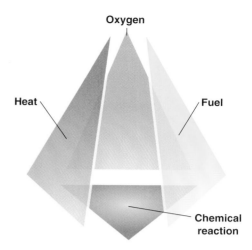

Removal of any side of the fire tetrahedron, that is: fuel, heat, oxygen or the chain reaction, results in extinguishment of the fire.

FIGURE 6-9   The fire tetrahedron and fire extinguishment.

by cooling the burning material, so it is best fought by cooling the fuel below its ignition temperature. A Class B fire is usually extinguished by isolating the fuel from the oxygen source or smothering it with a chemical or foam, so Class B fires are best fought by removing the source of oxygen. Class C fires involve energized electrical energy. The electricity usually is not the only element burning; however, everything will continue to burn as long as the electrical current applies energy to the fire. Therefore, the best way to extinguish a Class C fire is to stop the flow of electricity, which removes the heat source. Once the heat source has been removed from an electrical fire, any remaining fire involves either Class A or Class B combustible materials and should be extinguished accordingly (Figure 6-9).

The fact that we classify fires by the material that is burning also indicates where our firefighting efforts for small fires should be focused—on the burning material and not on the flames. Regardless of the classification of fire, the extinguishing agent should be applied at the base of the flames and on the material that is burning.

As we stated in the introduction to this text and in previous chapters, we are going to introduce you to the various tools, equipment, and operations in context. We start with simple scenarios and provide direction about the applications of the different tools, equipment, and techniques utilized to control a fire emergency in the scenario presented. Because each scenario builds upon the previous one, as you progress through the content and advance in your training, it is extremely important that you read the fire emergency scenarios in order.

Types of Small Fires

Small fires include trash fires, burning liquids, electrical fires, and dumpster fires. Each type of fire requires a different method of extinguishment.

Trash Fires

Trash fires typically involve Class A materials. The extinguishing agent best suited for these materials are water or Class A foam extinguishing agents. We will discuss Class A foam in a later chapter, so for now we'll concentrate on water from a water extinguisher and hose lines.

 View It!

Go to the DVD, navigate to Chapter 6, and select *Class A Trash Fire, Water Extinguisher.*

 Practice It!

Using a Water-Type Fire Extinguisher

To extinguish a simple trash fire involving mainly Class A materials, a firefighter may first use a water fire extinguisher, following these basic steps:

1. Pull the extinguisher off its mounting and pull the safety pin located in the operating handle (Figure 6-10).

   FIGURE 6-10

2. Approach the fire from a safe position with the wind to your back (Figure 6-11). *Never* let the fire get between you and your exit point.

   FIGURE 6-11

3. Point the nozzle at the base of the fire and depress the operating handle. Direct the water onto the burning materials until the fire is extinguished (Figure 6-12). Use your finger over the nozzle to break up the stream slightly. This will help avoid spreading the fuel around and will allow the water to better absorb the heat.

   FIGURE 6-12

—Continued

4. After use, the water extinguisher should be marked as "empty" so others will know it is not ready to be used again. Then at the fire station, the water extinguisher should be refilled and recharged (Figure 6-13). Your department will have specific procedures for indicating that an extinguisher is empty and for refilling a discharged water pressure fire extinguisher.

FIGURE 6-13

The General Care and Maintenance of Fire Extinguishers

The general care and maintenance of all fire extinguishers can be accomplished by visually inspecting them using the following steps:

1. Inspect the operating handles and cylinders of the fire extinguisher for physical damage (Figure 6-14). Damaged fire extinguishers should be immediately removed from service and documented. You should also notify your Company Officer.

FIGURE 6-14

2. Check the hydrostatic date and report any out-of-date extinguisher to your Company Officer (Figure 6-15).

FIGURE 6-15

3. Look for an inspection tag (except on water pressure fire extinguishers). (Figure 6-16.) Make sure that it is up to date. Out-of-date fire extinguishers should be immediately reported to your Company Officer.

FIGURE 6-16

—Continued

4. Make sure that the extinguisher is properly mounted, whether in the fire station or on the fire apparatus (Figures 6-17 and 6-18).

FIGURE 6-17

FIGURE 6-18

⇨ Practice It!

Extinguishing a Trash Fire with a Small Attack Line

One-inch attack lines used to extinguish trash fires include booster lines and single-jacketed lines. Use these steps to extinguish a trash fire with a small attack line:

1. Grab the nozzle and advance the line toward the fire. If someone else is advancing with the nozzle, grab the hose about 25 feet behind him or her and help pull the line (Figure 6-19).

FIGURE 6-19

2. Point the nozzle at the ground, slowly open it, and adjust the spray pattern (Figure 6-20). Bleeding the nozzle ensures that you have water at the nozzle before approaching the fire.

FIGURE 6-20

—Continued

3. Shut off the flow of water at the nozzle, hold the line and nozzle under your arm with both hands, and approach the fire (Figure 6-21).

FIGURE 6-21

4. Flow water onto the base of the trash fire, which will quickly extinguish the fire. For a trash fire, start with a straight stream and continue cooling it with a wide-pattern fog stream (Figure 6-22).

FIGURE 6-22

5. Flow water until the fire is completely extinguished (Figure 6-23). With some trash fires, the debris will need to be turned in order for the water to reach hidden fires.

FIGURE 6-23

Burning Liquids

The extinguishing agents best suited for small fires involving flammable liquids work by smothering the flames. Common examples of small, burning liquid fires include cooking oil fires and fires involving spilled gasoline around lawn mowers (Figure 6-24). Anything larger than these types of fires is beyond the capabilities of most portable fire extinguishers. Class B fire extinguishers include a carbon dioxide (CO_2) extinguisher and a dry chemical extinguisher. Most dry chemical extinguishers are useful for both Class A and Class B fires.

FIGURE 6-24 Class B fire extinguishers can be used on small, burning liquid fires.

When the burning liquid has spread out on level ground and the fuel that is burning is only a millimeter or so deep, the fire will usually go out and stay out when you apply the extinguishing agent as long as the extinguishing agent stays in place until the fuel cools down.

When the fire involves a liquid that is deeper than a millimeter or so, applying the extinguishing agent with too much force can make the liquid spread or splash out of its container. Burning liquids can be spread when the nozzle from the fire extinguisher is too close to the burning liquid. Another problem with burning liquids is that they are affected by gravity. Until the source of a burning liquid is either controlled or exhausted, the fire will flow downhill. Running liquid fires are much larger than can be handled with portable fire extinguishers, so if the fire moves, evacuate the area and don't try to fight it.

The most important principle to follow when extinguishing a liquid fire is to approach it from the upwind and/or uphill side. Start at one side of the fire and allow the extinguishing agent to push its way across the surface of the fire (Figure 6-25).

Carbon Dioxide Fire Extinguisher

As its name implies, a carbon dioxide (CO_2) fire extinguisher is filled with pressurized carbon dioxide. When applied to a burning liquid, it smothers the flames by dispersing the available oxygen, replacing it with carbon dioxide, which does not support combustion. The large horn at the end of the hose best differentiates a CO_2 extinguisher from a typical dry chemical extinguisher. This horn allows the carbon dioxide gas to expand slightly as it directs the gas to the flames (Figure 6-26). Because the carbon dioxide gas is under pressure, you must take care to avoid blowing the burning fuel out of its container, thus spreading the fire.

Because a CO_2 extinguisher uses a gas as the primary extinguishing agent, it leaves no contaminating residue to be cleaned up. However, this feature of a CO_2 extinguisher provides both an advantage and a disadvantage. CO_2 dissipates rapidly and doesn't require clean up, but it often dissipates before the flammable liquid is allowed to cool; therefore, the liquid often re-ignites.

FIGURE 6-25 When extinguishing a liquid fire, approach it from the upwind and uphill side. Start at one side of the fire, allowing the extinguishing agent to push its way across the surface of the fire.

FIGURE 6-26 Carbon dioxide fire extinguisher.

View It!

Go to the DVD, navigate to Chapter 6, and select *Carbon Dioxide Fire Extinguisher.*

Practice It!

Using a Carbon Dioxide Fire Extinguisher

To extinguish a small fire involving Class B materials, a firefighter can use a carbon dioxide extinguisher, following these basic steps:

1. Pull the extinguisher off its mounting and pull the safety pin located in the operating handle (Figure 6-27).

FIGURE 6-27

2. Approach the fire from a safe position with the wind to your back (Figure 6-28). *Never* let the fire get between you and your exit point.

FIGURE 6-28

3. Point the nozzle at the base of the fire and depress the operating handle. Direct the agent onto the burning materials until the fire is extinguished (Figure 6-29).

FIGURE 6-29

Dry Chemical Extinguisher

Dry chemical extinguishers contain a nonflammable, powdered chemical that is expelled by a harmless gas when you squeeze the trigger of the extinguisher. The chemical coats the surface area of the burning material to break the connection between the fuel and heat. This type of extinguisher works on the chemical reaction side of the fire tetrahedron (Figure 6-30). Because the extinguishing agent is expelled under pressure, a dry chemical extinguisher can spread a fire involving a puddle of a burning liquid if you aren't careful when you operate the device.

As with the other portable extinguishers we have discussed, approach the fire from an upwind, safe area and start applying the dry chemical from a safe distance, moving in on the fire as the flames subside.

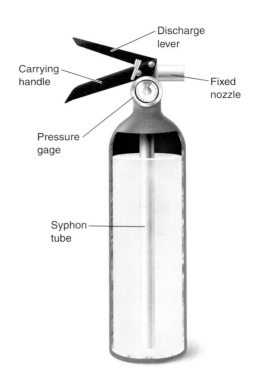

FIGURE 6-30   Dry chemical fire extinguisher.

 **View It!**

Go to the DVD, navigate to Chapter 6, and select *Dry Chemical Fire Extinguisher.*

Practice It!

Using a Dry Chemical Fire Extinguisher

To extinguish a small fire involving Class A, B, or C materials using a dry chemical extinguisher, following these basic steps:

1. Pull the extinguisher off its mounting and pull the safety pin located in the operating handle (Figure 6-31).

FIGURE 6-31

2. Approach the fire from a safe position with the wind to your back (Figure 6-32). *Never* let the fire get between you and your exit point.

FIGURE 6-32

—Continued

3. Point the nozzle at the base of the fire and depress the operating handle. Direct the agent onto the burning materials until the fire is extinguished (Figure 6-33).

FIGURE 6-33

Electrical Fires

Although many types of fire extinguishers are rated for Class C fires involving energized electrical equipment, the best approach to an electrical fire is from the heat side of the fire tetrahedron. An energized electrical fire receives its main heat source from electricity and not from what is burning. For example, if a small electrical appliance is on fire, switching off the electrical source at the circuit breaker will usually stop the fire or at least decrease the fire from a Class C fire to a lower-grade fire. By stopping the electrical current, the fire can be switched from a Class C to a Class A or Class B fire, depending on the material that is left burning. In addition to extinguishing the fire, your concern is for individuals' safety from the hazard that the electrical current presents. Therefore, isolating the electrical source is an important measure.

Isolating the electrical source from a small appliance is simple enough when you can safely unplug the cord or switch off a circuit breaker (Figure 6-34). However, if the electrical fire involves anything more than a small appliance (for example, a downed power line), then controlling the electricity should be left to the power company. You need to secure the area and stay away!

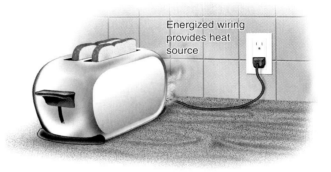

Energized wiring provides heat source

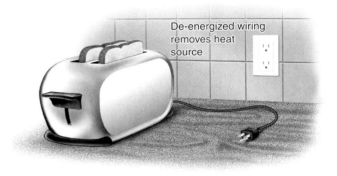

De-energized wiring removes heat source

FIGURE 6-34   Turn off the electricity!

Dumpster Fires

There are many types of trash containers that you will encounter in responding to trash fires. The most common trash containers at commercial businesses and construction sites are dumpsters. Dumpsters are commonly metal containers of various sizes that have a metal or plastic lid. They may or may not be locked and might be situated next to a large trash compactor.

You will use the same tools and techniques on a dumpster fire as you will with any trash fire, with few exceptions. Be ready to place a small ladder to

get access to the top of the dumpster. You may need to force entry to any locked access doors. You may also need a larger flow of water through large hose lines and nozzles due to the increased amount of the material inside the dumpster.

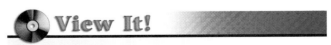

View It!

Go to the DVD, navigate to Chapter 6, and select *Dumpster Fires*.

Safety Tips!

Use the following precautions when extinguishing a dumpster fire:

- Always wear full PPE, including an SCBA (Figure 6-35).

FIGURE 6-35

- Fires in metal dumpsters are hot, so remember not to touch the metal surfaces.
- Always approach a dumpster fire with caution, because you do not know what is burning in the dumpster. Stay protected and have a good water supply (Figure 6-36).

FIGURE 6-36

- Large, roll-off type dumpsters with trash compactors have other hazards, including pressurized hydraulic lines and electrical hazards. Consider these to be large machinery fires that present additional hazards not expected at a normal dumpster fire.
- Never climb inside a dumpster!

Do It!

Extinguishing Small Fires Safely

As a firefighter, you need to know how fire burns and how the materials burning affect the way you extinguish the fire. You should know how to use a fire extinguisher or a small attack line to extinguish a trash fire and a dumpster fire. You should also remember the characteristics of burning liquid and electrical fires. Always remember that whatever the size of the fire or the materials burning, all fires can be dangerous. Wear appropriate personal protective equipment at all times when working to control these incidents.

Prove It

Knowledge Assessment

Signed Documentation Tear-Out Sheet

Exterior Operations Level Firefighter—Chapter 6

Name: _____

Fill out the ten-question quiz below, the Knowledge Assessment Sheet, by circling the correct answer for each question. When finished, sign it and give to your instructor/Company Officer for his or her signature. Turn in this Knowledge Assessment Sheet to the proper person as part of the documentation that you have completed your training for this chapter.

1. Four things need to come together for combustion to occur: fuel, heat, _____ , and the chemical reaction.
   a. carbon dioxide
   b. water
   c. oxygen
   d. nitrogen

2. A fire grows in size based on the amount of _____ there is to burn.
   a. oxygen
   b. nitrogen
   c. fuel
   d. air

3. _____ doesn't depend on air currents or direct contact with flames to spread a fire.
   a. Radiation
   b. Convection
   c. Conduction
   d. Fire spread

4. A water extinguisher would work best on a _____ fire.
   a. Class A
   b. Class B
   c. Class C
   d. Class K

5. An example of a small, burning liquid fire would be _____ .
   a. a spill and fire at an oil refinery
   b. a burning gasoline tanker on a highway
   c. spilled gasoline around a lawn mower
   d. magnesium metal shavings burning outside a machinist shop

6. In most small fires, the extinguishing agent should usually be applied to the _____ of the fire.
   a. top
   b. back
   c. front
   d. base

7. Energized electrical fires receive their main heat source from _____ .
    a. oxygen
    b. electricity
    c. nitrogen
    d. radiation

8. Fire extinguishers rated for use on Class B fires include carbon dioxide and _____ extinguishers.
    a. water
    b. dry chemical
    c. light water
    d. heavy chemical

9. Dumpsters are the most common type of trash containers located outside of commercial businesses.
    a. True
    b. False

10. Full PPE is NOT required for dumpster fires because they are so small.
    a. True
    b. False

Student Signature and Date _____   Instructor/Company Officer Signature and Date _____

146

Prove It

Skills Assessment
Signed Documentation Tear-Out Sheet
Exterior Operations Level Firefighter—Chapter 6

Name: _____

Fill out the Skills Assessment Sheet below. Have your instructor/Company Officer check off and initial each skill you demonstrate. When finished, sign it and give to your instructor/Company Officer for his or her signature. Turn in this Skills Assessment Sheet to the proper person as part of the documentation that you have completed your training for this chapter.

Skill	Completed	Initials
1. Employ a pressurized water extinguisher.	_____	_____
2. Employ a carbon dioxide water extinguisher.	_____	_____
3. Employ a dry chemical fire extinguisher.	_____	_____
4. Deploy and use a booster line.	_____	_____

Student Signature and Date _____   Instructor/Company Officer Signature and Date _____

7

Ground Cover Fires

What You Will Learn in This Chapter

In this chapter we will discuss ground cover firefighting and introduce you to basic aspects of wildland or brush fires. We will explain some of the terminology that is unique to these types of fire operations. You will learn about ground cover fire movement and behavior along with some extinguishing methods. You will also learn about the black-line approach, protective clothing, and personnel accountability systems used at a typical brush fire operation. Finally, you will learn about tools, equipment, and brush truck operations.

What You Will Be Able to Do

After reading this chapter, you will be asked to tour the fire station so that you know where to find items that are important to your safety. After reading the chapter and taking the tour, you will be able to

1. Define basic terms used at brush fire incidents.
2. Describe the basic parts of a typical brush fire.
3. Explain how to safely approach a brush fire.
4. Explain your part in a brush fire accountability system.
5. Demonstrate the proper donning of the brush fire protective clothing your agency uses.
6. Explain the "black-line" firefighting approach.
7. Demonstrate the use of various hand tools associated with brush fire operations.
8. Describe the fire movement and assessment safety issues that pertain to brush fires.
9. Given the brush fire apparatus your agency uses, demonstrate how to safely ride on it, deploy and extend hose lines, and utilize tools and equipment carried on the apparatus for fighting a small brush fire.

Safety Lesson: A NIOSH Report

Wear Your Gear, Even on Small Fires!

On August 1, 2002, a firefighter in South Dakota was severely burned while fighting a fire that was consuming a wheat field. He had responded directly to the fire in his personal vehicle (POV) where he met up with another firefighter whose POV, a pickup truck, was equipped with a 75-gallon water tank and a gasoline-driven pump. According to the NIOSH report, although numerous firefighters responded to the scene, there was no Incident Command System established. The firefighters on the scene dispersed on their own as they arrived on the scene. The victim and the firefighter with the pickup truck talked on the scene and agreed that the victim would spray water from the bed of the truck while the other firefighter drove.

The two firefighters proceeded through a gate and into the field near the encroaching head of the fire. While fighting the fire, the victim was wearing tennis shoes, denim jeans, a T-shirt, and a baseball cap. A sudden gust of wind blew fire and smoke over the truck. The driver immediately pulled the truck forward and to the right. It is unknown if the victim fell from the truck as a result of being overcome by the fire and smoke or from the sudden forward movement of the truck. He ran about 200 yards, where he encountered a barbed wire fence and became entangled in the barbed wire. Other firefighters rushed to his aid, and the victim was evacuated by a medical helicopter to the burn center, where he died 5 days later from his injuries.

Follow-Up

NIOSH Report #F2002-37

After this incident was reviewed and evaluated, the NIOSH investigative report recommended that the following practices be implemented:

- Ensure that firefighters follow established procedures for combating ground cover fires.
- Develop and implement an Incident Command System.
- Provide firefighters with personal protective equipment (PPE) that is appropriate for wildland fires and is also NFPA 1977 compliant.
- Provide firefighters with appropriate wildland firefighter training.

Small Ground Cover Fires

Firefighters are called upon to perform many different jobs, including extinguishing **ground cover fires.** Ground cover fires occur in grassy vacant lots, rural wooded areas, parks, and even in the median areas on roadways (Figure 7-1). These fires are quite different from building fires. Ground cover fires are more like large Class A trash fires in that the fuel is spread out over a wider area. The tactics that firefighters use to extinguish these fires must take into consideration such elements as weather conditions, the humidity level, the type and arrangement of foliage, natural and manmade **firebreaks,** and the direction the fire travels as it burns.

In the United States, urban and suburban areas have been encroaching more and more on the wildland areas surrounding them. This spread is referred to as the **wildland/urban interface.** In this interface there is little or no separation between homes and even commercial buildings and the heavily wooded areas they are near. Property loss often results when large wildfires occur.

At this point in your training, we are going to limit our discussion to small ground cover fires. Even though we see and hear about the massive fires that occur in vast wildland areas, most ground cover fires are less than an acre in size and are controlled by a small crew

FIGURE 7-1 Ground cover fires are very common, even in urban areas. Most are small enough to be extinguished with a small hose line.

of firefighters. These smaller fires occur everywhere—in big cities and in small, rural communities.

KEY WORDS

firebreak An area, either manmade or natural, that provides no fuel for a spreading ground cover fire. Firebreaks are used to halt the spread of and assist in controlling ground cover fires.

ground cover fire A category of brush fire that is smaller than a wildfire—usually less than an acre in size and handled by one firefighting crew. The majority of brush fires in the United States fit this description.

wildland/urban interface The situation in which urban and suburban growth has intruded into open wildland areas, increasing the exposure to wildfires to homes and businesses in the area.

Wildfires

Firefighters who work routinely on **wildfires** in wildland areas receive additional training specific to these very different and much larger fire incidents. The operations for wildfires involve an extensive Incident Management System (IMS) and different firefighting apparatus, such as air **tankers** and fire-line tractors. These fires are major events and require some prequalification training in order to understand their scope and to understand and participate in tactical operations (Figure 7-2). This special training can result in certification and becoming a "red-card" status **wildland firefighter.** Though structural firefighters will respond to and assist in these events, you will be assigned duties within your scope of training and your capabilities, as established by your agency.

FIGURE 7-2 Large brush fires require extensive training and are coordinated through an Incident Management System.

KEY WORDS

tanker An airplane equipped to deliver large amounts of water or other extinguishing agents to a ground cover fire via an air drop.

wildfire A large ground cover fire that involves many acres of open wildland.

wildland firefighter A firefighter trained for fighting fires in open wildland areas.

Fire Movement and Behavior

Ground cover fires involve natural plant growth fuels burning in an open area. These fuels can be grass, brush, and even trees, as well as combinations of these items. These fires are usually handled by one or two firefighting crews.

Depending on wind direction, the topography of the landscape, and the dryness and arrangement of the ground cover growth involved, the fire tends to spread outward. As it burns, it moves in the direction of the wind. In hilly or mountainous areas, the fire tends to burn up a slope toward the unburned area until it is affected by winds at the top of the hill or mountain (Figure 7-3).

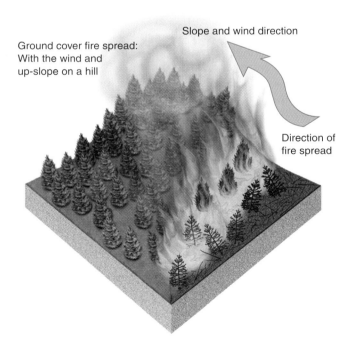

Slope and wind direction

Ground cover fire spread: With the wind and up-slope on a hill

Direction of fire spread

FIGURE 7-3 Fire tends to move downwind and uphill. A fire burning up the side of a hill will move until it is affected by winds at the top of the hill.

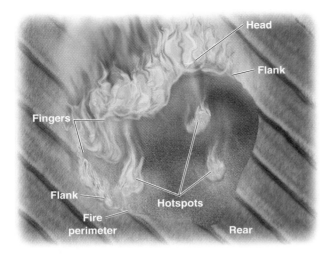

FIGURE 7-4 Parts of a ground cover fire. The fastest moving part of a brush fire is called the head, the sides are the flanks, and the point opposite the head is the rear.

Common Fire Terms

There is usually a concentrated, heavy involvement at the leading edge of a fire. This part of the fire is known as the **head** of the fire and is the most rapidly moving area of the fire. The parts of the fire on either side of the head are known as the **flanks** of the fire. The edge of the burned fire area opposite the head is known as the **rear** (Figure 7-4). The area around the edge of the entire fire area, including both the burned and the still burning areas, is known as the **fire perimeter.** As the fire burns, involved areas can extend beyond the main perimeter in narrow burning areas called **fingers**. The ground cover fire may also feature an area called a **hotspot** that is located inside the burned area. The hotspot may continue to burn because it has more fuel than the surrounding brush. Hotspots can also be located outside the original fire area due to hot embers falling from the main body of the fire. Finally, a rapidly spreading ground cover fire with a well-defined head is said to be **running.**

▬▬ KEY WORDS ▬▬

fingers   Small extensions of fire growth that protrude from the main body of a ground cover fire.

fire perimeter   The outside edge of the entire ground cover fire. The inside of the fire perimeter contains the burned area while the area outside the perimeter is unburned.

flanks   The smaller fire-involved areas on either side of the head of a ground cover fire.

head   The main burning area of a brush fire that occurs on the perimeter of the fire. It is located on the side in the direction in which the fire is moving and will have the most intense fire characteristics.

hotspot   An area of burning located either within the burned perimeter of a brush fire or outside the fire perimeter where fire has jumped over from the main body of fire. A hotspot continues to burn inside a burned-out area of a ground cover fire. Hotspots can also develop from hot ashes and burning embers that drop from the fire, landing outside the fire area and starting a small fire or hotspot.

rear   The edge of the burned fire area opposite the head.

running   Rapid movement of a ground cover fire.

Extinguishing Ground Cover Fires

Extinguishment Methods

Ground cover fires can be extinguished in three main ways: (1) with water and other extinguishing agents, (2) with firebreaks, and (3) with a combination of these items. Whatever method is used, the head and flanks of the fire should always be extinguished from the burned side of the fire. Because ground cover fires can suddenly change intensity and direction, approaching them from the burned side reduces exposure to an uncontrolled and often deadly onrush of fire. This approach should be used even on small grass fires that are extinguished with a small booster line connected to a pumper.

Water and Other Extinguishing Agents

If the fire is small enough and a water supply is available, the fire can be extinguished directly with the application of water or another extinguishing agent like a Class A foam. Class A foams are usually added to the attack-line water supply. Because these types of foam agents allow the water to be more easily absorbed by the natural wood and brush materials, they provide more extinguishing capability to the water as it is applied. Water can be applied with a booster line or a trash-line hose connected to a standard fire pumper, a **brush truck,** or a **tender (water tanker)** (Figure 7-5).

brush truck A specialized piece of fire apparatus designed to deliver tools, manpower, and some water to the scene of a ground cover fire. It may or may not have off-road capability and can be used to extinguish smaller fires as well as to protect equipment, personnel, and fire lines on larger wildland fire operations.

tender A piece of specialized firefighting apparatus designed to deliver large amounts of water to a fire scene where a water supply is not readily available. Under the National Incident Management System, wheeled apparatus that had previously been called a tanker is now called a tender. The term *tanker* is now used to refer to an airplane that delivers water or other extinguishing agents via an air drop.

water tanker Under the National Incident Management System, this apparatus is now called a *tender*.

Firebreaks

Ground cover fires can be extinguished by preparing the unburned area as the fire burns, steering the fire by the use of firebreaks, both manmade and natural. Examples of natural firebreaks include rivers, lakes, streams, and sparsely vegetated areas. Examples of manmade firebreaks include roadways, parking lots, and farmlands. Manmade firebreaks also include trenches made by teams of fire crews using hand tools or specially designed forestry tractors in areas well ahead of the fire. Foliage can also be cleared utilizing a backfire technique. It involves intentionally but carefully setting fire to foliage ahead of the running head of a fire to slow its progress. This technique requires special training and must be performed by qualified personnel.

Firebreaks can also be prepared by applying fire retardant agents delivered by air drop or sprayed by hose lines. The fire burns up to the firebreak, stops, and burns the remaining fuel inside the perimeter. The work area around the fire that is prepared as a firebreak is known as the **fire line** (Figure 7-6). After

(a)

(b)

(c)

FIGURE 7-5 (a) Engine, (b) brush truck, and (c) tender.

FIGURE 7-6 A firebreak can be created by scraping away any flammable ground cover until mineral soil is exposed.

creating firebreaks, firefighters then monitor them and quickly extinguish any small spot fires that may spread beyond the firebreaks.

fire line The work area around the body of a ground cover fire.

Combination Method

The third method of extinguishing ground cover fires is a combination of the previous two methods—stabilizing the firebreaks and extinguishing the head and flanks of the fire with water or other extinguishing agents (Figure 7-7). Even a small ground cover fire can be dangerous. The combination method of extinguishing a ground cover fire is considered an advanced method and should not be attempted without proper supervision and support from experienced crews.

The Black-Line Approach

If left unchecked, most ground cover fires burn until they run out of readily consumable fuel. The **black-line approach** is a method of controlling ground cover fires by allowing the fire to burn to a natural or manmade firebreak where it runs out of fuel. Typically, a fire that is running through

light fuels, such as tall grass or knee-high vegetation, burns until it reaches an open field of grass, a plowed field, or a road, where it slows down or self-extinguishes (Figure 7-8). Use this dynamic to your advantage by approaching the fire from the burned side or by letting the fire burn across open areas until it reaches a road or plowed firebreak. When the fire reaches short grass, the intensity diminishes and a simple dousing with water takes care of the fire at that point. This isn't to say that a wildfire won't jump a firebreak or road, but remember, for our purposes we are concerned with fires in light fuels, such as knee-high grass, weeds, or crops. Any fires that start outside the fire area due to hot ashes and burning firebrands dropping down result in spot-over fires. Spot-over fires are handled quickly with available water.

black-line approach A method of controlling ground cover fires that allows the fire to burn to a natural or manmade firebreak, where it runs out of fuel.

Protective Clothing: Wildland Gear

Protective clothing for structural firefighting is often sufficient for the short term in ground cover firefighting operations. In some areas of the country,

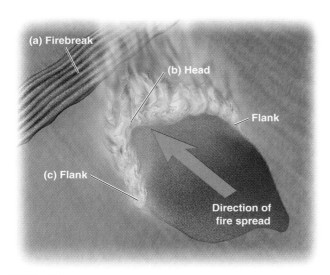

FIGURE 7-7 Firebreaks, head, and flank of a groundcover fire. (a) Firebreak, (b) head, and (c) flank.

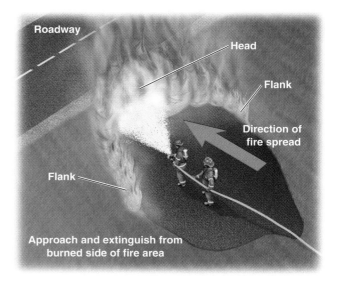

FIGURE 7-8 The black-line approach takes advantage of natural breaks, such as roadways, to allow the intensity of the fire to diminish naturally.

structural firefighters may be assigned wildland fire-fighting protective clothing. This clothing is lighter weight and is designed for longer-term firefighting operations at wildland fires. Be sure to wear the appropriate gear as designated by your agency's policy and your Company Officer.

A typical wildland firefighter's personal protective clothing includes the following items (Figure 7-9):

- Head protection, provided by an approved light-weight helmet
- Eye protection, provided by approved goggles and a face shield
- Additional head protection, provided by a face and neck shroud (such as fire-resistant material attached to the helmet)
- A face protector, independent of the helmet
- Body protection, provided by an approved two-piece garment (pants and coat) or an approved one-piece jumpsuit
- Hand protection, provided by approved gloves
- Approved footwear

Accessories may also be used, including belts, clips, and small tools. Small, personal, fireproof enclosures called fire shelters may also be included. If you are issued protective clothing, become familiar with properly donning it for ground cover fire operations.

Tools and Equipment

In fighting ground cover fires, it is important to establish a small firebreak around the perimeter of the fire to help ensure that a rekindling does not occur. To establish a firebreak, you can use several common ground cover firefighting tools:

- *Shovel.* Used to clear an area of vegetation around the fire perimeter (Figure 7-10).
- **Council rake.** Used for clearing vegetation and debris (Figure 7-11).
- **Brush axe.** Used to cut down small bushes and shrubs that may provide fuel for a rekindling (Figure 7-12). It is important that you carry any axe

FIGURE 7-10   Shovel.

FIGURE 7-9   A typical wildland firefighter's personal protective clothing: (a) head protection, (b) eye protection, (c) face and neck shroud, (d) face protector, (e) body protection, (f) hand protection, and (g) foot protection.

FIGURE 7-11   Council rake.

safely. Carry it with the point down and throw the tool clear if you stumble or fall.

- *Backpack-style water extinguisher.* A backpack that holds up to 5 gallons of water that is sprayed with a hand-operated pump sprayer (Figure 7-13). It is a good tool to handle small spot-fires and to overhaul small areas.

KEY WORDS

council rake   A specialized tool used by firefighters to clear undergrowth and debris in order to create a fire-break at a ground cover fire.

brush axe   A brush-clearing tool used by firefighters in preparing firebreaks.

FIGURE 7-12   Brush axe.

FIGURE 7-13   Backpack-style water extinguisher.

Ground Cover Fire Operations

Alarm Response

When you receive an alarm to respond to a ground cover fire, your response and arrival are no different than for any other type of fire. You may be responding on a regular structural fire pumper, a tender, or even a specially designed brush truck. Regardless of the type of apparatus, the safety rules are the same: you should wear your seatbelt, sit in a designated seat, and put on your gear either before leaving the station or after arriving on the scene.

If you are responding to the ground cover incident in your private vehicle, make sure to park it where you can leave the area quickly if necessary. Also, carry your keys in your pocket or consider leaving them in your car. Be aware of the firefighting operations and be ready to move your vehicle if necessary.

Scene Arrival and Assessment

When your unit arrives on the scene, your Company Officer will perform a rapid size-up of the fire-involved area, looking for the extent of the involvement, the type of ground cover burning, and how fast and in which direction it is spreading (Figure 7-14). Any exposures to the fire as well as safety hazards are noted as the assessment progresses. Your Company Officer will then develop a plan and advise dispatch of both the situation and the initial actions your crew will be taking and establish Incident Command.

The personnel accountability systems used in ground cover fires are similar those used in structural fire operations. If the incident is large and requires multiple units and agencies, the PAS tags are given to the Incident Commander so that the locations of

FIGURE 7-14   The first step to developing a plan is to size up the situation.

the firefighters are monitored according to wildland firefighting procedures.

Extending Hose Lines and Fire Extinguishment

The most important thing to remember when extending a line to extinguish a brush fire is to remain constantly aware of your surroundings. Be aware of the limited extinguishing capabilities of a small fire attack line and nozzle. Stay out of brush and ground cover that is higher than your knees. The fuel in higher brush and in trees exceeds the extinguishing capabilities of the line.

Enter the fire area from the burned side and knock down the head first, especially if the fire is spreading rapidly (Figure 7-15). Watch for trip hazards as you extend the line through the ground cover. Continue applying water down one flank and then down the other.

Next, extinguish the fire along the rest of the perimeter. Make sure the fire perimeter has been completely extinguished and then wet down the unburned area adjacent to the perimeter and completely around the fire area (Figure 7-16).

Finish with the interior of the fire perimeter, extinguishing any hotspots in the burned area (Figure 7-17).

Brush Truck Operations

Some fire apparatus is designed especially for fighting ground cover fires (Figure 7-18). These units are usually designed with a small amount of water on

FIGURE 7-16 Extinguish the flanks to stop the spread of the fire.

FIGURE 7-17 Mop up any remaining hotspots to reduce the chance of another fire.

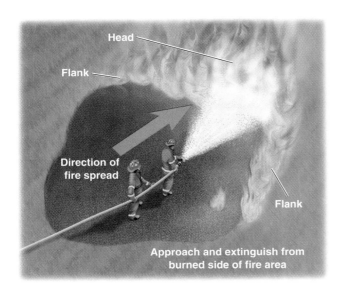

FIGURE 7-15 Knock down the fire at the head first to stop the fire's travel.

FIGURE 7-18 Brush trucks are specifically designed for off-road work.

board; they are also designed for off-road capability. They contain pumps and hose lines for attacking ground cover fires that are easily accessible and deployable. Brush trucks also have an array of brush firefighting tools, a first aid kit, and perhaps some drinking water.

As we stated before, you should respond on these units in a safe and designated seat, with your seatbelt in place. Whether these units are traveling on or off the roadway, we do not recommend riding on the front or the rear. Doing so is unsafe.

The unit will respond to the brush fire. You will deploy a small attack hose line and extinguish the fire as you would any ground cover fire. If the unit goes into the fire perimeter, it will approach it from the burned side, away from the direction the head of the fire is traveling in. The brush truck should never be positioned in front of the head of the fire (Figure 7-19).

In larger wildland incidents, brush trucks are used to protect exposures, monitor the perimeter of the fire and the fire-line area, extinguish spot-over fires, and protect other fire equipment (Figure 7-20).

The water tanks of brush trucks are refilled similarly to those on regular fire pumpers, with a fill hose at a fire hydrant. If the ground cover fire is in a remote area, the brush truck may need to be refilled by tenders. Again, the refilling procedure is basically the same, except that you will connect the brush truck refill hose into the discharge port of a tender's pump. The tender driver will then coordinate with the brush truck driver to discharge and refill the brush truck's water tank (Figure 7-21).

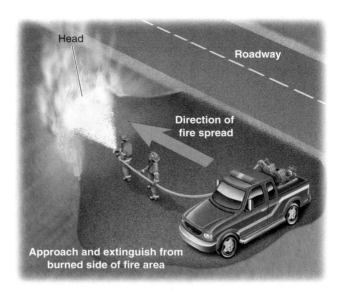

FIGURE 7-19   On small, low, ground cover fires, a brush truck may be positioned so that you can work inside the blackened area.

Brush trucks are very effective for the rapid knockdown and extinguishment of ground cover fires and can be a great asset for protection on larger wildland fires. Always be extremely careful when working around these vehicles as they travel in and around the fire area. If you are on foot, the driver may not be able to see you; therefore, stay clear of these units while they are moving (Figure 7-22).

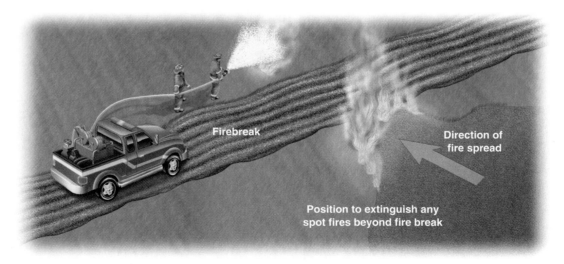

FIGURE 7-20   On larger fires, the brush truck may be positioned at a fire break to be ready to extinguish spot fires ahead of the blaze.

Evolution 7-1

Extinguishing a Ground Cover Fire

Training Area: Open area, preferably with trees and other obstacles

Equipment: Pumper or brush truck with small-diameter hose line

At least 10 targets (traffic cones or 2-liter plastic soda bottles filled with water)

PPE: Head, eye, hand, and foot protection is suggested, but follow your department's policy. ***This is*** **<u>not</u>** ***a live-fire drill.***

1. Mark off a perimeter approximately 50 feet in diameter. Arrange the targets around the perimeter, grouping 4 together at the far end of the circle to simulate the head of the fire, 2 on each flank, and setting 2 targets about 10 feet apart to simulate the rear. It is preferable if there are some trees or bushes inside the "burn area" that will offer obstacles to the hose team. If more targets are available, set them in clumps 15 or 20 feet outside the circle to simulate fingers burning outside the perimeter of a fire.

2. Each member of the crew takes a turn pulling the hose line, snaking it into the burn area from the rear. The object is to knock over all the targets at the head, then at the flanks, and then to extinguish any remaining hotspots along the entire perimeter of the fire area. Guard against horseplay and running with the hose line over uneven ground. The object of this practice drill is to teach, not to injure.

It is important that the crewmembers function as a team during this drill and follow these drill components:

- Crew members should practice spacing evenly along the hose line as it is deployed.

- A firefighter should take a position at each obstacle to keep the line moving and to prevent kinks in the hose.

- Each firefighter should rotate through all the positions in the line.

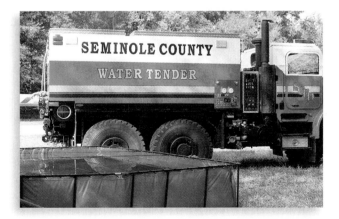

FIGURE 7-21   Tenders are usually positioned in safe areas where the brush trucks can return for more water when needed.

FIGURE 7-22   Because they are large, some brush trucks and tenders prevent the driver from seeing the area close to the unit. For your safety, stay clear of moving apparatus.

Making a Firebreak

Training Area: Open area, preferably with trees and other obstacles

Equipment: Necessary tools may include a shovel, a council rake, and some sort of axe

PPE: Head, eye, hand, and foot protection is suggested, but follow your department's policy. ***This is <u>not</u> a live-fire drill.***

1. Firebreak tools are assigned to clear away the ground cover in order to establish a firebreak around the perimeter of a ground cover fire.

2. Discuss the various methods and techniques for using each tool to rake back the ground cover in order to expose mineral soil around the entire perimeter of a burn area. If the area can be cleared, demonstrate the techniques for clearing a firebreak. If the training area is in an open area where damage to the landscape is a concern, do not perform the exercise but simply discuss the tools and tactics you will use.

3. Demonstrate and explain overhauling the burn area.

4. Finally, after the fire is declared under control and has been put out, replace your tools and equipment on the unit and return to the fire station.

5. Some agencies may require checking the fire a few times after the incident, looking for any rekindling of the fire. This practice is particularly important during hot and dry weather conditions when blowing embers can quickly start a spot fire outside the fire perimeter (Figure 7-23).

FIGURE 7-23 It is important to check for any rekindling of a fire, especially during hot and dry weather conditions.

Respecting Ground Cover Fires

Brush fire operations involve their own set of extinguishing tactics and practices. These firefighting skills are just as dangerous as any other firefighting skill you will learn. Having a serious respect for ground cover fires will enhance your safety while operating at these fire incidents.

In this chapter, we discussed ground cover firefighting and introduced wildfire incidents while explaining some of the terminology that is unique to these types of fire operations. We explained ground cover fire movement and behavior along with some extinguishing tactics. You learned about the black-line approach, protective clothing, and the personnel accountability systems used at a typical brush fire operation. You also learned about tools and equipment, and about brush truck operations. You should use everything you learned in this chapter to safely extinguish ground cover fires.

Prove It

Knowledge Assessment

Signed Documentation Tear-Out Sheet

Exterior Operations Level Firefighter—Chapter 7

Name: _____

Fill out the ten-question quiz below, the Knowledge Assessment Sheet, by circling the correct answer for each question. When finished, sign it and give to your instructor/Company Officer for his or her signature. Turn in this Knowledge Assessment Sheet to the proper person as part of the documentation that you have completed your training for this chapter.

1. The majority of ground cover fires are _____ in size.
   a. more than half of an acre
   b. less than an acre
   c. more than one tenth of an acre
   d. more than an acre

2. In hilly or mountainous areas, a ground cover fire tends to burn _____ .
   a. up the slope
   b. down the slope
   c. at an angle to the slope
   d. in a circular direction on the slope

3. A concentrated area of heavy fire involvement at the leading edge of a ground cover fire is referred to as the _____ .
   a. firebreak
   b. base
   c. flank
   d. head

4. The _____ is the area around the edge of the entire ground cover fire area.
   a. flank
   b. fire perimeter
   c. finger area
   d. fire base

5. A roadway would be an example of a _____ .
   a. natural wind break
   b. wildland fire line
   c. manmade firebreak
   d. poor firebreak

6. In many cases, it is much safer to allow a brush fire to burn to a firebreak, such as a roadway, than to extinguish any spot-over fires.
   a. True
   b. False

7. It is acceptable to put on safety gear while responding on a brush truck to a ground cover fire.
   a. True
   b. False

8. When using small-diameter fire attack lines, stay out of brush _____ .
   a. that is higher than your chest
   b. that is higher than your knees
   c. that is higher than your ankles
   d. at all times

9. A good tool for clearing ground vegetation and debris at a ground cover fire is a _____ .
   a. pike pole
   b. flat-head axe
   c. council rake
   d. Halligan bar

10. Brush trucks enter the fire area and fight the brush fire from the _____ .
    a. burned side of the fire
    b. unburned side of the fire
    c. uphill side of the fire
    d. unburned side of the head of the fire

Prove It

Skills Assessment

Signed Documentation Tear-Out Sheet

Exterior Operations Level Firefighter—Chapter 7

Name: _____

Fill out the Skills Assessment Sheet below. Have your instructor/Company Officer check off and initial each skill you demonstrate. When finished, sign it and give to your instructor/Company Officer for his or her signature. Turn in this Skills Assessment Sheet to the proper person as part of the documentation that you have completed your training for this chapter.

Skill	Completed	Initials
1. Define some basic terms used at brush fire incidents.	_____	_____
2. Describe the basic parts of a typical brush fire.	_____	_____
3. Explain how to safely approach a brush fire.	_____	_____
4. Explain your part in a brush fire accountability system.	_____	_____
5. Demonstrate the proper donning of the protective clothing used by your agency for brush fires.	_____	_____
6. Explain the black-line firefighting approach.	_____	_____
7. Demonstrate the use of various hand tools associated with brush fire operations.	_____	_____
8. Describe fire movement and assessment safety issues as they pertain to brush fires.	_____	_____
9. Demonstrate how to safely ride on the brush fire apparatus used by your agency.	_____	_____
10. Demonstrate how to deploy and extend hose lines on the apparatus for fighting a small brush fire.	_____	_____

Student Signature and Date _____   Instructor/Company Officer Signature and Date _____

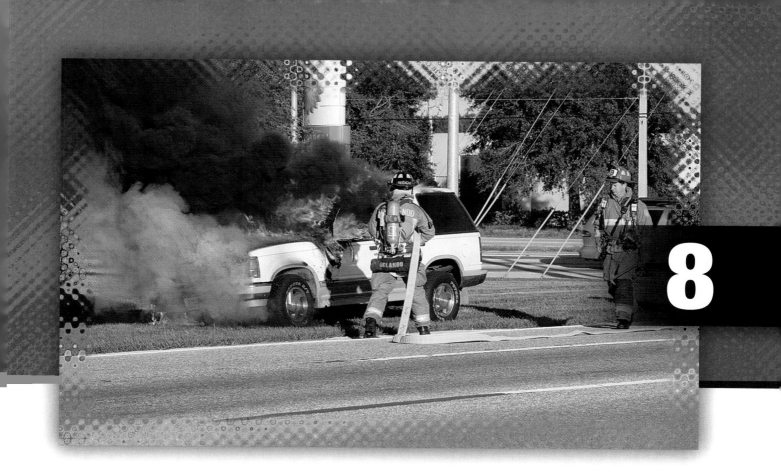

8

Passenger Vehicle Fires

What You Will Learn in This Chapter

In this chapter we will introduce you to vehicle fire operations, starting with personal protective equipment (PPE) and proper safety zones at vehicle fires. Then we will discuss vehicle design and burn characteristics. We will conclude the chapter with extinguishment techniques for vehicle fires.

We should also mention what you will *not* learn in this chapter. Fighting fires that involve a single automobile or light truck is much different from fighting fires in cargo-type vehicles or large, over-the-road equipment. Large vehicles often carry dangerous cargo and, at the very least, large amounts of flammable fuels that require a skill set that goes beyond the scope of this introductory chapter. For now, we will keep our focus on automobiles and light trucks, such as passenger vans, pickup trucks, and sport utility vehicles (SUVs).

What You Will Be Able to Do

After reading this chapter and participating in the practical skills sessions, you will be able to

1. Participate as a team member in setting up a typical safety zone and the traffic control needed at the scene of a vehicle fire.
2. Demonstrate how to chock the wheels and remove the keys of a vehicle involved in a fire.
3. Explain the safety risks of a vehicle fire and the importance of wearing full PPE and SCBA at a vehicle fire.
4. Describe the burn characteristics of the passenger, engine, and cargo compartment areas of a vehicle.
5. Demonstrate how to safely approach a vehicle fire with a small attack hose line.

6. Demonstrate the methods for safely extinguishing a fire in the passenger compartment of a vehicle.

7. Demonstrate the methods for safely accessing and extinguishing a fire in the engine compartment area of a vehicle.

8. Demonstrate the methods for safely accessing and extinguishing a fire in the cargo compartment of a vehicle.

9. Participate as a member of a two-member team demonstrating proper hose line stretch and control.

10. Participate as a member of a two-member team demonstrating proper charged hose line movement and nozzle control.

11. Demonstrate safely advancing a charged, small attack hose line.

12. Demonstrate safely performing overhaul operations on a vehicle that has been involved in a fire.

Putting a Vehicle Fire into Perspective

Most vehicle fires that you will respond to are a lost cause from the very start. Therefore, the risks from aggressive extinguishment are seldom justified by the potential for a favorable outcome. Traffic is usually the most significant danger you will encounter anytime you are working in a street. However, toxic smoke, the potential for exploding car components, and rapidly advancing flames are all very real hazards that must be addressed while fighting a car fire. The reality is that any significant fire in a car or light truck usually results in a total loss of the vehicle. Your efforts should be scaled accordingly.

Although rare, there are occasions when a person is trapped in a burning car. In these instances, your rapid action can make the difference between life and death. However, anyone trapped in a fully involved car fire most likely will not survive. Therefore, firefighters should not take excessive risks in an attempt to rescue the victim. The goal for fighting a well-involved vehicle fire is to overwhelm it early with a large amount of water applied from a safe distance. This action cools the flames to a safe level before you approach the vehicle.

Vehicle Fires

Vehicle fires are common, representing about 200,000 fires (or 17% of the fires) in the United States each year. You will probably respond to more vehicle fires than structural fires. In this chapter, we present a set of new skills that build upon the skills we have already covered.

Safety Zones at Vehicle Fires

Vehicle fires present significant hazards to firefighters, many of which are not obvious at first glance. Although any smoke is hazardous and should not be breathed, the toxic gases created when an automobile burns contain more **hydrogen cyanide** than any other type of fire. Therefore, it is important that you use a self-contained breathing apparatus (SCBA) whenever you are near a burning vehicle (Figure 8-1).

In addition to the **traffic control area,** the hazards associated with a burning vehicle require observation of a wide area as a safety zone around the burning car. The following represent rapidly changing conditions or hazards that can potentially harm anyone within 50 feet of a burning automobile:

- Fuel spills or the potential for a burning or melting fuel tank that will dump highly flammable liquids
- The potential for exploding components such as pressurized cylinders used to assist in opening doors, the hood, and airbags

FIGURE 8-1 Because vehicle fires are very hazardous, full PPE, including an SCBA, is the minimum required protection for firefighters.

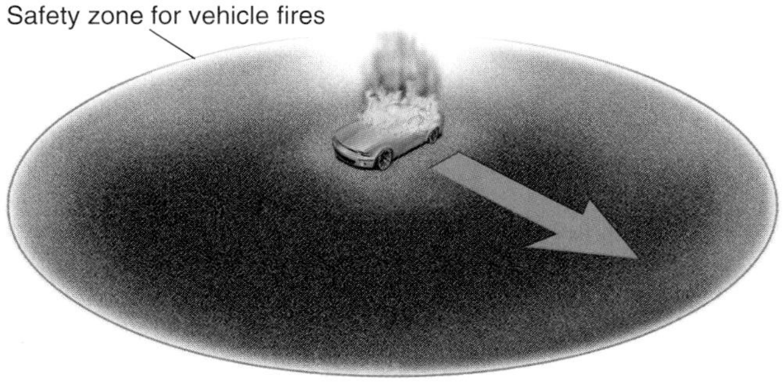

Safety zone for vehicle fires

Initially 50 feet in all directions

FIGURE 8-2 Safety zones for vehicle fires initially extend 50 feet in all directions from the burning vehicle.

Anyone working within 50 feet of a car or light truck that is well-involved in fire must be properly protected with full PPE, including breathing apparatus (Figure 8-2). It is never a good idea to breathe smoke, especially when you consider the products of combustion that are liberated from the burning plastics and other manmade materials in a motor vehicle.

▨▨ KEY WORDS ▨▨▨▨▨▨

hydrogen cyanide   A highly poisonous gas created when plastic materials burn. This gas is present in the immediate area anytime plastics burn. It mixes with other dangerous gases that are by-products of fires involving flammable liquids and caustics.

traffic control area   The area around a vehicle crash or vehicle fire incident in which any traffic passing through is safely directed by personnel or traffic cones away from the safety zone.

Traffic Control

A burning car on the side of a road is particularly distracting to drivers in the area, especially when the brilliant flames light the area on a dark night. Because of this distraction, working near traffic at the scene of a vehicle fire is particularly dangerous. Therefore, controlling the traffic flow should be your first action in stabilizing the scene. Remember, if the vehicle is well-involved in fire and it is obvious that it is unoc-cupied or the fire is not survivable, then there is no need to take a chance of being struck by traffic.

Safe Working Zones

The procedures for establishing a **safe working zone** around a burning vehicle are the same as those presented in Chapter 5, with one exception: The entire roadway or at least the lanes of travel on a divided highway that are within 50 feet of the fire should be totally blocked while the fire is actively burning. The potential is great for projectiles to fly under pressure when components of a burning car explode. The struts from pressurized cylinders used to assist in opening hoods and rear cargo lids, airbags, bumpers, and other objects explode when heated by fire. Equally hazardous is the potential for a pressurized fire from a venting fuel tank. Traffic flow can be released around an established safe working area once the fire has been controlled and the overhaul phase begins.

▨▨ KEY WORD ▨▨▨▨▨▨

safe working zone   The designated safety area around a burning vehicle that includes the entire roadway or at least the lanes of travel on a divided highway that are within 50 feet of the fire. This area should be totally blocked while the fire is actively burning.

Chocking Wheels and Removing Keys

To protect yourself from being struck by the car, chock the vehicle's wheels as soon as possible and before moving to a position in front of or behind the vehicle. A burning vehicle should not be considered safe from unintentional movement until the electrical system has been neutralized and the wheels chocked.

Another component that will concern you is the burning vehicle itself. It is not unusual for a car engine to start on its own when the electrical system has been compromised by fire. Shorted wires can also short-circuit any vehicle safety systems that prevent the car from starting while in gear, so don't take a chance on having the car lurch forward or backward, striking you during the firefight. If the passenger compartment is not involved in fire, confirm that the ignition switch is in the *off* position and the keys are removed.

⇨ Practice It!

Methods of Chocking Wheels and Removing Keys at a Vehicle Fire
Use the following steps to chock the wheels and remove keys from a vehicle that is or has been involved in fire:

1. Position a 4 x 4 inch piece of cribbing in front of and behind one wheel of the vehicle.
2. Safely access the interior of the vehicle. The method of access depends on the extent of fire involvement and the resulting damage.
3. Reach in and turn off the ignition, if needed, and then remove the keys.
4. Place the keys in your pocket or hand them to your Company Officer.

Vehicle Design and Burn Characteristics

Passenger cars, vans, SUVs, and light trucks can be divided into two or three distinct segments: the engine and the passenger and cargo compartments. Obviously, any motor vehicle has an engine and passenger compartment, and most passenger cars and pickup trucks have a separation between the passenger compartment and the cargo area. Passenger vans, SUVs, and station wagon style vehicles usually do not have a separation between the passenger and cargo areas. The significance of dividing the vehicle into compartments is that each compartment presents a different set of inherent hazards as well as a different challenge in accessing the seat of the fire.

The Engine Compartment

Most accidental fires involving light vehicles start in the engine compartment area (Figure 8-3). The engine compartment is where all the electronics and fuels come together in a single location; therefore, this can be the most dangerous area when on fire. Most hazards associated with the engine compartment are due to the following four items:

- The deadly smoke liberated by burning plastics
- Exploding batteries, which result in eye and skin injuries
- Melted **radiator** or heater hoses, which cause steam burns
- Projectiles that can fly from heated struts, such as the lift-assist cylinders that help open and close the hood of a car

The main defenses against these hazards are your PPE, copious amounts of flowing water for cooling these items, and a prudent approach to the area.

▨ KEY WORD ▨

radiator A part of any water-cooled internal combustion engine that provides a coil and air vents to cool fluids that in turn cool the engine as it operates. In most vehicles, the radiator is located at the front of the engine compartment.

FIGURE 8-3 In light vehicles, the engine compartment is the area most likely area to have an accidental fire. It is also the most dangerous area when it is on fire.

Never Breathe Smoke

The fluids and manmade materials that burn in the engine area liberate thick, black, choking smoke that can incapacitate you with a single breath. Large amounts of deadly gases, including hydrogen cyanide, are present in the immediate area anytime plastics burn. These gases mix with the other dangerous gases that are by-products of fires involving flammable liquids and caustics. Because vehicle fires usually occur outdoors, many firefighters are tempted to simply approach the fire from upwind of the incident, relying on a breeze or wind to blow the smoke away. This approach is extremely dangerous, as a momentary shift of wind or position will expose you to deadly gases. Wear your SCBA with the mask in place whenever you are near a burning or even smoldering vehicle. Proper PPE is essential.

Lead-acid batteries are usually found in the engine area. In some models, this type of battery may be located elsewhere, such as in the rear cargo compartment or even underneath the back seat of some sedans. The plastic case of a lead-acid battery usually burns and melts during a fire, spilling the caustic acid. However, it is not uncommon for a battery to explode when heated or when the wires short out elsewhere during a fire involving the vehicle's electrical system.

If the battery has not been involved in fire and is accessible, it is necessary to disconnect the electrical battery cables. Doing so reduces the chance of a secondary fire from the vehicle's battery power. It also helps to eliminate the possibility of an accidental restart of the vehicle's motor. Disconnecting the electrical battery cables is also the primary step toward preventing the accidental deployment of any nondeployed airbags. Be extremely careful when disconnecting the cables and continue to wear your full PPE during the procedure. Start with the ground (negative) side and then proceed to the positive side of the battery. If you cannot reach the bolts that connect the leads to the battery, use a pair of insulated cable cutters to cut a section out of each wire—again, starting with the negative side first. Making a single cut in each wire is not sufficient because it allows a chance for the wires to accidentally touch and re-energize the circuits. Cutting out at least an inch-long section of wire and covering the exposed ends with electrical tape helps prevent this hazard (Figure 8-4).

Steam and pressurized fluids released from small leaks in the hoses within the engine compartment present an immediate hazard to exposed skin. Many pressurized fluids, such as transmission fluid or engine oil, are highly flammable when atomized under pressure. These fluids present a significant exposure to re-ignition when the atomized, flammable fluids make contact with hot objects in the area. Once again, the best defense against this hazard is full PPE and the application of copious amounts of water to cool the area.

The Passenger Compartment

The hazards associated with the passenger compartment of light vehicles currently manufactured have changed in recent years. As with any other part of the car, burning plastics present the most obvious threat

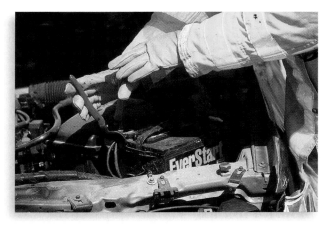

FIGURE 8-4 If cutting battery cables, start with the negative cable and cut out a 1-inch section of the cable, leaving a gap.

FIGURE 8-5 Burning plastics present the primary respiratory health hazard in the passenger compartment of light vehicles.

FIGURE 8-6 Airbag systems that deploy during a passenger compartment fire present the main strike hazard for firefighters during a vehicle fire in this area.

to your respiratory system (Figure 8-5). The changes in hazards are due to the potential strike hazards associated with the passive-restraint systems (airbags and **seatbelt pretensioners**) in modern cars and light trucks (Figure 8-6).

The elements that deploy most airbags found in the dash and seatbacks are flammable products that burn rapidly at a relatively low temperature. Side-curtain airbags are usually inflated with an inert gas that is contained in a pressurized cylinder, which can be contained in the A **post,** the C post, or even the roof rail on some model cars. When the vehicle's passenger compartment is well-involved in fire, the airbags often deploy from the heat, sounding like a shotgun blast. In rare cases, these pressure releases have caused either burning materials from the airbag or some small hard components of the assembly to fly out of the passenger compartment, often traveling several feet in the air.

A fire that does not involve the passenger compartment can also cause an unintentional deployment of one or more airbags if the circuits short as wires melt. Therefore, it is extremely important that the electrical system be neutralized anytime a fire occurs in a passenger vehicle that is equipped with passive-restraint systems.

▰ KEY WORDS ▰

posts The parts of a vehicle's construction that connect the roof of the vehicle to the body. They are constructed of rolled sheet metal and are given alphabetical labels, starting with A at the front and continuing with B and C for each of the next posts on the same side of the vehicle.

seatbelt pretensioner A device designed to automatically retract a seatbelt to better secure the user during a collision.

The Cargo Compartment

A fire that involves the cargo compartment of a car is a very unpredictable event because the material that is burning is an unknown. As an example, picture a fire involving a cargo compartment that contains clothing the driver purchased during a shopping trip to the local mall. Now picture the same car and the same driver as he or she is returning from the local garden center with three bags of fertilizer and a bottle of concentrated pesticide. The types of smoke and vapors liberated from a cotton shirt differ greatly from the smoke and vapors liberated from the pesticide. In the case of fertilizer, the contents can become explosive when mixed with other materials, like a plastic bottle of motor oil that the driver was also carrying and had forgotten about.

The cargo compartment can also become unpredictable because the fuel tank of most cars is near the cargo area. In addition, aftermarket alternative fuels

FIGURE 8-7 The fuel tank is normally located under the rear cargo area. Some vehicles are equipped with alternative fuel systems whose fuel tanks are located inside the trunk area.

such as **propane** or **compressed natural gas** might be located in the cargo compartment (Figure 8-7).

Again, the common element to your personal safety with any vehicle fire is exactly like that of any significant fire: Wear your PPE in the proper manner, no exceptions!

▰ KEY WORDS ▰

compressed natural gas A type of fuel found as a gas in nature that is liquefied and stored in compressed gas cylinders for use. As a gas, it is lighter than air and will rise when released. It can be used as an alternative fuel for a gasoline-powered internal combustion engine.

propane A type of fuel found as a gas in nature that is liquefied and stored in compressed gas cylinders for use. As a gas, it is heavier than air and will seek its lowest level when released. This material can be used as an alternative fuel for a gasoline-powered internal combustion engine.

Hybrid Vehicles

Hybrid vehicles, which use both a conventional gasoline motor and a high-voltage electric motor for propulsion, are becoming more common with each model year. The high-voltage circuits derive their power from banks of dry-cell batteries, very similar to flashlight batteries. However, unlike a flashlight that uses two or three 1.2-volt batteries for power, the rechargeable batteries in a hybrid vehicle are assembled in a series,

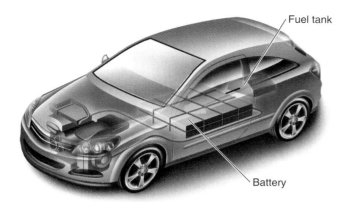

FIGURE 8-8   The battery cell in a hybrid car. Hybrid vehicles have large banks of batteries that deliver high voltages of electricity. These batteries disconnect when the ignition is shut off, the normal engine battery is disconnected, or a fuse is activated.

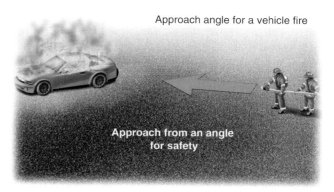

FIGURE 8-9   For safety, approach a vehicle fire at an angle.

which means that their voltage is multiplied. The entire battery cell in a typical hybrid vehicle can deliver more than 400 volts of power (Figure 8-8).

The high-voltage circuit on a hybrid vehicle is protected by fuses that are designed to interrupt power in the event of a short circuit. The high-voltage circuit is also designed to be disconnected when the ignition key is switched off and any time the low-voltage, conventional battery is disconnected. The high-voltage wires on a hybrid vehicle are clearly covered with a bright, orange-colored wrapping. Avoid coming into contact with any of these wires when you are working near a hybrid vehicle. It is also wise to avoid contact with any substance leaking around the batteries in any type of vehicle, including a hybrid.

Extinguishing Vehicle Fires

For your immediate safety, fires of any significance involving a passenger vehicle require a hose line capable of at least a 95-gpm flow and should be backed up with a hose line of equal capacity. Because most light-vehicle fires are quickly extinguished with less than 100 gallons of water, there is usually no reason to connect to a sustained water supply for the operation. However, it is a good idea to locate a water source, just in case something changes during the fire that requires more water than the booster tank carries.

Passenger Compartment Fires

Choose your approach path wisely when deploying the hose line to extinguish a vehicle fire. You should take into consideration three main factors: the wind,

the terrain, and the vehicle. Even when wearing full PPE and breathing fresh air from an SCBA, it is a good idea to approach the burning vehicle from the upwind and uphill side whenever practical. The upwind approach allows the wind to blow the thick smoke away from you, greatly improving your visibility. The uphill approach also helps prevent any flammable runoff from flowing toward you and your apparatus during the approach.

It is most often advisable that you approach the vehicle from an angle rather than moving directly in line with the front or rear of the car, or perpendicular to the side (Figure 8-9). The front or rear approach can put you in line with most of the struts or other components that can eject from the car during a free-burning fire. The perpendicular approach can put you in the path of a fireball as it erupts from a venting gasoline fill spout.

Begin flowing water from at least 30 feet away when approaching a well-involved fire, using a tight pattern to reach the seat of the fire and overwhelming it with force. First direct the stream toward any fire that is near the fuel tank and then concentrate on each of the three compartments as you go. The passenger compartment will emit a large volume of fire that can be knocked down quickly with a tight stream from a relatively safe position. As you approach the car, widen the stream to keep from "overshooting" the blaze. As you approach, play the water in a sweeping motion underneath the car.

Break any glass that prevents you from applying water to the seat of the fire and also to release trapped smoke. A striking tool, like an axe or a Halligan bar, works well for this purpose. If the passenger compartment is well-involved in fire, then a short **ceiling hook** used at a distance of approximately 6 feet can also be used to break the **tempered glass** on the sides and rear of the car from a safer distance than the shorter **Halligan bar** or an axe allows.

A fire in the passenger compartment can be quickly extinguished, but the area underneath the dash will probably continue to burn. This is due to the fuel load (the coatings on wires and plastic components). The area beneath the dash will also burn because any fire in the engine compartment will probably travel through the so-called firewall until it can be controlled.

KEY WORDS

ceiling hook   A common hand tool used by firefighters to access inside wall and ceiling areas in light vehicles. It has a handle with a specialized head on one end of the handle that is used to puncture and then cut and pull interior ceiling and wall coverings.

Halligan bar   A specialized firefighter's hand tool made up of a handle with a pry fork at one end and a combination adze and pick at the opposite end. This tool was developed to aid in forcing entry into buildings through door and window openings. It has since been adapted for many other uses in the Fire Service.

tempered glass   A type of glass commonly used in the construction of side and rear vehicle windows. This type of glass is heat-treated and tempered, which add strength to the glass. It is broken by applying a small point of contact with a large amount of force, which breaks it into many small pieces.

View It!

Go to the DVD, navigate to Chapter 8, and select *Extinguishing a Passenger Vehicle Fire.*

Practice It!

Extinguishing a Passenger Compartment Fire

Use the following method to approach and extinguish a fire in the passenger compartment of a vehicle:

1. Approach a burning vehicle from the upwind and uphill side when possible, and begin flowing water from about 30 feet away, using a tight stream pattern (Figure 8-10).

Use a tight stream pattern starting 30 feet away

Approach from upwind and uphill side

FIGURE 8-10

2. With a well-involved vehicle fire, first apply water near the fuel tank area and then to the three compartment areas. Widen the stream pattern as you get closer to the vehicle, using a sweeping motion (Figure 8-11).

First apply water to fuel tank area, use a wider stream pattern

Approach from upwind and uphill side

FIGURE 8-11

3. If you cannot open the doors of the passenger compartment and all the windows are closed, you can remove the side and rear windows by using a striking tool to break the tempered glass. To break the glass, use a ceiling hook from approximately 6 feet away or a Halligan bar at a closer distance (Figure 8-12).

4. Complete the process by extinguishing the rest of the vehicle as necessary.

FIGURE 8-12

Engine Compartment Fires

The main obstacle to controlling a fire in the engine compartment is the lack of access to the area. Fires in the engine compartment can be knocked down to some extent by flowing water through the wheel wells. Most passenger vehicles have plastic inner liners placed on their fenders in the engine compartment that usually burn out of the way, making this area a quick path for applying water. Another method, which is less effective, is to train a tight stream through the front grille and radiator area. This method won't extinguish the fire, but it may buy you some time until the hood can be opened.

 Safety Tip!

WARNING: Opening the hood while the engine compartment is burning can cause a rush of fresh air to reach the seat of the fire, producing a rush of heat and flame. You can prepare yourself for this by wearing your full PPE and breathing from your SCBA.

Opening the hood of a burned car can be a frustrating exercise. More often than not, the hood release cable or mechanism has burned away in the passenger compartment near the dash, making the conventional method of "popping the hood" ineffective. Because it will take a few minutes to open the hood, it is usually most effective to simply use a pry bar to pry open a small access point on the side of the hood between the hood and the fender. Once this access point is created, flow plenty of water into the area to cool it (Figure 8-13).

FIGURE 8-13 As an opening is made into the engine compartment, make sure to flow plenty of water into it.

There are a couple of steps you can take to open a hood after most of the operating cable has burned away. First, break away any grille that is in your way and locate the remaining hood release cable, which should be in front of the radiator just behind the grille. A quick tug on this cable usually operates the first position of the hood latch. If you cannot reach the cable with your gloved hand, use the forked end of a Halligan bar to catch the cable and then twist it, wrapping it around the forked end until the latch operates. The secondary latch operates normally with a gloved hand.

More often than not, the plastic clips that hold the insulation blanket that lines the underside of the hood will have melted away, causing the blanket to drop down over the motor. Be careful when removing the blanket, taking care to wet it first. Use a long-handled tool such as a pike pole to drag the blanket out of the way as another firefighter stands by with a charged hose line to take care of any flare-ups.

Practice It!

Accessing and Controlling an Engine Compartment Fire

Use the following steps to access and control a fire in the engine compartment of a vehicle:

1. As with passenger compartment fires, approach an engine compartment fire at an angle. Use a tight-pattern stream of water and widen it as you get closer.

FIGURE 8-14

2. When you are at the engine compartment area, apply water into the wheel well or to the front grille (Figure 8-14).

3. To open the front hood, access the cable in the passenger compartment or break out the front grille with a Halligan bar. Locate the latch-operating cable with your gloved hand and pull it outward (Figure 8-15).

FIGURE 8-15

4. An alternative method for operating the cable is to twist the cable with the forked end of the Halligan bar (Figure 8-16).

FIGURE 8-16

5. Carefully raise the hood and be ready to extinguish any additional fire that develops when more air reaches the engine compartment fire (Figure 8-17).

FIGURE 8-17

Cargo Compartment Fires

As with engine compartment fires, the main obstacle to controlling a fire in the cargo compartment is the lack of access to the area. In addition, fires in the cargo area will present their own set of access obstacles that will vary, depending on the style and model of vehicle that is burning. Many cars have fold-down rear seats or small access panels that allow long objects to pass into the passenger compartment. These areas make great access points for directing water to the seat of a cargo compartment fire. However, there are some alternative actions you can take if you are unable to readily access the compartment and keys are not available to operate the latch in the conventional manner.

First, cool the cargo area as much as possible by breaking out a taillight assembly and flowing water in. This action usually takes care of any active fire. To force entry to the cargo area, use the pick-end of a Halligan bar to punch out the key cylinder and then use a small tool such as a screwdriver to turn the latch assembly, unlocking the trunk.

Practice It!

Accessing and Controlling a Cargo Compartment Fire

Use the following steps to access and control a fire in the cargo compartment of a vehicle:

1. Approach the cargo compartment fire from an angle as you would a passenger compartment fire, using a tight-pattern stream until you get closer to the cargo area and then widening the stream pattern.

   FIGURE 8-18

2. Next, cool the cargo area by breaking out a taillight and flowing water in (Figure 8-18).

3. Access the cargo compartment by using the pick-end of a Halligan bar to punch out the key cylinder. Then, using a small tool like a screwdriver, turn the latch assembly, unlocking the trunk lid (Figure 8-19).

   FIGURE 8-19

View It!

Go to the DVD, navigate to Chapter 8, and select *Stretching a Dry Hose Line and Nozzle Control.*

Evolution 8-1

Stretching a Dry Hose Line and Nozzle Control

Training Area: Open area; level ground free of trip hazards

Equipment: Equipped pumper

   3 targets (traffic cones weighted on the bottom or 2-liter plastic soda bottles filled with water)

PPE: Full protective clothing and SCBA. ***This is <u>not</u> a live-fire drill.***

1. Mark off an area approximately 150 feet in length. Arrange the targets approximately 50 feet apart at one end of the training area (Figure 8-20).

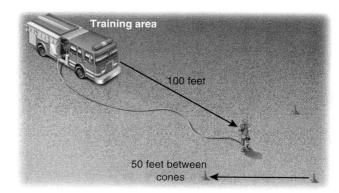

2. Position the pumper approximately 100 feet from the targets.

FIGURE 8-20

FIGURE 8-21

3. Working in teams of at least two, the simulated crew takes a turn pulling a preconnected hose line, stretching it to the target area (Figure 8-21). They then signal for the line to be charged. Once the line is stretched, practice flowing it for at least 4 minutes, flowing various patterns. Then use a narrow stream pattern to knock down all 3 targets. The additional team member should be positioned as a backup person, taking much of the load off the nozzle person. Guard against horseplay. The object of all practice drills is to teach, not to injure.

 **View It!**

Go to the DVD, navigate to Chapter 8, and select *Advancing a Charged Hose Line and Nozzle Control—2-Person Drill.*

Evolution 8-2

Advancing a Charged Hose Line and Nozzle Control—2-Person Drill

Training Area: Open area; level ground free of trip hazards

Equipment: Equipped pumper

3 targets (traffic cones weighted on the bottom or 2-liter plastic soda bottles filled with water)

PPE: Full protective clothing and SCBA. ***This is <u>not</u> a live-fire drill.***

1. Mark off an area approximately 150 feet in length. Arrange the targets approximately 50 feet apart at one end of the training area.

2. Position the pumper approximately 100 feet from the targets.

3. Working in teams of two, the crew takes a turn pulling a preconnected hose line, stretching it enough to allow the line to be charged and then advancing it at least 75 feet while charged. Once the line is stretched, the team works together to knock down all 3 targets using a narrow stream (Figure 8-22).

FIGURE 8-22

View It!

Go to the DVD, navigate to Chapter 8, and select *Advancing a Charged Hose Line and Nozzle Control—1-Person Drill.*

Evolution 8-3

Advancing a Charged Hose Line and Nozzle Control—1-Person Drill

NOTE: This is an optional drill at the Exterior Operations level.

Training Area: Open area; level ground free of trip hazards

Equipment: Equipped pumper

3 targets (traffic cones weighted on the bottom or 2-liter plastic soda bottles filled with water)

PPE: Full protective clothing and SCBA. *This is __not__ a live-fire drill.*

1. Mark off an area approximately 150 feet in length. Arrange the targets approximately 50 feet apart at one end of the training area.

2. Position the pumper approximately 100 feet from the targets.

3. Each member of the simulated crew takes a turn pulling a preconnected hose line, stretching it enough to allow the line to be charged and then advancing it at least 75 feet while charged. Once the line is stretched, each crew member should take turns knocking down all 3 targets using a narrow stream (Figure 8-23). Guard against horseplay and running with the hose line. The object of this practice drill is to teach, not to injure.

FIGURE 8-23

Vehicle Fire Overhaul

Overhaul is the process of systematically looking for any hidden fire or hot areas and taking measures to completely extinguish any of these remaining problems. Overhaul begins once the main body of the fire has been extinguished and continues until there is no chance of an accidental re-ignition. Overhaul is an important process in any fire operation; it is the best defense to prevent a rekindling of the original blaze (Figure 8-24). It is often best to let the vehicle cool down for a few minutes to let any hidden hotspots either die out or re-ignite so that you will know where to look for any hidden fires that remain.

FIGURE 8-24 Proper overhauling prevents rekindling of a vehicle fire.

Because smoke and products of combustion are released until the car is completely cooled, it is important that you keep your air mask on during overhaul. It is also important that your hands are protected by gloves and that all of your remaining PPE remains in place. The metal on the car will be very hot for a few minutes after the fire has been extinguished. Therefore, there is an obvious chance of accidental burns to exposed skin from contact with hot objects.

Overhauling a vehicle fire is usually best accomplished by flowing a lot of water, flushing out any hidden embers. Open every compartment, including the glove box. Because it is common for most drivers to carry important papers such as insurance records and vehicle registration documents in their glove box, open it first and salvage anything you can before flooding that area. If smoke is still issuing from underneath the dashboard area, water can be trained down through the defroster vents. If more room is needed for water flow, the entire glove box can be removed with a little force from a Halligan bar so that water can be applied directly to the fire source or area of smoldering.

Upholstered and padded areas in a car can sometimes smolder for quite a while, so the Company Officer or pump operator may decide to put an additive called **Class A foam** into the water. This additive allows the water to soak into the padded areas to better extinguish any deep-seated fire or embers. You will notice a foamy consistency as it strikes the surface of wherever you are directing the fire stream; however, there is no difference in the way you will handle the nozzle and hose line (Figure 8-25). Just be aware

that when you see the foam, the Class A additive is working.

■■ KEY WORD ■■

Class A foam A fire-extinguishing additive applied to fires involving Class A materials. It provides additional absorption capability to the water to which it is added.

Overhauling a Vehicle Fire

After the vehicle fire has been initially extinguished, use the following steps to extinguish any remaining fires:

1. With PPE and SCBA still in place, open all compartments and look for hidden fires and hotspots. Flow water onto them to extinguish them.
2. If the dashboard is still smoldering, flow water down into the defroster vents or remove the glove box with a Halligan bar.
3. In order to provide better soaking capability to upholstered seats and other areas inside the vehicle, your supervisor may add a Class A fire foam agent to your water supply. Douse the areas the same as you would with plain water.

Do It!

Managing Vehicle Fires Safely

Vehicle fires require taking all the safety and protection precautions necessary for any other fire event. The importance of having adequate protection, using proper PPE and SCBA, and controlling traffic cannot be overemphasized. Remember to always have an adequate-size fire attack hose line and water supply. Apply the water from a distance first and approach at an angle as well as from uphill and upwind when possible. Keep in mind the potential dangers involved in vehicle fires, stay alert, and work as an effective firefighting team member.

FIGURE 8-25 Applying a Class A foam agent during the overhaul of a passenger compartment can be more effective than simply applying water to smoldering upholstery.

Knowledge Assessment

Signed Documentation Tear-Out Sheet

Exterior Operations Level Firefighter—Chapter 8

Name: _____

Fill out the ten-question quiz below, the Knowledge Assessment Sheet, by circling the correct answer for each question. When finished, sign it and give to your instructor/Company Officer for his or her signature. Turn in this Knowledge Assessment Sheet to the proper person as part of the documentation that you have completed your training for this chapter.

1. Vehicle fires are common, representing about _____ of the fires throughout the United States each year.
   a. 77%
   b. 50%
   c. 25%
   d. 17%

2. Anyone working within _____ feet of a car or light truck that is well-involved in fire must be properly protected with full personal protective equipment, including breathing apparatus.
   a. 150
   b. 50
   c. 100
   d. 30

3. Most accidental fires in light vehicles start in the _____ compartment area.
   a. cargo
   b. rear seat
   c. passenger
   d. engine

4. Large amounts of the deadly gas hydrogen cyanide are present in the immediate area anytime plastics burn and mix with other dangerous gases that are by-products of fires involving flammable liquids and caustics.
   a. True
   b. False

5. When the vehicle's passenger compartment is well-involved in fire, the airbags will often _____ from the heat.
   a. melt
   b. remain unaffected
   c. deploy
   d. shrink

6. Fire in the _____ compartment can be unpredictable because the fuel tank of most cars is near this area.
   a. cargo
   b. passenger
   c. engine
   d. glove

7. The entire battery cell in a typical hybrid vehicle can deliver more than _____ volts of power.

   a. 400
   b. 600
   c. 800
   d. 900

8. Begin flowing water from at least _____ away when approaching a well-involved fire, using a tight pattern to reach the seat of the fire and overwhelming it with force.

   a. 100 feet
   b. 30 feet
   c. 75 feet
   d. 10 feet

9. Fires in the engine compartment can be knocked down to some extent by flowing water through the wheel wells.

   a. True
   b. False

10. _____ begins once the main body of the fire has been extinguished and continues until there is no chance of an accidental re-ignition.

    a. A vehicle fires
    b. The donning of PPE
    c. Flowing water
    d. Overhaul

Student Signature and Date _____   Instructor/Company Officer Signature and Date _____

182

Prove It

Skills Assessment
Signed Documentation Tear-Out Sheet
Exterior Operations Level Firefighter—Chapter 8

Name: _____

Fill out the Skills Assessment Sheet below. Have your instructor/Company Officer check off and initial each skill you demonstrate. When finished, sign it and give to your instructor/Company Officer for his or her signature. Turn in this Skills Assessment Sheet to the proper person as part of the documentation that you have completed your training for this chapter.

Skill	Completed	Initials
1. Participate as a team member in setting up a typical safety zone and the traffic control needed at the scene of a vehicle fire.	_____	_____
2. Demonstrate how to chock the wheels and remove the keys of a vehicle involved in a fire.	_____	_____
3. Explain the safety risks of a vehicle fire and the importance of wearing full PPE and SCBA at a vehicle fire.	_____	_____
4. Describe the burn characteristics of the passenger, engine, and cargo compartments of a vehicle.	_____	_____
5. Demonstrate how to safely approach a vehicle fire with a small attack hose line.	_____	_____
6. Demonstrate the methods for safely extinguishing a fire in the passenger compartment of a vehicle.	_____	_____
7. Demonstrate the methods for safely accessing and extinguishing a fire in the engine compartment area of a vehicle.	_____	_____
8. Demonstrate the methods for safely accessing and extinguishing a fire in the cargo compartment of a vehicle.	_____	_____
9. Participate as a member of a two-member team demonstrating proper hose line stretch and control.	_____	_____
10. Participate as a member of a two-member team demonstrating proper charged hose line movement and nozzle control.	_____	_____
11. Demonstrate safely advancing a charged, small attack hose line.	_____	_____
12. Demonstrate safely performing overhaul operations on a vehicle that has been involved in a fire.	_____	_____

Student Signature and Date _____   Instructor/Company Officer Signature and Date _____

9

Supply Hose Lines

What You Will Learn in This Chapter

This chapter will introduce you to the elements of a proper water supply for fighting fires. We will explain the initial water supply that is carried to the fire by the apparatus and sustained water supplies. In addition, we will discuss the water supply that is adequate and non-interruptible. You will also learn the methods used to assist with developing and utilizing the different types of water sources.

What You Be Able to Do

After reading this chapter and participating in the practical skills sessions, you will be able to

1. Explain the elements of an initial and a sustained water supply.
2. Help establish a water supply from various static sources, including portable tanks, lakes, and streams.

3. Work safely around a static water supply.
4. Help refill a booster tank and a tanker truck.
5. Operate a fire hydrant.
6. Assist in establishing a drafting operation.
7. Assist in establishing a sustained water supply from a hydrant using various hose configurations and layouts.
8. Explain the differences among hard suction hose, conventional supply hose, and large-diameter supply hose.

Water Supply—A Critical Firefighting Factor

When most citizens think of firefighters, they immediately conjure an image of heroic acts in which a greater-than-life hero is walking from a burning inferno carrying a just-rescued child in his or her arms.

185

FIGURE 9-1 A good supply of water is essential to any fire operation.

plies. Water can be obtained from a piped-in water main system in which water is under pressure and fire hydrants are attached as access points for use by the Fire Service.

Generally speaking, the water supply on most fire scenes comes from a combination of sources. Most often, water is initially brought to the scene by a fire apparatus. This **initial water supply** is often replaced by a **sustained water supply,** which comes from a more substantial source of water.

███ **KEY WORDS** ███

initial water supply   The first supply of water that is accessed for extinguishing a fire. This water supply is usually established prior to a sustained water supply. It is usually carried to the scene by the fire apparatus or specially designed tenders.

sustained water supply   The water supply established with a substantial water supply system or source, like a municipal water system or a large static water resource, such as a stream or a lake.

Certainly, there are extraordinary acts of humanity performed daily by firefighters everywhere, but the reality is that fighting fires is *always* a team effort. No single job is more or less important to the safety and efficiency of the mission than others; however, some tasks are absolutely critical to a mission. So while the news cameras are trained on the firefighters who are moving in and out of a burn area, flowing large amounts of water on the blaze, an educated firefighter knows that somewhere in the scheme of things all of that water has come from somewhere. Although one would seldom think it a meritorious act, simply connecting the hose to a fire hydrant and charging the line at the proper time is often critical to the entire operation (Figure 9-1). No positive actions on the fireground will take place very long without an adequate supply of water to flow through the lines.

Water Supplies

Firefighters cannot extinguish fires with their hose lines if they do not have an adequate water supply. This fact has never changed for the Fire Service. The water supply needed can be brought to the scene on the fire apparatus along with the hose and other firefighting tools and personnel. It can arrive on a specialized tender unit that is specially designed to haul large amounts of water to the fire scene. A supply of water can be obtained from a static water supply. Static water supplies are not under pressure. A lake, stream, river, swimming pool, and water storage tank at ground level are good examples of static water sup-

Initial Water Supply

The initial water supply is usually developed from water carried on an engine in its **booster tank** (Figure 9-2). It can also be supplied by a second fire apparatus on the scene through an engine-to-engine water supply operation. Many fires can be adequately handled with an initial water supply. Often a sustained water supply is developed as a safety backup for the initial water supply but is not put into use.

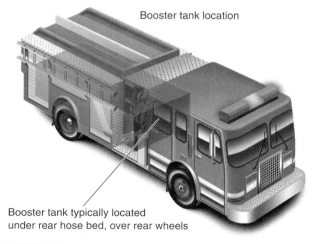

Booster tank location

Booster tank typically located under rear hose bed, over rear wheels

FIGURE 9-2 Booster tanks are not visible on most fire apparatus. They can carry between 250 and 1000 gallons of water, depending on their design.

booster tank   The onboard water supply tank on a fire apparatus usually used as an initial water supply at a fire scene.

Booster Tanks

A water supply that arrives on a fire apparatus is usually 250 to 1000 gallons, depending on the needs of the fire department and the design of the fire apparatus. If a small fire attack line flows 100 gpm on a fire, then it is easy to estimate that the fire apparatus has about 5 minutes of water supply with one small fire attack line flowing. The water on a fire apparatus can be refilled from any type of water source. This onboard water supply is commonly referred to as the booster tank.

Engine-to-Engine Water Supply

There are instances in which one fire engine uses all of the water in its booster tank on a fire and needs more water supplied from a second fire engine on the scene. The second engine provides water to the first engine by connecting its water tank to the first engine through its pump. In this instance, the first engine, which is supplying water to the nozzles, is called the **attack pumper.** The engine that is delivering its

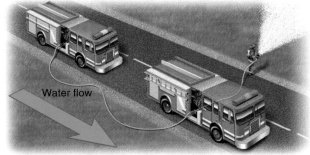

(b) Supply pumper

Water flow

(a) Attack pumper

FIGURE 9-3   (a) Attack pumper and (b) supply pumper.

booster tank of water to the attack pumper is called the **supply pumper** (Figure 9-3).

KEY WORDS

attack pumper   A fire truck located at the fire scene to which water is supplied from a sustained source during the firefighting operation. This fire truck distributes the supplied water to the fire attack hose lines at the fire.

supply pumper   The fire truck that provides water to the attack pumper, either from its own booster tank or by pumping water in water supply hose lines to the attack pumper.

 View It!

Go to the DVD, navigate to Chapter 9, and select *Engine-to-Engine Water Supply.*

➥ Practice It!

Establishing an Engine-to-Engine Water Supply

When fire engines connect to each other to transfer a booster tank water supply, they usually use a section of a 2½- or 3-inch hose. Use the following procedure to assist in making the connection:

1. Remove a section of supply hose from one of the fire engine hose beds. Connect the female end of the supply hose to a discharge outlet on the fire engine providing the water supply (Figure 9-4).

FIGURE 9-4

—Continued

2. Connect the male end to an intake outlet on the fire engine that is taking in the water supply (Figure 9-5).

FIGURE 9-5

3. Advise both pump operators that the supply line is properly connected to each pumper. Walk the hose line, loosening any kinks in the charged line (Figure 9-6).

FIGURE 9-6

Fire Hydrants

Fire hydrants are simply valves that firefighters open and close to provide the water supply from a water main system for fire department operations (Figure 9-7). A typical fire hydrant has two or three outlet ports. These ports have male thread ends with female caps. The top of the hydrant features an operating nut. The tool used to open the hydrant is called the hydrant wrench. This wrench is adjustable and is designed to open and close the valve inside the fire hydrant. Nearly all fire hydrants open in a counterclockwise direction and close in a clockwise direction. For our purposes, we will assume that the hydrants we use

open and close in this manner. An arrow on or near the operating nut on every hydrant indicates the operating direction (Figure 9-8). Open a hydrant slowly to avoid a water hammer at the other end.

In climates that experience freezing weather, dry-barrel hydrants are used. A dry-barrel hydrant has a long stem that operates a valve well below the freeze line in the ground, so the part of the hydrant that is above the freeze line remains dry. There is a drain valve at the base of the hydrant that remains open unless the hydrant is under pressure. Because it takes pressure to close this valve, the hydrant should be fully opened when used and fully closed when not in use—otherwise the drain valve can leak and cause the ground around the hydrant to erode away. Sus-

FIGURE 9-7 A typical fire hydrant has two 2½ connections and one 4½ connection.

FIGURE 9-8 The operating nut has an arrow that indicates the direction to turn the valve.

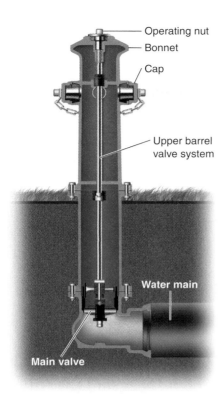

FIGURE 9-9   Dry-barrel hydrant.

FIGURE 9-10   Wet-barrel hydrant.

pect that the drain valve has a problem anytime you open a port on a dry-barrel hydrant and find water at the cap or when you see a leaking cap on a hydrant that is fully closed off. Report this to your Company Officer so that arrangements can be made to repair the hydrant (Figure 9-9).

▬ KEY WORD ▬

fire hydrant   A valve opened and closed by a firefighter that provides the water supply from a water main system for fire department operations. A typical fire hydrant has two or three outlet ports that have male thread ends with female caps. An operating nut on top of the hydrant opens and closes the water flow from the appliance.

To check the drain valve on a hydrant, cap all but one of the ports and flow some water. When the water is shut down, hold your hand over the uncapped port. You should feel the hydrant "suck" on your hand as the water inside the barrel drains.

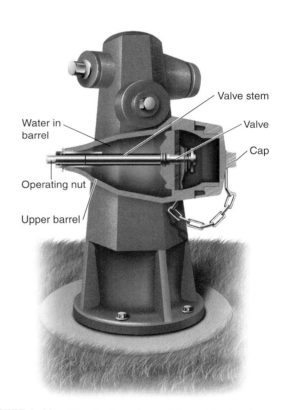

FIGURE 9-11   The design of a wet-barrel hydrant.

Wet-barrel hydrants are typically used only where there is no chance of freezing weather (Figure 9-10). A wet-barrel hydrant remains full of water that is under pressure to a point just behind the port. A wet-barrel hydrant operates by opening a valve directly behind the port (Figure 9-11).

 **View It!**

Go to the DVD, navigate to Chapter 9, and select *Fire Hydrants*.

Practice It!

Opening and Closing a Fire Hydrant

Use the following procedure to open and close a fire hydrant:

1. Remove one of the discharge outlet caps. If needed, use the hydrant wrench to loosen the cap (Figure 9-12).

FIGURE 9-12

2. Place the hydrant wrench on top of the operating nut of the hydrant and slowly turn it in a counterclockwise direction until water flows out of the open discharge outlet (Figure 9-13).

FIGURE 9-13

3. Finally, close the hydrant valve with the wrench. Turn the operating nut in a clockwise direction with the hydrant wrench (Figure 9-14).

FIGURE 9-14

Booster Tank Refill

When you extinguish a fire and utilize water straight from the fire apparatus with no outside water supply, you will need to refill the apparatus with water. For this reason, you need to learn how to use a fire hydrant to refill the booster tank of the fire apparatus.

Usually you will use a 2½- or 3-inch supply hose line to refill the booster tank on a fire apparatus. There may be a short section of this hose on the fire apparatus that is usually used to refill the booster tank. This procedure can also be used for other water supply sources by following Steps 2 through 5 in "Practice It! Refilling a Booster Tank."

 View It!

Go to the DVD, navigate to Chapter 9, and select *Booster Tank Refill.*

Practice It!

Refilling a Booster Tank

Follow these steps to use a fire hydrant to refill the booster tank on a fire apparatus:

1. With the supply hose laid out to the fire apparatus, use the hydrant wrench to remove at least one of the hydrant caps. To clear the waterway of any debris or contaminants in the water as well as to ensure proper operation of the hydrant, open the hydrant slowly and only partially, and flow some water (Figure 9-15). Shut off the hydrant so you can attach the fill hose.

FIGURE 9-15

—Continued

2. Attach the supply refill hose to the hydrant discharge using the female end of the coupling (Figure 9-16). Tighten to hand-tight. Attach the male end of the hose to the intake gate on the fire apparatus (Figure 9-17). The intake gates have various designs and are found in various locations, depending on the apparatus design.

FIGURE 9-16

3. The driver will open the tank refill valve on the fire apparatus and signal to you when he or she is ready for you to slowly open the hydrant. When opening the hydrant, use the hydrant wrench to turn the operating nut counterclockwise until it stops turning.

FIGURE 9-17

4. Maintain eye contact with the driver at the pump panel. The driver will signal when the tank is full so that you can close the valve (Figure 9-18). To close the valve, turn it clockwise with the hydrant wrench.

FIGURE 9-18

5. Properly detach the hose line, hand-tighten the discharge cap on the hydrant, and roll up the refill supply hose line. Put the hose back onto the fire apparatus and return the hydrant wrench to its correct storage location.

Sustained Water Supply

As the fire progresses, the fire department busily starts setting up and establishing a sustained water supply. The sustained water supply replaces the initial water supply, which ensures that adequate water is available to extinguish the fire.

Tenders (Water Tankers)

Depending on your location, the trucks that bring an additional water supply to the fire are called *tenders* or *water tankers.* The term *tanker* has now been given to airplanes that drop large amounts of water on forest fires. For our use, the terms *tender* and *water tanker* are interchangeable. Use the term that your instructor says is appropriate for your area.

These apparatus can carry from 1000 to more than 8000 gallons of water. Tenders can be connected into the fire pumper on the scene as a water supply. They can even be used in conjunction with portable water tanks, set up on the scene as water reservoirs. Tenders connected into pumpers can have pumps that supply the water to the pumper or they can allow a gravity-fed supply.

Fire departments utilize several tenders in rotation to supply the fire scene. Refilling a tender is similar to refilling a booster tank on a fire apparatus. Each tender is refilled as the other deploys its load of water, thus establishing a sustained water supply.

This operation is commonly referred to as a **tender water shuttle operation** (Figure 9-19).

FIGURE 9-19 Multiple tenders can be used to shuttle water from the supply source to the fire scene.

▷ Practice It!

Hooking into a Tender

When a tender apparatus connects to a pumper to provide a water supply, a section of 2½- or 3-inch hose is usually used. Use the following procedure to assist in making the connection:

1. Remove a section of supply hose from the fire engine or tender apparatus.

2. Connect the female end of the supply hose to a discharge outlet on the tender that is providing the water supply (Figure 9-20).

3. Connect the male end to an intake outlet on the fire engine that is taking in the water supply.

4. Advise both driver-pump operators that the supply line is properly connected to each pumper. Walk the hose line, loosening any kinks in the charged line.

FIGURE 9-20

Static Water Supplies

Natural bodies of water, such as streams, rivers, ponds, and lakes, provide substantial water supply resources. Additional static water resources include manmade reservoirs, swimming pools, and above- and below-ground water tanks. An above-ground water tank is considered a static supply when it is at ground level. Anytime the tank is elevated above the ground, it becomes a pressurized water supply. The fire department may also have portable water tanks that are set up for use during a fire. These static water supply resources can be accessed by portable fire pumps placed nearby. They can also be set up before-hand with special hydrants, called **drafting hydrants.** Fire apparatus can also directly access a static water supply with a water drafting operation.

Drafting Water from Natural Sources

Most fire department pumpers can be set up near a natural source of a static water supply. They have a specially designed fire hose referred to as **hard suction hose.** When deployed into a body of water, hard suction hose can draw water into a pumper, providing a sustained water supply for the fire scene (Figure 9-21).

▮▮ KEY WORD ▮▮

hard suction hose A specially designed fire hose that is deployed into a body of water to draw water into the fire apparatus pump and provide a sustained water supply for the fire scene.

FIGURE 9-21 A drafting operation allows us to take advantage of static water supplies.

 View It!

Go to the DVD, navigate to Chapter 9, and select *Drafting Operations.*

⇨ Practice It!

Participating in Drafting Operations

Follow the procedure below to assist with setting up a drafting operation:

1. The crew places drafting hose lines (hard suction hose) into the static water supply source with a drafting strainer attached to the end (Figure 9-22). This strainer assures that chunks of debris do not enter the fire pump during drafting operations.

FIGURE 9-22

2. The strainer end of the hard suction hose is secured to the pumper with ropes in order to suspend the strainer in the water supply. It is important to maintain a good depth within the water supply. This also keeps the strainer end off the bottom of the water supply and from potential clogging materials that may be sucked into the strainer during drafting operations.

The fire apparatus pump creates a negative pressure in the hard suction hose and water is lifted into the pump. Water is then supplied to the fire scene with a supply hose line or it is directly applied onto the fire through fire attack lines.

WARNING: Conventional PPE for firefighters is bulky and cumbersome and can be deadly if you accidentally fall into the water. Consider this any time you are working around an open static water source, and avoid wearing full gear around the water whenever possible. Some agencies require that life jackets be worn while working near open water. Follow your agency's protocols.

View It!

Go to the DVD, navigate to Chapter 9, and select *Drafting Hydrants.*

Practice It!

Assisting with Drafting Hydrant Water Supply Operations

Follow the procedure below to assist with setting up a drafting hydrant water supply:

1. With the fire apparatus positioned within reach of the drafting hydrant with hard suction supply hose, the crew removes the hard suction hose from the apparatus (Figure 9-23).

FIGURE 9-23

2. Attach the female end of the hard suction hose to the drafting hydrant (Figure 9-24).

FIGURE 9-24

3. Attach the other end of the hard suction hose to the fire apparatus pump. This end of the hard suction hose may have a large male threaded end or it may have a double female adapter if it is being attached to the large port on the pump.

The fire apparatus pump creates a negative pressure in the hard suction hose and water is lifted into the pump. Water is then supplied to the fire scene with a supply hose line or it is directly applied onto the fire through fire attack lines.

Portable Water Tanks

Because they are constantly being refilled by tenders, portable water tanks allow a fire pumper to draw from a steady supply of water. The fire apparatus uses drafting operations to draw the water and develop a sustained water supply through a rotation of units. A sustained water supply can also be created by laying a supply hose line from the portable tank to the apparatus needing water on the fire scene (Figure 9-25).

FIGURE 9-25 Portable water tanks provide a reservoir of water for drafting operations where a natural body of water doesn't exist.

 **View It!**

Go to the DVD, navigate to Chapter 9, and select *Portable Water Tank Operations.*

➡ Practice It!

Setting Up a Portable Water Tank

Use the following procedure to assist in setting up a portable water tank:

1. Position a team member at the apparatus carrying the portable water tank. Assist in disconnecting any straps, hooks, or openings on the compartment area.

2. Using good body positioning, carefully assist removing the unit from the apparatus (Figure 9-26).

FIGURE 9-26

3. Assist in unfolding the unit. Position it on an area that is as level and as safely accessible as possible. Check the water drain, making sure that it is closed. Position the tank so that the drain is at the lowest point to help drain the tank later, when the operation is complete. It is now ready to receive water and act as a water supply source for the fire operation (Figure 9-27).

FIGURE 9-27

Portable Fire Pumps

Portable pumps are carried on some fire apparatus and deployed at the water source. They come in two basic styles: land-based and floating. These pumps are usually used to refill tenders or to supply a fire apparatus at a fire scene. If the portable pump is land-based, then a drafting operation is set up using hard suction hose to draw water from a static source into the portable pump. A supply line is then hooked into the portable pump. If the portable pump is a floating type, then it floats on the surface of the water source and supplies water through a supply line to where it is needed.

Portable pumps do not provide a great deal of water but are adequate for filling booster tanks and attacking small fires. The main difference between a land-based portable pump and a float pump is that the float pump has no hard suction hose attached. It simply draws the water from beneath it as it floats on the surface.

Practice It!

Setting Up a Floating Fire Pump

Use the following steps to assist in setting up a float pump:

1. Assemble the crew at the float pump on the fire apparatus. Remember to use good body mechanics and posture when lifting. Float pumps are usually heavy and require two or more people to safely unload and move. Assist in a coordinated lift and removal of the pump (Figure 9-28).

FIGURE 9-28

2. Place the pump on a level area at the water's edge. Connect the hose to the pump's outlet and float the pump onto the water (Figure 9-29).

FIGURE 9-29

3. The pump operator will start the engine power unit, and the pump will draft water into itself. The pump will discharge water from the outlet side of the pump either to the fire apparatus needing to be refilled or to the fire apparatus on the fire scene (Figure 9-30).

FIGURE 9-30

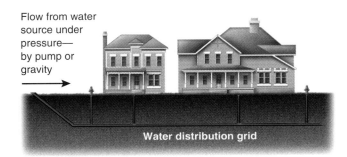

FIGURE 9-31 A typical water main system.

Flow from water source under pressure— by pump or gravity →

Water distribution grid

Water Main Systems

One of the best sources of a water supply for fire operations is the water main system. This system is composed of a water source that is placed under pressure by either gravity or pumps. The water is distributed to the community through a system of valves and pipes. The fire department accesses this water source via fire hydrants that are installed at specified intervals throughout the system (Figure 9-31).

Supply Hose

Most fire apparatus designed as the first-in (first-arriving) fire attack units carry water supply fire hose that is loaded so that it is ready for deployment on a fire scene. The sections are connected together in preset lengths, but the hose is not connected to the pump. Perhaps you have seen firefighters laying out their hose as they approach a building fire in a neighborhood. This hose is carried on the hose bed of the fire apparatus and deploys (flakes off) the back of the fire apparatus as it slowly drives from the water supply to the fire (Figure 9-32). Typical supply hose is 2½ to 3 inches in diameter. Hose of this size usually comes in 50-foot lengths. Supply hose that is 2½ to 3 inches in length can also be used as an attack line, which we will discuss in detail in Chapter 10. Large-diameter supply hose, which is between 4 and 6 inches in diameter, is explained later in this chapter in the section "Large-Diameter Supply Hose."

FIGURE 9-32 Because the supply hose is connected together in the hosebed, the pumper can lay the supply hose out as it goes from the water source to the fire.

 **Tip!**

If you are hooking only one line to a hydrant, take a moment to connect a gate valve to the unused hydrant port before charging the line. By doing so, you can attach another line later without having to shut off the hydrant. Remember, open and close the gate valve slowly to avoid a water hammer.

Gated Manifold Appliances

One supply line can be made into two or more smaller supply lines by using a **gated manifold appliance** (Figure 9-33). Some gated manifold appliances are designed for use with large-diameter supply hose. For example, a 5-inch manifold appliance may branch into two 2½-inch supply lines, each with its own gated valve for operation.

▰▰ KEY WORDS ▰▰

appliance Any Fire Service–related device through which water flows. These devices include manifolds, master stream appliances, adapters, and others.

gated manifold appliance An appliance designed for use with large-diameter supply hose. It allows one

FIGURE 9-33 Gated manifold appliance.

FIGURE 9-34 Siamese appliance.

large supply hose to be branched into two or more smaller supply hose lines. For example, a 5-inch manifold appliance may branch into four 2½-inch supply lines, each with its own gated valve for operation.

Siamese Appliances

Siamese appliances take two or more supply lines and join them into one supply line (Figure 9-34). These appliances typically have a clapper valve inside each intake opening that shuts off if only one line connected to the appliance is flowing water. These appliances allow two or more supply lines to combine to provide more water flow and pressure to one supply line, a fire attack line, or a master stream appliance.

KEY WORD

Siamese appliance A hose appliance that combines two or more supply lines into one supply line. Normally, this appliance has a clapper valve inside each intake opening that shuts off if only one line coming into the appliance is flowing water. This appliance allows two or more supply lines to combine to provide more water flow and pressure to one supply line, a fire attack line, or a master stream appliance.

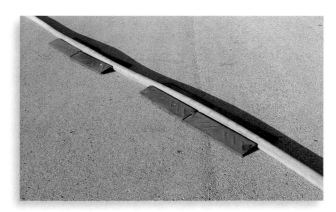

FIGURE 9-35 Never drive directly over an unprotected, charged hose line. Hose bridges allow for traffic to pass slowly over a supply hose.

Hose Bridges

Many times supply hose lines are laid out in neighborhood streets or across highways. Vehicles should never be allowed to drive over charged hose lines. If traffic is going to be allowed to pass over these supply hose lines, specially designed hose bridges should be used (Figure 9-35). These bridges provide protection for the charged supply hose lines.

Supply Hose Loads

A supply hose is usually laid out from a fire apparatus in two primary directions: (1) *to* the fire (a forward lay) or (2) *away from* the fire and toward the water supply (a reverse lay). The supply hose can be loaded on the fire apparatus in several ways. Variations to these basic loads are many and are specific to the needs of your community and the design of the fire apparatus.

 **View It!**

Go to the DVD, navigate to Chapter 9, and select *Loading Supply Hose.*

Practice It!

Loading Supply Hose

Use the following steps to assist in loading supply hose:

1. Drain and lay flat the fire hose section that will be loaded as a supply hose.

2. Position yourself to assist in the hose load. This positioning will be on the hose bed, on the tailboard of the fire apparatus, or on the ground behind the apparatus (Figure 9-36).

3. As the section is loaded, stop as you get to the end of the section and allow the next section to be connected (Figure 9-37).

4. If the apparatus must be moved, step down from it and remain clear of the apparatus until it is finished being repositioned. Then return to loading the hose.

FIGURE 9-36

FIGURE 9-37

Safety Tip!

One, and only one, person should be designated as the safety person who signals the driver to move the vehicle. That person should remain visible in the driver's rearview mirror at all times. However, anyone near the truck should be aware of the dangers and should yell **Stop!** if necessary.

Large-Diameter Supply Hose

The large-diameter fire hose designed for water supply is typically 4 to 6 inches in diameter (Figure 9-38). This type of hose may have quick-connect couplings. All these couplings are identical—that is, there is no male–female differentiation. In addition, they connect with a quarter turn. Small locking mechanisms on each coupling usually secure the couplings together. A large-diameter fire hose (LDH) usually

FIGURE 9-38   A large-diameter fire hose.

FIGURE 9-39   A typical quick-connect coupling: (a) lugs, (b) gasket, and (c) locking mechanism.

comes in sections that are 50 to 100 feet in length. This type of hose is heavy and sometimes cumbersome, but it can supply large amounts of water to the fire scene very quickly.

Quick-Connect Hose Couplings

Quick-connect couplings attach to each other differently than threaded couplings do. Because the two ends of a quick-connect coupling are identical, there is no need to find matching ends. These couplings are primarily found on large-diameter hose (Figure 9-39). The gaskets in a quick-connect coupling should be lubricated per the manufacturer's instructions so that the coupling works freely. A dried-out gasket makes it very hard to couple or uncouple the fittings.

 **Safety Tip!**

It is very important that quick-connect couplings be fully connected and locked in place before pressurizing the hose. You should hear and feel a solid "click" when the coupling is made.

 View It!

Go to the DVD, navigate to Chapter 9, and select *Quick-Connect Couplings.*

 Practice It!

Coupling and Uncoupling Quick-Connect Hose Couplings

The following procedures can be used to connect and disconnect hose sections. Separate procedures are provided for one firefighter and for two firefighters.

Coupling and uncoupling quick-connect hose couplings with one firefighter:

FIGURE 9-40

1. Hold one hose section end in place on the ground with your knee and foot (Figure 9-40).

—Continued

2. Take the end of the second section, placing it into the end of the first section. Turn the end of the first section until it clicks into place and locks (Figure 9-41).

FIGURE 9-41

3. Before disconnecting the couplings, assure that the water pressure is released from the supply line and no water is flowing. To disconnect the couplings, place spanner wrenches on each coupling and turn them in a counterclockwise direction. You should operate the coupling lock releases at the same time (Figure 9-42).

FIGURE 9-42

Coupling and uncoupling quick-connect hose couplings with two firefighters:

FIGURE 9-43

1. With two people, bring each end together and fit the couplings into the reception slots (Figure 9-43).

2. Turn the couplings in a clockwise direction to connect them (Figure 9-44). The couplings will fit together snugly, clicking as the locks on each coupling snap into place. If necessary, use spanner wrenches to turn the couplings.

FIGURE 9-44

3. To disconnect the couplings, make sure that all water flow has been discontinued to the lines and that the water pressure has been released from them. Each firefighter holds the locking mechanisms down and turns them counterclockwise, releasing each coupling (Figure 9-45).

FIGURE 9-45

Safety Tip!

Never uncouple supply hose unless you are sure it is not pressurized and water is not flowing. Severe injury can occur with a sudden release of water pressure if the hose is uncoupled while under pressure. Always check with the pump operator and release any pressure by opening the nozzle at the end of the attack line.

View It!

Go to the DVD, navigate to Chapter 9, and select *Loading Large-Diameter Supply Hose.*

Practice It!

Loading Large-Diameter Supply Hose

Large-diameter hose, like regular supply hose, can be loaded in several configurations. Use the following steps as a guideline for loading large-diameter supply hose:

1. Follow the directions of the Company Officer when loading large-diameter hose. He or she will direct you regarding the proper placement of each section as it is loaded (Figure 9-46).

FIGURE 9-46

2. Large-diameter hose is usually loaded one section at a time, with each section connected to the next section at the back of the fire apparatus. Position yourself at the back of the apparatus, on the tailboard of the apparatus, or on the hose bed of the apparatus to help feed and place each section of hose (Figure 9-47).

FIGURE 9-47

—Continued

3. The sections of hose must be loaded so that they will deploy (flake off) easily during the hose lay. In addition, the hose couplings need to be positioned in the load so that they fit. Both of these items require a short fold known as a *Dutchman* to occasionally be placed in the load (Figure 9-48).

FIGURE 9-48

4. The load is finished by placing the last coupling into position. Secure the last coupling in the manner approved by your department (Figure 9-49).

FIGURE 9-49

Safety Tip!

When climbing onto the hose bed of a fire apparatus, always use the handholds provided for that purpose. Always check overhead when mounting the top of the hose bed. Look for obstructions and overhead electrical power wires. Never touch these items. If the apparatus needs to move during the reloading process, dismount it, staying clear of it and any traffic lanes that may be present. When the apparatus has repositioned, go back to your previous spot and continue loading the hose.

Supply Hose Layouts

When fire apparatus start arriving on the scene of an active fire, among the first things to be accomplished is the rapid establishment of an initial water supply and a sustained firefighting water supply. The initial supply will more than likely come from the booster tank on your apparatus. The sustained water supply may come from hooking your apparatus into a substantial water supply, laying the water supply line to the fire scene. Alternately, another apparatus can lay a water supply line from a substantial water supply to your unit on the scene, flowing water to the initial fire attack lines. The two general ways to lay supply hose are with a forward lay and a reverse lay.

Forward Lay

A forward lay of supply hose is a very common fire ground operation. It involves the apparatus stopping at the water supply source and leaving a firefighter, who takes a supply line hose end and a hydrant wrench off the hose bed of the apparatus and secures the hose end at the water source.

Tip!

Many agencies keep a bag of tools they call the *hydrant bag* on or near the tailboard. This bag makes it easy to grab the hydrant wrench and any other tools, such as a rope, spanners, or adapters, as you remove the line from the rig.

The fire apparatus then proceeds to the desired location at the fire scene as the hose deploys off the back of the hose bed. Simultaneously, the firefighter at the water source connects the end of the supply hose at his location into the water supply source. This water supply can be a fire hydrant on a water main system, a portable pump or tank, or another fire apparatus. On a signal from the apparatus that laid out the supply hose, the firefighter opens the water source. Water flows to the fire scene and apparatus from the water source, and a sustained water supply is established.

View It!

Go to the DVD, navigate to Chapter 9, and select *Forward Lay from a Hydrant.*

Practice It!

Forward Lay from a Hydrant

Probably the most common method of establishing a sustained water supply system on a fire scene is laying hose from a fire hydrant to the scene of the fire. This operation can be accomplished by doing the following:

1. As the firefighter designated to make the hydrant connection, you must wait for the apparatus to come to a full stop. Check for traffic hazards, dismount the fire apparatus, and proceed to the hose bed area.

FIGURE 9-50

2. Grasp the designated supply line. Loop the hose end around the fire hydrant starting from the street side, and stop on the backside of the hydrant barrel. Position yourself away from the street and place a foot on the end of the looped hose end where it crosses the hose line, a few feet down from the hydrant (Figure 9-50).

FIGURE 9-51

3. When you are ready, signal the apparatus driver to proceed toward the fire scene. The supply hose lines will flake off the rear of the apparatus hose bed (Figure 9-51).

FIGURE 9-52

4. You can step off the hose section after a few sections have cleared the rear of the hose bed. Take a cap off one of the small discharge outlets on the hydrant. Open the hydrant with the hydrant wrench until some water flows and shut off the hydrant (Figure 9-52). Note that this step is precautionary. It assures that the hydrant works and that it is free of debris that could clog the line.

—Continued

5. Connect the supply hose line to the hydrant. Wait for either a predesignated signal or a radio transmission from the apparatus driver requesting that the hydrant and supply hose line be charged with water. On his or her signal, open the hydrant completely and walk with the hose line back to the apparatus, checking for and undoing any kinks in the supply hose line (Figure 9-53).

FIGURE 9-53

Reverse Lay

A reverse lay involves laying a water supply line from the scene back to the water supply source. This source may be a fire hydrant on a water main system or another apparatus. In this instance, a firefighter may or may not be dropped off at the fire scene to assist the crew in securing the end of the supply line as it is laid out. To secure the line, the hose end can be chocked under a front or rear tire of an apparatus remaining on the scene. When a few hose line sections have come off the apparatus, pull the line from under the truck's tire and connect it to the supply intake outlet on the apparatus at the scene.

View It!

Go to the DVD, navigate to Chapter 9, and select *Reverse Lay*.

Practice It!

Reverse Lay

Use the following steps when laying a supply hose line from a fire scene to the fire hydrant water source:

1. Your apparatus will come to a stop at the fire scene where another apparatus needing water will be. Alternately, it will stop at a spot where the supply hose line will be used as a fire attack line. Safely dismount the apparatus, checking for traffic hazards. Gather several loops of the supply hose and pull them from the hose bed (Figure 9-54).

2. If you are connecting to another fire apparatus on the scene, pass the hose to the operator of the apparatus and she will slide the hose under a wheel of her apparatus. When you have remounted your apparatus, the operator of the other apparatus will signal for the hose lay to begin.

FIGURE 9-54

—Continued

3. If you are merely leaving the supply line at the scene to be later used to connect to attack hose lines and nozzles, pull the loops of supply hose to the street behind the apparatus. Then turn them over to a firefighter on the scene to anchor with one knee. On his signal, your apparatus should proceed to the fire hydrant (Figure 9-55).

FIGURE 9-55

4. Make the connection to the fire hydrant. Alternately, if the line was laid to the attack pumper, hand the supply hose to that pumper's engineer (Figure 9-56).

FIGURE 9-56

View It!

Go to the DVD, navigate to Chapter 9, and select *Large-Diameter Supply Hose Lay.*

Practice It!

Laying Large-Diameter Supply Hose

The steps for assisting with laying a large-diameter supply hose are similar to the procedures outlined for laying a smaller-diameter hose, with the following exceptions:

Forward lay:

1. The hydrant wrap can be accomplished by wrapping the hydrant as described. To secure the hose while the apparatus begins the lay, you may use a hose-pulling rope or strap handle to hook the hydrant (Figure 9-57).

FIGURE 9-57

—Continued

2. With a large-diameter hose, there may or may not be a hydrant valve that needs to be hooked into the hydrant (Figures 9-58 and 9-59).

FIGURE 9-58 A hydrant without the hydrant valve attached.

FIGURE 9-59 A hydrant with the hydrant valve attached.

3. The large-diameter hose is hooked into the large discharge opening of the hydrant (Figure 9-60).

Reverse lay:

1. Use the same procedure that is used for regular-diameter hose lines. However, at the fire scene, the large-diameter hose may be connected into a manifold that will reduce the line to several smaller-diameter hose lines.

2. The large-diameter hose may be connected into a fitting on the apparatus at the water supply. If the apparatus is not able to discharge one large-diameter hose line from its pump panel, the fitting will take in two smaller supply lines, combining them into one large-diameter line.

FIGURE 9-60

Hydrant Valves

Hydrant valves are appliances that allow a fire apparatus to hook into the water supply at the fire hydrant without interrupting the flow of water to the fire scene. These valves are commonly used with large-diameter water supply hose but can also be provided on smaller-diameter water supply hose (Figure 9-61). These appliances are attached to the large discharge opening on the fire hydrant, before the first section of supply hose is attached. They can be preconnected to the first section of hose coming off the hose bed. Once they are in place and the water supply from the fire hydrant is turned on, the fire apparatus can return to

FIGURE 9-61   A Humat valve is a type of hydrant valve used for large-diameter hose.

the hydrant and hook into the hydrant valve. This arrangement allows the apparatus to become an in-line pump, which increases the flow of water through the supply line. This setup is good for fires that require a larger water supply to be controlled. It is also useful if the supply line is a longer layout to the fire scene.

View It!

Go to the DVD, navigate to Chapter 9, and select *Hydrant Valves.*

Practice It!

Applying Hydrant Valves

Use the following procedure to connect a large-diameter hose hydrant valve to a fire hydrant:

1. After the fire apparatus has come to a stop, safely dismount the apparatus and go to the rear hose bed area. Remove the hydrant valve and hose line, looping the hydrant as previously described (see the section "Laying Large-Diameter Supply Hose").

2. Remove the large-diameter discharge outlet cap and flow a small amount of water, checking for any debris inside the opening. Shut down the hydrant and connect the hydrant valve (Figure 9-62).

FIGURE 9-62

—Continued

FIGURE 9-63

3. Make sure that the hydrant valve is connected properly and is in line with the large-diameter hose. Also ensure that the valve is in the proper position to supply the hose line from the hydrant (Figure 9-63). On signal, charge the hose line with the hydrant.

4. Walk along the supply line to the fire, checking for and undoing any kinks in the supply hose line. If needed, you may be required to remain at the fire hydrant so that you can assist the apparatus driver with connecting the supply line to the hydrant valve. Follow your department's operating practices and guidelines for this procedure.

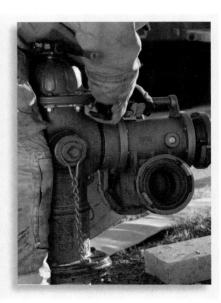

Hose Clamps for Supply Hose

As with fire attack hose lines, there may be times when a section of pressurized supply hose needs to be replaced or extended during a fire and the water cannot be shut off from the pump or water supply. For this reason, hose clamps have been designed to help shut off a hose line in order to stop the flow of water (Figures 9-64 and 9-65). These clamps can be used as a clamping device, operating as a lever with a handle that closes over the hose and locks into place. They can also be used as a screw-down clamp that stops the flow of water. As with all Fire Service tools, hose clamps can be dangerous if not used properly. Be sure to practice and train with them often.

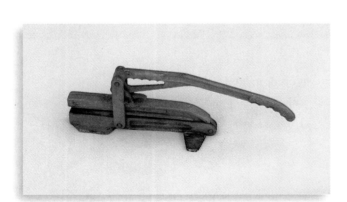

FIGURE 9-64 A level-style hose clamp.

FIGURE 9-65 A screw-style hose clamp.

View It!

Go to the DVD, navigate to Chapter 9, and select *Hose Clamps for Supply Hose.*

Practice It!

Applying a Hose Clamp to Supply Hose

Use the following procedure to apply a hose clamp on a supply side hose line:

1. Apply the hose clamp at least 5 feet from the couplings, toward the supply side of the hose line (not toward the fire attack side). Place the appropriate size clamp so that all of the hose will fit inside the hose clamp when it is applied (Figure 9-66).

2. To avoid creating a water hammer in the supply system, slowly apply the hose clamp. When it is fully applied, remove the section of hose, nozzle, or appliance and replace it with the desired replacement.

3. When ready, slowly open the hose clamp to allow the water supply to flow freely again. Make sure your body is not directly over a lever-type clamp when you open it, as the lever can spring up suddenly, causing significant injury.

FIGURE 9-66

Do It!

Practicing Skills Related to Securing a Water Supply

No single job is more or less important to the safety and efficiency of the mission than others. However, few tasks are more critical during a fire than developing a proper water supply to protect firefighters, contain and extinguish the fire, and protect adjacent property. Practice the steps described in this chapter until you can perform them safely and without hesitation. Practice each step periodically to hone your skills so that, when the need arises, you can safely work as a valuable team member in establishing the water supply needed to extinguish the fire.

Prove It

Knowledge Assessment

Signed Documentation Tear-Out Sheet

Exterior Operations Level Firefighter—Chapter 9

Name: _____

Fill out the ten-question quiz below, the Knowledge Assessment Sheet, by circling the correct answer for each question. When finished, sign it and give to your instructor/Company Officer for his or her signature. Turn in this Knowledge Assessment Sheet to the proper person as part of the documentation that you have completed your training for this chapter.

1. The water supply that is carried on the fire apparatus in what is generally referred to as a _____ .
   a. holding tank
   b. booster tank
   c. hose bed
   d. portable tank

2. The fire truck that pumps the water to the fire attack hose lines at the fire is commonly called the _____ pumper.
   a. first-due
   b. supply
   c. initial
   d. attack

3. On a typical fire hydrant, there will be two or three _____ ports.
   a. intake
   b. inspection
   c. suction
   d. outlet

4. Some fire departments utilize tender water shuttle operations in which several tenders in rotation supply the fire scene, each refilling as the other deploys its load of water, thus establishing a sustained water supply.
   a. True
   b. False

5. _____ hose is a specially designed fire hose that, when deployed into the body of water, can draw water to provide a sustained water supply for the fire scene.
   a. Soft suction
   b. Large-diameter
   c. Hard suction
   d. Fiber jacketed

6. The main difference between a portable pump and a float pump is that the float pump has no _____ hose attached.
   a. soft suction
   b. large-diameter
   c. hard suction
   c. fiber jacketed

7. Firefighters can use a _____ to divide one supply line into two smaller supply lines.
   a. gated manifold appliance
   b. hydrant valve
   c. gated hydrant valve
   d. hard suction hose

8. A supply hose layout operation that begins at the fire and proceeds toward the water supply is called a _____ lay.
   a. supply
   b. reverse
   c. forward
   d. preconnected

9. A 3- to 6-inch-diameter supply hose is considered large-diameter supply hose.
   a. True
   b. False

10. _____ are appliances that allow a fire apparatus to hook into the water supply at the fire hydrant without interrupting the flow of water to the fire scene.
    a. Gated manifolds
    b. Siamese appliances
    c. Hydrant valves
    d. Hose straps

Student Signature and Date _____   Instructor/Company Officer Signature and Date _____

Prove It

Skills Assessment
Signed Documentation Tear-Out Sheet
Exterior Operations Level Firefighter—Chapter 9

Name: _____

Fill out the Skills Assessment Sheet below. Have your instructor/Company Officer check off and initial each skill you demonstrate. When finished, sign it and give to your instructor/Company Officer for his or her signature. Turn in this Skills Assessment Sheet to the proper person as part of the documentation that you have completed your training for this chapter.

Skill	Completed	Initials
1. Explain the elements of an initial and a sustained water supply.	_____	_____
2. Help establish a water supply from different static sources, including portable tanks, lakes, and streams.	_____	_____
3. Describe how to work safely around a static water supply.	_____	_____
4. Work as a member of a team to refill a booster tank.	_____	_____
5. Operate a fire hydrant.	_____	_____
6. Work as a member of a team to establish a drafting operation.	_____	_____
7. Work as a member of a team to establish a sustained water supply from a hydrant using various hose configurations and layouts.	_____	_____
8. Explain the differences among hard suction hose, conventional supply hose, and large-diameter supply hose.	_____	_____
9. Demonstrate setting up a floating portable pump (if applicable).	_____	_____
10. Work as a team member loading 2½- or 3-inch supply hose.	_____	_____
11. Demonstrate safe procedures for coupling and uncoupling quick-connect hose couplings.	_____	_____
12. Work as a team member loading large-diameter supply hose.	_____	_____
13. Demonstrate safe procedure for applying a hydrant valve.	_____	_____
14. Demonstrate how to apply a hose clamp to a hose line.	_____	_____
15. Work as a team member hooking into a water tender for a water supply.	_____	_____

Student Signature and Date _____   Instructor/Company Officer Signature and Date _____

Large Attack Lines

What You Will Learn in This Chapter

In this chapter you will learn about the fire hose lines used to deliver large amounts of water onto large fires. We'll discuss how to pull and stretch large hose lines as well as methods for assembling and extending them. We will also present steps for handling these large and heavy hose lines as well as drills so that you can practice for loading large attack hose lines onto the fire apparatus. Finally, we will introduce you to some basics of master stream appliances.

What You Will Be Able to Do

After reading this chapter and practicing the skills in a classroom setting, you will be able to

1. Demonstrate how to pull and stretch a large preconnected attack hose line.
2. Demonstrate how to assemble a large attack hose line.

3. Explain and demonstrate the steps for flowing a large attack line, one-person method.
4. Explain and demonstrate the steps for looping a large attack line, one-person method.
5. Discuss and demonstrate the steps for advancing a large attack line as a hose team member.
6. Discuss and demonstrate how multiple firefighters, as hose team members, handle a large attack line in the kneeling position.
7. Demonstrate and explain how to extend a line with a gated wye.
8. Demonstrate how to extend a charged hose line with a hose clamp.
9. Demonstrate how to extend a line through the nozzle.
10. Explain and demonstrate how to set up a monitor-deck gun master stream appliance.

Exterior Fire Attack—Large Attack Lines

There is an old saying in the Fire Service: "Big fire, big water." This phrase is a very commonsense approach to basic fire facts. Simply put, the larger the fire and therefore the greater the release of heat, the more water that is needed to be applied to the fire in order to absorb the heat. Fire attack lines for "big water" are generally 2½- to 3-inch diameter hose lines with associated nozzles. As with small fire attack lines, the nozzles are either fog or smoothbore type and operate similarly. One of the main differences between large and small attack lines is that large attack lines flow much more water volume and require more people to operate them safely. Their reach is farther and they can extinguish much more fire. They also use up the water supply much faster and should therefore be connected to a sustained water supply as soon as possible after they are deployed and operated.

Pulling and Stretching Large Attack Lines

Maneuvering a large attack line is much more cumbersome than using a small attack line. A charged large attack line can be moved, but you will probably need more help to do it (Figure 10-1). These attack lines are often used on exterior fire attacks due to their capacity to flow large amounts of water on **exposures** to the original fire as well as rapidly extinguish fires. When extended to the interior of a structural fire, they can flow much more water. However, they use up manpower and can be difficult to maneuver inside the building.

Large attack lines can be configured in two main ways: (1) they can be preconnected, like small attack lines, or (2) they can be put together as needed off the supply hose bed of the fire apparatus. We will discuss the various methods of establishing a large attack line utilizing both configurations.

▬ KEY WORDS ▬

exposure   Anything that has the potential of catching fire as a result of its proximity to something that is already on fire.

Preconnected Large Attack Lines

Often referred to as blitz lines, preconnected large fire attack lines are loaded in a similar manner as small attack lines. Because of the increased size and overall weight of the hose, you should consider getting help to pull the preconnected load (Figure 10-2). Getting assistance is especially important if you need to move a *charged* hose line to a certain placement to apply a fire stream. However, pulling an *uncharged* line across level ground with no obstructions can be accomplished by one firefighter.

FIGURE 10-1   Large attack lines are more cumbersome and require more people to maneuver than small attack lines.

FIGURE 10-2   Preconnected, large attack lines are often referred to as *blitz lines.*

TABLE 10-1	Weights of Uncharged and Charged Fire Hoses		
Hose Size (in inches)	Hose and Coupling Weight (in pounds)	Water Weight (in pounds)	Total Weight (in pounds)
1.5	30	80	110
1.75	35	105	140
2	40	135	175
2.5	55	225	280
3	70	305	375
4	85	545	630
5	100	850	950

Safety Tip!

Obviously, the larger the hose line, the heavier it is, especially when it is filled with water. Strained muscles and sprained joints can occur when we underestimate the weights we are working with and try to do too much without asking for help. Look at Table 10-1 to get an idea of exactly how the diameter of the hose affects its weight when it is charged and ready to flow. The weights given have been rounded off to the nearest 5 pounds and are for each 100 feet of hose.

View It!

Go to the DVD, navigate to Chapter 10, and select *Stretching a Preconnected Large Attack Line.*

Practice It!

Stretching a Preconnected Large Attack Line

Use the following general steps when pulling and deploying any large preconnected attack hose line:

1. Go to the hose bed where the preconnected load is located. Grab the nozzle and one or two loops of hose line, and turn. As you turn, position the hose over one shoulder (Figure 10-3).

2. With the nozzle and hose loops over your shoulder and facing in your direction of travel, walk in that desired direction, feeding off the loops when you feel a substantial tug in the hose. Quickly check to see that the hose is stretched out with no kinks in the line. Also make sure that the hose is not passing under, over, or against any obstructions that may restrict water flow.

FIGURE 10-3

—Continued

3. Get into position to support the nozzle and hose, and signal the pump operator to charge the attack line (Figure 10-4). If possible, plan to have at least one other person assist in holding and maneuvering the charged attack line. Without the help of another firefighter, you will need to slowly shut down the flow at the nozzle, reposition the hose, and then slowly reopen the nozzle flow.

FIGURE 10-4

Assembling a Large Attack Line

Oftentimes, the large attack line must be assembled from lengths of hose from the supply hose bed on the apparatus and a large attack nozzle located on the apparatus. This assembly is usually more the norm rather than the exception, so you must know how to quickly assemble these parts to make it work.

Practice It!

Assembling a Large Attack Line

Follow these steps when assembling a large fire attack line on the fire scene:

1. Grab a large attack nozzle from the apparatus. From the supply hose bed, pull enough of the desired amount of hose to complete the stretch. Place the hose sections over your shoulder as you remove them from the hose bed (Figure 10-5). Disconnect the hose at the last coupling.

FIGURE 10-5

2. Hand the female end to the pump operator, who will connect it to a discharge port on the truck.

3. Continue by carrying the hose, flaking it off as you proceed, to near the area where you want to start flowing water. The male coupling should lead to the fire. Drop the last section of hose and connect the nozzle to the hose line (Figure 10-6).

FIGURE 10-6

4. Open the nozzle about halfway, pointing it away from any other firefighters, and signal the pump operator to charge the line. Bleed off excess air, adjust the nozzle to the desired pattern, shut it off, and get into position (Figure 10-7). If possible, get a second or third firefighter to assist you in holding the large attack line.

FIGURE 10-7

Tip!

When assembling any attack line, make sure you have more than enough hose played out to reach your target and to move around a little. Otherwise, once the hose is stretched full length, you will be held in one spot.

Flowing Large Attack Lines

Large attack lines flow much more water than small attack lines. However, the result is a higher gpm rate of water delivered to the seat of the fire. The greater flow rate means that more people are needed to operate and maneuver the flowing lines. In addition, a more substantial sustained water supply is needed to keep it flowing. Remember that the reaction forces at the nozzle from the larger volumes of flowing water tend to create a greater kickback on the nozzle team.

We'll present steps for positioning and flowing large attack lines with a single firefighter, with multiple firefighters, and in standing and kneeling positions. We will also present looping techniques for line operation.

View It!

Go to the DVD, navigate to Chapter 10, and select *Flowing a Large Attack Line—Single Firefighter.*

Practice It!

Flowing a Large Attack Line—Single Firefighter

Use the following steps as a guide when flowing and operating a large attack line alone:

1. Position the hose under your arm, using your hip and leg as support for the line. Grasp the nozzle at the handle with one hand and the operating gate valve with the other. Keep your feet at a comfortable width and stay well balanced (Figure 10-8). The nozzle should be a little bit ahead of you so that you will have room to move it up, down, and sideways without having to turn your body.

FIGURE 10-8

2. The rest of the attack line should be in a half loop behind you, on the ground. This position provides some slack for a little bit of maneuvering. Slowly open the gate valve on the nozzle until the desired flow is reached and the valve is entirely open. Adjust the gallons-per-minute flow if available and the pattern (if a fog nozzle) as needed. If the reaction force is too great, you can partially close the gate valve and then ask the pump operator to reduce the flow pressure on your attack line. Remember—reducing the flow reduces the amount of water reaching the fire and can produce less extinguishment than desired.

FIGURE 10-9

3. Move the nozzle back and forth or up and down as desired while water is flowing. Lean into the line with your hip and leg (Figure 10-9).

Safety Tip!

Remember: While flowing a large attack line by yourself, you are stuck in the spot where you are standing. Don't try to walk with a large line while it is flowing. Shut down the flow, move, and then start the flow again. Keep the nozzle a little bit ahead of you and the hose close to your body so that you can maneuver the nozzle without twisting your body. This positioning will go a long way toward preventing back strain.

Looping a Large Attack Line

If a large attack line is being used by one or two firefighters, is going to be mostly stationary, and is a safe distance from the fire, the hose line can be looped on the ground. This positioning saves the firefighter's energy and allows for a longer application of water using one firefighter (Figure 10-10).

FIGURE 10-10 Looping a large attack line allows for positioning one firefighter on the line.

View It!

Go to the DVD, navigate to Chapter 10, and select *Ground Loop—Single Firefighter.*

Practice It!

Ground Loop—Single Firefighter

Use the following steps to create a loop while operating a large attack hose line:

1. Shut down the flow of water at the nozzle and walk the line in a curve over itself, creating a loop that is about 10 feet in diameter (Figure 10-11).

   FIGURE 10-11

2. Slip the nozzle end under the running end of the hose line where it crosses over it (Figure 10-12). Pull through the nozzle end with about 2 feet of line.

   FIGURE 10-12

—Continued

3. Sit on the hose on top of the nozzle end. Get into a comfortable position and open the nozzle slowly. To properly apply the water stream, adjust the nozzle flow, the pattern, and the direction as needed (Figure 10-13).

FIGURE 10-13

Safety Tip!

Use the loop method only when you are located in a safe area. Stay away from building collapse zones. Be alert. If you are called upon to retreat rapidly, be ready to shut down the line and leave it.

Advancing Large Attack Lines

When large attack lines need to be advanced to different positions, it is best to have a two- to three-firefighter crew attending the line. As we mentioned earlier, these lines flow tremendous amounts of water and, due to their increased diameter and volume, these lines can become very unwieldy for one firefighter.

View It!

Go to the DVD, navigate to Chapter 10, and select *Advancing Large Attack Lines—Multiple Firefighters.*

Practice It!

Advancing a Large Attack Line—Multiple Firefighters

The following steps can be used to maneuver a large attack line with multiple firefighters:

1. The firefighter at the nozzle is positioned as described in "Practice It! Flowing a Large Attack Line—Single Firefighter."

2. A second firefighter positions himself behind the first firefighter on the same side of the hose line. The second firefighter leans into the first firefighter as he bends the hose line over his hip. He should assist the firefighter on the nozzle to maneuver the hose as the first firefighter aims the nozzle (Figure 10-14). The second firefighter should take as much weight of the hose as possible so that the person at the nozzle can concentrate on controlling and directing the stream.

FIGURE 10-14

3. A third firefighter can also assist by positioning himself on the same side of the hose line a few feet behind the second firefighter. In this position he can handle the trailing line as well as assist in aiming the hose line with the firefighter at the nozzle (Figure 10-15).

4. On a signal from the firefighter at the nozzle, the large attack line is advanced carefully.

FIGURE 10-15

 Safety Tip!

It is always better to shut down the nozzle on a large fire attack line before repositioning the line. However, there are occasions when doing so is not possible. If the line must be moved while flowing, the firefighter at the nozzle should be ready to shut down the nozzle if he or she stumbles or loses balance.

 View It!

Go to the DVD, navigate to Chapter 10, and select *Kneeling Position on a Large Attack Line—Multiple Firefighters.*

 Practice It!

Using a Kneeling Position for a Large Attack Line—Multiple Firefighters

Use the following steps to position yourself in a kneeling position with other firefighters on a large attack line:

1. The first firefighter positions himself at the nozzle as described previously, assuming a kneeling position. The nozzle and line should still be positioned to one side, under the firefighter's arm and on his hip (Figure 10-16).

FIGURE 10-16

2. A second firefighter positions himself behind the first firefighter, in a kneeling position and on the same side. The second firefighter should be close enough to provide backup assistance in holding the hose line, taking as much of the weight as possible (Figure 10-17).

FIGURE 10-17

—Continued

3. A third firefighter positions a few feet behind the first two firefighters, in a kneeling position and on the same side of the hose line. From this position he can maneuver the trailing hose line and assist the first two firefighters with maneuvering the nozzle and hose line (Figure 10-18).

FIGURE 10-18

Extending a Line Using a Gated Wye

Large attack lines can also be used to extend the reach of smaller lines when a **gated wye** is used at the end. A gated wye is an appliance that takes in water from a large attack line and then distributes it through two outlets that are controlled by gate valves (Figure 10-19). A typical gated wye has a 2½-inch inlet and two 1½-inch outlets.

Many areas call this operation a garden apartment stretch because the evolution is frequently used to reach courtyard areas and long corridors in garden apartment buildings. However, this evolution is useful almost anytime the fire is beyond the reach of the preconnected attack lines on the pumper.

A gated wye uses quarter-turn valves. When a handle on the appliance is in line with the discharge port, the valve is open and the water is flowing. When the handle is perpendicular to the discharge port, the valve is closed and no water will flow. As with any other valve, open these valves slowly to avoid creating a water hammer.

Some departments have an appliance that closely resembles the gated wye, but in addition to the two 1½-inch discharge ports, it has a single 2½-inch discharge port in the middle. This appliance is called a **water thief.** The water thief allows you to stretch to a certain point, deploy two small attack lines, and then extend further with more large attack lines where either another gated wye or a nozzle is attached. A firefighter should be stationed at each appliance to control the valves (Figure 10-20).

▨ KEY WORDS ▨

gated wye   An appliance that takes in water from a large attack line and then distributes it through two outlets that are controlled by gate valves.

water thief   An appliance that closely resembles a gated wye. In addition to the two 1½-inch discharge ports, it has a single 2½-inch discharge port in the middle.

FIGURE 10-19   Gated wye.

FIGURE 10-20   Water thief.

View It!

Go to the DVD, navigate to Chapter 10, and select *Extending a Line with a Gated Wye.*

Practice It!

Extending a Line with a Gated Wye

Use the following steps to extend a line with a gated wye:

1. Assemble and extend a large attack line to the connection point—usually within 50 feet of the fire.

2. Attach a gated wye or water thief and attach at least two lengths of small attack line with a nozzle attached (Figure 10-21).

FIGURE 10-21

3. Assure that the valves are closed and signal to the pump operator to start the water flow.

4. Once the line is charged, open the appropriate valves slowly (Figure 10-22).

FIGURE 10-22

Extending Large Attack Lines— Hose Clamp Method

When you find that the length of line you are flowing falls short, extending its length is a fairly straightforward task. The simplest method to extend the line is to have the pump operator shut down the line, bleed off the pressure at the nozzle, add a section or two of hose, reconnect the nozzle, have the pump operator charge the line, and go back to work. However, this is time-consuming and sometimes impractical. This is where using a hose clamp comes into play.

Go to the DVD, navigate to Chapter 10, and select *Extending a Line—Hose-Clamp Method.*

Practice It!

Extending a Line—Hose-Clamp Method

Use the following steps to extend a line using a hose clamp:

1. Lay out the appropriate amount of hose you want to add to the line so that the female end is 4 or 5 feet behind the nozzle where it is presently located (Figure 10-23). This gives you enough slack in the hose to make the connection.

FIGURE 10-23

2. Position the hose clamp one section back on the charged line, making sure that the clamp is positioned just to the "engine" side of the coupling (Figure 10-24).

FIGURE 10-24

3. When ready, clamp the line, bleed the pressure and remove the nozzle, attach the extended hose, and place the nozzle at the end of the new line (Figure 10-25).

FIGURE 10-25

4. Assure that the nozzle is closed and open the hose clamp slowly, reestablishing flow to the nozzle (Figure 10-26).

FIGURE 10-26

Safety Tip!

Never stand over a lever-type hose clamp. Make sure your body is not in line with the handle, especially when opening the clamp, so that it doesn't fly up and hit you in the chest or face.

Extending Large Attack Lines— Through-the-Nozzle Method

Once a fire is knocked down, it is often time to switch from a large attack line to a smaller one. Since the large line is already in place, it is often better to simply extend the smaller line from the large one instead of pulling a preconnected line all the way from the engine to the fire. This is especially easy if the nozzle you are using is designed to break down at the tip. The gate valve on a typical large stream has a 2½ inch inlet and a 1½ inch outlet. This allows you to simply close the gate valve, remove the nozzle's tip, and replace it with the smaller attack line.

View It!

Go to the DVD, navigate to Chapter 10, and select *Extending a Line—Through-the-Nozzle Method.*

Practice It!

Extending a Line—Through-the-Nozzle Method

Use the following steps to extend a line with a smaller line:

1. Lay out the appropriate amount of hose you want to add to the line so that the female end is 4 or 5 feet behind the nozzle where it is presently located (Figure 10-27). This gives you enough slack in the hose to make the connection. This smaller line should have a nozzle attached that is in the off position.

FIGURE 10-27

—Continued

2. Stop the flow at the large nozzle and remove the nozzle's tip (Figure 10-28). That nozzle now becomes both a gate valve and a reducer. Attach the smaller line to the male coupling on this gate valve (Figure 10-29).

FIGURE 10-28

FIGURE 10-29

3. Reestablish the flow to the nozzle by opening the gate valve (Figure 10-30).

FIGURE 10-30

Loading Large Attack Lines

As we mentioned earlier in this chapter, large attack lines are either preconnected or they are assembled as needed from the supply hose on the fire apparatus. After the incident is over, the hose should be reloaded onto the apparatus. As with all fire hose that has been charged with water on the fire incident, large attack lines must be shut down at the pump discharge gate valve, pressure must be relieved at the nozzle, and the hose sections must be disconnected. Each section of hose is then drained and the nozzle is placed at the apparatus in preparation for reloading the hose.

View It!

Go to the DVD, navigate to Chapter 10, and select *Loading Large Attack Lines.*

Practice It!

Loading Large Attack Lines

Use the following steps to load a preconnected large attack line:

1. With the hose drained and disconnected, start at the female end of a section of hose at the apparatus and stretch it away from the opening of the hose bed section into which it is to be loaded (Figure 10-31).

FIGURE 10-31

2. Reconnect the female end to the discharge port of the preconnected hose bed. Load the hose, folding it at each end of the hosebed and reconnecting each section as you go, until all the hose is lying in a single stack, flat loaded (Figure 10-32).

FIGURE 10-32

—Continued

3. Reattach the nozzle and take up any slack in the last section of hose (Figure 10-33).

FIGURE 10-33

Every department has its own methods of loading preconnected large attack lines. Learn and follow the guidelines that your department utilizes.

If the large attack line was assembled from supply hose on the apparatus, do the following:

1. With the hose drained and disconnected, start at the female end of a section of hose at the apparatus and stretch it away from the opening of the hose bed section into which it is to be loaded. Reconnect each section.

2. Connect the female coupling to the male coupling on the supply hose bed on the apparatus and reload the hose sections (Figure 10-34).

FIGURE 10-34

3. When this has been done, return the large attack line nozzle to its storage place on the apparatus (Figure 10-35).

FIGURE 10-35

Master Stream Appliances

When a large fire occurs and the greatest possible volume of water must be applied to cover exposures, confine the fire, and extinguish it, master streams are put into action (Figure 10-36). Any appliance that flows over 500 gpm is considered to be a master stream appliance. These large-volume streams of water can be delivered by any one of several appliances. Master stream appliances can be positioned and flowed from the ground, from preconnected positions on an engine, or from an elevated position, such as the end of an aerial ladder apparatus. A master stream appliance that is portable and can be located on the ground is often called a *deluge gun*. A master stream appliance located on an engine is often called a *deck gun*. A master stream appliance connected to an aerial ladder or platform is usually called an *aerial stream*. As a member of the outside firefighting team,

FIGURE 10-36 A master stream appliance flowing water to protect an exposure.

FIGURE 10-37 Deluge gun.

you may be assigned to set up and operate a master stream appliance located on ground level or to assist in flowing a master stream appliance that is on the fire apparatus. Operating master stream devices from aerial ladders is a more advanced skill that is unique to each type of aerial apparatus.

Ground-Level Master Stream Appliances—Deluge Gun

The **deluge gun** (also called a *monitor*) is a master stream appliance set up primarily for use at ground level (Figure 10-37). It has a base with two or three inlets (with female swivels) and a swivel nozzle mount. Attached to the nozzle mount is a nozzle—either an adjustable fog nozzle or an open-tip master stream

nozzle. Supply lines (usually large attack lines) are attached from the pump panel discharge outlets into the base of the unit and charged when ready.

Master Stream Nozzles

Master stream nozzles are similar to fire attack line nozzles (Figure 10-38). They deliver much higher volumes of water at a far greater distance than other types of nozzles. The firefighter can easily adjust the nozzle pattern (on adjustable-flow fog nozzles), aiming the fire stream by raising and lowering the nozzle and rotating the nozzle from side to side. Master stream nozzles provide a great deal of reach for the master stream and deliver large volumes of water to the desired location.

Master Stream Deployment

Once placed into position and operational, master streams can provide excellent exposure protection at large fire scenes in which exposures to the original fire are at risk. Because they are intended to stay in place while flowing, master streams can be attended by only one firefighter after they are set up. This is their most common application.

FIGURE 10-38 Master stream nozzles provide a great deal of reach for the master stream and deliver large volumes of water to the desired location.

They can also be set up and then left working in place, which is useful with fires of long duration and especially with hazardous fire situations (Figure 10-39).

Any significant change in location requires the master stream appliance to be shut down and relocated to the next position. It may also require the lines to be extended. In addition, it requires the hose lines supplying the appliance to be shut down, drained of pressure, disconnected, and extended after the appliance is repositioned.

FIGURE 10-39   Unattended master stream.

 View It!

Go to the DVD, navigate to Chapter 10, and select *Setting Up a Monitor-Deck Gun.*

Practice It!

Setting Up a Monitor-Deck Gun

Use the following steps when setting up the deluge gun for operation:

1. Remove the deck gun from its storage place on the fire apparatus and place it where it will provide the best coverage for the effect desired (Figure 10-40).

FIGURE 10-40

2. Remove and extend large attack lines or supply lines and attach them to the deck gun intake openings and the fire apparatus discharge gates (Figure 10-41). Walk the lines to remove any kinks or obstructions.

FIGURE 10-41

3. Signal the pump operator to charge the lines, aiming the stream away from any firefighters nearby. After the air has been bled from the deck gun and hose, position the height and direction of the master stream and adjust the flow of the nozzle and pattern (with an adjustable fog nozzle) (Figure 10-42).

FIGURE 10-42

 ## Safety Tip!

Due to the volume and force of the water coming out of any master stream appliance, you must avoid allowing the stream of water to hit other firefighters. These streams can also knock down weakened building structural parts and push loose debris long distances. In addition, the volume of water can add significant weight to the location it is applied, increasing the chances of structural collapse in fire-weakened buildings. These streams are usually applied to structural fire areas evacuated of any firefighters.

 ## Do It!

Deploying and Operating Large Attack Lines

Deploying and operating large attack lines is always a team effort. A charged line holds quite a volume of water and is heavy. In addition, the backpressure of a nozzle flowing a large amount of water can be straining. Practice working as a team and rotate positions often to conserve your energy when working with these lines. One of the main values of using a large attack line is found in the reach they have when flowing water. The extended distance between you and the fire makes the large-diameter line a good choice during a defensive fire attack; this distance keeps firefighters clear of the collapse zone. Take advantage of this safety feature and do not "creep" closer to the fire than necessary. Like any other aspect of fireground operations, working with large attack lines takes practice, so practice often.

Prove It

Knowledge Assessment

Signed Documentation Tear-Out Sheet

Exterior Operations Level Firefighter—Chapter 10

Name: _____

Fill out the ten-question quiz below, the Knowledge Assessment Sheet, by circling the correct answer for each question. When finished, sign it and give to your instructor/Company Officer for his or her signature. Turn in this Knowledge Assessment Sheet to the proper person as part of the documentation that you have completed your training for this chapter.

1. Large fire attack lines are generally _____ diameter hose lines with associated nozzles.
   a. 1- to 3-inch
   b. 2½- to 3-inch
   c. 1½-inch
   d. 5-inch

2. Large, preconnected fire attack lines can also be referred to as _____ lines.
   a. red
   b. quick
   c. blitz
   d. black

3. Large attack lines deliver a greater gallons-per-minute rate of water to the seat of the fire. The greater flow rate means that more people are needed to operate and maneuver the flowing lines. A sustained water supply is also needed to keep it flowing.
   a. True
   b. False

4. If a large attack line is being used by one or two firefighters, is going to be mostly stationary, and is at a safe distance from the fire, the hose line can be _____ on the ground.
   a. twisted
   b. held
   c. flaked
   d. looped

5. When large attack lines need to be advanced to different positions, it is best to have one firefighter attending the line.
   a. True
   b. False

6. If the line must be moved while flowing, the firefighter at the nozzle should be ready to _____ if he or she stumbles or loses balance.
   a. shut down the nozzle
   b. reloop the hose line
   c. advance the hose line
   d. open the nozzle

7. A _____ is an appliance that closely resembles the gated wye, but in addition to the two 1½-inch discharge ports, it has a single 2½-inch discharge port in the middle.
   a. deck gun
   b. water thief
   c. monitor
   d. hydrant valve

8. A typical _____ has a 2½-inch inlet and two 1½-inch outlets.
   a. water thief
   b. deck gun
   c. gated wye
   d. hose clamp

9. Operating _____ from aerial ladders is a more advanced skill that is unique to each type of aerial apparatus.
   a. small attack lines
   b. master stream appliances
   c. a gated wye appliance
   d. a water thief

10. _____ are intended to stay in place while flowing. They can be attended by only one firefighter after they are set up.
   a. Large fire attack hose lines
   b. Gated wye appliances
   c. Water thief appliances
   d. Master streams

Student Signature and Date _____   Instructor/Company Officer Signature and Date _____

238

Prove It

Skills Assessment

Signed Documentation Tear-Out Sheet

Exterior Operations Level Firefighter—Chapter 10

Name: _____

Fill out the Skills Assessment Sheet below. Have your instructor/Company Officer check off and initial each skill you demonstrate. When finished, sign it and give to your instructor/Company Officer for his or her signature. Turn in this Skills Assessment Sheet to the proper person as part of the documentation that you have completed your training for this chapter.

Skill	Completed	Initials
1. Demonstrate how to pull and stretch a large preconnected hose line.	_____	_____
2. Demonstrate how to assemble a large attack line.	_____	_____
3. Explain and demonstrate the steps for flowing a large attack line, one-person method.	_____	_____
4. Explain and demonstrate the steps looping a large attack line, one-person method.	_____	_____
5. Discuss and demonstrate the steps for advancing a large attack line as a hose team member.	_____	_____
6. Discuss and demonstrate how multiple firefighters handle a large attack line in the kneeling position.	_____	_____
7. Demonstrate and explain how to extend a line with a gated wye.	_____	_____
8. Demonstrate and explain the hose-clamp method for extending a line.	_____	_____
9. Demonstrate and explain how to extend a line using the through-the-nozzle method.	_____	_____
10. Explain and demonstrate how to set up a master stream appliance.	_____	_____

Student Signature and Date _____   Instructor/Company Officer Signature and Date _____

11

Single-Family-Dwelling Fires

What You Will Learn in This Chapter

In this chapter you will be introduced to one of the most common fire situations faced by today's firefighters, the single-family-dwelling fire. We will introduce you to some construction and burn characteristics of manufactured housing and site-built structures. You will review safe response and arrival practices as well as command personnel accountability needs. Safety practices on the dwelling fire scene will be discussed. We will explain the fire attack team and the various jobs that they may be assigned. You will learn about roof and extension ladders, which are commonly carried and used by engine company units. We'll talk about exposures and making an exterior fire attack on a dwelling fire situation. Finally, you will practice what you have learned with three drills for dwelling fire situations.

What You Will Be Able to Do

After reading this chapter and practicing the skills in a classroom setting, you will be able to

1. Explain the differences between manufactured and site-built dwellings as they relate to construction and fire conditions.

2. Describe safety zones on the dwelling fire emergency scene.

3. Explain how to check in with command using your fire department's personnel accountability system (PAS).

4. Define the different job functions that a typical fire attack team may be called upon to perform on the scene of a dwelling fire.

5. Demonstrate forcible entry techniques on an exterior door that swings inward.

6. Demonstrate forcible entry techniques on an exterior door that swings outward.

7. Explain techniques for using a Halligan bar and flathead axe to force a lock.

8. Explain how to assist interior firefighters with extending hose while stationed at the doorway to a dwelling.

9. Describe how to safely break and clear glass from a window frame on a dwelling.

10. Define what is meant by the term *intervention team*.

11. Describe how and where a tool staging area might be set up and its main purpose on the dwelling fire scene.

12. Demonstrate how to place ventilation fans for negative- and positive-pressure ventilation on a single-family dwelling.

13. Describe a lockout/tagout system and how it is used on the fire ground.

14. Demonstrate how to control utilities in a dwelling.

15. Demonstrate how to deploy, place, and stow a roof ladder.

16. Demonstrate how to prepare a roof ladder for use on a roof.

17. Demonstrate how to deploy, place, and stow an extension ladder.

18. Explain what is meant by the term *exposure* and the best methods of protecting an exposure with an attack line stream.

19. Demonstrate dwelling fire operations for Exterior Operations level firefighters as a member of a fire attack team.

20. Demonstrate dwelling fire support operations for Exterior Operations level firefighters.

Structural Firefighting and Teamwork

Some of the most complex and inherently dangerous operations a fire department undertakes involve the duties associated with a structural fire. A lot goes on during the first few minutes after the Fire Department arrives on the scene, and for someone uninformed about Fire Department procedure, at first glance our actions can appear chaotic. However, nothing could be farther from the truth. The safety and success of everyone on the scene of a structural fire is dependent on an integrated system of safety, equipment, tools, and the actions of teams of people working as part of a command structure toward the common goal—to save *savable* lives and protect *savable* property. Nothing on a properly staffed and controlled fire scene is accomplished through an individual effort. Safe firefighters work in teams of two or more, depending on the task, and are actively involved in either directly extinguishing the fire or supporting those who are. There is no room for any freelance operations on a fire scene. For everyone's safety, all activities *MUST* be coordinated

FIGURE 11-1 An Incident Commander is essential on any fire scene.

through the Incident Commander, who orchestrates the actions (Figure 11-1).

Because this is your initial exposure to working at a structural fire, your training at this point will focus on the functions that are conducted *outside* the burning structure—in this case, a single-story, single-family dwelling. A fire in a single-family dwelling is the most common type of structural fire to which we respond. Those who enter the dangerous atmosphere contained in a burning structure should be trained to at least the Level 1 standard. However, there are dozens of essential actions that you can perform outside the building in support of the interior attack team.

Single-Family-Dwelling Fires

The most common kind of structural fire you will respond to as a firefighter is fire in a single-family dwelling. These buildings are where most people live and, consequently, where most structural fires occur. Vast areas of subdivisions surround densely populated cities in the United States. There are also large areas where homes are intermingled with wildland areas, where the risk of a structural fire is no less common.

The normal routine for the Fire Service is to make an aggressive interior fire attack on these structures when the risk is justified by the potential to save a life or to save *savable* property (Figure 11-2). If there are unburned areas in the structure where fire victims may be located, or if the fire is small and the building can be saved for repair, then this option is usually

FIGURE 11-2 An aggressive interior fire attack is often referred to as an offensive fire attack.

KEY WORD

defensive fire attack A term used during fireground operations for a building fire that has extended throughout the structure, necessitating an exterior fire attack.

Manufactured Homes

In the years since its inception, the house trailer evolved into the mobile home and has now evolved further into today's **manufactured home.** A manufactured home that was built after the mid-1990s meets a strict building code that makes it much safer than its predecessors. However, there are plenty of the older mobile homes still in use. The greatest difference between the two types is in the time it takes for the fire to travel through the structure. In today's better-built manufactured home, a fire is often contained in one or two rooms inside the structure. Before the code changes, mobile homes were likely to be totally engulfed by rapidly spreading fire.

Manufactured homes usually have an exterior metal cladding and are built with a wood frame and floor. They are mounted on a chassis that allows the home to be transported from the manufacturer to the final home site (Figure 11-3). The chassis arrangement means that the finished floor can be 2 or 3 feet above grade level, with a large void space underneath the home. When properly installed, the manufactured

called for. This practice is referred to as an offensive fire attack.

An Exterior Operations level firefighter does not have the training to enter a burning structural fire. You must first successfully complete the next curriculum, Level 1, to be able to take part in an interior offensive fire attack.

However, as an Exterior Operations level firefighter, you are able to assist an interior fire attack operation from the outside. Essential work is needed on the outside to support interior firefighting crews. After completing this training section, you will be able to assist fire crews in opening locked or blocked doors (forcible entry) as well as removing glass from windows from the outside. During a fire, secondary fire attack hose lines need to be deployed and all hose lines need to be set up and advanced into the structure from the outside. Supply hose lines need to be set into operation and ladders raised (especially on multistory dwellings). All of these jobs can be accomplished by the Exterior Operations level firefighter.

In addition, when the building fire has extended throughout the structure and an exterior fire attack, also referred to a **defensive fire attack,** has been called for, then you will be able to use your skills to extinguish the fire as a member of the exterior firefighting team.

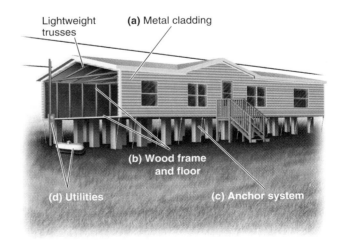

Manufactured home

FIGURE 11-3 A typical modern manufactured home consists of the following elements: (a) metal cladding, (b) wood frame and floor, (c) anchor system, and (d) utilities.

home is held in place by ground anchors and straps that help prevent wind damage to the structure. Just like a site-built home, most manufactured homes are served by electricity, water, and propane or natural gas utilities.

▰▰ KEY WORD ▰▰

manufactured home A building that is assembled in a factory and then transported to its final location for use as a single-family dwelling. This type of building can also be used as nonpermanent housing.

Site-Built Homes

Most single-family dwellings are built on site (Figure 11-4). **Site-built single-family homes** can range from small wood-framed buildings that are less than 1000 square feet in size to vast estates with multiple buildings enclosing many thousands of square feet. They may have large basement areas, multiple levels above ground, and open attic areas under the roof. The fires you encounter involving single-family dwellings will vary greatly between incidents, so our focus at this point is on the skills and abilities that are common to fighting most single-story, single-family-dwelling fires.

▰▰ KEY WORD ▰▰

site-built single-family home A building that is built on the site location. This type of building is not designed to be moved and is therefore a permanent structure used for single-family dwelling.

FIGURE 11-4 Single family site built homes are very common throughout North America.

Safe Response and Arrival

When the alarm sounds, dispatching units to a structural fire, it is only natural that your adrenaline flows and you get excited, especially if this type of work is new to you. However, it is extremely important that everyone focuses on the firefighter's first responsibility for any mission: to get to the scene safely. We discussed the steps for a safe response in Chapter 5. However, it cannot be stressed enough that one of the most dangerous aspects of any emergency work is the response phase. Whether you are responding from the fire station to the incident, from home to the fire station, or from home directly to the incident, your safety is your responsibility. ***Wear your seatbelt, and focus on the traffic and safe driving.***

If you respond directly to the scene in your personally owned vehicle (POV), make sure to park your vehicle out of the way when you arrive. Keep in mind that other arriving vehicles may need room to stretch supply hose from the hydrant to the fire and to deploy attack lines, ladders and equipment. Therefore, they need as much room in the street or road as they can get. Remember to remain aware of your surroundings when choosing the proper parking spot for your POV. Keep away from overhead power lines that stretch from the power pole to the burning structure. It is very common for a line to burn free from the house and drop to the ground, creating an extreme electrical hazard to anyone below or near the energized wires.

Incident Command Framework

The elements of a good Incident Command System call for the first trained person who arrives on the scene to establish command of the incident. This person is usually the Company Officer of the first arriving unit. However, it could very well be you if you are the first to arrive in your POV. Your role in this case is to gather information and be prepared to relay that information to the first arriving crew. In most instances, however, you will arrive as part of a crew or after the first responding unit arrives and establishes command. In this case, report to the Incident Commander and wait for instructions before taking any action. There is no room for freelancing on any fire scene, so expect to be teamed up with other firefighters or crews.

One of the most important elements of a command structure is the personnel accountability system (PAS). This system enables the Commander to know where on the fire scene each individual firefighter is working and what they are doing at any given time

FIGURE 11-5 Personnel accountability systems are important for firefighter safety on the fire scene.

FIGURE 11-6 The interior of a burning building is considered an atmosphere that is Immediately Dangerous to Life and Health (IDLH).

during the operation. It is important that you take whatever action is required by your department's procedures for "tagging in" with the Personnel Accountability Officer and then stay with your assigned crew throughout the incident (Figure 11-5).

Overall Scene Safety

For our purposes at this point, we will divide the job assignments for a dwelling fire into two categories: exterior and interior. Individuals who work inside a burning building are working in an atmosphere that is **Immediately Dangerous to Life and Health (IDLH)** (Figure 11-6). However, this isn't the only hazard they face. Many of the line-of-duty deaths of firefighters working inside a structure occur when the firefighter becomes disoriented and runs out of fresh air supplied by his or her SCBA. Therefore, just knowing how to wear PPE and breathe from an SCBA does not qualify a person to work inside a structural fire. This type of competency will come later, during your Level 1 training. For the rest of this chapter we will focus on exterior operations.

By now you are probably noticing a common theme to most emergency operations we discuss in this book. Everyone's safety at most incidents depends on a few common factors: a safe response, a safe arrival and setup, the observation of safety zones around the hazard, and the proper use and wearing of PPE. Working at a structural fire is no different in this respect. We must observe traffic safety zones in the street around the apparatus. We must also observe the hot, warm, and cold zones around the structure so that everyone is working where they should be and employing the proper level of PPE according to their job task.

KEY WORD

Immediately Dangerous to Life and Health (IDLH) A term used to define for firefighters the conditions of an atmosphere in a confined area, like a building fire, that can result in serious injury or death.

Traffic Control Zone

The traffic control zone for a structural fire is not much different from a vehicle crash. The main differences are the amount of apparatus staged in the work area and the length of the control zone that is necessary for the supply hose stretched from one or more hydrants (Figure 11-7).

In many areas, laws make it illegal for a civilian to even drive on the same block as a parked fire truck that is working at a fire. However, very few people are aware of such laws. The reality is that most people become excited when they see the activity around a fire and the fire itself. They often drive in an erratic manner, very close to you and the hose or apparatus—so be especially careful.

Onlookers gather at any type of emergency and can become a problem if they are allowed to venture too close to the action. It is best that you speak in a respectful but firm tone when asking bystanders to step back and remain out of the way. The key is to ask for their help and not shout out any orders. And, for the most part, you will get the cooperation you are seeking. Establish a clear, safe area using banner tape when possible, and seek the assistance of law enforcement personnel to control the crowds that gather at the scene.

Safety Zones

The hot, warm, and cold zones associated with a structural fire vary in size and shape depending on the size structure and fire. The zones also differ according to whether the fire attack is offensive or defensive. These zones should be designated by the Incident Commander on each emergency (Figure 11-8).

The Hot Zone

During an offensive, interior attack, the hot zone usually includes any area inside the structure where an IDLH incident in an enclosed area is encountered. Any-

Supply hose in the street

Staged apparatus

FIGURE 11-7 The traffic control zone for a structural fire includes (a) staged apparatus and (b) a supply hose in the street.

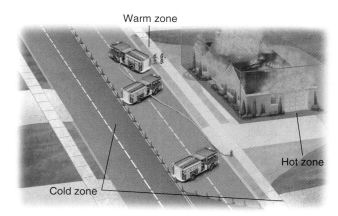

Warm zone

Cold zone

Hot zone

FIGURE 11-8 The safety zones for a typical single-family-dwelling fire consist of (a) the hot zone, (b) the warm zone, and (c) the cold zone.

one working in the hot zone should be fully protected with PPE and a charged hose line. These individuals should also be trained to the Level 1 standard.

If the fire is well-advanced and the fire attack becomes defensive, the hot zone is expanded to anything within the area that could be hazardous if the building was to collapse.

There are conflicting opinions as to how large this area should be, but for safety's sake we consider the collapse area to extend out for a distance of twice the height of the building. Walls seldom fall out any farther than their height, but doubling that potential allows for any errors in judgment.

Another exception to the hot zone area includes areas around any downed or dangerous electrical lines that could possibly fall to the ground as they burn away from the structure. Keep clear of these areas by a distance of at least the length of the wire in all directions. Because the hot zone can be irregular in shape and size, many agencies mark the dangerous areas with traffic cones early in the operation as a warning to firefighters working in the area.

The Warm Zone

In a single-story, single-family-dwelling fire in a residential area, the warm zone typically starts at the doorway and extends outward several feet. The warm zone is usually anything on the property, extending to and including the traffic control areas outside the property line boundaries. Anyone working in the warm zone should also be protected in full PPE during the active fire. However, because a firefighter may work in a support role independent of a charged hose line, once the fire has been controlled the PPE requirements can be relaxed at the Incident Commander's order.

The Cold Zone

The cold zone is obviously anything outside the hot and warm zones. This area is any place beyond the scope and control of the Incident Commander. Therefore, it is generally of no concern to you. Although the PPE requirements for the warm zone are relaxed once the fire has been controlled, the warm zone does not convert to a "cold zone" due to the need to restrict civilian access to the area around the equipment and the hazards that may remain.

Unit Assignments

The type and amount of equipment dispatched to a single-family-dwelling fire varies drastically throughout North America. Fire departments in urban areas tend to send more equipment of various types to a house fire than departments in rural areas because the equipment available in a rural setting is often more limited. Our focus here will not be on the type of truck or trucks that respond to the scene, but on the number of firefighters that should respond and their job functions on the scene.

Any work done on a fire scene should be accomplished in teams of at least two individuals. The work is assigned by the type of job the team is charged to perform. For example, the **fire attack team** is charged with forcing open any locked doors that are in the way of the advancing hose team, while the ventilation team is responsible for opening windows to vent the smoke and hot gases from inside the structure. More than one job can be assigned to a team. In the absence of extra support staff on the scene in the first moments of the fire, the initial hose team may be assigned the tasks of both the fire attack team and the ventilation team so that these important functions are not overlooked. When staffing permits, most of these jobs are performed simultaneously.

■■ KEY WORD ■■

fire attack team A group of firefighters who perform various firefighting functions on the scene of a fire emergency in order to mitigate the situation and return it to a safe condition.

Fire Attack Team

The fire attack team is responsible for deploying the proper size hose line, forcing open any locked doors or windows (forcible entry), and advancing a hose line to the seat of the fire. If the scope of the fire calls for an offensive, interior attack, the team operates inside the burning structure. Although the Exterior Operations level firefighter's job stops at the front door, there are several duties you can perform to assist with the fire attack team's mission. Forcing a locked door, helping to straighten any kinks in the hose line, and feeding hose from the outside to the fire attack crew can help conserve the fire attack team's energy for the hose work inside.

If the fire attack team is working in a defensive, exterior mode, then their duties are performed outside the structure. The Exterior Operations level firefighter may therefore be called upon to help staff the hose line or operate the nozzle (Figure 11-9).

Forcible Entry

The most common tools used to force a door are the flathead axe and the Halligan bar. The flathead axe used for the Fire Service has both a cutting surface and a pound-

FIGURE 11-9 An Exterior Operations level firefighter may be working on a hose line while other firefighters work on forcing the door.

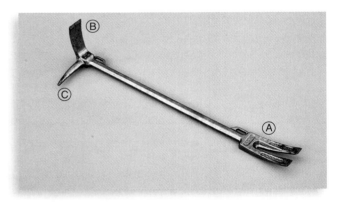

FIGURE 11-10 Halligan bar: (a) forked end, (b) adze, and (c) pick.

ing surface. The Halligan bar is a tool that was specially designed for forcible entry. The Halligan tool is forked on one end and has an adze and pick on the other end. Each of these features can be adapted to almost any use (Figure 11-10). A typical Halligan-style bar provides quite a bit of leverage, so prying a door is well within the range of the tool and a person of average strength. The flathead axe serves as a pounding tool to pound the Halligan bar into place, which then allows the leverage provided by the bar to pry open the door. It is important that you view these two tools as being almost "married" together as a two-piece tool. You should carry them together whenever you are assigned the duty of performing forcible entry. A good way to carry these two tools is to "marry" them together by placing the forked end of the Halligan bar over the axe blade and folding the bar against the axe handle so that you can pick up both tools in one hand (Figure 11-11).

Forcible entry is a skill worthy of an entire textbook of its own. There are two basic maneuvers that help you force open most conventional residential doors; the method used depends on the direction in which the door swings. When sizing up a door that you are about

FIGURE 11-11 The Halligan bar and axe "married" together.

to force open, look closely at whether the door swings inward (away from you) or outward (toward you). Generally, if the hinges are visible on the outside, the door swings outward. Next, try the doorknob. The door may not be locked; if it isn't, report this to your team's Officer and be ready for another order. If the door is locked, then be prepared to force entry when told to do so and not before. Before you take action, it is important that a charged hose line is in place and that the fire attack team is ready for the door to be opened.

 View It!

Go to the DVD, navigate to Chapter 11, and select *Forcible Entry—Inward-Swinging Door.*

Practice It!

Forcible Entry—Inward-Swinging Door

Working as part of a two-person team, use a flathead axe and Halligan bar to perform the following steps:

1. Size up the door, and check to see if it is locked, the direction it swings, and the location of the lock(s) (Figure 11-12).

FIGURE 11-12

2. Confirm that the hose team is in place with a charged line and is ready for the door to be forced.

3. Position the adze end of the Halligan tool in the gap between the jamb and the door, just above or below the lock(s) (Figure 11-13).

FIGURE 11-13

4. Use the flat of the axe to pound the adze end in place until it is well seated between the door and the jamb (Figure 11-14).

FIGURE 11-14

5. Apply force to the bar, moving the bar toward the door until the door opens (Figure 11-15).

FIGURE 11-15

Go to the DVD, navigate to Chapter 11, and select *Forcible Entry—Outward-Swinging Door.*

Practice It!

Forcible Entry—Outward-Swinging Door

Working as part of a two-person team, use a flathead axe and Halligan bar to perform the following steps:

1. Size up the door, assuring that it is locked, the direction it swings, and the location of the lock(s).

   FIGURE 11-16

2. Confirm that the hose team is in place with a charged line and is ready for the door to be forced.

3. Position the adze end of the Halligan tool in the gap between the jamb and the door, just above or below the lock(s) (Figure 11-16).

   FIGURE 11-17

4. Pound the adze in place until it is well seated between the door and the jamb (Figure 11-17).

5. Apply force to the bar, pulling the bar outward until the door opens (Figure 11-18).

   FIGURE 11-18

Forcing Locks

Doors to outbuildings, such as storage sheds or barns, may be locked with a padlock and hasp. The pick feature of the Halligan bar is useful when you encounter this situation. While the lock seldom breaks under the force of the Halligan bar, it makes a good purchase point for the Halligan bar to apply force on the hasp. Place the pick into the lock's shackle and pound down sharply on the back of the Halligan tool (Figure 11-19). This action usually strips away any screws that are holding the hasp in place, breaking the assembly free and thus opening the door.

 Safety Tip!

Anytime you use a striking or prying tool, always wear full protective gear, including eye protection. Forcible entry during fire conditions should be performed wearing full PPE with an SCBA in place. Stand to one side of the door and avoid standing directly in the doorway to avoid the hot smoke and flames that may come from the opened door. Stay as low as possible and apply just enough force to open the door, controlling the door so that it doesn't fly open. It is not uncommon to find a victim collapsed just inside a locked door, so be prepared as the door opens.

FIGURE 11-19 When you encounter a padlock and hasp, place the pick of the Halligan bar in the shackle and strike the back of the tool with the flat side of an axe.

Advancing Hose

Once the door is opened, the fire attack team advances toward the fire. As an Exterior Operations level firefighter, you won't be part of the crew inside but you are still part of the team. Dragging a charged hose line through a house is difficult, especially if the interior crew is crawling on their hands and knees. This task can be made quite a bit easier if someone stages at the doorway, outside the building and the IDLH environment, to feed the hose into the building. This helps the interior team because they will only have to drag the 20 or so feet of line that is inside the building and not the entire 150 to 200 feet of charged hose line that extends all the way back to the pumper.

It is also important that the hose line be free of kinks and snags. Get in the habit of straightening any kinks in the line so that the maximum water flow is available at the nozzle when needed. Snags occur when the hose is dragged around obstacles such as fence posts, trees, plants, and even the wheels of the pumper. Pull the line free of any obstacles before the line becomes snagged and the interior crew is forced to stop (Figure 11-20).

FIGURE 11-20 At the doorway, straighten any kinks and assure that the line is free of obstacles that may snag it while it is being pulled inside.

Ventilation Team

The ventilation team is responsible for opening windows to vent the smoke and hot gases from inside the structure. They may also place specialized fans to ventilate smoke-filled areas.

Although some ventilation methods involve working on a roof, the Exterior Operations level activities are limited to ventilation techniques that can be accomplished from the ground and from outside the building.

Ventilation

The smoke and hot fire gases inside a structure can be more dangerous to the firefighters and occupants inside the structure than the flames. The products of combustion not only are toxic but can be explosive under certain conditions. It is important that the heat and smoke be ventilated from the structure. This ventilation is often accomplished by breaking glass or opening windows in a controlled and systematic manner. The ventilation efforts may occur through the natural process of the hot, pressurized gases that move from the building to the cooler, lower pressure outside. Alternately, ventilation may be augmented by the use of large fans that can either add pressure and fresh air to the structure or, when possible, pull the smoke out.

 Safety Tip!

Ventilation is conducted under the control and orders of the Incident Commander. Several factors are considered when the order is given to ventilate the structure, including hose line placement, team positions, and the location of the fire inside the structure. *DO NOT* ventilate the structure without an order to do so. The Incident Commander gives the order to ventilate and advises about the location of the openings and the type of ventilation that is to be used.

Breaking Glass   At first glance, it may seem to be excessive damage to break the glass in a window to vent the smoke from a building. If the fire is small enough and the smoke is fairly cool inside, the Incident Commander may give the order for the interior team to just open the windows from the inside as they proceed through the structure. This is usually the case when the fire is confined to a mattress or a pot on the stove in the kitchen. However, when the fire involves one or more rooms inside, the volume of smoke and heat far exceeds the amount that can be ventilated through a small, open window. In this case, the Incident Commander may call for exterior ventilation, which can

FIGURE 11-21   Positioning with a ceiling hook to break glass.

usually be conducted by crews standing in a safe area on the ground outside the building.

The tools of choice for outside ventilation through windows include an axe, a Halligan bar, and a ceiling hook. As a rule of thumb, the ceiling hook is usually the better choice because it allows you a chance to stand to one side of the window, preferably upwind, and keep your hands away from the glass shards that fall when you strike the window. Regardless of the tool used, keep your hands as far away from the glass as possible. Remember to keep the tool as close to horizontal as you can so that glass shards don't slide down the handle of the tool, striking you or gathering inside your coat sleeve. It takes a little force to break the glass, especially if it is mounted in a thermal-pane window in which the glass is thicker and possibly made of double layers. Strike the glass with minimal force at first and swing the tool quicker with subsequent blows if it doesn't break the first time (Figure 11-21).

Take the time to clear out all of the glass in the window by raking the tool around the window frame. This action removes the sharp, jagged edges that could injure someone later. Many agencies prefer that you simply pull the entire window assembly out of the frame so that the hole left behind can be used as an emergency escape route for the interior crew if something goes wrong. In reality, once you break the glass out of a typical residential window, the damage has been done and the most cost effective way to repair the window later is to replace the entire assembly. Therefore, no further damage is done when you pull the entire assembly out of the frame.

Once the glass and window frame have been cleared, use the tool to reach in and clear away any window treatments that can block smoke, such as curtains or blinds. Even something as porous as a wire screen across a window can hold back a lot of smoke, especially when it becomes clogged with soot, so clear away anything that can slow the ventilation process or get in the way of an exiting firefighter.

Ventilation Fans Ventilation fans come in two basic styles: gasoline powered and electric powered. Like all other aspects of the ventilation process, the placement and use of these fans is conducted only under the direct orders of the Incident Commander.

Negative-Pressure Ventilation Fans Electric-powered ventilation fans are most often used for **negative-pressure ventilation.** The fan is set up in a window or doorway with the inlet side facing toward the fire and the outlet side facing toward the open air. This type of fan is also called a **smoke ejector.** Smoke ejectors have hooks on cables and can be secured in place using an expanding door bar, hanging from a door or ladder, or by being placed on the ground. The key is to place the fan in as small an opening as pos-sible so that the air pulled into the inlet comes from inside the structure and is not simply recirculated air from outside the building.

KEY WORDS

negative-pressure ventilation A method of ventilation used to remove smoke from a building. An electric-powered fan is set up facing out of a building's opening. The fan is then activated to draw out smoke from inside the building.

smoke ejector A type of electrically powered smoke ventilation fan used on buildings for negative-pressure ventilation.

View It!

Go to the DVD, navigate to Chapter 11, and select *Negative-Pressure Ventilation.*

Practice It!

Negative-Pressure Ventilation

Use the following steps to position a smoke ejector fan for negative-pressure ventilation:

1. Remove the electric smoke ejector fan from the apparatus and plug it into the power cord from the apparatus generator. Turn it on and off quickly to check for operation. Then carry it to the desired location as directed by your Company Officer.

2. Hook the fan onto an open door, to an expanding door bar, or place it securely in a window (Figure 11-22). Switch it on.

3. Advise your Company Officer that you have accomplished the assignment.

FIGURE 11-22

Positive-Pressure Ventilation Fans Gasoline-powered fans are usually much more powerful than the electric versions and are also heavier in weight. Therefore, these fans are almost exclusively restricted to remaining on the ground outside the structure. They blow inward to fill the building with fresh air and positive pressure that forces the smoke and gases out of the building. You will also hear these fans referred to as **PPV (positive-pressure ventilation)** fans. When using a PPV fan on a typical structure, position it about 10 or 12 feet from the doorway so that the "cone" of air exiting the fan fills the entire doorway, forming a positive-pressure seal. This seal, in turn, forces more of the bad air out of the building through the other openings. Setting the PPV fan too close to the doorway causes the inlet air to fill only part of the doorway, allowing smoke to exit the upper part of the door, which is then sucked into the fan and recirculated back into the structure.

KEY WORD

positive-pressure ventilation (PPV) A method of ventilation used to push smoke out and fresh air into a building. A specially designed fan is positioned outside the building at an opening, facing into the building. The fan is then operated and the building fills with fresh air under pressure, pushing out the smoke and gases.

Go to the DVD, navigate to Chapter 11, and select *Positive-Pressure Ventilation.*

⇨ Practice It!

Positive-Pressure Ventilation

Use the following steps to position a gasoline-powered fan for positive-pressure ventilation:

1. Remove the fan from the apparatus and carry it to the desired location as directed by your Company Officer. This location is usually 10 to 12 feet from a doorway (Figure 11-23).

FIGURE 11-23

2. Turn the fan to one side, away from the doorway, and start it, checking its operation.

FIGURE 11-24

3. Turn the fan so that it is blowing air toward the doorway and into the structure (Figure 11-24).

4. Advise the Company Officer that you have accomplished the assignment.

Intervention Team

In an effort to provide backup and protection on the fire scene, the Fire Service has developed the concept of an Intervention Team. This team consists of a small group of firefighters who stand by in the warm zone outside the fire area with full PPE, tools, and attack hose line. They are prepared to quickly enter the fire area to locate, defend, and rescue any downed firefighters inside (Figure 11-25). This team has become a very important aspect of the fire control operation. It provides rescue and safety backup for the firefighting team inside.

Tool Staging

There may be several places on the emergency fire scene where tools and equipment are placed either for use by firefighting teams or returned to after their use. These areas are referred to as tool staging areas. They are provided for the inside firefighting teams, the outside firefighting teams, and the rescue and intervention teams. These staging areas are placed near a fire truck located at the fire scene.

The tool staging areas are where tools and equipment from one or several fire trucks can be placed for later use by firefighters as needed. They are also

FIGURE 11-25 Intervention teams are prepared to enter the fire area to locate, defend, and rescue any downed firefighters.

FIGURE 11-26 Outside firefighters assist in setting up the tool staging area.

a place that tools and equipment can be returned for replacement onto the fire trucks after the emergency is over. In this way, staging areas help organize tools and equipment as well as allow an organized movement of these items from the fire apparatus to the staging area to the fire scene and back again.

Part of your job as an outside firefighter is to assist in setting up the staging area, and moving tools from the apparatus to the tool staging area and back to the apparatus (Figure 11-26). Examples of tools that may be placed in these areas include forcible entry tools, ventilation tools, spare SCBA air bottles as well as exhausted SCBA air bottles, salvage tarps, and any other tools deemed necessary by the Company Officer. You must learn the location and types of tools and equipment located on the apparatus to which you are assigned.

When you arrive at the scene of a house fire, your Company Officer and driver will determine the location of the tool staging area as well the types and amount of tools to be placed there. You can be assigned to assist in staging these tools. Generally, a tarp is laid out as an indicator of a tool staging area, and the tools and equipment are placed on the tarp. It is important that you listen closely to your Company Officer and apparatus driver and quickly get the tools out and ready for use.

When the fire emergency is over, you must return the tools and equipment to the tarp and then to the fire apparatus. It is critical that you inspect each tool and piece of equipment for damage as you return it to the apparatus from the tool staging area. It is also very important that the apparatus driver be told that the tool has been placed back into its proper location on the apparatus.

Utilities Control

Almost every building has some sort of utility connection that may need to be controlled during the fire emergency. This control usually means shutting off the utility in some manner. As an outside team member, the utilities that you might encounter and be asked to assist in controlling are the electrical system, gas service, fuel oil supply, and water main.

Safety Tip!

When dealing with flammable or energized utilities it is important to remember to wear full PPE.

Lockout/Tagout Systems Some utility or electrical companies use a utility security system called lockout/tagout. This system ensures that any switch or valve that is meant to remain in its present position is locked into that position with a lock. The person locking the valve is identified on a tag that is attached to the locking device (Figure 11-27). If you encounter these locks and tags when asked to control utilities on a dwelling fire, don't take any action until you check with your Company Officer for advice on whether to break the lock and tag and move the switch or valve to a new position (Figure 11-28).

FIGURE 11-27 A typical lockout/tagout kit.

FIGURE 11-28 A lock and tag applied to a switch.

Electricity The electricity provided to most dwellings in the United States is 110 and 240 volts, alternating current. This electricity is delivered to most homes via aboveground or belowground electrical main feeds coming into or near the power meter, which usually is located on the outside of the building. There should be a main disconnect switch that can be switched into the *off* position to cut off power to the building. This disconnect switch is usually near the power meter.

Safety Tip!

Pulling the power meter to disconnect the power is a technique that is best left to the power company. Typically, firefighters do not have the proper safety equipment to pull a meter safely and should avoid this dangerous practice.

The circuit breaker box inside the building is another place switches to cut the power can be found. This box has several individual switches that control power to various room circuits in the home. All of these switches should be placed in the *off* position to cut off power to the dwelling. Because you are not able to enter a burning building with Exterior Operations level skills, this will be assigned to a firefighter with Level 1 skills.

Because after-construction electrical circuits may have been added or alterations may have been made to the electrical system, you should always remember that disconnecting the electrical power to the building in the ways just described may *NOT* ensure that the power has been completely disconnected. Therefore, any wiring that you encounter should be dealt with as if it is still live.

It is also important to remember that main electrical feeds coming into the house from outside power lines are still energized. Any overhead electrical wires should be avoided and their location relayed to the Incident Commander or your Company Officer. In severe building fires, these electrical feeds can disconnect and fall away from the burning building. For this reason, it is important to mark the location of these feeds during the fire emergency. Use fire-line tape or traffic cones to do this. If the power line does fall on the ground, widen your security around the wire and notify your Company Officer or Incident Commander of the downed wire and its location.

Practice It!

Controlling Electrical Utilities

The electrical power service for most single-family homes is commonly located at the outside meter box. Use the following steps to control the electrical power service to a dwelling:

1. When given direction by your Company Officer, locate the electrical meter and service junction outside the building. If the electrical service is provided by an overhead power line, follow it as it will direct you to the most likely area of the meter on the outside wall (Figure 11-29).

FIGURE 11-29

2. Take a good look at the meter and breaker box area. If it is flooded with water or the ground below it is wet, do not touch the main switch. Also, look for a lockout/tagout. If either of these conditions is present, do nothing and report the situation to your Company Officer.

3. If the meter and breaker box area are clear, then shut down the main switch. Report to your Company Officer that you accomplished the task. Remember, full protective clothing should be in place prior to performing this function (Figure 11-30).

FIGURE 11-30

 Safety Tip!

Remember that any energized electrical equipment can kill and should be handled with extreme care. Water conducts electrical current very well, so never handle electrically energized equipment that is wet. Don't stand in water or snow while doing any of these procedures. Always consider all electrical wiring as energized unless you know for sure that it is not.

Gas Many homes in North America have gas service that is used for heating and cooking as well as for hot water heaters. The type of gas provided is usually natural gas that is piped in or liquid propane gas that is stored in a gas tank on the property. We'll take a look at each of these types of gas and discuss the methods used to shut them down.

Natural gas is a flammable gas that is lighter than air. It is delivered to the dwelling by in-ground pipelines. Because natural gas is lighter than air, it rises when released into the air. The gas feeds to the building are normally located outside along an exterior wall of the house. A meter and/or pressure-regulator diaphragm and cutoff valve is usually placed above or below ground level, where the gas line enters the building. If the valve is belowground, an access cover has to be opened to get to the valve. The valves have a flange that operates the valve. When the flange is turned so that it is perpendicular to the gas piping, the flow is shut off.

Liquid propane gas is also a flammable gas but it is heavier than air. Because of this, liquid propane gas seeks its lowest level when released into the atmosphere. As a liquid, propane is extremely cold. This type of gas is usually contained in pressurized storage tanks, either aboveground or belowground on the dwelling property. These tanks contain liquid propane at the bottom of the tank and gaseous propane above the liquid. The top of the tank features a relief valve as well as a fill valve. The shutoff control valve is located near the fill valve on the top of the storage tank. Turn this valve clockwise to shut off the flow of gas.

KEY WORDS

liquid propane gas A flammable gas that is heavier than air. Because of its weight, this gas seeks its lowest level when released into the atmosphere. As a liquid, propane is extremely cold. This type of gas is usually contained in pressurized storage tanks, either aboveground or belowground on the dwelling property.

natural gas A flammable gas that is lighter than air. Because of its weight, this gas rises when released into the air. It is delivered to a dwelling by in-ground pipelines.

View It!

Go to the DVD, navigate to Chapter 11, and select *Controlling Utilities—Gas.*

Practice It!

Controlling Gas Service

Use the following steps to shut off the flow of natural gas:

1. Locate the service meter and flow-regulator piping on the property (Figure 11-31). These items are usually found along an exterior wall. If the meter and piping are belowground, there will be an access lid on the property.

FIGURE 11-31

2. Find the valve on the piping. Turn the valve so that the valve flange is perpendicular to the flow pipe. To do this, you may need a hand tool, like a pair of large pliers (Figure 11-32). Most spanner wrenches have a slot designed to fit over a gas valve.

3. Notify your Company Officer when you have accomplished this task.

FIGURE 11-32

Use the following steps to shut off the flow of liquid propane gas:

1. Locate the gas tank. It will be next to the building or elsewhere on the property. If it is safe to approach, do so from the side. Make sure to wear full protective clothing.

2. Lift the access lid on the tank and locate the shutoff valve. Turn it in a clockwise direction to shut down the flow (Figure 11-33).

3. Notify your Company Officer when you have accomplished this task.

FIGURE 11-33

Safety Tip!

Flammable gas is very dangerous for firefighters, especially if it is located nearby and is an exposure to a burning building. During a building fire, always wear full PPE when working around these tanks. Stay clear of the ends of aboveground tanks and approach from the side. If fire is near the tank or if the tank is being heated by the building fire, do nothing. Retreat and immediately notify your Company Officer of the situation, including that you did not shut down the gas flow.

Fuel Oil Many dwellings use fuel oil heaters for warmth. This type of heating is most prevalent in the northeastern United States, where 7.7 million homes heat with oil. Fuel oil is lighter than water and floats on any water surface. The fuel oil provided for these heaters is usually stored in an outdoor storage tank. However, the tank can also be located in the basement. This tank can be aboveground or belowground. Aboveground tanks have a shutoff valve located at the bottom, at one end of the tank. Turn this valve clockwise to shut off the fuel flow. Belowground tanks have an access lid and the fuel may be pumped out of the tank at this lid. A shutoff valve may be located in this area. Turn the valve clockwise to stop the flow of fuel. Because the fuel is pumped from a belowground tank, shutting off the electricity to the home usually stops the flow from a belowground tank and no further action is necessary (Figure 11-34).

Safety Tip!

Fuel oil can be very dangerous for firefighters, especially if it is located nearby and is an exposure to a burning dwelling. During a building fire, always wear full PPE when working around these tanks. Stay clear of the ends of aboveground tanks and approach from the side. If fire is near the tank or if the tank is being heated by the building fire, do nothing. Retreat and notify your Company Officer of the situation, including that you did not shut down the oil flow.

Water Controlling the water supply to a burning dwelling may seem a bit odd. However, the damage from water to a dwelling can be just as severe and costly as damage from fire. Water pipes in a home are often broken during the fire and water flows freely. The easiest way to control the water service to the home is to locate the water meter. These meters are usually located toward the street or on the side of the home facing the local water main distribution system. They are belowground and can be located under a water department lid. Raise the lid and you will see a small water meter and a shutoff valve. Move the valve so that the operating flange is perpendicular to the water service pipeline (Figure 11-35). Some water service valves require a special tool called a **water key**

FIGURE 11-34 Fuel oil tank and shutoff valve.

FIGURE 11-35 Move the water valve handle perpendicular to the pipeline.

to operate the valve flange. Your fire apparatus may carry the proper size water key.

KEY WORD

water key A special tool used to operate shutoff valves on municipal water systems.

Controlling Water Service

Use the following steps to control the water service to a dwelling:

1. Find the water service meter and control valve. They are usually located toward the street or on the side of the home facing the local water main distribution system. They are belowground and can be located under a water department lid. Raise the lid to locate a small water meter and a shutoff valve (Figure 11-36).

FIGURE 11-36

2. Move the valve so that the operating flange is perpendicular to the water service pipeline (Figure 11-37). Some water service valves require a special tool called a water key to operate the valve flange. Your fire apparatus may carry the proper size water key onboard.

FIGURE 11-37

3. Notify your Company Officer when you have accomplished this task.

Safety Tip!

Always notify your Company Officer or the Incident Commander when you have shut down any utilities to the dwelling. It is equally important to notify your Company Officer if you are unable to shut down the utility.

Scene Lighting

Most fire units are equipped with portable generators and powerful lights that are used to illuminate the scene and the interior of the structure. It is important to everyone's safety that these lights are deployed early during a nighttime operation. Even during daylight fires, it can become very dark inside a burned building, even after the fire has been knocked down and the smoke has cleared. Everything inside be-

FIGURE 11-38 Most fire units are equipped with portable generators and powerful lights that are used to illuminate the scene and the interior of the structure.

comes charred or covered in a flat, black soot that absorbs light. Therefore, most emergency scene lights we use employ light bulbs that are between 250 and 500 watts (Figure 11-38). These bulbs produce a lot of heat and should not be placed within 12 inches of flammable products. In addition, the lights are not safe to use in flammable or explosive atmospheres.

The generators we use can be very powerful, so don't underestimate the danger of the electrical shock they can provide just because they look like a small device powered by a small engine.

Portable Lighting Exterior lights used to illuminate a scene are usually positioned on all four sides of the structure, if possible. Be careful when dragging long cords from the generator. Keep connections away from accumulating water. Inspect the cords for frays or loose connections before you pick them up. It is often a good idea to plug the cord and light into the generator to be sure that the light operates before you take it to where it is needed. This action not only saves you a trip back to the truck for another light, but it also allows you to illuminate your way as you go (Figure 11-39).

Interior lights should be deployed as soon as possible. If possible, deploy a working light with the initial fire attack crew or as soon as possible after they enter. As an Exterior Operations level firefighter, you can accomplish this by taking a working light to the point of entry and pulling loops of extra cord so that the interior crew can take the light without much effort on their part.

FIGURE 11-39 Plug in the floodlight to see that it works. You can then use it to illuminate your way into position.

Ladders at Dwelling Fires

Firefighters often need to access elevated areas in a dwelling fire. They may need to provide an emergency escape route for interior firefighters in a multilevel building or they may need to rescue occupants from upper levels. Ladders can also be placed to position firefighters for ventilation and fire extinguishing work. For Exterior Operations level firefighters, we are going to limit our discussion of ladders to roof access of single-story dwellings and window access of two-story dwellings. Most engine company apparatus carry a **roof ladder** and an **extension ladder**. At this point in your training, we will limit our discussion to these two types of ladders.

KEY WORDS

extension ladder A specialized Fire Service ladder used for greater height capability by firefighters accessing and working in upper levels of a building fire.

roof ladder A specially designed straight ladder that has two rails connected by rungs and specialized folding hooks at the tip. These hooks are moved to the open position when the ladder is to be placed on a roof surface and hooked over the ridge of the roof. This type of ladder provides access support for firefighters working on a roof.

Ladder Basics

Ladders are made up of rails and rungs (Figure 11-40). The rails run along the sides and are connected by the rungs that are the steps of the ladder. The top end of the ladder is called the tip. The bottom end of the ladder is called the butt.

Ladders are provided in many configurations. Some are single, straight ladders with two rails connected by rungs. Straight ladders can also feature special designs. For example, a roof ladder is a straight ladder with folding hooks at the tip. These ladders are used to hook the ladder in place on a rooftop.

Extension ladders have two or more sets of straight ladders, called **fly sections,** with ropes and pulleys used to extend the fly sections (Figure 11-41). The rope on extension ladders is the **halyard.** Pulling the halyard extends or retracts the fly sections. Ladder-locking devices located on each rail are referred to as dogs or pawls. The fly sections are locked into place by the dogs.

Whether Exterior Operations level firefighters work alone or as part of a team, they need to be able to remove a ladder from its storage location on the fire apparatus, carry the ladder to the desired location under the direction of a Company Officer, and place the ladder for the desired use on a single-family dwelling. Firefighters must also be able to safely replace ladders onto the fire apparatus after use. This needs to be done in a safe manner, using proper body positioning. A good rule of thumb for determining the number of people needed to place a ladder is to check the ladder length tags at the ends of the ladder rail. The first digit indicates the number of people needed to handle the ladder. A

14-foot roof ladder requires one person, a 35-foot extension ladder requires three people, and so on.

Ladders are stored in many different configurations and places on fire apparatus. Be sure to review with your instructor safe methods for removing, deploying, and reloading ladders from the fire appara-

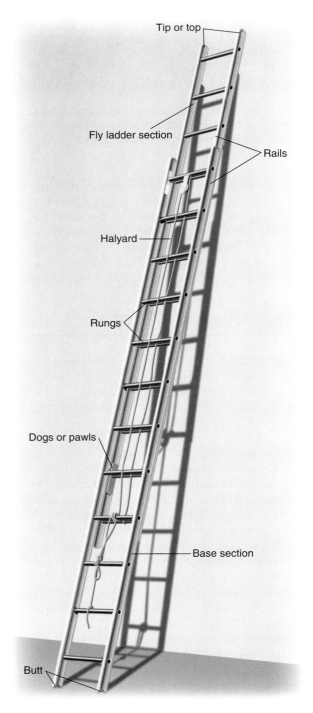

FIGURE 11-41 Parts of an extension ladder: (a) tip, (b) butt, (c) rails, (d) rungs, (e) fly section, (f) base section, (g) halyard, (h) dogs or pawls.

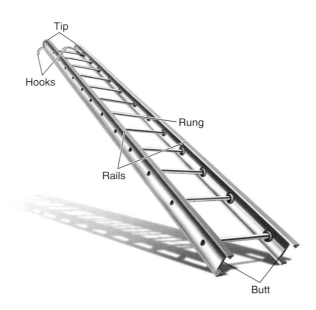

FIGURE 11-40 Parts of a roof ladder: (a) tip, (b) butt, (c) rails, (d) rungs, and (e) folding hooks.

tus you will be using for training. If you need further assistance, the driver should be well informed about ladder removal as well as storage on the apparatus.

KEY WORDS

fly sections Additional ladder sections combined on a single ladder to create an extension ladder. They are the parts of an extension ladder that extend and retract.

halyard A rope located on an extension ladder used for raising and lowering the fly sections of the ladder.

Safety Tip!

Wear the proper safety gear when handling ladders, even during practice. A helmet, eye protection, gloves, and foot protection are the minimum safety equipment to wear during ladder drills.

View It!

Go to the DVD, navigate to Chapter 11, and select *Removing and Stowing Ladders*.

Practice It!

Removing and Stowing Ladders

Use the following steps when removing ladders from fire apparatus:

1. Unlatch any restraining devices that hold the ladder in place on the apparaturs.

FIGURE 11-42

2. If you are alone, find the balance point of the roof ladder by positioning yourself at its center. Lift the ladder from the rack and, bending your knees, place it on the ground next to the apparatus.

3. Pick up the roof ladder at the center. Place your carrying arm and shoulder between the rungs and grasp one rung ahead to control it (Figure 11-42). This technique is commonly referred to as a shoulder carry (Figure 11-43). Carry the roof ladder to the desired location.

FIGURE 11-43

Stow the ladders onto the apparatus using the following steps:

1. Lift the ladder and place it back into its storage rack. Remember proper body positioning. Your feet should be placed shoulder-width apart, with your arms and hands close to the body for support.

—Continued

2. Latch any securing devices (Figure 11-44).

FIGURE 11-44

Straight Ladders and Roof Ladders

View It!

Go to the DVD, navigate to Chapter 11, and select *Straight Ladders.*

Practice It!

Straight Ladders

Use the following steps to place a straight ladder:

1. Check for overhead power lines and obstructions. Then place the ladder flat (against the building), with the butt touching the building.

FIGURE 11-45

2. Grasp the rung closest to the tip and move toward the building, walking hand over hand on the rungs as you raise the ladder over your head (Figure 11-45).

3. Adjust the ladder for climbing by moving the butt away from the building by about one-fourth of the ladder's height from the building. Place the butt of the ladder at your feet, grasping the rung nearest shoulder height at arm's length (Figure 11-46). This should be the proper climbing angle.

4. If requested, you can support the ladder in place by positioning yourself outside the ladder with your feet at the butt of each rail and your hands straight out on each rail (Figure 11-47). This will help protect your face from falling debris.

Take down a straight ladder using the following steps:

1. Check again for any overhead obstructions and then adjust the ladder by scooting the butt up to the wall.
2. Move to the outside of the ladder and slowly back away from the building using the hand-over-hand method on the rungs as you lower the ladder.
3. At the tip, grasp the last rung and lower the ladder flat on the ground.
4. Pick up the ladder at the center. Place your carrying arm and shoulder between the rungs and rest the rail on your shoulder. Grasp one rung ahead for control. Carry it back to the apparatus.

FIGURE 11-46

FIGURE 11-47

 **View It!**

Go to the DVD, navigate to Chapter 11, and select *Roof Ladders*.

Practice It!

Deploying a Roof Ladder

Use the following steps to deploy a roof ladder for use on the roof:

1. At the desired location, place the roof ladder on the ground and open the two roof hooks located at the tip (Figure 11-48).

FIGURE 11-48

—Continued

2. Lift at the tip and carefully pass this end to a firefighter positioned in place on the ladder (Figure 11-49). The roof ladder will be passed on, hooks away from the building, and positioned by other firefighters at the roof.

FIGURE 11-49

3. The firefighters slide the roof ladder up the slope of the roof with hooks at the top, facing upward. The ladder is adjusted and then turned over, with the hooks beyond the ridge of the roof. The roof ladder is pulled back with the hooks securing the ladder at the ridge (Figure 11-50).

FIGURE 11-50

View It!

Go to the DVD, navigate to Chapter 11, and select *Extension Ladder—Single Firefighter*

Practice It!

Extension Ladder—Single Firefighter

The following steps can be used by a single firefighter to place an extension ladder:

1. Pick up the extension ladder at the center. Place your carrying arm and shoulder between the rungs and rest the rail on your shoulder, grasping one rung ahead for control. Proceed to the building (Figure 11-51).

FIGURE 11-51

2. Check for overhead power lines and obstructions. Place the extension ladder flat on the ground. Grasp the extension ladder rung at the tip of the ladder and move toward the building. Walk hand over hand on the rungs as you raise the ladder over your head toward the building until it is flat against the wall.

3. At this point, position yourself at the rungs with the extension ladder between you and the building. Pull the butt of the ladder a couple feet from the wall. Untie the halyard, pull the tip away from the wall, and raise the fly section to the desired height (Figure 11-52). Support the ladder with your shoulder and hip while extending it. At the desired height, allow the fly section to lock into the dogs and tie the halyard in place in the middle of a rung in front of you.

FIGURE 11-52

4. Adjust the extension ladder for climbing by positioning about one fourth of the ladder's height from the building (Figure 11-53). Place the butt of the ladder at your feet, grasping the rung nearest shoulder height at arm's length. This should be the proper climbing angle. If needed, you can support the ladder in place by positioning yourself outside the ladder with your feet at the butt of each rail and your hands straight out on each rail. Don't look up.

FIGURE 11-53

The following steps can be used by a single firefighter to take down an extension ladder:

1. Check again for overhead obstructions and adjust the butt of the ladder inward to within a couple feet of the wall.
2. Untie the halyard and position the ladder the same way as when you extended the fly section. Pull the halyard to raise the fly section slightly to unlock it from the dogs (Figure 11-54). Then lower the fly section into place for storage and retie the halyard if necessary.
3. Push the butt of the ladder against the building and lower the extension ladder. Slowly back away from the building using the hand-over-hand method on the rungs as you lower the ladder. At the tip, grasp the last rung and lower the ladder flat on the ground.
4. Pick up the extension ladder at its center. Place your carrying arm and shoulder between the rungs, resting the rail on your shoulder. Then grasp one rung ahead for control. Carry it back to the apparatus.

FIGURE 11-54

View It!

Go to the DVD, navigate to Chapter 11, and select *Extension Ladder—Two Firefighters.*

Practice It!

Extension Ladder—Two Firefighters

The following steps can be used by two firefighters to place an extension ladder:

1. Position on the same side of the ladder, facing the same direction. The firefighter at the tip gives all of the commands. Pick up the extension ladder, placing your carrying arms and shoulder between the rungs. Rest the rail on your shoulders, grasping one rung ahead for control (Figure 11-55). This action can be better coordinated with a simple command such as *"Ready, lift."* Now proceed to the building.

FIGURE 11-55

2. Check for overhead power lines and obstructions as you walk toward the building. Lay the ladder flat on the ground with the fly section on the bottom. Position at the tip, on the outside of each rail. Grasping the rung closest to the tip, lift the end of the extension ladder and move toward the building, walking hand over hand on the rungs and rails until the ladder is flat against the wall (Figure 11-56). A good signal to coordinate this move is, *"Ready, raise."*

FIGURE 11-56

3. Both firefighters position to the side, supporting one rail of the extension ladder. Pull the butt of the ladder a couple feet from the wall. Untie the halyard, pull the tip away from the wall, and raise the fly section to the desired height, allowing the fly section to lock into the dogs. Remember to support the ladder with a shoulder and hip as you pull the halyard (Figure 11-57). Tie the halyard in place in the middle of a rung near waist level.

FIGURE 11-57

4. Adjust the extension ladder for climbing by positioning about one-fourth of the ladder's height from the building and placing the butt of the ladder at your feet. This should be the proper climbing angle. If needed, one of you can support the ladder in place by positioning outside the ladder, your feet at the butt of each rail, and hands straight out on each rail. Don't look up.

The following steps can be used by two firefighters to take down an extension ladder:

1. Position on each side of the extension ladder at the rails. Check again for overhead obstructions and adjust the butt of the extension ladder inward to within a couple feet of the wall (Figure 11-58).

2. Pull the halyard to raise the fly section slightly in order to unlock it from the dogs. Lower the fly section into place for storage and retie the halyard if necessary.

3. Push the butt of the extension ladder against the building and lower the extension ladder. Slowly back away from the building, using the hand-over-hand method on the rungs and rails to lower the ladder. Grasp the last rung and lower the ladder flat on the ground.

4. Position at each end and pick up the extension ladder. While resting the rail on your shoulder, grasp one rung ahead for control. A good signal for this is for the firefighter at the tip to say, "*Ready, lift*." Now take the ladder back to the apparatus.

FIGURE 11-58

Protecting Exposures

Any material that ignites as a result of fire coming from another source is technically an exposure fire. An **exposure** is anything that has the potential of catching fire due to its proximity to something that is already on fire. In building fires, an exposure is an item in a room that has the potential of catching fire because it is exposed to something already on fire in the room. This definition can be expanded to large fires in a building that have the potential of spreading to adjacent buildings. The adjacent buildings become exposures to the original building fire and must be protected *before* they catch fire.

There are situations in which the fire is so big that the fire department units on the scene do not have the resources to extinguish the fire or the original building is beyond saving. It may be determined that it is best to allow this building to burn while firefighting efforts shift to keep the fire from spreading to exposures around it. Fire attack hose lines are deployed to flow water onto exposures until the fire burns enough of the fuel so that it begins to lessen in intensity. Attack hose lines can then again be applied directly on the fire to extinguish it (Figure 11-59).

Because heat spreads in more than one way (refer to Chapter 6), including by conduction, convection,

FIGURE 11-59 If the fire is beyond the extinguishing capability of the fire department, water may be flowed onto exposures to keep the fire from spreading.

and radiation, applying a water stream is important in protecting exposures. As an outside team member, you may be assigned to deploy a fire attack hose line to protect an exterior exposure. Protecting an exposure by applying water cools it, keeping the temperature of the exposure below the temperature necessary for fire ignition.

It is also important to position in a **safe area** while protecting exposures. A safe area is any place that is free of hazards to you and your team. Many hazards can result from your position yourself too close to the fire. The building can collapse as it weakens and is consumed by fire. Other hose streams can unintentionally be directed toward you, causing you serious injury. Heat from the fire can be so intense that you can become an exposure yourself and receive thermal burns, even if you have full PPE in place. If you do not have your SCBA on and in use, intense, low-lying smoke can become a health hazard. When possible, Exterior Operations level firefighters should remain in safe areas on the fire scene.

KEY WORDS

exposure Anything that has the potential of catching fire as a result of its proximity to something that is already on fire. In building fires, an exposure is an item in a room that has the potential of catching fire because it is exposed to something already on fire in the room. This definition can be expanded to large fires in a building that have the potential of spreading to adjacent buildings. The adjacent buildings become exposures to the original building fire and must be protected *before* they catch fire.

safe area Any place on an emergency scene that is free of hazards to you and your team.

Exterior Fire Attack

As a member of the firefighting team outside the building, at times you may be directed to apply water from the exterior of a dwelling fire. Always follow your Company Officer's directions regarding the pattern, shape, and direction of the water stream (Figure 11-60). If you need to protect yourself from the heat of the fire, either switch the pattern to a wide-angle fog on the line or back away from the fire, still flowing water toward the fire. Again, Exterior Operations level firefighters should remain in safe areas during firefighting operations on dwelling fires.

FIGURE 11-60 Follow the Company Officer's orders regarding the pattern, shape, and direction of the fire stream.

Do It!

Performing Safely at Single-Family-Dwelling Fires

Everyone working at the scene of a structural fire has a responsibility for the safety of the operation. By this point in your training, you should be able to perform well as an effective member of a team, performing several of the functions that are inherent to a safe, efficient operation. The key word to remember is *team*. Nothing on a safety-conscious operation is an individual effort, nor is it performed freelance, without the knowledge and direction of the Incident Commander. Your role starts with a safe response, arrival, and proper tagging in to the personnel accountability system. It continues with the efficient and proper use of tools and equipment to support the fire attack crews working inside the structure. Performing all of these tasks takes practice and repetition. Listen to your instructors and to more experienced firefighters, absorbing their knowledge.

There is plenty to be done between now and your first actual fire. Spend time learning all about the tools on the rigs in your station. Participate in all the drills and read everything you can about the Fire Service—twice. The learning process is never-ending, especially when public safety is concerned.

Evolution 11-1

Maneuvering a Small Attack Line During an Exterior Attack

This drill has been developed to practice the skills necessary to establish a water supply and to apply water from the exterior to a simulated single-family-dwelling fire using a small attack line. The firefighters will be working either to establish the water supply or to deploy, set up, and apply a fire stream to the simulated building fire (Figure 11-61). The drill should be repeated, switching firefighter positions so that each person can practice the training drill in both positions.

Training Area: Open area; level ground free of trip hazards

Equipment: Equipped pumper

Training burn building or other acquired building

Sustained water supply source, or static or water main system with hydrant

PPE: Full protective clothing and scba, on and ready for use

1. A fully equipped pumper with a crew consisting of a driver, a Company Officer, and two firefighters is positioned away from the water supply and simulated dwelling fire. All individuals are appropriately protected in PPE with their seatbelts on and ready to respond. A signal is given and the pumper responds to the simulated fire.

2. The pumper positions at the water supply source. A firefighter dismounts safely and removes any equipment necessary to establish a connection to the water supply, including supply hose lines. The firefighter signals for the pumper to proceed with a layout of supply hose while approaching and positioning at the simulated fire.

3. When the pumper positions at the fire, the second firefighter safely dismounts and receives orders from the Company Officer to deploy a small attack line and prepare to flow water onto the building from a safe area.

4. After establishing a connection to the water source, the first firefighter walks next to the supply hose line, straightening it out as he or she approaches the fire scene. This firefighter then arrives at the fire scene, locates the Company Officer, and receives orders to assist the second firefighter on the small attack line.

FIGURE 11-61 Using a small attack line, firefighters will establish a water supply or apply water to a simulated building fire from the outside.

5. While the two firefighters are flowing water from the small attack line, they are directed to reposition it several times. They will also be directed to change the flow pattern of the stream.

6. When the drill has been completed, the crew will properly relieve pressure, disconnect, drain, and reload all the supply and attack hose. They should trade positions and repeat the drill.

Evolution 11-2

Maneuvering a Large Attack Line During an Exterior Attack

This drill has been developed to practice the skills necessary to establish a water supply and apply water from the exterior to a simulated single-family-dwelling fire using a large attack line. The firefighters will be working either to establish the water supply or to deploy, set up, and apply a fire stream to the simulated building fire (Figure 11-62). The drill should be repeated, switching firefighter positions so that each person can practice the training drill in both positions.

Training Area: Open area; level ground free of trip hazards

Equipment: Equipped pumper

Training burn building or other acquired building

Sustained water supply source, or static or water main system with hydrant

PPE: Full protective clothing and SCBA, on and ready for use

1. A fully equipped pumper with a crew consisting of a driver, a Company Officer, and two firefighters is positioned away from the water supply and simulated dwelling fire. All individuals are appropriately protected in PPE with their seatbelts on and ready to respond. A signal is given and the pumper responds to the simulated fire.

2. The pumper positions at the water supply source. A firefighter dismounts safely and removes any equipment necessary to establish a connection to the water supply, including supply hose lines. The firefighter signals for the pumper to proceed with a layout of supply hose while approaching and positioning at the simulated fire.

3. When the pumper positions at the fire, the second firefighter safely dismounts and receives orders from the Company Officer to deploy a large attack line, place it in a looped configuration, and prepare to flow water onto the building from a safe area.

4. After establishing a connection to the water source, the first firefighter walks next to the supply hose line, straightening it out as he or she approaches the fire scene. This firefighter then arrives at the fire scene, locates the Company Officer, and receives orders to assist the second firefighter on the large attack line.

5. As the two firefighters are flowing water from the large attack line, they are directed to reposition it several times. They will also be directed to change the flow pattern of the stream.

FIGURE 11-62 Using a large attack line, firefighters will establish a water supply or apply water to a simulated building fire from the outside.

6. When the drill has been completed, the crew will properly relieve pressure, disconnect, drain, and reload all the supply and large attack hose. They trade positions and the drill is repeated.

Evolution 11-3

Other Functions During an Exterior Attack

This drill has been developed to practice the skills necessary to demonstrate many of the other functions an Exterior Operations level firefighter will perform at a simulated, typical dwelling fire. The firefighters will be working to assist in forcible entry, stretching a line into a doorway, setting up ventilation, placing ladders, and staging tools for a simulated building fire (Figure 11-63).

Training Area: Open area; level ground free of trip hazards

Equipment: Equipped pumper

Training burn building or other acquired building

Sustained water supply source, or static or water main system with hydrant

PPE: Full protective clothing and SCBA, on and ready for use

1. A fully equipped pumper with a crew consisting of a driver, a Company Officer, and two firefighters is positioned away from the simulated dwelling fire. All individuals are appropriately protected in PPE with their seatbelts on and ready to respond. A signal is given and the pumper responds to the simulated fire.

2. The pumper arrives and is designated to assist in exterior preparations and activities. The crew reports to command and turns over passes for the accountability system.

3. The Company Officer first directs the firefighters to deploy a small attack line from the pumper and stretch it to the simulated front door. He then directs the firefighters to force open the door.

4. A interior fire attack crew pulls the attack line into the building and the firefighters assist until given another assignment by their Company officer.

5. The Company Officer then assigns the firefighters to place ventilation fans for negative or positive ventilation in the doorway area.

FIGURE 11-63   Assisting with other functions at a simulated building fire from the outside.

6. The firefighters are next assigned to place an extension ladder against the building and prepare a roof ladder for use on the roof, at the extension ladder.

7. Finally, the Company Officer directs the firefighters to set up a tool staging area near the pumper for use by crews operating at the scene. They will stage tools as directed by the Company Officer.

Knowledge Assessment

Signed Documentation Tear-Out Sheet

Exterior Operations Level Firefighter—Chapter 11

Name: _____

Fill out the ten-question quiz below, the Knowledge Assessment Sheet, by circling the correct answer for each question. When finished, sign it and give to your instructor/Company Officer for his or her signature. Turn in this Knowledge Assessment Sheet to the proper person as part of the documentation that you have completed your training for this chapter.

1. Many of the line-of-duty deaths of firefighters working inside a structure happen when the firefighter becomes disoriented and runs out of fresh air supplied by his or her SCBA.
    a. True
    b. False

2. Any firefighter working in the hot zone at a structural fire should be fully protected with PPE and a charged hose line. The firefighter should be trained to the _____ standard.
    a. Level 2
    b. Level 3
    c. Level 1
    d. Exterior Operations level

3. If the door of a burning dwelling is locked, firefighters should be prepared to _____ when told to do so and not before.
    a. ventilate
    b. force entry
    c. control utilities
    d. attack the fire

4. Dragging a charged hose line through a house is an easy job, especially if the interior crew is crawling on their hands and knees.
    a. True
    b. False

5. _____ are placed outside a building, blowing inward to fill the structure with fresh air and forcing the smoke and gases outward.
    a. Smoke ejector fans
    b. Negative-pressure fans
    c. Negative-pressure, gasoline-powered fans
    d. Positive-pressure fans

6. A system used to ensure that a switch or valve is secured in its present position is known as a _____ system.
   a. lockout/tagout
   b. lockout/tag-in
   c. lock-in/tagout
   c. personnel accountability

7. If a power line falls on the ground, widen your security around the wire and notify your Company Officer or command of the downed wire and its location.
   a. True
   b. False

8. Most engine company apparatus carry a roof ladder and a(n) _____ ladder.
   a. folding
   b. A-frame
   c. extension
   c. attic

9. By positioning a ladder at about one-fourth of the ladder's height from the building and placing the butt of the ladder at your feet, if you grasp the rung nearest shoulder height at arm's length, you will place the ladder _____.
   a. too vertical for safe climbing
   b. at the proper climbing angle
   c. at an improper climbing angle
   d. at too low a climbing angle

10. Anything that has the potential of catching fire due to its proximity to something that is already on fire is known as _____.
    a. the seat of the fire
    b. an ignition factor
    c. an exposure
    c. a safe position

Student Signature and Date _____   Instructor/Company Officer Signature and Date _____

Prove It

Skills Assessment

Signed Documentation Tear-Out Sheet

Exterior Operations Level Firefighter—Chapter 11

Name: _____

Fill out the Skills Assessment Sheet below. Have your instructor/Company Officer check off and initial each skill you demonstrate. When finished, sign it and give to your instructor/Company Officer for his or her signature. Turn in this Skills Assessment Sheet to the proper person as part of the documentation that you have completed your training for this chapter.

Skill	Completed	Initials
1. Explain the difference between manufactured and site-built dwellings as they relate to construction and fire conditions.	_____	_____
3. Describe safety zones on the dwelling fire emergency scene.	_____	_____
3. Explain how to check in to command using your fire department's personnel accountability system (PAS).	_____	_____
4. Define the different job functions that a typical fire attack team may be called upon to perform on the scene of a dwelling fire.	_____	_____
5. Demonstrate forcible entry techniques on an exterior door that swings inward.	_____	_____
6. Demonstrate forcible entry techniques on an exterior door that swings outward.	_____	_____
7. Explain techniques for using a Halligan bar and flathead axe to force a lock.	_____	_____
8. Explain how to assist interior firefighters with extending hose while stationed at the doorway to a dwelling.	_____	_____
9. Describe how to safely break and clear out glass in a window frame on a dwelling.	_____	_____
10. Define what is meant by the term *Intervention Team*.	_____	_____
11. Describe how and where a tool staging area might be set up and its main purpose on the dwelling fire scene.	_____	_____
12. Demonstrate how to place ventilation fans for negative- and positive-pressure ventilation in a single-family dwelling.	_____	_____
13. Describe a lockout/tagout system and how it is used on the fireground.	_____	_____
14. Demonstrate how to control utilities in a dwelling.	_____	_____
15. Demonstrate how to deploy, place, and stow a roof ladder.	_____	_____
16. Demonstrate how to prepare a roof ladder for use on a roof.	_____	_____
17. Demonstrate how to deploy, place, and stow an extension ladder.	_____	_____
18. Explain what is meant by the term *exposure* and the best methods of protecting an exposure with an attack-line stream.	_____	_____

19. Demonstrate dwelling fire operations for Exterior Operations level firefighters as a member of a fire attack team.   _____   _____

20. Demonstrate dwelling fire support operations for Exterior Operations level firefighters.   _____   _____

The Level I Firefighter

What You Will Learn in This Chapter

This chapter will introduce you to the second level in our program, the Level I Firefighter, and will define the role of the Level I firefighter. You will learn the rules for safe engagement for this level of firefighting, which will define your role in the Fire Service. You will also learn the philosophies for being prepared for your next step in fighting fires, the step that takes you inside the burning structure.

What You Will Be Able to Do

After reading this chapter, you will be able to:

1. Define the Level I firefighter's role on a hose team.
2. Define the type of communication that is required between a Level I firefighter and the immediate supervisor of an interior attack team.

3. Describe the importance of physical fitness for a Level I firefighter.
4. Describe the "rehab" cycle during a structural fire.
5. Explain the main reasons some firefighters are injured or killed while on duty, and describe some of the steps to take to prevent becoming one of these statistics.
6. Define the basic tenet of safe firefighting.
7. Define the "two-in/two-out" rule and describe how it works in a practical setting.
8. Describe risk assessment as it relates to fighting structural fires or hazardous rescues.
9. Describe the 10 Rules of Engagement for Structural Firefighting as defined by the International Association of Fire Chiefs.
10. List and describe four safety tips for working within an Incident Command System in an IDLH atmosphere.

Reality!

It is often dangerous to fight fires and work in high-risk environments during rescues that require strenuous activity performed at a rapid pace. However, when we fully analyze the statistics for death and injury to firefighters, weighing them against the remarkable work we do, it is apparent that the Fire Service is working hard to address everyone's safety on the fireground. Published standards and laws have been adopted that help guide the overall fireground operations, giving us a good sound base for our actions. Technology gives us high-quality personal protective equipment, tools to help us get the job done in a timely manner, and apparatus that has been designed to keep us safe while responding to calls for help. Research and the review of our procedures is ongoing, helping to provide education and training in the safest and most efficient methods to cover every aspect of our job.

Sadly, though, about 100 firefighters die each year. In addition, each year about 50,000 of us are injured while on duty, both on and off the fireground. Even sadder, many of these deaths and injuries could have been prevented by following basic rules and guidelines, employing the most basic technology and basic Fire Service training.

It is our goal to help you to stay safe while serving the public. However, the reality is that most of the responsibility lies with you. Far too many firefighters with previously known cardiac problems die each year from sudden cardiac arrest (Table 12-1).

Make sure you are physically up to the challenge of firefighting by receiving a full physical examination from a physician who understands the type of activity firefighters engage in. **National Fire Protection Association (NFPA)** 1582, *Standard on Medical Requirements for Firefighters and Information for Fire Department Physicians,* specifies the medical requirements for firefighters.

Most fire departments need many tasks performed that allow you to contribute in ways other than fighting fires. Fire prevention activities, public education, dispatching, and administrative duties are all crucial to the overall mission and may be more suitable for you if you have known cardiac-related issues.

Developing a safe attitude toward the job will go a long way in keeping you safe. Without exception, employ all of the personal safety equipment that is available to you, including buckling your seatbelt before you respond. Remain vigilant against unsafe practices while training and on the fireground, and watch out for each other. And never stop training.

▰ KEY WORD ▰

National Fire Protection Association (NFPA) An organization that sets fire codes and standards. It is recognized by most Fire Department organizations in the United States.

The Level I Program

Safe Firefighting has been designed as a progressive training system in which each level builds upon the skills of the previous program. Therefore, this program, Level I, is not stand-alone, and must follow the successful completion of the Exterior Operations Level program. The Level I program is the intermediate level of recruit training, preparing you to be fully qualified to fight an interior structure fire as part of a team. Once you have completed this level of training, you will still be expected to work under direct supervision during firefighting operations.

This program is a more in-depth look at handling more types of fire and rescue emergencies than covered in the Exterior Operations Level program. At the end of the Level I program, our goal is for you to be able to work well with the firefighting crew; use safe, effective techniques; recognize dangerous situations;

TABLE 12-1	Firefighter Deaths by Nature of Injury (2004)	
Nature of Injury	**Deaths**	**Percentage**
Stress	52	50.5
Struck by/contact with object	29	28.2
Caught or trapped	12	11.7
Fell or jumped	6	5.8
Drug overdose	1	1.0
Embolism	1	1.0
Infection	1	1.0
Gunshot	1	1.0
Total	**103**	**100.0**

FIGURE 12-1 This training will help you focus on the skills and abilities that will allow you to participate as part of the entry team at a structure fire.

and respond in a manner that is safe for yourself and the public (Figure 12-1).

Interior Firefighting Teamwork

The step from working on the outside of a burning structure to working inside that same structure is a big one. This step should be taken only after you complete this training, and then only as part of a qualified team. All interior work is done as part of a **buddy system** in which teams of two or more firefighters stick together for safety. Working as part of a team inside a burning structure will require you to stay in close contact with other team members at all times and to work under the direct supervision of a more qualified team member. A typical example of this type of teamwork is a three-person hose team with two Level I firefighters and one Level II qualified firefighter serving as the team's leader. The three people on the hose team stick together at all times while inside the fire area to allow communication by both voice and touch while advancing the hose line and attacking the fire. Because portable radios can be unreliable, they are not acceptable as the only method of communication among team members.

The team leader works under the supervision of an officer who is usually outside the fire, and communications between them are conducted via a portable radio. This system of teamwork hinges on personnel accountability in which the **Incident Commander** knows where everyone is operating all of the time. It allows no room for **freelancing** on the fireground if everyone is to remain safe during the operation.

KEY WORDS

buddy system   The act of working in teams of at least two whenever engaged in a hazardous activity.

freelancing   The act of working outside the purview of the Incident Management System, and without the knowledge of everyone responsible.

Incident Commander (IC)   The person in charge of an emergency operation command structure and therefore the individual in charge of the emergency incident at hand.

Fitness

Any physical activity requires a level of fitness that allows you to do that activity well and reduces your chance of being injured. Fighting fires requires us to be physically strong enough to handle the heavy equipment safely. It also necessitates that we have a fit cardiovascular system that provides us the energy to do heavy work in quick bursts over a fairly long period of time, often in adverse weather conditions. Pick a physical fitness program that addresses both strength and cardiovascular training and stick to it. Regardless of departmental rules or standards, peer pressure, and other motivations, the choice to succeed in maintaining an adequate level of physical fitness is yours. You will succeed only if you make the personal commitment to remain fit (Figure 12-2).

Rehabilitation

Even during a cool day, the inside of a burning structure is a high-heat environment that will sap your energy before you realize you're tired. Therefore, much of our work is conducted in short cycles in which we work until relieved, go to a rehabilitation area (**rehab**) for rest and rehydration, and then return for another work cycle. The length of time you spend working or in rehab will depend on the type of activity and weather conditions (Figure 12-3).

FIGURE 12-2 Make the commitment now to stay physically fit for a lifetime, not just long enough to complete your training.

FIGURE 12-3 It is essential that you rest and rehydrate BEFORE you are exhausted.

Expect to work as a team and rehab as a team. Take the time in rehab to cool down (or warm up), rest, and take in fluids so that you are prepared for another work cycle. The **personnel accountability system (PAS)** should track you as a team while in rehab. Your Company Officer will advise the **Person-**nel Accountability Officer when your team is ready to return to work.

One of the most dangerous things you can do is to ignore your need for rehab on the fireground. Tell your Company Officer if you are experiencing any signs of heat stress, such as dizziness, nausea, confusion, or a headache. It is much more efficient to go to rehab *before* you need it than to wait until exhaustion sets in. A drink of water or a sports drink, a chance to cool off in the summer or get warm in the winter, and a few minutes of rest will usually allow your energy to return for another work cycle. However, if it doesn't, tell your Officer.

KEY WORDS

Personnel Accountability Officer The person working within the Incident Command System who is in charge of tracking the locations and activities of team members during an emergency.

personnel accountability system (PAS) A system used as part of an Incident Command System to track the location and activities of team members during an emergency.

rehab The controlled area where firefighters go to recover and rehydrate after intense physical activity on an emergency scene; the act of rehydrating and recovering from intense physical activity.

Attitude

Review *Safe Firefighting: First Things First,* Chapter 5, *"Response Safety and Vehicle Crashes."*

Most firefighters who die on duty do not die on the fireground. The majority of on-duty fatalities are the result of vehicle crashes while responding to or returning from the alarm, being struck by a vehicle while working on an alarm, or cardiac-related events. Far too many of the firefighters who crash a vehicle while responding to an alarm are driving carelessly, often because of adrenaline and the desire to be "first on the scene" of the emergency (Figure 12-4). To be safe, we must develop a mature attitude and healthy respect for the power of a speeding vehicle. You will greatly enhance your personal safety simply by driving at a safe speed; stopping at all stop signs, red lights, and unprotected railroad crossings; and taking care of your physical health.

FIGURE 12-4 Drive with a mature attitude and a healthy respect for the power of a speeding vehicle.

FIGURE 12-5 The "two-in/two-out" rule provides a crew working on the outside, watching for signs of potential collapse and standing ready to rescue interior firefighters if necessary.

Most firefighters who are injured on duty suffer their injuries on the fireground. Strains, cuts, and broken bones are often the result of taking on a heavy task without enough help. Again, a mature attitude about the job at hand will help reduce these types of injuries. Ask for help when lifting a heavy object to help prevent a back strain. Walk, don't run, on the fireground to help prevent trips and sprained ankles. Take a moment to look around for hazards before moving toward the fire. Although as a Level I firefighter you won't be in charge of the work team, everyone is responsible for looking after each other and should be empowered to call attention to any hazards that may be present.

Two-In/Two-Out Rule

All firefighting, rescue, and Emergency Medical Services (EMS) activities carry an inherent level of risk to everyone involved. The most basic tenet of safe firefighting is that *no property, regardless of value, is worth the life of a firefighter*. This belief is the foundation of what has become known as the ***two-in/two-out rule.*** Simply stated, the two-in/two-out rule says that unless there is a known life hazard, no interior firefighting will occur until there are at least four trained and equipped firefighters on the scene. Two firefighters work inside while two remain outside the structure to watch for signs of collapse and to stand ready to rescue the firefighters inside (Figure 12-5). This ruling applies to any area that is deemed immediately dangerous to life and health (IDLH) and is law in most areas, required by the **Occupational Safety and Health Administration (OSHA)** (29 CFR 1910.155) and prescribed by NFPA 1500. These OSHA requirements apply to paid and volunteer firefighters as well as to those who work in the private or industrial fire brigade setting.

The two-in/two-out rule applies to any activity that involves fighting fire inside the structure when the fire has grown beyond the incipient stage. In other words, for any fire larger than a trash basket fire that can be controlled with a pressurized water extinguisher, the two-in/two-out rule must be followed. The only exception to this rule is if a known life hazard is involved. The two-in/two-out rule is not designed to prevent us from doing our jobs, but to allow us to *survive* the job. If there is a known and immediate danger to someone's life, then yes, we can do what is necessary to save a *savable* life. However, if it is obvious that the fire is of a magnitude that is not survivable, then chances are that we cannot enter the structure until the fire has been knocked down and more help is on the scene.

OSHA also requires that any work done in an IDLH atmosphere be performed while wearing the proper respiratory protection. In other words, wear your air pack and don't breathe smoke (Figure 12-6). There is no reason to expose your respiratory system to the products of combustion and heated air.

OSHA regulations do not require that a separate "two-out" team be established for each entry team. However, a prudent Incident Commander will establish a **Rapid Intervention Crew (RIC)** to stand by for a quick rescue, assigning more firefighters to that team. A Rapid Intervention Crew's only assignment is to stand by, with rescue tools staged, to rescue a firefighter if the need arises (Figure 12-7).

The two-in/two-out rule works! For the first time since they began keeping statistics of firefighter

FIGURE 12-6 Never breathe smoke.

FIGURE 12-7 A rapid intervention crew augments the original "two-out" crew as more help arrives on the fire scene.

deaths, the NFPA reported that in 2004 no firefighters were killed in a fire involving a vacant building. This citing is more than just a blip in the statistics, as the number of firefighters who died working in vacant buildings went from an annual high of 37 during the late 1970s to less than 8 during the past few years. This positive trend directly reflects a change in firefighters' attitudes toward assessing risk versus potential gain on the fireground.

Risk Assessment

The ability to assess the level of risk involved with a given task or situation is an ability that one acquires with education and hones with experience. Unfortunately, those of us who work in areas low in fire activity will not have the opportunity to hone our risk-assessment skills through practical experience. Therefore, our perception of the degree of danger related to a given fireground task may cause us to underestimate the hazard.

The International Association of Fire Chiefs (IAFC) Health and Safety Committee has published *The 10 Rules of Engagement for Structural Firefighting and the Acceptability of Risk.* This short, straightforward document breaks risk down into two simple principles:

- A basic level of risk is recognized and accepted, in a measured and controlled manner, in efforts that are routinely employed to save lives and property. ***These risks are not acceptable in situations where there is no potential to save lives or property.***

- A higher level of risk is acceptable only in situations in which there is a ***realistic potential*** to save known endangered lives. This elevated risk must be limited to operations that are ***specifically directed toward rescue*** and in which there is a ***realistic potential to save the person(s) known to be in danger.*** (Source: *The 10 Rules of Engagement for Structural Firefighting and the Acceptability of Risk,* IAFC, August 2001)

The 10 Rules of Engagement for Structural Firefighting are broken into two categories: acceptance of risk and risk assessment.

Acceptance of Risk

The acceptance of risk is defined as the following:

1. No building or property is worth the life of a firefighter.
2. All interior firefighting involves an inherent risk.

3. Some risk is acceptable, in a measured and controlled manner.

4. No level of risk is acceptable when there is no potential to save lives or savable property.

5. Firefighters shall not be committed to interior offensive firefighting operations in abandoned or derelict buildings.

Risk Assessment

Risk assessment is defined as the following:

1. All feasible measures shall be taken to limit or avoid risks through risk assessment by a qualified officer.

2. It is the responsibility of the Incident Commander to evaluate the level of risk in every situation.

3. Risk assessment is a continuous process for the entire duration of each incident.

4. If conditions change and risk increases, change strategy and tactics.

5. No building or property is worth the life of a firefighter.

Personnel Accountability

Review *Safe Firefighting: First Things First,* Chapter 3, *"Personnel Accountability."*

The safety of anyone who works on an emergency scene hinges on communications and a working command system. It is imperative that the Incident Commander be able to account for each working company on the scene, but this is impractical without a system in place that breaks down this task into manageable groups. To make any accountability system work, it is extremely important that every firefighter remains with his or her assigned company on the fireground (Figure 12-8). There are several types of personnel accountability systems used throughout the Fire Service. These systems employ all levels of technology, from simple paper and pencil to sophisticated computer systems. All of them work on the principle of tracking every firefighter. They are therefore only as good as the individual firefighter's participation in the system.

The personnel accountability system is only one element of your accountability on the scene. Everyone on the firefighting team is responsible for safety at all times, and a good **Incident Command System (ICS)** will empower everyone on the scene to call attention to a safety problem. Here are a few tips to help avoid safety problems:

1. Make sure you clearly understand all orders you receive.

FIGURE 12-8 The Personnel Accountability Officer works with the Incident Commander and the Branch and Company Officers to systematically track every working firefighter on the scene.

2. Don't do anything alone while in an IDLH atmosphere or in the hot zone.

3. Make sure the Incident Commander knows where you are at all times.

4. Stop before entering any hazardous area and do a visual safety check of each other's protective equipment before proceeding. Look for exposed skin and dangling straps that could catch on something inside. Also make sure all of the appropriate equipment is in place.

KEY WORD

Incident Command System (ICS) A system of organization at an emergency that designates supervisory levels and responsibility.

Prepare Yourself

It is our sincere hope that you accept the challenge to advance in the Fire Service by completing this program safely and with a high degree of success. Set yourself on a regimen that will help you gain and maintain the level of physical fitness to allow you to work safely for an entire career of firefighting. You should also train hard to develop the skills and abilities to work safely as a firefighter. Pay close attention to your personal safety and to the safety of those around you. Make safe firefighting a habit by developing a safety-conscious attitude toward the work.

Knowledge Assessment

Signed Documentation Tear-Out Sheet

The Level I Firefighter—Chapter 12

Name: _____

Fill out the ten-question quiz below, the Knowledge Assessment Sheet, by circling the correct answer for each question. When finished, sign it and give it to your instructor/Company Officer for his or her signature. Turn in this Knowledge Assessment Sheet to the proper person as part of the documentation that you have completed your training for this chapter.

1. NFPA _____ specifies the medical requirements for firefighters.
   a. 1500
   b. 1582
   c. 1001
   d. 1002

2. Interior firefighters work as part of a buddy system, in which teams of _____ or more people stick together for safety.
   a. 2
   b. 3
   c. 4
   d. 5

3. A portable radio is NOT acceptable as the only method of communication among team members working as a hose team inside a burning building.
   a. True
   b. False

4. What system is used on the fireground to track individual firefighters and their assignments?
   a. Incident Command System
   b. Buddy system
   c. Personnel accountability system
   d. Company management system

5. Part of the work cycle on a fire or emergency allows time for rest and rehydration. This cycle is called the _____ cycle.
   a. rest
   b. recuperation
   c. recovery
   d. rehab

6. Firefighters are assigned, as individuals, to the cycle defined in Question 5 and are replaced on the work team so the team constantly has at least 3 members working.
   a. True
   b. False

7. All of the following are signs of heat stress *except*
   a. dizziness.
   b. nausea.
   c. confusion.
   d. a slow pulse rate.

8. Most firefighters who die in the line of duty do so on the emergency scene.
   a. True
   b. False

9. Who is responsible for calling attention to any hazards on the emergency scene?
   a. Company Officer
   b. Incident Commander
   c. Safety Officer
   d. Everyone should be empowered to call attention to hazards

10. Because the two-in/two-out rule is a mandate of OSHA, it does NOT apply to volunteer firefighters.
    a. True
    b. False

Level I

Student Signature and Date _____   Instructor/Company Officer Signature and Date _____

Skills Assessment

The Level I Firefighter—Chapter 12

There are no specific skills related to this chapter.

Student Signature and Date _____ Instructor/Company Officer Signature and Date _____

13

Response Readiness

What You Will Learn in This Chapter

In this chapter you will learn about the importance of keeping your personal protective gear ready for the next response and how to assist in doing a routine apparatus check. You will also learn how to inventory, inspect, and maintain the tools, equipment, hose, and appliances on the fire apparatus. We will finish by discussing the importance of proper documentation for this kind of preparation work.

What You Will Be Able to Do

After reading this chapter and practicing the skills, you will be able to:

1. Explain the procedure for checking your personal protective equipment and the area around your riding position on the fire apparatus.

2. Demonstrate how to assist in a routine apparatus check.

3. Demonstrate how to document a routine apparatus check on an appropriate form.

4. Describe how to inspect and maintain hand tools with handles.

5. Explain how to check and what to look for with electric-powered tools and equipment.

6. Demonstrate how to properly remove and check gasoline-powered tools and equipment.

7. Explain how to check and maintain pneumatic tools.

8. Describe an inventory form and an out-of-service tag.

9. Explain the importance of being prepared for the next emergency response.

Reality!

How Important Is It?

You are driving down the road in your own private vehicle and you suddenly realize you have a flat tire. You pull over to the side of the road and stop. Next you open the trunk, take out the spare tire, and get the jack out. Then you look for the jack handle and it is not there. Think about what your options are. Call a garage to come out and help you? Call home and have someone bring you another jack? Or do you lift your front hood and hope someone stops to give you a hand?

Now imagine that you are part of a firefighting team that has just arrived at a house that is completely engulfed in flames. People are shouting at you when you get off the fire truck. They are screaming for you to do something fast before the fire spreads to the neighboring houses. You go to the rear of the fire truck and pull a preconnected attack line as the driver sets up the fire pump for operation. Your Company Officer is waiting at the front door of the burning house, looking back at you impatiently.

You stretch the hose line to the front door of the house. It is then that you realize there is no nozzle on the end of the hose line. Where is it? Who checked it last? Who is going to help you now? You will have to get someone to get the nozzle for you. Or you may have to get it yourself, if it is on the fire truck. Maybe you will have to pull another preconnected attack hose line.

The point here is simple: The emergency, whether it is a flat tire on your private vehicle or at the doorway of a burning house, is not the time to realize you are not prepared. The opportunity for becoming prepared is before the need arises. This aspect is vitally important in emergency service organizations, and much time is devoted to maintaining a high state of readiness to respond to an emergency that can occur at any time, day or night. If you are not prepared prior to the emergency, the consequences can include further property loss, injuries, and even worse.

Preparation and Readiness

A firefighter's working life is generally divided into two main categories. The first is responding to emergencies. The second is preparing to respond to emergencies. You will likely spend most of your firefighting career preparing and being ready to respond. A much smaller portion of your time will be spent actually responding to emergencies. There will, of course, be exceptions to this rule; some Fire Service response

areas generate a much larger load of emergency calls than others do. But for most of us, most of our time will be spent in preparation.

Preparation primarily involves training and maintaining equipment and apparatus. Your own self-preparation is also important, including making sure you are physically and mentally prepared to fight fire. You are preparing in part for response right now by participating in this training. Rest assured that you will train and practice your skills many times over the course of your career. This training is just the beginning.

We'll talk now about how you will make sure you and your tools, equipment, and apparatus are prepared and made ready for response. So let's get started.

Routine Preparations

All scheduled or planned tool, equipment, or apparatus inspections and preparations are considered routine. Many departments designate certain days of the month or week for this work to be performed. During these inspections and preparations, you will be expected to be able to check for the location, operation, and proper maintenance of your tools and the equipment for which you are responsible. It is an important aspect of your job to be able to safely inspect, maintain, and properly document tools and equipment during routine preparations.

Quick Checks After Emergency Use

All tools and equipment that were used on an emergency scene should be quickly checked for damage, reset, and made ready for operation. They should then be placed back on the fire apparatus. This should be done immediately after every use and before leaving the emergency scene. Remember, your next alarm may occur before you make it back to the station. Quick checks after emergency use are much faster than routine checks. After the apparatus has returned to the fire station, a more thorough check and maintenance is performed on any tools and equipment that were used (Figure 13-1).

Personal Protective Equipment (PPE)

Your personal protective equipment (PPE) is probably the single most important gear that you will inventory, maintain, and repair. This equipment must be ready for use because the failure of any

FIGURE 13-1 Make a quick check of your tools at the scene before you place them back on the apparatus.

FIGURE 13-2 Personal Protective Clothing bag, also called a gear bag.

component can cause serious injury or even death. Because gloves and protective hoods are small, it is easy to lose them. Therefore, many firefighters keep their personal protective clothing (PPC) in "gear bags." These bags are large, duffle-type bags that keep all your gear together and make it easier to transport. You may be with a department working as a volunteer where you must respond directly to the emergency scene. If you keep your PPC in a bag, it will help you keep everything together and ready for use (Figure 13-2).

Safety Tip!

Keep a dry T-shirt or sweatshirt and socks in a plastic bag inside the duffle bag so that you can keep warm after a fire on a cold day.

When you report for duty, the very first thing you should do after being assigned to an apparatus is to gather your personal protective clothing and place it appropriately on or near the apparatus, according to department practice. At this time, you should look at each piece and make sure your set of protective clothing is complete. Check the self-contained breathing apparatus (SCBA) you are using. Make sure it is all there and ready for use.

Review It!

Review *Safe Firefighting: First Things First,* Chapter 3, "*Protective Equipment,*" and review the DVD from *Safe Firefighting: First Things First*, Chapter 3, "*Visual Inspection of SCBA.*"

In addition, you should check the area on the apparatus in which you will be riding when an emergency call comes in. Are all the hand tools present that are typically located in that space? Do they need any cleaning or maintenance? Does your seatbelt work properly? If applicable, check your communications headset. Is proper hearing protection available nearby if needed?

Apparatus, Tools, and Equipment

Once your personal protective equipment and clothing has been inventoried, checked, and properly placed on or near the apparatus, you may be required to assist in performing a routine apparatus inventory and check. This check involves two main areas of consideration. The first is the apparatus itself. The second is the tools and equipment carried on the apparatus. We'll begin by discussing a routine inventory and check of the apparatus itself.

Apparatus Check

Your department will have a policy dictating when routine apparatus checks are to be conducted. In some departments, this check is done on a daily basis, with one day a week devoted to a more thorough inventory and check. In other departments, the routine check may be only once a week. The policy will vary with the needs of each fire department.

As a firefighter, it is important to remember that you most likely will not be responsible for the apparatus. The apparatus is usually handled by the designated driver-operator and, ultimately, the supervisor on the apparatus. However, you will more likely be assigned to *assist* the driver-operator in routinely checking the fire apparatus. A routine apparatus check typically involves taking an inventory of the small tools and equipment, performing minor maintenance, and immediately reporting any needed repairs to the apparatus driver. A routine check also includes checking the functions and fluid levels of the apparatus drive train, inspecting the tires for wear and proper air pressure,

and checking peripherals such as the booster water tank and all of the lights and electronics.

Fire departments require that every routine apparatus check be documented by filling out a check-off form as the inspection and maintenance is performed. The form typically covers the areas to be checked as completed by the driver and the firefighters on the apparatus.

➡ Practice It!

Apparatus Check

The firefighter assists the driver in the routine apparatus check by doing the following:

1. Inventory all compartment, storage, and passenger areas of the vehicle.
2. Assist the driver in checking all emergency lights and audible signals for proper operation (Figure 13-3).
3. Assist in checking the headlights, brake lights, and signal lights for operation.
4. Make sure that the vehicle backup alarm sounds.
5. Check the windshield wipers for operation as well as their condition.
6. Ensure that the wheels are chocked whenever the vehicle is parked (Figure 13-4).
7. Safely check the operation of the emergency brake.
8. Check the fluid levels in the engine compartment. This check includes the engine oil, power steering fluid, and radiator water levels.
9. Check the hydraulic fluid levels on the apparatus if applicable.
10. Check the booster water tank, ensuring that it is full of water.
11. Check any pre-plumbed foam tank systems for proper readiness and fill levels.
12. Inspect the tires, looking for proper tire pressure and checking for any damage to the tires, including nails or screws embedded in the tires (Figure 13-5). Also check for tire wear. Most tires have wear bars to indicate excessive tire wear.

FIGURE 13-3

FIGURE 13-4

FIGURE 13-5

—Continued

13. Check for roadside warning devices such as flares and other warning devices (Figure 13-6).

FIGURE 13-6

 Safety Tip!

Use extreme caution when working near a hot engine. Be aware that there may be many hot surfaces and the fluids may also be hot. Before leaning into the engine compartment area, properly lock any engine cowling or tilt cab as recommended by the manufacturer. Wear gloves and safety glasses when near these areas.

Equipment Inventory and Maintenance

After checking the apparatus thoroughly, the next step is to inventory, maintain, and repair hand tools, equipment, nozzles, and hose appliances either located in the storage compartments or attached to the exterior areas of the apparatus. We will look at each tool and equipment category separately; however, you will most likely perform the actual inventory and maintenance as you go through each compartment and storage area on the apparatus. As with the apparatus check, your department may require documentation that you performed the checks and may have you complete an appropriate form.

Whenever you remove any item from a fire apparatus, you must replace it in the exact spot where you found it. The only exceptions are when equipment is being relocated by the department or is out of service

for repairs or replacement. Even then, the department and apparatus crews must be notified in writing when this is done. Every tool and piece of equipment has a vital role on that apparatus. When someone from the crew goes to get that tool or piece of equipment during an emergency, it must be in place and ready for use.

When checking any compartment or storage area on a fire apparatus, it is important to refer to a written inventory (Figure 13-7). This inventory is particularly important if you are new to the apparatus. If there is a tool listed that is not present, you need to notify the apparatus driver and document the missing item. If

FIGURE 13-7 Typical apparatus check sheet.

there is a tool present that is not listed, then the tool has been misplaced there. Again, check with the apparatus driver or inventory listing to see where that tool needs to be located.

We are going to go into more detail about the care and maintenance of all these tools later in this book. However, here are a few pointers for the different tools and equipment that you should consider during a routine apparatus check.

Hand Tools

Hand tools are any tools on the apparatus that are operated manually. They do not use any power, such as electric- or gasoline-powered motors, for operation. We'll list typical types of hand tools located on a fire apparatus, what to check, and any special maintenance you need to perform on them.

Tools with Handles   These tools include pike poles, axes, Halligan bars, bolt cutters, ceiling hooks, sledgehammers, battering rams, and others. They generally have no working parts—just a handle with a specialized head designed for particular jobs on the fire scene.

Check the handles of these tools for a tight fit. Any tools with loose handles should be removed from service and repaired properly or replaced. Look for any cracks or distortions in the handles. Even though wood-handled tools are becoming a rare sight, they may still be on some fire apparatus. Again, check these tools for looseness, wear, splintering, cracks, and overall condition. They can be wiped down with a lightly oiled cloth (using linseed oil).

Safety Tip!

Always safely discard linseed-oil-soaked rags properly in an approved container (Figure 13-8).

Inspect the heads for damage, including cracks, gouges, and bends in the metal. Some hand tools rust. Be sure any rust is cleaned off the tool by either wiping it down with a very lightly oiled rag or painting the tool, according to the manufacturer's recommendation and Fire Department practice.

Small Hand Tools   These tools include pliers, screwdrivers, ratchet sets, hydrant wrenches, spanner wrenches, and others. They generally should be checked for operation and any damage or rust. Clean any rust found and remove any tools that are broken or do not work properly. Immediately replace the tool and make sure to properly document that it has been removed or replaced and the reason for doing so.

FIGURE 13-8   Check tools with wooden handles for looseness, wear, splintering, cracks, and their overall condition. They can be wiped down with a lightly oiled cloth (using linseed oil). Oily cloths are combustible—always dispose of them properly.

Powered Tools and Equipment

Powered tools are those that are powered by electrical motors, gasoline engines, or compressed air. Examples of these types of tools and equipment are portable generators, ventilation fans, air chisel tools, and electrical- and gasoline-powered cutting saws, among others. We will look at the general checking and maintenance of these tools and equipment according to their power sources.

Safety Tip!

It is important for you to remember to always check any powered tool according to your department's guidelines and the recommendations of the manufacturer. Deviating from these good practices can cause injury to yourself or another firefighter. Always wear appropriate safety protection when operating and checking powered tools. This protection should include eye and hand protection, as well as hearing protection if necessary.

Electric-Powered Tool Check   A wide variety of electric-powered tools might be located on any given fire apparatus. The type of tool depends on the job functions that the fire department has determined that firefighting unit is capable of performing. These tools can be as small as a **reciprocal saw** and as large as a ventilation fan. In addition to tools, an assortment of extension cords are used to extend the electrical power from the source to the tool. An electrical source will also be included. This source may be an on-board power converter on the fire truck or a portable gasoline-fueled generator located in a compartment.

Safety Tip!

Whenever you are checking electrical equipment that is energized or potentially energized, use the following safety precautions:

1. Always check these items in a dry area. When inspecting these tools while they are energized, never stand in pooled water or snow.

2. All plugs, adapters, and equipment should be provided with a ground wire. If this wire is missing or broken, it is not safe to operate the tool and the tool should be removed from service and repaired.

3. It is best to plug in and unplug electrical extension cords and tools with the power source in the "off" position. If this is not possible, make sure to check that the tool or appliance is switched off and you are not standing in water when you plug these items into the power source.

4. Do not use any electrical equipment in an explosive atmosphere.

Generators that are powered by a small gasoline engine should be checked in the same way as any gasoline-powered equipment. Begin your check of a generator by inspecting the electrical receptacle panels for any damage, such as broken cover plates or frayed and exposed wiring (Figure 13-9). Check the fuel level and then start the generator. Plug an extension cord end into each receptacle to check for proper fit. Attach an electrical tool or floodlight to check for electrical power at the receptacle outlet.

There may also be small extension cord wires with different ends provided with the generator and extension cords (Figure 13-10). These ends are usually referred to as **pigtail adapters**. They are electrical plug devices that may be necessary to adapt different types of plug ends and receptacles. Cords and plugs used for emergency services may feature a twist connection that locks them together, or they may be regular household plugs, especially on small electrical tools with the traditional three-prong plug. Also check these cords and plugs for damage and exposed, frayed wiring.

Extension cords should be completely extended and visually inspected for damage at each end as well as along the entire length of the insulation. Plug each cord into an electrical source and operate an electrical tool to check for a complete electrical circuit. There may also be specialized junction boxes provided with

the extension cord system that allow for plugging more than one tool into the cord at the same time. These boxes should be Fire Service designed with

FIGURE 13-9 Begin checking a generator by inspecting the electrical receptacle panels for any damage, such as broken cover plates or frayed and exposed wiring.

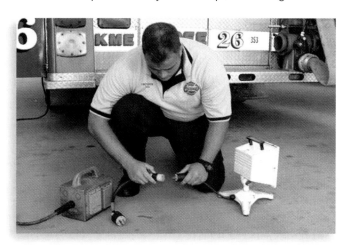

FIGURE 13-10 Pigtail adapters.

FIGURE 13-11 Typical junction box for Fire Service use.

FIGURE 13-12 Check electric-powered tools according to manufacturer recommendations.

FIGURE 13-13 Batteries should be stored and recharged according to the manufacturer's recommendations. Heat is the primary cause of damage to rechargeable batteries, including the batteries of portable radios.

twist-lock connections (Figure 13-11). They may be provided with a small indicator light that shows the box is energized. The junction boxes may be located at the far end of an extension cord; therefore, the indicator light is the only way to know that the box is energized. Again, these need to be checked for damage and proper operation.

Individual electric-powered tools should be checked and maintained according to department practice and manufacturer recommendations (Figure 13-12). Each tool should be plugged into an electrical source and operated. After checking for proper operation, unplug the tool and place it back in its original location.

Any tool or other piece of electrical equipment that is found to be defective should be removed from service immediately for repair. Remember to properly notify the apparatus driver and supervisor that it has been removed and make proper documentation if required.

KEY WORDS

pigtail adapter Electrical plug devices that are necessary to adapt different types of plug ends and receptacles.

reciprocal saw A powered saw, usually electric, in which the blade is driven by a motor. The blades move in and out to provide cutting action.

 Safety Tip!

Make sure to don appropriate safety gear when operating any electrical tools and equipment. This equipment may include eye and hand protection as well as hearing protection as needed.

Electrical tools that are battery powered should be checked frequently (Figure 13-13). Batteries should be stored and recharged according to the manufacturer's recommendations. Heat is the primary cause of damage to rechargeable batteries, including the batteries of portable radios. For this reason, the tools and extra batteries should be stored in a cool place, far from exposure to engine heat or hot outside temperatures. Some departments charge the batteries in the fire station and ride the spare charged batteries with the tool on the apparatus.

When using any battery-powered tool, it is important that you do not put undue strain on the motor, which causes excessive heat and stopping of the motor. This will quickly drain the battery. Check any battery charger connections and make sure they are operating properly. Remove from service any batteries that do not recharge properly. Keep the best battery in the tool ready for use.

Gasoline-Powered Tool Check There are many types of gasoline-powered tools and equipment used in the Fire Service. As with all tools, the mission of the individual fire apparatus will dictate the number and type of tools carried. These tools and equipment can include saws and generators as well as positive-pressure ventilation (PPV) fans.

It is a good idea to have the apparatus driver or an experienced firefighter demonstrate the proper way to start and check any power tool for the first time. Every tool is different and has different starting and running procedures.

When checking a gasoline-powered tool, the very first step is to check for any fluids leaking from the tool. Start by looking at the surface of the storage area or the compartment where the tool is kept. Leave the tool in place while looking for oil or fuel puddles underneath it. Attempt to determine the source of the leaks by looking at the tool surfaces above the puddles for leaks or wet spots. If you find any excessive pooling of fluids under the tool as it sits in the compartment, show the apparatus driver what you have discovered.

Next, remove the tool and place it on the ground. If the tool is too heavy for you, get some help when removing it. Use proper body position, lifting and lowering with your legs when possible. Check for the levels of fuel and engine case oil. Make sure these fuels are filled to levels recommended by the manufacturer and as required by the Fire Department. Always use the proper fuels and fluids. Some small engines require a specific mixture of gasoline and oil.

After checking fuels and fluids, the tool or piece of equipment should then be started and operated to ensure that it is working properly. Take the tool outside to do this—starting gasoline-powered tools in the vehicle bay area releases carbon monoxide inside the fire station and is quite noisy. Remember that each tool will have a different starting procedure. Some will have a manual choke, which is used for the initial startup process. Others may have a throttle that is automatically set. Always run the tools according to the manufacturer's recommendations. It is generally best to run the tool's engine until it is warmed up before shutting it down. Always use the recommended shutdown procedure for the tool. Never flood the tool by

Safety Tip!

Any portable fuel cans carried on board the fire apparatus should be approved safety containers. These containers are specifically designed to be safely used with portable gasoline-powered equipment and tools. Always have an appropriate fire extinguisher handy when filling and checking any gasoline-fueled tools and equipment. Before starting gasoline-powered equipment, be sure you are wearing appropriate personal protective clothing, including hand and eye protection. Hearing protection may also be appropriate for gas-powered tool operations.

using the choke to shut it down. Doing so may prevent the next user—possibly at an emergency scene—from being able to start the tool.

Check the tool accessories to see that they are present and in working order. Resupply any expendable supplies like saw blades and tool bits.

Remember that any tools that cannot be started should be placed out of service and the apparatus driver and supervisor notified immediately. Replace the tool with a spare and make sure to document what has been done.

Practice It!

Gasoline-Powered Tool Check

Use the following milestones to properly check a gasoline-powered tool:

1. Check for fuel leakage (Figure 13-14).

FIGURE 13-14

2. Remove the tool and place it on the ground.
3. Check the levels of fuel and engine oil (Figure 13-15).

FIGURE 13-15

—Continued

4. Safely refill any low fuel or oil to the recommended levels (Figure 13-16).

FIGURE 13-16

5. Start and operate the tool.
6. Check accessories and expendable items like blades.
7. Properly shut down the tool and replace it on the apparatus.

Pneumatic Tool Checks Many departments use specialized tools that utilize compressed-air pressure as a power source. These tools may run off a compressed-air supply that is carried on board the apparatus itself or contained in SCBA bottles. These tools include air chisels, special saws, drills, and **rescue air bag systems.**

The general rules for caring for and checking any compressed-air tool or equipment are to keep the tools clean, check for damage and wear to the compressed-air couplings and fittings, and check for operation according to the manufacturer's recommendations and department practices. Any tools or equipment that utilize moving pistons should be well lubricated. Look for cracks and wear on rescue air bags. Check operating gates and regulator systems for damage, such as broken gauges and handles (Figure 13-17).

▮ KEY WORD ▮

rescue air bag system A specialized rescue tool used for lifting heavy loads with pneumatic air pressure. This system is composed of sets of air bladders with connecting hoses, an air pressure regulator, control valves, and a compressed-air source.

FIGURE 13-17 Keep air-operated tools clean, check for damage and wear to the compressed air couplings and fittings, and check for operation according to the manufacturer's recommendations and department practices. Any tools or equipment that utilize moving pistons should be well lubricated.

Safety Tip!

When checking or operating any tool or piece of equipment that is powered by compressed air, it is extremely important to use the proper air pressure. Never operate any of these tools at an air pressure above what is designated by the tool manufacturer. Tool failure and severe injury can result.

Nozzles

Perhaps the most neglected piece of equipment, and one of the most important to us, is the nozzle. Fire apparatus can carry as many as seven or eight nozzles, ranging in size from 1 to 3 inches in diameter. The types of nozzles vary and include small and large fire attack nozzles, solid bore nozzles, foam nozzles, automatic gallonage, master stream, and high-rise pack nozzles.

Practice It!

Nozzle Check and Maintenance

You should use the following steps to inspect and maintain a nozzle:

1. Inspect the nozzle for damage, both interior and exterior, and look for and remove any debris inside the nozzle. Inspect the swivel gasket for damage (Figure 13-18).

2. Soak the nozzle in warm water and a mild soap solution for about 10 minutes and then scrub it with a soft bristle brush. Remove and rinse the nozzle and wipe it dry.

3. Look at the nozzle and operate the valve handle, checking for tightness. Operate fog stream and gallonage adjusters, making sure they rotate easily on the nozzle (Figure 13-19). If equipped, check the pistol grip or handles for tightness.

4. Check the interior of the nozzle. If it is equipped with a **rotary vane**, check it for looseness. Make sure the **ball valve** operates freely (Figure 13-20). Check interior stream straighteners and baffles for tightness.

5. Lubricate the nozzle as recommended by the manufacturer. Make sure to wipe the nozzle once more after lubricating, as excess lubricant can attract grit and dirt.

FIGURE 13-18

FIGURE 13-19

FIGURE 13-20

KEY WORDS

ball valve   Located inside the gate valve assembly on a typical fire nozzle, this ball has an opening that rotates with the gate valve handle to open and close the flow of water through the nozzle.

rotary vane   A circular swivel located on the end of a fog nozzle that aids in properly shaping the fog pattern as water flows out of the nozzle end.

Appliances

These devices include hydrant valves, water thieves, manifolds, gated wyes, coupling adapters, Siamese adapters, and reducers. They are located in compartment storage areas, are attached to running boards, or are in line with preconnected hose in the hose bed area.

These devices should be inspected for obvious physical damage and deformity. Check for any missing gaskets and operate any gate valves to check for ease of operation. Some of these appliances will have **clapper valves**. Check for any missing or inoperable clapper valves (Figure 13-21). They should be cleaned periodically and maintained according to manufacturer's recommendations. General cleaning includes soaking and washing them in warm, soapy water. They should be rinsed and wiped clean afterward.

KEY WORD

clapper valves   Small, sealed metal parts that act as stoppers on the interior of one intake of a hose appliance when water is flowing through a hose connected to the other intake of a dual-intake appliance, such as a Siamese adapter.

Hose

One of the most vital tools carried on any fire apparatus is the fire hose. It is difficult to check and maintain because it is carried in the hose bed areas of the fire truck. It will be checked at much longer intervals. However, all fire hose must be tested by the Fire Department at least once a year. The department will have schedules and testing procedures that you will follow when the time comes. Usually the hose is stretched out in sections and tested to a predetermined pressure for a certain length of time. The hose lines are checked for any leaks in the hose jacket and at the couplings. Hose that leaks excessively or bursts during the annual test is removed from service for immediate repair. The hose is also checked for any looseness at each coupling.

FIGURE 13-21   Be sure to check any appliances equipped with clapper valves for proper operation.

Hose Coupling Construction

Standard Threaded Couplings

Standard threaded couplings are made up of threaded male and female couplings that attach to each other. The male coupling has a single-piece coupling housing with the male threads on the outside (Figure 13-22). A sleeve fits inside the coupling hosing and holds the coupling in place on the fire hose. The threads of the male coupling should be inspected for damage and deformity.

The female coupling is made up of the coupling body and the swivel with its threads inside (Figure 13-23). There is also an expansion ring provided to hold the hose end into the coupling. The swivel also holds the gasket for the seal of the coupling connection to the male coupling end. These should be inspected for missing gaskets, damage, and deformity.

Any damaged couplings should be removed from service, and the hose section should be repaired or replaced.

Quick-Connect Couplings

Quick-connect couplings are identical couplings on each end of a hose section that connect together and twist one-quarter turn clockwise to make a connection (Figure 13-24). They may or may not have coupling locks on each coupling to ensure that they stay together after being connected. They have a coupling body and swivel along with a gasket on each one. This type of coupling should be checked for any deformity, damage, faulty locking devices, and missing or damaged gaskets.

Any hose with damaged couplings should be removed from service and replaced or repaired.

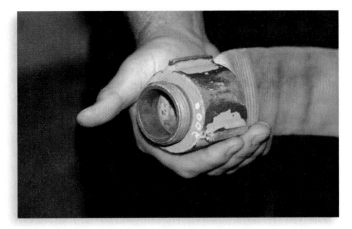

FIGURE 13-22 Check male couplings for damaged or deformed threads.

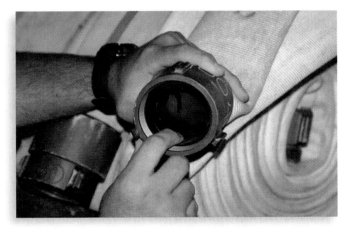

FIGURE 13-23 Check female coupling swivels for a gasket, any deformity, and thread damage.

FIGURE 13-24 Quick-connect couplings should be checked for any deformity, damage, faulty locking devices, and missing or damaged gaskets.

FIGURE 13-25 Fire hose should be checked for any damage, abrasion wear, burns to the jacket, and holes.

Fire hose should be checked for any damage, abrasion wear, burns to the jacket, and holes (Figure 13-25). Generally, after it has been deployed, fire hose is given a very quick visual inspection during reloading either for training or at an emergency. A closer inspection takes place during any removal or change of hose loads; items such as hose cleaning and hose inventory are done at this time. Hose is inventoried at intervals and with procedures that will be determined by your department's practices.

Any repairs of fire hose and couplings should be done by properly trained personnel with approved equipment and tools. Your department will have a procedure for replacing any hose that has been removed from service.

Fire hose can be cleaned with soapy water and then rinsed with clean water (Figure 13-26). It is then laid on edge in a secure area to dry prior to being stored or reloaded on the fire apparatus. Some types of fire hose can be reloaded wet, at the fire scene, and be ready for use at the next emergency. Your department will have a standard policy for the cleaning and care of their fire hose.

Documentation

The Fire Department will have a procedure for properly documenting and tracking the apparatus inventory and checks. The fire apparatus may have a vehicle checklist and inventory with check-off sheets. The department may have a system of out-of-service tagging that identifies items, such as equipment, tools, or hose, that have been removed for repair. These tags have a place to describe the problem and identify which fire apparatus it came from.

FIGURE 13-26 Fire hose can be cleaned with soapy water and then rinsed with clean water.

Documentation is usually the responsibility of the apparatus operator or supervisor. However, you may be made responsible for filling out at least some of the documentation.

 **Safety Tip!**

Always remember to tell the apparatus operator when you find a problem with any tools or equipment on the apparatus. It is also important that you notify anyone who may be relieving you on that apparatus. This notification can be made verbally or on a station status board. It is extremely dangerous for a crew to think a piece of equipment is on board and working properly when it is out of service for repairs.

 **Do It!**

Be Ready

You will probably spend a great deal of time preparing for your next emergency response. This readiness includes constant checks and maintenance of apparatus, tools, and equipment. Unlike in most other occupations, in the Fire Service a missing or broken tool or piece of equipment is not a mere inconvenience—instead, it can potentially cause a great deal of danger. Because we may have only one shot at making a successful rescue or at extinguishment or hazard control, we cannot afford to not be ready 100% of the time. It is an important part of your job to be prepared.

Prove It

Knowledge Assessment

Response Readiness—Chapter 13

Name: _____

Fill out the ten-question quiz below, the Knowledge Assessment Sheet, by circling the correct answer for each question. When finished, sign it and give it to your instructor/Company Officer for his or her signature. Turn in this Knowledge Assessment Sheet to the proper person as part of the documentation that you have completed your training for this chapter.

1. In the Fire Service, _____ primarily involves training and maintaining equipment and apparatus.
   a. recruit preparation
   b. preparation
   c. off-duty time
   d. very little time

2. When you report for duty and are assigned an apparatus, the first thing you should do is to _____.
   a. complete an apparatus check
   b. check the brakes on the apparatus
   c. gather your gear and place it appropriately on the apparatus
   d. wait for the next call to come in

3. A routine apparatus check includes checking the functions and fluid levels of the apparatus drive train.
   a. True
   b. False

4. Tires should be inspected for _____.
   a. damage
   b. wear
   c. the proper inflation of air pressure
   d. all of the above

5. Hand tools are any tools that are operated _____.
   a. by a gasoline motor
   b. by an electrical motor
   c. by a pneumatic power source
   d. manually

6. The type of electric-powered tool carried on a fire apparatus depends upon the _____ of the fire department.
   a. job functions and capability requirements
   b. expense capability
   c. number of users
   d. number of the same type of tools

7. It is best to plug in and unplug electrical extension cords and tools with the power source in the "on" position.

   a. True

   b. False

8. The very first thing to check when you access a gasoline-powered tool in the storage compartment is _____.

   a. the fuel level

   b. fluid leakage

   c. frayed wiring

   d. bent throttle switches

9. It is best to check a gasoline-powered tool by starting and running it _____. Doing so reduces noise and dangerous fumes for fellow workers.

   a. in the vehicle bays

   b. in a special closed room

   c. at the workbench in the vehicle bay

   d. outside

10. Service tests for fire hose are conducted _____.

   a. semiannually

   b. bimonthly

   c. annually

   d. every other year

Student Signature and Date _____ Instructor/Company Officer Signature and Date _____

Skills Assessment

Signed Documentation Tear-Out Sheet

Response Readiness—Chapter 13

Name: _____

Fill out the Skills Assessment Sheet below. Have your instructor/Company Officer check off and initial each skill you demonstrate. When you are finished, sign this page and give to your instructor/Company Officer for his or her signature. Turn in this Skills Assessment Sheet to the proper person as part of the documentation that you have completed your training for this chapter.

Skill	Completed	Initials
1. Explain the procedure for checking your personal protective equipment and the area around your riding position on the fire apparatus.	_____	_____
2. Demonstrate how to assist in a routine apparatus check.	_____	_____
3. Demonstrate how to document a typical apparatus check on an appropriate form.	_____	_____
4. Describe how to inspect and maintain hand tools with handles.	_____	_____
5. Explain how to check and what to look for with electric-powered tools and equipment.	_____	_____
6. Demonstrate how to properly remove and check gasoline-powered tools and equipment.	_____	_____
7. Explain how to check and maintain pneumatic tools.	_____	_____
8. Describe an inventory form and an out-of-service tag.	_____	_____
9. Explain the importance of being prepared for the next emergency response.	_____	_____

Student Signature and Date _____   Instructor/Company Officer Signature and Date _____

Ropes and Knots for the Fire Service

What You Will Learn in This Chapter

This chapter will define the characteristics of a utility rope and a life safety rope. You will learn about how these types of ropes are made, how to care for them, and the safety considerations for working with rope. You will also learn the basic knots used in the Fire Service and some practical applications for these knots.

What You Will Be Able to Do

After reading this chapter and practicing the skills described, you will be able to:

1. Describe utility rope and its uses.
2. Describe life safety rope and its uses.
3. Describe some of the drawbacks of using natural fiber ropes.

4. State some of the reasons we use synthetic rope in the Fire Service.
5. Describe the construction characteristics of twisted rope.
6. Describe the construction characteristics of braided rope.
7. Describe the construction characteristics braid-on-braid rope.
8. Describe the construction characteristics of kernmantle rope.
9. Define the required safety factor of life safety rope.
10. Define a shock load (accidental dynamic load).
11. Describe a static rope and its use.
12. Describe a dynamic rope and its use.
13. Define a fall protection line.
14. State 8 principles of caring for a synthetic rope.

15. Describe the "look, feel, and read" method of inspecting a rope.
16. State the information that is contained in a rope record.
17. Define when it is necessary to retire a rope from service as a life safety rope.
18. Define the three elements of a knot.
19. Describe the uses of and successfully tie the following knots in a 1/2-inch kernmantle rope while wearing gloves:
    a. Overhand safety knot
    b. Bowline
    c. Clove hitch
    d. Clove hitch around an object
    e. Figure eight on a bight
    f. Becket bend (sheet bend)
    g. Half-hitch
20. Using two utility lines, secure the following tools for hoisting:
    a. Axe
    b. Roof ladder
    c. Uncharged hose line
    d. Charge hose line
    e. Long-handled tools
    f. Heavy equipment

Reality!

Ropes Are Tools

For most of us, the mention of ropes for the Fire Department conjures up images of daring rescues conducted while dangling hundreds of feet from a building or sophisticated rope rescue systems stretched across the raging waters of a flooded river to help us reach a stranded victim on a clump of trees. While these very real scenarios occur, for most of us ropes are more of a utility tool, allowing us to hoist tools and equipment up a couple of floors so we won't have to carry them up a ladder. They also serve as a search line that can guide us back out of a smoke-filled structure. When we actually tie a person to a rope, it is usually for use as a fall protection device rather than a technical rescue system.

If and when you undergo training as a Rescue Technician, the basics of ropes and knots used in the Fire Service will serve you well because the basic knots and concepts of rope work you will learn in this chapter are the core components of any rope rescue activities. We will mention rope work several times in the remainder of this text, building on the foundation you learn in this chapter with other uses such

as search lines and fall protection. For now, we will concentrate on the fundamentals for the majority of the Fire Service work that involves ropes.

Rope

Ropes used for our purposes are separated into two general categories: utility rope and lifeline rope. **Utility rope** is used for such things as hoisting tools and equipment, tying off loads, serving as ladder halyards, serving as guide ropes during a search, and roping off dangerous areas to prevent a fall or an accident. Because it is the most frequently used type of rope, utility rope is subjected to damage from dirt and grit, moving over sharp objects, heavy loads of unknown weight, and potential contamination from damaging fluids, such as those found at the scene of an auto accident. Because of these factors, ropes that have been designated for utility purposes should *NEVER* be used to support a human load (Figure 14-1).

Rope designated from the beginning as **life safety rope** is used exclusively for supporting human loads,

FIGURE 14-1   A utility rope in use.

FIGURE 14-2   A life safety rope in use.

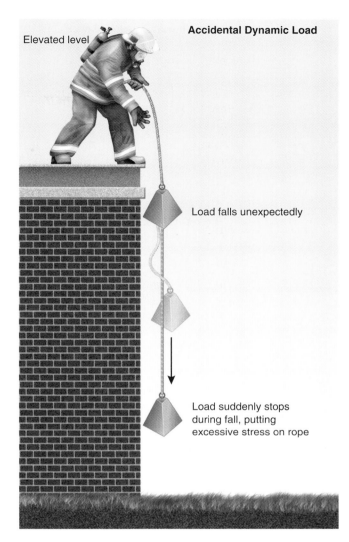

Accidental Dynamic Load

Elevated level

Load falls unexpectedly

Load suddenly stops during fall, putting excessive stress on rope

FIGURE 14-3   Inconsequential shock load.

during an emergency and during training sessions. A life safety rope should never be used as a utility rope. If it is used once as a utility rope, usually during an emergency situation where a utility line is not available, then it is never again to be used as a life safety rope and must be replaced (Figure 14-2).

▦ KEY WORDS ▦

life safety rope   Rope that meets the standards set by NFPA 1983 and is used exclusively to support a human load.

utility rope   Rope that is used for any use other than supporting a human load.

Fire Service Rope Requirements

Because the ropes used for fire and rescue work are often used under extreme conditions, the construction of the rope we use differs greatly from the rope that is commonly available for purchase at a hardware store. Although ordinary ropes are similar in appearance to the ropes we use, any rope used for Fire Service work must meet very specific standards as outlined in NFPA 1983, *Standard on Fire Service Life Safety Rope and Components.*

When it comes to strength, life safety rope must have a built-in 15:1 safety factor to allow for the stresses a rope can undergo if a load suddenly moves or falls and then stops suddenly. These stresses are called **shock loads.** It is normal for a load to move and stop while suspended from a rope. This type of dynamic loading occurs when you are hoisting a tool or piece of equipment to the roof of a building, for example. Every time you change hands to pull up another length of the rope, the load will stop and then start its upward movement again. This type of dynamic loading is expected and is inconsequential (Figure 14-3). However, whenever an object falls, even for a short distance of a few feet, and is stopped by the rope, it is called an **accidental dynamic load**

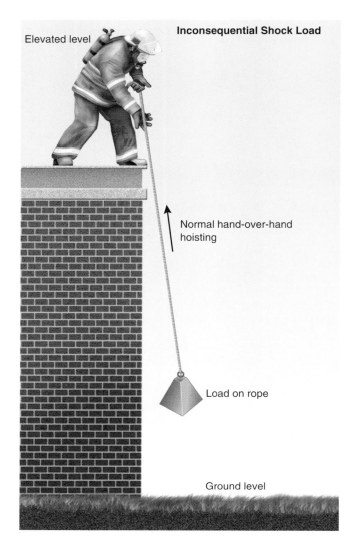

Inconsequential Shock Load

Elevated level

Normal hand-over-hand hoisting

Load on rope

Ground level

FIGURE 14-4 Accidental dynamic load.

FIGURE 14-5 Natural fiber and synthetic fiber ropes.

██ KEY WORDS ██

accidental dynamic load A type of shock load in which an object that accidentally falls, even for a few feet, is stopped by a rope.

shock load The stress placed on a rope when a load that's being held by the rope moves or falls and then stops suddenly.

Rope Materials

The ropes we use in the Fire Service are made of synthetic (manmade) fibers. We have moved away from using natural fibers, such as sisal or hemp, because they are prone to rot and mildew. In addition, the natural fibers soak up water and lose as much as 50% of their strength when wet. Instead, both utility and life safety ropes are made of much stronger synthetic fibers, such as nylon or polyester (Figure 14-5). These materials offer a great deal of strength in a relatively small size, so the ropes can be smaller in diameter and lighter in weight than those made of natural fibers.

Although synthetics are much stronger than natural fibers, they are still subject to damage caused by exposure to sunlight, chemicals, and abrasion caused by friction. It is very important that you become familiar with the manufacturer's recommendations for cleaning and storing rope.

Rope Construction

Even though their fibers may be the same, ropes can have very different characteristics, depending on the type of construction used in making the rope. For the most part, rope construction falls into two categories:

(Figure 14-4). It is a type of shock load. Because there is no way of determining the amount of stress an accidental dynamic load has placed on a rope, any rope subjected to an accidental shock load should be retired, especially if it is a life safety rope.

Whenever a load moves and stops suddenly on a rope, whether it is an accidental dynamic load or the load from a normal start-and-stop action, the stress that the load's weight exerts on the rope is drastically increased for just a moment. A substandard rope can fail in that moment. For rating purposes, each person on a rope is considered to be 300 pounds. Therefore, a life safety rope rated for a single-person load must be able to support a stationary (static) load of at least 4500 pounds. A life safety rope rated for a two-person load must be able to support a static load of at least 9000 pounds.

FIGURE 14-6 Twisted rope construction.

twisted and braided. The different types of construction makes these ropes suited for different jobs.

Twisted Rope

Twisted rope is the oldest style of rope construction. In this type of rope, the strands of fibers are twisted by machines into yarns and then twisted repeatedly in layers to form a rope. Twisted rope is also referred to as *laid rope* or *hawser-laid rope.* Laid or hawser-laid rope is a type of rope used for nautical applications. This rope is composed of three strands, each of which has been made by twisting the strands in a left-handed direction. This type of rope should be avoided for use as a lifeline because the layers can "untwist" easily as the rope travels around an object or a heavy load is applied. However, laid rope is very strong, relatively inexpensive, and well suited as utility line (Figure 14-6).

Another disadvantage of using laid rope is that all of the fibers are exposed to the outer layer at random points along the rope's length. Therefore, they have the potential to be exposed to damage from abrasion from friction. They can also be degraded from exposure to sunlight, which will obviously reduce the rope's strength over time.

▰ KEY WORD ▰

twisted rope   A type of rope construction in which fibers are twisted into yarns and then the yarns are twisted repeatedly in layers to form the rope.

Braided Rope

Another common rope construction technique is braiding, which eliminates many of the disadvantages of twisted rope. **Braided rope** is made by weaving the strands together to interconnect them into a common length of rope (Figure 14-7). Braiding alone will make a rope strong. Also, because the strands are interwoven instead of twisted together, they remain locked and are not subject to having layers "untwist" as is common with laid rope. However, a simple braided rope still exposes all of its fibers to the outer layer at random points along the rope's length, so it can be subjected to abrasion or other damage. Like a laid rope, if a braided rope shows any signs of questionable wear along its length, then the rope should be retired.

A more sturdy braided type of rope is the **braid-on-braid** style, which is sometimes called a **double-braided** rope. Braid-on-braid rope resembles two ropes in one package: A braided rope is wrapped in a braided sheath that gives the rope some added strength. This type of rope also has the advantage of protecting the inner braided strands from abrasion and other external damages. Braid-on-braid rope is very strong for its size and is well suited for use as a utility line (Figure 14-8).

▰ KEY WORDS ▰

braided rope   A type of rope construction in which the strands are woven together to interconnect them into a common length of rope.

braid-on-braid rope (double-braided rope)   A type of rope construction in which a braided rope is wrapped in a braided sheath.

FIGURE 14-7 Braided rope construction.

FIGURE 14-8 Double-braided rope construction.

FIGURE 14-9 Kernmantle rope construction.

Kernmantle Rope

Kernmantle is a German term meaning "core and sheath." **Kernmantle rope** is the type of rope most often used for life safety rope. The core (kern) of a kernmantle rope is made of very long, continuous strands of synthetic materials that run the entire length of the rope without knots or splices. The core gives the rope most of its strength. The sheath (mantle) of the rope is a braided sleeve that gives the rope its shape and protects the core from external damage (Figure 14-9).

Because kernmantle rope is very strong for its size, most Fire Service life safety lines can be small in diameter, usually either 7/16 inch (11 mm) or 1/2 inch (12.5 mm) in diameter. Most 1/2-inch kernmantle ropes of quality construction meet the 9000-pound safety rating required for a two-person load. However, this rating should be confirmed by the manufacturer and should not be taken for granted. A rope used for life safety purposes will come with a rating tag attached that gives the specific information related to that particular rope.

Rope Characteristics

Because rope is used in so many different ways in the Fire Service, there is no single size and type of rope that is best suited for every application. Many of the styles of ropes available can appear similar in construction type and size. However, they can still have very different performance characteristics.

Some ropes are designed to provide very little stretch, so that when the load is applied to the rope, the rope secures the load in place. This type of rope is referred to as **static rope** because, as the name suggests, the load doesn't move when suspended by it. By design, the static ropes used in the Fire Service aren't totally free of stretch under a load, so they offer some shock-absorbing capability. Although it is possible to weave a rope that doesn't stretch at all under a load, the loads placed on a Fire Service rope are seldom totally static and usually involve some movement. Therefore, Fire Service ropes that are considered to be static ropes still offer about 2% stretch capability to help absorb shock loads.

Other ropes are designed to stretch so that they can absorb the shock of a moving load that is subject to a sudden stop. This type of rope is called a **dynamic rope.** The load will move when subjected to a sudden stop due to the stretching of the rope. It is important that the stretch factor in a dynamic rope can be as much as 20%, so the final stopping point of the load can be as much as 20% lower than what is expected with a static rope. The normal stretch factor of a dynamic rope with a single-person load applied is actually around 4% to 8%, making it a good shock absorber. Because of this, most dynamic rope used in the Fire and Rescue Services is used as a **fall protection line** and not for the primary lifeline rope. A fall protection line is used as a lifeline rope whenever possible and does not support a load unless an accidental fall occurs. Then the dynamic rope used as a fall protection line will stretch to absorb the shock load, helping to protect both the rope and the person on the rope from the energy of a sudden stop.

KEY WORDS

dynamic rope   A rope designed to stretch to absorb the shock of a moving load that is subject to a sudden stop. This type of rope offers as much as 20% stretch capability.

fall protection line   A safety rope used as a backup to a rope rescue system to provide redundant protection from falls for rescue personnel. Most fall protection lines are dynamic ropes and do not normally carry any loads in use. The only time there is a load on a fall protection rope is if a person on the rope system falls—this rope will stop their fall.

Caring for Rope

Most ropes used in the Fire Service have a relatively long service life, depending on several factors. Damage due to abrasion, heat, contamination, sunlight, and heavy loads can cut short this service life. Basic rope care can prolong the service life. This care includes keeping all rope clean and dry. Dirt can shorten the life of the rope by working its way into the fibers and cutting some of the small strands inside the rope. Most ropes can be washed occasionally in cold water with a mild soap. Never use harsh detergents or bleach on a rope. Allow the rope to air-dry away from direct sunlight, and do not place the rope in a heated dryer.

Here are some simple, commonsense steps that will help you extend the life of the ropes you use:

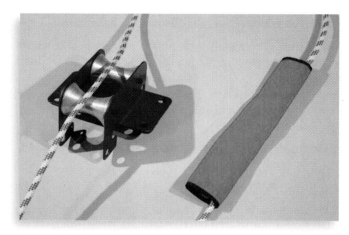

FIGURE 14-10   An edge pad and a rope roller.

- *Follow the manufacturer's guidelines!*
- *Protect the rope from abrasion.* Abrasion occurs any time you drag a rope over a rough surface or allow it to move over a sharp edge. Also, tight bends in a rope can cause a certain amount of abrasion to occur. Use an **edge pad** or a **rope roller** to avoid friction and to help "round out" tight bends when using a rope over an edge (Figure 14-10).
- *Never step on a rope.* Stepping on a rope can cause a great deal of damage to the rope's fibers. It can also grind dirt and grime into the fibers, which can cut the strands.
- *Keep the rope cool.* Any rope, especially synthetic fiber rope, can burn or melt. Carry and store the rope so that it is protected from open flame and high temperatures. Never smoke around a rope.
- *Keep the rope clean and dry.* Wash synthetic fiber rope with a mild soap and cold water, and allow it to air-dry away from direct sunlight. Do *NOT* place a rope in a clothes dryer or a heated hose dryer.
- *Store the rope properly.* Rope should be stored in a well-ventilated storage bag that is kept in a dry compartment on the truck, isolated from gasoline fumes, oils, and other contaminants. Instead of trying to neatly coil the rope, stuff it into the bag. Attempts to coil the rope usually result in tangles when the rope is played out of the bag later.
- *Avoid sunlight.* Synthetic fibers break down from long exposure to ultraviolet light. Whenever a rope is not in use, it should be stored away from exposure to direct sunlight.
- *Protect the rope from chemicals.* Any type of acid, alkali, oxidizer, or bleaching agent will degrade a rope's fibers. Keep the rope away from battery acid or acid fumes, and avoid using harsh detergents or bleach on any rope.

edge pad A padded form that is placed over a sharp edge or angle to protect a rope from abrasion or other damage.

rope roller A device that allows a rope to move over rollers instead of a sharp edge to reduce friction and wear on the rope.

Inspecting Rope

The inspection procedures for ropes are similar for every manufacturer, but it is a good idea to consult the manufacturer's recommendations for specific inspection methods for each particular rope. Ropes should be inspected on a regular basis—at least once every 3 months—by a qualified person. Inspect any rope before and after every use, whether it was used on an incident or during training. The decision to use a rope is based on this inspection process. A good method for inspecting a rope is the "look, feel, and read" method (Figure 14-11):

- *Look.* Take a slow, deliberate look at every inch of the rope, looking for visible signs of damage, abrasions, discoloration, and signs of contamination by any chemical agent. It is normal for a used rope to appear a little "fuzzy." However, if this fuzz appears to be excessive, consult the Company Officer for assistance in evaluating the rope more closely.

- *Feel.* Because a visual inspection covers only the outer sheath of a rope, squeeze the rope between your fingers all along its length, checking for depressions and separations of the rope's core. Check the cleanliness of the rope as it passes through your hands. If the rope is excessively dirty or gritty, then it should not be used until it is cleaned and inspected again.

- *Read.* Check the rope's history. Has it been subjected to any chemicals? A shock load? Heat or a direct flame impingement? Does the record card show that the rope has been retired from service as a lifeline and has been redesignated a utility rope?

Rope Records

A permanent record of a rope's service history, the **rope log,** should be kept on every rope used for life safety purposes. Many departments require this record to be kept on utility rope as well. The rope record will include the rope's basic information, including the name of the manufacturer and the type, size, and color of the rope. It will also indicate the rope's pur-

FIGURE 14-11 A firefighter inspecting a rope.

pose (life safety or utility). Note every use, every inspection, and any pertinent events in the rope log, such as potential exposure to heat, direct flames, or harsh chemicals. It is important that you refer to the rope record before *every* use of a rope as a life safety line. Because this isn't practical at the emergency scene, review the rope log for each rope during the daily apparatus check (Figure 14-12).

rope log A permanent record of a rope's service history.

Retiring a Rope

It is often necessary to retire a rope that at first glance looks perfectly good and strong but fails to pass a closer inspection. Don't take any chances on a suspected rope. There are several factors that can cause a rope, especially a lifeline rope, to be retired from

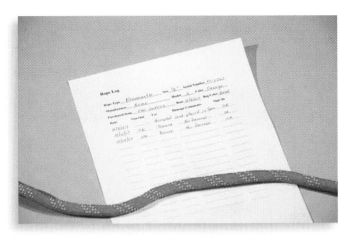

FIGURE 14-12 An example of a rope record.

service. However, the most important factor to consider is whether you have faith in the rope. *If you lose faith in the rope for any reason, bring it to the attention of your Company Officer and strongly consider retiring the rope.*

If your rope has any of the following issues, then it *MUST* be retired:

- If the core is exposed or more than half of the outer sheath is abraded or excessively "fuzzy," then *retire the rope.*
- If any of the strands on the outer sheath are broken or frayed, then chances are that the rope has been overloaded or the abrasion is severe. *Retire the rope.*
- If the rope's original color has changed, then it may have been overexposed to ultraviolet light. *Retire the rope.*
- If any of the rope's core fibers are exposed anywhere along the length of the rope, then the sheath has suffered severe damage. *Retire the rope.*
- If the rope's diameter is no longer uniform along the entire length, or if you feel depressions or lumps anywhere in the rope, then the core has been damaged. Remember, 70% of a kernmantle rope's strength comes from its core. *Retire the rope.*
- If the rope is old, then it has served its purpose. Ropes lose strength with age, even when properly stored and not used. If a rope is 10 years old, then it is worn out regardless of the amount of use. *Retire the rope.*

Knots

Knots are used to put a loop in a rope and/or to secure a rope to an object. It is important that you know how to consistently tie and untie the proper knot for the

given job. It takes a lot of practice to learn, and to retain your proficiency in, knot work. Knowing how to tie a given knot is only part of the process. It is equally important that you know which knot or knots to tie for a given job.

Anytime you put a tight bend in a rope, the rope loses a bit of its strength at that bend. On the very rare occasion that a rope fails, the failure most often occurs near a knot. More problems come from improperly tied knots than from failures due to the stresses placed on the rope by the tight bends in a knot. While there are literally hundreds of knots that can be tied in a rope, we will concentrate on the basic knots that will serve you well for fire and rescue purposes. These knots are strong, place acceptable (minimal) amounts of stress on the rope, and are easy to tie.

Go to the DVD, navigate to Chapter 14, select "Knots," and navigate to each knot you would like to review.

Elements of a Knot

Every knot we tie can be broken down into three movements: the bight, the loop, and the round turn. A bight is simply a bend in the rope. A loop is one full turn in a rope, and a round turn is one and a half turns in the rope, so that the traveling end of the rope reverses direction. Any knots noted in this chapter are the result of a combination of the bight, the loop, and the round turn (Figure 14-13).

For orientation purposes, we call the tip of the rope that is moved and manipulated to make a knot the **working end.** The part of the rope that is left over is called the **standing part.** This information means little once you

FIGURE 14-13 A bight, a loop, and a round turn.

get the knack of how to tie a given knot, but the language makes it easier to explain the motions when teaching someone how to tie a knot (Figure 14-14).

KEY WORDS

standing part The part of the rope between the end of the rope with the knot and the opposite end of the rope (without the knot).

working end The end of the rope that is moved and manipulated to form a knot.

Types of Knots

Overhand Safety Knot

An overhand safety knot is a knot used to keep another knot secure. This knot is very simple to tie and is used with nearly every other knot you will use.

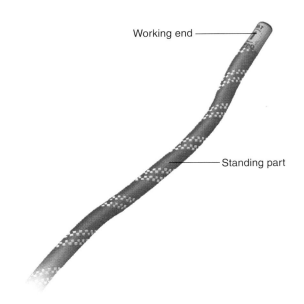

Working end ———

Standing part

FIGURE 14-14 The working end and standing part of a rope.

Practice It!

Overhand Safety Knot

To tie an overhand safety knot, follow these steps:

1. Make a round turn in the end of the rope so that the loop that is formed passes around the running part of the rope (Figure 14-15).

FIGURE 14-15

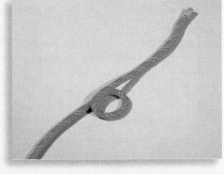

2. Now pass the working end through the loop and pull on both sides of the knot to cinch it down (Figure 14-16).

FIGURE 14-16

Bowline

A bowline is a very strong knot used to form a loop in the end of a rope. This loop can be formed around an object as the bowline is tied. Alternately, it can be a freestanding loop at the end of the rope to which something else can be attached. Whether the bowline is tied around an object or as a loop, the motions are the same.

Clove Hitch

A clove hitch is used to secure a rope around a round object. It can be tied around an object, such as the base of a tree, or formed in the air and then draped over the object and cinched down, as you would around the end of a pipe. Some good qualities of a properly tied clove hitch are that it will tighten when the rope is pulled from either end and the knot is easy to tie and untie, making it well suited for securing equipment to be hoisted.

➡ Practice It!

Bowline

To tie a bowline, follow these steps:

1. Make a loop in the rope a foot or two from the end. Pass the working end up through the loop, pass it around the rope, and push it back down through the loop (Figures 14-17 to 14-19).

FIGURE 14-17

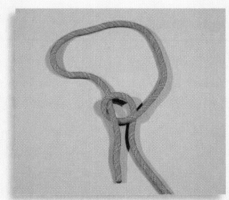

FIGURE 14-18

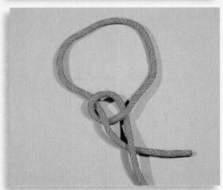

FIGURE 14-19

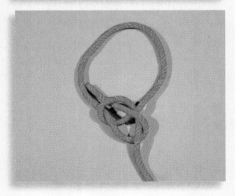

—Continued

2. Cinch down the knot and secure it with an overhand safety knot (Figure 14-20).

FIGURE 14-20

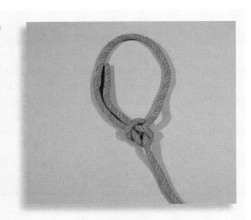

➡ Practice It!

Clove Hitch

To tie a clove hitch, follow these steps:

1. Start with an overhand loop in your left hand (Figure 14-21).

FIGURE 14-21

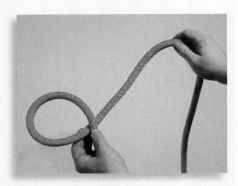

2. Form another overhand loop in your right hand beside the first one and place it over the top of the first loop (Figure 14-22).

FIGURE 14-22

3. Now simply drape both loops over the round object and pull both sides of the rope to cinch the knot, and finish with an overhand safety knot (Figure 14-23).

FIGURE 14-23

Clove Hitch Around an Object

To tie a clove hitch around an object, follow these steps:

1. Drape the rope over the object and pass the working end around the right side of the standing part of the rope, forming a round turn (Figure 14-24).

   FIGURE 14-24

2. Now make another round turn on the left side of the first, and bring the working end up and through the cross that has formed in the rope at the object (Figure 14-25).

   FIGURE 14-25

3. Pull both sides to cinch the knot, and finish with an overhand safety knot (Figure 14-26).

   FIGURE 14-26

Figure Eight Stopper Knot

A figure eight stopper knot is the fundamental first step in tying any knot in the "family of eights" series. It is often tied in the bitter end (also called the terminal end) of a rope to keep something from slipping off the end, and as the base for tying another version of a figure eight (for example, a figure eight on a bight).

 Practice It!

Figure Eight Stopper Knot

To tie a figure eight stopper knot, follow these steps:

1. Make a round turn at one end of the rope (Figure 14-27).

   FIGURE 14-27

—*Continued*

Level I

2. Pass the end of the rope behind the standing part, bringing it back toward the loop (Figure 14-28).

FIGURE 14-28

3. Pass the end through the loop and cinch down the knot (Figure 14-29).

FIGURE 14-29

Figure Eight on a Bight

Similar to a bowline, a figure eight on a bight knot is also used to form a loop at the end of a rope. This loop can be tied around an object to attach the rope, or it can be formed in the air as a loop to secure an object with the rope.

➡ Practice It!

Figure Eight on a Bight

To form a figure eight on a bight knot, follow these steps:

1. Start by forming a large bight in the rope near the end (Figure 14-30).

FIGURE 14-30

2. Pass the bend of the rope around the running part (Figure 14-31).

FIGURE 14-31

3. Now pass the bend back up through the hole created by the first bight (Figure 14-32).

FIGURE 14-32

4. Cinch the knot down and finish with an overhand safety knot in the working end for security (Figure 14-33).

FIGURE 14-33

Becket Bend (Sheet Bend)

A becket bend, also known as a sheet bend, is used to connect two ropes of unequal diameter. This knot is good for a quick connection on a rope that is used for hoisting light objects. However, it is not strong enough to use for human loads.

⮕ Practice It!

Becket Bend (Sheet Bend)

To tie a becket bend (sheet bend), follow these steps:

1. Start by forming a bight in the larger rope (Figure 14-34).

FIGURE 14-34

2. Now pass the working end of the smaller rope through the bight, and pass it around both parts of the bight (Figure 14-35).

FIGURE 14-35

3. Tuck the working end of the smaller rope behind its own standing part and over the top of the bight (Figure 14-36).

FIGURE 14-36

4. Now draw the knot tight and finish with overhand safety knots at the end of both ropes (Figure 14-37).

FIGURE 14-37

Half-Hitch

A half-hitch is not actually a knot because it does not secure anything to a rope by itself. A half-hitch is used to snug down a rope and help keep the item that has been secured by a more substantial knot in line with the rope. Half-hitches are very useful when a long tool is being hoisted.

Half-Hitch

To form a half-hitch, use the following steps:

1. Make a loop in the rope and pass it over the end of the item that is being secured (Figure 14-38).

FIGURE 14-38

2. Pull on the standing end of the rope to draw the half-hitch tight. Several half-hitches may be used in a row if needed (Figure 14-39).

FIGURE 14-39

Support Activities Using Rope

Ropes are used for many things on the fireground or rescue scene. Hoisting tools and equipment, securing a heavy load, extending a ladder, providing a guide back to the door of a smoke-filled building, and serving as a fall protection line while working on a roof are all duties in which ropes are used. Accomplishing these tasks in a safe, efficient manner takes a lot of practice and careful forethought as to which type of knot or knots to tie for a given task. In this section we will focus on hoisting tools and equipment.

Review It!

Go to the DVD, navigate to Chapter 14, select *"Hoisting,"* and navigate to each tool to be hoisted that you would like to review.

Hoisting Tools and Equipment

Most tools and equipment that are hoisted by a rope are secured using a series of knots. In the interest of safety, many agencies have a prescribed set of knots and methods that they require for each type of tool that is to be hoisted. A falling tool can be lethal if it hits someone. At the very least, it will almost always result in damage to the tool, rendering it useless on the fire.

Often there are two different ropes attached to a tool before it is hoisted. The hoisting line is used to raise the tool, while the person on the ground staffs the tag line to help guide the tool along the way. This is very useful if the tool is being raised through tree limbs or around building features that jut out, such as a ledge or cornice.

Tag lines can be tied directly to the tool or can be attached using a "wrap-and-snap" method. The wrap-and-snap method uses a metal **snap link** (carabineer) attached to the line with a secure loop, such as a bowline or figure eight on a bight. Because this line will bear little or no weight, the snap link can be relatively light in construction. However, it should always be a rated carabineer that is capable of supporting the same amount of load as the rope to which it is attached. Avoid using cheap snap links found at the hardware store to hoist tools.

To attach the tag line using a wrap and snap, simply wrap the rope around the object three or four times and snap the carabineer back onto the standing part of the rope. This rope will cinch down and grip the tool tight enough to serve well as a tag line. The clear advantage of using the wrap-and-snap method for securing the tag line is that it is quick to construct and easy to untie, so it is an efficient method to use when time is of the essence.

■ KEY WORD

snap link (carabineer) A metal connector that has a locking gate that allows the connector to pass over a rope, locking it in place.

➡ Practice It!

Hoisting an Axe

To use a rope to hoist an axe, use the following steps:

1. Start with a clove hitch around the handle, near the axe head (Figure 14-40).

FIGURE 14-40

2. Pass the rope around the head and secure it in position with an overhand safety knot formed using the working end of the rope (Figure 14-41).

FIGURE 14-41

3. Now add one or two half-hitches along the handle. The axe should be hoisted with the head down and the handle up (Figure 14-42).

FIGURE 14-42

4. Use either a wrap-and-snap method or another clove hitch to secure the tag line to the axe just above the first clove hitch on the handle (Figure 14-43).

FIGURE 14-43

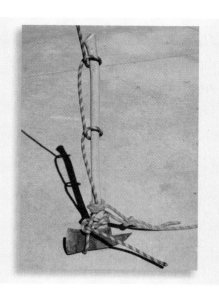

⮕ Practice It!

Hoisting a Roof Ladder

To use a rope to hoist a roof ladder, use the following steps:

1. Form a large loop at the end of the hoisting rope. This knot can be either a bowline or a figure eight on a bight. Either knot is sufficient and should be secured with an overhand safety knot tied in the working end of the rope (Figure 14-44).

FIGURE 14-44

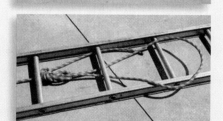

2. Pass the knot behind the ladder about a third of the way down (Figure 14-45).

FIGURE 14-45

3. Bring the loop up between the rungs and pass it over the ladder's tip, forming a large hitch over the ladder (Figure 14-46).

FIGURE 14-46

4. Attach a tag line to the bottom rung using an appropriate method (Figure 14-47).

FIGURE 14-47

⮕ Practice It!

Hoisting an Uncharged Hose Line

When hoisting an uncharged hose line, it is important to protect the hose coupling from damage.

1. Fold the hose line twice about 3 or 4 feet from the end (Figure 14-48).

FIGURE 14-48

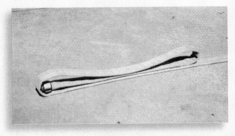

2. Tie a clove hitch with an overhand safety knot around the base of those folds, followed with a half-hitch midway to the end and another half-hitch at the end of the rope (Figure 14-49).

FIGURE 14-49

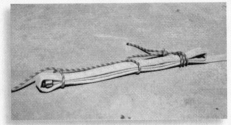

Hoisting Hose Lines, Alternate Method

If time is of the essence, the wrap-and-snap method can be used to secure the hoisting rope to the end of the hose line. This method is not prescribed by most formal establishments, but it is very effective and there has never been a documented failure using a properly tied wrap-and-snap method to hoist a hose, whether charged or uncharged (Figures 14-50 and 14-51).

FIGURE 14-50 Attach a carabineer to the end of a line using a bowline or figure eight on a bight. Wrap the line around the object several times.

FIGURE 14-51 Snap the carabineer around the standing part of the rope and cinch down to complete the wrap-and-snap.

Practice It!

Hoisting a Charged Hose Line

To hoist a charged hose line, use the following steps:

1. Tie a clove hitch about 3 or 4 feet down from the nozzle (Figure 14-52).

FIGURE 14-52

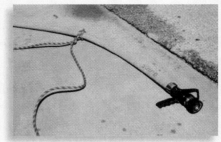

2. Place a half-hitch a foot or two behind the nozzle, and then pass a second half-hitch through the nozzle's bale so that the standing part of the rope passes over top of the closed bale, keeping it closed while hoisting (Figure 14-53).

FIGURE 14-53

 ## Practice It!

Hoisting a Long-Handled Tool

Long-handled tools, such as long ceiling hooks, should be hoisted with the head pointing up.

1. Place a clove hitch and overhand safety knot near the butt of the handle, followed with a half-hitch placed every 3 or 4 feet along the handle, with a final half-hitch just behind the tool's head (Figure 14-54).

FIGURE 14-54

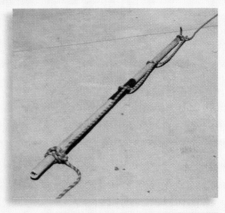

2. Secure a tag line with either a clove hitch or the wrap-and-snap method. Be sure to secure the tag line above the first clove hitch to keep it from slipping off the end of the handle as the tool is hoisted (Figure 14-55).

FIGURE 14-55

Level I

Heavy Equipment

It is usually safer to raise a heavy item, like a smoke ejector or hose appliance, by using a rope rather than by carrying it up a ground ladder. However, there is a limit to what can be safely pulled up using a rope. Some gasoline-powered smoke ejectors can weigh in excess of 100 pounds and can be very heavy and cumbersome when swinging from a rope. So first consider the weight and the alternative methods of hoisting an item before you start the operation. If the tool is heavy, it is usually best to secure more than one hoisting rope and use more than one firefighter to share the weight of hoisting the tool.

Most heavy equipment can be secured to the hoisting rope or ropes using a bowline or a figure eight on a bight. As always, secure the primary knot with an overhand safety knot for good measure. Tag lines can be secured using the same method or the wrap-and-snap method, whichever you prefer and is authorized by your agency (Figure 14-56).

The Practical Use of Ropes

Although this chapter on ropes and knots hasn't prepared you for a complex technical rescue, the material you have read and the skills you will practice serve as the foundation for any rope rescue work you do in the future. A majority of the rope work you will do in the Fire Service will be accomplished using utility ropes for hoisting tools and equipment, securing heavy loads, and using life safety rope to provide fall protection when working above ground level. Practice the knots constantly so that you can tie them consistently, even while wearing gloves and under adverse conditions. And practice good rope safety by taking exceptional care of all of the ropes and associated equipment.

FIGURE 14-56   Have help when hoisting heavy equipment.

Prove It

Knowledge Assessment
Signed Documentation Tear-Out Sheet
Ropes and Knots for the Fire Service—Chapter 14

Name: _____

Fill out the ten-question quiz below, the Knowledge Assessment Sheet, by circling the correct answer for each question. When finished, sign it and give it to your instructor/Company Officer for his or her signature. Turn in this Knowledge Assessment Sheet to the proper person as part of the documentation that you have completed your training for this chapter.

1. Once a rope has been used as a utility line, it can be later used as a life safety rope if it passes inspection and meets the specifications for a life safety rope.
   a. True
   b. False

2. Utility rope that meets the specifications for use as life safety rope can be used as a life safety rope for training purposes.
   a. True
   b. False

3. Life safety rope must have a built-in _____ safety factor.
   a. 10:1
   b. 20:1
   c. 15:1
   d. 5:1

4. When a load suspended from a rope is moving and it comes to a sudden stop, the resulting stresses on the rope are called _____.
   a. shock loads
   b. drop loads
   c. static loads
   d. inconsequential loads

5. Laid rope is another name for _____ rope.
   a. braided
   b. braid-on-braid
   c. kernmantle
   d. twisted

6. The type of rope most commonly used for life safety purposes is _____ rope.
   a. braided
   b. braid-on-braid
   c. kernmantle
   d. twisted

7. A life safety rope that meets the standard for a single-person load must have a breaking strength of at least _____ pounds.

　　a. 300

　　b. 600

　　c. 4500

　　d. 9000

8. A(n) _____ knot is used to form a secure loop at the end of a rope.

　　a. overhand safety knot

　　b. bowline

　　c. clove hitch

　　d. becket bend

9. A(n) _____ knot is used to secure a rope around a round object.

　　a. becket bend

　　b. overhand safety

　　c. sheet bend

　　d. clove hitch

10. A(n) _____ knot is the first knot tied to a long-handled tool that is to be hoisted.

　　a. becket bend

　　b. clove hitch

　　c. overhand safety

　　d. half-hitch

Student Signature and Date _____　　Instructor/Company Officer Signature and Date _____

330

Prove It

Skills Assessment
Signed Documentation Tear-Out Sheet
Ropes and Knots for the Fire Service—Chapter 14

Name: _____

Fill out the Skills Assessment Sheet below. Have your instructor/Company Officer check off and initial each skill you demonstrate. When you are finished, sign this page and give to your instructor/Company Officer for his or her signature. Turn in this Skills Assessment Sheet to the proper person as part of the documentation that you have completed your training for this chapter.

Skill	Completed	Initials
1. When given a choice of the two, properly identify a life safety rope and a utility rope.	_____	_____
2. Identify the working end and the standing part of a rope.	_____	_____
3. Perform a proper rope inspection.	_____	_____
4. Complete a rope record.	_____	_____
5. Tie an overhand safety knot.	_____	_____
6. Tie a bowline.	_____	_____
7. Tie a clove hitch.	_____	_____
8. Tie a clove hitch around an object.	_____	_____
9. Tie a figure eight on a bight.	_____	_____
10. Tie a becket bend (sheet bend).	_____	_____
11. Tie a half-hitch.	_____	_____
12. Secure an axe for hoisting.	_____	_____
13. Secure a roof ladder for hoisting.	_____	_____
14. Secure an uncharged hose line for hoisting.	_____	_____
15. Secure an uncharged hose line using a "wrap and snap."	_____	_____
16. Secure a charged hose line for hoisting.	_____	_____
17. Secure a long-handled tool for hoisting.	_____	_____
18. Secure a piece of heavy equipment (smoke ejector) for hoisting.	_____	_____

Student Signature and Date _____   Instructor/Company Officer Signature and Date _____

Forcible Entry and Exit

What You Will Learn in This Chapter

This chapter is intended to help you understand the tools and techniques used to create openings in buildings to access the building, attack the fire, and rescue victims. Having in-depth information about the various construction methods used for doors, windows, and walls you can expect to encounter in residential and commercial applications will help you overcome the challenges of forcing entry during an emergency.

What You Will Be Able to Do

After reading this chapter and practicing the skills described, you will be able to employ various forcible entry tools to safely:

1. Identify and explain the uses for multiuse forcible entry tools, striking tools, power tools, lock pullers, and several miscellaneous hand tools used to create openings in buildings.
2. Explain the types of doors and locks used in typical residential construction.
3. Force open residential doors that swing inward and outward, using more than one method.
4. Force open residential garage doors using more than one method.
5. Force open residential windows using more than one method.
6. Clear an entire opening around a residential-style window for rescue or fire attack.
7. Cut or force a padlock, hasp, and chain.
8. Demonstrate through-the-lock entry through tubular-, rim-, and mortise-style locks.

9. Force entry through a fortified door.
10. Force open or create an opening in overhead rolling doors and grates.

Reality!

Security Slows Down Firefighters!

Considering the level of crime in all areas of the world today, there are very few places left where people leave their doors and windows unlocked, especially at night. Essentially every commercial occupancy will go to great lengths to lock and even barricade their business from the threat of thieves after normal working hours. In addition, some types of businesses operate in a secure setting that requires the building's doors to be locked at all times.

When a fire breaks out in an occupied building, every moment spent trying to force doors or windows means time added to the trapped person's exposure to heat and toxic smoke. Hose crews and search teams standing ready to enter the building become anxious and frustrated, making any delay in forcing open a door seem to take hours. With practice and a little forethought, forcing entry into nearly any building can be accomplished in a matter of moments rather than several minutes.

The time factor for forcing open a door or window really comes into play when you are inside a structure and want to get out. Forcible *exit* is usually accomplished using the same techniques as forcible entry; however, the work is done in more cramped surroundings and often under conditions that offer poor or no visibility. Forcible exit is discussed in depth in Chapter 19, where you will practice forcing doors under many different conditions rather than in the clinical setting of a training academy.

The ability to efficiently force entry isn't restricted to just those structures that are burning. There are times when someone becomes incapacitated, requiring emergency medical care, but is unable to open the doors to allow EMS personnel inside. Other modes of forcible entry do not involve a building at all, such as fences, padlocks, and other obstructions that can prevent our being able to deliver emergency service.

After reading this chapter and practicing the skills, you will probably look at doors and windows much differently than before. That's good! Constantly size up doors and windows in the buildings you are in during the normal course of a day. Pay close attention to how they operate and run through a mental plan of how you would overcome them if they were to present an obstacle to your access to or egress from the building.

Creating Openings in Buildings

One of the most important keys to a successful entry through a locked door or window is to properly size up the situation. There are several reasons to create openings in a building. You may force open a locked door or window to create a path of access to the building to attack a fire or effect a rescue. You may need to create a path of egress for the occupants to evacuate a hazardous area. Windows and doors may need to be completely opened to evacuate smoke or hot gases from a building, which is making openings for **ventilation** purposes. We will look closely at the ventilation process in Chapter 18 to better understand how any openings we create in a burning building will affect the fire. For now, we will concentrate on the skills necessary to force entry properly and safely (Figure 15-1).

Because any opening we create in a burning building will affect the fire, it is extremely important that the Incident Commander knows which door or window you are about to open and when you open it. This will give the Incident Commander time to consider the effect that the opened door will have on the fire. In addition, by relaying over the radio the locations of openings as they are created, everyone on the scene will know where alternate paths of access and egress exist.

KEY WORD

ventilation   The deliberate and well-planned act of removing smoke and heat from a burning building.

FIGURE 15-1   Opening the door to a smoke-filled area can affect the fire.

Safety Tip!

Because most of the skills used for forcible entry involve striking and breaking objects, there is a very high potential for eye and hand injury. Whenever you are observing or performing forcible entry, whether during training or at an emergency scene, it is extremely important that you wear the proper personal protective equipment. This includes head, eye, hand, foot, and body protection.

Forcible Entry Tools

Nearly any heavy tool that is designed to pound something and has a long handle can accomplish some sort of forcible entry into most structures. So why not simply bash in every door with a huge sledgehammer? Because that method doesn't always work and because it can destroy the door or knock it off its hinges, making it impossible to close the door if needed. A good choice of forcible entry tools will allow you to force the door. It will also allow you to control the door to keep it from swinging violently open, where it could strike a victim just inside the door. In addition, it will allow you to close the door, if necessary, to restrict flame travel. Some typical tools for forcible entry include:

- Multiuse forcible entry tools
- Striking tools
- Power tools
- Small hand tools
- Lock pullers

Multiuse Forcible Entry Tools

Because quality tools used for prying and chopping are often heavy, it is important that every tool we carry can perform more than one function. For this reason, most of the tools designed for firefighters for forcible entry are **multiuse forcible entry tools**—they have specifically designed components that are useful for more than one job. These tools include the Halligan tool, the Hooligan tool, the Kelly bar, and many more.

▨ KEY WORD ▨

multiuse forcible entry tools Tools designed to perform more than one function for forcing entry through a door or window. Examples of these tools are the Halligan, Hooligan, and Kelly tools.

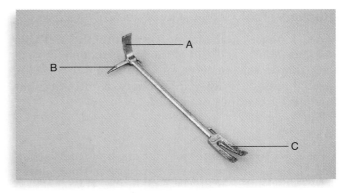

FIGURE 15-2 (a) Adze, (b) pick, and (c) fork.

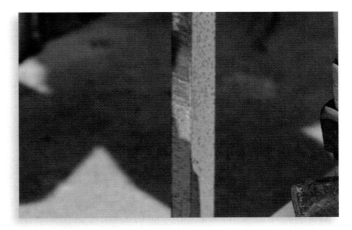

FIGURE 15-3 A good multipurpose tool is useful for more than one job. Here the gas supply to a building is being controlled with the fork end of a Halligan bar.

Halligan Tool

One of the most popular tools for forcible entry is the Halligan tool. The Halligan was specifically designed for Fire Service work. Every component of the Halligan has been designed to serve multiple purposes (Figure 15-2). The forked end is great for prying, and for shutting off a gas meter. The **adze** on the other end provides a great deal of leverage for prying open doors and windows. The pick is good for anchoring in a padlock to force it off a hasp, and it works great as a fulcrum when prying with the adze. An average firefighter using a Halligan bar for leverage can usually apply between 800 pounds and 1200 pounds of force at the tip of the adze when prying. A good Halligan bar is built with one-piece forged construction and can last a lifetime (Figure 15-3).

▨ KEY WORD ▨

adze The arched blade that is set at a right angle to the handle of a tool used for prying or chopping.

Level I

Hooligan Tool

The Hooligan tool closely resembles the Halligan tool, but the forked end of the tool can come in various shapes that make it suitable for cutting metal, prying cylinders away from doors, shutting off gas meters, and various other jobs.

Kelly Tool

The Kelly tool is more popular on the West Coast of the United States than in other parts of the country. The Kelly has an adze and striking surface on one end and a fork on the other. This tool is good for striking, chopping, and prying.

Striking Tools

Striking tools work using a very basic principle: If you make something hard and heavy move fast enough, anything it hits will break. While not an actual scientific statement, you get the picture.

Prying tools are seldom useful alone and should be accompanied by a **striking tool,** such as a flat axe or sledgehammer. Most prying tools will need to be forced between a door and the doorjamb, and this is best accomplished by pounding them into place. When matched together, the prying tool and striking tool in combination are referred to as "the irons." An easy way to carry a Halligan or Hooligan with an axe is to "marry" the two by sliding the forked end of the pry tool over the axe head and aligning the tools' handles so that they can be carried in one hand (Figure 15-4). You should make it a practice to never carry one of these tools without the other so that you are prepared for striking, prying, or both.

▰ KEY WORD ▰

striking tools   Tools used for breaking, breaching, or driving a prying tool into a gap. Examples are the sledgehammer and flathead axe.

Axe

Fire Service axes come in two general types: pickhead and flathead (Figure 15-5). The pickhead axe is a good tool for breaking through wood. On the opposite side of the axe, it has a pick for light prying and punching holes through wood or light steel. While the pickhead axe is a good tool, it provides no surface for striking another tool, such as a Halligan, into place. A flathead axe used in the Fire Service has a flat surface opposite the blade that makes it a good striking tool as well as a good cutting tool. Most flathead axes used in the Fire Service have a heavy head, and the

FIGURE 15-4   When carried together, the axe and Halligan combination is referred to as "the irons."

FIGURE 15-5   (a) Pickhead axe and (b) flat axe.

handle is either hardwood or a composite material such as fiberglass.

Sledgehammer

Sledgehammers used in the Fire Service range in weight from 6 to 12 pounds. Most sledgehammers have a composite handle, which greatly reduces the

FIGURE 15-6 Sledgehammer.

chance of breaking the handle with a missed swing (Figure 15-6). Obviously the bigger the head on the hammer, the more force produced with each swing; however, the added weight can become tiresome to carry during a long operation.

Sledgehammers are good tools for breaking through doors, especially when you are faced with a lot of doors to force open in a hurry, as you would expect to encounter at a hotel or office complex. One good swing on a single deadbolt lock and the door will usually fly open. Sledgehammers are also great tools for breaching a masonry wall.

 Safety Tip!

While bashing in a door with a sledgehammer is a very effective way to quickly open the door, this method usually results in destroying the locking mechanism and will often bend or splinter the door beyond repair. It is very hard to control a door's swing when using a pounding method to force it open, and the resulting damage will make it hard or even impossible to close the door, if needed, to control the fire.

FIGURE 15-7 Battering ram.

Battering Ram

Because of its heavy weight, a battering ram will provide even more force with each swing than a sledgehammer. Battering rams make short work of most doors and walls. However, because of their weight and the energy required to carry and swing them, battering rams are rarely used for conventional forcible entry. They are more often used for breaching walls.

Safe operation of a battering ram requires two firefighters. Another drawback to battering rams is that they are useful for only one purpose—breaking things. Unlike most other forcible entry tools, battering rams cannot be used to close a gas valve, pry a lock, or punch a small hole in metal (Figure 15-7).

Power Tools

Most **power tools** that we use in the Fire Service have been designed for other purposes, usually the construction trades. Gasoline-powered circular saws, chain saws, and hydraulic tools all fall under the category of power tools.

▮▮▮ KEY WORD ▮▮▮

power tools Tools that derive their operating power from a gasoline, electric, or pneumatic motor. Examples of power tools are the gasoline-operated circular saw for cutting metal and concrete, a chainsaw designed for cutting wood, and an electric reciprocal saw designed for cutting most types of materials.

Circular Saw

Gasoline-powered circular saws are extremely useful for cutting away steel bars, steel garage-style doors, and large locks that cannot be cut with bolt cutters. When equipped with an aluminum oxide composite disk instead of a wood-cutting blade, a circular saw will slice quickly through most metals used for doors

FIGURE 15-8 Circular saw.

FIGURE 15-9 Chain saw.

and burglar bars. With a quick change of the disk to one designed for masonry, the circular saw can work through concrete. Although the circular saw is only used for cutting, it is a very versatile tool in this respect (Figure 15-8).

Chain Saws

Chain saws are useful for cutting through wooden doors, especially garage-style doors. Most chain saws used for our purposes have a carbide-tipped chain specially designed for the type of materials we encounter when cutting doors and roofs (Figure 15-9).

 **Safety Tip!**

Always follow the manufacturer's instructions and safety guidelines when using any power tool.

Hydraulic Tools

Specially designed hydraulic tools are available for forcible entry work. Most work only on doors that open inward and away from the user, by jamming the "jaws" of the tool between the door and the door stop, and applying hydraulic force with a hand-operated pump to break the lock free (Figure 15-10).

Lock Puller

Lock pullers are tools that are designed to extract the cylinder of a door lock, allowing us access to the inner mechanism of the lock for further manipulation and opening. This type of forcible entry is called the *through-the-lock* method. Some lock pullers are small and are designed to work with the adze of a prying tool so that when driven down across the cylinder's

FIGURE 15-10 A Rabbet Tool uses hydraulic power supplied by a hand pump to force open a door that swings away from the user.

rim, the tool extracts the lock's cylinder from the frame. An example of this type of tool is the K-Tool, which gets its name from the shape of the blades on the pulling side of the tool (Figure 15-11). Other types of lock pullers have their own pry bar attached or are built into the forked end of a Hooligan tool.

KEY WORD

lock pullers Tools specifically designed to extract the key cylinder from a lock.

Other Forcible Entry Tools

We have been discussing tools specially designed for forcible entry. In addition to these tools, there are several hand-operated tools that, while not specifically designed for forcible entry, can be very useful.

FIGURE 15-11 A K-Tool is a common lock-pulling device.

FIGURE 15-12 Other forcible entry tools include bolt cutters, a pry axe, and a flat pry bar.

Bolt cutters, for example, are extremely useful for cutting chains and padlocks. Bolt cutters come in several sizes, and bigger is not always better in this case. Large bolt cutters, with handles longer than 36 inches, provide a great deal of power to the blades, but they are heavy and unwieldy for cutting small or average-size locks. Smaller bolt cutters are good for common locks and chains but they will fail to cut thick, heavy chains or locks (Figure 15-12).

There are several **small hand tools** that are useful for light-duty forcible entry, including small axes and small, construction-style pry bars. Some of these tools have specially designed ends for cutting sheet metal, operating gas valves, and other special purposes. These tools are useful in tight areas in which a larger tool cannot be used. The disadvantages to using them are that they provide much less leverage when prying as well as less impact with each swing. Because tools of this type are small and lightweight, many firefighters carry one on a tool belt as a backup to the larger tools. However, they are usually too small for general forcible entry duties and should not be considered a replacement for larger, heavier tools.

Forcible Entry—Residential Buildings

Forcible entry, like any strategy we undertake in emergency services, begins with a size-up of the situation. The size-up for forcible entry starts with the location of the door or window, and how opening the building at that point will affect the fire. When forcing a window, look for smoke seeping around the window frame or from the eaves at the roofline. Opening this window will probably have a ventilation effect on the fire. Feel the door for heat with the back of your ungloved hand or wrist. Do not use the palm of your hand for this because the skin is thicker and tougher on the palm, and it may not allow you to detect subtle heat changes. Look for signs of smoke seeping around any cracks around the door or windows.

Because the heat from the fire increases the pressure of the smoke and other gases in a burning building, making an opening can draw the fire toward the opening. However, if the wind is considerable, then opening a door or window can cause the fire to push toward other parts of the building, which may be unburned or contain victims (Figure 15-13).

 **Safety Tip!**

Have a charged hose line staffed and ready whenever opening a door to a high-heat area. It is very important that you stand to one side of a door or window when forcing it open if there is any heat or smoke in the building. The sudden rush of fresh air can cause a flashover or a sudden and violent ignition of the unburned gases and flammable smoke in the building. If you can't stand completely out of the way, then crouch low when forcing a door.

While you are looking at the door, look for alternate means of entry. Is there any adjacent glass around the doorway or even in the door that you can break to reach in and unlock the door? Is there another door that is unlocked? Remember, people who are running from a burning building seldom stop to lock the door behind them, so the door through which they exited may be unlocked.

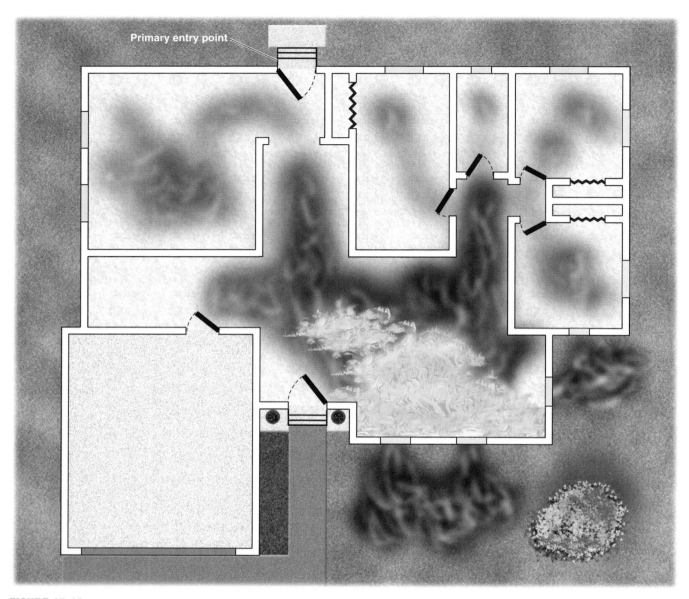

FIGURE 15-13 The primary point of entry is determined by the available points of entry and the fire/smoke conditions.

Residential Doors

Residential doors have several key features that you should size up. The door lock (doorknob) will usually conduct heat much quicker than an insulated or wooden door, so be careful when touching the metal knob. You can probably feel the warmth through your gloved hand when you try to turn the knob to be sure that the door is indeed locked. The old adage *"Try before you pry"* is a good one to remember to save you a lot of work and embarrassment that would come with pounding away on an unlocked door.

The next thing to look for when sizing up a door is how the door is built. Residential exterior doors are usually solid core, steel clad, or fiberglass. All of these doors are very sturdy and will hold up well under prying forces. Most residential exterior doors swing into the building, away from you when forcing entry. (Conversely, most exterior doors to commercial buildings swing outward to serve as exit doors.) Because residential doors swing inward, the hinges are usually on the inside for security. Therefore, simply removing the hinge pins to remove the door isn't usually an option.

Safety Tip!

It is best if you have a means to control a swinging door, especially if it swings inward toward the fire, so you can close it to hold the fire in check if needed. Many people use a rope, nylon strap, or chain attached to the doorknob to do this. Maintain plenty of slack in the rope, strap, or chain to allow the door to swing open, and if you encounter heavy fire, quickly pull it closed until the nozzle person is ready to attack the fire.

A door comes to rest against some sort of stop on the **doorjamb.** A stop that is nailed on is called a **stopped jamb.** More often the stop is a ledge that is formed when a groove is cut or formed into the doorjamb. This type of doorjamb is called a **rabbeted jamb.** In the case of a stopped jamb, it is relatively simple to peel back the thin wood to form a gap for a **purchase point** for your forcible entry tool. However, working around a rabbeted jamb isn't really a problem, so don't spend a lot of time if the type of jamb isn't quickly apparent to you due to thick coats of paint or poor light conditions (Figure 15-14a, b).

▰▰ KEY WORDS ▰▰▰▰

doorjamb The frame into which the door's hinges and lock receiver are set.

purchase point A gap or opening where a firefighter can place a prying or cutting tool's working surface to gain a firm grip for prying or cutting action.

rabbeted jamb A style of doorjamb in which the ledge that seals the edges of the closed door is cut into the wood or formed in the steel of the jamb.

stopped jam A style of doorjamb in which thin strips of wood are nailed into place to serve as the ledge that seals the edges of the door when it is closed.

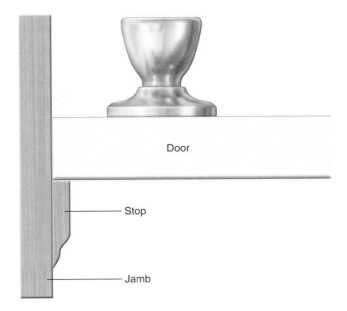

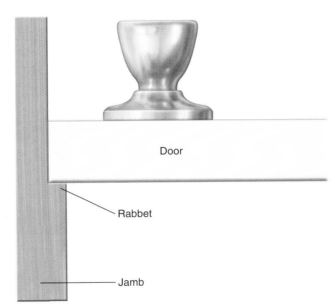

FIGURE 15-14   (a) Stopped jamb, and (b) rabbeted jamb.

Residential Locks

The next thing to consider when sizing up the door is the type and locations of the locks. Residential door locks are usually either a tubular- or rim-type lock. Tubular locks are installed in a hole drilled in the door, while rim locks are held on the inside surface of the door with screws. A tubular lock may or may not have a key cylinder showing on the outside of the door. A normal doorknob found in most residential applications operates a tubular latch that is beveled on one side so that it closes with little effort (Figure 15-15a, b).

A deadbolt lock will protrude into the jamb and is operated with a key or possibly a twist knob on the inside of the door. The lock is not beveled, so it does not lock automatically when the door is closed. Inspect the outside of the door to locate the locks. Is there more than one lock showing above the door knob? How about below it? Tubular deadbolt locks often extend from 3/4 to 1 inch into the doorjamb.

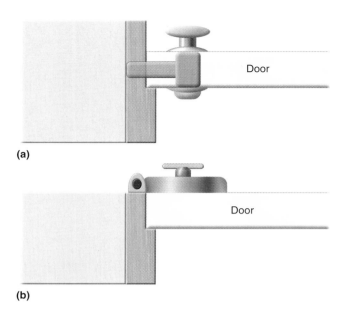

(a)

(b)

FIGURE 15-15 (a) Tubular lock, and (b) rim lock.

This means that a gap of about the same measure must be created between the door and the jamb before the door will swing open. This is where the "force" part of forcible entry comes in (Figure 15-16a, b).

(a) Beveled latch

(b) Deadbolt lock

FIGURE 15-16 (a) Beveled latch, and (b) deadbolt lock.

Review It!

Go to the DVD, navigate to Chapter 15, select *"Forcing a Residential Door,"* and navigate to the door type you would like to review.

Practice It!

Forcing an Inward-Swinging Door

Working as a two-person team, use the following method to force a door that swings away from you:

1. Inspect the door to be sure it is locked, and feel for heat (Figure 15-17). Radio to the Incident Commander the location of the door you are going to force and receive confirmation that it should be forced.

FIGURE 15-17

2. Select the purchase point and position the adze of the tool between the door and the jamb (Figure 15-18). Drive the tool into place if necessary.

FIGURE 15-18

3. Rotate the tool toward the center of the door to force the door open (Figure 15-19).

FIGURE 15-19

If the door is set against a stopped jamb, the stop will break off before the door or lock gives way if you use it as a prying surface. To overcome this, drive the pick end of the Halligan securely into the jamb. This will leave the adze flush against the door or, if possible, the door lock. Now pull upward or downward, depending on the side of the door you are on, to pivot the adze against the door, forcing it open (Figure 15-20). The amount of leverage afforded by a Halligan against the tip of the adze is phenomenal and will make short work of most doors attacked in this manner.

Another, less graceful way to force a door that swings away from you is to use a sledgehammer or battering ram to bash through the door. Simply aim your swing toward the lock or the part of the door closest to the jamb on the lock side and it will usually fly open with one or two hard blows

(Figure 15-21). However, this method will certainly break something, making it nearly impossible to secure the door if the need arises to close it. It will also cause the door to swing violently open, striking anything in its path. It is very common to encounter a victim on the floor next to a locked door, so this violent swinging of the door can cause further harm to a patient in its path.

 **Safety Tip!**

If you encounter any resistance to opening a door that is freed from the lock and should otherwise open, push it gently but firmly until it is open enough for you to feel behind the door for a victim.

FIGURE 15-20 The pick, when driven into a jamb, provides a great fulcrum for forcing open an inward-swinging door.

FIGURE 15-21 A door usually opens with one or two blows to the lock. This method makes it hard to control the door, but it is effective when there are several doors to force.

Review It!

Go to the DVD, navigate to Chapter 15, select "*Forcing a Residential Door,*" and navigate to the door type you would like to review.

Practice It!

Forcing an Outward-Swinging Door

Working as part of a two-person team, use a flathead axe and a Halligan bar to perform the following steps:

1. Size up the door, ensuring that it is locked and noting the direction in which it swings and the location of the lock(s).

2. Confirm that the hose team is in place with a charged line and is ready for the door to be forced.

3. Position the adze end of the Halligan tool in the gap between the jamb and the door, just above or below the lock(s) (Figure 15-22).

FIGURE 15-22

4. Pound the adze into place until it is well seated between the door and the jamb (Figure 15-23).

FIGURE 15-23

5. Apply force to the bar, pulling the bar outward until the door opens (Figure 15-24).

FIGURE 15-24

Level I

FIGURE 15-25 Push the forked end of a prying tool securely behind the hinge pin when forcing the hinge side of a door.

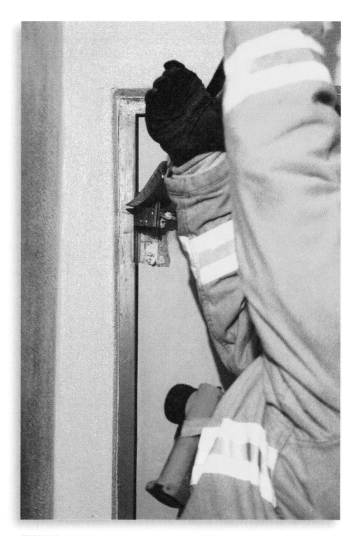

FIGURE 15-26 The screws offer little resistance to the force generated by a prying tool.

Hinge Side Method

An alternate method for forcing an outward-swinging door is to attack the exposed hinges. This method is especially useful if the door is secured by more than two locks, which is common in high-crime areas and many commercial buildings. The latch side of the door is well secured, but each hinge is held in place by only 6 to 8 screws, which can be easily forced free with a pry tool.

To force the hinges free, hook the forked end of a multipurpose prying tool behind the hinge so it locks behind the rounded hinge pin (Figure 15-25). Now simply apply outward pressure to the prying tool and the screws will strip free, pulling the entire hinge free from the door (Figure 15-26). Repeat the process until the hinges are removed and pry the door free from the jamb, allowing the locks to slip out of their keepers.

Residential Garage Doors

Residential garage doors are most often a folding panel type of door that travels up and down on rollers set in tracks. The door can be made out of steel, fiberglass, or wood (Figure 15-27). This type of door can be secured in several ways:

- By an electric door opener
- With a latch on each side that is operated individually from the inside
- By operating mechanisms on the outside that resemble a T-shaped handle
- By a single mechanism in the center of the door that, when rotated, unlocks both of the locks simultaneously

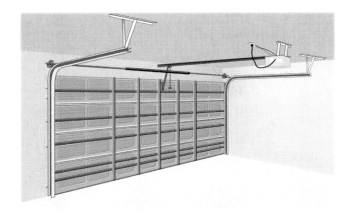

FIGURE 15-27 A typical garage door is made of hinged panels that travel on rollers set in tracks.

FIGURE 15-28 A triangular cut is very efficient for making an opening in a garage door when operating a heavy saw.

FIGURE 15-29 The release on a typical garage door opener is operated by pulling a rope.

When exposed to fire, the door mechanisms that open a garage door usually warp and the door must be forced. The quickest way to overcome this obstacle is usually to cut the door with a gasoline-powered circular saw using an aluminum oxide cutting disc. One popular method is to cut a large, triangular opening in the center of the door. Cutting a triangle-shaped opening allows you to make an adequate opening with only two cuts, as the metal will usually fall to the ground as you cut it away. However, it may be necessary to pull the cut pieces out of the way with a long-handled tool of some sort (Figure 15-28).

If the door isn't directly exposed to fire, it can usually be opened easily. First, size up the door, look-ing for external signs of locks. Cut an access opening near the lock so that you can reach in and operate the mechanism. If the door is a wood panel design, knock out a panel near the lock to do this.

If there are no external signs of locks on the garage door, then it is probably secured by an electric door opener. If this is the case, knock out a panel near the top center of the door or cut an access opening near the top if the door is made of steel so that you can reach in and pull the emergency release rope that should be hanging from the release latch near the door. A sharp tug downward is usually all it takes to release the latch. If the rope is not present, the latch can be operated by hand or pulled with a ceiling hook if it is hard to reach. The door will travel freely upward once the latch has been released (Figure 15-29).

Block any overhead door once it is opened. The door can be propped open with a long-handled tool

FIGURE 15-30 A long-handled tool, jammed in the track, will help secure a garage door in an open position.

FIGURE 15-31 Locking pliers work well for securing open a garage door.

placed in the track (Figure 15-30). A pair of locking pliers, if available, can be attached to the track near a wheel so that it blocks the door's travel as an alternative to leaving a firefighting tool behind just to block a door (Figure 15-31). These heavy doors are assisted upward and held in place by a very strong spring that can be damaged in a fire, or may simply be weak or broken from wear. If the spring isn't working properly, the door can fall violently, causing injury or trapping firefighters inside the structure when the door breaks and jams from the fall.

Residential Windows

Residential windows are usually forced by breaking the glass and clearing out the window's frame so that a large opening for ventilation as well as rescue and emergency access/egress is available during the operation. This may seem excessive, but it is important that the opening be large enough to easily pass through while wearing full protective equipment, including an SCBA. In reality, whenever we break a window, the repair usually involves replacing the entire assembly rather than the glass because it is usually more cost effective in residential construction. Therefore, clearing out the entire frame is not excessive and is important to everyone's safety.

Residential Window Construction

Residential windows usually differ from those used in commercial buildings, so we will discuss each style separately. Residential windows come in many styles. The **glazing,** which is the part of the window that allows the light to enter, is most often made of glass. However, not all glass is alike. The window assembly includes the window **sash(es),** frame, operating mechanism, and lock(s). A sash is the frame that holds the glass. There may be one or two sashes in a single window. The frame is the part of the window that is attached to the building and holds the sash(es). The operating mechanism is a mechanical crank-and-lever mechanism that opens and closes the window sash. Most residential window locks are a simple thumb latch that slides into place to secure the window (Figure 15-32).

Checkrail windows have a sash that is divided into smaller panes in a grid. The rails are made of the same material as the window frame (wood or metal). Checkrail windows are often imitated in look by the addition of ornamental "rails" that simply decorate a single pane of glass, so inspect the window closely before assuming that it is truly a checkrail style (Figure 15-33).

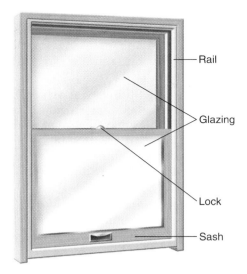

FIGURE 15-32   (a) Sash, (b) lock, (c) rail, and (d) glazing.

FIGURE 15-33   A checkrail window.

Residential Glazing   The most common type of glass used for window glazing is regular **plate glass.** Plate glass has been hardened to withstand weather and other elements. However, it breaks with little effort into large, sharp pieces when hit with a striking tool or when fire heats it. Most plate glass breaks into fragments that leave sharp, knifelike pieces hanging from the window frame. Expect to find plate glass in most residential windows.

Tempered glass is glass that has undergone a high-heat process that leaves it very strong and much more resistant to our attempts to break it with conventional striking tools. When tempered glass breaks, it shatters into hundreds of small, almost rounded pieces that fall to the ground. The principle for breaking tempered glass is to apply enough force in pounds per square inch to the surface so that the glass gives way. This takes a lot of force distributed over a square inch (about 10,000 pounds per square inch). Therefore, it's best to use a sharp tool, such as the pick of an axe or a Halligan-type tool, to reduce the amount of area to which you are applying force. Because you are reducing the surface area to a fraction of an inch, then a fraction of the force is needed to break the entire pane of tempered glass. You can expect to find tempered glass in sliding glass doors and many sliding windows.

Safety Tip!

Breaking glass is a dangerous but necessary part of our job. Wear full PPE and protect your eyes and hands whenever you break glass. Stand on the upwind side of any window you are breaking and take a moment to shake any broken pieces of glass off your gear before moving to the next window. To keep the shards away from you and your hands, use as long a tool as possible to break the glass. If possible, position your hands higher than the head of the tool as you strike the glass to prevent pieces of glass from traveling down the handle and striking your hands.

Level I

Polycarbonate glazing is a very hard, strong, and clear plastic material that is more commonly referred to by the trade name Lexan. Polycarbonate glazing is used from time to time in residential construction, especially as a replacement glazing for broken windows. It is less expensive and easier to work with for the "do-it-yourselfer" than regular glass. Polycarbonate glazing does not break or cut easily with hand tools. The best way to get around this is either to use a carbide-type circular saw to cut the glazing or to attack the window frame, driving the glazing out of the opening.

Residential Window Types Most windows used in residential construction have either a wood or an aluminum frame. Both are fairly easy to break with conventional tools. They come in several styles that are classified by the way they open. These styles include:

- *Single-hung windows*—These windows have a fixed pane glass, usually on top, and a lower sash that slides vertically. The lock may be in the center, or two locks may be spaced evenly along the center frame (Figure 15-34).
- *Double-hung windows*—Both the upper and the lower sashes in a double-hung window slide vertically. Most of these windows have locks on each side of the sash (Figure 15-35).
- *Awning windows*—These windows have mechanisms that, when operated, allow one or more sashes to pivot on hinges so that the sash swings out. There may not be a lock on this type of window because the cranking mechanism is designed to hold the window sash in position (Figure 15-36).
- *Sliding windows*—Sliding windows will have one or more sashes that slide horizontally in a track. This type of window may have one or more locks. They are often secured with a piece of wood or metal that is dropped into the sliding track at the bottom, preventing the window from traveling along the track (Figure 15-37).
- *Thermal pane windows*—Energy-efficient windows have two panes of glass in each sash and may be of any of the above types of windows.

FIGURE 15-35 Both sashes travel up and down on a double-hung window.

FIGURE 15-34 A single-hung window has only one sash that travels up and down.

FIGURE 15-36 An awning window.

FIGURE 15-37 A sliding window with a drop lock in place.

FIGURE 15-38 Thermal pane windows have more than one pane of glass, and will not show signs of heat as quickly as a single window pane.

Thermal pane windows are very resistant to heat. They conceal the amount of heat inside a burning room from anyone outside who feels the outer glass pane to check for heat (Figure 15-38).

- *Jalousie windows*—This type of window has small panes of glass that are connected to the cranking mechanism by small frames on either end of the glass. The panes of glass do not seal well and are seldom used in modern construction. The glazing may be tempered glass or plate glass in jalousie windows. Because little is gained from forcing jalousie windows, the best course of action is to simply clear the entire window opening by breaking the glass and clearing the opening of any remaining debris (Figure 15-39).

Forcing Residential Windows

Generally speaking, there are two types of forcible entry through a residential window. If there is no fire or there is any reason that breaking the glass is not desirable, then *forcing* the window is the best course of action. Forcing involves breaking the latch free and sliding the window open. This type of entry can be used to clear residual smoke or access the home during an EMS incident in which the patient cannot get to the door to unlock it for your entry. Forcing involves using a prying tool to apply pressure to the moving sash. The goal is to break the locks free from their latch and operate the window in a conventional manner.

FIGURE 15-39 Jalousie windows are best forced by simply breaking the glass and cleaning away any sharp edges.

If the need is for a large, clear opening for entry or emergency egress from a burning building, then forcing a window most often involves breaking the glass and clearing out the entire window frame. We refer to this action as *clearing* the window opening. It is best accomplished using a long-handled tool such as a ceiling hook while standing on the upwind side of the window. Clearing requires striking the glass near the center of each sash. Aluminum-framed windows can be cleared quickly from the frame by striking the center frame in the middle with a sharp, downward motion. This usually causes the outer frame to pull away from the structure. The entire assembly can then be pulled free using the leverage provided by the ceiling hook. Wood-framed windows will take a little more force to clear than aluminum-framed windows. You should deliver the force with a heavy tool such as an axe or a Halligan bar rather than a ceiling hook.

Review It!

Go to the DVD, navigate to Chapter 15, select *"Forcing a Residential Window,"* and navigate to the window type you would like to review.

Practice It!

Forcing a Residential Window—Single- or Double-Hung and Sliding Type

Working as part of a two-person team, use a flathead axe and a Halligan bar to perform the following steps:

1. Size up the window, ensuring that it is locked and noting the location of the lock(s).
2. Confirm that the hose team is in place with a charged line and is ready for the window to be forced.
3. Position the forked end of the Halligan tool in the gap between the windowsill and the sash (Figure 15-40).

FIGURE 15-40

4. Pound the fork into place until it is well seated (Figure 15-41).

FIGURE 15-41

5. Apply steady force to the Halligan bar until the locks break free (Figure 15-42).

FIGURE 15-42

Go to the DVD, navigate to Chapter 15, select *"Forcing a Residential Window,"* and navigate to the window type you would like to review.

Practice It!

Clearing a Residential Window

Working as part of a two-person team, use a long-handled tool to perform the following steps:

1. Size up the window, ensuring that it is locked and noting the location of the lock(s).

2. Confirm that the hose team is in place with a charged line and is ready for the window to be forced.

3. Stand to the upwind side of the window, with full personal protective equipment in place.

4. Swing the heavy end of the tool so that it strikes the upper pane of glass near the center, and then swing it to strike the lower pane (Figure 15-43).

FIGURE 15-43

5. Strike the center rail near the center to break it free (Figure 15-44).

FIGURE 15-44

6. Pull the entire window frame clear of the building, creating a large opening free of glass shards (Figure 15-45).

FIGURE 15-45

Level I

 **Review It!**

Go to DVD, navigate to Chapter 15, select *"Forcing a Residential Window,"* and navigate to the window type you would like to review.

Practice It!

Forcing a Residential Window—Awning Type

Working as part of a two-person team, use a flathead axe and a Halligan bar to perform the following steps:

1. Size up the window, ensuring that it is locked and noting the location of the lock(s).

2. Confirm that the hose team is in place with a charged line and is ready for the window to be forced.

3. Standing on the upwind side, break the pane of glass closest to the cranking mechanism. Clear the entire window frame of any sharp shards of glass that remain (Figure 15-46).

FIGURE 15-46

4. Reach in and operate the window mechanism with a gloved hand (Figure 15-47).

FIGURE 15-47

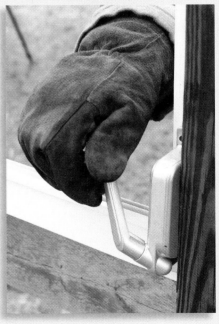

Padlocks and Chains

The most basic type of security device we encounter is the simple lock and hasp. Padlocks come in several styles and are made of different types of materials, some of which are extremely hard to cut.

When a padlock is used to secure a chain around a fence or a gate, for example, it is often easier to cut the chain than to cut the padlock itself. Bolt cutters usually make easy work of this process. When cutting a chain, try to cut a link very close to the lock. The chain should remain long enough to encircle the object it is securing so that the property owner can resecure the object by simply placing a new lock in the next link of the chain (Figure 15-48).

 **Tip!**

If possible, have a padlock available so that you can secure the property if the owner cannot respond to the scene to lock the gate or secure the other object with a lock and chain. Pass the lock through the shackle of the original lock and the next link of the chain. That way the property owner can still access the area later using the original lock.

When cutting a padlock attached to a hasp, place the **shackle** as deeply as possible in the bolt cutter's jaws and apply force. The pieces of the lock can fly when the shackle breaks, so be sure that all of your personal protective equipment is in place.

It is often quicker and easier to break away the entire lock and hasp than to cut the lock. To do this, place the pick end of a Halligan-type bar in the lock's shackle and pound it with a striking tool until the hasp and lock pulls free from the door.

▰▰ KEY WORD ▰▰

shackle The U-shaped portion of a padlock that moves from a locked to an unlocked position.

Forcible Entry—Commercial Buildings

Because the building codes and security requirements for commercial buildings differ from those for residential buildings, the steps we take to force entry into commercial buildings also differ. In general, the locks found in a typical commercial door are heavier and stronger. Similarly, the glazing in the doors and windows is thicker, stronger, and set in stronger frames with more secure locks than we will expect to encounter in residential applications. Many businesses use additional security measures after normal operating hours, including iron grates, steel overhead rolling doors, and thick steel bars, to secure their businesses against thieves. All of these impede our access and egress from a burning structure, and should be considered early in any operation.

FIGURE 15-48 Cut a link in the chain closest to the padlock so it can be secured later.

FIGURE 15-49 A mortise lock will usually have the latch and locking bolt in the same mechanism.

Through-the-Lock Entry

Most commercial entry doors have a very strong lock, called a *mortise lock,* set in a strong frame. Mortise locks fit into a large cavity that is formed in the door when it is manufactured. The locking mechanism in a commercial mortise lock may be a deadbolt, in which the locking bolt travels horizontally into the doorjamb, similar to a tubular deadbolt. Alternately, it may feature a pendant-style lock that swings vertically into the opening. A mortise-style lock may also have the latch and the locking bolt in the same mechanism, both operating from a single key (Figure 15-49).

The through-the-lock method for forcing this type of door involves extracting the key cylinder from the door and manipulating the internal mechanism to unlock the door. Glass entry doors commonly used in commercial applications have a thick tempered glass glazing and usually have a heavy metal push bar across the center. It is much safer to force the door open so that it swings freely on its hinges, rather than simply smashing the glass and ducking underneath the push bar. An added advantage to forcing the door to swing is that it remains intact, allowing the doorway to be secured after the incident, if necessary.

The tools of choice for extracting the key cylinder are the K-Tool, a lock puller, or even a good pair of pliers or a pipe wrench. The K-Tool and other types of lock pullers work by driving the extracting part of the tool over the key cylinder and applying pressure to extract the cylinder. Pliers and pipe wrenches work by locking down on the cylinder and turning it coun-terclockwise. In most cases, the only damage done is to the soft brass lock cylinder, which is relatively inexpensive and can be quickly replaced (Figure 15-50).

Key tools are used to manipulate the locking mechanism. These tools come in different shapes, each designed for a specific type of lock. The flat key tool has a curved, pointed end and is useful for manipulating most mortise locks, while the pointed straight end works well with several types of tubular or rim locks. The square tool works for tubular- and rim-style locks that have a square opening for the key cylinder or doorknob (Figure 15-51).

FIGURE 15-50   A K-Tool or a pair of pliers can be used to extract the cylinder to allow you access to the locking mechanism.

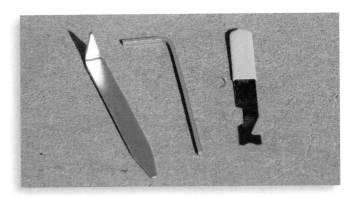

FIGURE 15-51   Various types of key tools are used to manipulate the lock's mechanism to open the door.

⇨ Practice It!

Through-the-Lock Method—Extracting the Key Cylinder

Working as a two-person team, use the following method for through-the-lock entry:

1. Inspect the door to be sure it is locked and feel for heat.
2. Radio to the Incident Commander the location of the door you are going to force and receive confirmation that it should be forced.

3. Place the lock-pulling tool over the cylinder until it "bites." Drive the tool over the cylinder and extract it from the lock, exposing the mechanism (Figures 15-52 and 15-53).

FIGURE 15-52

FIGURE 15-53

Variation: Use pliers or a pipe wrench to remove the cylinder.

Review It!

Go to the DVD, navigate to Chapter 15, select *"Forcing a Commercial Door,"* and navigate to the method you would like to review.

Practice It!

Manipulating a Locking Mechanism

Use the following method for through-the-lock entry, starting with the key cylinder already extracted:

1. Look into the opening and determine the location of the locking mechanism.

2. For a mortise-type lock, insert the angled end of the key tool and depress the roller cam or other type of spring-type latch that allows the lock to move. Move the locking mechanism to either the "5 o'clock" or the "7 o'clock" position to open the lock (Figure 15-54).

3. For a rim or tubular lock, insert the appropriate type of key tool and twist the mechanism to operate the lock (Figure 15-55).

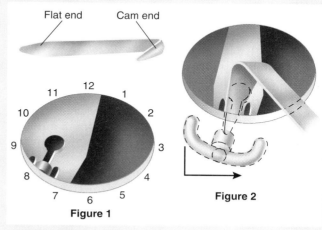

FIGURE 15-54

FIGURE 15-55

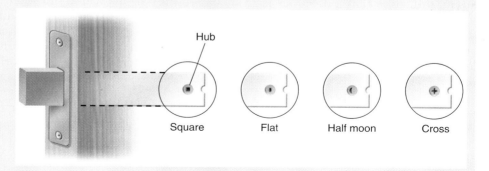

Level I

Fortified Doors

Because the rear doors to most mercantile and many other types of commercial occupancies are out of plain view, these doors are most often the most fortified against crime. Most life safety codes require that these doors be operable as emergency exits during normal operating hours. However, most business use added measures to secure them after hours, and we can't assume that these measures have been removed when the occupant is open for business.

One device commonly used to fortify these doors is the drop bar. A drop bar may be made of wood or steel. It rests in saddles that have been attached to the door to hold the drop bar across the entire door opening. The drop bar prevents the door from swinging open, even when unlocked by normal means. Some indicators that a drop bar is in place are the rounded heads of bolt showing on the outside of the door. However, because many of these saddles are welded to the interior surface of the door, there may be no outward signs that a drop bar is in place (Figure 15-56).

FIGURE 15-56 A drop bar can be made of wood or steel. There may be no outward signs that indicate the presence of a drop bar.

If you suspect that a drop bar is in place, it is often possible to cut an access hole in the door using a circular saw. This allows you to reach in and remove the bar. Still, as an added measure, it is common to find the drop bar secured in place with padlocks on either side to prevent this type of entry. If a quick entry is desired, then cutting the door from top to bottom, directly through the center of the door and the drop bar, may be your best choice of entry method.

Overhead Rolling Doors and Security Gates

Overhead rolling doors made of steel slats are used as outer security doors after business hours for many commercial applications. They may also be found inside large commercial buildings where they are locked in a closed position after hours to segregate high-security areas inside the building. These steel doors might be operated by a motorized opening device. They might also be manually operated by a chain that rolls the door up on a large drum attached to the door header. This chain is usually secured with a padlock. Even though the chain appears smaller and easier to cut than the padlock, do not cut the chain—if you cut it, you will not be able to easily open the door (Figure 15-57).

The most effective way to overcome overhead rolling doors is to make two diagonal and intersecting cuts from top to bottom to create a triangular opening. Remember, as you cut away the steel slats, the door becomes lighter. This is important because overhead rolling doors have very strong springs to assist the normal operating process. Once the door has been cut, make sure to keep it secured in the down position to prevent the rest of the door from flying violently upward. Security gates are often seen inside shopping malls after business hours. The steel mesh grids work on a mechanism very similar to the mechanism for overhead rolling doors. Through-the-lock entry is usually a good method for overcoming these types of doors. Cutting with a circular saw is also an option (Figure 15-58).

FIGURE 15-57 Do not cut the chain on an overhead rolling door or it will be very difficult to open the door.

FIGURE 15-58 Security gates are typically found in shopping malls.

Making Access

You have probably noticed that there are several methods to choose from when creating access to a structure. Not every method will work every time or for every firefighter. Access problems may prevent you from positioning in a way that allows you to use one method, so an alternative may be necessary. Personal size and strength may prevent you from using brute force to overcome a tough door. However, the leverage provided by a tool, when applied with a technique that you master through practice, will help you overcome the situation. The first step is to practice every technique until you have mastered forcible entry. Next, mentally size up the buildings in your area, considering the types of openings (or potential openings) that may be necessary to access a victim or rescue a trapped firefighter or—even more importantly—to get you and your team *out* of a burning building when something goes wrong.

Knowledge Assessment

Signed Documentation Tear-Out Sheet

Forcible Entry and Exit—Chapter 15

Name: _____

Fill out the ten-question quiz below, the Knowledge Assessment Sheet, by circling the correct answer for each question. When finished, sign it and give it to your instructor/Company Officer for his or her signature. Turn in this Knowledge Assessment Sheet to the proper person as part of the documentation that you have completed your training for this chapter.

1. All of the following are examples of multiuse forcible entry tools *except* the _____.
   a. Halligan tool
   b. Hooligan tool
   c. K-Tool
   d. Kelly bar

2. When paired with a Halligan tool, a pickhead axe is a good striking tool for forcible entry.
   a. True
   b. False

3. Which tool is best designed for through-the-lock forcible entry?
   a. Halligan tool
   b. Hooligan tool
   c. K-Tool
   d. Kelly bar

4. Which way do exterior residential doors usually swing?
   a. Inward
   b. Outward
   c. Both inward and outward
   d. This is of no concern for forcing entry

5. Residential exterior door locks are most commonly of the following types *except* _____.
   a. tubular
   b. rim
   c. mortise
   d. deadbolt

6. Which part of a Halligan bar is usually used to apply direct force to an inward-swinging door?
   a. Fork
   b. Pick
   c. Adze
   d. Flat

7. The locking mechanism in a mortise-type lock operates either the deadbolt or the latch, but never both.

   a. True
   b. False

8. All of the following tools are useful for through-the-lock forcible entry *except* the _____.

   a. K-Tool
   b. Halligan bar
   c. flat axe
   d. pick axe

9. Through-the-lock entry is a very effective method for opening the rear door on a commercial structure that has a drop bar in place.

   a. True
   b. False

10. Which is the best tool for forcing a commercial door that is reinforced with a drop-bar lock?

   a. K-Tool
   b. Hydraulic door opener
   c. Chain saw
   d. Circular saw

Student Signature and Date _____   Instructor/Company Officer Signature and Date _____

Skills Assessment

Signed Documentation Tear-Out Sheet

Forcible Entry and Exit—Chapter 15

Name: _____

Fill out the Skills Assessment Sheet below. Have your instructor/Company Officer check off and initial each skill you demonstrate. When you are finished, sign this page and give to your instructor/Company Officer for his or her signature. Turn in this Skills Assessment Sheet to the proper person as part of the documentation that you have completed your training for this chapter.

Skill	Completed	Initials
1. When given a choice of several forcible entry tools, identify each type.	_____	_____
2. Identify by example the types of doors and locks used in residential construction.	_____	_____
3. Force a simulated residential door that swings inward.	_____	_____
4. Force a simulated residential door that swings outward.	_____	_____
5. Force a residential-style casement window.	_____	_____
6. Force a residential-style awning window.	_____	_____
7. Demonstrate through-the-lock entry methods.	_____	_____
8. Operate a gasoline-powered circular saw.	_____	_____

Student Signature and Date _____   Instructor/Company Officer Signature and Date _____

Ladders

What You Will Learn in This Chapter

In this chapter we will talk about the different types of ladders and their use. Then we will demonstrate basic laddering practices. We'll discuss the strategies and tactics for deciding where and how to place ladders on an emergency scene. Finally, we'll cover the care and maintenance of these important access tools.

What You Will Be Able to Do

After reading this chapter and practicing the skills in a classroom setting, you will be able to:

1. Describe a straight ladder design.
2. Describe a typical roof ladder design.
3. Explain the different working parts of a typical extension ladder.

4. Describe how attic ladders are used on a structural fire.
5. Briefly describe the general construction of Fire Service ladders, including the duty ratings of straight, roof, and extension ladders.
6. Explain what is meant by the proper climbing angle for ladders.
7. Demonstrate a beam raise using a straight or extension ladder.
8. Demonstrate how to position a roof ladder on a roof for use as a work platform.
9. Demonstrate how to properly tie a halyard on an extended extension ladder.
10. Demonstrate how to work as a member of a three- or four-firefighter team to flat-carry and raise an extension ladder.
11. As a member of a firefighter team, demonstrate a method for carrying and raising an extension ladder equipped with staypoles.

12. Explain what to look for in stable surfaces to rest the tip and butt of a ladder when placing it against a building.

13. Discuss the rule of thumb for selecting the right height ladder.

14. Explain the four main reasons ladders are placed on the scene of an emergency.

15. Demonstrate how to lock in and work from a ladder.

16. Demonstrate various methods for moving conscious and unconscious victims down a ladder for rescue.

17. Describe how to use a ladder as a support for tools and equipment and as an anchor point for hoisting equipment.

18. Explain how to inspect a ladder for damage and how to perform routine maintenance for a ladder.

About Ladders

One of the most important access tools that firefighters can use on the emergency scene is the ladder. Ladders allow you to reach upward as well as downward on the fireground in order to access another level for firefighting or rescue, or to perhaps create an additional access and exit point for crews already inside a structure. There are many types and configurations of ladders, depending on their intended use. Ladders that are designed for Fire Service must meet minimum construction requirements and are very safe when properly used.

If safely removed, carried, and raised, ladders can become lifesavers on the emergency scene. Ladders have saved countless firefighters' lives, allowing them to quickly escape a building when things went bad inside during a fire operation. Your job will be to learn ladder basics that will help you understand and be able to use the most common types of Fire Service ladders. As a firefighter, you must be proficient in using and caring for the Fire Service ladders that your fire department has available to use on the emergency scene.

General Ladder Design and Construction

Fire Service ladders are designed to be used for rescue, firefighting, and training. They should not be used for any other purpose. They can be constructed of metal, wood, or fiberglass.

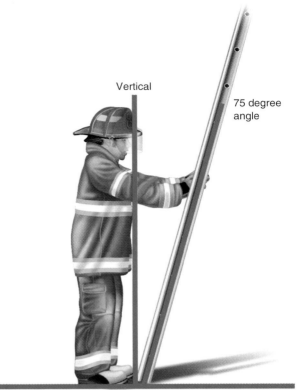

Correct climbing angle for a ladder

FIGURE 16-1 The proper climbing angle for straight and extension ladders.

Ladders are composed of a set of steps called *rungs* that are held in place by two side beams (or rails). The top of the ladder is called the *tip* and the bottom of the ladder is called the *heel* or the *butt*. Spurs or footpads are located at the butt of the ladder.

All Fire Service ladders, with the exception of folding ladders, are rated for 750 pounds of weight. This rating is called the *duty rating* or the *duty load rating* of the ladder. Folding ladders are duty rated at 300 pounds. This duty rating includes all personnel, hose lines, tools, and equipment placed on the ladder at any one time. Note that the duty load rating is only applicable if the ladder is positioned at the correct climbing angle.

The proper climbing angle for all extension and straight ladders is 70 to 76 degrees, with 75 degrees being the best angle. All ladders should be secured at the top by tying off the tip or at the bottom (butted or heeled by a firefighter) (Figure 16-1).

Heat sensor labels are located on the side beams below the second rung from the tip of the ladder and also in the middle of the ladder. These labels change color when exposed to extreme heat and indicate

FIGURE 16-2 Heat sensor labels are located on the side beams below the second rung from the tip of the ladder and also in the middle of the ladder.

potential heat damage to the ladder (Figure 16-2). There are also testing certification labels on approved Fire Service ladders. These should be clearly visible on one of the beams.

 Safety Tip!

All ladders, regardless of construction materials, can potentially conduct electricity. Metal naturally conducts electricity, and any wet wood or fiberglass can also conduct electricity. For this reason, you should always use extreme caution when placing any ladder. Check for overhead electrical service lines and avoid these areas with all ladders.

Types of Ladders

There are many types of ladders available today. The Fire Service can employ any of several types on a fire scene. The ladders required to be carried on engine and truck companies are mandated by NFPA 1901, *Standard for Automotive Fire Apparatus.* Engine companies are presently required to carry a minimum of one roof ladder, one extension ladder, and one attic ladder. Truck companies are required to carry a minimum of 115 feet of ladders (not including the aerial ladder). These ladders include one attic ladder, two roof ladders, and two extension ladders. However, you should remember that these standards are revised every several years and can change.

FIGURE 16-3 Straight ladder.

Straight Ladders

Straight ladders have one continuous section of **rungs** connecting two **beams.** They can range from 10 to 20 feet in length (Figure 16-3).

■ KEY WORDS ■

beams The side pieces of a ladder that run from the tip to the butt of the ladder. They are held in place by rungs that are positioned at equal intervals between the two beams and that serve as steps for the ladder.

rungs The steps of a ladder that connect the two ladder beams. They are located at regular intervals on the ladder running parallel to the ground.

Roof Ladders

Roof ladders are basically straight ladders with folding hooks added at the tip. They are designed for reach and support on roof areas. Generally speaking, Engine companies carry a minimum of one 14-foot roof ladder (Figure 16-4).

FIGURE 16-4 Roof ladder.

Extension Ladders

Engine companies carry at least one extension ladder, which can be 24 to 35 feet in length, depending on the needs of the fire department. Extension ladders are made up of a **base section** as well as one or two **fly sections** of decreasing width so that one fits inside the other and both fit inside the base section. Each section is essentially a straight ladder (Figure 16-5). The base section has a pulley and **halyard rope** that is used to extend the fly section or sections (Figure 16-6). Each fly section has locking devices called pawls (or dogs), which secure the section to a rung of another section when it is extended to the desired height (Figure 16-7). These are located on the inside of each side beam of the fly section. The base and the fly sections are held in place by guides or brackets in which they slide. The fly sections also have a pulley with a halyard rope attached. A pulley and the rest of the halyard rope are connected to the base section. As the halyard is pulled, the fly sections extend upward from the base section to the desired height.

In addition, you may come across extension ladders more than 40 feet long, which are referred to as pole (or bangor) ladders. These ladders have addi-

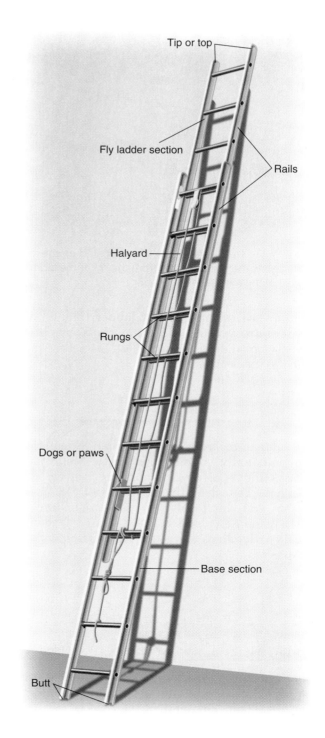

FIGURE 16-5 Extension ladder parts.

tional devices called **staypoles** (or tormentor poles) attached to the outside of each base section beam. Staypoles are used to assist in stabilizing these large extension ladders while the ladder is extended and positioned into place on a building (Figure 16-8).

FIGURE 16-6   Halyard and pulley.

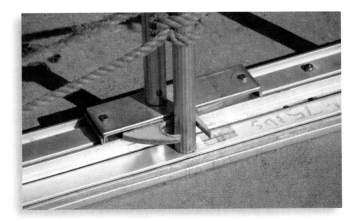

FIGURE 16-7   Pawls, which are also called dogs.

FIGURE 16-8   Extension ladder with staypoles.

KEY WORDS

base section   The widest and sturdiest section of an extension ladder in which the other sections (fly sections) move up and down to extend the reach of the ladder. The base section includes the butt end of the ladder, which features butt spurs and pads that rest on the ground as the ladder is raised into place.

fly sections   The sections of an extension ladder that are located inside the base section. They extend the length of the extension ladder from its base section as the halyard rope is pulled.

halyard rope   A rope that is used to raise and lower fly sections on an extension ladder. The rope is connected through pulleys to all the sections of the extension ladder so that, when it is pulled, the fly sections of the ladder rise into place.

staypoles   Devices located on larger extension ladders that assist in stabilizing the ladder after it has been extended and lowered into place on a building. They are connected to the outside of each beam of the base section of the extension ladder.

FIGURE 16-9   Attic ladder.

Specialized Ladders

This category of ladders includes **attic ladders** (folding ladders) and **combination ladders** (Figures 16-9 and 16-10). Specialized ladders can also include any utility ladder, like a folding A-frame ladder that may be carried on a fire apparatus.

FIGURE 16-10   Combination ladder.

FIGURE 16-11   Attic ladders are carried into the structure and unfolded as they are lifted into the attic or ceiling overhead access opening.

Attic Ladders

Attic ladders are the primary type of folding ladders you will use on a structural fire incident. They are made up of two beams that are grooved so that the connecting rungs can swivel into the side beams. This feature allows the ladder to fold into one long, narrow piece for easier access into a structure for use accessing attic areas. They are duty rated at a 300-pound capacity, meaning one person at a time on the ladder. However, you must still have one firefighter support the ladder while a firefighter climbs it.

Attic ladders can be used for quick access to elevated areas outside a building. However, they are mainly designed for use inside a building to access above the ceiling spaces for investigation and extinguishment purposes. They are carried into the struc-

ture and unfolded as they are lifted into the attic or ceiling overhead access opening. You should be sure they are placed tip up and locked into the open position. Also, be sure the tip is resting on a solid area like a rafter or a joist. Remember to have someone secure the butt while you are ascending or descending the ladder (Figure 16-11).

▓ KEY WORD ▓

attic ladders   These ladders are used to access interior ceiling openings leading to attic spaces above. They have two beams connected by rungs, which fold into the beams and collapse the ladder into a narrow configuration for ease of use inside a building. These are duty rated at 300 pounds.

Combination Ladders

Combination ladders are very handy and adaptable at a fire incident. They are usually made of two small sections of ladder, each 6 to 8 feet in length. These

FIGURE 16-12 A combination ladder set up as a small extension ladder.

sections can be extended like a small utility extension ladder as well as configured in an A-frame style so that firefighters can go up and over an obstruction. Again, as with all ladders, be sure someone is supporting the ladder as it is being used. Combination ladders are also duty rated at 300 pounds (Figures 16-12 and 16-13).

KEY WORD

combination ladders Specially designed ladders made up of two short sections of ladder. This type of ladder can be used as a small extension ladder or folded into a small A-frame configuration.

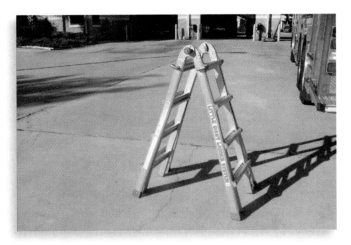

FIGURE 16-13 A combination ladder set up as an A-frame ladder.

Basic Laddering Practices

In our first text, *Safe Firefighting: First Things First*, Chapter 11, we covered how to assist in removing, carrying, and placing straight, roof, and extension ladders on the outside of a building. In this text, *Safe Firefighting: Inside Operations*, you are required to learn some more details about carrying, placing, and climbing various ladders on the fire scene, including the following skills:

- Beam raise
- Roof ladders for roof work
- Tying a halyard
- Extension ladder—three- or four-firefighter flat carry
- Extension ladder—three- or four-firefighter raise
- Carrying and raising extension ladders equipped with staypoles climbing ladders

Review It!

Review *Safe Firefighting: First Things First,* Chapter 11, "Single-Family-Dwelling Fires," and also review the *Safe Firefighting: First Things First* DVD, Chapter 11, "Removing and Stowing Ladders, Straight Ladders, Roof Ladders, Extension Ladder—Single Firefighter, and Extension Ladder— Two Firefighters."

Small Ladder Raise

As an alternative to the flat raise, you can also position any ladder—straight, roof, or extension ladder—in one smooth motion without setting the ladder down and repositioning for the raise.

View It!

Go to the DVD, navigate to Chapter 16, and select *"Beam Raise."*

 Practice It!

Small Ladder Raise

Use the following steps to raise the ladder:

1. As you approach the building with the ladder in a shoulder carry position spike the ladder next to the building and use the building to steady the butt of the ladder. Raise the ladder directly from your shoulder in one smooth motion.

2. Place the ladder at a safe climbing angle as discussed earlier and secure the ladder.

FIGURE 16-14

Roof Ladders for Roof Work

If a roof ladder is to be placed for use as a foothold or work platform on a roof, then the hooks should be in the open position. The ladder is passed up by firefighters already positioned on another ladder and slid into place with the hooks finally flipped down into position so they can grasp the ridge line of the roof surface.

 View It!

Go to the DVD, navigate to Chapter 16, and select *"Roof Ladders for Roof Work."*

 Practice It!

Roof Ladders for Roof Work

Use the following method to place a roof ladder as a foothold and work platform on a roof area:

1. Unfold the hooks (Figure 16-15). Then pass the roof ladder up to the roof area by giving it to the firefighters located on the ladder already in place.

FIGURE 16-15

2. Push up the roof ladder to the roof ridge, with the hooks pointing up (Figure 16-16).

FIGURE 16-16

3. When the ladder is positioned, turn it over so the hooks can grasp the roof ridge, securing the tip of the ladder into place (Figure 16-17).

4. You can now move up the roof ladder and use it as a foothold or a platform to perform jobs with greater safety.

FIGURE 16-17

Safety Tip!

Never place the roof ladder over hot or damaged areas on a roof. If the roof is damaged near the ladder, it is not safe to go on the roof. Advise your Company Officer and move to a safe area or consider a safer option.

Tying a Halyard

When an extension ladder is extended, there is excess halyard rope at the base of the ladder that should be tied both to secure the ladder's height and to keep the halyard aligned and neat to avoid a tripping hazard.

View It!

Go to the DVD, navigate to Chapter 16, and select "*Tying a Halyard.*"

Practice It!

Tying a Halyard

Use the following method to tie a halyard:

1. Standing at the bottom of the ladder, gather the slack in the halyard rope and wrap it around the two rungs directly in front of you on the ladder.

—Continued

2. Next, tie a clove hitch knot in the excess halyard rope onto the upper most of the two rungs.

3. Finish by tying a safety knot in the doubled halyard rope (Figure 16-18).

FIGURE 16-18

Extension Ladder—Three- or Four-Firefighter Flat Carry

When larger extension ladders are used, such as those that are 35 feet or longer, it may be necessary to have three or four firefighters to carry the ladder. With more than two firefighters, a flat carry is more effective.

 View It!

Go to the DVD, navigate to Chapter 16, and select "*Extension Ladder—Three- or Four-Firefighter Flat Carry.*"

Practice It!

Extension Ladder—Three- or Four-Firefighter Flat Carry

Use the following guidelines for a flat carry of an extension ladder with more than two firefighters:

1. Position the ladder flat with the butt facing the building. Check for any overhead obstructions or electrical hazards. Advise the team members where the ladder is to be placed.

2. With three firefighters, position one at each end on the same side and the third firefighter in the middle on the opposite side, all kneeling and facing away from the building (Figure 16-19).

FIGURE 16-19

3. On the command *"Ready, lift"* from the firefighter in charge at the butt, grasp the rung near the beam closest to you. Then lift and swing your opposite shoulder under the beam as you all stand up, all in one motion (Figure 16-20).

4. When you are all in position at the building with the ladder, the firefighter in command calls out, *"Ready, lower."* All firefighters grasp the nearest rung and swing out from under the ladder and lower it to the ground, all in one motion.

FIGURE 16-20

With four firefighters, position one at each end or beam and use the same commands. Maneuver to place the ladder flat on your shoulders. Carry and place it at the building (Figure 16-21).

FIGURE 16-21

Extension Ladder—Three- or Four-Firefighter Raise

As a member of a team of more than two firefighters raising an extension ladder, consider a well-coordinated effort. This will make your efforts much easier and more effective.

 **View It!**

Go to the DVD, navigate to Chapter 16, and select *"Extension Ladder—Three- or Four-Firefighter Raise."*

➡ **Practice It!**

Extension Ladder—Three- or Four-Firefighter Raise

Use the following methods to raise an extension ladder using three or four firefighters:

1. With the ladder positioned at the building on the ground, two firefighters lift the ladder and proceed hand under hand. The other one or two firefighters act as safety on either side of the ladder, ready to grasp the ladder if it starts to fall. As an alternative, the two firefighters not lifting the ladder can anchor the butt end as demonstrated earlier.

2. If the three- or four-member team has just arrived at the building with the ladder, they can elect to place the ladder and raise it in one motion without completely placing the ladder on the ground first. The one or two firefighters at the butt end of the

—Continued

ladder simply swing out and lower their end down to the bottom of the building wall. Alternately, they can anchor the butt end as the one or two firefighters at the tip continue under the ladder, raising it as they progress hand under hand on the rungs or on the beams (Figure 16-22).

FIGURE 16-22

3. The two firefighters who were at the butt during the lift reposition, one at the outside of each beam, as one firefighter uses the halyard to extend the extension ladder into place.

4. Position the ladder at the proper climbing angle, tie the halyard, and pivot and secure the ladder in place.

Safety Tip!

When steadying an extension ladder by holding the beam, always keep your hands and fingers away from the track or guides in the base and fly beams. Severe injury can result if your fingers or hands are snagged or caught by a fly section in the beam.

Carrying and Raising Extension Ladders Equipped with Staypoles

Extension ladders equipped with staypoles are more than 40 feet in length. These ladders usually have three fly sections with staypoles on the outside of either beam of the base section. Many times, fire departments must use these large extension ladders as a substitute when aerial apparatus are not available to the community. These ladders will be quite heavy and may require up to six people to safely carry them and raise them into place.

 Practice It!

Carrying and Raising Extension Ladders Equipped with Staypoles

Working as a member of a team, use the following procedure to carry and raise a staypole ladder:

1. Position the ladder with the butt facing the building. The team first checks for overhead obstructions and electrical hazards. Then they discuss where they are going to place the ladder at the building.

2. Six firefighters position themselves, kneeling (with three along each beam, facing away from the butt).

3. The command "*Ready, lift*" is given and the team lifts the ladder and swings their shoulders under the beam, the same as in the flat carry with the smaller extension ladder (Figure 16-23).

4. They carry the ladder into position at the building, with the butt a few feet away from the structure. On the command "*Ready, lower,*" they swing out from under the ladder, grasping the nearest rung, and lower the ladder.

FIGURE 16-23

5. Two firefighters position at the butt to anchor it as two firefighters position at the tip, ready to lift the ladder. The two firefighters midway on each beam, reposition at the staypoles on either beam. The staypoles are extended away from the beams. On the command "*Ready, lift,*" the two firefighters at the tip begin to raise the ladder, hand under hand (Figure 16-24). Simultaneously, the two firefighters at the staypoles push up to take some weight off the beams as the ladder raises into position.

FIGURE 16-24

6. When the ladder has been positioned for raising the fly, the firefighters on the staypoles position themselves, one in line with the ladder rungs and one perpendicular to the ladder rungs. This positioning provides maximum stabilization while the flies are extended by the two firefighters who just raised the ladder from the tip (Figure 16-25).

7. The two firefighters who anchored the ladder assist with holding the ladder at each beam as the ladder flies are extended to the desired height. The ladder is lowered into place with the proper climbing angle established.

FIGURE 16-25

—Continued

8. The final step is to secure the ladder in place at the tip or butt and rotate the staypoles in toward the building, setting them for climbing. Tie the halyard, and the ladder is ready for climbing (Figure 16-26).

FIGURE 16-26

Climbing Ladders

Properly placed ladders are very safe for climbing. Always pay attention to what you are doing and always be deliberate with your techniques.

Normal Climbing

After checking for any overhead obstructions and electrical hazards, step on the first rung as you grasp the rung directly in front of you and begin to climb. The overall object of climbing without a tool is to keep three points of contact with your hands and feet as you climb. You can also grasp the side beams and slide along them with your hands as you climb. Keep your body perpendicular to the ground or very slightly leaning in toward the ladder as you ascend and descend the ladder (Figure 16-27).

 Safety Tip!

Any time you are on a Fire Service ladder, you should have either the tip or the butt end of the ladder secured. Otherwise, the ladder could shift dangerously to one side or the other, resulting in serious injury.

FIGURE 16-27 The overall goal of climbing without a tool is to keep three points of contact with your hands and feet as you climb.

Encumbered Climb

If you need to carry a tool in one hand as you climb up or down a ladder, grasp the beam with your free hand and slide your hand up or down as needed, not releasing your grip. The weight of the tool may also cause you to lean a little inward toward the ladder as you move (Figure 16-28). Keep in mind that you can also climb to the elevated location and drop a utility rope to a firefighter below, hoisting your tool to your location as an alternative to carrying the tool.

For placement on fire escapes, rooftops, and balconies, the ladder tip should extend four to five rungs above the edge of the level on which you wish to step off. This upward extension also provides a good handhold for you. For window openings, place the ladder so that the tip rests on the window sill. When you reach the desired location and wish to step off onto the roof or into a balcony, be sure to check the surface you are about to step on before making that first step. Use a Halligan bar, an axe, or a ceiling hook to do this check, tapping the surface to check for stability and solidness.

Ladder Placement Strategy

We have discussed how to remove, carry, raise, and climb several different types of ladders with various numbers of firefighters. Now we will talk about the different ways in which ladders are positioned on the emergency fire scene. The intended use of the ladder at the scene dictates where and in what special position the ladder is placed on the building.

Ladders are placed for four primary reasons:

1. To access and egress upper or lower levels
2. To allow firefighters to work from elevated exterior areas of a building fire
3. To rescue trapped fire victims
4. As a support for tools and equipment

Your fire department may have a standard guideline for the initial placement all ladders. Many departments initially place ladders for rescue on the fire scene. They then adjust the ladders for access and egress, and to work from them as the fire extinguishment operation progresses.

FIGURE 16-28 An encumbered climb.

Ladder Selection Guidelines

When selecting a ladder to reach different heights on a typical building, use the following rules of thumb (Figure 16-29):

- For access to the roof of the first floor, use a 16- to 20-foot straight ladder, or a 24-foot extension ladder.
- To safely reach a second-floor window or roof, use a 24-foot extension ladder.
- To access a third-floor window or roof, use a 35-foot extension ladder.

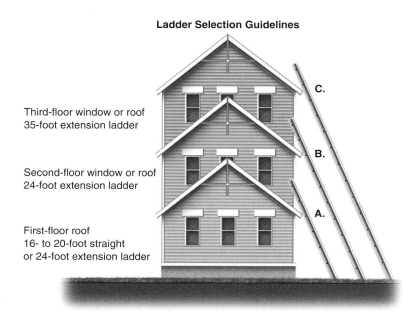

Ladder Selection Guidelines

Third-floor window or roof
35-foot extension ladder

Second-floor window or roof
24-foot extension ladder

First-floor roof
16- to 20-foot straight
or 24-foot extension ladder

C.

B.

A.

FIGURE 16-29 (a) For access to the roof of the first floor, use a 16- to 20-foot straight ladder, or a 24-foot extension ladder.
(b) To safely reach a second-floor window or roof, use a 24-foot extension ladder.
(c) To access to a third-floor window or roof, use a 35-foot extension ladder.

Ladders Placed for Access and Egress

The first major reason ladders are placed on a building is to provide firefighters a means to access and egress the building during firefighting operations. These tools give firefighters an important alternative way to enter upper floors during a fire. They also give them an emergency exit if needed during the fire. Ladders placed for access and egress are placed the same as for rescue: with the tips resting on the window-sill slightly above the edge. You should remember to make sure the ladder is secure by tying the tip or positioning a firefighter to support the ladder at the butt (Figures 16-30 and 16-31).

Ladders Placed for Firefighting Functions

Many times a ladder is used to provide a way for a firefighter to work in an elevated position. This can be to open windows for ventilation or flow water from a nozzle for fire extinguishment. To do this, you must use a leg lock on a ladder rung to secure yourself onto the ladder.

FIGURE 16-30 Ladder placed for access/egress from a window.

FIGURE 16-31 Ladder placed for access/egress from a rooftop.

 **View It!**

Go to the DVD, navigate to Chapter 16, and select *"Locking In to Work from a Ladder."*

Practice It!

Locking in to Work from a Ladder

If you are carrying a tool up a ladder to work from the ladder itself, you should use the following procedure to use a leg lock to secure yourself on the ladder:

1. Climb the ladder to the location where the work will be performed.

2. Grasp the ladder beam with your free hand. With your other hand, support the tool and run this hand along the other beam as you climb. Note that a long tool should be carried up in the hand opposite the side where you will be working. This

—Continued

Ladder Placement Strategy   **381**

will enable you to extend the tool in front of you after you are locked into place (Figure 16-32).

3. Advance one rung up from the level at which you want to work and insert over the rung the leg opposite the side of the ladder you will be working from. Hook your leg in place, under the rung below or around the beam, and step down with your free foot to the rung below.

4. Now your hands will be free to work from the side of the ladder as your leg keeps you safely locked in place on the ladder.

FIGURE 16-32

Flowing Water from a Ladder

Flowing water into an opening or onto an upper level from a ladder should also be done using the leg-lock method of securing yourself onto the ladder. The hose line is stretched up the ladder with no water flowing until you are in place. The hose line should be supported by being tied in by hose straps or held by firefighters below on the ladder (Figure 16-33).

Stretching a Charged Hose Line up a Ladder

There will be times when your team will be asked to extend a hose line up a ladder and into a window opening or rooftop area. When you do this, it is best to pass the charged hose line to a couple of firefighters stationed on the ladder. They will then pass the hose line up the ladder from one firefighter to the next. After the hose line has been fully stretched, you can secure it with a hose strap and leave it in place.

Creating Ventilation Openings

At times during firefighting operations, upper-level windows need to be opened for ventilation of the building's interior. Place the ladder tip three or four rungs above the level where you want to work, on the upwind side of the window. You should position yourself on the ladder so you are level with or above the window.

With shorter tools like an axe or a Halligan bar, grasp the tool in the hand on the same side that you are working from. When you reach your work level, you can easily lock in and work from that same side (Figure 16-34).

FIGURE 16-33 Flowing water into an opening or onto an upper level from a ladder should be done using the leg-lock method of securing yourself onto the ladder.

FIGURE 16-34   Working with a tool while on a ladder.

Warn any firefighters below, and then use your tool to break out the window glass. The smoke and gases will exit the window and blow away from your location.

Ladders Placed for Rescue

Ladders that are placed in a window for rescue should be positioned with the tips resting on the windowsill, slightly above the edge. Ladders placed for rescue off a rooftop, balcony, or fire escape should be placed with the tip four or five rungs above the edge. With this positioning, a safe handhold is provided for the victim to mount the ladder.

 Safety Tip!

If victims are visible in a window or other elevated area as you are placing the ladder, set the butt of the ladder four or five feet from the building. With a firefighter anchoring it at that point, raise the ladder out from the building. When vertical, slowly lower the tip to the edge. This will help to prevent premature mounting of the ladder by any distressed fire victims before the ladder is in place and secure.

 View It!

Go to the DVD, navigate to Chapter 16, and select *"Assisting a Conscious, Ambulatory Victim Down a Ladder."*

Practice It!

Ladder Rescue: Assisting a Conscious, Ambulatory Victim Down a Ladder

To assist a conscious, ambulatory victim down a ladder, use the following method:

1. Check first that the ladder is clear of hazards, and is secure and safe to ascend.
2. With the victim on the ladder, assure him that you are there to help and will be coming up to assist him.
3. Climb to the rung below the victim and grasp each beam, enclosing the victim inside your arms.
4. Reassure the victim and verbally guide him down the ladder one step at a time (Figure 16-35).

FIGURE 16-35

 View It!

Go to the DVD, navigate to Chapter 16, and select *"Assisting a Conscious to Unconscious Victim."*

⇨ Practice It!

Ladder Rescue: Assisting a Conscious to Unconscious Victim

Many times a victim may start out descending the ladder alert and conscious, only to lose consciousness on the way down. Use the following rescue method if this occurs:

1. Make sure the ladder is safe and secure to climb.
2. With the victim located on the ladder, call out and assure the victim that you are going to assist her. Tell her to wait where she is until you reach her.
3. Climb to the rung below the victim and begin to talk the victim down as you descend, hands on the beams, around the victim.
4. If the victim becomes unconscious, press in closer to the victim to hold her in place as you reach down and move her feet and legs outside the beams of the ladder.
5. Support her weight with your knees as you climb down the ladder, keeping her body between your arms and hands (Figure 16-36).

FIGURE 16-36

 View It!

Go to the DVD, navigate to Chapter 16, and select *"Assisting an Unconscious Victim, Facing Away."*

⇨ Practice It!

Ladder Rescue: Assisting an Unconscious Victim Facing Away from the Firefighter

Use the following method to lower down a ladder an unconscious victim who is facing away from you:

1. Make sure the ladder is safe and secure to climb.
2. Two rescuers will pass the victim to you from inside the building.
3. Guide the victim down onto your knee, placing her feet on the beams. She will be facing the ladder. Keep the victim between your arms.
4. Keep your hands on the beams as you descend and shift the victim's weight from knee to knee as you descend (Figure 16-37).

FIGURE 16-37

View It!

Go to the DVD, navigate to Chapter 16, and select "*Assisting an Unconscious Victim Facing the Firefighter.*"

Practice It!

Ladder Rescue: Assisting an Unconscious Victim Facing the Firefighter

The following method should be used to lower down a ladder a victim who is facing you:

FIGURE 16-38

1. Make sure the ladder is safe and secure to climb.
2. Two rescuers will pass the victim to you from inside the building.
3. Guide the victim down onto your knee, placing her feet on the beams. She will be facing you. Keep the victim between your arms.
4. Keep your hands on the beams as you descend, and shift the victim's weight from knee to knee as you descend (Figure 16-38).

View It!

Go to the DVD, navigate to Chapter 16, and select "*Cradle Method.*"

Practice It!

Ladder Rescue: Cradle Method

Use the cradle method as an alternate method of moving a victim down a ladder. Follow these steps:

FIGURE 16-39

1. Make sure the ladder is safe and secure to climb.
2. Two rescuers will pass the victim out to you on the ladder.
3. Position the victim's legs over your shoulders with the victim's back against the ladder.
4. Position your arms underneath the patient's armpits to support the patient. This positioning cradles the victim between you and the ladder.
5. Descend the ladder, sliding your hands down the beams (Figure 16-39).

Go to the DVD, navigate to Chapter 16, and select *"Cross-Arm Method."*

⇨ Practice It!

Ladder Rescue: Cross-Arm Method

The cross-arm method for moving a victim down a ladder places the victim sideways across both of your arms. Use the following steps to accomplish this:

1. Make sure the ladder is safe and secure to climb.
2. Two rescuers will pass the victim out to you when you are positioned on the ladder.
3. Position the victim so that the victim's legs straddle one of your arms, allowing the victim's torso to rest across your other arm, which is positioned underneath the victim's armpit.
4. Keep your hands on the ladder's beams as you descend (Figure 16-40).

FIGURE 16-40

Ladders Placed as Supports

Ladders can also be used as improvised support for various job functions. Be careful not to go beyond the ladders' duty load rating when using them in this way. Ladders should also never be placed and used where there is an excessive twisting action on the beams and rungs.

Support negative-pressure ventilation fans on the exterior of a building window by placing the ladder tips one or two rungs above the window opening. Then hang the negative-pressure fan so that it blows away from the window opening (Figure 16-41).

Using the same placement, ladders can be used as an anchor point for hoisting tools and equipment. Start by wrapping a utility rope around the rung nearest the window opening. Place one end inside the window for an interior firefighter to pull in order to hoist up a tool that is tied to the other end on the ground. An alternate method is to wrap the utility rope around the rung at the window and again around the bottom rung, leaving both ends on the ground. Tie the tool or equipment to the free end of the rope hanging between the building and the ladder. Hoist the tool using the rope that is coming from the wrap at the lower rung (Figure 16-42).

Ladders can be placed at upper-level openings and inside buildings to be used as a base for a water chute. This is accomplished by rolling a salvage tarp from both sides and placing it on a ladder. Then position the ladder where the water is flowing to guide

FIGURE 16-41 Support negative-pressure ventilation fans on the exterior of a building window by placing the ladder tips one or two rungs above the window opening.

it to another part of the building or to the outside (Figure 16-43).

Ladder Inspection and Testing

Ladders should be checked once a month, after every use, after any unusual use, and after any repairs have been made to the ladder. It is also recommended that all Fire Service ladders be tested annually, after

FIGURE 16-42 Using the same placement, ladders can be used as an anchor point for hoisting tools and equipment.

FIGURE 16-43 Ladders can be placed at upper-level openings and inside buildings to be used as a base for a water chute.

failing a visual inspection, when a ladder has been overloaded, when a ladder has been used out of its normal operating range, after any repairs, and after a ladder has been exposed to excessive heat.

Ladder Maintenance and Care

Ladders should be washed on a regular basis and after each use at a fire incident. Use a mild soap and water with a truck brush. Wood ladders should be wiped dry after washing. All moving ladder parts should be lubricated. Follow the manufacturer's recommendations for cleaning and lubrication. An entire ladder should never be painted. However, it is acceptable to paint the tip of a ladder for better visibility.

Wood and fiberglass ladders should not be exposed to the direct sun for extended periods of time. Wood ladders should be taken out of service if dark

Ladder Inspection Guidelines

Use the following guidelines to inspect ladders:

1. Ensure that all connecting bolts and rivets are tight and secure.
2. Look for cracking in any welds.
3. Check rungs and beams for bends, cracks, gouges, and any other distortions.
4. If present, check the heat labels on metal, fiberglass, and wood ladders for exposure to excessive heat.
5. Look for bent, missing, or damaged butt spurs.
6. Operate the roof hooks on a roof ladder to ensure proper operation.
7. Check the pawls and halyard pulleys on extension ladders for operation and damage. Inspect the halyard rope to be sure it is not frayed or worn.

streaks appear in the wood. Ladders taken out of service must be service-tested by the fire department before being placed back into full emergency service. They should also be protected with at least two coats of varnish.

Laddering Skills and Knowledge

You must learn how, when, and where to apply all of the types of ladders that your department uses. In this chapter, we discussed the various types and construction of Fire Service ladders. Then we demonstrated how to remove, carry, and raise different types of ladders that may be available to you in your fire department. Finally, we discussed how to inspect and care for various types and configurations of ladders.

The importance of being well versed in both the practical as well as the tactical skills of Fire Service ladder use cannot be stressed enough. To maintain their laddering skills, firefighters should train periodically with all the ladders carried on their fire apparatus. You will use these important tools again and again during your career—one may even save your life or the life of a fellow firefighter.

Resources

Additional Readings and Resources

NFPA 1931   *Standard for Manufacturer's Design of Fire Department Ground Ladders*

NFPA 1932   *Standard on Use, Maintenance, and Service Testing of In-Service Fire Department Ground Ladders*

NFPA 1901   *Standard for Automotive Fire Apparatus*

Knowledge Assessment

Signed Documentation Tear-Out Sheet

Ladders—Chapter 16

Name: _____

Fill out the ten-question quiz below, the Knowledge Assessment Sheet, by circling the correct answer for each question. When finished, sign it and give it to your instructor/Company Officer for his or her signature. Turn in this Knowledge Assessment Sheet to the proper person as part of the documentation that you have completed your training for this chapter.

1. Roof ladders are basically _____ ladders with folding hooks added at the tip.
   a. extension
   b. combination
   c. straight
   d. folding

2. Extension ladders are made up of a _____ section and one or two _____ sections.
   a. base, fly
   b. hooked, pawl
   c. base, extension
   d. combination, fly

3. Specialized ladders include all of the following types *except* _____ ladders.
   a. attic
   b. combination
   c. utility
   d. straight

4. A new Fire Service roof ladder has a duty rating of _____ pounds.
   a. 500
   b. 750
   c. 300
   d. 450

5. All ladders should be secured at the top by tying off the tip or at the bottom by a firefighter.
   a. True
   b. False

6. A good rule of thumb is that the number of firefighters needed to carry a ladder is the same as the first digit in the ladder's length in feet (a 35-foot ladder should be carried by at least 3 firefighters).
   a. True
   b. False

7. When placing a ladder on a building, it is important to place the _____ on a firm, even surface and the _____ on a secure edge.
   a. tip, butt
   b. beam, rung
   c. butt, tip
   d. pawl, butt

8. Placing a ladder on the ground parallel to the building, resting it on one beam, and then raising it starting at the tip using a hand-under-hand method is called a _____ raise.
   a. hand-under-hand
   b. overhead
   c. beam
   d. flat

9. Ladders are placed for four primary reasons. Which of the following is NOT one of the primary reasons for placing a ladder?
   a. To access and egress upper or lower levels
   b. To allow firefighters to work from elevated exterior areas of a building fire
   c. To rescue trapped fire victims
   d. To block access and egress

10. Ladders placed to provide emergency egress from a window opening should be placed the same as for _____ out of that same window, with its tips showing slightly at the windowsill edge so they are visible to the firefighters inside.
   a. roof access
   b. rescue
   c. climbing
   d. supporting equipment and tools

Prove It

Skills Assessment
Signed Documentation Tear-Out Sheet
Ladders—Chapter 16

Name: _____

Fill out the Skills Assessment Sheet below. Have your instructor/Company Officer check off and initial each skill you demonstrate. When you are finished, sign this page and give to your instructor/Company Officer for his or her signature. Turn in this Skills Assessment Sheet to the proper person as part of the documentation that you have completed your training for this chapter.

Skill	Completed	Initials
1. Describe a straight ladder design.	_____	_____
2. Describe a typical roof ladder design.	_____	_____
3. Explain the different working parts of a typical extension ladder.	_____	_____
4. Describe how attic ladders are used on a structural fire.	_____	_____
5. Briefly describe the general construction of Fire Service ladders, including the duty ratings of straight, roof, and extension ladders.	_____	_____
6. Explain what is meant by the proper climbing angle for ladders.	_____	_____
7. Demonstrate a beam raise using a straight or extension ladder.	_____	_____
8. Demonstrate how to position a roof ladder on a roof for use as a work platform.	_____	_____
9. Demonstrate how to properly tie a halyard on an extended extension ladder.	_____	_____
10. Demonstrate how to work as a member of a three- or four-firefighter team to flat-carry and raise an extension ladder.	_____	_____
11. As a member of a firefighter team, demonstrate a method for carrying and raising an extension ladder equipped with staypoles.	_____	_____
12. Explain what to look for in stable surfaces to rest the tip and butt of a ladder when placing it against a building.	_____	_____
13. Discuss the rule of thumb for selecting the right length of ladder for the height in reach needed.	_____	_____
14. Explain the four main reasons ladders are placed on the scene of an emergency.	_____	_____
15. Demonstrate how to lock in and work from a ladder.	_____	_____
16. Demonstrate various methods for moving conscious and unconscious victims down a ladder for rescue.	_____	_____
17. Describe how to use a ladder as a support for tools and equipment and as an anchor point for hoisting equipment.	_____	_____
18. Explain how to inspect a ladder for damage and how to care for a ladder for routine maintenance.	_____	_____

Student Signature and Date _____   Instructor/Company Officer Signature and Date _____

Building Construction

What You Will Learn in This Chapter

This chapter will help you understand many of the common construction types used in buildings built over the past century. We will discuss how the components of a building are designed to help withstand a collapse and how fire can attack those components, causing them to fail.

What You Will Be Able to Do

After reading this chapter and practicing the skills described, you will be able to:

1. Describe the characteristics of various materials used in building construction.
2. Recognize and describe a dead load, a live load, and an environmental load.
3. Recognize and describe a column, a beam, and a girder.
4. Recognize and describe the five construction types.
5. Recognize and describe the various components of residential buildings, including:
   - Foundations
   - Load-bearing walls
   - Non-load-bearing walls
   - Platform-type construction
   - Balloon-frame construction
   - Roofs and ceilings
   - Lightweight trusses
6. Recognize and describe some essential components of commercial buildings, including:
   - Roof components
   - Columns
   - Reinforced concrete walls
   - Tilt-slab construction

Reality!

Know Building Construction!

On February 14, 2000, members of the Houston (Texas) Fire Department responded to an early-morning arson fire in a McDonald's restaurant. Upon their arrival, they reported that fire was showing through the roof of the building. Later accounts indicated that the fire gave the appearance of being a grease fire in a vent hood. The Captain of the first arriving company, Engine 76, announced via his radio that his company was going to complete a "fast attack" on the fire. The crew entered the building and reported very little heat at the floor level. Soon thereafter the conditions changed. Smoke and heat banked to the floor, and the Incident Commander ordered that everyone evacuate the building and assume a defensive attack. At about the same time, the restaurant's roof collapsed.

Unfortunately, two of the firefighters from Engine 76 never exited the building. It was later determined that both died of asphyxia due to being trapped by falling debris when the roof collapsed around them. As with any tragedy involving firefighters, there was a thorough review of the operation and recommendations were made to help prevent such a tragedy from occurring again. The National Institute for Occupational Safety and Health (NIOSH) report for this incident made 16 recommendations. Many of these emphasized the importance of having an acute awareness of building construction and how fire affects a building's ability to remain standing. Following are some of the NIOSH report's recommendations:

- Fire departments should ensure that Incident Command conducts an initial size-up of the incident before initiating firefighting efforts and continually evaluates the risk versus gain during operations at an incident. This recommendation goes on to list important factors to be considered in the size-up, including:
  - *The type of occupancy involved* and how it can affect aspects of the fire attack;
  - *Smoke conditions* and how they can indicate the type of material that is burning;
  - *The type of construction* and how buildings of the same type tend to hold up under fire conditions;
  - *The type of roof system* and how it will perform during a fire;

- *The age of the structure* and what the building's age indicates about the building's construction type and integrity;
  - *Time considerations.* How long the building has been burning before the fire department's arrival is very important for determining the wisdom of an interior attack.
- Fire departments should ensure that firefighters are trained to identify truss roof systems.
- Fire departments should ensure that firefighters use extreme caution when operating on or under a lightweight truss roof and should develop standard operating procedures for buildings with lightweight roof trusses.
- Fire departments should ensure that firefighters performing firefighting operations under or above trusses are evacuated as soon as it is determined that the trusses are exposed to fire.
- Fire departments should explore using a thermal imaging camera as part of the exterior size-up.

The NIOSH report detailed other recommendations, involving procedural and training issues. But it is clear that it is crucial to firefighter safety to have a thorough knowledge of how a building's construction characteristics will affect the building's performance during a fire. Planning and command decisions rely on this knowledge. In addition, each individual firefighter should be able to recognize the building's type of construction and have an idea of how the construction type will affect the safety of extinguishment or rescue activities.

Building Design

Buildings are designed to protect their contents from nature, to offer a climate-controlled environment for the occupants, and to support the weight of the building's components, occupants, and contents. To do this, the building's designers carefully engineer the construction type and select the materials used for each of the building's components, such as floors, walls, and roof, so that the building will withstand a reasonable amount of force imposed by the environment. Unfortunately, fires often attack the structural components that hold a building together, and part or all of the building collapses as a result of the fire.

Tip!

Buildings are built to support different types of loads. The weight of the building materials and anything permanently attached to a building is called the **dead load.** The occupants and movable objects in or on a building represent a **live load.** Any stresses added to a building by nature (snow, wind, earthquake, etc.) are called **environmental loads.** Buildings are seldom designed with consideration for the added weight of water used to fight a fire inside a building (Figure 17-1).

Level I

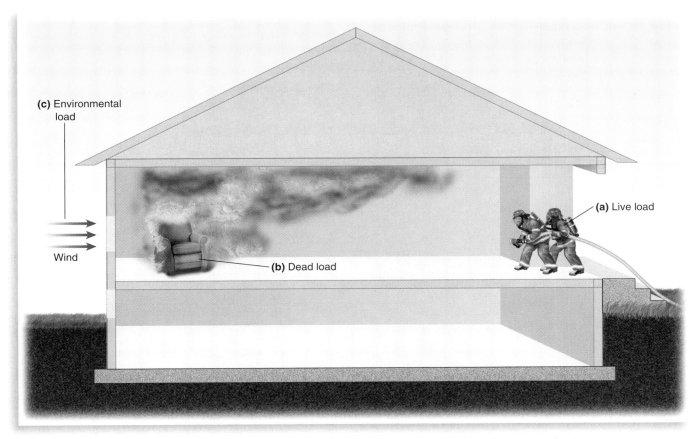

FIGURE 17-1   Different types of building loads: (a) live load, (b) dead load, and (c) environmental load.

Building Materials

Many types of materials are used to build buildings, and each type has advantages and disadvantages that are considered in the design and construction phase of a building (see Table 17-1). As firefighters, we would like to see all buildings built like a bank vault—totally encased in steel-reinforced concrete and resistant to fire, wind, earthquakes, and small explosions. But this is impractical. Even concrete weakens during a significant fire, so we must contend with the characteristics of the buildings we find in our area.

Construction materials and techniques are constantly evolving. The brick, mortar, and heavy timbers used to build most of the buildings in the first half of the last century have been replaced with engineered components made of wood or thin metal. The **lightweight wooden truss** or the **wooden I-beam** are examples of engineered components often used in newer residential construction (buildings built after the mid-1960s), in place of heavier solid wood members that support the floors and roofs of older buildings. Steel is often used to replace wood in the **trusses** and the structural support of commercial buildings. Plastics are often used as decorative trim, replacing the plaster and concrete decorations that adorned buildings years ago.

KEY WORDS

lightweight wooden truss An assembly of wood members that can span a gap and serve as a beam or as a combination rafter and ceiling joist.

truss An assembly of components that can serve as a beam for a roof or a floor, or as part of an entire roof and ceiling support. Trusses rely on the combined strength of a top and bottom chord, and the web of material that bridges the two together.

wooden I-beam A beam with a top and a bottom chord connected by a plywood center that stands on edge, forming an "I" shape.

TABLE 17-1 Characteristics of Building Materials		
Material	**Uses**	**Hazards to Firefighters**
Wood	Wall supports, roof supports, doors, wall coverings, trim	Burns quickly, loses structural integrity as it deteriorates, adds to the volume of fire and smoke
Masonry (bricks, concrete blocks, and stone)	Walls, exterior wall coverings	**Spalls** (loses surface material) when exposed to fire
Mortar	The "glue" for unreinforced masonry (bricks, concrete blocks, stone)	Can dissolve with heavy applications of water, may expand with heat or freezing
Cast iron	Support columns in buildings constructed in the last century	Becomes brittle when heated, fractures when cooled rapidly
Steel	Structural supports	Conducts heat, expands and fails at about 1000°F to 1100°F; a major concern is that structural steel will elongate when heated, pushing walls outward and causing an early failure of the building
Thin-gauge steel	Wall studs	Conducts heat and electricity, fails at a relatively low temperature
Concrete	Walls, floors, roofs	Can spall and fail
Gypsum (wallboard, drywall, and sheetrock)	Wall and ceiling coverings, protection for structural steel	Absorbs heat and protects for a time, but starts to break down with heat; gypsum boards (drywall) absorb water and fail quickly when wet
Reinforced, impact-resistant drywall	For high-traffic areas of commercial buildings and secure facilities	Absorbs heat, protects like typical wallboard, but extremely resistant to penetration from tools typically carried by firefighters
Waterproof membranes	Roof coverings in commercial buildings to shed water	Shedding water can often hamper an exterior attack by preventing the water from reaching the fire
Aluminum	Roofs and window frames	Melts quickly at ordinary fire temperatures
Glass	Windows, ornamental walls (glass block), and lighting fixtures	Fails under high temperatures and under the increased pressures caused by a confined fire
Plastics	Laminates, lighting fixtures, and trim	Melt and burn at relatively low temperatures, liberating dense, black smoke

FIGURE 17-2 A column supports a load along its length, carrying the load from one end to the other.

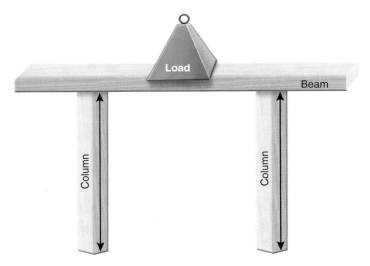

FIGURE 17-3 A beam carries the load between two points.

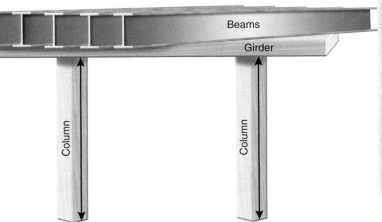

FIGURE 17-4 A girder supports other beams.

The most important principle to remember in any type of construction is that the building uses the mass of various materials to transfer the weight of the roof and upper floors to the ground. Where the load meets the ground, it is distributed to the greater mass of the earth so that the building remains in place and doesn't fall. Gravity is always at work, trying to bring everything down to the lowest point. Gravity works in a straight line, so any stationary object above the earth falls straight down unless it is supported by something strong enough to hold it in place.

A **column** is a common building component that carries the load of something heavy to the ground. A column has enough mass to resist the compressive force of the weight above it. It transfers the weight of objects above it to the building's foundation (Figure 17-2). Columns can be made of wood, steel, reinforced concrete, cast iron, or other materials.

A **beam** carries the load it supports between two horizontal points (Figure 17-3). Beams usually rest on walls or columns. Beams can be made of almost any material, but they are commonly made of wood, steel, or reinforced concrete. A **girder** is any beam that supports other beams (Figure 17-4).

Resisting the downward force of gravity involves more than simply supporting a load from beneath or suspending it from above. Imagine a beam sitting on top of two unsupported columns. The columns may be strong enough to support the beam's weight. However, if they are unsupported, the entire assembly simply topples over in a wind. To overcome this, the columns and beams in a building are connected in a system that provides **structure** to the assembly (Figure 17-5). For this reason,

FIGURE 17-5 When columns, beams, and girders are connected, they form a structure that allows the components to support each other.

when a beam and columns are affected by a lateral force, such as wind, the force is supported horizontally by the other beams and columns within the structure.

A structure's strength relies mostly on three very important things: beams, columns, and the connecting points that hold them together. When fire attacks a structure, the flames weaken steel, spall concrete, and burn away the mass of wood components. As the fire continues to attack the structure, the entire assembly becomes weaker and fails.

KEY WORDS

beam   A building component made of any material that spans a gap between two points and is supported on either end.

column   A building component made of any material that supports a load along the component's length.

girder   Any beam that supports other beams.

structure   The entire assembly of building components that supports the load. Studs, trusses, beams, and columns are part of the structure, while carpeting, paint, and wallpaper are not.

Safety Tip!

Look for obvious and sometimes not so obvious beams and columns within a structure. Consider the effect the fire is having on them, and decide on a defensive attack if the fire involves the actual structure. Once the fire is extinguished, survey the building closely before beginning overhaul activities. Identify the structural components and avoid doing anything that would compromise their integrity. If the structural components have lost mass or changed shape, do not go inside the collapse zone.

Construction Types

When the structural components that support a building's roof and walls are attacked by fire, they can deteriorate quickly and fail miserably. Because buildings are built to last a long time, we are likely to encounter fires in nearly any type of building. Therefore, it is important that firefighters study old and new construction materials and techniques.

Buildings are generally classified into five types, based on the type of materials used in their construction. By understanding the type of building construction used, we can get a general idea of how well the building will withstand a fire inside.

Tip!

Don't be fooled by the name associated with the construction type. Just because a building's construction type is called *noncombustible*, it doesn't mean the building can't have a significant fire followed by a total structural collapse. There are many variables that apply to the cause and type of fire in a building, and how the building behaves while involved in a fire. And be aware: Any given building can have a combination of any of these classifications.

Type I: Fire Resistive

The walls of a Type I (fire-resistive) building are built of noncombustible materials, such as reinforced concrete or masonry, with metal components used to support the roof and/or interior walls (Figure 17-6). No wood is used in the construction, and all metal components are properly "fireproofed" by a noncombustible covering

FIGURE 17-6   The structural components in a fire-resistive (Type I) building are protected from fire.

that insulates the metal from fire. The potential for collapse in a Type I building is delayed somewhat because the noncombustible components are insulated from the heat of a fire.

Type I construction is used in commercial buildings that are occupied by large numbers of people or hazardous contents. Shopping centers, high-rise buildings, movie theaters, and large warehouses are examples of buildings that are usually built of fire-resistive construction.

Type II: Noncombustible

A Type II (noncombustible) building is built of the same type of materials as a Type I building, but the metal structural components that support the roof and upper floors are not insulated or protected from open flame (Figure 17-7). Don't be fooled by the name *noncombustible*. Even though the structural members supporting the roof won't readily burn, they fail in a very short time when exposed to open flame. Noncombustible buildings with any significant interior fire do not support interior firefighting efforts.

Noncombustible construction is used regularly for buildings that serve as warehouses, offices, and some "big-box" type stores.

Type III: Ordinary

Type III (ordinary) buildings have walls made of reinforced or **unreinforced masonry** (concrete blocks, bricks, or stone) and wood or other combustible materials for roof and floor supports (Figure 17-8). The wall construction can be hidden by a coat of cement called *stucco*, which is a texture that is often applied to masonry as well as to wood, making it hard to tell at first glance if the building is made of masonry or wood.

FIGURE 17-7 The structural components in a noncombustible (Type II) building are not insulated or protected from open flame.

FIGURE 17-8 Although the walls are made of steel, wood, or masonry, the wooden roof structure is what makes this building an ordinary construction type (Type III).

A quick way to tell the difference between masonry and wood buildings covered in stucco is to look at the windows. If the window is set a few inches from the wall's exterior surface and the windowsill is concrete, then it's likely that the wall is made of unreinforced masonry. If the window is set near the wall's exterior surface and the windowsill is small and made of wood, then the wall is probably made of wood with a brick veneer.

Ordinary construction is used most often for residential and small commercial buildings.

KEY WORD

unreinforced masonry Brick, concrete blocks, or a combination of both assembled with mortar joints to form a wall.

Type IV: Heavy Timber

The supporting structure of a Type IV (heavy timber) building is made of substantial wood elements (at least 8 x 8 inches) that have enough mass to resist failure from fire for up to one hour. The exterior walls of a Type IV building can be made of unreinforced masonry; however, heavy timbers are used as structural columns, roof supports, and upper floor supports (Figure 17-9).

Heavy timber construction is not used today as often as it was during the first half of the 20th century. Expect to encounter this type of construction in older buildings that were first built to serve as warehouses and factories. Many of these buildings are now used for other purposes, including restaurants, nightclubs, mercantile, and even residential occupancies.

FIGURE 17-9 The heavy timbers used in Type IV construction carry the load. The masonry walls are not part of the support structure.

FIGURE 17-10 The wood frame of a Type V building is protected by siding on the exterior walls and gypsum board on the interior walls.

Type V: Wood Frame

Type V (wood-frame) construction is, as its name implies, a building that is built either entirely or partially of wood structural supports. To resist a fire, the wooden components are covered with noncombustible materials, usually **gypsum board** (**drywall**) (Figure 17-10). Wood-frame construction is relatively lightweight construction and collapses rapidly whenever the structural components are exposed to fire.

Wood-frame construction is used in residential and light commercial applications, and can be found in buildings up to four stories in height.

KEY WORD

gypsum board A fire-resistive material that is used to cover interior walls and ceilings. Also called *drywall* or *sheetrock.*

Residential Buildings

Buildings are designed for a specific purpose and therefore meet a different standard than those built for other types of use. Residential buildings, such as a single-family house, are built of relatively light construction materials when compared to commercial structures like a warehouse or shopping center.

The average single-family home is one or two stories in height and is usually built from wood, unreinforced masonry, or both. When the main supporting components of a building are made of wood, it is called wood-frame construction. The unreinforced masonry used in modern residential construction is usually concrete blocks stacked with mortar joints and tied together across the top and at the corners of the building with steel and concrete. The roof structure of unreinforced residential buildings is usually made of wood components. This type of construction is commonly called ordinary construction.

We all recognize the obvious components of a building. Walls, floors, and a roof make up a building, right? As firefighters, we must learn to mentally remove the exterior surface of a building to see what is really underneath so that we can understand what is actually supporting the load.

Building Foundations

Any building needs a strong foundation if it is expected to last very long. The type of building foundation depends on the type of construction used. Most modern residential construction is built on one of two types of foundations: a monolith or a stem wall. **Monolith foundations** are most often used when a building has no basement, and the concrete for the floor and foundation are poured as a single slab. Walls are then built directly over the reinforced and thickened edges of the monolith slab, which transfers the weight of the building to the earth (Figure 17-11).

Stem-wall foundations are used for buildings with basements or crawl spaces beneath the first floor. First a footing of concrete and steel is poured, and then a small wall, called a *stem wall,* is built to support the floor. **Floor joists** span the gaps between the stem walls, serving as beams and transferring the load to the stem walls. The stem walls now serve as the columns to carry the load to the footings, which are supported by the earth (Figure 17-12).

FIGURE 17-11 A monolith foundation is a single slab of reinforced concrete with thickened edges that serve as the footing.

FIGURE 17-12 A stem-wall foundation carries the load to the footing.

Older houses may be built using a technique called **platform construction.** The foundation for a building built this way is a series of strategically placed concrete and steel footings. Concrete blocks or bricks are stacked on the footings to form **piers**. The entire floor system is then built using wood components, as a single platform on top of the piers. In this type of foundation, the floor joists are the beams and the piers are the columns that carry the load to the footings and then to the earth (Figure 17-13).

■■■ KEY WORDS ■■■

floor joist A solid beam that supports a finished floor.

monolith foundation A type of foundation in which the foundation and the floor are formed from a single slab of reinforced concrete that is thickened at the edges to support the exterior walls.

pier A short column that rests on a footing and supports the floor in a platform-type foundation.

platform construction A construction technique in which each floor is built as an independent platform that rests on the load-bearing walls below, or on piers and/or stem walls beneath the bottom floor.

stem-wall foundation A type of foundation in which a short wall is built on a reinforced footing and then a platform or slab is poured on top.

FIGURE 17-13 Brick or block piers carry the load from the floor to small footings in a platform-style building foundation.

 Safety Tip!

It was common in the early 20th century for the footings used under the piers of a platform-style building foundation to be made of tiers of bricks instead of solid concrete. Beware that water from fire streams can wash away the earth around these weak foundations or can collect and freeze in extremely cold weather, causing the building to collapse.

Types of Walls

The types of walls in a building can fall into many different categories. For our purposes, we will focus on their structural function and how their materials behave during a fire. Structurally, a wall either bears the load above, or it supports nothing but itself, serving as a partition.

Load-Bearing Walls

The exterior walls of a house (and some interior walls) are built to carry the weight of the remaining structure to the foundation, where it is supported by the mass of the earth. These walls are **load-bearing walls.** To support the massive weight of a building, load-bearing walls are built with substantially more mass than a typical interior **partition wall.** It is the load-bearing walls' mass that gives a building its structure and its ability to withstand the forces and weight that the building was designed to support (Figure 17-14).

FIGURE 17-14 This wood-frame wall has substantial supports added to help carry the load of what will be a three-story building.

FIGURE 17-15 A lintel carries the weight of the blocks and roof, distributing that weight to the columns on either side of a door or window.

Masonry Walls Typical masonry walls withstand fire well and offer the mass needed to support the load. However, unreinforced masonry alone fails easily when subjected to a lateral force, such as a strong wind or earthquake, unless it is tied in to the foundation and roof structure, and reinforced in strategic areas with concrete and steel. A typical concrete block wall has hollow cells inside the block. The cells on or near the corners of a concrete block building have steel tied into the foundation's steel. These cells are poured solid with concrete, which fortifies the structure. Cells near windows, doors, and throughout a concrete block structure are reinforced in the same way as the corners.

Reinforced concrete **lintels** (also called headers) are used to overcome the gaps in a masonry wall that are necessary for windows and doors. A lintel spans the gap and transfers the load above to the blocks on either side of the window or door. In effect, the lintel serves as a beam, while the blocks on either side of the window serve as columns to carry the load to the foundation (Figure 17-15).

Brick buildings may have a lintel over the windows. More commonly, they have either a steel header that supports the brick above or an arch built of bricks to carry the load of the bricks above to those on either side of the window (Figure 17-16).

FIGURE 17-16 Bricks are often laid in an arch over a door or window. They rely on the strength of the bricks to resist compression as they distribute the load to either side of the opening.

A masonry wall is tied together at the top with concrete and steel that forms a reinforced concrete beam around the outer walls of a building. Special concrete blocks are used for the top course of blocks in a concrete block wall, and the steel and concrete are placed and poured inside these blocks. Therefore, at first glance from outside the building, it may not be evident that the top lintel beam is present. A **top plate,** made of one or more layers of wood, is secured to large bolts that are embedded in the concrete lintel when it is poured. This top plate makes it possible to secure the wood supports for the roof structure directly to the walls, tying the entire structure together as a single unit.

KEY WORDS

lintel A reinforced concrete beam used over window and door openings.

top plate The top components that run horizontally across a wall.

 Safety Tip!

It is common to find that older brick buildings are supported by long steel rods called *spreaders* that span either from one side to the other or from the front to the back of the building. These spreaders are noticeable on the outside of the building and are often decorated with iron stars or steel S-shaped plates. If you see these rods, remember that they are not simply decorations, and that what is underneath them is a very important component that helps to support the building (Figure 17-17).

Wood-Frame Walls Wood used in building construction is a very strong natural product that holds up well to the forces and weight applied to the structure. Unlike masonry products, bare wood burns easily and adds to the volume of fire and smoke as it burns. Therefore, the structural wood used in load-bearing walls is covered with protective materials that can be made of more wood, gypsum, concrete, metal, or brick. To help us identify the beams and columns hidden behind these wall coverings, we must learn to mentally remove the exterior surface of a building in order to visualize exactly what is underneath.

FIGURE 17-17 Example of a stretcher as seen from outside the building.

 **Tip!**

At first glance, wood-frame and masonry walls covered with a thin layer of stucco look nearly alike. Look at the windows to determine at a glance if the structure underneath the foundation is wood or masonry. A window set in a wood-framed wall is nailed to the surface and has a small metal or wooden sill. A window set in a masonry wall is set back a few inches from the outer surface of the wall and usually has a large concrete sill.

Load-bearing, wood-frame walls are tied to the foundation with bolts that are set in the concrete when it is poured. The bottom of the wall is called the **sole plate.** The sole plate transfers the weight carried by the **studs** to the footings, which in turn transfer the load to the earth. The studs in a wood-frame wall are the columns and are commonly spaced 16 or 24 inches apart.

At the top of a wood-frame wall is the *top plate.* It is sometimes called a double top plate, because the top plate for most residential uses is made of two pieces of wood but the term *top plate* refers to the entire assembly, regardless of how many layers of wood there are. The top plate serves as the beam that carries the load to the columns (studs), which carry the load to the earth.

Siding is used to cover the outside walls. This siding can be a single layer of plywood. It may also consist of some sort of wood product as a base that is covered with a vapor barrier and decorative material, such as metal, vinyl, or wood siding. Stucco and even brick are common types of exterior wall coverings.

KEY WORDS

sole plate The wooden member at the bottom of a wood-frame wall.

studs Wood or metal components that serve as columns in a framed wall.

Non-Load-Bearing Walls

Many interior walls in a building are built to simply break the interior space into smaller compartments. These walls are usually designed to support their own weight and nothing more. These walls are called *non-load-bearing* walls. The studs in a non-load-bearing wall are usually spaced every 16 inches and are used more as support to the gypsum drywall covering than as a column. Non-load-bearing walls are reinforced around doorways so that they can support the door; however, very little support is offered elsewhere in the wall (Figure 17-18).

Construction Styles

Platform Construction

In a single-story, wood-frame building, the roof assembly is attached to the top plate and the structure's framework is complete. In a typical multistory wood-frame building, each floor is built as a platform that rests on the load-bearing walls underneath it. This is called platform construction. Each platform provides a very strong support system that ties the structure together at each level. This system serves as a barrier to any fire that enters an exterior wall, so that a fire from a lower floor doesn't quickly travel to the attic. Platform construction is the most common type of wood-frame construction used today (Figure 17-19).

Balloon-Frame Construction

Before the second half of the 20th century, it was common to use a technique called **balloon-frame construction** when building wood-frame buildings.

FIGURE 17-19 In a multistory building that incorporates a platform design, each floor provides a natural break in the exterior walls so that fire doesn't travel easily from the foundation to the attic.

This type of construction involves using very long timbers, which span two floors, as the studs for exterior walls, leaving hollow gaps between the studs that run from the foundation to the attic area. The floor joists for each floor are nailed into the long studs. It is very common to have fire and smoke travel upward between the studs in a balloon-frame wall, quickly engulfing the attic in fire (Figure 17-20).

▓ KEY WORD ▓

balloon-frame construction A construction technique usually associated with older two-story buildings that uses long timbers as a continuous wall stud, leaving no fire separation between the foundation and the attic.

 *Tip!*

Not all older wood-frame buildings are balloon-frame construction. If you notice that the windows on the upper and lower floors on an old wood-frame building are in perfect alignment, one over the other, then suspect balloon-frame construction.

Roofs and Ceilings

The obvious purpose of a roof is to shed water and protect us from the sun. Because they are seldom used to carry a live load, residential roofs are designed to

FIGURE 17-18 A non-load-bearing wall is reinforced at the door openings but otherwise is designed to support only its own weight.

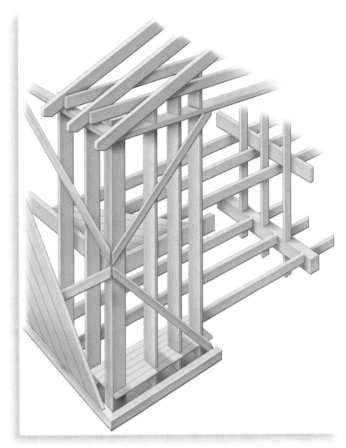

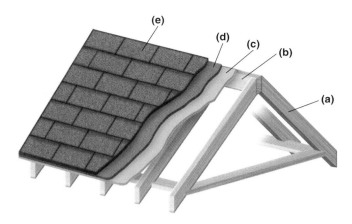

FIGURE 17-21   Parts of a residential, rafter-style roof:
a.   rafter
b.   ridge pole
c.   sheathing
d.   roofing paper
e.   roof covering
f.   ceiling joist
g.   ceiling

FIGURE 17-20   Balloon frame construction provides vertical shafts that allow fire and smoke an unimpeded path of travel all the way to the attic area.

support the weight of a dead load and a reasonable amount of environmental load (water or snow).

Rafters

A conventional residential roof system uses **rafters** to support the roof deck. Because they span a wide area, rafters are made of thicker wood so that they have the strength to carry the load to the walls. The rafters are attached to the walls at the top plates. They are held in place with nails and metal clips that help prevent the roof from blowing off during a heavy wind. **Sheathing** covers the support structure and serves as a base for the top layers of the roof (Figure 17-21).

A bottom layer of roofing materials provides a waterproof membrane. A top layer of roofing materials, such as shingles, tiles, or tar and gravel, are added to protect the roof deck. While it is important to know all of the components of a roof, it is most important to understand what supports the roof's structure and how fire can cause that structure to fail.

Wood beams called *ceiling joists* support ceilings on a conventional roof system. Ceiling joists span between load-bearing walls, and drywall is secured to the underside of the joists. This drywall barrier protects, for a limited amount of time, both the ceiling joists and the rafter system from a room and contents fire below them.

KEY WORDS

rafter   A wooden beam that supports the roof deck.

sheathing   Wood or metal used to cover a roof's support system.

Wood Trusses

Over the last three or four decades, wood trusses have been used in place of rafters for most roof supports. A wood truss is an engineered system that uses multiple spans to carry the load to the support walls on either end. A truss has a top and a bottom chord that are connected at various points by components that allow both chords to work together to share the load the truss is supporting. The top chord of a truss serves as a rafter, and the bottom chord as a ceiling joist. However, unlike a typical rafter-style roof, the bottom chord of a wood truss is a vital part of the roof's support system.

Trusses come in many different shapes and styles. They are usually custom built to meet the needs of the particular application. A truss roof can be pitched, flat, or arched, and various components may be any of the three. Trusses aren't restricted to just serving as a part of the roof structure in a building. Flat trusses, known as *parallel chord trusses*, are often used to replace floor joists in modern construction.

Gussets made of stamped sheet metal are used to help strengthen each connecting point on a truss. Small, sharp edges resulting from the stamping process press into the wood, and nails are often added to help hold the gussets in place (Figure 17-22). Trusses are often protected from a contents fire below with drywall; however, fire can find its way quickly to the attic space, burning as a "hidden" fire above your head. When exposed to the heat of a fire, these gussets quickly conduct the heat to the wood surrounding the thin metal teeth that hold the gusset in place, causing it to loosen and fall away. This leaves nothing to hold the truss together, so it fails quickly and often without warning.

Because wood truss roofs are designed as a roof support system, the ability of a single truss to support the load it carries is shared by the trusses on either side. If a single truss fails, then the weight is added to the adjacent trusses. Roof trusses seldom fail alone—they usually involve several surrounding trusses. This means that a total roof collapse is likely when just one or two trusses fail.

▨▨ KEY WORD ▨▨

gusset   A metal plate that connects the components of a truss. Also called a *gang-nail*.

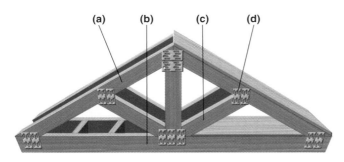

FIGURE 17-22   Parts of a residential, wood-truss-style roof:
a. top chord
b. bottom chord
c. web
d. gusset

Let this safety tip serve as your warning! A lightweight wood truss will fail if exposed to high heat or fire, even for a very short period of time. ***Beware of lightweight wood truss roofs.*** Many firefighters have been killed or have suffered life-changing injuries from roof collapses attributed to the early failure of a wood truss roof. Do not work on or below a wood truss roof that has been damaged by fire.

Another problem with truss roofs is that there is no ridge board running down the center. If the roof deck burns away from a conventional roof, a roof ladder's hooks still have the ridge board to grip. Not so with a truss roof.

Commercial Buildings

Commercial occupancies usually require larger, more open spaces than residential buildings. To accommodate the need for greater space, heavier materials such as reinforced concrete or steel are often used in load-bearing walls. In addition, a series of beams and girders may also be used to help transfer the load from the roof to the walls (Figure 17-23).

Building Components

Unreinforced masonry is often used in modern commercial buildings simply to fill in the gaps between the reinforced columns and the beams that actually support the structure. Because unreinforced masonry can only be stacked a certain height without support, intermediate beams greater than 10 feet in height are located in exterior walls to help carry this load. Columns inside the open structure help support beams and girders that support upper floors and the roof.

Roofs and Ceilings

Steel trusses, called **bar joists,** are commonly used as the roof structure in fire-resistive buildings. Bar joists are used when a building has a flat roof (Figure 17-24). They help support additional dead loads commonly added to a commercial building with a flat roof, such as air conditioners and refrigeration units. These bar joists are often left exposed in a warehouse-type structure. If there is a ceiling underneath a steel bar joist roof, it is usually suspended by thin wires attached to the bottom chord of the bar joists. This type of ceiling is commonly called a *drop,* or *suspended, ceiling.* Insulation, heating, and air conditioning ductwork and telephone wires are usually found above a drop ceiling (Figure 17-25).

Light corrugated metal often serves as the roof deck on a flat commercial roof. This decking may be covered with insulation or even a lightweight concrete material. The waterproofing may come from tar and gravel or a waterproof membrane material.

Wood or lightweight metal trusses in commercial structures often support pitched roofs. Don't assume that just because a building's structure is made of steel or reinforced concrete, the roof over your head is not a wood truss. If you notice that the ceiling in a commercial building is smooth and lacks the metal grid used in suspended ceilings, then suspect a wood or light metal truss roof.

▨ KEY WORD ▨

bar joist   A parallel chord truss made of steel and used most often as a roof support in commercial-style construction.

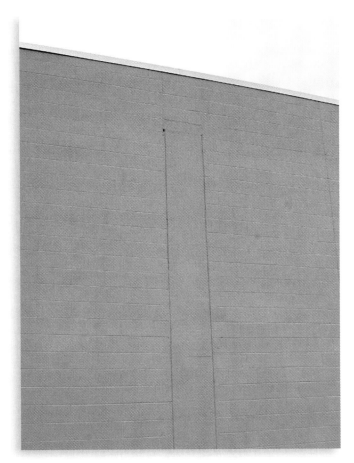

FIGURE 17-23   This commercial building has a series of columns and beams formed as part of the system of load-bearing walls. The concrete blocks in this example add no overall strength to the wall.

FIGURE 17-24   Steel bar joists are a type of truss used mainly in commercial construction with a flat roof.

FIGURE 17-25   Drop ceilings are suspended from bar joists by wires. They can conceal a great deal of ductwork, machinery, and wires.

Survey the exterior of a commercial building closely. Notice its height. It is a common practice to build a "structure within a structure" in warehouse-type buildings. While the overall ceiling height in a building may be more than 16 feet, the front office area is often made with non-load-bearing walls and simple ceiling joists (Figure 17-26). The rear of this type of occupancy may be open and used for warehouse space. When you enter this type of building, there will be a very large space over your head that can conceal a great deal of fire that originates in the rear of the structure and travels to the front of the building. As you enter a burning commercial building, check above the ceiling to be sure there is no fire in the space overhead.

Tilt-Slab Construction

Another popular style of construction used today is commonly called **tilt-slab construction.** The exterior walls of a tilt-slab building are made of high-strength reinforced concrete that is lifted into place and held upright by staypoles during the construction process. Steel plates embedded in the concrete are welded at critical points to connect the walls together. Steel girders or bar joists are welded to other plates in the walls so that the building has enough structure to keep the walls upright. Once the structure is complete, the staypoles are removed.

The window and door openings in a tilt-slab building are either formed as the walls are poured or cut out later as needed. These openings require no headers or lintels because the reinforced concrete is self-supporting (Figure 17-27).

KEY WORD

tilt-slab construction A construction technique in which the exterior walls are formed and poured out of reinforced concrete, and then lifted into position as a single unit when installed.

FIGURE 17-26 The office inside this warehouse-style building is essentially a structure within a structure.

FIGURE 17-27 The walls of a tilt-slab building are lifted into place by a crane. To hold the walls in place, the remaining structural members are welded to steel plates embedded in the concrete, forming a self-supporting structure.

Safety Tip!

Pay very close attention to the height of a tilt-slab building and respect the collapse zone during a defensive attack. Tilt-slab walls do not crumble when they fail. What makes a tilt-slab building fall is the weakening of the steel support structure inside. Once the connections fail, the walls may topple inward or outward, crushing anything in their way.

Interior Finishes

The interior walls of a commercial structure are often made of light metal studs. Drywall is attached to the studs with screws. These partition walls seldom support ceiling joists. Drop ceilings are common in commercial-style buildings.

High-traffic areas, such as hallways in schools and hotels and some minimum-security facilities, are now equipped with **reinforced drywall** that resists impact. This reinforced drywall will resist fire the same as regular drywall; however, it is reinforced on the back with a very strong woven plastic that holds the drywall together when it is impacted. This type of drywall will resist several poundings from a sledge, a maul, or an axe. The best way to overcome this type of material is with a saw, such as a drywall saw or a reciprocal saw.

Do It!

Understand Building Construction!

Make it a point to study building construction in close detail. The best time to understand how a building is designed and built to resist the force of gravity is before a fire, not after. Make it a point to visit any structures under construction in your area, and pay close attention to the components and how they interconnect to form a building. Look at the buildings already in place and identify the construction type and design features common to your area. Share your observations with those you work with so you can all be aware of the hazards you may face in any building fire you will be asked to control.

Level I

Prove It

Knowledge Assessment

Signed Documentation Tear-Out Sheet

Building Construction—Chapter 17

Name: _____

Fill out the ten-question quiz below, the Knowledge Assessment Sheet, by circling the correct answer for each question. When finished, sign it and give it to your instructor/Company Officer for his or her signature. Turn in this Knowledge Assessment Sheet to the proper person as part of the documentation that you have completed your training for this chapter.

1. Any single-piece component that spans the distance between two points and supports a load is called a _____.
   a. truss
   b. column
   c. joist
   d. beam

2. A component must be made of steel to be considered a beam or girder.
   a. True
   b. False

3. A building made with protected metal components and no wood is an example of what type of construction?
   a. Ordinary
   b. Noncombustible
   c. Fire resistive
   d. Commercial

4. A building made with masonry exterior walls, metal interior wall studs, and a wood truss roof support system is what type of construction?
   a. Ordinary
   b. Noncombustible
   c. Fire resistive
   d. Residential

5. A lintel is an example of a _____.
   a. beam
   b. column
   c. truss
   d. pier

6. A steel bar joist is an example of a truss.
   a. True
   b. False

7. The stamped sheet metal components used to connect the web and chords of a truss are called _____.

　　a. clips

　　b. gussets

　　c. clamps

　　d. plates

8. A building that features substantial wood elements as the structural support system and unreinforced masonry exterior walls is an example of _____ construction.

　　a. heavy timber

　　b. ordinary

　　c. fire-resistive

　　d. masonry

9. Wood-frame construction is used for residential buildings only.

　　a. True

　　b. False

10. All of the following are examples of engineered building components *except* _____.

　　a. truss

　　b. wooden I-beam

　　c. wood rafter

　　d. steel bar joist

Student Signature and Date _____ Instructor/Company Officer Signature and Date _____

412

Prove It

Skills Assessment

Building Construction—Chapter 17

Name: _____

There are no specific skills associated with this chapter.

Student Signature and Date _____   Instructor/Company Officer Signature and Date _____

413

Ventilation and Fire Behavior

What You Will Learn in This Chapter

This chapter will help you better understand how fires grow and react to being confined inside a structure. We will discuss the steps we use to systematically create openings in buildings to direct heat, smoke, and fire out of a burning building.

What You Will Be Able to Do

After reading this chapter and practicing the skills described, you will be able to:

1. Describe and recognize certain types of fire behavior associated with building fires, including exposed fire growth, hidden fire growth, flashover, and backdraft conditions.
2. Describe ventilation for fire control and ventilation for life safety.

3. Safely break a ground-level window for ventilation.
4. Safely break a window from a ladder.
5. Explain and perform horizontal ventilation using natural methods.
6. Explain and perform negative-pressure mechanical ventilation.
7. Explain and perform positive-pressure ventilation.
8. Work safely on a flat roof.
9. Work safely on a pitched roof using a roof ladder.
10. Hoist ventilation tools to a roof using a utility rope.
11. Start and operate ventilation saws.
12. Create a vertical ventilation path using natural openings in a roof.
13. Create forced openings in a flat and a pitched roof.
14. Create natural and forced openings to ventilate a basement fire.

Review It!

Before reading this chapter, we suggest that you review *Safe Firefighting: First Things First,* Chapter 6, to refresh your memory about basic fire chemistry.

Reality!

Safety Lesson: A NIOSH Report

Ventilation Saves Lives!

On the morning of March 21, 2003, firefighters in Ohio responded to a single-family house fire. The first arriving firefighters had trouble determining which house was on fire as they arrived on the block because thick, heavy smoke obscured their view from the street. Engine company firefighters pulled hose lines to mount an interior attack while the ladder company began ventilation activities. The hose lines became kinked in the front yard, and the entry team entered the fire before the lines became fully charged and operational.

The entry team had entered a dangerous situation without the protection of a fully operational hose line and without fully coordinating with the ventilation team. Their entry occurred before the ventilation team had completed their task, resulting in their operating in a high-heat and smoke-charged environment.

As a firefighter from the first arriving ladder truck went to the roof to cut a ventilation hole, windows on the second floor broke and flames burst out when the smoke and heated gases inside the building ignited in very dangerous condition called a *flashover.* In a flashover, flammable smoke and heated gases suddenly ignite, raising the temperature inside a building to a nonsurvivable level. One firefighter on the entry team was killed and two were injured as they narrowly escaped.

Follow-Up

NIOSH Report #2003-12

NIOSH investigated the incident and concluded that, along with several other related procedures, fire departments should ensure that ventilation is closely coordinated with interior operations. The NIOSH report also recommended that standard operating procedures for structural firefighting ensure that firefighters enter burning structures with charged hose lines.

Fire Behavior in Buildings

When a material is heated, it expands. When the same material erupts in flame, it releases **thermal energy** and generates smoke and other dangerous gases. As the amount of fuel feeding the flames increases, so does the amount of thermal energy and smoke. If the burning material is outdoors, unconfined, and not affected by a strong wind, the smoke will rise because, as we learned in elementary school, hot air rises. We also learned that anything in motion remains in motion until a greater force acts upon it. In other words, everything tends to naturally move toward the path of least resistance. So, unconfined and outdoors, the smoke will continue to rise into the atmosphere, where it is steered away and dispersed by natural air currents. If a strong wind is present at ground level, the smoke will move horizontally instead of upward. The path of least resistance determines the direction of the smoke, which is downwind instead of upwind.

When a fire occurs inside a structure, the heat and smoke are confined. Imagine a small fire that starts in an overstuffed chair in a tightly sealed room. Heat, flames, and smoke are present first, during the growth phase of the fire. The heat allows the smoke to travel upward until it hits the ceiling. If the fire runs out of fuel at that point, the heat will remain at the ceiling level and keep the smoke there in a **thermal layer** (Figure 18-1).

▓ KEY WORDS ▓

thermal energy   The force exerted from heat. Thermal energy gives smoke motion.

thermal layer   A layer of smoke and gases that is created when heat reaches a natural level within a space, usually near the ceiling, and the smoke and gases linger at that level.

Flashover

If the fire continues to grow, the heat and smoke will push upward until they meet the ceiling. The ceiling interrupts the natural process of heat rising and redirects the heat and smoke outward. Because the fire is still adding energy, the smoke gains velocity (speed) as it travels across the ceiling to the walls. The smoke and heat are confined by the walls, so they change direction once again, traveling along the path of least resistance, which is downward to the floor, where they make another turn and head back to the seat of the fire. As the flames build to the fully

FIGURE 18-1 Heated smoke will tend to remain in a thermal layer when the fire runs out of fuel, but the smoke is confined.

developed phase, they follow the same path as the smoke—up, across, and down. Because the smoke and gases that are generated by the burning process are flammable, fires that start in a confined area, such as a building, go through an additional phase called **flashover.** During flashover, the smoke and heated gases combine with the right amount of heat and oxygen to ignite suddenly in a very intense fire (Figure 18-2).

Some indicators that a flashover is about to occur include

- High heat pushing out of the structure
- Intense smoke conditions
- Turbulent smoke that is moving rapidly

FIGURE 18-3 Fire travels through openings, both horizontally and vertically, as it seeks a path of least resistance.

- Brown- or yellow-stained smoke, which indicates incomplete combustion

The cycle continues until the room is full of smoke and the available oxygen is consumed, or the fuel is consumed and the fire enters the decay phase. Although the flames are gone, the heat (thermal energy) is still confined in the room. The scenario of a tightly sealed room is somewhat theoretical. Most buildings have several rooms with doors, windows, vents, and other openings, so as the thermal energy released by the flames builds pressure inside the building, it pushes the smoke to other parts of the building (Figure 18-3).

FIGURE 18-2 Thick, dark, turbulent smoke issuing from a confined area is one indicator that flashover is about to occur.

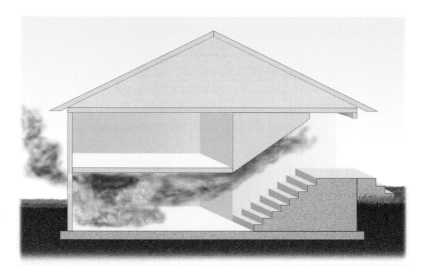

KEY WORD

flashover A dangerous situation in which the smoke and fire gases in a room suddenly ignite, causing the entire room to burn in an instant.

Backdraft

There are times when the heat and fire gases fill an entire space and the flames diminish because the available oxygen inside the space is consumed during the burning process. Enough heat is present to ignite the smoke, gases, and contents of the space, but there simply isn't enough oxygen to sustain an open flame. This is a very dangerous situation because oxygen will rush into the space when we enter the structure, allowing a very violent explosion to occur. This phenomenon is called a **backdraft** (or smoke explosion). The difference between a backdraft and a flashover is in the presence of an explosion. A flashover ignites the smoke and contents in a sudden way, but there is no loud explosion, just a rapid ignition. A backdraft can destroy the structure with a violent explosion. Although the differences between a flashover and a backdraft are subtle, both are deadly.

Some indicators that a backdraft condition may be present include

- A tightly sealed building with little or no smoke showing
- High heat conditions—glass and doors very hot to the touch, but little or no smoke issuing from the structure
- Hot smoke pushing rapidly from a small opening in the building, but no visible flames

KEY WORD

backdraft A violent explosion of unburned gases and superheated smoke resulting from the sudden introduction of oxygen to an otherwise oxygen-deprived, confined area.

Exposed Growth

Unlike our theoretical room that is totally sealed and contains only a single chair, most buildings are filled with a lot of stuff. Most of the items in today's buildings are flammable, and most fires in buildings spread first through the contents of the building and then to the structure. Radiant heat from flames can heat a nearby chair, causing it to erupt in fire. Convection

heat can travel across the room to window curtains, resulting in another fire on the other side of the room. All of the contents in a room, including the paint, carpet, wallpaper, and fixtures, will add fuel to the fire as the fire grows in intensity. Most of these interior contents are made largely of manmade materials (such as plastics). When these items burn, the smoke they give off contains a lot of carbon particles and **carbon monoxide**. Carbon particles and carbon monoxide in the smoke burn well and contribute greatly to the flashover potential in a structural fire.

As the fire burns across the ceiling, the radiant heat from the flames and the increased confined thermal energy heats the exposed surfaces of the contents below. This phenomenon is sometimes referred to as **thermal feedback**. Because the heat is confined, the building heat adds to the fire's intensity. If the contents are made of like materials, they will erupt into fire at almost the same instant. This phenomenon is called a **flameover.** When flameover occurs, the entire contents of the room ignite almost simultaneously into a raging fire (Figure 18-4).

As the pressure created by a fire increases within a space, the heat and smoke continue to seek the path of least resistance. The thermal energy pushes the heat and smoke into every opening in a room, allowing them to travel down a hallway, to other rooms, or out an open window. This causes the fire to spread throughout the building.

KEY WORDS

carbon monoxide A colorless, odorless gas that is produced during incomplete combustion. At certain percentages in the air, carbon monoxide is deadly to breathe and can be explosive.

flameover A situation in which the surfaces of combustible materials in a room reach ignition temperature at the same time, causing them to burst into flames at nearly the same moment.

thermal feedback A situation in which convection causes the heat from a fire in a room to circulate back to the seat of the fire, adding to the intensity of the fire.

Hidden Growth

Because rooms have doors, windows, and ventilation shafts, smoke and heat can easily push into a hidden area through any openings they can find. A good example of this is when a fire breaks out in an attached garage in a typical single-family house. Many of these garages have a pull-down stairway that provides easy access to the attic area above. These

FIGURE 18-4 When the contents of a room are heated at the same rate and are made of the same material, they will ignite simultaneously. This phenomenon is called a flameover.

pull-down stairways are often backed with a thin layer of plywood that burns quickly, providing an opening for the fire and smoke to travel into the attic. This situation allows the fire to grow overhead in a hidden area and build to a dangerous level, undetected by the occupants of the house below. The fire will eventually burn through the roof or exit through a roof vent until it reaches the unconfined space outdoors (Figure 18-5).

Smoke, heat, and fire will find any opening that is present and, if left unchecked, will create new openings. Any penetration through the walls or ceiling can allow a fire to move from an open area to a hidden space. It is very common to have clear, fully visible conditions in the living space of a building while a fire rages overhead. Fire can also originate in a hidden space, where it can grow undetected. Electrical fires that start in walls and attic spaces are examples of this type of hidden growth.

Ventilation

Ventilation procedures on a structural fire are just as critical to the extinguishment of the fire as applying water. The goal of ventilating a fire is to create a path

FIGURE 18-5 Fire can grow undetected in a hidden area such as an attic space, between wall studs, and around pipes.

of least resistance in the most desirable location so that accumulated heat and smoke can leave the building. Ventilation also allows fresh air back into the building. **Ventilation** is a task that is accomplished by various methods, all applied in a well-coordinated way under the full control of the Incident Management System (IMS) that is working on the fireground. Ventilation tasks are conducted using basic tools to enhance natural openings that are already present, such as doors and windows, or to create openings in a structure by cutting or breaking through barriers.

Ventilation continues naturally until the rate of heat released from the building equals the amount of heat produced. As water reaches the fire, the rate of heat that is being produced diminishes and eventually stops. A large amount of the remaining smoke naturally leaves the building, but once it cools down, smoke lingers inside unless there is a strong breeze flowing through the building. Heat gives smoke velocity while the fire is ongoing. Once the fire is extinguished, the velocity ceases. Mechanical aids, including **smoke ejectors** and large fans, help move more of the bad air out of a building and the good air into it by giving smoke the velocity to leave the building (Figure 18-6).

When most types of plastic burn, large amounts of smoke and toxic gases are given off by a relatively small fire. Because a small fire doesn't produce enough heat to give smoke the velocity it needs to travel, it lingers. Food burning on a stove also produces the same quality of slow-moving smoke. This phenomenon is often called a **cold smoke condition**. It requires **mechanical ventilation** or a very strong breeze to give the smoke enough velocity to exit the building.

FIGURE 18-6 Smoke ejectors and gasoline-powered fans are used to give velocity and direction to static smoke.

▆▆ KEY WORDS ▆▆

cold smoke condition A condition in which, after flames reach the decay phase or the fire is small relative to the building size, the smoke lingers after the thermal energy has diminished.

mechanical ventilation The use of a specially designed fan to draw smoke from a building or pull fresh air in to force smoke out in order to assist the natural ventilation process.

smoke ejector A large, electric-powered fan specially designed for Fire Service use in mechanical ventilation.

ventilation The controlled, coordinated, and systematic removal of heat, smoke, and/or gases from a confined area, and the replacement of those undesirable conditions with fresh air.

Ventilation for Fire Control

When we arrive at most significant structural fires, the lack of adequate ventilation controls the fire by denying oxygen to the flames. Or it may add to the intensity of the fire as the heat builds, directing the fire to other parts of the building. Ventilation is a crucial step in accomplishing most of our basic

firefighting objectives because it helps slow a fire's growth rate. Venting a fire can decrease the rate of fire growth by allowing the building to lose heat instead of containing it. When properly used, ventilation results in a fire with less heat, a slower flame spread, and overall safer conditions. When venting is improperly performed, it can result in uncontrolled fire growth or possibly a deadly explosion. This is why it is critical that ventilation never be conducted without strongly considering the effect it will have on the fire. Charged and properly staffed hose lines must be in position to protect firefighters and to attack the fire.

Ventilating a fire safely nearly always involves doing some damage to the building. Breaking windows, forcing doors, and cutting holes in a building can seem excessive. However, hesitating to do a little damage at this point in the fire usually results in a greater fire loss, so the damage is well justified.

Ventilation for Life Safety

Venting a fire can change the conditions inside a building from nonsurvivable to survivable by removing heat and toxins, thus enhancing a victim's chance for surviving the fire. Venting a fire enhances the visibility inside, making the entry team safer and more efficient as they conduct a search for victims and the seat of the fire.

The goal of venting for life safety is to draw the heat and toxins away from trapped victims and also away from the entry point that firefighters use to attack the fire. When a vent point is opened near the seat of the fire and firefighters enter from the unburned side of the building, smoke and heat are drawn away from the entry point and the fresh replacement air enters through the entry door, providing a much clearer atmosphere for the entry team. Venting a fire, even at

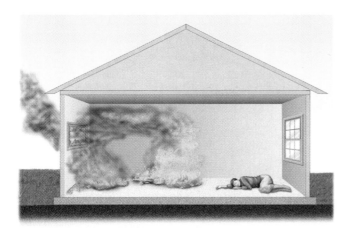

FIGURE 18-7 Ventilation for life safety is often performed at the risk of spreading the fire in the building to draw it away from a trapped victim.

the risk of spreading the flames to unoccupied parts of a building, is often necessary to make the conditions inside the building more survivable for occupants and firefighters (Figure 18-7).

 **Safety Tip!**

Just because proper ventilation of a fire has created clear visibility conditions inside the structure, don't assume that the interior of the structure is free of dangerous gases. Carbon monoxide is colorless and odorless, and lingers in an atmosphere. Keep your SCBA in place until a clear, non-IDLH atmosphere has been verified with the proper gas detection device.

Natural Ventilation

When a fire burns, the heat and smoke that accumulates inside the structure are usually at a higher pressure than the outside air. Therefore, they naturally tend to leave the building when given an opening. Convection moves the smoke naturally upward, and the thermal energy from the fire moves it naturally outward in all directions. **Natural ventilation** is a process in which we simply provide the proper size openings in the most desirable locations along the exterior of a building to let convection and thermal energy move the smoke outside. This can be done horizontally, so that windows, doors, and other openings along the walls are used as paths of egress for the smoke. It can also be done vertically, so that openings are created on or near the roof.

KEY WORD

natural ventilation A type of ventilation accomplished by making openings in a building at strategic locations to allow natural convection to vent the building.

 **Tip!**

Good ventilation activities start with locating the fire as best as we can from outside the building. Smoke, darkness, building design, and other factors can hamper our ability to quickly locate a fire within a building. A thermal imaging camera (TIC) is a great tool to help overcome many obstacles so that we can try to determine the best ventilation points for a structure. Use a TIC to determine which windows are the hottest, or where the hottest point is on a wall or a roof. Think of a TIC as "firefighter's radar" and use it to your advantage.

Horizontal Ventilation

Ventilation depends on velocity to carry smoke out of the structure. **Horizontal ventilation** is the type most often used in residential firefighting. If the building is charged with heat and smoke from a significant fire inside, removing the windows nearest the seat of the fire will rapidly improve the conditions inside for trapped victims and the firefighters on the entry team. As the entry team enters from the other side of the structure, a natural current of air will start to flow (Figure 18-8).

FIGURE 18-8 Horizontal ventilation takes advantage of natural openings in a building's walls, the thermal energy added by the fire, and the energy added by wind.

The first points to consider when selecting the most desirable ventilation point are wind speed and direction, and the effect the wind will have on the fire. When the wind outside a building is calm or light, smoke will naturally exit through the opening we make. Fresh air will enter through the remote point where the entry team enters the structure. If a strong wind blows toward the vent opening, it will add to the velocity given off by the heat. The wind will push the smoke and fire back into the structure and directly toward the entry team as if the fire was coming from a blowtorch. When a strong wind blows toward the entry side of the building, it adds more energy and helps evacuate the smoke from the downwind side, even as the fire cools and the rate of released heat diminishes. It is very important to open the downwind-side windows first so that the smoke and heat have somewhere to go when you open the upwind side. Otherwise, the added wind pressure from the upwind side will churn the smoke inside and help spread the fire throughout the building (Figure 18-9).

The next point to consider is where the heat will go once you create the opening. Convection naturally sends heat, smoke, and flames upward. When making an opening in the roof of a building, convection works in our favor to allow smoke and heat to leave the building. However, when opening a window, the same smoke and heat can leave the building and travel vertically into the attic if there is a large roof overhang or it can spread to an exposure near the opening. Plan for this and have a charged hose line available to take care of this problem.

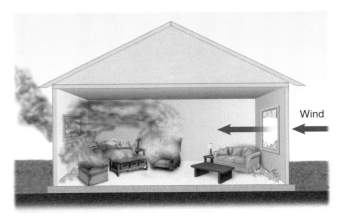

FIGURE 18-9 Whenever possible, vent the downwind side first and then open the upwind side.

Vent-point ignition is a condition in which the heated smoke bursts into heavy flames as it exits a building and reaches fresh air. Consider the exposures to the smoke as you vent, and *never* stand in the smoke column as it exits a building.

KEY WORDS

horizontal ventilation The act of creating openings along the exterior walls of a structure to allow smoke and heat to escape.

vent-point ignition The sudden ignition of heated smoke and gases as they exit a building at the ventilation opening.

Practice It!

Breaking Windows in High-Heat Conditions

Using a ceiling hook at least 6 feet long, or an axe or a prying tool, do the following:
1. Identify the wind direction and the appropriate window to force, and position on the upwind side of the window (Figure 18-10).

FIGURE 18-10

2. Perform a mental survey of your personal safety gear, ensuring that your PPE is in place. Notify the next-highest ranking person above you in the IMS that you are ready to vent the building. Wait for his or her confirmation before proceeding to break the glass. Before proceeding, check for anyone in the area who could be struck by broken glass or affected by the heat and smoke (Figure 18-11).

FIGURE 18-11

3. If at all possible, hold the striking tool with your hands above the head of the tool to help avoid having glass travel down the handle toward you. If the window is above your eye level, use a long-handled tool such as a long ceiling hook instead of an axe or a Halligan bar (Figure 18-12).

FIGURE 18-12

4. Break the glass, clearing away all of the glass, screen, and window treatments inside if possible (Figure 18-13).

FIGURE 18-13

Safety Tip!

Many instructors insist that you stand with your back against the wall, facing outward, when you break a window. While this is probably the safest stance to take, it is seldom practical in the field due to ground obstructions, landscaping, and other obstacles. Also, standing underneath the drip-edge of a pitched roof will often expose you to hot tar dripping from the roof. Breaking glass with an axe or a Halligan bar is acceptable. However, using a long-handled tool such as a long ceiling hook will provide you more distance from the hazards and, subsequently, more safety.

Horizontal ventilation works well for multistory buildings. When venting a multistory building, open the fire floor first before opening the lower windows. This order will take advantage of the natural convection and will allow the heat and smoke to lift instead of churning throughout the structure. When the windows on several floors need to be opened, work from the top down.

Breaking Windows from a Ladder

Using a ground ladder along with a ceiling hook at least 6 feet long, or an axe or other striking tool, do the following:

1. Identify the wind direction and the appropriate window to force, and position the ladder off to the side on the upwind side of the window (Figure 18-14).

FIGURE 18-14

2. Perform a mental survey of your personal safety gear, ensuring that your PPE is in place. Notify the next-highest ranking person above you in the IMS that you are ready to vent the building. Wait for his or her confirmation that you can proceed with breaking the glass. Before proceeding, check for anyone in the area who could be struck by broken glass or affected by the heat and smoke (Figure 18-15).

FIGURE 18-15

3. Ascend the ladder and lock in to secure your working position on the ladder (Figure 18-16).

FIGURE 18-16

4. If at all possible, hold the striking tool with your hands above the head of the tool to help avoid having glass travel down the handle toward you. If the window is above your eye level, use a long-handled tool such as a long ceiling hook instead of an axe or a Halligan bar to break the glass (Figure 18-17).

FIGURE 18-17

5. Break the glass, clearing away all of the glass, screen, and window treatments inside if possible (Figure 18-18).

FIGURE 18-18

Level I

At first glance, it may seem excessive to remove an entire window frame while venting a window. Breaking window glass and leaving the center rail or other trim features will usually do the job for removing smoke. However, it is important to remember that the opening you are creating may later be used as an escape path for interior firefighters or as a point of entry for a rescue. So make it a habit to remove the entire window, frame and all, for enhanced firefighter safety.

Mechanical Ventilation

In the absence of a strong breeze, natural ventilation stops when the fire is knocked down and the temperature of the smoke and gases inside the building drop to nearly the same temperature as outside. Mechanical ventilation, using high-velocity fans to either draw smoke from the building or pull fresh air in to force the smoke out, overcomes the lack of naturally occurring ventilation.

Negative-pressure ventilation is accomplished using specially designed electric fans that move approximately 5000 cubic feet of air per minute. When these fans are positioned at windows and door openings, the products of combustion are drawn out of the structure and fresh air naturally flows into the building in their place. This exchange of air is best accomplished when the negative pressure around the fan is maintained by sealing the area around the window or door opening so that the air around the door doesn't "short circuit" at the doorway. If sealing the entire doorway or window isn't practical, place the smoke ejector as high as possible in the opening, where it will encounter the most smoke (the thermal layer) (Figure 18-19).

KEY WORD

negative-pressure ventilation The use of a smoke ejector to draw smoke and heat from a building, pulling fresh air into the building in the process.

Review It!

Negative-pressure ventilation skills were practiced in *Safe Firefighting: First Things First,* Chapter 11. We suggest that you review and practice this technique if you feel the need to do so.

FIGURE 18-19 If you can't seal the area around a smoke ejector, place the ejector high in the smoke column to take advantage of the thermal layer.

Because negative-pressure ventilation requires you to work close to the building, these techniques are designed to work *after* the fire has been knocked down and the atmosphere inside the structure has started to cool. During the growth phase of a fire, do not attempt to augment naturally occurring ventilation with negative-pressure ventilation. Stay out of the hot smoke that exits a structure from naturally occurring velocity, because it often ignites in flames as it exits the building.

Hydraulic Ventilation

Once the fire has been knocked down, interior firefighters can create a form of negative-pressure ventilation by directing a fog stream from the attack line through a window. This process is called **hydraulic ventilation.** When properly applied, the rushing fire stream moves quite a bit of air through an open window, creating a negative-pressure situation in the room that naturally pulls in fresh air from the entry point.

To perform hydraulic ventilation, position across the room from an open window or about 10 to 15 feet

FIGURE 18-20 Hydraulic ventilation is more efficient if you position across the room from an open window and fill the opening with a narrow fog pattern from the hose line.

FIGURE 18-21 Place a PPV fan at least 10 feet from a doorway to "fill" the opening with a cone of air.

back if you are in a large room and direct a fog pattern through the window to the outside. Adjust the nozzle pattern so that it just fills the window, sealing it so that the smoke doesn't circulate back into the room. When hydraulic ventilation is properly applied, you will feel the room cool quickly and the smoke conditions will improve greatly (Figure 18-20).

KEY WORD

hydraulic ventilation The act of directing a fog stream from inside a building, through a window, to the outdoors to pull smoke from the building.

Positive-Pressure Ventilation (PPV)

Positive-pressure ventilation (PPV) is a method of ventilation that uses large-capacity fans (PPV fans) to introduce large volumes of fresh air into a structure through an entry point. This type of ventilation gives the smoke and hot air inside more velocity and direction toward the desired vent point. When the PPV fan's airflow is directed into the structure, it creates a slight rise in interior pressure. However, the main reason PPV is an effective ventilation method is that it adds velocity to the smoke (Figure 18-21).

For PPV to be effective, the vent points should be no more than 1 3/4 times the size of the air entrance opening. As a rule of thumb for an average size house, this means that no more than two or three windows should be opened when the fan is placed at the front door. However, in most house fires, the fire area is broken into several rooms, connected by a hallway and segregated by doors. If more than two or three rooms are involved or charged with smoke, then they all need to be vented. Opening and closing selected doors along the hallway will accomplish this.

Many progressive fire departments now employ PPV as part of their fire attack plan. Think of the

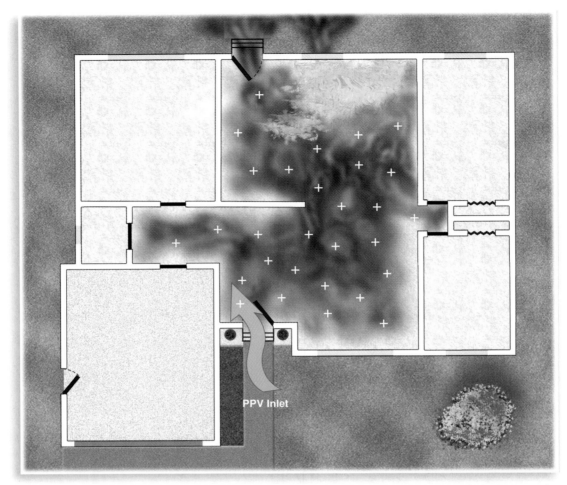

PPV Inlet

FIGURE 18-22 Maintain an adequate flow of air through the fire attack corridor by opening and closing one door at a time as you proceed.

hallway as a fire attack corridor and each room as a separate compartment. As long as there is an opening on the other end for the heat and smoke to escape, the velocity of the inward-rushing fresh air will drop the temperature and improve the visibility in the fire attack corridor. Closing the doors in the corridor acts as a damper, stopping the flow of air. By opening the doors as they encounter them, the interior team can selectively vent the rooms adjacent to the fire attack corridor as they go. Once the room is cooled and there is no fire, the attack team can close the door and move to the next door to repeat the process. As the team progresses along the corridor, the air quality and visibility conditions will improve (Figure 18-22).

■■■ KEY WORD ■■■■■■■■■

positive-pressure ventilation (PPV) The use of a specially designed fan directed into a structure to add velocity to smoke and direct it to a strategically placed opening (vent point) in an exterior wall.

 **Review It!**

Positive-pressure ventilation skills were practiced in *Safe Firefighting: First Things First,* Chapter 11, "Single-Family-Dwelling Fires." We suggest that you review and practice this technique if you feel the need to do so.

Vertical Ventilation

Vertical ventilation is the most efficient way to vent a structural fire. In this process, an opening is made in the roof to allow the heat of a fire to naturally vent the structure while fresh air enters through openings at the bottom. However, safe vertical ventilation operations depend on several factors, including adequate fireground staffing and building construction that supports this option. Vertical ventilation relies on the same principles as the chimney in a fireplace—hot air rises, and very hot air rises quickly. Successful vertical ventilation depends on two things: an opening for the heat to escape and an opening for fresh air to enter the space. Without the ability to draw in fresh air, vertical ventilation will not be effective. So it is important that, as with any ventilation operation, vertical ventilation be conducted as part of a coordinated fireground effort and not as an independent activity.

KEY WORD

vertical ventilation The act of creating openings in the roof of a structure to allow smoke and heat to escape.

Roof Operations

The two most important aspects of venting any roof are to know the condition of the roof's deck and support structure before you put your weight on them, and to immediately leave the roof once the job is done. It is unwise to linger on a roof as the fire attacks the structure that is supporting your weight. Roof activities should not be conducted unless it is confirmed that the roof structure can support the operation *and* adequate staffing is on the scene to support all essential fireground activities (Figure 18-23). Truss roofs have no distinguishing characteristics that are visible from the outside, so confirm the type of roof structure before climbing out onto a roof. Truss roofs, when made of wood or exposed steel trusses, will fail rapidly when exposed to fire. Do not perform roof operations on truss roofs if there is any suspicion that the trusses are exposed to fire.

 Safety Tip!

If it cannot be confirmed that the condition of the roof's structure can support the weight of a roof team working above the fire, then conventional vertical ventilation activities are no longer an option unless a sufficient platform can be provided by an aerial ladder. Do not risk falling through a weak roof. Instead, be patient. The fire will burn its own ventilation point soon enough.

 **Review It!**

Review Chapter 17, "Building Construction," paying close attention to the section on truss roofs.

Before going out on a roof, it is often a good idea to make a small inspection hole near the roof's edge

FIGURE 18-23 Roof operations are performed as a team and not as an individual effort.

FIGURE 18-24 A kerf cut is simply a single slice the same width of a saw blade that allows you to watch for smoke and fire.

FIGURE 18-25 A small triangular hole in the roof deck makes a good inspection opening.

to determine how much smoke and fire are present in the attic space. Start with a single cut the width of the saw's blade, called a **kerf cut**. If heavy smoke or fire pushes out, then you know that the fire is attacking the roof supports. If you need more access to inspect the attic area, make an inspection hole by adding two more intersecting cuts to form a small, triangular-shaped opening about 1 foot long on each side (Figures 18-24 and 18-25).

When walking out onto a flat roof, stop at the roof's edge and, while still supported by the ladder, sound out the roof by thumping it with a heavy tool. This thumping allows you to check the roof for the location of supports and to determine if the roof deck

FIGURE 18-26 "Thumping" a roof will help you identify the location of roof supports underneath.

is strong enough to support your weight. You will hear and feel a substantial difference between where the roof support beams are located and where the roof deck is unsupported. This will tell you which way the roof supports are running. Sound out the roof as you go, checking it for soft spots that would indicate a need to evacuate the roof (Figure 18-26). Some indications of a possible roof collapse include distortion in the roof's surface, smoke or fire coming from cracks and spaces in the roof covering, sagging, and melted roof coatings. Watch for these indications and evacuate the roof immediately if you encounter any indication of possible roof collapse. Your best defense is to know the type of roof you are working

on and the fire conditions you will be working over before walking out on a roof.

If the roof is pitched in any way, it is best that you use a roof ladder, hooked over the ridge, to support your weight and provide secure footing as you go. For safety, keep your weight distributed on the ladder and not on the roof deck. If you must reach out beyond your normal reach and step off the roof ladder, use a second ladder.

KEY WORD

kerf cut A slice cut that is just the width of a saw blade. This cut is made in a roof to check for fire or smoke conditions in an attic space.

Roof operations are inherently dangerous and should be done as a team, not as an individual, under the full support of the Incident Management System. A charged hose line should be staffed and ready to protect anyone on the roof. Beware of changing fire conditions underneath you and be prepared to immediately evacuate the roof. In case conditions worsen, have at least two ways to evacuate the roof. A second ladder from another location will give you a secondary means of escape if fire cuts you off from the ladder you used to access the roof. A fire escape ladder attached to the building is another means of egress. However, you should inspect the fire escape for damage or decay before you designate it as your secondary means of escape.

Practice It!

Working from a Roof Ladder

Using a ceiling hook at least 6 feet long, or an axe or a prying tool, do the following:

1. Identify the wind direction and the appropriate window to force. Position the ladder on the upwind side of the building (Figure 18-27).

FIGURE 18-27

2. Perform a mental survey of your personal safety gear, ensuring that your PPE is in place (Figure 18-28).

FIGURE 18-28

3. Notify the next-highest ranking person above you in the IMS that your team has laddered the building and is proceeding to the roof.

4. Sound out the roof structure. Ladder the roof with the hooks of the roof ladder secured over the peak and the ladder on the upwind side of where you will be creating an opening (Figure 18-29).

FIGURE 18-29

5. Keep your feet in contact with the roof ladder. If it is necessary to step out from the ladder, use a second roof ladder to secure your footing (Figure 18-30).

FIGURE 18-30

6. Notify the next-highest ranking person above you in the IMS that you are leaving the roof and notify him or her again when you are safely on the ground (Figure 18-31).

FIGURE 18-31

Tip!

Use a Roof Rope

Saws and other equipment can be heavy and cumbersome to carry up a ground ladder. It is usually far easier to carry a light rope to the roof, drop it to a firefighter below, and hoist the tools to the roof (Figure 18-32). Review and practice the knots you learned in Chapter 14 with this tip in mind.

FIGURE 18-32 Check that a saw will start. However, shut it off before hoisting it to the roof.

Natural Roof Openings

Natural roof openings are often the best outlet for vertical ventilation. This type of roof opening includes gable vents, roof vents, roof hatches, and skylights. Although they are situated on the side of a building, gable vents are directly underneath the roof line and offer a good opportunity to vent an attic area of smoke and heat without climbing on the roof. Therefore, they are considered to be a natural roof opening.

Although you may notice heavy smoke issuing from a gable vent, these vents usually have a screen backing that restricts the flow of smoke from them. Most gable vents can be easily removed while standing firmly on the ground by using a long ceiling hook (Figure 18-33). Start by checking for overhead obstructions and hazards, such as wires. Now jam the tool's head between the louvers near the top of the vent and pull down and out. If the vent doesn't pull out easily, push the tool's head in a little so you can gain some momentum and strike the vent with more force, breaking it free.

Roof vents are often available along the ridge, just off of the ridge, or along the roofline. These vents already have an opening underneath, with a light metal covering that is designed to keep rain out of the structure. Some roof vents have a wind-driven turbine that twirls in the breeze, acting as a fan to theoretically remove heat from the attic space. Breaking away this metal covering will help the heat and smoke flow freely (Figure 18-34).

Roof hatches that are part of a roof access scuttle opening on a commercial building make great vertical ventilation shafts for the upper floor. These scuttles often have a protected shaft that prevents the heat and smoke from entering the attic space, venting the smoke and heat from the top floor directly outside. Most roof hatches are locked. They will take forcible

FIGURE 18-33 The louvers and screen on a gable end vent restrict the flow of smoke. Remove the vent to provide the best ventilation.

FIGURE 18-34 Roof vents will draw smoke naturally. However, the vent covering should be removed when it is safe to go to the roof.

entry work to cut them open from the roof side. When a roof scuttle is used as a vent point, it is no longer available as a secondary means for escaping the roof if the need arises, so be sure to have a second ladder in place.

Skylights are also good options for vertical ventilation. To remove most skylights, stand on the upwind side of the skylight and strip away any metal trim that may be around the rim. Then pry the skylight from the roof or curb. Turn the skylight upside down on the roof. Place it on the upwind side of the opening to serve as a warning to other firefighters working on the roof that there is an opening in the roof. Many firefighters have been injured when they stepped into an opening while walking through thick smoke on a roof. Be sure everyone knows that the skylight has been removed and that there is a hole in the roof.

Forced Roof Openings

Although natural roof openings allow for quick ventilation, it is quite often necessary to create an opening in the roof deck. The type of material that is used as sheeting for the roof deck and roofing materials often dictates the type of tools you use. Conventional sheeting on modern residential structures is usually a variation of plywood, particle board, or oriented strand board. Residential construction during the first half of the 20th century often has 12-inch-wide boards used as sheeting to make the roof deck. Either type of deck is covered with a layer of waterproofing material called roof felt and then another layer of asphalt shingles. If wood, concrete tile, or slate is used as shingles, then the roof may not have a conventional deck at all. Instead, 6-inch-wide boards might be used as laths, spaced at crucial points to support the shingles. If this is the case, expect fire to rapidly attack the laths, causing a rapid collapse of the entire roof structure.

Cutting through the roof deck to create a vent point is usually done with a power saw and ceiling hooks. On older roofs with conventional boards for a deck, chopping through the roof deck with an axe is an option, but this is time-consuming and very labor intensive.

Keep the following points in mind before going to the roof to create a ventilation opening:

- Be sure you have at least two separate ways to get off the roof and that everyone understands the evacuation plan.
- Choose the right tools for the type of roof construction you are about to cut.

- Be sure to take the appropriate tools for pulling away debris from the opening and to punch through a ceiling layer beneath the opening.
- Be sure the saw starts and runs well before taking it to the roof.
- Have a charged hose line available.
- Notify the next level of IMS that your team is going to the roof, when their job is complete, and when you are off the roof and safely on the ground.

Gasoline-Powered Saws

When faced with cutting a hole through a roof, gasoline-powered saws give us a great advantage over an axe. They are the tools most commonly used for roof ventilation operations. The two main types of saws used for roof ventilation are the circular saw and the chain saw. Each type of saw has advantages and disadvantages, but of the two, a chain saw that has been designed for Fire Service ventilation is the most versatile type for roof work. This is not an ordinary chain saw that one would use for tree trimming. The chain saw that is designed for ventilation purposes is generally referred to as a **ventilation saw** (Figure 18-35).

■■■ KEY WORD ■■■

ventilation saw   A chainsaw that is specially equipped with a powerful motor, a carbide-tipped chain, and a bar that is designed specifically for cutting into roofs.

Circular Saws   Circular saws use a composite disc that is designed for specialized use. A disc designed for metal cutting will not work well when cutting concrete, and vice versa. Specialized discs are available that offer multi-cutting capabilities, including wood, metal, and concrete. However, most fire departments keep their circular saws equipped with a metal-cutting disc for forcible entry through bars. If this is the practice in your fire department, then more often than not roof ventilation with a circular saw will start with the time-consuming task of changing the cutting disc for one designed for the type of roof deck you will be cutting. Following the manufacturer's directions, be sure to practice changing the cutting disc on the type and model of circular saw your jurisdiction uses.

Ventilation Saws   Ventilation saws have specially designed, carbide-tipped chains and short cutting bars designed to cut through the roof deck. Some models have a specially designed cutting bar that is

FIGURE 18-35 Gasoline-powered saws: (a) circular saw, and (b) ventilation saw.

FIGURE 18-36 A ventilation saw has several specially designed features that assist in cutting into a roof to the proper depth.

TABLE 18-1 Uses of Circular and Ventilation Saws		
Use	Circular Saw	Ventilation Saw
Wood roof decks	Yes	Yes
Light metal roof decks	Yes	Yes
Light concrete over corrugated metal roof decks	Yes	Yes
Concrete roof decks	Yes	No

angled to allow the user to keep the motor level at a comfortable height while cutting through the roof deck. Other models have adjustable guides on the bars that control the depth of the cut by stopping the bar from plunging too deeply. This safety feature helps prevent cutting through rafters underneath the roof deck (Figure 18-36).

Table 18-1 lists the uses of gasoline-powered circular and ventilation saws.

Power-Saw Operations Circular and chain saws are driven by similar two-stroke motors. Two-stroke motors run on a gasoline-oil mixture that lubricates the motor as it runs. Be sure to follow the manufacturer's instructions when mixing the fuel-oil combination so that the proper ratio is achieved. A well-maintained two-stroke motor is very dependable. However, starting one can be a bit tricky at times. The most common problems that make a saw hard to start include

- Stale fuel
- Flooding due to overchoking the motor
- A clogged air filter
- A fouled spark plug

Take the time to read the instructions for your specific saw and learn how to troubleshoot the motor when it doesn't start. There is no substitute for proper maintenance for any Fire Service tool, which is especially important for small, gasoline-powered motors.

General Guidelines for Operating a Power Saw

Using either type of power saw, follow the manufacturer's instructions to do the following:

1. Identify the type of fuel mixture and check that the saw is properly filled with fresh fuel.

2. If using a chainsaw, check that the saw is properly filled with bar oil for lubricating the chain (Figure 18-37).

FIGURE 18-37

3. Visually inspect the chain or cutting disc for deformities and proper tightness.

4. Ensure that the air filter is present and clean (Figure 18-38).

FIGURE 18-38

5. Have the appropriate PPE in place before starting the saw.

6. If the saw is equipped with a run/stop switch, move it to the run position (Figure 18-39).

FIGURE 18-39

—Continued

Level I

7. Cold start: Pull the choke out fully. Warm start: Pull the choke to the half-stop position. Hot start: Leave the choke alone (Figure 18-40).

FIGURE 18-40

8. Lock the throttle trigger in the start position.
9. With the saw firmly on the deck, brace the saw with your foot or knee and pull the rope sharply until it starts. Immediately put the choke in the off position and move the trigger to the idle position, letting the saw warm to the proper running temperature before shutting it off (Figure 18-41).

FIGURE 18-41

Tip!

Pull the throttle and then make the cut. The most common mistake a novice makes when initially cutting with a power saw is making contact with the cutting surface and the material, and then hitting the throttle. Take advantage of the power and momentum of a high-speed blade or chain, and rev the motor before putting the blade to the roof deck. Otherwise, you will probably stall the motor, causing a delay in the operation and causing yourself some frustration.

Ventilating a Flat Roof

The general approach when cutting a ventilation hole in a flat roof is to make one large hole rather than several small holes. Not only does the larger hole have more area for the smoke to escape, it also allows for a quicker operation, which means less time spent on a dangerous roof. A good starting point is to make a 4-by-4-foot square opening. This size opening takes advantage of the 24-inch spacing between rafters that is found in many roofs and provides a good opening that can be extended in size with three cuts if necessary.

To make a rectangular cut in a flat roof, start by sounding out the roof to determine which way the roof supports are running. It may be necessary to cut a small inspection opening to determine this. If the roof covering is simply asphalt shingles or some other soft material, cut through the material rather than taking the time to strip it back. If the roof material is concrete or slate, you may have to strip it away before making a cut. Make the first cut along the inside of one of the rafters, followed by cuts across the rafters at either end. Take special care to avoid cutting through the roof supports when you encounter them. You should feel a change in the cutting speed when you touch the supports. Simply rock the saw back or lift it so that you are just cutting through the roof deck as you cross the center support. Stop just short of the last roof support. Now complete the cut with a long cut parallel to the remaining roof support. The goal is to have the remaining piece of roof deck supported by only one rafter at this point (Figure 18-42).

You now have two general options for removing the remaining section of roof to create the opening: Pull out the material or create a louver. Pulling the material may require one extra small cut across a corner of the material to allow access to the opening. If you anticipate this need, you may cut a corner as you make the initial cuts in the roof. Now you can simply pull or pry away at the roofing to make the opening.

Instead of pulling and prying, some firefighters prefer to punch down on one side of the opening, taking advantage of leverage and using the center rafter as a fulcrum. It may not be necessary to pull the debris completely away from the hole if it is still supported by the center rafter. Just leave it in place as a louver and get off the roof.

Once the debris is out of the way and the roof is open, evaluate the results and notify the appropriate person in the IMS of your results. It may be necessary to punch an opening through the ceiling layer to allow the upper floor to vent. To do this, use a long-

FIGURE 18-42 Making a rectangular roof opening on a flat roof.

handled tool, such as a ceiling hook, dropping the tool's handle end into the hole. If you use the head of the tool, it can easily become entangled in debris and wires in the attic space. Using the smooth handle end will help prevent this.

 ## View It!

Go to the DVD, navigate to Chapter 18, and select *"Rectangular Roof Cuts."*

➥ Practice It!

Making Rectangular Roof Cuts

Using a gasoline-powered ventilation saw, do the following:

1. Check and run the saw on the ground before hoisting it to the roof (Figure 18-43). (*Note:* Do not hoist a running saw.)

2. Check your PPE and also check your partner's PPE before climbing to the roof. Notify the appropriate level of the IMS that you are going to the roof.

FIGURE 18-43

—Continued

3. Sound out the roof supports and mark the area you plan to cut (Figure 18-44).

FIGURE 18-44

4. Confirm that IMS is ready for the opening to be made.

5. Make the cuts, starting along the inside of the first rafter and moving across both ends and along the inner edge of the last rafter (Figure 18-45).

FIGURE 18-45

6. Remove the debris or make a louver to create the opening (Figure 18-46).

FIGURE 18-46

7. Use a long-handled tool, handle end first, to punch through any ceiling materials if this is needed (Figure 18-47).

8. Notify IMS that the opening has been created, evaluate the results, and get off the roof if no more roof work is needed.

FIGURE 18-47

Once the primary opening has been made, it is usually far easier to extend the size of that opening than to create a new hole in the roof. To enlarge the opening, simply extend any two of the original cuts and make an intersecting cut across the end, pulling away the debris and punching through the ceiling as necessary.

Stay back from the opening. Never look directly into a vent opening. Keep your face and body back when punching through the ceiling layer, taking advantage of a long-handled tool to maintain a safe distance from the rising heat and smoke.

Ventilating a Pitched Roof

Pitched roof ventilation has the added obstacle of working on a slope instead of a flat surface. However, by working from a roof ladder, the principles for making a rectangular hole as a primary opening requires the same steps as if you were working on a flat roof. Sound out the roof supports and make an inspection hole near the edge. Cut the far side of the opening along the inside of the rafter and a diagonal notch on one corner. Cut across both ends and make the final cut along the inside of the closest rafter. Doing so will allow you to either punch the closest edge of the debris downward to create a louver or pull the far corner of the debris to strip it away. Once the opening has been created, punch through the ceiling layer as described before to allow the smoke and heat to rise from the top floor of the structure (Figure 18-48).

The primary opening can be expanded with two or three cuts, depending on the type of roof deck you are cutting. If the sheeting is plywood, expect to make three cuts because the size opening will seldom fall at a joint in the plywood. If the sheeting is horizontal 12-inch-wide boards, the two cuts along the rafters will make quicker work of extending the opening, taking advantage of the spaces between the boards.

Ventilating a Basement

Basement fires present a very dangerous, tough situation because there is usually a lack of windows or adequate natural openings for ventilation. Also, many basements have only one entry point, which means that you will have only one exit point once you are in the basement. Therefore, quite often the only natural ventilation point will also be the access point, which puts firefighters and hot smoke in the same opening if a remote vent point isn't established. The goal is to provide a ventilation point away from the entry point so that the heat and smoke draft away from the entry team as they make their way to the basement. Although some heat and smoke will exit the staircase that is used for the fire attack, ventilation often al-

FIGURE 18-48 Pitched roof ventilation.

lows the heat to rise, so that the entry team can crawl down the stairs, feet first, while staying beneath the thermal layer.

Of all the types of fires we face, basement fires usually require the most damage to be done to the building to provide adequate ventilation for fire control and life safety. The first choice for venting a basement is usually the windows or exterior access points, if available. Although basement windows are small, they are a good place to start venting a small fire. Often the basement wall is made of concrete or cinder block that extends above ground level. If this is the case, breaching the wall is a viable option for creating a vent point.

A method of last resort for ventilating a basement fire is to create a vent point through the floor near a window, allowing the heat to enter the first-floor living space. This requires extensive coordination between hose teams and the vent team, and it will require a hose team dedicated to the vent point before making the opening. Start by moving any furniture in the area and stripping back any flammable floor coverings such as carpeting or an area rug. Clear the window of glass and remove the entire window frame to provide as large an opening as possible. Take down any window treatments such as curtains or blinds, even if they do not obstruct the window opening. Now cut away the flooring as if it were a roof. The finished opening should be nearly the same size as the window you are using to vent the heat. The hose team should remain in place to monitor the opening for fire, and to use hydraulic ventilation techniques to help push the venting smoke and heat out of the window.

Trench Ventilation

Trench ventilation, or trenching, is a method of secondary ventilation that can be used to limit fire spread in a large but narrow building or portion of a building. The main intent of trench ventilation is to provide a firebreak similar to a break around a grass fire, where the fuel is limited and the heat and smoke can escape. An additional advantage of trenching is that it allows fresh air to enter an attic from a remote area in order to replace venting smoke and heat from the primary vent point.

▰▰▰ KEY WORD ▰▰▰

trench ventilation　A vertical ventilation technique in which a long, narrow opening is extended between the exterior walls in a larger, narrow building.

Safety Tip!

Because a trench cut usually extends from one wall to the other, it will cut off your escape path if you are standing on one side of the trench and your primary escape ladder is on the other side. Plan every step of the process well, and provide for at least two paths of escape from the side of the trench you are standing on, which should be the side away from the main body of fire. Everyone involved in the trench operation should work from the same side of the opening for safety.

When trenching a flat roof, start with a cut along the wall and another cut about 4 feet long extending from the wall. If you are trenching a pitched roof, start at the peak and work downward. The first long cut should be along the side of the trench that is farthest from your escape path. Now make the second long cut and another across the end of the opening to create

FIGURE 18-49　A trench cut is useful to limit fire spread in a long, narrow building.

the first segment of the trench. Continue extending the trench in 4-foot segments until the trench extends from one wall to the other, or from the peak to the edge of a pitched roof on either side of the ridge (Figure 18-49).

Do It!

Ventilate Safely!

Ventilation is a fireground action that is just as crucial to safely extinguishing a fire as applying water. To safely vent a fire, we must practice the skills often, keep our equipment in excellent running condition, and work within the Incident Management System so that our efforts are coordinated with the entire fire attack. Rusty skills, dull or poorly running tools, and freelancing on the fire scene while ventilating a fire will create an unsafe and potentially deadly situation. Make ventilation as important a part of your personal strategy as pulling hose, operating a nozzle, and maintaining your breathing apparatus.

Knowledge Assessment

Signed Documentation Tear-Out Sheet

Ventilation and Fire Behavior—Chapter 18

Name: _____

Fill out the ten-question quiz below, the Knowledge Assessment Sheet, by circling the correct answer for each question. When finished, sign it and give it to your instructor/Company Officer for his or her signature. Turn in this Knowledge Assessment Sheet to the proper person as part of the documentation that you have completed your training for this chapter.

1. When a fire in a room runs out of fuel before overheating the room, the smoke remains at the ceiling level. This is called a _____.
   a. backdraft
   b. thermal layer
   c. flashover
   d. flameover

2. A condition in which the smoke and heated gases in a confined area combine with the right amount of heat and oxygen to ignite suddenly in a very intense fire is called a _____.
   a. backdraft
   b. thermal layer
   c. flashover
   d. flameover

3. A sudden explosion of superheated smoke and gases in a confined space is called a _____.
   a. backdraft
   b. thermal layer
   c. flashover
   d. flameover

4. In a structural fire, ventilation procedures are secondary in the extinguishment process to the application of water on the flames.
   a. True
   b. False

5. The use of fans to remove warm smoke from a building is called _____.
   a. vertical ventilation
   b. horizontal ventilation
   c. forced ventilation
   d. mechanical ventilation

6. _____ is a condition in which the heated smoke from a vented structure bursts into heavy flames as it exits a building and reaches fresh air.

    a. Flashover

    b. Vent-point ignition

    c. Backdraft

    d. Flameover

7. If a smoke ejector is hung from a door and the exhaust side of the fan is directed outward, it is set up to perform _____ ventilation.

    a. negative-pressure

    b. positive-pressure

    c. vertical

    d. hydraulic

8. A cut in a roof that is the width of a saw blade, and is used to determine how much smoke and fire is present below the roof team, is called a(n) _____ cut.

    a. relief

    b. kerf

    c. inspection

    d. pressure

9. When ventilating through a roof, it is more efficient to make several small openings in the roof rather than one large opening.

    a. True

    b. False

10. In a long, narrow building, a _____ cut helps limit the horizontal flame spread.

    a. relief

    b. kerf

    c. trench

    d. rectangular

Student Signature and Date _____   Instructor/Company Officer Signature and Date _____

442

Prove It

Skills Assessment

Ventilation and Fire Behavior—Chapter 18

Name: _____

Fill out the Skills Assessment Sheet below. Have your instructor/Company Officer check off and initial each skill you demonstrate. When you are finished, sign this page and give to your instructor/Company Officer for his or her signature. Turn in this Skills Assessment Sheet to the proper person as part of the documentation that you have completed your training for this chapter.

Skill	Completed	Initials
1. Safely break a ground-level window for ventilation.	_____	_____
2. Safely break a window from a ladder.	_____	_____
3. Perform negative-pressure ventilation.	_____	_____
4. Perform positive-pressure ventilation.	_____	_____
5. Work safely on a flat roof.	_____	_____
6. Work safely on a pitched roof using a roof ladder.	_____	_____
7. Hoist ventilation tools to the roof using a utility rope.	_____	_____
8. Start and operate ventilation saws.	_____	_____

Level I

Student Signature and Date _____   Instructor/Company Officer Signature and Date _____

Safety and Survival for Interior Firefighters

What You Will Learn in This Chapter

This chapter will introduce you to a very critical step in firefighting, the step you take to cross the threshold of a burning building—the step that takes you inside the hazard zone and an atmosphere that is immediately dangerous to life and health (IDLH). Our philosophy at this point in your training is simple: We want you to know how to use all of your PPE to safely navigate through the smoke and heat as a team, to efficiently search for and rescue a victim, and to be able to react properly if you or another crew member gets in trouble. This chapter is filled with important drills that will help you build some fundamental habits you will need whenever working inside.

What You Will Be Able to Do

After reading this chapter and practicing the skills described, you will be able to:

1. Describe some of the hazards to look for when making the decision to enter a burning structure.
2. Safely use a portable electrical generator and Fire Department–issued floodlighting to light the scene and interior of a building for safety.
3. Describe the hazards associated with, and safety procedures to use while working around, stacked materials.
4. Explain the role that personnel accountability plays in the safety of crews working inside an IDLH atmosphere, and the responsibility of every firefighter working within a proper personnel accountability system.
5. Explain a Personnel Accountability Report and when it is used.
6. Perform controlled breathing techniques while wearing an SCBA.
7. Describe and perform all the skills necessary to work as part of the interior team while searching, fighting fire, and exiting the structure.

445

8. Recognize and take appropriate actions when your low-air warning signal activates.

9. Recognize various problems with the function of your SCBA and take appropriate action, including using the purge valve when necessary.

10. Describe and perform emergency evacuation procedures, including self-rescue techniques, emergency evacuations, ladder use, and methods for seeking refuge as necessary.

11. Effectively communicate if a problem arises while working inside a burning structure or other IDLH environment.

12. Effectively free yourself from entanglement if necessary.

13. Navigate with obscured vision inside a structure.

14. Perform a primary and a secondary search of a structure.

15. Describe and perform the basics of operating a thermal imaging camera.

16. Describe and perform various techniques for locating and rescuing a civilian from a burning structure.

17. Describe and perform various techniques for locating and rescuing a fellow firefighter from a burning structure.

Our Common Goal: Everyone Goes Home!

A common term heard around most progressive firehouses these days is *EGH—Everyone Goes Home!* This simple idea should be the essence of everything we do, and the philosophical center of every decision we make. The reality is that we continue to have thousands of needless injuries and over 100 firefighter deaths in the United States each year. More than half of the deaths are medically related, and many are related to age, lifestyle choices that lead to poor physical condition, obesity, and other factors that have been discussed previously. The focus of this chapter is on the many preventable traumatic injuries and deaths to firefighters.

As Monday-morning quarterbacks, we know that most injuries and traumatic deaths to firefighters could have been prevented. However, the distractions of the emergency often pull our focus away from safety. The old term for this was "candle-moth syndrome"—a moth is drawn to the flame on a burning candle, only to die when it flies into the light. Experience will help you overcome this problem, allowing you to concentrate on what is really important—your safety and the safety of the other firefighters around you. The bottom line is that it's your responsibility to be safe

and to survive. To do this takes endless training and conditioning so that you have the skills and ingrained habits that allow you to recognize the hazard, formulate a safe plan of action, and react appropriately when something doesn't go as planned. With that in mind, this chapter relies on several practice sessions to help you develop, and in some cases reinforce, good habits that will help you survive those things that will affect your immediate safety, as well as helping reduce the long-term exposure to your health. Both are consequences of being a firefighter.

Hazard Recognition

One may think that, as a Level I firefighter, your safety is the responsibility of the Company Officer. This is partially true, but it doesn't leave much room for error. The overall safety of the crew is always the Company Officer's responsibility, but in reality, the more eyes that look at a problem and the more brains that work on a solution, the better the outcome will be. Everyone on the fireground should have the power to call attention to a hazard and to stop an unsafe practice. There is a fine line between a thinking firefighter and an insubordinate firefighter. However, blind obedience is dangerous and should not be part of the safety plan on any emergency scene. Stop and think: *Does the order I just received make sense and do I see something that the Officer may not have seen?* Awareness of your surroundings and changing conditions is the most basic element of making sure that Everyone Goes Home!

The decision to enter a hazardous area, such as a burning structure, is reached after all of the known hazards have been addressed (Figure 19-1). Obviously, when the hazard is a burning structure or other situation involving fire, the method we use to address the level of hazard is to don all of our PPE, have the proper staffing in place, make sure an adequate and uninterruptible water supply is established, and ensure that ventilation and adequately charged and staffed hose lines are in place before we make entry. But the question remains: Does the type of construction combined with the fire conditions support a reasonable margin of safety for an entry team?

Immediate Hazards

The hard fact is that when fighting a structural fire, things can go from reasonably safe to deadly in a moment. This entire book is designed to help you gain the knowledge and skills you need to recognize and overcome some of the hazards that can keep you from going

FIGURE 19-1 The decision to enter a burning building is an informed decision, not an automatic reflex. Know as much as possible about what you are getting into before going inside.

FIGURE 19-2 The smoke issuing from this building is dark and turbulent, signaling the possibility that a flashover is about to occur.

FIGURE 19-3 Adequate lighting should be deployed on all sides of a building and anywhere in the interior where firefighters will be working.

home after the fire is out. Knowing the construction characteristics of a building, and how fire and smoke behave during a structural fire, have been discussed in previous chapters. A major factor to consider in your decision to enter a burning structure is the smoke and fire behavior you observe before making entry. Heavy fire showing from a structure is an obvious sign that at least part of the structure is untenable. But what about the remaining structure? Is thick, dark smoke issuing from every opening in the building? If so, then flashover is likely to follow (Figure 19-2). Is the smoke sluggish and light in color? Then chances are that in portions of the structure the conditions are survivable for a victim who is likely to be inside.

Reading smoke and fire conditions is a skill that is best gained through experience. Rely on the opinions of your Company Officer and the more experienced members of your crew, and ask plenty of questions after each fire to help hone these skills. If you have any doubts about the importance of this skill, review Chapters 17 and 18 before attempting the drills in this chapter.

Emergency Lighting

Many factors that are critical to our initial size-up of an emergency can remain hidden in darkness unless we provide adequate lighting. Lighting the scene should be an initial safety measure, not an afterthought. A large fire provides plenty of light as it burns, but the objective is to extinguish this light source, so plan ahead and provide light for the scene before you need it. Even during daylight operations, the inside of a building can be a dark place. Make it a habit to take lighting inside as you go. Personal flashlights are a great secondary source of light; however, they cannot

compete with the bright illumination of a 500-watt light that is powered by the generator on your truck. Most fire departments also have truck-mounted lights that allow us to illuminate the exterior of a building at night (Figure 19-3).

 Safety Tip!

With all the tools and equipment we carry to a fire, it is often hard to drag along a floodlight and cord. If this is a problem, make it standard procedure to have one of the support people outside the building bring the light to the entry point as you enter, with the light pointing into the building. This will illuminate the initial area and, more importantly, serve as a beacon to mark the exit as you search through limited visibility conditions.

Working with a generator can be hazardous. The cords, lights, and circuit protection on the generator should be designed for Fire Service use. Most fire departments use twist-lock style electrical connections instead of the standard three-prong household type you would purchase at the hardware store. A twist-lock connection allows you to drag the cord behind you as you go, without having to worry about pulling the plug free at each connection in a cord. The circuits on a generator should be equipped with a circuit breaker and a **ground-fault interrupter (GFI).** Circuit breakers sense an overloaded circuit. When too many things are plugged into the same circuit, the breaker trips to prevent a fire. A GFI is a safety measure that protects humans from electrical shock. A GFI senses a difference in current between the positive and negative terminals in an electrical circuit. Normally the current is the same between both as it flows. When there is a break in a cord, or if someone comes into contact with the current, the flow changes and becomes unequal, tripping the GFI circuit before it reaches the circuit breaker. GFI outlets are equipped with a test button that should be activated when doing a routine equipment check of a generator.

▰ KEY WORD ▰

ground-fault interrupter (GFI) A specially designed circuit breaker that senses an overloaded circuit. When too many things are plugged into the same circuit, the breaker trips to prevent a fire. The GFI is a safety measure that protects humans from electrical shock.

Portable Generator Safety

Remember that just because the electricity is being generated by a small, gasoline-powered device, electrical voltage is still present and can be deadly. Follow these tips when working with a portable generator:

1. Use the generator outdoors and away from doors, windows, and vents to avoid carbon monoxide buildup. Keep the generator dry and protected from rain while it's running (Figure 19-4).
2. Dry your hands before touching a running generator or before plugging in any attachments connected to the generator. It is best to make connections before you start the generator (Figure 19-5).
3. Never plug the generator into a wall outlet to "back-feed" power to the rest of the building.
4. Let the generator cool before refilling the tank. If this is impractical because of the type of emergency service the generator is providing, then follow all fire precautions and wear PPE when refilling it (Figure 19-6).

Utilities

It is common for firefighters to punch holes in walls and ceilings to locate hidden fires (Figure 19-9). You will learn about this in the next chapter. Behind the wallboard and above the ceiling is electrical wiring.

FIGURE 19-4

FIGURE 19-5

FIGURE 19-6

Providing Adequate Light

Using the portable generator, and lighting equipment provided, do the following:

1. Locate all of the cords, adapters, and ancillary lighting equipment, and practice operating each type (Figure 19-7).

FIGURE 19-7

2. Clean and store all electrical equipment in a ready-for-use position on the apparatus (Figure 19-8).

FIGURE 19-8

You may encounter water and gas pipes as well. So it is important that the utilities are controlled early at any structural fire. This is best done by an outside team of firefighters before the interior team makes entry. There are times when this isn't practical, such as when there is a reasonable belief that someone is trapped inside and the utilities control points are located where they can't be readily accessed. There may be someone trapped in a house fire that originated in the garage, where the electrical power disconnect switch is inside the garage. It is important that everyone know when the utilities have been controlled and, more importantly, when there is a delay in controlling the utilities in the operation.

FIGURE 19-9 Expect hidden hazards inside walls and above the ceiling.

FIGURE 19-10 Stacked materials are common in commercial buildings, especially in the warehouse area.

Stacked Materials

A typical residential occupancy has a certain level of hazards that we come to expect in the Fire Service. Utilities, some pesticides or flammable liquids in the garage or basement, and storage in an attic, among other things, are all expected to be part of any residential fire. Commercial occupancies can present several immediate hazards that go beyond the typical residential fire. For example, instead of nicely arranged furnishings that we encounter in a typical living room, a large warehouse has heavy merchandise stacked at heights well above our heads (Figure 19-10). As fire burns away at the wooden pallets or shelving, the merchandise will collapse and tumble, trapping or crushing anyone underneath. Even when untouched by fire, the added weight of water from a sprinkler system or from our fire streams can cause stacked materials to collapse unexpectedly. Be aware of this potential hazard and maintain an adequate safety zone that equals the height of the storage in all directions.

Buildings Under Construction

When buildings under construction burn, they present some added hazards to firefighters beyond what we would expect to encounter in a typical fire in a completed structure of similar construction type. Exposed structural members in an unfinished building are attacked immediately by heat and fire, and fail much sooner during the fire than if they were protected by the finished building. Open shafts, pits, and stairs that don't have railings are dangerous to navigate in smoke-filled areas. The pits can also fill with water, creating a severe submersion hazard. Never walk through standing water unless you are sure of its depth. Use a tool to probe ahead as you go, checking the depth of the water before you walk through it (Figure 19-11).

Unfinished buildings often rely on **wood shoring** to hold upper floors in place until load-bearing walls are built underneath. The shoring will burn away and the building will collapse.

The area outside a building that is under construction is also a hazardous environment. Pulling hose lines around the obstructions, stacked materials,

Probing debris during overhaul

FIGURE 19-11 Probe ahead as you go when crossing wet areas to avoid tripping or becoming submerged in water.

heavy equipment, and fuels for the equipment all present a challenge to safe operations. Be aware of these problems and plan on working in a defensive mode at a construction site.

KEY WORD

wood shoring A type of support used during building construction to hold upper floors in place until load-bearing walls are built underneath them.

Going Inside

The last step before going inside a burning structure is to ensure that you have an adequate supply of clean air to breathe and that all of your PPE is in place, making sure that there is no skin exposed to the heat you are about to encounter. Take a moment to check your air gauge and to look at your other team members as a quick crosscheck of your PPE. Far too many injuries occur because of forgotten gloves, improperly worn protective hoods, and exposed skin around the neck and wrists. Taking a quick moment at the door to check yourself and your other crew members goes a long way toward preventing these needless injuries (Figure 19-12).

FIGURE 19-12 Pause momentarily to cross-check each other's PPE before entering a hazardous area.

Safety Tip!

Some departments allow an air cylinder to be used as long as it contains at least 90% of its air capacity. It is not a good idea to make this procedure a habit. You may need that extra few minutes of air to survive, so be sure to have a full tank of air whenever possible.

Personnel Accountability

A major component of any Incident Management System is personnel accountability. We discuss this frequently throughout this text because it is important enough to your safety to bear repeating. When you "go on air," you are preparing yourself to enter a hazardous area that is **immediately dangerous to life and health (IDLH).** It is imperative that the Incident Commander (IC) or a designated **Accountability Officer** knows who is entering the IDLH area, when they began breathing compressed air, their point of entry, and their mission. Your Company Officer will transmit this notice as you enter and again as you exit.

Periodically, the Accountability Officer or the Incident Commander requests a Personnel Accountability Report (PAR) from every Company Officer. Your Company Officer is responsible for your whereabouts, so it is imperative that he or she not only knows where you are at all times, but can physically see and account for you if you are working in an IDLH area. There should be no exceptions to this rule.

Expect to hear a call for a PAR when the fire is knocked down, the emergency has been controlled, or anytime an emergency evacuation of the area is called for. These are not the only times a PAR is called for, but they are the major milestones that trigger a PAR.

KEY WORDS

Accountability Officer A person in the Incident Command chain of command who has the responsibility to manage the accounting of all fire department personnel on the scene of an emergency.

immediately dangerous to life and health (IDLH) As defined by OSHA, an atmosphere that contains a concentration of any toxic, corrosive, or asphyxiate substance that poses an immediate threat to life; would cause irreversible or delayed adverse health effects; or would interfere with an individual's ability to escape from a dangerous atmosphere.

Breathing Safe Air

We take breathing for granted until something interrupts our ability to exchange air or limits the amount of air we have to breathe. Then panic sets in. Unless you practice with an SCBA and have confidence in your ability to get fresh air, your stress level will cause you to breathe rapidly, consuming all the air in your cylinder prematurely. Even seasoned firefighters experience some degree of nervous tension when they enter a smoke-filled atmosphere. Limited visibility, inability to feel what is around you, and heavy equipment that muffles your hearing all add to the tension, causing your breathing to speed up and deepen. The fight-or-flight reflex kicks into high gear and, before you know it, you're out of air. All of this can be controlled through training and practice, allowing you to get the most breathing time possible from each air cylinder, which increases your survival time if the need arises. Confidence comes with familiarity, so practice with the SCBA as much as possible during your entire career.

Several drills follow that are designed to help you gain confidence in your ability to work while in full PPE and while breathing compressed air from your SCBA. They are not intended to serve as an endurance test, so be sure to rest and rehabilitate yourself between each drill so you can concentrate on the techniques of the drill.

➥ Practice It!

Controlled Breathing Techniques

This drill is intended to help you establish a baseline of air consumption, and is conducted in a clean, nonhazardous atmosphere. Don your full PPE ensemble and prepare to breathe from the air supply when instructed to do so.

1. Record your air pressure before going on air (Figure 19-13).

FIGURE 19-13

2. When instructed, connect your air supply and try to breathe normally for 5 minutes while walking at a slow, steady pace (Figure 19-14).

FIGURE 19-14

3. At the end of the allotted time, disconnect your air regulator and record the remaining air pressure in the tank, making note of how much air you consumed (Figure 19-15).

FIGURE 19-15

After 10 minutes of rest, repeat the drill, making an effort to control the pace of your breathing, taking slow, steady breaths as you walk. The goal is to use less air than in the first step of the drill by simply being aware of your breathing pace.

Working as a Team

The foundation of firefighter safety is to maintain the integrity of the team whenever working in a hazardous area. Everyone watches for the other's safety, so everyone goes home. Therefore, whenever we enter a hazardous area as a team, it is imperative that we leave the area as a team, leaving no one behind and not allowing anyone to exit by themselves as the others remain inside.

 Safety Tip!

Don't wait until the low-air warning sounds before leaving an IDLH atmosphere. Maintain a constant awareness of your air supply and let your Company Officer know when you have reached the halfway point so he or she can start the exit plan.

The next two drills are designed to help you hone the skill of maintaining the team's integrity as you work in full PPE.

Practice It!

Exiting as a Team

This drill is designed to help you to practice a constant awareness of your air consumption while working as a team. This drill is to be conducted in a safe atmosphere and in a well-lighted area free of hazards. Identify a starting point to the drill as a "safe area" and designate an imaginary "hazard zone" where you will work while on air.

1. Don your entire PPE and SCBA, and assemble at the designated "safe area." The instructor will tell you when to go on air, and will give you a set of tasks to be performed while you are working in the "hazard zone" (Figure 19-16).

FIGURE 19-16

2. Remain constantly aware of your breathing while you are working, and maintain a steady pace. Check your air pressure gauge periodically and maintain a constant awareness of how much air you are consuming as you go (Figure 19-17).

FIGURE 19-17

3. When any crew member's air level reaches the halfway point, stop what you are doing and move to the safe area as a team (Figure 19-18).

FIGURE 19-18

Once in the "safe area," take a quick note of how much air you have remaining in the cylinder, comparing the remaining air levels with the other crew members from the drill.

Practice It!

Low-Air Warnings

Low-air warnings are provided on any SCBA that is certified for Fire Service use. This drill is designed to help you to become familiar with these warnings and the limited time they allow you to exit a hazardous atmosphere. It will be conducted in a safe atmosphere and in a well-lighted area free of hazards.

Identify a starting point to the drill as a "safe area" and designate an imaginary "hazard zone" where you will work while on air. Don your entire PPE and SCBA, and assemble at the designated "safe area." The instructor will tell you when to go on air and will give you a set of tasks to be performed while you are working in the "hazard zone." Remain constantly aware of your breathing while working, and maintain a steady pace. Check your air pressure gauge periodically and maintain a constant awareness of how much air you are consuming as you go. When any crew member's low-air warning signal activates, stop what you are doing and move to the safe area as a team.

Once in the "safe-area," take a quick note of how much air you have remaining in the cylinder, comparing the remaining air levels with the other crew members from the drill.

FIGURE 19-19

➡ Practice It!

Emergency SCBA Procedures

The SCBA's regulator is equipped with a safety feature that, when activated, allows air to free-flow past the regulator directly to the facemask. This emergency purge valve feature depletes the air cylinder quickly. Don your PPE and SCBA, and begin one of the air consumption drills you have already practiced. The instructor will tell you that your SCBA has malfunctioned and you are to initiate emergency procedures. Do the following:

1. Inspect your facemask with your hand. Is it positioned properly and intact? Most air leaks can be fixed by adjusting the facemask (Figure 19-20).

FIGURE 19-20

—Continued

2. Check the air lines to be sure they are not kinked (Figure 19-21).

FIGURE 19-21

3. Turn the emergency purge valve so it is slightly opened, regulating the amount of air entering the facemask at a comfortable level (Figure 19-22).

FIGURE 19-22

4. If the emergency purge valve fails to deliver air, immediately check your tank valve and make sure that it is opened fully and that you have air pressure showing on the pressure gauge (Figure 19-23).

FIGURE 19-23

5. Signal to the others on your team that you are in trouble, and work as a team to exit the "hazard zone" (Figure 19-24).

FIGURE 19-24

 Safety Tip!

Many SCBA manufacturers offer a "**buddy-breathing**" feature that allows you to share breathing air between two firefighters if one experiences a breathing apparatus failure. Buddy-breathing is outside the scope of the NFPA standards as written at the time of this publication. However, we highly suggest that you practice often, following the manufacturer's guidelines, every emergency maneuver that the manufacturer prescribes for their particular breathing apparatus (Figure 19-25). The goal is to make sure your respiratory protection remains uncompromised.

FIGURE 19-25

buddy-breathing A rescue air-breathing technique that uses an adapter provided by the SCBA manufacturer so that one firefighter can share his or her air supply with another firefighter who has run out of air. This procedure is outside the scope of the NFPA standards as written at the time of this publication. However, we strongly suggest that, following the manufacturer's guidelines, you practice often every emergency maneuver that they prescribe for their particular breathing apparatus.

Emergency Evacuation Procedures

We all hope that you never get into a predicament in which you become lost inside a building during a fire. All our training is done to teach you how to stay out of these situations using your skills and knowledge of firefighting and safety. However, there may come a time when the worst happens and you and your crew are cut off from everyone else. This can be due to rapidly changing conditions like an unexpected building collapse, poor communications between crew members, or becoming trapped by debris. In all such situations, you need to remain calm and use the following procedures to get help as soon as possible.

 **Safety Tip!**

Know the Emergency Evacuation Signal

Most fire departments have a universal signal that is sounded when someone detects the need to immediately evacuate the structure or hazardous area. This may be a continual blast of air horns, sirens, a specialized radio signal and transmission, or a combination of all of the above. Know the signal and practice all of the following activities to help you survive as you make an immediate exit from the building or hazard zone.

Communicate

Many firefighters have died because no one else at the scene knew the firefighters were in trouble or missing until long after they became lost or trapped. The emergency sequence should be to communicate

that you are in trouble, and then attempt to get yourself to safety. The initial communication gets help started on the way as you are trying to get to safety. You can always stop the help from coming if you get to a safe area.

The very first thing to do is to communicate to those around you and to Command that you are in trouble and need help. Your department has a standard emergency signal on your portable radio to use for a firefighter in distress. The most recognized way to call for help over the radio is to say the word "**Mayday**" three times, then identify yourself and your location as best as you can. The IC and rescue crews also need to know how you are stuck or injured. If you can, update Command about your progress so that rescue crews can be coordinated as they work to your location. Every time you talk on the radio, call out your remaining air supply level so that ensuring your uncompromised breathing is addressed as part of the plan.

Next, call out to those around you and listen for a reply. A fellow firefighter may be just outside the door or across the room. Maybe he or she will hear your call for help and be able to get to you quickly. Also, rescue crews will soon be in the area, and they will be listening for any calls for help as they search.

After calling out for help, sound your personal alert safety system (PASS) device by turning it manually to the emergency signal. Turn it to the automatic mode every so often for a few seconds to listen for any firefighters who are approaching or calling out.

Use your flashlight to illuminate your location. This will make it easier for rescuers to locate you (Figure 19-26). Occasionally look for a light as firefighters get nearer.

FIGURE 19-26 Flashlight beams will bounce off smoke, making it easier for searching firefighters to find you.

Mayday The universal radio signal that you, or someone with you, is trapped or in grave danger.

 Tip!

Use the Correct Terminology

- "Mayday"—The universal radio signal that you, or someone with you, is trapped or in grave danger.
- "Emergency Traffic" and "Priority Traffic"—Terms used to gain priority attention on the radio frequency so that you can transmit a clear and urgent message about the safety and health of working firefighters. An example of "emergency traffic" would be a message calling attention to a potential building collapse.

Take Action

Now it is time to take action. You have communicated your situation and need for help. You need to get to a safe area outside or seek a **safe haven** to wait for help to get to you. Locating a wall and communicating that you are at the wall will give those searching for you an important clue as to where to find you.

If you are still with your crew, it is always best to exit as a team if you are making an emergency evacuation. Stay together as a team at all times.

KEY WORD

safe haven A place inside a structure that is free of fire and hazards, and that provides some protection until help arrives.

View It!

Go to the DVD, navigate to Chapter 19, and select *"Emergency Evacuation—Rope to Hose."*

Practice It!

Emergency Evacuation—Rope to Hose

It is important to practice an emergency evacuation using your search rope and hose line as a guide to the outside of a building. A charged hose line is positioned inside a simulated building fire. Firefighters position away from the hose line but are connected with search rope. Their vision is impeded, either by a darkened SCBA mask or a darkened building. Use the following steps to practice this skill:

1. First, communicate your emergency using your portable radio, or calling to your Company Officer or other firefighters. If you are with your crew, you should take an accounting of all your members. Stay together and begin your exit (Figure 19-27).

FIGURE 19-27

—Continued

Level I

2. Follow the search rope to the hose line (Figure 19-28). Remember to stay low.

FIGURE 19-28

3. When you reach the hose line, follow it until you reach a coupling. Feel the coupling or, if possible, shine your light on it to see which side has the female end. The female end of a hose line usually leads to the outside of the building. Follow the hose line in that direction to the outside of the building and report to Command (Figure 19-29).

FIGURE 19-29

Ladders as Emergency Exits

During any fire in a multistory building, ladders are placed at windows to provide access to upper floors, both as emergency exits and to rescue civilians and firefighting crews inside. When placed in these positions, the tip of the ladder is located just above the windowsill. Command will be notified of the ladders' positions. These locations are relayed to everyone on the scene via portable radio from Command. In addition, the locations of the ladders may be marked with portable lights or small marker lights just inside the window. (See Chapter 16, "Ladders," for specific procedures for placing a ladder for rescue).

When you are making an emergency evacuation from an interior of a burning building from upper floors, you may need to use one of these ladders. If you do not have a search line or a hose line, the general rule is to locate an exterior wall and follow it until you find a window. If there is a ladder at that window, then make your escape. Stay below any heat and smoke pouring out of the window. Once you grip the ladder, maintain your grip and contact with the ladder at all times. Swing your leg over the sill and out the window. Descend the ladder to safety below and report to Command.

Ladder Escape

Use the following steps to practice locating and using a ladder as an escape route from the upper floor of a simulated building fire:

1. When you need to make an emergency escape, notify Command of your situation and location, call out for your fellow team members, and start your escape (Figure 19-30).

FIGURE 19-30

2. Search for and find a wall. Follow the wall until you locate a window. Check for a ladder placed at the window. Grip the ladder and maintain your grip at all times (Figure 19-31).

FIGURE 19-31

3. Stay low and swing one leg over the sill, placing your foot onto a ladder rung (Figure 19-32).

FIGURE 19-32

4. Move the rest of the way out of the window and descend the ladder to safety (Figure 19-33). Report to Command.

FIGURE 19-33

Level I

Self-Rescue

In more severe situations in which you or your team have been cut off and cannot evacuate the building, you may need to seek a safe haven. These are places inside the structure free of fire and hazards that provide some protection until help arrives.

If you are cut off, call Command and announce a Mayday for yourself. Provide Command with your approximate location and situation, if possible. Call out for the rest of your team. If your hose line is still charged, keep it available. Tie off your search line to the hose and, if possible, locate a wall to find an exterior window. Open the window or break it out with your tool. Attempt to signal firefighters outside from the window. In finding a safe haven, it is always best to locate near a window. Be sure to locate any open doors to the room and close them for protection. Wait for help to arrive, conserving your air and communicating with Command if you can. Operate your PASS by manually switching on your emergency signal. Keep your flashlight on. Listen for rescue crews as they approach. If you hear them calling out, be sure to answer them.

⮕ Practice It!

Shelter in Place

It is important to practice sheltering in place—moving to a safe area to protect yourself and waiting for rescue. Use the following steps to train for doing this survival technique:

1. When you realize you are separated and cut off from making an emergency evacuation, transmit the emergency radio signal to bring attention to Command and other crews that you are in need of help. Provide Command with a description of your location and your situation. Call out for the rest of your crew and activate your PASS emergency signal (Figure 19-34).

FIGURE 19-34

2. Move to a wall and follow it until you find a window. For added protection, close any doors to the room as you go (Figure 19-35).

FIGURE 19-35

3. Open the window and exit if you can, or signal for help (Figure 19-36). Call Command again and advise where you are located.

FIGURE 19-36

View It!

Go to the DVD, navigate to Chapter 19, and select *"Seek Refuge."*

Practice It!

Seek Refuge

Once fire has entered the room you are in, you only have moments left to get out unless you have a means to extinguish the fire. If you are cut off from escape and there is no way to shelter in place, then it is time to seek refuge elsewhere. This often involves breeching an interior wall so that you can quickly move to an uninvolved room. To do this, practice the following drill:

1. Use any tool you have with you to quickly punch a small opening between the wall studs, making an opening near the floor that is only large enough to crawl through (Figure 19-37).

FIGURE 19-37

—Continued

2. Loosen the waist and shoulder straps on your SCBA, *BUT DO NOT REMOVE THE SCBA* (Figure 19-38). Rotate the backpack to one side, allowing you to streamline your profile so that you can slip between the wall studs, which are usually spaced 16 inches apart (Figure 19-39).

FIGURE 19-38

FIGURE 19-39

3. Once through the opening, properly reposition your SCBA and retighten the waist and shoulder straps, transmit a signal over the radio that you have moved to another room, and look for another way out of the building (Figure 19-40).

FIGURE 19-40

Disentanglement

Because of our bulky equipment and limited visibility, it is very easy to become entangled in all sorts of debris and contents inside a building (Figure 19-41). If you haven't practiced untangling yourself from this sort of entrapment ahead of time, then chances are that you will panic and try to muscle your way through whatever has entangled you. This will only make things worse by tightening everything around you. Think about the last time you worked with an extension cord that had not been coiled properly. You probably tried to pull the ends apart, hoping to straighten the cord so you could use it, only to have knots and loops tighten into a mess. It is the same sort of thing when you become entangled in debris: You have to stop, signal for help, clear the entanglement, and move on.

A building fire is full of entanglement hazards. Burned-out bedsprings and furniture can trap your feet. A common problem in modern construction is the type of ductwork that runs through the attic space above you. The flexible piping has a helix-coil wire inside it that, once the insulation burns away, resembles a big, sloppy spring. As you pull the ceiling to

Hidden hazards during a search

Duct work

Wiring

Burned out furniture

FIGURE 19-41 Duct work, electrical wiring, and burned furniture all can easily entangle you during a search.

check for hidden fire, this ductwork will often fall, becoming entangled in your backpack and air cylinder. Electrical wires and other hazards also drop down and will entangle you. It is a good idea to carry quality wire cutters in your bunker gear pocket so you can cut your way free of these entanglement hazards.

View It!

Go to the DVD, navigate to Chapter 19, and select *"Disentanglement."*

Practice It!

Disentanglement

This drill is designed to help you practice clearing your SCBA of an entanglement. The entanglement in this case will be a small rope, wire, or helix-coil spring. The goal is to clear yourself of the entanglement without compromising your flow of clean breathing air.

1. Stop moving the moment you realize you are trapped, signal a Mayday, and activate your PASS (Figure 19-42).

FIGURE 19-42

—Continued

2. Back up to see if you can simply slip away from the wires. If possible, pick another direction of travel to avoid the wires (Figure 19-43).

FIGURE 19-43

3. If the wires are in your only path of travel and can't be avoided, lie flat, or if possible roll to your side or back, and push your arms forward underneath the wires as if you were "swimming." As you push your arms forward, the wires often will gather on top of your arms. Then you can lift them up and over yourself as you go (Figure 19-44).

FIGURE 19-44

4. Feel around and determine where you are entangled and determine what you will need to free yourself (Figure 19-45).

FIGURE 19-45

5. If the entanglement is around the air cylinder or on your back, you will need to loosen the harness and rotate it around so that the backpack is resting on your chest (Figure 19-46). It is best if you can first remove your arm from the side of the harness that does not contain the high-pressure air line so you can maintain control of the regulator (Figure 19-47).

FIGURE 19-46

FIGURE 19-47

6. Clear the entanglement and immediately move at least 6 inches away from where you were entangled before you don the SCBA in its normal position (Figure 19-48). This will help you avoid becoming entangled again.

FIGURE 19-48

7. Check your air supply, signal that you are clear, and rejoin your team or make an emergency exit of the area (Figure 19-49).

FIGURE 19-49

Level I

 ## Safety Tip!

If you are assisting a firefighter who is trapped by wires or helix coils, be aware of where the obstruction will move when you cut it. Be sure you don't become entangled from the debris as you work. Also, avoid pulling on the wires. You will be working in poor visibility conditions and you could possibly pull a heavy object that is attached to the other end of the wire, causing it to fall on you.

Navigating with Obscured Vision

When you are inside a building full of smoke, looking for either the fire or fire victims, you need to use all your senses. Unfortunately, most of your senses will be partially obscured by the smoke and fire as well as the noises from your equipment and those around you. Your PPE also has an encapsulating effect, limiting your ability to feel the heat of the fire.

For these reasons, you need to be more alert of your surroundings. For example, if you cannot see in the dense smoke, then you must listen and feel more intently. Listen for the sound of the fire as it burns and for any calls of distress from trapped victims. Feel your way ahead with your gloved hands and a tool as you move along (Figure 19-50). Monitor the tempera-

FIGURE 19-50 Use your senses of touch and hearing to help you navigate through the smoke. Remember, your vision may be useless and your other senses dulled by your heavy PPE.

ture. You need to stop and back up if you start feeling extreme heat. Even in the smoke and darkness, you will still probably be able to faintly see open flame.

Searching for the Fire

The best time to start looking for the location of a fire in a building is during your approach on the fire truck. Even though this initial search may not pinpoint the exact location, it can tell you which way to go when you enter the building. Any heavy smoke or flames will also give you an idea of the intensity of the fire inside. We will go into more detail for entering and extinguishing an interior fire in Chapter 20 of this text.

Listen for the sounds of the fire burning, debris falling, and glass breaking. These can all point to an actively burning fire inside a structure. Look for the glow of the flames burning. Remember, you should always have a charged attack line with you when you enter any interior area to search for the fire. Be ready to cool the ceiling.

 **Safety Tip!**

Keep in mind the dangers of flashover. You should flow some short blasts of water at the ceiling as you approach the fire. In a large, open-area building, you can be standing inside with smoke high above you and still be under a threat of a severe flashover fire without warning.

In multistory buildings, the location of the fire can be difficult to narrow down during your search. Fires in a basement can cause smoke to come out of the upper floors or the attic. If you are searching for a fire upstairs and cannot locate any heat or fire, think about the lower levels. An undiscovered fire can be directly beneath you.

Use care when opening doors to look for fires inside a room. When you open the door, always stand to one side with the hose line ready to flow water.

If you and another firefighter must leave the hose line to check an area, be sure to connect your search line to the hose line. Conduct your search, leaving the rope limp on the floor as you go. When you return to the hose line, gather the search line.

Searching for Victims

The same safety rules apply when you are searching for fire victims. Though a firefighting team may be assigned specifically to conduct a search, they should always have a charged attack line available. There are two main search operations used on a building fire that utilize two distinct search methods. These are the primary and secondary searches.

Primary Search

The primary search is done as the fire is being extinguished by interior firefighting crews. Everyone fighting the fire should always be looking for fire victims, even as they stretch hose lines and look for the fire.

However, there is usually a crew assigned to the specific task of primary search. This search is rapid, but must be done as thoroughly as fire conditions permit. This initial search provides the best opportunity to save lives from the fire.

To do a primary search of an area, firefighters in teams of two enter the building behind the fire attack crews and start moving to the right or to the left, performing a right-handed or left-handed search pattern as they go from room to room. The decision on which pattern to use is based on the fire conditions and the probable locations of any victims. For example, if a fire is in the middle of the night, trapped victims would more likely be in the bedroom areas of a home. If these are to the right as you enter, then that is the search pattern direction you will use.

Firefighters conducting the search should each be carrying a tool to provide reach in larger rooms, under furniture, and into small spaces. These tools are also used to force open locked spaces. The tools can be used to sweep the search area, feeling and looking for any possible fire victims.

Stay low, crawling on all fours in heavy smoke and heat conditions. One firefighter maintains contact with a side wall as the second firefighter maintains contact with him. The second firefighter reaches toward the center of the room. Check under tables, beds, and chairs. Move lighter debris and furniture and check underneath. In larger rooms, the firefighters can cover more area by having one firefighter follow the wall, reaching into the room with his tool while the second firefighter grabs the end of that tool and extends into the floor space. This firefighter can even extend her or his tool into the space for maximum coverage.

 **Safety Tip!**

Whenever you are in contact with a wall, make an effort to count the doors and windows you pass during the search. This will help you remain aware of your position so that you can retrace your movements back to the exit, quickly find an alternate exit, or better describe your position to a search team if you get in trouble while inside.

Any objects found should be checked to eliminate the possibility that they are a fire victim. Remember to listen for any cries for help. The object of this search is to check survivable areas quickly yet thoroughly. In buildings with multiple floors, check floors above and then below the fire using the same pattern.

Larger spaces may necessitate the team going back and forth over the entire floor from one end of the room to the other, maintaining visual and audible contact with each other (Figure 19-51). Use a search line, hooking onto an entrance door, and extend into the open space as you move along a wall. To do this, tie your line onto a lower hinge of the open entrance door. Do not pull the search line taut above the floor as this may cause a trip hazard for other firefighters working in the area. Do not leave too much slack in the search line either, as a slack line can easily become entangled in objects and other firefighters working inside with you. Remember to extend, using your tools as you go. To leave the area, simply follow your search line to the door. Larger buildings will also require more firefighters and search crews to conduct a primary search.

Some departments use a system of markings or tags to indicate when a room has been searched. This can be done with a marker crayon, making an "X" on the door, or the use of tags on the doorknob. Both of these indicate the room has been searched.

As with all functions at the fire, Command should be kept informed of the progress of the search and any fire victims located. Maintain visual and audible contact at all times with each team member conducting the search. Monitor your air supply. If it runs low, leave as a team and be sure to advise any crews taking over your search about where you stopped your efforts. Barring any immediate hazards and as long as an adequate, safe air supply is available, the team should continue searching until the entire building is searched, another search team relieves them, or they locate a fire victim.

If you find a victim, inform Command. Relay the victim's condition and where you will be exiting, so that the Incident Commander will have appropriate help ready for you at the exit point.

FIGURE 19-51 It is extremely difficult to maintain contact with the other crew members while searching in heavy smoke conditions, so maintain constant contact with each other as you go.

View It!

Go to the DVD, navigate to Chapter 19, and select *"Primary Search."*

Practice It!

Primary Search

An optimum training simulation will provide various sizes of rooms to search, with opened and closed doors. This ensures that the crew will need to use a search line and also practice extending out into a larger open space as they work. Furniture and obstructions will also add to the training. The rooms should be darkened so that crews will have to feel their way around as they work.

—Continued

Before the simulation begins, a two-firefighter search crew should assemble outside the training building. All PPE and tools should be in place. A fire attack crew enters the simulated building to locate and extinguish the fire. The search crew then performs the following steps to practice doing a primary search inside a building with two-firefighter search teams:

1. Determine the search pattern and, if needed, anchor a search line at the door. Give a radio report to Command that you are entering the building. Enter and begin searching for a simulated victim inside (Figure 19-52).

FIGURE 19-52

2. Mark the doors to each room as you finish searching (Figure 19-53).

FIGURE 19-53

3. Stay on task and continue the primary search until you have finished searching the whole building, are relieved by another crew, or locate a fire victim. Then exit as a team (Figure 19-54).

FIGURE 19-54

Secondary Search

Soon after the fire has been controlled and knocked down and the visibility has improved, either from daylight or floodlights inside, Command will call for a secondary search of the building. This search is a more methodical and thorough search process than the primary search. If possible, different firefighters will make up the secondary search crew. This allows for a fresh look to the area during the search.

The secondary search team uses the same tools as the first search team and wears full PPE while they perform their search. The actual process of the search is similar to the primary search with the exception that the team will have much better search conditions. They will be able to stand up because the heat from the fire will be mostly gone. They will also have much better vision because smoke will

be vented out of the structure and portable lighting will be in place. Crews should still perform a search pattern in the room, but they will be able to see and talk to each other and coordinate their search as they go. This is the time to check again under all furniture, as well as to check debris and closed or hidden spaces. Everything must be checked again to ensure that no victims were missed during the primary search. More rarely, a third search may be conducted, especially if all the occupants are not accounted for after the fire.

Thermal Imaging Cameras

Because we are encapsulated by our protective equipment and are working in a high-noise environment with little or no visibility, navigating through a smoke-filled building is a slow, dangerous, and yet

FIGURE 19-55 A thermal imager, or TIC, works as "firefighter's radar" to help you navigate through the smoke.

essential fireground operation. One of the greatest technological advances in the Fire Service is the thermal imager. A **thermal imaging camera**, commonly referred to as a **TIC**, is a rugged instrument that enhances our sight, making what is normally invisible information visible (Figure 19-55). Although a TIC is easy to operate, with only a button or two to power it up, it still takes training and practice to use it efficiently. Interpreting the picture you see in a thermal imager often depends on your knowledge of building construction or your familiarization with the objects you are viewing. For instance, a hole in a floor can appear through a thermal imager as a dark spot, and to an inexperienced user it might even look like it is boarded over. Steps can look like level ground if you aren't used to interpreting the visual image in the scope. The bottom line: We must constantly practice with the TIC to remain proficient in its use.

Thermal imagers are useful tools for much more than searching a smoke-filled building for a victim. Searching for hidden fires, overheated mechanical devices, spilled hazardous materials, and victims that have wandered away from an automobile crash are just a few potential uses of a thermal imager.

Search teams working with a thermal imager seldom have more than one camera per team. Therefore, the person with the TIC serves as the "eyes" for the entire team. While your first instinct may be to have the person with enhanced vision move in front of the rest of the team, this usually isn't the most efficient way to operate. Instead, the person with the TIC should be farther back in the line of firefighters so that he or she not only can look for victims, but also can keep an eye on the team members. Think of it this way: Wouldn't it be easier to direct another person's actions if you could see them do the task rather than have them standing behind you?

KEY WORD

thermal imaging camera (TIC) A rugged instrument that enhances our sight, making normally invisible information visible. It creates a visual image of the different temperatures in the area viewed. It is an excellent tool for finding missing or trapped firefighters and fire victims as well as hot spots in concealed spaces.

Safety Tip!

Thermal imagers are electronic instruments that are rugged and designed to withstand the rigors of our work. However, like any electronic equipment, even TICs are susceptible to problems. Make it a habit to scan the room before you enter it, and scan the entire room periodically as you go. This will help you maintain your orientation in case the TIC fails to operate.

The most common cause of a TIC failure is a depleted battery. Make it a habit to put a spare CHARGED battery in your pocket when you are assigned to the TIC, and know how to change the battery without the luxury of being able to see what you are doing.

➡ Practice It!

Operating a Thermal Imaging Camera

This drill is designed to give the TIC operator an opportunity to serve as the eyes of the search team in zero-visibility conditions. Outfitted with the appropriate PPE, search team members put their protective hoods on *backward*. This will do two things: obscure their vision and remind them that they should wash their hoods more often. The person operating the TIC won't be wearing a hood but will drape a large towel over his head, wrapping it around the TIC in such a way as to obscure any peripheral vision, making him rely solely on the TIC for vision (Figure 19-56). The apparatus bay will be your search area, which can become surprisingly confusing to the blindfolded search team, even though they are quite familiar with the surroundings.

The instructor will repeat the drill until everyone in your team has had a chance to be the TIC operator. To mix things up a bit, the instructor may sound an evacuation alarm and have your team practice an emergency evacuation of the fire area, using the closest exit rather than their original point of entry. By now you should see that communication between your fellow team members is crucial to the operation. Work on ways to keep confusion to a minimum by controlling the amount of unnecessary talk between yourself and other team members.

FIGURE 19-56

Like all of our practical training, the drill you just practiced is about building good habits. As you enter the structure, immediately look up, down, and sideways to scan the ceiling for signs of fire or excessive heat over your head, as well as the room for victims. As you navigate inside the structure with a thermal imager, keep an account of everyone on your team. Periodically count heads if necessary. And when you leave the structure or move from room to room as you go, stop at the doorway to make one last scan of the room to be sure you have not accidentally left someone behind. The TIC operator should be the last person out of the search area.

➡ Practice It!

Searching for Subtle Heat Sources

The key to using a TIC is the ability to detect subtle differences in heat sources. Place several small containers of warm-to-hot water around the training area and take turns using the TIC to locate them in conditions as dark as possible. Metal cans conduct the water's heat well, so they work very well for this drill. Move the cans around from time to time so the TIC operator can identify where the heat sources are as well as where they were located prior to being moved, based on the residual heat signature they leave behind (Figure 19-57).

FIGURE 19-57

Rescuing a Civilian Victim Horizontally

Once a victim is located by the search team, you should notify Command. Then it is time to do a rapid assessment of the victim's condition, develop a rescue plan, and quickly move the victim out to a safe area for emergency medical treatment. This should all be accomplished as quickly as possible because under fire conditions the victim is in a severe life-threatening situation. The victim will die soon if not removed to the outside and fresh air.

The primary purpose of the following victim rescue techniques are for life rescue, not injury treatment. Victims need to be taken outside so that emergency medical personnel can begin proper assessment and life-saving first aid to prepare them for rapid transportation to a medical facility.

If the victim is ambulatory and conditions permit, simply guide her out of the building and leave her with medical personnel outside for further assessment. Ask the victim if anyone else is inside and, if so, where they might be. You can assist an injured adult patient in walking out by placing one of the victim's arms over your shoulder, and walking the victim out of the building, taking weight off the victim's injured side.

A patient who is unconscious or unable to walk will need to be carried or dragged. There are three common ways for firefighters to move victims: (1) the cross-chest carry, (2) the blanket carry, and (3) the victim's clothing drag.

Cross-Chest Carry

The cross-chest carry involves lifting the victim to a sitting position, positioning behind the victim, and grabbing both arms from behind as they are crossed in front of the victim. A second firefighter grabs the victim's legs, and the crew carries the victim out of the building. If two victims are located, each firefighter can grab one of the victims in a cross-chest method and drag the victim out. Keep in mind that fire victims are very often slippery and very hard to grasp, especially if they are unconscious.

⇨ Practice It!

Victim Removal—Cross-Chest Carry, Two Firefighters

After locating the victim, notify Command of your discovery, rapidly assess the victim, and develop a plan to remove the victim. Use the following procedure to lift and carry a fire victim using the cross-chest method:

1. The first firefighter moves the victim to a sitting-up position from the prone position and remains behind her while kneeling on one leg (Figure 19-58).

FIGURE 19-58

2. This rescuer reaches around the victim, under one arm, and grabs the victim's opposite arm at the wrist. He or she then does the same with the other arm, grasping it at the wrist (Figure 19-59).

FIGURE 19-59

—Continued

3. A second firefighter kneels between the victim's legs, facing away, and grasps the victim's legs under the knees. On a signal from the rescuer behind the victim, both rescuers then stand up together, with their backs straight and lifting with their legs (Figure 19-60).

FIGURE 19-60

4. They then walk out of the building with the victim and take her to a safe area where she can be evaluated by emergency medical personnel (Figure 19-61).

FIGURE 19-61

Alternate Method—One Firefighter:

a. The firefighter moves the victim to a sitting-up position from the supine position and remains behind him, kneeling on one leg (Figure 19-62).

FIGURE 19-62

b. The rescuer reaches around the victim, under one arm, and grabs the victim's opposite arm at the wrist. He or she then does the same with the other arm, grasping it at the wrist (Figure 19-63).

FIGURE 19-63

c. With back straight and feet at shoulder width, the firefighter stands up and walks backward, pulling the victim along (Figure 19-64).

FIGURE 19-64

Blanket Carry

Another method for moving a fire victim rapidly is the blanket carry. This method is accomplished by two firefighters moving an unresponsive patient to a blanket or sheet. They then roll the blanket inward on all sides. This creates handholds on the blanket around the patient. The firefighters kneel, grab the handholds, and stand up. They can then rapidly carry the patient to a safe area outside the building for further assessment and treatment.

➡ Practice It!

Victim Removal—Blanket Carry

After locating the victim, notify Command of your discovery, rapidly assess the victim, and develop a plan to remove the victim. Use the following steps to carry a fire victim using a blanket carry:

1. Position the unresponsive patient on a blanket, sheet, or small tarp and roll the edges inward (Figure 19-65).

FIGURE 19-65

2. Next, position at each end of the victim, facing the direction of travel. Then kneel at each end, grasping the rolled edge. With feet shoulder width apart and backs straight, lift the victim using your legs (Figure 19-66).

FIGURE 19-66

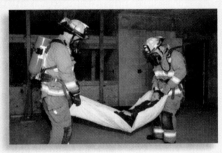

Victim's Clothing Drag

If you and a fellow firefighter come across two fire victims during a search, you can drag both victims out quickly, each of you using a clothing drag to pull the victims to a safe area. You can also use this method when fire conditions are still critical, when heat is building up in the area. In these circumstances, you will need to stay low, keeping the victim below the heat of the fire as you drag him to safety.

Once the victim is located, move him onto his back and position with your knees at the victim's head. Grasp the victim's clothing at the collar and shoulder areas, and drag him along the floor.

➡ Practice It!

Victim Removal—Victim's Clothing Drag

After locating the victim, notify Command of your discovery, rapidly assess the victim, and develop a plan to remove the victim. Use the following steps to remove a fire victim using the victim's clothing drag:

a. Roll the victim onto her back and position at the victim's head (Figure 19-67).

FIGURE 19-67

—Continued

b. Grasp the victim's clothing at the collar and shoulder area, and drag the victim along the floor, staying low (Figure 19-68).

FIGURE 19-68

Rescuing a Civilian Victim Vertically

When a fire victim is on upper or lower levels of a building, he or she needs to be moved up or down and then out of the building to a safe area. There are many ways to do this. Again, we need to remember that these types of rescues are for fire victims who will probably die if they remain where they are. These are life-saving carry and drag rescue techniques. The victims will be assessed and treated by emergency medical personnel when they reach a safe area.

In Chapter 16 of this text, we demonstrated ladder rescue techniques for lowering both ambulatory and unresponsive fire victims from the upper levels of a building. To demonstrate how to move a fire victim up and down a stairway during a fire, we'll continue here using the three basic horizontal rescue methods: (1) the cross-chest carry, (2) the blanket carry, and (3) the victim's clothing drag.

➡ Practice It!

Victim Removal—Cross-Chest Carry on Stairways

After locating the victim, notify Command of your discovery, rapidly assess the victim, and develop a plan to remove the victim. Use the following methods to move an unresponsive fire victim up or down a stairway.

To go down stairs:

FIGURE 19-69

- Two firefighters carefully go down the stairs, carrying the victim feet first and taking one step at a time until they reach the next landing. They repeat this process until they reach the bottom of the stairway (Figure 19-69).

To go up stairs:

FIGURE 19-70

- To go up stairs, the firefighters position at the bottom landing. The firefighter at the feet positions facing the firefighter at the head. They turn and go up, carrying the victim head first, one step at a time, until they reach the desired level (Figure 19-70).

⇨ Practice It!

Victim Removal—Blanket Carry on Stairways

After locating the victim, notify Command of your discovery, rapidly assess the victim, and develop a plan to remove the victim. Use the following method to move an unresponsive fire victim up or down a stairway using the blanket carry.

To go down stairs:

- The two firefighters approach the top of the stairway, carrying the victim in the blanket. The firefighter at the feet positions facing the firefighter at the head (Figure 19-71).
- They then carefully go down the stairs with victim's feet first, taking one step at a time until they reach the bottom of the stairway (Figure 19-72).

To go up stairs:

- Two firefighters position at the bottom landing and then go up one step at a time, victim's head first, until they reach the desired level.

FIGURE 19-71

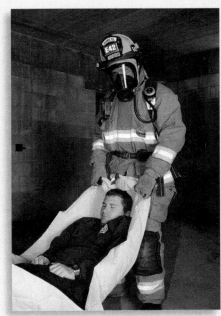

FIGURE 19-72

⇨ Practice It!

Victim Removal—Clothing Drag on Stairways

After locating the victim, notify Command of your discovery, rapidly assess the victim, and develop a plan to remove the victim. Use the following method to move an unresponsive fire victim up or down a stairway using the victim's clothing drag.

To go down stairs:

- The firefighter approaches the top of the stairway, dragging the victim head first, using the victim's clothing (Figure 19-73).
- Staying low, the firefighter drags the fire victim down the stairs, protecting the victim's head at each step as she proceeds. She repeats this process until they reach the bottom of the stairway (Figure 19-74).

To go up stairs:

- The firefighter positions the same at the bottom landing, with the victim's head first. She then goes up one step at a time until she reaches the desired level.

FIGURE 19-73

FIGURE 19-74

Searching for a Firefighter in Trouble

The chaotic and stressful work that often occurs at emergency fire scenes can at times result in missing, trapped, or injured personnel. When this occurs, it takes a well-organized effort by fellow team members to effect a quick rescue of fire personnel. Your quick yet well-coordinated work will save a life. It is imperative that we continue to work as a team while we locate, treat, and rescue a firefighter in trouble.

Searching for a Lost Firefighter

The first step toward a safe outcome for a lost or trapped firefighter is to acknowledge his or her call for help. Gather as much information as you can to assist the rescue team in locating the lost firefighter. The next step is to make sure the building is safe enough to support a rescue attempt. Far too often, additional rescuers have been injured or killed because they entered the structure to make a rescue attempt, only to fall to the same fate as the original lost firefighter.

It may take a few moments to make the situation safe, but the time spent will help ensure your safety as well as the safety of the trapped firefighter.

Landmarks inside a building may be hard to see in heavy smoke conditions, so the lost firefighter's best guess of his location is usually only that, a guess. If the firefighter was part of a hose team, then follow the hose to the end. If he was part of a search team, look for his search line. Determine whether he was attempting a right-handed or left-handed search so that you have a general idea of his direction of travel before he became lost.

To speed up the search process, use a thermal imager if possible. The heat signature of a firefighter trapped in a high-heat area may be a bit faint to see because our gear withstands a lot of heat, so be aware of subtle differences in the TIC's image.

Call out and listen while searching. A firefighter's PASS alarm may be sounding but muffled by something covering it, perhaps because the firefighter is lying on top of the alarm. Listen closely for a PASS, call out the firefighter's name, and listen for a reply. Look for a flashlight beam or any other clue as you search.

Listen for radio transmissions coming from the firefighter's radio. Also listen for a "squeal" sound of feedback when you talk on your radio. If you are close to the firefighter, you may experience this feed-back sound before you see the victim. You can also improvise this type of sound by holding two radios close together and depressing the microphone on one radio. This will cause everyone's radio to "squeal," including the victim's. Turn down the volume on your radio momentarily and listen for this signal.

View It!

Go to the DVD, navigate to Chapter 19, and select *"Searching for a Lost Firefighter."*

Practice It!

Searching for a Lost Firefighter

Working as a team, practice the following drill:

1. Acknowledge the distress call and get as much information as you can.

2. Evaluate the situation for safety and survivability, and make the decision to either enter or control the hazards before making entry.

3. Use all of the previously described methods to locate the victim (Figure 19-75).

4. Once the firefighter is located, rapidly establish a fresh air supply to the victim's facemask before taking further action (Figure 19-76).

5. Report to Command that you have located the firefighter and also your location.

6. Quickly determine the condition of the firefighter. Fire conditions are often the least ideal for assessing an injured firefighter. There may be intense heat and smoke. You may even need to move the injured firefighter a short distance before you can safely do a quick evaluation. If the injured firefighter is lying facedown, carefully roll him onto his side for assessment. Be careful with his head and cervical spine.

FIGURE 19-75

FIGURE 19-76

—Continued

7. Reset the injured firefighter's PASS. It may be set to emergency operation, so reset it to normal. Listen for breathing sounds coming from his regulator. See if you can get a response from him. Assess the victim to see if he is trapped in any way, and free the patient as necessary (Figure 19-77).

FIGURE 19-77

Assisting a Firefighter with a Compromised Breathing Apparatus

Most firefighters who are in trouble are also out of, or nearly out of, breathable air. Along with any rescue tools you take with you on the search, it is absolutely essential that you carry an extra, complete SCBA to the rescue. Once you locate the firefighter, immediately assess his situation and breathing. If his air supply has been depleted or the SCBA isn't functioning, simply remove his regulator, leaving his facemask in place, and clip the working SCBA's regulator into his facemask. You should practice doing this in your training until you can accomplish the change within 10 seconds of locating a downed firefighter.

If the firefighter has lost his SCBA or, for that matter, if the victim is a civilian who does not have any means of respiratory protection, then place the spare mask on the victim's face, holding it in place as you adjust the head gear for a proper fit.

Deciding How to Move an Injured Firefighter

Perhaps the best decision for the survival of injured firefighters is to get them away from the danger as quickly as possible. There are a few basic ways to move disabled firefighters. The idea here is to determine the very fastest route to get your victim to a safe area where his gear can be removed and he can be properly evaluated, treated, and placed on a cervical-spine immobilization system.

Drag Rescue Devices Newer firefighting bunker coats have a built-in rescue strap called a drag rescue device, or DRD. These straps must be accessible from the outside of the coat and are provided to give a quick handhold for fellow firefighters to grab and drag the incapacitated firefighter to a safe area during a fire emergency. They are NOT designed to be used for vertical lifting or as tie-off points for raising or lowering an injured firefighter using rescue rope rigging techniques. These simple-to-use devices allow firefighters to access a strap, built into the bunker coat, and pull the victim along the floor or ground (Figure 19-78). If you must drag a firefighter to safety during an emergency, always check for a DRD in their bunker coat. These devices normally are located at the back exterior of the coat, below the middle of the rear of the coat's collar. As you pull the strap, it will tighten underneath the injured firefighter's arms, and around the shoulders, as some slack will extend out from the DRD opening.

If the firefighter is trapped or the rescue team is cut off from a safe exit by fire or building collapse conditions, it may be necessary to stay in position and defend the patient and rescuers with additional fire streams and personnel. There may be times

FIGURE 19-78 Always check for a drag rescue device in the coat to use as a handle to drag the firefighter.

FIGURE 19-79 Try to move the victim in line with his spine, trying to maintain cervical alignment as you go.

when retreating to a safe area is all rescuers can do with the firefighter until help arrives and a safe route can be established. A balcony or window may be the only place that provides immediate safety until more help can be provided. Get the firefighter ready to go by lining him up, head first in the direction of travel, and try to maintain cervical-spine alignment while doing this (Figure 19-79).

Finally, once you've taken the preparations above, it will be time to organize and move out. Remember, this is an emergency operation. The safety of the rescuers, as well as of the firefighter, is in question, so we need to be fast and efficient. We move injured firefighters in three basic directions on the fire scene: horizontally, up, and down. You will need to remember a few variables to determine the methods chosen for the rescue:

- How big is the firefighter?
- How many rescuers are available to make the move?
- What is the best method for both rescuers and the firefighter?
- How much time do you have?

In all the operations, rescuers need to advise Command that they are beginning to move the patient and their destination. In this way, Command can adapt to the plan and get you more help.

Go to the DVD, navigate to Chapter 19, and select *"Horizontal SCBA Harness Drag Drill."*

Practice It!

Horizontal SCBA Harness Drag Drill

A good tactic for moving a firefighter is to use the SCBA harness straps as handles. The rescuer grasps the harness shoulder straps on the injured firefighter's SCBA and drags him to safety. Note that if the firefighter's SCBA is disconnected at the waist or has a damaged harness strap, this method may not work. Always check for a drag rescue device in the firefighter's coat, and use it if possible.

Practice this drill with one rescuer and then two rescuers performing the drag, using the following steps:

FIGURE 19-80

1. Unbuckle the victim's waist strap, pass the strap between his legs, and reconnect it at the buckle. This will keep the SCBA from slipping upward during the drag (Figure 19-80).

2. Move the victim at least 25 feet without stopping (Figure 19-81).

FIGURE 19-81

 ## View It!

Go to the DVD, navigate to Chapter 19, and select *"Rope Drag Drill."*

 ## Practice It!

Rope Drag Drill

You can also move a firefighter horizontally by attaching a length of rope or webbing strap to the injured firefighter and pulling him along. Always check for a drag rescue device in the firefighter's coat, and use it if possible.

1. Attach the rope or webbing to the shoulder straps of the firefighter's SCBA. Cross the lines under the firefighter's head and pull the firefighter as shown previously (Figure 19-82).

FIGURE 19-82

2. If three or more rescuers are available, one rescuer will guide the firefighter as the others pull (Figure 19-83).

FIGURE 19-83

Level I

 View It!

Go to the DVD, navigate to Chapter 19, and select *"Moving on Injured Firefighter on Stairs, Harness Drag."*

Practice It!

Moving an Injured Firefighter on Stairs, Harness Drag

1. Position the injured firefighter head first up the stairway.
2. Always check for a drag rescue device in the firefighter's coat, and use it if possible.
3. Be sure the injured firefighter's air pack harness is securely attached with the waist strap passed between his legs and secured (Figure 19-84).

FIGURE 19-84

—Continued

4. Sit on the first step and position your feet on either side of the victim.

5. Grasp the shoulder harness and pull up, pushing off with your feet and lifting the patient one step at a time. Be sure to keep your feet even as you pull each time, slowly going up as you go up the stairs. This will take some time to accomplish. If the injured firefighter is a bigger person, this will be time-consuming and difficult for a single firefighter (Figure 19-85).

FIGURE 19-85

If you have two firefighters, work together and use a cadence to coordinate both of your lifting actions. Something like, "Ready–Lift" will work well.

Do It!

We have covered a lot of critical information in this chapter. Working inside a burning building is inherently dangerous and requires the discipline of a well-trained team. Be sure that this is not the last time you practice each of the skills you have learned. Regardless of your level of experience, entering a burning structure to fight a fire or to search for a victim is strenuous and stressful. We cannot maintain these skills solely through our work at fire scenes. Therefore, it is important to practice these skills as often as you can so that you will be able to perform them efficiently and safely as you work inside a burning structure. More importantly, practice so you will respond appropriately if the time comes that your own life or the life of your fellow crew members depend on it.

Prove It

Knowledge Assessment
Signed Documentation Tear-Out Sheet
Safety and Survival for Interior Firefighters—Chapter 19

Name: _____

Fill out the ten-question quiz below, the Knowledge Assessment Sheet, by circling the correct answer for each question. When finished, sign it and give it to your instructor/Company Officer for his or her signature. Turn in this Knowledge Assessment Sheet to the proper person as part of the documentation that you have completed your training for this chapter.

1. *EGH* is a common term heard around most progressive firehouses these days. This simple idea should be the essence of everything we do, and the philosophical center of every decision we make. What does *EGH* stand for?
   a. Extremely Good Hazard
   b. Everyone Goes Home
   c. Everything Gets Hot
   d. Everyone Gets Hurt

2. All Fire Service generators should be equipped with a _____ to help protect humans from electrical shock.
   a. ground-fault interrupter
   b. ground-wire connection indicator
   c. circuit-fault indicator

3. The most recognized way to call for help over the radio is to use the word _____.
   a. *help*
   b. *delta*
   c. *emergency*
   d. *Mayday*

4. An example of an "Emergency Traffic" message on the radio would be a warning of a potential building collapse.
   a. True
   b. False

5. In multistory buildings, a hidden fire in a basement can be indicated by smoke coming from the _____.
   a. basement
   b. attic
   c. first floor
   d. all of the above

6. The type of search operation that has the most potential for saving the lives of fire victims is the _____.
   a. third search
   b. secondary search
   c. primary search
   d. overhaul search

7. A thermal imaging camera (TIC) produces exact images of the scene ahead. It simply eliminates the smoke from the image.

  a. True

  b. False

8. The _____ carry involves lifting the victim to a sitting position, positioning behind the victim, and grabbing both of the victim's arms from behind as they are crossed in front of the victim. A second firefighter grabs the victim's legs, and the crew carries the victim out of the building.

  a. cross-back

  b. cross-chest

  c. blanket

  d. victim's clothes

9. The first step to locating a lost firefighter is to acknowledge his call for help and gather as much _____ as you can to assist the rescue team.

  a. equipment

  b. SCBA bottles

  c. information

  d. hose lines

10. Firefighters should practice changing a downed firefighter's mask from his nonfunctioning regulator to a working regulator so that they can accomplish it in _____.

  a. 10 seconds

  b. 30 seconds

  c. 10 minutes

  d. 1 minute

Student Signature and Date _____   Instructor/Company Officer Signature and Date _____

486

Prove It

Skills Assessment

Signed Documentation Tear-Out Sheet

Safety and Survival for Interior Firefighters—Chapter 19

Name: _____

Fill out the Skills Assessment Sheet below. Have your instructor/Company Officer check off and initial each skill you demonstrate. When you are finished, sign this page and give to your instructor/Company Officer for his or her signature. Turn in this Skills Assessment Sheet to the proper person as part of the documentation that you have completed your training for this chapter.

Skill	Completed	Initials
1. Describe some of the hazards to look for when making the decision to enter a burning structure.	_____	_____
2. Demonstrate how to safely use a portable electrical generator and Fire Department–issued floodlighting to light the scene and interior of a building for safety.	_____	_____
3. Describe the hazards associated with, and safety procedures to use while working around, stacked materials.	_____	_____
4. Explain the role that personnel accountability plays in the safety of crews working inside an IDLH atmosphere, and the responsibility of every firefighter working within a proper personnel accountability system (PAS).	_____	_____
5. Explain a Personnel Accountability Report and when it is used.	_____	_____
6. Perform controlled breathing techniques while wearing an SCBA.	_____	_____
7. Describe and perform all the skills necessary to work as part of the interior team while searching, fighting fire, and exiting the structure.	_____	_____
8. Recognize and take appropriate actions when the low-air warning signal activates.	_____	_____
9. Recognize various problems with the function of your SCBA and take appropriate action, including using the purge valve when necessary.	_____	_____
10. Describe and perform emergency evacuation procedures, including self-rescue techniques, emergency evacuations, ladder use, and methods for seeking refuge as necessary.	_____	_____
11. Effectively communicate a problem that arises while you are working inside a burning structure or other IDLH environment.	_____	_____
12. Effectively free yourself from an entanglement.	_____	_____
13. Navigate with obscured vision inside a structure.	_____	_____
14. Perform a primary and a secondary search of a structure.	_____	_____
15. Describe and perform the basics of operating a thermal imaging camera.	_____	_____
16. Describe and perform various techniques for locating and rescuing a civilian from a burning structure.	_____	_____
17. Describe and perform various techniques for locating and rescuing a fellow firefighter from a burning structure.	_____	_____

Student Signature and Date _____   Instructor/Company Officer Signature and Date _____

Residential Structure Fires

What You Will Learn in This Chapter

In this chapter we will introduce you to interior fire attack operations on residential structures. Common residential building layouts will be discussed. We will also discuss what to look for when you are on the scene of a smoke odor investigation or an incipient fire in a residential building. We will address advancing an attack line inside, as well as confining, knocking down, and extinguishing a fire. Fire overhaul and property conservation practices are explained. Finally, we will describe a defensive fire attack. As always, your safety and welfare will be stressed throughout the chapter.

What You Will Be Able to Do

After reading this chapter and practicing the skills described, you will be able to:

1. Describe some common building layouts of residential structures.
2. Participate as a team member when investigating a residential building for a smoke odor, a gas odor, and an activated smoke or carbon monoxide detector.
3. As a team member, assist in stretching a charged attack line into the interior of a residential building.
4. As a team member, assist in stretching a charged attack line up or down an interior or exterior stairway.
5. Describe pre- and post-flashover fire conditions.
6. Describe how to open walls, ceilings, and floors for further fire extinguishment and overhaul.
7. Describe initial and secondary search operations during a residential structure fire.
8. Explain the different considerations when fighting fires in multiple rooms, attics, basements, and garages in residential buildings.

9. Describe the laddering, fire spread, and potential for a large fire in apartments and row houses.
10. Describe a defensive fire attack.

Reality!

Firefighter Priorities at a Residential Fire

Residential fires start as a rescue operation. By this we mean that a fire is a threat first to life and then to property. Our priorities should always be first to protect life then to extinguish the fire to save property. The very first people whose lives we are concerned about are ourselves and our fellow firefighters. Next are people who are in a life-threatening situation and then those who might be injured. If we do nothing else but rescue all the occupants of a building fire and keep every firefighter alive and uninjured, then, at the end of the day, we have fulfilled the first priority of firefighting, saving lives. Even if the building burns to the ground and all the property is lost, lives were protected. The safety focus of all firefighters should be that *no building ever built is worth a firefighter's life.* You must always respect a building fire. Remember—you are entering a very hostile environment that can become deadly in an instant.

Safety Lesson: A NIOSH Report

Firefighters Die and Are Injured in a House Fire Flashover

On March 21, 2003, a 25-year-old male firefighter (the victim) was fatally injured in a flashover during a house fire. The victim and two other firefighters were on an interior attack crew and had just gone through the front door of a single-family residence. The hose line was uncharged and the crew was calling for water when a flashover occurred. The time between the victim's arrival on the scene and the flashover was approximately 4 minutes. After the flashover occurred, firefighters on the front porch witnessed the victim walk toward the front door and then turn and retreat into the structure. Two other firefighters on the interior crew exited through the front door. They were injured and transported to the hospital, where they were treated and released. The victim was located and removed from the structure within 10 minutes. He was transported via ambulance to the hospital, where he was pronounced dead.

Follow-Up

NIOSH Report #F2003-12

NIOSH investigators concluded that, to minimize the risk of similar occurrences, fire departments should do the following:

- Review and revise existing standard operating procedures (SOPs) for structural firefighting to ensure that firefighters enter burning structures with charged hose lines
- Ensure that a Rapid Intervention Team (RIT) is established and is in position prior to initiating an interior attack
- Ensure that ventilation is closely coordinated with interior operations
- Ensure that crew continuity is maintained on the fireground
- Ensure that the Incident Commander always maintains close accountability for all personnel operating on the fireground

Finally, NIOSH investigators determined that Emergency Dispatchers should obtain as much information as possible from the caller and report it to the responding firefighters.

Residential Structures

Residential structures encompass a wide variety of styles and building arrangements. People live in all kinds of structures, from mobile homes to high-rise apartments to huge mansions. For the purposes of this text, we will limit our discussion to the most common types of residential structures. These include one- and two-family dwellings and multifamily dwellings that are within reach of ground ladders, meaning residential buildings up to three stories in height (Figures 20-1 and 20-2). The techniques and practices we discuss here will apply to common residential structures. Other types of buildings will be covered in Chapter 21, "Large Buildings."

FIGURE 20-1 A typical two-story house.

Because people live in residential structures, these are the most numerous structures in a community. Therefore, they are also the most common type of structure to catch fire. You will respond to more residential fires than any other type of structural fire. Due to the frequency of fires in these structures, this is where the greatest loss of life and injury occurs to occupants as well as to firefighters.

One- and two-family dwellings include manufactured as well as site-built structures. Manufactured homes can be located in trailer parks, in urban/wildlife interface areas, and in rural locations. Site-built structures include single-family homes as well as duplex structures, and are usually located in subdivisions. They can also be located in urban/wildlife interface areas and rural locations. Multifamily dwellings include apartments, condominiums, and row houses. Vast areas of the country have large suburban areas filled with residential dwellings accessed by streets.

Common Residential Building Layouts

Residential structures have family areas within them. Family areas can consist of a common area or living room, a kitchen, bathroom(s), and bedroom(s). Other areas can include closets, storage areas, an extra family room, a home office, a garage, and utility rooms. These areas can be arranged in multiple levels or as a split-level. They can also include attics and basements.

A front entrance door is present in most cases. Rear or side doors may or may not be present. Normally, most rooms located along exterior walls will have at least one window. In multilevel structures, there may be balconies located off upper floor areas. Split-level structures may have more floor levels on one side than the other (Figure 20-3).

FIGURE 20-2 A multistory apartment building.

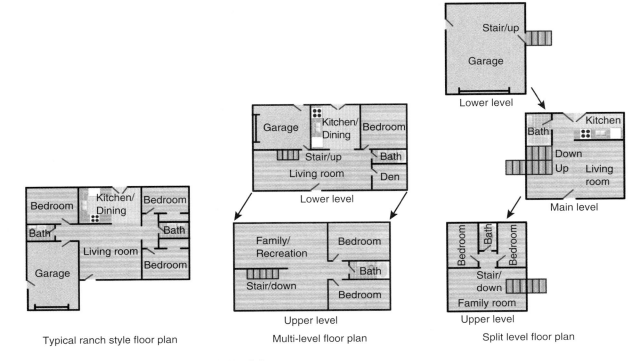

FIGURE 20-3 Typical layouts for residential buildings.

Investigating Smoke Odors and Incipient Fires

What if your crew is dispatched to investigate a residential structure in which there is only a slight smoke odor or a smoke alarm has gone off with no obvious fire? Perhaps there was a small fire that burned itself out or is still an incipient fire. These situations can occur from a lightning strike to the building, an electrical short of some kind, or even a child playing with matches in the home. Because of these varied origins, these types of calls can be very difficult to resolve. Your Company Officer will check with the occupant to try to narrow down the possible sources of the odor or smoke. You and the crew will be asked to help locate the source. The best method to use is the process of elimination. What type of smoke odor is it?

Thermal Imaging Cameras (TICs)

Modern technology has introduced heat-sensitive devices, known as thermal imaging cameras (TICs), for use by firefighters to locate hidden fires, hot areas, and even people and animals inside an otherwise invisible area. TICs produce a live image, showing the different temperatures of objects within the viewfinder. The picture resembles a negative image, with warmer surfaces being lighter or a different color than cooler surfaces. These devices have revolutionized firefighters' ability to locate other downed firefighters, fire victims, and hot spots in a fire situation. They are also invaluable tools for locating hot wiring or hidden fires under surfaces, like a wall or the covering of an appliance. If your department has one of these devices, you will receive training in its proper use (Figure 20-4).

Shorted Electrical Wiring Odor

To investigate an odor related to shorted electrical wiring, follow these steps:

1. Locate and take a look at the main circuit breaker or fuse box. Check to see if any circuit breaker switches are thrown or if the wiring to the box is hot (Figure 20-5). If the breakers or fuses are labeled correctly, they can help you locate the room or area in the home where the problem is.

2. Check all appliances in the building that are plugged into wall outlets. Are they or their wires hot or giving off the odor?

3. Find the inside air-handling units of the **HVAC** (heating, ventilation, and air conditioning) for the building. Check their operation and check for a smoke odor. You may have to remove a side panel to look at the unit's internal wiring (Figure 20-6). Be sure the main circuit breaker switch for the unit is in the "off" position before doing this.

4. Check any major appliances that run on electricity, such as stove, washer, dryer, and refrigerator.

5. Investigate any lamps, room lighting, computer equipment, TV sets, stereos, radios, and any other electrical appliances to see if they are overly hot.

6. Check any garage or workshop areas for tools or equipment that may have been used recently and could be the cause.

7. Check the area outside the house where the meter and the main electrical wiring feeds in from the utility pole or underground. These feeds must have all three wires connected to be safe. If one is shorted out or disconnected, it could cause a serious electrical short in any electrical equipment in the home.

8. Any appliances or electrical equipment found to be the source of the odor should be disconnected and removed from the building. If you

FIGURE 20-4 Some fire departments use a thermal imaging camera (TIC) to check for hot wiring on the other side of walls, ceilings, and floors.

FIGURE 20-5 Circuit breakers in a residential building.

FIGURE 20-6 The interior of an HVAC panel.

cannot locate the source of the electrical odor, then your Company Officer will advise the occupant of the next safety step. This step may include having a certified electrician carefully check the building.

KEY WORD

HVAC An abbreviation for the heating, ventilation, and air-conditioning system located within a structure.

Gas Odor

Remember that not all gas smells are natural gas. They may be propane (from a gas grill) or methane (from dried sewer traps). If you are at a multifamily dwelling, check the other living units.

To investigate a gas odor, follow these steps:

1. If there is a gas odor inside the building, the building should be immediately evacuated.
2. Your Company Officer may decide to shut off the gas service to the home at the main feed.
3. Do not operate any electrical switches, and ventilate the structure.
4. The main electrical power should be disconnected by the power company at the street or electrical main.

5. The gas service and all of the gas piping and appliances should then be checked by a gas company technician prior to gas service being restored. The gas company should also relight any pilot lights in these appliances after service has been restored.

Wood, Paper, or Plastic Smoke Odor

To investigate a smoke odor of wood, paper, or plastic, follow these steps:

1. Find out if anyone has been burning anything in or near the home.
2. Look in every room for evidence of a fire, being sure to check trash cans. Remember to check attic and basement areas.
3. Use a TIC to check the exterior roof area for any hot spots.
4. Determine if there could have been another fire in the area that is the source of the odor.
5. Find out if the occupant has recently been cooking or using the stovetop, oven, or microwave oven.
6. Find out if the occupant has recently been using the fireplace. Check whether the flue on the fireplace or wood-burning stove is open or closed.
7. Does the occupant have a dishwasher? Check it for plastic dishware in the heating element.

Activated Smoke Detector

Since smoke detectors are so common today, your department will respond to many activated smoke detectors to investigate the cause of the activation. If the detector is intermittently chirping, this indicates that the battery in the device is low. If the detector is sounding a steady tone, it can be due to several things. However, a steadily sounding detector is seldom a false alarm. Causes can include

- Cooking in the kitchen
- A hidden fire somewhere in the structure:
  - You will have to check the entire building, inside and out. Check darkened areas, like attics or basements by shining your flashlight into these areas, looking for light smoke.
  - If your department has a Thermal Imaging Camera, this would be a good time to use it to look for hidden hot spots.
- Dust or a defect in the detector

If nothing is found, your Company Officer will provide the occupant with suggestions developed by your fire department for this situation.

Activated Carbon Monoxide Detector

Like smoke detectors, carbon monoxide detectors are becoming increasingly common. This type of detector is activated by increased levels of carbon monoxide in the building. These increased levels can result from improperly vented equipment that burns fossil fuels, such as gas heaters or gas fireplaces. Carbon monoxide can also result from vehicle exhaust from cars running in an attached garage area.

Whatever the cause, your Company Officer will provide the occupant with guidelines developed by the fire department. These guidelines usually include checking for any symptoms of carbon monoxide poisoning in the occupants. Many fire departments have carbon monoxide detectors available to check inside buildings. This should be done prior to ventilating the structure. You should then thoroughly ventilate the residence by opening all windows and doors. When ventilation has been completed, check the structure again with a carbon monoxide detector. Remember, carbon monoxide is colorless and odorless, so you will need to check the atmosphere with a monitor before reentering the structure.

Incipient Fires

Smaller fires in or outside a structure that are attacked during their earlier stages are referred to as *incipient fires.* These fires may be smaller due to the limited fuel composition or supply of the materials on fire. As we discussed in Chapter 6 of *Safe Firefighting: First Things First*, incipient fires are usually handled by fire extinguishers. Review that chapter as necessary.

Review *Safe Firefighting: First Things First,* Chapter 6, "*Small Fires.*" Also review the Chapter 6 content on the DVD that accompanies that text.

Residential Fire Operations

There are two main fire attack operations to consider when a building is on fire: offensive and defensive fire attacks. An offensive fire attack involves entering the structure to rescue any trapped or injured fire victims as well as aggressively confining and extinguishing the fire. A defensive fire attack involves fighting the fire from the outside. This type of fire attack is used when the building is deemed too dangerous to enter and there are no survivable areas of the building to search. In these cases, the fire has progressed beyond any hope of safely salvaging the building and the risks of entering and extinguishing the fire within are far too great.

No Freelancing   To ensure your safety when working at any emergency scene, ask yourself these questions: *Does Command know where I am and what I am doing? Do I have backup support as I work?* Don't freelance on the scene and get yourself into trouble with no way out!

Offensive Fire Attack

We are now going to discuss how to offensively attack a few types of residential fires. These fires include room and contents fires, multiple-room fires, attic fires, basement fires, garage fires, apartment fires, and row house fires.

Room and Contents Fires

The steps necessary to handle a room and contents fire are common to most types of offensive attacks. They will simply be added to or adapted depending on the situation at hand. These steps are dictated by the situation and the conditions your Company Officer and crew find upon arriving at and assessing the scene. Your actions will be determined by the job given to you and your crew by your Company Officer and the Incident Commander. Your crew may pull an attack line and enter the structure to confine and extinguish the fire. Or you and your crew may pull a backup line to act as a safety outside the building or to use as you go inside and assist the interior crew. You may be told to ventilate the structure, provide ladders to upper levels, control utilities, or protect exposures. There are many jobs your crew will be expected to be able to perform. Our next discussion will focus on you and your crew being assigned to enter the building to confine and extinguish the fire.

Making Entry

You will probably start by entering an opening into the structure. In residential structures, this opening will usually be a front door, a window, or another door opening (Figure 20-7). Your Company Officer will coordinate with the driver and the Incident Commander to make sure a water supply has been established. Your Company Officer will also ensure that other actions are taken, such as making sure that ventilation and backup fire attack crews are in place for the entry to be made.

FIGURE 20-7 Entry is usually through a doorway, but it can also be through a window or other opening.

The backup crew should enter behind your team as soon as possible. They will have a charged attack line, providing a safety backup for your team.

The opening may have to be forced. This job can be done by your crew or members of another crew.

 Safety Tip!

Two-In/Two-Out and Intervention Teams The two-in/two-out safety rule states that if a fire crew arrives on the scene of a building fire and the interior contains an IDLH (immediately dangerous to life and health) atmosphere, and the crew has reasonable information that there is no one trapped inside, they must go in with at least two firefighters on the attack line to extinguish the fire. They also must have two firefighters standing by outside with a backup attack hose line before they enter the burning structure. This is a minimum requirement. It is always better to have additional firefighting crews, coordinated by an Incident Commander. The only exception to this rule is if there is the possibility that someone is trapped inside and must be rescued immediately. In this situation, the two-in/two-out rule can be suspended.

In many fire departments this requirement has evolved into the establishment of an Intervention Team (also called the Rapid Intervention Team or Rapid Intervention Crew). This team is responsible for firefighter rescue if the interior team gets into trouble. They will be standing by with tools, medical equipment, and a charged attack hose line ready to come to the aid of any interior attack crews or firefighters that are in need of emergency assistance (Figure 20-8).

FIGURE 20-8 A Rapid Intervention Team standing by outside a structural fire.

Before you enter a structural fire, check with your Company Officer to see that he or she is ready and also take a quick look at your fellow crew member, checking for any PPE that is not in place. You should advise your team partner if he or she needs to adjust their PPE. Check your tools. If you are on the nozzle, then you should have your flashlight switched on and attached to your gear. If you are the backup firefighter on the hose line, you should be carrying a forcible entry tool that can be used to gain access to locked areas, to help with searching larger areas, or for forcible exit in an emergency. A ceiling hook should be carried in by a crew member for opening walls and ceiling areas overhead to check for heavy smoke and fire conditions. Your Company Officer may or may not be bringing in a tool. Many fire departments provide portable radios for all firefighters inside a building fire; however, yours might not. Your Company Officer will at least have a portable radio. If no one has a radio, then you must maintain visual and audible contact with the safety crew outside the structure.

Never enter a burning building with an attack line unless you know you have a sustained water supply to that line. Before you enter, check for water pressure by opening the nozzle outside the structure, bleeding air from the line, and adjusting the nozzle pattern. As you

FIGURE 20-9 Never enter a building with an attack line unless you know you have a sustained water supply to that line.

FIGURE 20-10 Rapid ventilation openings are essential for a safe and quick fire knockdown and extinguishment.

open the door, anticipate heat by standing to one side, using the exterior wall for protection (Figure 20-9).

Ventilation efforts will likely be in progress as you prepare to enter the building. When another crew ventilates a room and contents fire from the outside, they will create openings first in the fire room. They will then continue to create openings, working their way outward from the fire room in either direction. Rapid ventilation openings are essential for a safe and quick fire knockdown and extinguishment (Figure 20-10).

Positive-pressure ventilation (PPV) may be set up and initiated as the door opens and you enter. A crew will be at the front door with the PPV fan running, but it will be turned away from the door. When your crew gets the door open and is ready to enter, they will turn the operating PPV fan toward the open doorway, positioning it for maximum effect. Proper ventilation reduces the chance for a flashover from a confined fire. Details of this kind of PPV are covered in Chapter 18 of this text.

If there is a known attic fire or smoke is coming from the attic, be sure to check the ceiling area just inside the front door before advancing the attack line inside. While standing in the doorway to the room, one firefighter from the entry team should make an inspection hole in the ceiling with a ceiling hook in order to check for heavy smoke or fire in the attic. The firefighter stands in the doorway for protection in case the ceiling collapses during this operation (Figure 20-11).

Stretching Attack Lines Inside As you enter with your Company Officer, fellow crew members, and the attack line, remember that you will all need to stay low because of excessive heat that builds at the ceiling and works its way down. Most firefighting inside a building takes place on your knees, below the heat

FIGURE 20-11 One firefighter from the entry team should make an inspection hole in the ceiling with a ceiling hook in order to check for heavy smoke or fire in the attic.

and heavy smoke. You will be crawling to the fire area through the smoke. During this advance, you and your crew will have to extend or stretch the attack line into position. At first, this would seem to be a simple function, but it can be very difficult. Attack lines that are charged and not flowing water can be very hard to maneuver through doorways, over furniture and debris, around corners, and into individual rooms. At every corner where the line is bent, someone will need to pull the line in as the crew moves forward. When the crew reaches another corner or obstruction, that firefighter repositions to that point and pulls more hose for slack, the same as before. If you must go through a doorway, you will have to be sure to use a door wedge to keep the door from closing. Hose lines can become wedged in a doorway if an unsecured door tries to close behind you. If there is an uncharged hose under a door that has closed, it may be pinched off when the line is charged with water.

View It!

Go to the DVD, navigate to Chapter 20, and select *"Stretching Attack Lines Inside."*

Practice It!

Stretching Attack Lines Inside

When stretching an attack line inside a residential structure, perform the following steps:

1. At the entrance point to the structure, check your attack line to see that it is charged with water. Gather enough extra line in large loops. These loops will be your slack line to be pulled in as you advance.

2. On the order of your Company Officer, enter the building with the nozzle and the line. One member of your team will station at the entranceway to feed the line in as you advance (Figure 20-12).

FIGURE 20-12

3. Inside a corner where the line is bent, another team member will position and pull sufficient slack, again feeding the attack line ahead as it is pulled. The firefighter at the entranceway can follow the line and relieve the firefighter at the first corner (Figure 20-13).

FIGURE 20-13

4. The firefighter who was relieved at the first corner follows the line to the next corner or obstruction and continues to feed the attack line as the hose is stretched. This leapfrog operation continues until the crew is in position to attack the fire. Remember, if you must go through a doorway, use a door wedge to keep the door from closing. An uncharged hose under a door that has closed can be pinched off when the line is charged with water (Figure 20-14).

FIGURE 20-14

Safety Tip!

Maneuvering Hose on Stairways If the fire is located in a room requiring access either up or down a stairway, there are a couple of methods for maneuvering the hose line. First, check the stairway for any fire damage before using it to access the other floor level. If the stairway is damaged, you may have to access the other floor from the exterior using a ladder or another safe stairway. If advancing up a stairway, first curl and loop the hose at the bottom. Doing so will allow you plenty of extra hose line for your advance to the fire room. Then, with your team, advance carefully until you reach the top. At this point, gather more slack hose before advancing to the fire room.

On exterior stairways, you can use the same methods to advance a hose line. Alternately, you can use a rope, a strap, or even a ceiling hook to move the hose and nozzle to the next level. To do this, one firefighter goes to the upper landing and drops one end of a rope or strap to a second firefighter at the nozzle below. The second firefighter ties a quick knot around the nozzle and the first firefighter pulls the hose line to the upper level. If you use a ceiling hook, simply reach down with the ceiling hook and allow the firefighter on the nozzle to hook the bale. You can then raise the nozzle and line to your level. Finish both of these methods by pulling enough hose to reach the upper level. Then use a hose strap or rope to secure the hose line to the stairway railing. This method is also very effective for raising a hose line to a balcony.

View It!

Go to the DVD, navigate to Chapter 20, and select *"Maneuvering Hose on Stairways."*

Practice It!

Maneuvering Hose on Stairways

When stretching an attack line up or down a stairway, perform the steps below.

Interior Stairways

1. First check the stairway for any fire damage before using it to access the other floor level. If the stairway is damaged, you may have to access the other floor from the exterior using a ladder or another safe stairway.

2. Gather plenty of extra hose line for your advance and extension to the fire room, curling and looping the hose. If you are going up the stairs, station a firefighter at the bottom to feed you line as you and your team advance to the next landing (Figure 20-15).

3. At this point, gather extra hose to either advance to the fire on that level or to advance up to the next landing above, depending on the location of the fire and the configuration of the stairs.

4. Use the same technique for advancing down a stairway.

FIGURE 20-15

Exterior Stairways

On exterior stairways, you can use the same methods to advance a hose line or you can use a rope, strap, or even a ceiling hook to move the hose and nozzle to the next level.

1. One firefighter goes to the upper landing and drops one end of a rope or strap to a second firefighter at the nozzle below.

FIGURE 20-16

2. The second firefighter ties a quick knot around the nozzle, and the first firefighter pulls the hose line to the upper level (Figure 20-16). An alternate method is to use a ceiling hook. Simply reach down with the ceiling hook and allow the firefighter on the nozzle to hook the bale of the nozzle on the attack line. You can then raise the nozzle and line to your level (Figure 20-17).

FIGURE 20-17

3. Finish both of these methods by pulling slack hose to reach the upper level and use a hose strap or rope to secure the hose line to the stairway railing (Figure 20-18). This method is also very effective for raising a hose line up to a balcony.

FIGURE 20-18

Level I

Conducting an Initial Search All firefighting personnel inside and outside the fire building should always be looking for fire victims. If there is any chance of finding survivors inside, Command will direct a search crew to enter the building. The first tactic is to rescue any fire victims from survivable areas of the building. This may involve removing the victims, cutting off the advance of the fire, or both. We need to get the people that are still inside the building to a safe area outside.

Even if you are with the inside firefighting crew, you should still be doing quick searches as you proceed. Use care when opening any interior doors, especially if they won't swing inward after you start to open them. There may be an unconscious victim blocking the door from the other side. As you attack the fire, check inside closets, behind furniture, under beds, and under windows for fire victims. In all cases, if you locate one, be sure to notify your Company Officer and Command, and immediately evacuate the victim to a safe area with fresh air. Review Chapter 19 of this text for additional details regarding search methods.

Confining the Fire Command may decide to try to cut off the spread of the fire in order to provide time for evacuations or searches. We can cut off the fire spread by confining the fire to the burned areas of the building. Confinement requires that we isolate the destructive fire to areas already involved, saving the survivable areas for a quick search and evacuation of fire victims, even if it is just a temporary measure.

Interior firefighting is usually done from the unburned interior areas toward the burned areas. However, there are exceptions to this rule. Sometimes the layout of the building or windy conditions will not allow firefighters to do this. Entering a burning building from the downwind side when there is a strong wind can be very dangerous. You may have to enter from the burning side, upwind, and extinguish the fire as quickly as possible. If no people are at risk, this situation may call be a defensive attack for safety reasons.

Achieving an Initial Fire Knockdown One of the best methods of saving lives is to extinguish the fire as soon as possible. Once the fire is confined, the next move is to position yourself to knock down and extinguish the fire. The initial knockdown can usually be accomplished by flowing a quick blast of water in a medium-pattern stream at the ceiling (Figure 20-19). This action will reduce the chance of flashover by cooling the superheated gases at the ceiling and allow water to rain down on the fire below.

After directing a short blast at the ceiling, aim the water stream at the base of the fire, eventually narrowing the stream. Flow the nozzle and sweep across the

FIGURE 20-19 Flowing a quick blast of water at the ceiling area will help reduce the chance of a flashover.

burning materials until the flames are extinguished. There will be extensive smoke and steam as the water absorbs the heat of the fire and turns to steam. Narrow or straight streams are good for penetrating the seat of the fire as well as for blowing through debris and opening weakened ceiling and wall areas.

Medium fog patterns are effective for general extinguishment and to cool down the room and contents. They also work well for venting through an open window and providing hydraulic ventilation.

Tip!

Pre-Flashover

A typical fire inside any structure starts as an incipient fire and then spreads to adjacent fuels as it increases in size and intensity. This is the pre-flashover phase. If you find a fire in a room with heavy, heated smoke at the ceiling level and objects across from the fire are smoldering but are not yet burning, it is important to reduce the possibility of a flashover fire by cooling the ceiling and fire while rapidly ventilating the room and building (Figure 20-20).

Post-Flashover

If you enter a building area and find the fire raging at the ceiling area and throughout the room, then you are probably looking at a post-flashover fire. You will need a narrower fire stream to penetrate the extreme heat being generated by the free burning. Keep your distance and flow plenty of water both at the ceiling and onto the fire (Figure 20-21).

Pre-flashover room and contents fire

FIGURE 20-20 In the pre-flashover phase, cool the ceiling and fire while rapidly ventilating the room and building.

FIGURE 20-21 During a post-flashover fire, flow a narrower fire stream onto the ceiling and the fire.

The Weight of Water

A gallon of water weighs about 8.3 pounds. It can injure a firefighter if he or she is hit by your flowing stream. The weight of water also means that water will add weight to the load on the floor you are working on. If you are flowing 100 to 150 gallons per minute from your nozzle, you are adding hundreds of pounds of weight to a floor that may already be weakened by fire.

Heat Absorption

A gallon of water absorbs about 9000 **British thermal units (Btus)** of heat while changing from a liquid to a vapor (steam). This is why we use water to extinguish fires—it is a good heat-absorbing agent, and it is also relatively plentiful in most areas.

Water Expansion

When water absorbs heat, changing from a liquid state into a gaseous state (steam), it expands to up to 1700 times its original volume. This characteristic explains why a fog pattern absorbs heat and expands to steam so readily. The small droplets of the fog pattern provide a greater surface area to absorb the heat more efficiently than a solid stream pattern would.

The Effects of Gravity

Gravity acts on water as it does on other physical objects. For firefighters, this means that water will flow down through a structure during the firefighting process. If you are on an upper floor, the more water you flow, the greater the potential for water damage to floors below your level.

KEY WORD

British thermal unit (Btu)   The total amount of thermal energy needed to raise the temperature of one pound of water by one degree Fahrenheit at the temperature at which water is at its greatest density (39 degrees Fahrenheit).

Completing the Extinguishment   After knocking down the fire, extinguishment is completed by checking for any fire extension to other areas of the building through hidden spaces and openings. Fire can travel into hidden areas through hollow wall spaces and openings in the floor and ceiling. These areas need to be opened and checked. Because the fixed electrical wiring of a structure is located inside wall, ceiling, and floor areas, your Company Officer will coordinate with Command to make sure power is off before opening hidden areas. Water pipes and other utility chases are also located in these areas.

Openings are made in walls, starting near the burned area and working outward. The wall coverings are pulled away until no embers, smoke, and charring are found. Use a short ceiling hook, an axe, or a Halligan bar to do this. Jab the sharp end of the tool into a hollow area between wall studs and pull outward.

Ceilings are best opened using a long ceiling hook. Jab the hook end through the ceiling between the rafters and pull downward. Make sure the area under the ceiling is clear of firefighters. Whole sections of ceiling panels can fall at once, especially if they have been damaged by fire.

The majority of newer residential structures are finished with gypsum board (drywall) (Figure 20-22). However, you may come across older structures with plaster over wood lath walls and ceiling coverings. These are much harder to open and will take more effort. You may also find wood and Masonite-type paneling covering the walls. These will also take

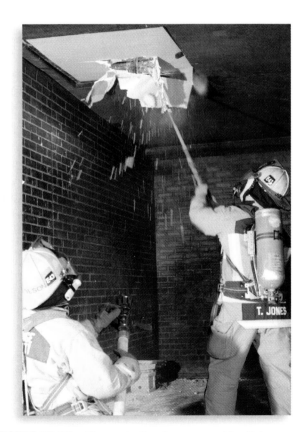

FIGURE 20-22   The majority of newer residential structures are finished with gypsum board.

much more effort to remove when checking for fire extension.

Check for fire extension in wood floors by going to the floor below and opening the ceiling to check the floor above. If there is no floor level below, you may need to cut inspection holes with a circular saw or chainsaw. Look for embers in dark areas and then use your flashlight to check for charring and smoke.

View It!

Go to the DVD, navigate to Chapter 20, and select *"Room and Contents Fire Extinguishment."*

Practice It!

Extinguishing a Room and Contents Fire

Use the following method to practice extinguishing a typical room and contents fire:

1. After ensuring that you and your team are in proper PPE, a second team with a backup attack line is in position, proper ventilation of the fire has been accomplished, and your attack line is charged with water and ready, enter the fire building, staying low. Assist your team in stretching the attack line into position at the entrance to the room on fire (Figure 20-23).

FIGURE 20-23

2. On the command of your Company Officer, go to a safe position to one side of the doorway to the room and push it open. Take a look inside to check the extension and location of the fire. If it is safe, position in the doorway to apply water.

FIGURE 20-24

3. From the doorway, flow short blasts of water to the ceiling, then narrow your stream and sweep across the burning materials in the room. Continue to flow water until all the fire has been knocked down and darkened (Figure 20-24).

FIGURE 20-25

4. Staying low, approach the area where the fire was burning and continue to flow water, further cooling the area. Monitor the ceiling above for any additional fire.

5. Finally, go to an open window or door to the outside and position on the inside about 4 or 5 feet from the opening. Flow water out of the window to assist smoke and heat removal. Use a fog pattern that just fills the inside of opening but allows smoke and heat to flow out with the water stream (Figure 20-25).

Training for interior fire attack is dangerous work. You should train for this only in an approved training facility. However, on occasion, acquired buildings are also used for this type of training. In either instance, these should be prepared prior to the training in accordance with your fire department's safety standards and in compliance with NFPA Standard 1403, *Live Fire Training Evolutions.* All fire training should also be conducted in accordance with safe practices and backup safety crews as noted in NFPA Standard 1403.

Conducting a Secondary Search When the fire has been extinguished and smoke is clearing from the structure, Command will most likely order a second search. This secondary search will entail a much more thorough search of the building. It will be conducted in a more methodical fashion by a different crew than the one that did the initial search. If your crew is given this task, you will be asked by your Company Officer to search for fire victims in all areas of the building, including areas destroyed by fire. You may also be looking for any pets that are suspected to still be inside the structure.

As you search, use adequate lighting—either your own flashlight or portable floodlights set up inside each search area. Look inside, underneath, and around everything. This includes piles of debris, furniture, and bedding. Closets and bathrooms need to be checked very closely. Even garage and storage areas need to be closely checked.

There will be instances when a third search may be directed by Command. The need to be thorough during these searches cannot be stressed enough. The Fire Department must be certain that all fire victims have been located. Search procedures are covered extensively in Chapter 19 of this text.

Overhauling the Fire Area The next step in the fire operation is thoroughly overhauling the fire area, ensuring that the fire has been completely extinguished. This part of firefighting is very important because a rekindled building fire can be even more dangerous to extinguish than the original fire. Overhaul involves flowing more water onto piles of debris. This is done as a team. One firefighter flows water as other team members use tools like a ceiling hook to pull and lift debris for better access and extinguishment. It may also include moving smoldering furniture and other contents to the outside of the building, where they can be soaked with water (Figure 20-26).

Another job started during the overhaul of a building fire is assessing the origin of the fire. Two of the methods for doing this are to look for burn patterns and check for the extent of charring damage from the fire.

Burn patterns may be left visible on walls and other surfaces. These burn patterns will be a different color than the surrounding surface and will usually be in a "V" pattern, with the bottom of the "V" indicating a possible origination area of the fire. If you find a "V" pattern during the overhaul of a fire, report this immediately to your Company Officer for further investigation.

Charring is another indicator of a fire's origin. The charring of wood objects and building features is deeper in depth and more evident the closer you get to the location of the original fire. The damage from charring is also more extensive closer to the origination area.

All of these indicators are important to the investigation of the cause and origin of the fire. You may even be asked to hold up further overhaul until your Company Officer or a fire investigator checks the area. He or she will advise you on the care you need to take to preserve any evidence during this time.

During overhaul, firefighters make the building as safe as possible. You may be directed by your Company Officer to help pull down damaged parts of the building, such as ceilings and wall coverings, and to check the stability of interior floors, interior walls, and stairways. Any dangerous conditions should be reported to your Company Officer and isolated with fire-line tape.

FIGURE 20-26 Overhaul also involves flowing more water onto piles of debris.

Safety Tip!

Wear PPE During Overhaul It is tempting to remove your PPE, especially your SCBA, during overhaul operations. This is a bad practice. Always wear your full PPE, including SCBA, while doing overhaul work. There is still plenty of hazardous smoke and gases from incomplete combustion, and these are just as dangerous to your health as the gases released during an actively burning interior fire. Many fire departments use carbon monoxide detectors to check levels inside buildings after the fire has been extinguished.

There will also be plenty of sharp edges in a fire-damaged building. Nails, screws, and other building parts that were safe before the fire will have been exposed.

Use care when overhauling a fire area inside a building. Keep in mind there may be unstable areas of the structure, including the roof, ceilings, walls, and floors. These areas may collapse and may pose fall hazards. Floors can have unexpected holes in them, either from the fire or from the extinguishment and overhaul processes. Stairways and railings, both inside and outside the structure, can be very hazardous if they have been damaged by fire.

Conducting Salvage Operations Using water to attack and extinguish a fire inside a building is not the only method used to reduce property loss. Often, salvage operations are conducted in conjunction with fire-extinguishing operations. Salvage operations involve covering valuables inside a structure to protect them from water damage, routing the water runoff to the exterior of the building, and removing undamaged or exposed items to the outside of the building.

Salvage Tarps for Covering Valuables There are a couple types of salvage tarps used to cover valuables during and after a fire: commercially available tarps and plastic tarps. Tarps specifically made for Fire Service use are designed to withstand repeated use. They are puncture resistant, but not impervious to punctures or heat damage. Plastic tarps are carried in a roll of plastic and cut to size as needed. These provide minimal protection, and they are easily punctured and damaged by heat. Sometimes they are precut and folded for storage on the fire truck.

All tarps should be folded in a configuration that allows them to be easily unfolded when used to cover valuables at a fire.

Level I

Practice It!

Folding Salvage Tarps

Two firefighters can use the following method to fold a tarp used to cover valuables at a fire:

1. Lay the tarp out on a clean, flat surface. Position at each end of the tarp on the same side and pick up the corner. Walk to the center of the tarp and lay the corner down, creating an inward fold. Position this fold at the center, lengthwise (Figure 20-27).

2. Go to the other side of the tarp, grab the corners, and position this side the same as before, at the center.

FIGURE 20-27

—Continued

3. Repeat these steps until the tarp is 3 or 4 feet wide. Then make a final lengthwise fold, placing one side on top of the other (Figure 20-28).

FIGURE 20-28

4. Finally, fold the tarp at 1-foot increments accordion style, until the tarp is completely folded (Figure 20-29).

FIGURE 20-29

If your crew is assigned to cover a pile of valuables in a room exposed to damage from water or falling debris, your Company Officer will direct you regarding which method to use.

 Practice It!

Covering Stacked Valuables with a Salvage Tarp

In most cases, valuables are stacked in a safe area of the room and covered with a salvage tarp. Two firefighters can easily do this using the following steps:

1. One firefighter stands at one end with the tarp and the other firefighter stands at the opposite end of the pile. The firefighter with the tarp tosses it toward the other firefighter while grasping its edge.

FIGURE 20-30

2. The tarp will unfold as it moves toward the second firefighter. This firefighter then grasps the tarp and they both unfold it over the pile (Figure 20-30).

Floor runners are long, narrow tarps used to cover flooring. These runners protect flooring from falling debris and dirt caused by firefighters walking in and out of an undamaged area of a building. They are easily laid out prior to entering an area.

Catch-alls are specially designed tarps for carrying materials and debris. They are usually 4 × 6 feet wide with handles along the edges. Debris and materials can be placed on the tarp, and several firefighters can lift the tarp and carry the debris or materials to another location.

Routing Water Runoff You can divert water runoff by building a system of troughs using salvage tarps. Unfold a tarp to a size a little larger than the space to be covered. Roll the sides inward and place the tarp in a hallway or stairway. You can create better support under the tarp by placing it on a small, straight ladder. The tarp and ladder can be combined to create a canal that allows water to flow to the outside (Figure 20-31).

Removing Valuables There may be instances when your Company Officer asks you to remove valuables from a building as a part of a salvage operation. Remember your physical limits and always use good body mechanics when lifting. If needed, get another team member to assist you. Carry the items to a safe area as directed. A safe area may be another secure room that is not going to be damaged from further fire control efforts, or it may be an adjoining area or building. If possible, be careful with the items you are moving. We don't want to cause further damage.

Valuables like jewelry or money that are found should be turned over to your Company Officer or the Incident Commander immediately, with a witness present.

Protecting and Retrieving Possessions

"The Three Ps" is a rule firefighters should follow when retrieving or protecting an occupant's valuable possessions during or after a fire. Always remember to be on the lookout for Pets, Pictures, and Pills. These are very important to people.

Other Interior Fire Situations

We will continue your training on residential fires by exploring some other typical fire situations that you will be expected to handle when fighting interior fires on residential structures. These situations include multiple-room fires, attic fires, basement fires, and ga-

FIGURE 20-31 A water trough made with salvage tarps.

rage fires. The basic operations discussed in the section on room and contents fires applies to all residential building fires. In addition, we will discuss other considerations for fires found in these other fire situations.

Multiple-Room Fires

When your crew arrives and finds a fire that involves more than one room, there will be some differences in how the fire is handled and the hazards it poses, compared to a single-room fire. These differences include more than one attack line operating inside to attack the fire, vent-enter-search operations, and additional hazards to firefighters.

Multiple Attack Lines In a residential structure in which more than a room and its contents are involved in fire, two or three fire attack lines will be deployed inside to control the fire. The Company Officers of each firefighting team must carefully coordinate their teams to best confine, knock down, and extinguish the fire. The main danger here is the possibility of opposing fire streams. If you are at the nozzle and there are multiple attack lines flowing inside on the fire-involved area, be careful not to direct your stream against another attack stream. The streams should be directed together at generally the same direction to halt the spread of the fire and then to extinguish it. Opposing streams can force the fire onto the firefighters operating on one of the attack lines, exposing them to injury. It will also impede extinguishment of the fire (Figures 20-32 and 20-33).

Vent-Enter-Search Operations When there is a larger fire in a residential structure, the search to locate fire victims in survivable areas of the building may be hampered by a lack of access to interior areas. If your team has been assigned to perform exterior ventilation on this type of fire, you may come across a room with an exterior window that may have fire victims inside. Your Company Officer will coordinate any search efforts with the Incident Commander and will call for a vent-enter-search operation. This operation requires a team of at least two firefighters, preferably with an exterior attack line backup. To perform this operation, open the window and climb inside, leaving your partner at the window. Rapidly locate and close the door to the room to provide protection from the heat and smoke of the fire. Do a very fast right- or left-handed search of the room, maintaining visual and audible contact with your partner at all times. Quickly exit the room through the window opening and move on with your venting work.

Additional Hazards The main hazards a multiple-room fire presents to firefighters are the intensity of the fire and the real danger of a significant flashover that involves a larger area of the building. The longer a structural fire burns, the larger the fire and the greater its destruction. Therefore, with a larger fire, there is a greater possibility of major structural failure and collapse.

Safety Tip!

Hazards of Split-Level Building Fires Many times, particularly in hilly areas, residential structures are built on a slope where one side is higher than the other. When a fire occurs on one level of a split-level structure and entry or ventilation is made upwind or downwind on another level, a severe flashover fire can occur, causing injury and a tragic loss of life.

To safely ventilate and fight fires in split-level structures, the Fire Command and Company Officers must specially coordinate the actions of the firefighting teams. As a general rule, upper floors should be vented first and then lower floors.

FIGURE 20-32 Opposing streams can force the fire onto the firefighters. They will also impede extinguishment of the fire.

FIGURE 20-33 To halt the spread of fire, the streams should be directed together in generally the same direction.

Attic Fires

A fire located in the attic area of a residential structure may have originated in the attic or it may have spread to the attic from a room below. Because most attics cover the entire top of the structure and they are open (that is, not divided into rooms), a fire can easily spread throughout the attic area. In addition, if the attic area has an access opening, it is likely that the attic has been used to store belongings. Therefore, the fire load of the attic area can be greater than anticipated.

Because the structural support for the roof is located in the attic space, it is critical to quickly control any fires in this area. Normally, most attic spaces do not have an interior finish, like gypsum board, to protect combustible structural members. Therefore, fires in these areas can spread rapidly.

An attic fire can be attacked quickly by making an opening in the ceiling with a ceiling hook and directing an attack stream into the opening. Position under a doorway to the area as you do this, to avoid any ceiling collapse hazards.

If the fire is small, in its incipient phase, a folding attic ladder can be deployed at the opening to the attic, called the scuttle opening. A firefighter can advance an attack line up the ladder and into the attic, spraying water across the underside of the roof to the base of the fire.

An attic fire can also be extinguished with the use of a piercing nozzle. Piercing nozzles are specially designed to be pounded with a flathead axe into a concealed area like an attic, a floor, a wall, or even a pile of burning debris. They have a shaft, a gate valve or bale, and a striking plate. Once they are inserted through the ceiling and into the attic space, they are operated, allowing water to flow into the attic space (Figure 20-34).

Refer to Chapter 18 of this text for information about ventilating attic fires.

Safety Tip!

Use Care in an Attic Space   When working in an attic area, be sure to wear complete PPE, including your SCBA. Attics are full of exposed insulation that can pose a health hazard under fire conditions.

Also be careful if you are walking or crawling in an attic space. Always work within a team, maintaining visual and audible contact with each other. Be sure to watch where you step or place your knees as you crawl. You can easily step or fall through ceiling coverings from the attic area. Ceiling coverings are not designed to hold any substantial weight, so stay on the rafters as you move along. Be aware that damaged and exposed wiring may also be located in an attic area. Before you enter and work in an attic space to extinguish a fire, the power to the structure must be turned off (Figure 20-35).

Basement Fires

The basement area of a residential structure offers some unique problems for firefighting operations. These challenges include access and egress, ventilation, and extinguishment.

By their nature, basement areas have very limited access. They usually provide a place for utility and plumbing access as well as locations for water heaters and other building service appliances, such as central heating units. In single-family dwellings, these areas can also be converted into recreational rooms. In additions, occupants often use basements for extra storage. Rarely, two access and exit points may be provided.

Usually a basement can be accessed by a single interior or exterior stairway. A single access and egress

FIGURE 20-34   A piercing nozzle.

FIGURE 20-35   Damaged and exposed wiring can be found in an attic space during a fire.

point can be a very dangerous condition for firefighters attacking a basement fire. If you enter to fight the fire and are cut off from using the same stairs to exit, you can easily become trapped. Because heat will be traveling up the stairs as you make your way down, stay low (Figure 20-36).

Basement fires are often more intense than fires on other levels of a structure. This is because a fire can build up massive heat due to the insulation of the earth on all four sides. Ventilation is often difficult and is limited to small window openings. However, in order to successfully extinguish a basement fire, there must be adequate ventilation openings through which trapped heat and gases can escape as the fire is being extinguished (Figure 20-37).

In a basement fire, your work time will be limited due to the heat conditions you will encounter. You will probably need a solid stream to reach the seat of a substantial basement fire. You can also use a distributor nozzle through an opening in the floor above to apply

Stay low when advancing down basement stairways

FIGURE 20-36 Stay low as you advance down basement stairways.

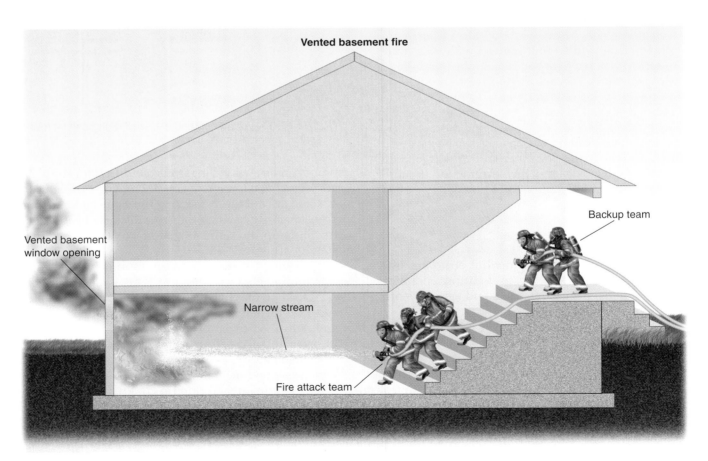

Vented basement fire

Backup team

Vented basement
window opening

Narrow stream

Fire attack team

FIGURE 20-37 A vented basement.

water spray to the fire area. Distributor nozzles consist of a rotating ball with a gate valve located on the end of an attack line (Figure 20-38). The rotating ball has several discharge openings that cause the ball to swivel and spray water when the valve is turned on.

Garage Fires

Many single-family dwellings also have a garage attached to the structure for housing vehicles. These areas can also contain utility appliances and HVAC air handling units. There may be a workbench, and flammable paints and gasoline often are stored in this area. Many times the scuttle access to the attic is located in the garage area. The circuit breaker switch panel box can also be located in the garage.

When a garage is involved in fire, it presents some unique problems for firefighting teams. First, the fire can be due to flammable liquids, a burning vehicle, natural gas, or an electrical appliance located within the garage. The fire will probably involve at least a couple of these fuels. This means that, once you access this area, you need to be prepared to fight a different type of fire than what you would encounter within the residence. There will be a greater and more varied fuel load in a garage.

In all cases, the main tactic is to access the garage, ventilate, and attack the fire with one or more attack hose lines. If you enter the garage through the overhead door, be sure to prop it open. Hot air from the fire can weaken the springs and cause the door to come down behind you or, worse, on top of you. There is also a good chance the fire will spread to the rest of the residence. Hose lines should therefore be placed inside the door to the garage from the structure to cut off any fire spread. Extinguishing agents for Class A, B, or C materials may also be needed to control fires in a garage (Figure 20-39). Because of their intensity, garage fires can spread quickly to the attic area or the floor above.

FIGURE 20-38 A distributor nozzle.

Apartments and Row House Fires

Multifamily residences include apartments (or condominiums) and row houses (or town homes), which are essentially single-family residences stacked next to and on top of each other. Your main concern will be the height of these complexes and the arrangement of the living units so close to each other.

As far as fighting interior fires inside an individual unit, the methods are the same. The differences will be in the access, the lengths of the attack lines, the ease of fire spread, and the potential size of the fire.

Accessing the Fire   These building complexes will be one to three stories in height, with attics and possibly a basement. They can also be located on a slope in a split-level configuration. There may be neighborhood streets bordering one side and parking lots within the complex.

Your team may be called upon to ladder these buildings for rescue, ventilation, or fire attack. If there is only one stairway up to the unit on fire, a second exit must be established by placing a ladder at a window

Garage fires
Class A – Interior finish, doors, etc.
Class B – Gas cans, fuel tank on car
Class C – Circuit breakers, HVAC unit

FIGURE 20-39   Garage fires can include Class A, B, and C combustibles.

FIGURE 20-40 Ladders can be placed to provide a secondary exit.

or balcony. Ladders may be placed to open windows or to flow water as needed (Figure 20-40).

Extending Attack Lines Attack lines will likely need to be extended to reach fires in these complexes, especially on upper floors. Review *Safe Firefighting: First Things First*, Chapter 10, for additional information about extending attack lines.

Review *Safe Firefighting: First Things First*, Chapter 10, "*Large Attack Lines.*" Also review the Chapter 10 content on the DVD that accompanies that text.

Assessing the Fire Spread In multiunit complexes, attic areas often cover several family living units. You may be told to assist your team in checking the attic or overhead breezeway area for fire extension, or to go to an adjacent apartment to pull the ceiling to check for extension (Figure 20-41). You will need an attack line available for either of these situations.

If your crew is assigned to search a multifamily apartment or condominium that is involved in fire,

FIGURE 20-41 Attic and breezeway overhead areas in apartment buildings can extend over several apartments.

search the apartment with the fire first. Then continue your search by checking the apartments above, below, and on each side of the unit on fire. Remember to have an attack line available as you search.

Assisting with Large Fires If there is a larger fire involving several living units, fire extinguishment will involve many attack lines and crews. Big fires call for big water to extinguish them effectively. If large attack lines or deck guns are flowing, you should be outside the building.

Defensive Fire Attack

As we stated earlier, a defensive fire attack operation involves fighting the fire from outside the structure because the building is too dangerous to enter and there are no survivable areas of the building to search. A defensive fire attack is used when the fire has progressed beyond any hope of safely salvaging the building and the risks of entering and extinguishing a fire from inside are far too great.

During a defensive fire operation, large flows of water from exterior attack lines are used to wet down the exposures to the original building fire as well as to buildings, objects, and materials outside the building to which the fire can spread (Figure 20-42). In some cases, larger attack lines or deck guns may also be placed to protect exposures. In this way, the structural fire is first confined. In addition, large deck guns or elevated fire streams from aerial ladder trucks may be used to cool the area above the fire to reduce the chance of exposure fires from hot embers.

FIGURE 20-42   Flowing water onto an exposure.

FIGURE 20-43   Large flows of water during a defensive fire operation.

 Safety Tip!

Residential Building Power-Line Feeds   When a structure is mostly involved in fire and is supplied by electricity from an overhead domestic feed coming from a power pole, there is a real danger of the wire burning off the structure and falling to the ground. Never position under these power lines. If one has fallen, notify Command immediately so that the rest of the fire crews can be made aware of its location. These lines are not safe until they are disconnected by the power company. Use cones and fire-line tape to isolate any downed wires. If possible, a firefighter should be stationed nearby to safeguard the public and other firefighters until the line has been rendered harmless.

The next step in a defensive fire operation is to deploy large attack lines to the structural fire itself. Water is applied from the same direction through openings like windows and doorways to begin extinguishment from a distance.

When the fire has been knocked down or the fire has consumed enough fuel to reduce the intensity of the fire, fire attack teams will make a coordinated move closer to the fire building. However, if warranted, they may maintain positions outside the collapse zone.

Finally, large amounts of water will be flowed on the rubble of the building until the fire has been extinguished (Figure 20-43).

 Safety Tip!

Wear PPE in Hot and Warm Safety Zones   If you are working as a team member on any lines or other activities inside the hot and warm zones around the fire, it is important that you keep your PPE in place. Your SCBA needs to be on but not necessarily in use. Your Company Officer will advise you when to operate your SCBA. If you have any doubts, use it.

In addition, areas inside the burned-out building as well as the collapse zone around any remaining walls are very dangerous places. Keep clear of these areas at all times, both during and after the fire.

Class A Foam Operations— Compressed Air Foam Systems (CAFS)

Compressed Air Foam Systems (CAFS) are being used by many fire departments in the United States. These systems use pre-plumbed compressed air foam delivery systems that are in line with the pump on the fire apparatus. They allow the firefighting team to deliver Class A foam (for Class A fires) onto structural fires. These systems have had good success and you may be assigned to a unit that uses them. If so, you will be given specialized training on how it is applied and all the benefits and risks involved. Our purpose here is to let you know that this new technology exists (Figure 20-44).

FIGURE 20-44 Compressed Air Foam Systems allow firefighters to deliver Class A foam onto structural fires.

Residential Structural Firefighting

With this chapter, we have finally gotten you inside a burning structure to extinguish specific types of fires. We showed you some common residential building layouts that you will encounter. We gave you information about how to help your team investigate smoke odor and detector activations when there is no apparent fire. Then we went into detail about the methods and techniques of working as a team member in handling different offensive fire attack operations inside a residential structure. We also discussed a general defensive fire attack and introduced Compressed Air Foam Systems.

You will gain experience as you respond to these structures and work as a member of the firefighting team. You need to remember that going inside is a big and dangerous step. You must to be extra alert for your safety and the safety of your fellow team members. You depend on each other for survival. Never lose respect for the dangers of a building fire.

Knowledge Assessment

Signed Documentation Tear-Out Sheet

Residential Structure Fires—Chapter 20

Name: _____

Fill out the ten-question quiz below, the Knowledge Assessment Sheet, by circling the correct answer for each question. When finished, sign it and give it to your instructor/Company Officer for his or her signature. Turn in this Knowledge Assessment Sheet to the proper person as part of the documentation that you have completed your training for this chapter.

1. Some fire departments have a thermal imaging camera (TIC) that can check the interiors of walls, ceilings, and floors for any hot wiring.
   a. True
   b. False

2. Which of the following fire attack operations involves entering the structure to rescue any trapped or injured fire victims as well as aggressively confining and extinguishing the fire?
   a. Exterior fire attack
   b. Exposure fire attack
   c. Offensive fire attack
   d. Defensive fire attack

3. Prior to entering a structure to fight a fire, your Company Officer will coordinate with the driver and _____ to make sure that a water supply has been established and that ventilation and backup fire attack crews are in place for the entry to be made.
   a. other crew members
   b. Incident Command
   c. Police Department
   d. rescue crews

4. If you are the backup firefighter on the interior attack line, which of the following should you be carrying?
   a. Extra water
   b. A tool
   c. An extra nozzle
   d. A salvage tarp

5. What is the first thing you should do before maneuvering a hose line up a stairway?
   a. Gather slack in the line
   b. Flow water at the ceiling
   c. Check with Command
   d. Check the stairway for any fire damage

6. When water absorbs heat, changing from a liquid state into a gaseous state (steam), it expands to up to 1700 times its original volume.
   a. True
   b. False

7. _____ nozzles consist of a rotating ball with several discharge openings and a gate valve located on the end of an attack line.

   a. Fog
   b. Distributor
   c. Solid-bore
   d. Foam

8. When an emergency evacuation signal has been sounded during an interior firefighting operation, you should first gather all of your equipment and hose lines and slowly retreat from the building, making sure you bring out everything.

   a. True
   b. False

9. When do firefighters conduct a much more thorough search of a building for possible trapped or injured fire victims?

   a. During the secondary search
   b. During the initial search
   c. Before attack lines are brought inside
   d. While a sustained water supply is being established

10. In basement fires, _____ is difficult and limited due to small window openings.

   a. laddering
   b. Incident Command
   c. ventilation
   d. assessment

Student Signature and Date _____   Instructor/Company Officer Signature and Date _____

516

Prove It

Skills Assessment

Signed Documentation Tear-Out Sheet

Residential Structure Fires—Chapter 20

Name: _____

Fill out the Skills Assessment Sheet below. Have your instructor/Company Officer check off and initial each skill you demonstrate. When you are finished, sign this page and give it to your instructor/Company Officer for his or her signature. Turn in this Skills Assessment Sheet to the proper person as part of the documentation that you have completed your training for this chapter.

Level 1

Skill	Completed	Initials
1. Describe some common building layouts of residential structures.	_____	_____
2. Participate as a team member when investigating a residential building for a smoke odor, a gas odor, and an activated smoke or carbon monoxide detector.	_____	_____
3. As a team member, assist in stretching a charged attack line into the interior of a residential building.	_____	_____
4. As a team member, assist in stretching a charged attack line up or down an interior or exterior stairway.	_____	_____
5. Describe pre- and post-flashover fire conditions.	_____	_____
6. Describe how to open walls, ceilings, and floors for further fire extinguishment and overhaul.	_____	_____
7. Describe initial and secondary search operations during a residential structure fire.	_____	_____
8. Explain the different considerations when fighting fires in multiple rooms, attics, basements, and garages in residential buildings.	_____	_____
9. Describe the possible laddering, fire spread, and potential for a large fire in apartments and row houses.	_____	_____
10. Describe a defensive fire attack.	_____	_____

Student Signature and Date _____   Instructor/Company Officer Signature and Date _____

Large Buildings

What You Will Learn in This Chapter

In this chapter we will discuss how to work as a firefighting team member during fire operations inside large buildings with open floor plans. First, we'll introduce you to general attributes of these buildings. Then we will explain how your team will respond to automatic fire alarms and work with fire detection and protection systems inside these buildings. This information is followed by offensive fire attack operations from the viewpoint of a team member. Finally, we'll talk about defensive fire attack operations on large buildings. As with all of our chapters, we will stress safety throughout the text.

What You Will Be Able to Do

After reading this chapter and practicing the skills described, you will be able to:

1. Explain the typical building features in large structures with open floor plans.
2. Describe the procedure for shutting off electrical, gas, and water utilities for large buildings.
3. Describe the arrangement and components of a typical heating, ventilation, and air-conditioning (HVAC) system for a large building.
4. List the 4 main types of automatic fire sprinkler systems.

5. Demonstrate hooking into a Fire Department connection on a sprinkler system.
6. Demonstrate shutting off the flow of a fire sprinkler head using a wooden wedge or a sprinkler tool.
7. Describe how to operate an outside screw and yoke (OS&Y) valve and a post indicator valve (PIV).
8. Demonstrate hooking an attack line into a standpipe system.
9. Describe what is meant by an offensive fire attack of a large building.
10. As a member of a team, demonstrate the alley lay for supply lines.
11. List the tools a member of the fire attack team should consider taking inside a large building.
12. Describe the advantages of using a thermal imaging camera (TIC) inside a large-building fire.
13. Describe how a combination fire attack works at a large-building fire.
14. Explain how a rehab area works.
15. Describe typical defensive, exterior fire attack considerations of a large-building fire.
16. Describe the collapse and safety zones of a large-building fire.
17. Explain the precautions to observe when working around large attack lines, ground monitors, deck guns, and elevated water streams during a large-building fire.

Safety Lesson: A NIOSH Report

Hazards of Large-Building Fires

On March 14, 2001, a 40-year-old male career firefighter/Paramedic died from carbon monoxide poisoning and thermal burns after running out of air and becoming disoriented while fighting a supermarket fire. Four other firefighters were injured, one critically, while fighting the fire or performing search and rescue for the victim. The fire started near a dumpster on the exterior of the structure. It extended through openings in the loading dock area into the storage area and then into the main shopping area of the supermarket. The fire progressed to five alarms and involved more than 100 personnel. Firefighters removed the victim from the structure and transported him to a local hospital, where he was pronounced dead.

Follow-Up

NIOSH Report #F2001-13

NIOSH investigators concluded that, to minimize the risk of similar occurrences, fire departments should:

- Ensure that the department's standard operating procedures (SOPs) are followed and continuous refresher training is provided.
- Ensure that a proper size-up, using common terminology, is conducted by all firefighters responsible for reporting interior/exterior conditions to the Incident Commander (IC).
- Ensure that preincident plans are established and updated on mercantile occupancies in their district.
- Ensure that firefighters manage their air supplies as warranted by the size of the structure involved.
- Instruct firefighters about and train them on initiating emergency traffic (Mayday), and also instruct them about the importance of activating their personal alert safety system (PASS) device when they become lost, disoriented, or trapped.
- Ensure that multiple Rapid Intervention Crews (RICs) are in place when an interior attack is being performed in a large structure with multiple points of entry.
- Consider placing firefighter identification emblems on the firefighters' helmets and turnout gear.
- Consider placing a bright, narrow-beamed light at all entry portals of a structure to assist lost or disoriented firefighters with emergency egress.

Additionally,

- Building owners should consider upgrading or modifying structures to incorporate new codes and standards to improve occupancy and firefighter safety.
- As a part of their preincident planning, fire departments should consider educating the public they serve about the importance of building owners, building personnel, or civilians immediately reporting any fire conditions to the first-arriving fire company on the scene.
- Manufacturers and research organizations should conduct research into refining existing and developing new technology to track the movement of firefighters inside structures.

Large-Building Fires

A category of building fire that you will commonly respond to in your career is the large-building fire. By "large building," we mean buildings that are within reach of ground ladders in height, but have large and relatively open floor plans. These include, but are not limited to, stores, factories, shopping malls, open-plan

FIGURE 21-1 Large buildings can have very large fires inside.

office spaces, public assembly buildings, vehicle maintenance buildings, and warehouses. In rural areas, these buildings also include large barns and stables.

The firefighting methods you use inside large buildings differ from residential buildings in the way you approach the interior fire, the number and size of the fire attack lines needed to extinguish the fire, and the complexity of working with many other firefighting teams.

Fires in these buildings can become well involved and large before you arrive (Figure 21-1). They often necessitate working with built-in fire protection systems to support the fire department's firefighting operation.

The vast majority of fire calls to large buildings are minor; however, there will be the "big one" that will challenge your team, requiring you to be even more conscious of the need to be safe, to work under the direction of an Incident Command System, and to work with a backup (Figure 21-2). Inside a large building you can easily become lost and outdistance your access to a safe area and fresh air. A large fire in a large building can also quickly overcome the initial fire attack lines deployed against them. Always have an escape plan for yourself when working inside.

This chapter will change the way you view large buildings and hopefully will increase your respect for the potential dangers they can present when they are involved in fire.

What's Inside

The interior layout of any large building largely depends on the way in which the building is being used. For example, a department store has a very different

FIGURE 21-2 At a large fire it is even more critical for firefighting teams to work under direction of an Incident Command System.

FIGURE 21-3 Lock boxes have access keys inside for the Company Officer to unlock the doors to a business.

layout than a warehouse. So we will go over the common characteristics first.

Entrances and Exits

Large buildings have one or more main entrances. These can be from the outside or the inside of a common mall area. In many fire department jurisdictions, access boxes called **key boxes** contain door keys (Figure 21-3).

These boxes have an access key available only to the Company Officer and the building management.

Large buildings also have emergency exit doors located at intervals as required by building code. These exit doors may be equipped with **panic hardware,** which allows occupants to open doors easily for a quick exit, yet the doors remain locked from the outside (Figure 21-4). In some places, these exit doors are monitored by an alarm system that sounds if the door is opened from the inside. Unfortunately, another feature all too often found on emergency exit doors are security bars that may or may not be locked in place. These are supposed to be unlocked and removed while the building is occupied, but this is not always the case. They present a challenge if you are assigned forcible entry of emergency exit doors from the outside.

Overhead doors are also common to large buildings. In stores and warehouses, they are necessary for the delivery of large amounts of stock at the rear or side of the structure. These doors can also be located inside a large structure, providing access between large spaces. We discussed how to force entry of this type of doors in Chapter 15, "Forcible Entry and Exit."

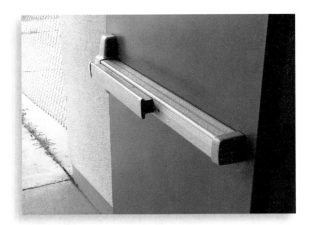

FIGURE 21-4 Panic hardware allows easy exit for occupants but remains locked from the outside.

▨ KEY WORDS ▨

key box A security device located on the outside of a building that provides an access key for Fire Service responders after normal operating hours. The box is normally connected to an alarm system and is opened by a special key given to the Fire Department. This box allows the Fire Department to access the building quickly if an alarm is received for a fire inside the structure.

panic hardware Special door handle hardware designed to allow rapid and simple opening of a designated exit door from the inside while still providing security from the exterior of the building. Many times doors equipped with panic hardware will be connected to an alarm that sounds when the door is opened from inside the building.

Windows

Window openings in large buildings are designed according to the use of the building and the needs of the occupant. Side and rear windows, which are not provided as a design enhancement, are probably much the same as any residential windows, with plate glass set in awning, sash, or similar frames.

Front windows or windows intended as a design element are usually set in a tightly closed frame and are made of tempered glass (Figure 21-5). Sharply breaking tempered glass in a corner of the window will probably shatter the glass into tiny pieces. Because windows in large buildings are usually larger than

FIGURE 21-5 Store front windows are commonly made of tempered glass.

residential windows, you need to be careful if you are assigned to vent or force entry through them.

Roof Access

Many large buildings have scuttles and ladders attached to them to provide interior or exterior access to roof areas (Figure 21-6). Interior roof access ladders go up to and through the roof. They are secured from the outside at roof level by a locked scuttle opening. Some scuttle openings are locked by an electromagnet device that releases when the fire alarm sounds, providing roof access and access to the interior from the roof in case of fire alarm activation. You may need the key or may have to cut the lock on scuttles secured by locks.

Open Areas

When you imagine the floor layout in any large building, remember that there are office areas and restrooms. Workshops and utility rooms may also be

FIGURE 21-6 An exterior roof access ladder.

FIGURE 21-7 A pre-hung ceiling.

present. These smaller rooms can be located inside the larger open area and at times can occupy more than one floor. They can also have their own dropped ceiling inside each space.

The main open area may include aisles of products, office cubicles, storage racks, or machinery, depending on the use of the building. In Chapter 22 of this book, we cover the preplanning operations that you will be involved in as part of your work in the Fire Department. Preplanning operations will help you gather information, and you will be allowed access to many areas of the building to get familiar with its layout.

You need to also develop the habit of looking at these buildings when you visit them, even when you are off duty. Take note of the floor layout, what is it used for, if it has a fire protection system, and where the exits are located. We don't mean for you to do a fire inspection, but you can make a few mental notes for when you might need to respond to a fire inside the building.

Ceiling Spaces

Looking up, you will see a large, open area that may have a suspended ceiling, like that used in an open office area, or the underside of the roof may be exposed with no ceiling, as in a warehouse building (Figure 21-7). The ceiling areas can have extensive permanent wiring chases, communications wiring, HVAC ductwork and air handling units, and even machinery (in factories).

Because large buildings cover such a large area, they can be equipped with **smoke curtains** and **automatic ventilation openings.** Smoke curtains are sections of noncombustible sheeting hung from the bottom of the roof. They are designed to slow the spread of smoke and heat from a fire below (Figure 21-8). Automatic ventilation openings are designed to automatically create openings in the roof of a large building so that heat and smoke can escape the building and slow a fire's spread. These openings can be as simple as plastic skylights designed to melt and fall out during a fire or fusible, link-controlled hatches that fall open when heated from a fire below.

KEY WORDS

automatic ventilation openings Building design features intended to automatically open the roof of a large building so that heat and smoke can escape the building and slow a fire's spread. Automatic ventilation openings can be as simple as plastic skylights designed to melt and fall out during a fire or fusible, link-controlled hatches that fall open when heated from a fire below.

smoke curtains Noncombustible panels installed in the exposed roof areas of large buildings with open areas. They are designed to slow the spread of heat and smoke from a fire below.

Smoke curtains

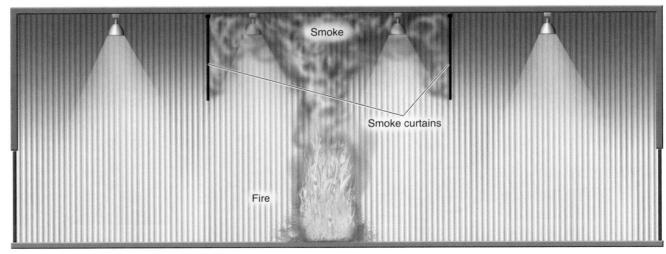

Large building (Side view)

FIGURE 21-8 Smoke curtains are sections of noncombustible sheeting hung from the bottom of the roof.

 Safety Tip!

Whenever working inside a large, open-area building during a fire, look above your head. You should check for the various features and equipment that can be located above you. Be aware of the collapse hazards of stacked materials inside any large building. These materials can be stock on sales floor display racks or storage on racks inside a warehouse (Figure 21-9). They can become prone to collapse after being involved in fire or when wet down during extinguishment operations.

Fire Walls

Large complexes of structures that are adjacent to each other and share a common wall are often required by building codes to be separated by special walls. These walls are referred to as **fire walls** and are designed to resist fire for up to 4 hours. A single large building that has been divided into more than one occupancy may also have a fire wall installed between each occupant, as required by fire and building codes.

Fire walls may be required to extend up to and out of the roof areas, creating a parapet between exterior roof spaces. Though designed to provide a 4-hour separation, these walls are too often breached with improper openings that compromise their ability to stop fire spread. Workers who need to run services in the attic areas or between occupancies often make access holes in the wall. Doorways may

FIGURE 21-9 Look for the various features and equipment that can be located above you. Be aware of the collapse hazards of stacked materials inside any large building.

be added as occupant needs change. In warehouses and factories, walls can become damaged by vehicles and machinery.

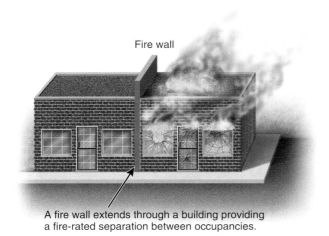

Fire wall

A fire wall extends through a building providing a fire-rated separation between occupancies.

FIGURE 21-10 Fire walls are designed to resist fire for up to 4 hours.

Because of all these factors, during a fire, you should note that fire walls are present, but you should never completely trust them to stop the spread of a fire. However, properly installed and maintained, fire walls work very well (Figure 21-10).

▨ KEY WORD ▨

fire wall A specially designed and built wall that separates spaces in a building. These walls are usually designed to provide a maximum 4-hour fire separation and can extend through and above the roof of the building. Their intent is to slow the spread of a fire from one building space to another until the site can be controlled and extinguished.

Utilities for Large Buildings

Just like any building occupied by people, large buildings need utility services like electricity, gas, and water. The main differences between the utilities used in large buildings and those used in other structures are the size and typical locations of the services, as well as the disconnect procedures.

Electricity

Because large buildings have a much bigger electrical supply requirement than smaller structures, they may have an electrical room. This room can be a small, closet-like room with a sign on the door indicating "Electrical Main Disconnect Inside." Main disconnect switches will be found inside the electrical room,

FIGURE 21-11 The main disconnect for the electrical system might not be located next to the circuit breaker switch boxes. If you switch off the electrical switches at the panel boxes, you may need to also switch off the main switch.

near the electrical panel boxes located inside a rear or side wall, or at a breakaway electrical shunt located on an outside wall of the building. In large buildings, the main disconnect for the electrical system may not be located next to the circuit breaker switch boxes. This means that if you switch off the electrical switches at the panel boxes, the main disconnect for the building may still be energized (Figure 21-11). Also, keep in mind that many large buildings have backup generator systems that automatically activate when the power is disconnected. These will need to be located and shut down for total power disconnect in a large building. At times, the local power company will be required to respond to a large-building fire to safely disconnect the electrical service.

 Safety Tip!

Never attempt to disconnect service to a large building unless it is equipped with an emergency shutoff switch or shunt. Do not touch electrical meters on a commercial building. The electrical service to a large building is much more powerful than that of a single family residence. If available, consider applying a lockout/tagout device to the electrical main switch once it has been shut off.

Gas

As with the electrical service to a large building, the gas service is larger in volume due to the needs of the occupant. The shutoff valves are located outside,

FIGURE 21-12 Gas service is larger in volume due to the needs of the occupant. The shutoff valves are located outside, on larger service feed piping.

FIGURE 21-13 An outside screw and yoke (OS&Y) valve.

FIGURE 21-14 An HVAC unit located on the roof of a large building.

on larger service feed piping. Remember to turn the valve so that it is perpendicular with the flow of gas through the pipe (Figure 21-12).

In large buildings that are using gas to operate machinery or cooking facilities, remember that shutting down the gas also shuts down the pilot lights on gas-operated equipment. Do not turn the gas back to the "on" position. This should be done by a certified technician from the gas company. If available, apply a lockout/tagout device to the gas valve once it has been shut off.

Water

Water service control valves to control the water supply to large buildings are usually located in underground vaults. These valves will require a special key tool to operate or there will be outside screw and yoke (OS&Y) type valves for opening and shutting down the water flow (Figure 21-13). In warmer climates, these valves may be located aboveground.

HVAC

Heating, ventilation, and air conditioning (HVAC) for large buildings presents significant challenges to firefighters working inside. HVAC systems can be used by the Fire Department to assist in the overall ventilation of a large building, particularly if there is smoke and no active fire.

Because of the volume of a large building space, there may be several large air-handling units that can be located inside the building, between the ceiling and the underside of the roof, on the roof itself, on the ground outside the building, or in special rooms inside the building (Figure 21-14). Most of these units

have a shutdown switch located nearby. You need to be sure that power is shut down to these units if you are opening up a side access panel to check for shorted wiring or a fan motor malfunction.

Because of their weight, you need to understand that these units can potentially fall through roof and ceiling areas damaged by fire or weakened by the water used to extinguish a fire.

Automatic Fire Suppression Systems

During the course of your responses to fires in large structures, you will find many buildings equipped with automatic fire alarm and **fire sprinkler systems.** Together these form the automatic fire suppression system of a building or property. You may be required to simply assist in checking a building for a fire after a detection device has activated the fire alarm system. Alternately, you may be required to help attach supply lines to a sprinkler system to augment the water flow to a fire inside a building.

It is important for you to have some understanding about what the different system components are and, if needed, how to use them. Remember: Any building or complex may have all or part of these systems located within, depending on the needs of the occupant and the fire code standard requirements.

▨▨ KEY WORD ▨▨

fire sprinkler system   A fire suppression system built into a building that consists of a water supply, valves, gauges, and water sprinkler heads with fusible links or other automatically operating devices. The sprinkler heads are heat activated and fall away from the head, allowing the flow of water onto the fire below.

Fire Detection and Alarm Systems

Fire detection and alarm systems may be as simple as a smoke or heat detector that sounds an alarm if fire or heat is detected. They may be complex detection systems that notify the occupants, as well as a fire alarm monitoring service, of any smoke or fire that is detected. They can also be designed to notify an alarm monitoring company that in turn notifies the fire department and building representatives of a fire in the building. In addition, fire detection and alarm systems can be used to activate fire suppression systems located in the building.

When a detector is activated, it sends a signal to a fire alarm control panel box located inside the building (Figure 21-15). This in turn sends a signal

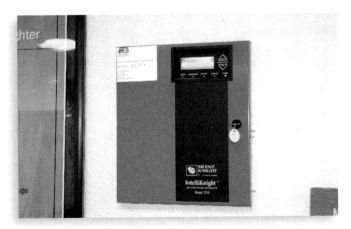

FIGURE 21-15   A typical fire alarm control panel box.

FIGURE 21-16   Some alarm systems have fire alarm notification lights as well as an audible alarm.

to the fire alarm monitoring company or the fire department to alert them of the fire alarm signal. This signal can be turned on and off or silenced from the fire alarm control panel. When the alarm is sounding and it has been determined that there has been a false alarm or an alarm malfunction, the system may need to be reset or turned off. It is best to have the building occupant reset or shut down the fire alarm control system. Your fire department has a standard operating practice to follow when handling building fire alarms (Figure 21-16).

The operating power of smoke and heat detectors used as part of a larger automatic fire suppression system is hardwired into the wiring system of the building, with a battery backup. Most smoke detectors designed for home use are battery powered. You may occasionally find home smoke detectors that are permanently wired into the electrical system of the home, with a battery backup.

Automatic Fire Sprinkler Systems

More than a hundred years ago, a system for providing built-in fire protection was developed: the automatic fire sprinkler system. This system is the single most effective and reliable fire protection system for buildings ever invented (Figure 21-17). It is the second part of a building's fire suppression system (the first being the fire detection and alarm system). Automatic fire sprinkler systems are found in almost every type of building. They can be located outside, under floors, in attic areas—wherever they are needed. Increasingly, fire sprinkler systems are being designed for use in residential single-family dwellings, providing

FIGURE 21-17 Automatic fire sprinkler system riser and controls.

excellent built-in fire protection. The extent and use of these systems are dependent on the building fire protection requirements of the community and the wishes of the building owner.

Components of Automatic Fire Sprinkler Systems

Automatic fire sprinkler systems are made up of some or all of the following parts:

- *Water Supply.* A water main pipe feed directly supplies the fire sprinkler system. It usually is a substantial water pipe supplied by a municipal or a private water system. The diameter of the pipe depends on the supply requirements of the sprinkler system.
- *Main Control Valve.* A main valve is located on the water supply main piping that is used to shut off the water supply to the sprinkler system.
- *Outside Screw and Yoke (OS&Y) Valve.* This device is a type of main control valve used in water systems. It consists of an inline valve operating as a fixed round handle. When it is turned, it pulls a screw through the handle. This action raises and lowers a gate to open and shut the flow of water. When the stem is not visible above the handwheel, the valve is shut (Figure 21-18).
- *Post Indicator Valve (PIV).* A type of water main control valve. It has a small window that features

FIGURE 21-18 Sprinkler system main control valve (in this case, an OS&Y valve).

the words *Open* and *Shut* to indicate that water flow to the system has been turned on or off (Figure 21-19).

- *Riser.* The main water supply to the branch lines of a fire sprinkler system, this device contains all the main valves and controls (Figure 21-20).
- *Check Valve.* A flapper-type valve located in the riser part of a fire sprinkler system. The check valve ensures that the water pressure above it is normally higher than the water pressure below it. When a sprinkler head activates and water pressure lowers above the check valve, water supplies the sprinkler system as it flows (Figure 21-21).
- *Water Gong.* A type of water flow alarm that is usually located on an exterior wall near the sprinkler system riser (Figure 21-22). It is operated mechanically by the flow of water in the operating sprinkler system.
- *Electrical Water Flow Detectors.* These electronic devices detect any movement of water in a fire sprinkler system (Figure 21-23). They activate a fire alarm system for the building,

FIGURE 21-19 Sprinkler system main control valve (in this case, a PIV valve).

FIGURE 21-20 A sprinkler system riser.

FIGURE 21-21 A check valve.

FIGURE 21-22 A water gong.

FIGURE 21-23 An electrical water flow detector.

notifying the occupants and fire department of a possible fire sprinkler operation and fire inside the building.

- *Water Pressure Gauges.* Two gauges located above and below the check valve on a fire sprinkler system riser that indicate the water pressure on each side of the check valve (Figure 21-24).
- *Fire Department Connections (FDC).* These connections serve as access points for augmenting the fire sprinkler system's water supply. They are female couplings with a cover that is easily broken off when tapped with a spanner or a hydrant

FIGURE 21-24 Water pressure gauges on a sprinkler system.

FIGURE 21-25 A Fire Department connection (FDC).

wrench (Figure 21-25). These connections are located on an exterior wall of the building or in an accessible area near the building.

- *Sprinkler Heads.* These water distribution devices are located along pipes that extend from the fire sprinkler system riser. Sprinkler heads are made of several types and configurations, depending on the protection they are designed to provide (Figure 21-26). These devices feature small openings through which water in the sprinkler system flows when the sprinkler is activated. They will have a fusible link or another activating device.

FIGURE 21-26 A sprinkler head.

When the fusible link or other activating device is heated, they fall away, releasing the flow of water through the sprinkler head. Each sprinkler head usually flows between 4 and 7 gallons of water per minute.

Types of Automatic Fire Sprinkler Systems

There are many types and configurations of automatic fire sprinkler systems. We'll describe a few of the main types that you may find in your fire department's area.

- Wet-pipe sprinkler system—This fire sprinkler system has water in all the pipes all of the time.
- Dry-pipe sprinkler system—This system has air or an inert gas in the pipes above the check valve. This type of system is mainly found anywhere that the sprinkler heads are likely to freeze.
- Deluge sprinkler system—The sprinkler heads in this type of system have no fusible links. When the system is activated, all the heads flow water at the same time. The heads are located wherever there is a potential for a sudden fire with high heat.
- Pre-action sprinkler system—This system allows for a time delay before the sprinkler head is activated with a water flow.

Fire Sprinkler System Operation

Because wet-pipe fire sprinkler systems are the most common type, we'll describe their operation. When a fire occurs in a building protected by an automatic fire sprinkler system, heat rises from the fire to the area where the sprinkler heads are located (Figure 21-27). When the fusible link device in the

Sprinkler head not flowing

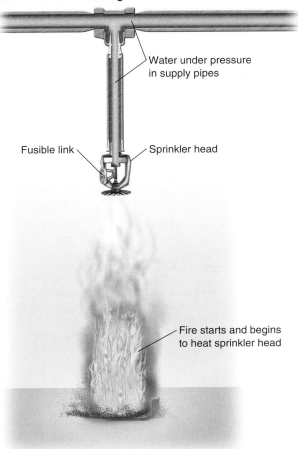

Water under pressure in supply pipes

Fusible link

Sprinkler head

Fire starts and begins to heat sprinkler head

FIGURE 21-27 When a fire occurs in a building protected by an automatic fire sprinkler system, heat rises from the fire to the area where the sprinkler heads are located.

Sprinkler head flowing

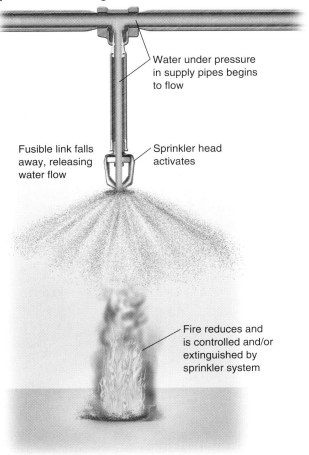

Water under pressure in supply pipes begins to flow

Fusible link falls away, releasing water flow

Sprinkler head activates

Fire reduces and is controlled and/or extinguished by sprinkler system

FIGURE 21-28 When the fusible link device in the sprinkler head reaches its designed activation temperature, the fusible link falls apart or breaks and the sprinkler head starts to flow water under pressure down onto the fire.

sprinkler head reaches its designed activation temperature, the fusible link falls apart or breaks and the sprinkler head starts to flow water under pressure down onto the fire (Figure 21-28). The sprinkler head is designed to distribute the water spray over and onto the fire below.

When a sprinkler head is activated, several things take place at the riser. The water pressure above the check valve drops as water flows through the piping and out of the sprinkler head. This activates a water motion detector in the riser, which in turn activates the automatic fire suppression system and the notification process. Simultaneously, water that is under pressure starts flowing into the sprinkler pipe. This pipe supplies the flow of water through the open sprinkler head (Figure 21-29). Addition-

ally, the local water gong alarm near the riser begins to ring, indicating that the system is activated with water flowing.

When activated, automatic fire suppression systems flow water until one of two things happen: (1) the fire is controlled and the system is shut down by the fire department or occupant at the main control valve (remember—this could be an OS&Y valve or PIV), or (2) the fire extends beyond the first sprinkler head and additional heads begin to open and flow water as the heat builds.

Statistically, buildings with automatic fire sprinkler systems control fire with one or two activated sprinkler heads. This is a long proven fact, so you can see the benefit of automatic fire sprinkler systems for the fire protection of a building.

Water flow to sprinkler head

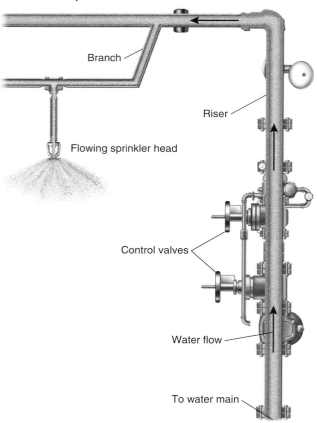

FIGURE 21-29 Water that is under pressure starts flowing into the sprinkler pipe. This pipe supplies the flow of water through the open sprinkler head.

Augmenting the Water Supply

When you arrive at a building with a flowing fire sprinkler system, you may be assigned to augment the system's water supply by hooking into it with one

FIGURE 21-30 We must provide an additional water supply and additional water pressure to the system to keep it at maximum effectiveness.

or two supply hose lines, usually 2½ to 3 inches in diameter, at the Fire Department connection (FDC). In order to establish a sustained water supply, you also need to connect a supply hose line to the engine attached to the sprinkler system FDC (Figure 21-30). Most sprinkler systems are designed to provide water to many but not all of the sprinkler heads in the system. For that reason, we must provide an additional water supply and additional water pressure to the system to keep it at maximum effectiveness.

Practice It!

Hooking Into an FDC Connection

In order to safely assist in hooking supply lines into a Fire Department connection (FDC), perform the following steps:

1. The driver of the apparatus positions within reach of two supply sections of fire hose at the FDC. A sustained supply of water to the apparatus needs to be established. Safely dismount and assist the driver in establishing this sustained water supply.

2. Next, get a tool to access the breakaway caps on the FDC. These caps are female connections. Tap one connection tab on the breakaway cap to snap it off (Figure 21-31). Check for any obstructions inside the FDC.

FIGURE 21-31

3. Locate and attach the male end of each supply line from the apparatus into the FDC (Figure 21-32).

4. Check with the driver to make sure that the lines are connected to the discharge ports on the apparatus. Then signal the driver to charge the lines. The driver will charge the supply lines to the required pressures.

FIGURE 21-32

Tip!

Residential Automatic Fire Sprinkler Systems

A quick note here about residential fire sprinkler systems. These systems are made of lighter-weight materials with controls located in small box panels inside or outside the residence. The FDC may be as small as a 1½-inch female coupling. However, the control of water flowing in these sprinkler heads and system is similar to that of commercial systems.

Stopping the Flow of Water in Sprinkler Heads

After a sprinkler head has been activated, there is nothing at the sprinkler head itself to shut off the flow of water. When directed to stop the flow of a sprinkler head by a Company Officer, firefighters use two small pieces of wood called sprinkler wedges. These wedges are placed between the water flow opening in the sprinkler and the deflector plate. Firefighters can also use a specialized sprinkler tool that also fits between the opening and the deflector plate. In both cases, insert the wedge or tool to hand-tightness only. Never pound these wedges or tools into place as the force may break the sprinkler head.

 Practice It!

Stopping a Sprinkler Head Flow

To stop the flow of water from a single fire sprinkler head, perform the following steps:

Using sprinkler wedges:

1. Keep your PPE in place and be sure you have two wedges available. Position yourself on an adequate ladder under the flowing sprinkler head.

2. Place both wedges between the water flow opening and the inside of the deflector plate (Figure 21-33).

3. Push the wedges until the flow stops and then carefully dismount the ladder.

Using a sprinkler tool:

1. Keep your PPE on and be sure you have the sprinkler tool with you. Position yourself properly on an adequate ladder under the flowing sprinkler head.

FIGURE 21-33

2. Operate the tool and place it inside the sprinkler head, between the water flow opening and the deflector plate, and release the tool (Figure 21-34). The flow of water should stop.

3. Carefully dismount the ladder.

FIGURE 21-34

Stopping the Flow of Water in a Fire Sprinkler System

If you are assigned to stop the flow of water to an entire sprinkler system, you will need to locate first the riser and then the main control valve. Remember—these larger valves will be either OS&Y valves or PIVs. They are usually secured in place by a breakaway lock and chain or other device. Once you have removed any security device, operate the valve. Be sure to operate the OS&Y valve until the screw disappears into the operating handle and it stops turning (Figure 21-35). Operate the PIV until the *Shut* indicator is fully visible and the handle stops. It is important to remain in radio contact with Command in case the water must be turned on again in a hurry.

Standpipe Systems

Some buildings may be required to provide firefighting hose, nozzles, and water to different interior areas. This combination of items is referred to as a standpipe system and it is made up of a nozzle and hose attached to a control valve and water supply pipe. These systems are usually located in cabinets or on hangars in the business and, in case of fire, may or may not be designed for use by the occupants (Figure 21-36). They are supplied by the fire department through

FIGURE 21-35 Once you have removed any security device, operate the valve. Be sure to operate the OS&Y valve until the screw disappears into the operating handle and it stops turning.

FIGURE 21-36 A standpipe hose station.

FIGURE 21-37 A high-rise pack.

FDC outside the building. The individual hose stations are located according to fire code requirements or the needs of the building occupant. In large, open areas, signs high above the standpipe hose stations indicate their location. In multistory buildings, they are commonly located in stairwells for easy access by firefighters.

Using Standpipe Systems

If you are assigned to use a hose line from a standpipe hose station, it is always best to use Fire Department hose and nozzle. You can do this by carrying a high-rise pack into the building (Figure 21-37). Depending on the department's needs, there are many configurations of high-rise packs. One type of pack consists of a 6-foot piece of 2½- to 3-inch hose with a gated wye

attached and one 100- to 150-foot small attack hose line with a nozzle attached. More than one nozzle and some other tools may be inside the pack. In addition, a 2½- to 1½-inch reducer is provided. All of this equipment is either carried in a specially designed pack or held together with straps.

If your department does not have high-rise packs, all of the parts can be assembled, loaded onto your shoulder, and then carried into the structure to the standpipe location. To do this, pull the preconnect attack line load, keeping the stack of hose on your shoulder as you pull away from the hose bed. Disconnect the line at the desired length, while it is still on the firefighter's shoulder in a stack. Gather the rest of the components, including a reducer and two spanner wrenches. The team is now ready to enter the building and hook into the standpipe system.

 View It!

Go to the DVD, navigate to Chapter 21, and select "Using a Standpipe Connection."

Practice It!

Hooking Into a Standpipe Connection

In order to safely assist in hooking attack lines into a standpipe connection, perform the following steps:

1. Carry the high-rise pack or hose load over your shoulder and go to the desired hose station. Lay it down and disconnect the occupant-provided hose line from the control valve.

2. Attach your short section of larger hose to the control valve, extend your hose, and open the

control valve. If you are using only a reducer with a hose load, attach the reducer to the standpipe and attach the hose load to the reducer (Figure 21-38).

FIGURE 21-38

3. Open the valve on the hose station valve to charge the attack line (Figure 21-39).

4. Before advancing toward the fire, be sure to bleed excess air from your line at the nozzle. For safety, wait for a second firefighter to assist you before you start to advance the line.

FIGURE 21-39

Other Building Fire Safety Systems

Some buildings have automatic smoke doors or stairway pressurization systems. The activation of the fire alarm causes automatic smoke doors to close and air to pressurize the stairways to help prevent the spread of heat and smoke into them. These devices are designed to protect occupants by isolating the spread of heat and smoke (automatic smoke doors) and to allow for a safe evacuation route down stairways (pressurized stairway systems).

Automatic smoke doors may be fitted with electromagnetic holders that keep the doors open under normal conditions (Figure 21-40). When a fire alarm sounds in the building, the electromagnetic holders are designed to turn off, releasing the doors to close.

Be aware that these doors can close behind firefighters as they work inside the building. Place a wedge under the door to keep it open if their closing will present a hazard to you.

In large storage facilities and industrial plants, there may also be automatic fire doors that close off big doorway openings between large floor areas or more hazardous areas (Figure 21-41). These are operated when a fusible link, holding a counterweight—which in turn holds the door open—is activated by heat and releases the counterweight. The fire door slides shut. These doors can be found in a rollup configuration from above the opening or a ramp configuration from the side of the opening. These fire doors can also pose a threat to firefighters working hose lines or conducting search and rescue functions inside a large building. They can isolate firefighters in unsafe areas of a building during a fire emergency.

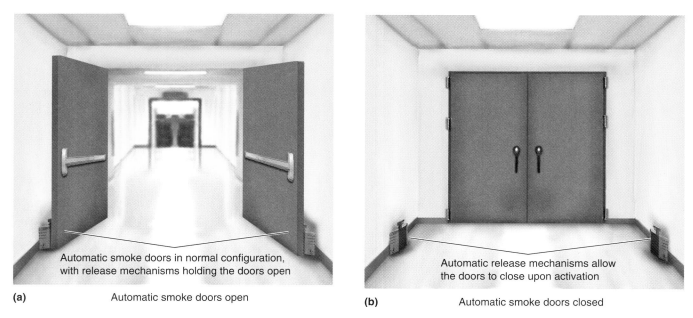

(a) Automatic smoke doors open

(b) Automatic smoke doors closed

FIGURE 21-40 (a) Automatic smoke doors may be fitted with electromagnetic holders when a fire alarm sounds. (b) These holders are designed to turn off, releasing the doors so they will close.

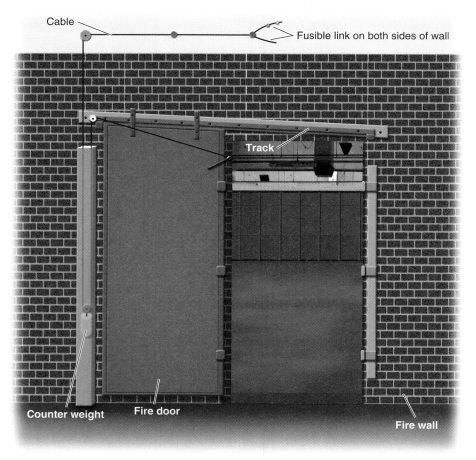

Sliding fire door

FIGURE 21-41 Automatic fire doors are operated when a fusible link, holding a counterweight, which in turn holds the door open, is activated by heat and releases the counterweight.

Smoke Investigations

Large buildings present special challenges for firefighters called to a smoke investigation. Their large size makes it very difficult to pinpoint the cause of any smoke inside. Possible sources to check are a defective HVAC system, a failure in some process or activity taking place inside, or an incipient fire.

If available, a thermal imaging camera works well for finding hidden fires and heat sources when checking a smoke-filled building. In addition, your Company Officer will work with a building representative to locate possible sources of the smoke.

Offensive Fire Attack in Large Buildings

An offensive fire attack on a large building is a big undertaking. Because the ceilings are often so high, and the buildings are so long and wide, you can easily go too far inside without the usual warning signs of imminent danger like a flashover. It takes much longer for a stack effect of heat buildup to reach the lower levels where firefighters are working, and a flashover can occur without warning. For this reason, early and adequate ventilation, as well as a coordinated fire attack effort closely supervised by the Incident Commander, are important.

Branches

In a large fire, offensive attack operations probably require a control operation involving several fire attack teams. Each team will work under the supervision of a Branch Officer. The Incident Commander will assign the command team members who are in charge of each branch. The most commonly used branches are named after the side of the building that the Branch Officer is supervising. It is important that you are familiar with the fireground IMS designation system used by your fire department.

The front of the building is side "A." Continuing clockwise around the building are sides "B," "C," and "D" (Figure 21-42). In some areas, these sectors are referred to as Alpha, Beta, Charlie, and Delta to help reduce confusion. These designations not only are important for your own reference if you are communicating your location inside the building, but they also are important when the Incident Commander gives directions during firefighting operations.

Example of side designations for a building fire

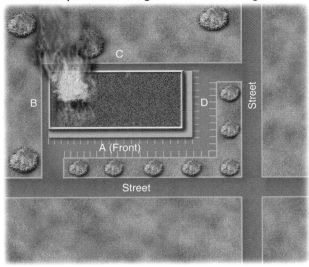

FIGURE 21-42 Sectors on a large-building fire.

Establishing a Water Supply

As you might expect, fires in large, open buildings have the potential to easily outgrow the onboard water supply of your engine. The common saying in the Fire Service is, "Big fire, big water." This means that if there is a sizeable fire in one of these structures, then a major effort must be made to quickly establish one or more sustained water supply operations. Your first job on the first-arriving engine may be to lay out your own supply line from a fire hydrant and then help your Company Officer assess the scene while waiting for more firefighting teams to arrive.

Because these structures are so large, they are commonly located in large complexes. The distances from the water supply to the engine at the interior access point and then from the interior access point to the fire inside are greater than those for a single-family-dwelling fire.

For this reason, your team will be required to be a bit more creative with supply hose lays. The most common difference will be the alley lay. An alley lay involves dropping a supply line at the entrance to the complex, or at a point where the engine leaves the common roadway or parking lot and continues to the access point for the attack lines. In this way, the engine that is laying a supply line from the hydrant (or other water source) can stop at the end of the first engine's supply line and hook into the line to supply water to the initial attack engine.

View It!

Go to the DVD, navigate to Chapter 21, and select *"Alley Lay."*

Practice It!

Making an Alley Lay

Use the following procedure to assist in making an alley lay at a large-structure fire:

1. The first engine stops at the desired entrance point, and a firefighter pulls the first coupling and section of supply off the truck. At this point, the firefighter kneels on the hose within view of the driver, or hooks a stationary object, such as a pole or post, and signals to the driver to proceed (Figure 21-43).

FIGURE 21-43

2. The second engine goes to the end of the supply line left by the first engine and attaches its own supply line from its hose bed. This crew continues to lay out supply hose (using a reverse lay) until they reach the water supply—in this case, a fire hydrant. They hook in and charge the supply line to the first engine at the building (Figure 21-44).

FIGURE 21-44

3. The supply line is charged at the hydrant, and the water supply is completed to the engine at the building.

Alternate method:

1. An alternate method of completing the alley lay is to lay out the supply line initially as before (Step 1, above).

2. A second engine stops at the nearest water supply—in this case, a fire hydrant—and lays out its supply hose until it reaches the firefighter and hose line at the end of the alley lay. The crew of this engine attaches the end of the first engine's supply hose to the discharge of the pump. They then attach the supply line from the fire hydrant to the intake port of their pump (Figure 21-45).

FIGURE 21-45

Stretching Attack Lines

There are three reasons to enter a large structure with attack hose lines: (1) to locate the fire and begin the extinguishing process, (2) to provide a safety backup, protecting the firefighters working inside who are either fighting the fire or performing rescue operations, and (3) to provide a lifeline to a safe area outside the building.

Your team will be stretching an attack line that needs to be long enough and have sufficient water flow capability to control and extinguish the fire. Because of this, you may be stretching a 2½- or 3-inch attack line into the building. This line may be used as it is set up or it may need to be divided into two smaller attack lines. Additionally, it may be extended for more reach to the fire.

In *Safe Firefighting: First Things First,* review Chapter 10, *"Extending Attack Lines."* Also insert the DVD from that text and review *"Extending a Line with a Gated Wye, Hose Clamp Method and Through-the-Nozzle Method."*

In this type of operation, it is critical to stay together and in contact with Command. As we have already stated in our training curriculum, freelancing on the fire scene is dangerous. If you cannot perform as a team member, then there is no need for you on the fire scene (Figure 21-46).

Remember your tools before you enter the building. Do a quick self-check and check your other team members to see that they are properly wearing all their PPE. Have your flashlights ready and be sure that at least one team member is carrying a long ceiling hook. Another team member needs to carry a flathead axe and a Halligan tool. All team members should have a search rope to use for navigation while inside the building. (Remember your navigating techniques from Chapter 19 of this text.) In addition, all the attack team members should each have a utility rope along with their other tools.

A firefighter on the nozzle and the Company Officer complete the team. Your Company Officer will notify Command that you are entering the building (Figure 21-47). There may be one or several intervention teams staged outside, depending on the needs dictated by the size of the fire and the number of fire crews working inside.

FIGURE 21-46 Good teamwork is critical at any fire emergency.

FIGURE 21-47 Your Company Officer will notify Command that you are entering the building.

Unlike a small building fire, the smoke and heat levels within a large building may be high above you due to the higher ceiling levels, so you may be able to easily walk into the structure at first. As you get closer to the fire and the smoke level drops, eventually you will be crawling inside. Firefighters will need to station at corners and obstructions to pull the line around them, the same as with a residential fire.

Level I

FIGURE 21-48 When entering a large, open room near the fire area, open an inspection hole in the ceiling with a long ceiling hook to check for any overhead fire or heavy smoke.

If you must enter a large, open area that is near the fire area, it is a good practice to open any ceiling area with a long ceiling hook to check for any overhead fire or heavy smoke (Figure 21-48). The presence of either indicates that it is dangerous to proceed. If heavy smoke or fire is found during this check, stop, stay in a safe area, and notify Command.

 **Safety Tip!**

Always stay in visual and audible contact with your fellow crew members. Monitor your air supply. *Remember:* When you get low on air, notify your Company Officer. You should return to the outside if your air gauge reads half-full. This ensures that you have enough air to reach the outside of a large building (half your air in/half your air out). If one member of the crew must leave the structure, the whole attack crew must leave. This action keeps the crew together. Another crew will then be assigned to relieve your team.

FIGURE 21-49 A thermal imaging camera (TIC).

 **Safety Tip!**

Using a TIC If available, a thermal imaging camera works very well in a large-building fire. In smoke and fire alarms, these cameras are useful for locating hot spots in hidden areas that can be the cause of the alarm (Figure 21-49). They can be used to help crews look for trapped fire victims, each other, and the fire. These devices are invaluable tools when used by the fire attack team, enhancing their ability to stay in visual contact. When the fire is knocked down, a TIC can be used for checking fire extension, providing valuable "eyes" to firefighters searching for hot spots and extended hidden fires.

When your team reaches the desired location inside the building, your Company Officer will notify Command of your location. With the line in place, you now have a safety guide to the outside: your hose line. Remember, when you find the hose couplings, the male coupling side and hose will lead to the outside. Follow the sections of hose: male end to hose to female end. The hose line is also a good anchor point for your search rope if you need to extend out into a dark and smoky area to do a search or some other job.

Setting Up Lighting

Setting up portable lighting inside a large-structure fire operation is an important safety consideration. These lights can illuminate the work area inside, exposing many hazards. Setting up portable lighting should be done quickly, along with stretching interior hose lines. If your team is assigned this job, hook the portable lights into the extension cords outside the building with the power on. Proceed with the lights, still lit, to the desired location for their placement, illuminating your way as you go.

 Safety Tip!

Portable lighting can become very hot when operating. Use caution as you carry the lights and place them into position. There is also the chance of water spray hitting the lights, which will explode a hot light bulb. Be sure to place portable lights in a dry area, away from water spray.

Tool Staging

Tool staging areas for a large-building fire are set up in various locations. They can be set up in front of the structure and may also be placed near access points around the structure. It is also possible that small tool staging areas will be set up inside the structure in a safe area that is well ventilated and well lit.

Confining the Fire

In a large firefighting operation, you will probably be working with other attack teams in confining and extinguishing the fire. As with any interior fire, you will work from the unburned side of the building. The tactics are to first isolate the fire and stop the spread, and then to attack the main body of the fire to achieve a knockdown (Figure 21-50).

If it is safe, fire crews will be on the roof, creating ventilation openings. These openings are created to reduce the chances of flashover and backdraft during interior firefighting operations. Ventilation openings also slow the progress of the fire, helping interior crews who are now placing water streams to confine the fire to the burned areas of the building.

Extinguishing the Fire

Once the fire is confined, crews begin to maneuver to knock down and extinguish the main fire. The simple fact with large fires is that you must apply enough water to absorb the heat being generated. Once that requirement is met, the fire begins to extinguish. In large-building fires, this takes a lot of water.

Combination Attack

A fire attack with hose lines in fog and straight stream patterns is most common in large buildings in which

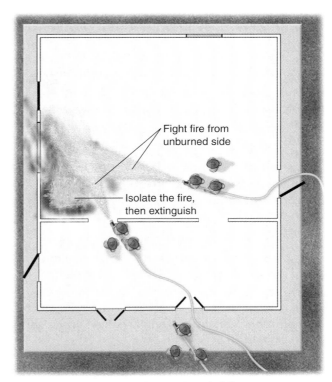

Confining a fire in a large building

FIGURE 21-50 Isolate the fire and stop the spread, and then attack the main body of the fire to achieve a knockdown.

there is a large fire area. A big fire inside a building gives off a tremendous amount of heat. The straight stream provides reach to the base of the fire and the fog pattern provides protection and cooling. You may be using large attack lines, so review Chapter 10 of *Safe Firefighting: First Things First* for handling techniques for a large fire attack line.

 **Review It!**

In *Safe Firefighting: First Things First*, review Chapter 10, *"Extending Attack Lines."* Also insert the DVD from that text and review all of the large attack line techniques.

 **Safety Tip!**

In large-building fires where we use large attack lines, it is even more important to avoid opposing water streams. These large streams can seriously injure firefighters.

Searching for Fire Extension

Once the fire has been knocked down, crews will start to look for small fires that have extended through walls, ceilings, and other parts of the building. A common area of fire extension in large buildings is the front **cockloft** area. The cockloft is the hidden space between the bottom of the roof and a hung ceiling in a building. A cockloft consists of a large, hollow space with little or no access. It must be checked for fire extension if the fire was near this area (Figure 21-51).

Other areas to check for fire extension are any rooms next to the fire area. Be sure to gain access to these areas before checking for fire extension.

Fire walls provide safety separation from adjacent businesses in the same building or complex. However, if there was a large fire directly next to a fire wall, you may be tasked with checking the unburned side of the fire wall for fire extension. These walls may have cracks or manmade openings created after the building was completed that provide opportunity for fire spread.

Fire can also extend to other areas of a large building through wire and utility chases and ventilation ductwork. These areas should be opened up close to the fire area and checked for extension.

Areas outside but adjacent to the fire building should also be opened up and checked. Heat could spread through exterior walls by conduction to adjacent rooms and materials, causing a hidden fire to spread.

▰ KEY WORD ▰

cockloft The concealed, empty space between the bottom of the roof structure and the top of a suspended ceiling in a building.

Safety Tip!

Rehab Area Since there are many more firefighters at a large-building fire operation, the rehab area will be much bigger and will be staffed by more people. You will probably be medically evaluated (vital signs taken) while you rest and recuperate at rehab. Be sure to remove as much of your PPE as possible, especially your helmet—your head releases a lot of body heat when uncovered. Have a seat and get comfortable. Take in a lot of good fluids to rehydrate yourself. Avoid caffeinated beverages like tea or coffee. The quicker you can regain your strength, the quicker you can get back to the fire as a team (Figure 21-52).

FIGURE 21-51 A cockloft area.

FIGURE 21-52 Rehab areas are critical on a large-building fire operation.

Overhauling a Large-Building Fire

After a fire has been extinguished and the building had been checked for fire extension, fire attack efforts turn to overhauling the fire area. Overhaul is a much bigger effort on a large-building fire than it is on a residential fire. There may be times when large machinery is brought in to move and separate damaged and undamaged materials. It takes much longer than efforts on a typical house fire and may even involve the building occupant's employees and equipment.

Salvage

Salvage at a large-building fire can also be a mammoth undertaking. These efforts can be started in one area of a large building even as extinguishing efforts are still under way in another area of the building. It is more common practice to salvage the contents by removing them as quickly as possible to the outside. In fact, in some instances, such as in a warehouse or big barn fire, part of the extinguishing tactic is to remove storage or hay to reduce the potential fuel from the fire in the building.

Normal salvage tarps are rapidly used up in a large-building fire. Many fire departments carry large rolls of plastic for this type of salvage operation. Stock on a large department store sales floor needs long covers. If you are assigned as a team to cover this type of exposure with rolled plastic, unroll the plastic the length to provide coverage, cut the piece, and unfold it over the stock. You can use the same plastic to cover floor areas and build water troughs as we discussed in the Chapter 20 for residential structures.

Defensive Fire Attack

There are times when the fire in a large building is beyond the extinguishing capability of an interior attack. This can happen before the arrival of the first fire department units, meaning that the Incident Commander immediately calls for an exterior defensive attack. Alternately, it can occur after initial interior operations fail to stop the spread of the fire and the building is no longer safe for firefighters. An evacuation signal is given, both from the apparatus and on the radio system, and all interior crews evacuate the building and change over from an offensive operation to a defensive operation.

In either situation, a defensive fire attack involves working hose lines and master stream devices to protect exposures and stop the spread of the fire. The final outcome of a defensive fire attack is to extinguish the fire from exterior positions. The building is considered a total loss when this type of fire attack is initiated (Figure 21-53).

Safety Tip!

Just a reminder here about evacuating a large building: You should leave with your crew *immediately* when the signal is sounded. Follow your hose line to the outside of the building; do not bring it out with you unless you need it for protection from the fire. Command will account for all personnel on the scene by requesting a PAR (Personnel Accountability Report) on each team of firefighters after the evacuation to ensure that everyone is present and safely outside.

Collapse and Safety Zones

While working in a defensive position on a large-building fire, it is important to remember the safety and collapse zones around the building. Usually the collapse zone is 1½ times the height of the building (Figure 21-54). A 30-foot-high building has a collapse zone of 45 feet that extends outward from the exterior walls.

Also consider any overhangs from which you should keep clear. These can be attached to outside walls and fail easily when involved in fire.

The safety zones extend all around the building. No one should be allowed in the hot or warm zone without full PPE and a purpose (working with a team).

FIGURE 21-53 A defensive fire attack usually means the building is considered a total loss.

Collapse zone for a large building fire

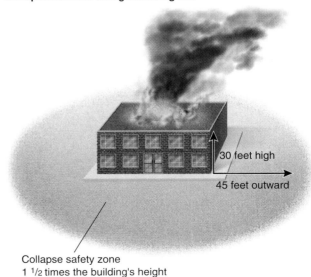

30 feet high

45 feet outward

Collapse safety zone
1 ½ times the building's height

FIGURE 21-54 A collapse zone.

Large Attack Lines

Due to the size of the fire and the distance of the collapse zones, you will need plenty of reach in your water stream to be effective on a large-building fire. If your team is assigned a large attack line, remember to use a narrow stream to provide reach. If you are assigned exposure protection, flow water onto the exposure to keep it cool. Always watch for drop-over fires behind you as embers fall from the main body of the fire.

Safety Tip!

Once you begin a defensive attack on a large building, keep it defensive. Resist the temptation to creep into the collapse zone to apply water to the part of the fire that is beyond the reach of your fire stream. The lack of windows and doorways on many sides of a "big-box" type of occupancy will often prevent you from being able to reach the fire with a fire stream, regardless of the size and type of line you use. STAY OUT OF THE COLLAPSE ZONE. The risk is not worth the potential gain at this point.

Even if you loop the large attack line and sit on it, be sure to have another firefighter with you to act as a backup and safety. Stay in visual or audible contact with your Company Officer at all times.

If you are directed to extinguish the fire with your stream, use your narrow stream from a distance. Then later, when the fire is reduced, you can approach the remaining fire to finish up the extinguishment.

Ground Monitors

A ground monitor provides a large flow of water through a master stream nozzle onto exposures and the fire (Figure 21-55). Just as with a large attack line, protect exposures by wetting them down during the fire.

Use a narrow stream to reach the seat of the fire if directed to apply water on the fire. As noted previously, watch out for opposing streams on the fire as these can be dangerous to firefighters operating them. If firefighters will be using a ground monitor, two firefighters should be stationed for safety. Remain in contact with your Company Officer at all times.

If necessary, a ground monitor can be set up and left flowing with no firefighters stationed with it.

Mounted Deck Guns

Many engines are provided with a deck gun mounted on top of the pump area behind the cab. These can be pre-plumbed with water supply pipes, or short sections of hose can be used to hook the device into the pump of the engine. They provide a very rapid method of attacking a large fire, using only a few firefighters (Figure 21-56).

FIGURE 21-55 Ground monitors provide a large flow of water through a master stream nozzle onto exposures and the fire.

FIGURE 21-56 Deck guns on a fire apparatus provide a very rapid method of attacking a large fire, using only a few firefighters.

A blitz attack is a common method of defensively attacking a fire in a small commercial structure with an open floor plan. This method often uses a preconnected apparatus-mounted deck gun to flow the contents of the booster tank onto the fire inside the building. At the same time, the rest of the crew hooks into a sustained water supply.

Elevated Master Streams

Another common sight at defensive attacks on large-building fires is the elevated master streams coming from aerial apparatus. These units are usually staffed by experienced firefighters who must be trained specifically on the aerial apparatus and the various other job functions that a truck company performs on the fire scene. Many of these apparatus carry their own water supply and have a pump; however, some are designed without water or a pump. Regardless, supplying water to them is similar to supplying any engine apparatus. The difference is whether or not your engine will be pumping the supply line (Figure 21-57).

 Do It!

Large-Building Firefighting Skills

We have reached the end of another chapter in your training. What have you learned? Hopefully, you've learned that large buildings require a different set of skills from firefighters. Large structures have bigger fires that involve many firefighters and require even more coordination by ICS. Firefighters should be aware that these buildings have a variety of built-in fire detection and suppression systems with which they will have to work. Because of the open floor plans, navigating in dark, smoky conditions is especially demanding and dangerous. Therefore, firefighters will have to make a special effort to stay together and with their Company Officer.

In general, during a defensive attack, bigger fires require large volumes of water flow from around the structure. Firefighters should avoid directing these streams onto other firefighters. They should also position safely out of the collapse areas around the building.

With good coordination, working consistently as part of a firefighting team, and following safe firefighting practices, you will do a good job at these incidents—and remain well and alive.

FIGURE 21-57 A common sight at defensive attacks on large-building fires is the elevated master streams coming from aerial apparatus.

Knowledge Assessment

Signed Documentation Tear-Out Sheet

Large Buildings—Chapter 21

Name: _____

Fill out the ten-question quiz below, the Knowledge Assessment Sheet, by circling the correct answer for each question. When finished, sign it and give it to your instructor/Company Officer for his or her signature. Turn in this Knowledge Assessment Sheet to the proper person as part of the documentation that you have completed your training for this chapter.

1. The firefighting methods you use inside large buildings differ from your methods for residential buildings in the way you approach the interior fire, the number and size of the fire attack lines needed to extinguish the fire, and the complexity of working with many other firefighting teams.
   a. True
   b. False

2. Sections of noncombustible sheeting hung from the bottom of the roof of a large building with an open floor plan that are designed to inhibit the spread of smoke are called _____.
   a. automatic ventilation curtains
   b. fire walls
   c. smoke curtains
   d. fire curtains

3. Fire walls work 100% of the time during a building fire.
   a. True
   b. False

4. The single most effective fire protection system for buildings ever developed is the _____.
   a. automatic ventilation curtain
   b. automatic fire sprinkler system
   c. fire extinguisher
   d. Class B foam system

5. _____ are access points for the fire department to augment the sprinkler system's water supply during a fire.
   a. Fire Department connections (FDC)
   b. Fire Department controls (FDC)
   c. Post indicator valves (PIV)
   d. Outside screw and yoke (OS&Y) valves

6. To stop the flow of water through a sprinkler head, you can place a _____ between the water flow opening and deflector plate of the sprinkler head.
   a. Halligan bar, pick end
   b. long ceiling hook
   c. screwdriver
   d. wooden sprinkler wedge

7. On a four-sided building, the side opposite the front of the building is labeled side _____.
   a. A
   b. B
   c. C
   d. D

8. During a large-building fire, if one member of the interior firefighting crew must go outside to a safe area, the rest of the crew remains inside to continue extinguishing the fire.
   a. True
   b. False

9. Large, hollow spaces between the hung ceiling and roof on a large building are often referred to as _____.
   a. attic spaces
   b. garret areas
   c. cocklofts
   d. hidden spaces

10. A building is considered a total loss when a defensive fire attack is initiated.
    a. True
    b. False

Student Signature and Date _____   Instructor/Company Officer Signature and Date _____

550

Prove It

Skills Assessment

Signed Documentation Tear-Out Sheet

Large Buildings—Chapter 21

Name: _____

Fill out the Skills Assessment Sheet below. Have your instructor/Company Officer check off and initial each skill you demonstrate. When you are finished, sign this page and give it to your instructor/Company Officer for his or her signature. Turn in this Skills Assessment Sheet to the proper person as part of the documentation that you have completed your training for this chapter.

Skill	Completed	Initials
1. Demonstrate hooking into a Fire Department connection on a sprinkler system.	_____	_____
2. Demonstrate shutting off the flow of a fire sprinkler head using a wooden wedge or a sprinkler tool.	_____	_____
3. Demonstrate hooking an attack line into a standpipe system.	_____	_____
4. As a member of a team, demonstrate the alley lay for supply lines.	_____	_____

Student Signature and Date _____   Instructor/Company Officer Signature and Date _____

Preplanning and Fire Prevention

What You Will Learn in This Chapter

In this chapter we'll cover preplanning activities, which include response area knowledge, building survey preplanning activities, and hazard recognition. Then we'll talk about your responsibility in being part of fire safety education programs at your fire department and how to conduct a fire station tour. Finally, the basic procedures for installing a smoke detector in a home will be explained, and tips for giving a short public fire safety talk will be given.

What You Will Be Able to Do

After reading this chapter and practicing the skills described, you will be able to:

1. Participate in a building survey as a firefighting team member, assisting as assigned by the Company Officer.

2. Identify life safety hazards and fire hazards, given a list of conditions found during a building survey.

3. Identify target hazards from a list of properties located in the first response area of the fire department.

4. Participate as a member of the firefighting team conducting a home fire safety survey.

5. List ten things to check when performing a home safety survey.

6. Describe how a smoke detector works, where smoke detectors should be located, and how many should be installed in a given building.

7. Conduct a station tour for a small group of adults or their children.

8. Describe the Stop, Drop, and Roll, and Operation EDITH Public Education Programs.

9. Discuss how to prepare for a Fire Education talk for a small group.

Preplanning and Fire Prevention

A career in the Fire Service is rewarding, and every day you work in the emergency services presents a new challenge. Thus far in your training you have learned about the work involved in controlling and extinguishing fires. A vital step in the preparation before the fire incident is to know the area in which you'll be responding. This means getting out into the community and becoming familiar with streets, neighborhoods, buildings, and hazards. If your job is to respond to emergencies, then you need to know how to get there and what type of environment to expect.

Firefighters should become experts about street and address locations as well as changes in their response areas. They should be aware of all buildings, hazardous processes, and other activities and occupancies that make up their community. It is an ever-evolving process and a very important one. This knowledge is a responsibility for everyone in the organization, from the newest firefighter to the Chief of the fire department.

Preventing fires through educating the community is also a big responsibility of firefighters. When you think about what you do in the Fire Service, you need to consider that the vast majority of fire and rescue situations are preventable.

A house catches fire and becomes well involved before the fire department is called to respond. Why? Perhaps there was no smoke detector.

Someone unfortunately dies in a building fire. Why? Perhaps they did not know or think about how they would escape if the building was on fire, or maybe it was a commercial structure and the exit signs and lighting did not work when the power went out.

In the Fire Service business, most of our emergency work could be avoided if we all did a better job of educating the public about fire hazards and fire safety, and enforced existing fire codes. The expense of prevention is much less than the cost in lives and property incurred during a fire.

Essentially, we are not putting fires out, we are limiting damage. We limit damage by extinguishing the fires to save as many of the people and as much of the building and contents as we can so to lessen the impact of the fire incident, both economically and socially. Imagine if the fire had never happened. There would be no impact and loss to the community. The expense of extinguishing the fire and returning the occupants to normalcy would be zero.

As a firefighter, part of your job is to be able to assist in the education of the public about fire hazards and the correct actions to take in case of a fire emer-

gency. You will be called upon to help install smoke detectors in homes, conduct fire station tours, be a part of fire safety education presentations, and discuss fire safety issues with members of your community. You will become ambassadors for public awareness and understanding of the dangers of fire as well as the importance of being responsible and safe.

Preplanning for Fire

There are several ways to preplan for fire operations. You will be required to study the layout of your response area, survey commercial buildings and target hazards, and learn to recognize common fire hazards in buildings. You will also need to know how to check building fire protection and fire alarm systems as well as conduct fire inspections.

Learning Your Response Area

The first step of preplanning is to personally become familiar with your response area. This entails learning the layout of the streets and highways in your area as well as the locations of fire hydrants and other water sources. Depending upon the policy of your fire department and your Company Officer, you may be required to pass periodic evaluations of your knowledge (Figure 22-1).

Your department will have maps designating streets, hydrants, and other water source information that you can study. There will be times when your crew will drive through the area to become familiar with the streets as well as to note any new construction or

FIGURE 22-1 The first step of preplanning is learning the layout of the streets and highways in your area as well as the locations of fire hydrants and other water sources.

road layout changes. Even though initially you won't be driving the apparatus to the emergency, you still should know where your unit is responding in case the driver becomes confused about the address and also so you can help guide others to the scene if necessary. This is a basic firefighter knowledge requirement.

Building Surveys

Another way to prepare for a fire emergency is to take part in building surveys. These are familiarization sessions in which the crews that will respond to a fire or other emergency in a building visit a business and tour their facility. These tours are an opportunity to become familiar with a building's layout and are a chance to meet the key people who will be affected in an emergency. The building survey is our chance to make a good impression on the building manager prior to an emergency.

It is very important that you present a professional appearance and conduct yourself in a businesslike manner anytime you interface with the public. This is especially important during a building survey. No matter how welcomed you are by the business manager, you are disrupting his or her normal business day, so your visit should leave the manager feeling that the time spent with the Fire Department was worthwhile. Keep your conversations with everyone at the business on-topic, and refrain from any horseplay whatsoever.

Survey Techniques

You will be scheduled to do a walkthrough survey of different buildings in your community. Usually these are public or commercial buildings and properties. (Private dwellings will be discussed later in this chapter in the section about prevention.) The purpose of the survey is to determine the basic layout of the property; gather any pertinent fire emergency information, such as emergency contact names and phone numbers; determine the occupancy use of the property; and become familiar with any hazardous processes or conditions at the property. Your crew should also take advantage of the survey to look at the types of existing openings, such as doorways and windows, to determine potential forcible entry points and ventilation openings. These should be noted on preplanning drawings and notes. Your fire department may also have your Company Officer inform the occupant of any obvious fire hazards that your crew encounters while surveying the property (Figure 22-2).

The survey process involves going to the building or property (preferably with an appointment), talking with the business or building representative, gathering information and making a rough sketch of the layout of the building and property, noting any obvious

FIGURE 22-2 Surveys determine the basic layout. Gather any pertinent emergency information, such as contact names and phone numbers. Also determine the use of the property and become familiar with any hazardous processes or conditions.

fire hazards, talking with the building representative again, and returning to the fire station. All the information gathered is documented on a pre-fire planning form and stored in the station or for reference on the fire apparatus if needed during an emergency. Your Company Officer will be responsible for the documentation, although you may be asked to assist.

In Fire Service vernacular, a building is simply a building. The construction of the building, which is the general makeup of the structure, is more important information.

Building Construction Types

We can start to define a building by generally classifying its construction type. This information was covered in detail in Chapter 17, "Building Construction," in this text. As a quick review, the construction types are as follows:

1. Type I: Fire Resistive
   - Made of steel, concrete, or gypsum board
   - Used in schools, hospitals, and high-rise buildings
   - Steel is protected
2. Type II: Noncombustible
   - Made of **noncombustible** structural materials
   - Used in warehouses, single-story buildings with steel frames; includes metal and concrete walls
   - Steel is unprotected
   - Some components may have a 1- or 2-hour protection

3. Type III: Ordinary
   - Used in buildings limited to 4 to 6 stories in height
   - Uses masonry exterior supporting walls
   - Uses wood for most interior walls, floors, and roof systems
   - Usually uses gypsum board or plaster to provide some fire resistance to the interior components
4. Type IV: Heavy Timber
   - Used for interior supports and floor decking
   - Uses masonry exterior walls
   - Contains no voids
   - Usually found in older buildings; today, buildings built for the same purpose are usually type I or II
5. Type V: Wood Frame
   - Most common type of construction
   - Used for residential and multifamily buildings as well as office buildings up to 4 stories
   - Uses plaster or gypsum board achieve fire-resistance ratings
   - Usually contains many voids
   - Quick to collapse, especially if a truss construction
   - Includes balloon-frame and platform construction

KEY WORD

noncombustible A term used to describe any material that, by itself, will not ignite or sustain combustion.

Review Chapter 17, "Building Construction."

The term *occupancy* further defines a building by telling us what that structure is used for. The occupancy of a building used as a restaurant would be classified as a Public Assembly occupancy. A warehouse used to store dry goods would be considered a Storage occupancy. Examples of occupancy classifications as defined in NFPA 101, *Life Safety Code,* are listed in Table 22-1.

After the building type and occupancy classification is determined and documented, your crew will now have a better idea of what may be required to check in the building during your survey. This will also give responding crews and Company Officers

TABLE 22-1 Examples of Building Occupancy Classifications

Classification	Examples
Assembly	Bars, restaurants, clubs
Educational	Schools, colleges
Health Care	Hospitals, clinics
Detention/Correctional	Prisons, jail facilities
Residential	Homes, duplexes, apartments
Mercantile	Stores, shops
Business	Offices, firms
Industrial	Factories, assembly plants
Storage	Warehouses
Mixed	Two or more different types of occupancies in the same building

insight into the potential fire problems at that building location.

Checking Building Fire Protection and Fire Alarm Systems

As we discussed in Chapter 21, "Large Buildings," many buildings, particularly larger commercial and residential structures and complexes, have **building fire protection and fire alarm systems.** These systems need to be maintained by the occupant of the building. As a part of your survey, you can give these systems a quick visual check, and you can give the occupant commonsense advice to encourage proper care.

Examples of building fire protection and fire alarm systems are:

- Fire alarm control panels
- Pull stations
- Fire sprinkler systems
- Private fire hydrants
- Fire Department connections to the systems
- Standpipe systems
- Specialized fire-extinguishing hood systems
- Auxiliary fire pumps
- Static water supply sources
- Fire extinguishers

Some common, general things to look for around any building fire protection and fire alarm systems are the following:

- Are the systems clean, uncluttered, and unobstructed for Fire Department access?
- Are they properly tagged with updated inspection documentation?

- Are any parts of the system damaged or shut down?
- Are Fire Department connections clearly marked and unobstructed?
- Are all standpipe hose stations accessible to the fire department?
- Are any fire sprinkler heads obstructed or damaged?

Building fire alarm systems are made up of a combination of fire, heat, and water flow detection devices and the fire alarm alerting system. During a building survey, they should be checked for the following:

- Is the fire alarm control panel box properly marked and the inspection updated?
- Does the building representative know how to reset the fire alarm box?
- Are all fire alarm pull stations reset for operation?
- Are any fire detection devices (for example, smoke, heat, or water flow detectors) damaged or disconnected?

In addition, the locations and type of building fire protection and fire alarm systems should be indicated on any drawings. This will help responding fire crews quickly locate the system controls during an emergency.

FIGURE 22-3 Hazard recognition on the firefighter level is really basic safety sense.

▨ KEY WORD ▨

building fire protection and fire alarm systems Any permanently installed devices or combination of devices and systems used for the detection, control, or extinguishment of fire in a building. These systems include but are not limited to heat and smoke detectors, fire alarm monitoring systems, cooking fire extinguishing systems, fire sprinkler and standpipe hose systems, and auxiliary fire pumps.

FIGURE 22-4 An exit door with sign.

Fire Hazard Recognition

When you participate in a building survey, you and your fellow crew members will assist your Company Officer in checking the occupancy for hazardous conditions as well as preplanning information. Hazard recognition on the firefighter level is really basic safety sense (Figure 22-3).

Life Safety Hazards

A life safety hazard represents a primary risk to life and limb. These are conditions that could potentially produce a large loss of life either at the occupancy or as an exposure to the surrounding community.

For example, a blocked designated building exit is a life safety hazard. This is because if a fire occurs, the occupants of the building may not be able to escape, creating a danger to life.

Examples of life safety hazards include but are not limited to:

- Blocked exits
- Locked **exit doors**
- Exit doors that are not clearly marked (Figure 22-4)
- **Exit signs** and **exit lighting** that are not working (Figure 22-5)

FIGURE 22-5 An illuminated exit sign and exit lighting.

FIGURE 22-6 Public assembly.

- Overcrowded public assembly areas (Figure 22-6)
- Nonfunctioning smoke detectors
- Inoperable or blocked **fire doors**
- Building fire protection and fire alarm systems that are inoperable or blocked (Figure 22-7)
- Missing or poorly maintained fire extinguishers (Figure 22-8)
- No posting of an **emergency evacuation plan**

KEY WORDS

emergency evacuation plan A drawing and legend that shows the viewer the safest exit route to take from the location of the drawing.

exit doors Doors that are located at the exterior walls of a structure. They are designed to open outward, providing an unobstructed opening and functioning as the exit path for building occupants.

exit lighting Special lighting units located along an exit path. They are designed to illuminate the exit route from a building if the power to the lights in the building is lost. They are installed with a battery backup. A small test button is located on the outside cover.

exit signs Signs specifically designed for use to indicate an exit or an exit door from inside a building. These signs may be either internally illuminated or brightly colored, as required by the local fire regulations.

fire doors Specially designed doors that are made of fire-resistant materials and designed to automatically close if a fire is detected in a building. They are used to slow the spread of smoke and fire in larger buildings.

FIGURE 22-7 Check to see that sprinkler risers are not blocked.

Fire Hazards

Fire hazards are conditions or practices in an occupancy that increase the potential risk of a fire. This type of hazard includes any condition or practice that presents the potential to start a fire.

FIGURE 22-8 Check for outdated or missing fire extinguisher inspection tags.

FIGURE 22-9 Trash and debris accumulation.

FIGURE 22-10 A UL-approved safety gas can.

Examples of fire hazards include the following:

- Trash and debris accumulation inside and next to the building (Figure 22-9)
- **Flammable liquids** stored in unapproved containers (for example, containers that are not **Underwriter's Laboratory [UL]** approved) (Figure 22-10)
- Smoking permitted near flammable materials or processes
- **Flexible wiring** (extension cords) substituted for **fixed wiring** (Figure 22-11)
- **Electrical receptacles** that are overloaded (for example, more than one plug per plug-in) (Figure 22-12)
- Fixed or flexible wiring that is frayed or damaged
- **Electrical system circuit breaker switches** that are taped or blocked (Figure 22-13)
- Other dangerous conditions or practices specific to each type occupancy or process that can potentially cause a fire

FIGURE 22-11 Check for excessive use of extension cords.

FIGURE 22-12 Look for overload plug-in receptacles.

FIGURE 22-13 Check for taped or blocked circuit breaker switches.

When life safety hazards or fire hazards are found during your building survey activities, your Company Officer will point out these hazards to the building occupancy representative before leaving. The Company Officer will document the problems and they will be turned over to fire code enforcement personnel. If the hazards are not considered severe, a resurvey of the building is done after the occupant has had time to remedy the documented hazards.

KEY WORDS

electrical receptacles Common electrical wall plug-in points located in any structure. They are a part of the permanent, fixed wiring of a building.

electrical system circuit breaker switches Electrical control switches that are located together in a specified area within a building. They are designed to switch to the *off* position automatically when the wiring circuit they are in becomes overloaded.

fixed wiring The electrical wiring that is a part of the finished structure of a building. It is installed in an approved manner and is designed to be permanent.

flammable liquids Material normally found in a liquid state that will ignite and support continuous combustion under normal atmospheric conditions.

flexible wiring Temporary electrical wiring, usually in the form of extension cords, that is used to connect a device or an appliance to a fixed wiring system of a building. This type of wiring should only be used briefly and should never be substituted for the fixed wiring of a building.

Underwriter's Laboratory (UL) A private testing organization that lists products as having passed a safety test.

Target Hazards

Some building and property occupancies in any given response area present more of a potential hazard to fire or life safety than is considered normal. These locations are referred to as target hazard occupancies. For example, if you have a fertilizer manufacturing plant in your response area, the potential for a small fire at this location to grow into a major fire and hazardous material release is far greater than a fire in a real estate office. The fertilizer manufacturing plant would definitely be a target hazard.

Another example of a target hazard is a large night club. If you have a fire in this type of occupancy when it is full of patrons, the potential for a large loss of life is far greater than we would expect at a single-family-dwelling fire.

Think about the community served by your fire department. Any occupancy that presents the potential for a large property loss or a large loss of life, or that can create a large loss of life in the surrounding community, can be classified as a target hazard. Examples of typical target hazards in a community include the following:

- Theaters, movie theaters, concert halls
- Hospitals
- Flammable liquid and gas storage complexes
- Schools
- Large manufacturing facilities
- Chemical processing plants and storage facilities
- Nightclubs
- Stadiums, coliseums, and convention centers
- High-rise buildings
- Communications facilities
- Large storage complexes
- Airports

Target hazards in the response area of the fire department will be more closely monitored by the department. You may be going to these places more often for building surveys, and you may also receive specific training for handling potential fire and rescue emergencies at these locations.

Fire Inspections

Normally, firefighting crews are not used for formal fire inspection work. This job is left to specially trained and certified fire inspectors provided by the Fire Department or by the local government. They will do a more in-depth inspection of the premises and will handle all sorts of complaints and fire problems. The fire department may have input into new construction building requirements and may inspect a building several times during its construction. Special installations, such as underground fuel tanks for gas stations, special industrial buildings, and plant facilities, may need to be inspected.

Fire inspectors use fire codes, adopted by the Fire Department or local government, that spell out specific requirements buildings and occupancies must follow. These codes can include the **National Life Safety Code** and the **National Fire Codes**, both assembled and published by the National Fire Protection Association (NFPA). All serious or difficult fire hazard situations should be documented and referred to a fire inspector for further action and remedy (Figure 22-14).

FIGURE 22-14 Fire inspectors use fire codes, adopted by the Fire Department or local government, that spells out specific requirements buildings and occupancies must follow.

KEY WORDS

National Fire Codes A set of nationally recognized standards that deal with a multitude of fire regulations. They also address fire department organizations, apparatus, and equipment as well as public and commercial facilities and processes. Local governments have the option of adopting these standards as fire regulations for their own communities.

National Life Safety Code A nationally recognized standard that deals primarily with life safety hazards in buildings. This standard deals with things such as exit access and egress, exit openings, and public safety in buildings.

Fire Prevention

As pointed out at the beginning of this chapter, fire prevention is much better for the community than extinguishing a fire after it has started. Another major aspect of the Fire Service's responsibility to the community is educating citizens about fire safety.

As a firefighter, you will play a big part in community educational activities. It is an integral part of your job. You will be required to take part in demonstrations, station tours, public fire prevention events, and home fire safety activities like smoke detector installations and home safety surveys. The extent that you take part is determined by the capability of your fire department and the needs of your community.

It is important to note that whenever you are working as a representative of your department for public fire education programs and duties, you must maintain a professional appearance and conduct yourself in a helpful, professional manner. You must always be courteous and a good listener. You are not expected to become an accomplished public speaker; however, you should be able to converse with the general public about fire hazards and fire safety practices (Figure 22-15).

Home Safety Surveys

The home safety survey is another type of building survey. This survey is usually requested by the homeowner; the fire department comes to the home and takes a look at the fire safety of the home. A home safety survey is an opportunity for you and your team to help members of your community maintain a house that is safe from the risk of fire, ideally preventing a future fire.

As with building surveys of public and commercial structures, you need to present a professional appearance and demeanor. Be sincere in your efforts

FIGURE 22-15 As a representative of your department for public fire education programs, you must maintain a professional appearance and conduct yourself in a helpful, professional manner. Always be courteous and a good listener.

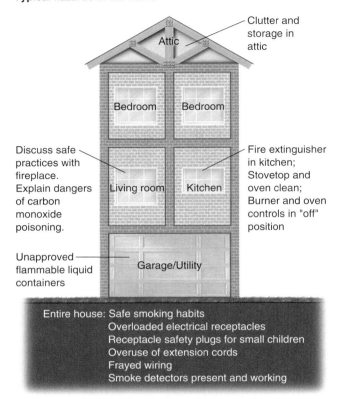

Typical hazards in the home

FIGURE 22-16 Typical fire hazards in the home.

and try to be as helpful as you can. Be prepared to point out fire hazards, explain why they are a hazard, and have a few suggestions for safely fixing the problem. If you do not have an answer for them, be prepared to refer them to your fire inspector or even another agency, if needed.

A home safety survey starts with an introduction by the Company Officer of your crew, a review with the homeowner of the purpose of your visit, and a walkthrough of areas as allowed by the homeowner. When you encounter a hazard, tell the homeowner how to remove it.

The following list provides suggestions of items to check during a home safety survey (Figure 22-16):

- Check for clutter and storage in the attic.
- Look for open or unapproved flammable liquid containers.
- If there are smokers in the house, discuss the need for safe smoking habits. Advise homeowners to never smoke in bed, always have ashtrays handy, and use care when emptying ashtrays.
- Look for overloaded electrical receptacle plugs.
- Advise homeowners to use safety plug covers if there are small children in the house.
- Look for the overuse of extension cords.
- Look for frayed wiring.
- Check for a fire extinguisher in the kitchen.
- Explain the importance of keeping the kitchen stovetop and oven clean.
- Demonstrate how to extinguish a cooking grease fire in a pan with both the fire extinguisher and by smothering (using the pan lid or another pan).

- Always check that burner and oven controls are in the *off* position.
- Discuss safe practices if a fireplace is used within the house.
- Explain the dangers of carbon monoxide poisoning whenever fossil fuels (coal, oil, and gas) are used in the house (for example, the car in the garage, the fireplace, or gas stoves or heaters).
- Check smoke detectors for operation and review with the homeowner when and how to change the batteries.
- If there is a pool or spa, advise the homeowner of the importance of keeping track of small children around their pool or spa. Tell them about any safety programs available for owners of pools and spas.

It is also important to discuss with the homeowner what to do in case they do have a fire in their home. Be sure to cover the following topics in your discussion:

- How to notify others in the house of a fire
- How to call the fire department for help (911)
- Having an emergency exit plan for the family, including designating a meeting place outside the home

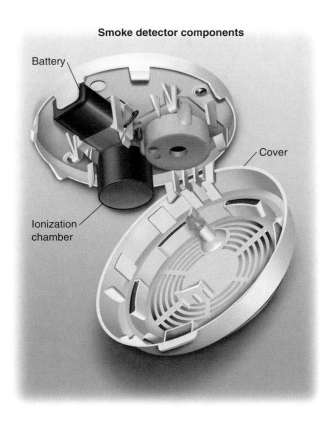

Smoke detector components

Battery

Cover

Ionization
chamber

FIGURE 22-17   A typical smoke detector features these
parts: (a) ionization chamber, (b) battery, and (c) cover.

- Practicing a fire drill with family members
- Rolling out of bed if you think there is a fire
- Crawling and not standing if the house is full of smoke
- Feeling interior doors before opening them, leaving them closed if they are hot and going to a window, and climbing out of the window; waiting for the fire department if you cannot climb out the window
- Always having two ways out of the house in case of a fire
- Never going back into a burning house

Installing Home Smoke Detectors

As part of a home safety survey program or as part of a service provided by your fire department, your crew may be called upon to install a battery-operated smoke detector in a home in your community. Even though most residential smoke detectors for single-family dwellings are battery operated, you may come across some home detectors that are installed into the electrical system of the home. You should only be called upon to install battery-operated units. These are truly lifesaving devices, so it is important that you know how to install them properly.

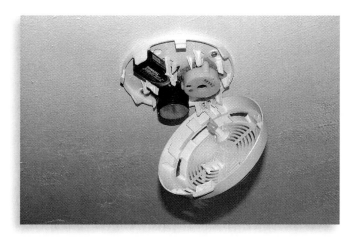

FIGURE 22-18   The Fire Service recommends that smoke detector batteries be changed when the time changes each fall and spring, and has undertaken a very successful media campaign called "Change your clock—Change your battery!"

Simply stated, some smoke detectors work by using a small chamber, called an **ionization chamber,** to detect tiny particles of smoke that are contained in any air that passes within it. Another type uses a photoelectric cell to detect particles of smoke from a rapidly growing fire when there is more fire than smoke. When particles are detected, the fire alarm sounds. They are usually powered by a 9-volt battery and today are not very expensive to purchase. Indeed, many fire departments have public safety programs that pay for one smoke detector to be installed in each home in the community (Figure 22-17).

The instruction sheet that comes with every smoke detector indicates the best location and number of smoke detectors needed in any one residence. We recommend that you follow the manufacturer's recommendations. However, it is generally recommended that there be one smoke detector installed on each living level in the home and between the sleeping areas and the rest of the home. They should be placed on the ceiling or close to the ceiling on the wall.

The battery should be replaced twice a year. The Fire Service recommends they be changed when the time changes, each fall and spring, and has undertaken a very successful media campaign called "Change your clock—Change your battery!" The fire alarm should be checked monthly. A manual test button is located on the outside cover of the detector. A continuous chirping sound coming from the detector in the absence of any fire or smoke usually indicates a low battery (Figure 22-18).

If the smoke detector sounds and there is smoke and heat, the homeowner should evacuate the family from the house and call the fire department from somewhere outside the home.

KEY WORD

ionization chamber The working part of a smoke detector that detects particles of combustion and activates the warning sound of the detector.

Typical Fire Education Programs

There are many fire education programs used in the Fire Service today. These programs can range from nationally available educational campaigns such as Stop, Drop, and Roll to local programs developed by members of your own fire department for the community (Figure 22-19).

Stop, Drop, and Roll

This program basically teaches children what to do if their clothes catch fire. It is easy to remember and the short title tells it all. If your clothes catch fire, be sure not to run—just stop, be sure to drop to the ground, and roll to help extinguish the fire. Some added tips are to show the children how to cover their faces with their hands and hold their breath as they roll. Stop, Drop, and Roll is the best way to teach a child to extinguish the fire if their clothes are burning, and it is easy enough for them to remember during an emergency.

When talking to any children about fire safety, it is very important to stress that they *never* play with matches or cigarette lighters. If they are around other children with matches or a lighter, they should immediately go home.

Operation EDITH

Operation EDITH is an acronym for *exit drills in the home.* It is a national campaign that encourages homeowners to practice evacuating their house and meet at

FIGURE 22-19 There are many fire safety education programs used by the Fire Service.

a designated safe area outside. It promotes preplanning the fire emergency and tells them what to do if they discover a fire in their home. As with all fire prevention, the protection of lives is always first and foremost. Buildings and property can eventually be replaced, but lives cannot. It teaches them to

- Have an exit plan.
- Appoint a "Fire Chief." This is an adult, babysitter, or older sibling who will be in charge during an emergency.
- Visit every room and pick two ways out—the "normal" exit and an emergency exit, such as a window.
- Plan how everyone can reach the ground through every exit.
- Decide on a meeting place, such as the driveway or the mailbox.
- Draw a diagram of the house and mark the exit routes in red.
- Call 911 from outside the home.

Station Tour

Probably one of the first public educational functions you will be given is a station tour. These are usually given to school-age children as part of a field trip, but they may also be requested of visitors of all ages to the fire station. If the tour involves young children, be sure they are managed by the adults for safety and that the adults know where to gather the children if an alarm sounds for a response. It is extremely important that the children are gathered and accounted for before moving the apparatus from the equipment bay.

You should begin by introducing yourself. Then talk about the history of your fire department, some of your activities at the fire station, and perhaps what it takes to become a firefighter. When describing becoming a firefighter, explain the training you have had and give them some attributes they will need, such as obtaining their education, being physically fit, having the ability to get along well with others, and, above all, being willing and eager to help the community. Stress that, today, anyone can become a firefighter who has the desire and the ability.

Next, conduct the walking tour, making sure you keep the tour participants together, especially smaller children. Explain the different apparatus and how each is used at a fire. It is never advisable to allow anyone to get on a fire apparatus. You can, however, allow them to see your PPE and how it is worn. Reinforce the point about the protection you need to enter a building on fire to emphasize the protection they don't have in a building fire. This will also allow smaller children to see what a firefighter may look like when he or she comes into the building to find them. Move slowly and gently, and try not to scare the children while you do this.

Complete the station tour with a closing discussion about how to call the fire department for an emergency and perhaps some discussion of Stop, Drop, and Roll for the children.

General Public Presentations

Your crew may be asked to go to community functions to show the fire truck, or to take part in a fire prevention week demonstration. In order to be able to give a short fire prevention presentation to a small group, you may want to use the following checklist:

1. *Prepare.* Review the topics you are going to cover. Perhaps outlining your thoughts on a 3 × 5 card would help.
2. *Be sincere.* Public fire education is serious stuff—it really can save a life.
3. *Be informative.* Try to get as much good information across to your audience as possible, but also keep it short and concise. Cover no more than three or four main points.
4. *Try to be at ease.* No one expects you to be an accomplished public speaker, but you should be able to talk to a small group of people about your job, the fire department, and fire safety.

There are several topics you can cover during a public fire safety presentation. Here are a few ideas of informative topics you could touch upon:

1. What to do in case of a home fire
2. The 911 system and how it operates
3. The points in Operation EDITH (*exit drills in the home*)
4. Stop, Drop, and Roll Safety
5. The job of today's firefighter
6. Smoke detectors—what they are and how to maintain them

Do It!

Saving Lives Without Fighting Fires

The training you have received at this level has given you the knowledge and skills to enter a burning building and extinguish a fire. There is still a great deal to learn about the job, and if you keep an open mind, you will keep learning throughout your career as a firefighter.

Hopefully, this chapter has shown you that there is much to be done to prepare for the next fire through preplanning, building surveys, and hazard recognition. Perhaps more importantly, we have opened your eyes to your public education responsibilities as a firefighter. You are the Fire Department's ambassador for public safety. You must prepare yourself to be able to conduct home safety surveys as a member of the firefighting team. You need to be able to explain the need for and maintenance of smoke detectors in the home. Finally, you should be able to briefly discuss fire safety with the citizens of your community.

No one knows how many lives and how much property have been saved through good public fire safety education programs. There is no number, but it must be significant. Our goal is to not have to respond to these tragic events. Our goal is to stop them before they happen.

Prove It

Knowledge Assessment
Signed Documentation Tear-Out Sheet
Preplanning and Fire Prevention—Chapter 22

Name: _____

Fill out the ten-question quiz below, the Knowledge Assessment Sheet, by circling the correct answer for each question. When finished, sign it and give it to your instructor/Company Officer for his or her signature. Turn in this Knowledge Assessment Sheet to the proper person as part of the documentation that you have completed your training for this chapter.

1. _____ are familiarization sessions in which the crews that respond to a fire or other emergency in a building visit a business and tour their facility.
   a. Public education sessions
   b. Building surveys
   c. Area street surveys
   d. Operation EDITH sessions

2. The purpose of the building survey is to _____.
   a. determine the basic layout of the property
   b. gather any pertinent fire emergency information
   c. determine the occupancy use of the property
   d. perform an official in-depth fire inspection

3. A typical three-bedroom, wood-frame home in a subdivision is considered a _____ construction.
   a. Type III
   b. Type V
   c. Type VI
   d. Type II

4. A blocked designated building exit is a life safety hazard.
   a. True
   b. False

5. Frayed or damaged wiring, both fixed and flexible, is considered a(n) _____.
   a. target hazard
   b. life safety hazard
   c. fire hazard
   d. acceptable hazard

6. Flammable liquid and gas storage complexes located in a fire department's response area are considered a _____.
   a. fire hazard
   b. target hazard
   c. life safety hazard
   d. property hazard

7. A _____ is usually requested by the homeowner for the fire department to come by and take a look at their home for fire safety.
   a. building survey
   b. public education presentation
   c. home safety survey
   d. fire inspection

8. Which of the following are *NOT* checked during a home safety survey?
   a. The presence of a fire extinguisher in the kitchen
   b. Overloaded electrical receptacle plugs
   c. The presence of leaky faucets
   d. The presence of open or unapproved flammable liquid containers

9. It is recommended that there always be at least two smoke detectors on every living level in a home.
   a. True
   b. False

10. Which of the following is *NOT* on the checklist for giving a good public fire education presentation?
    a. Being an accomplished public speaker
    b. Preparing and reviewing the topics you are going to cover
    c. Being sincere regarding the serious nature of public fire education topics
    d. Being informative by trying to get as much good information across to your audience as possible while also keeping it short and concise

Student Signature and Date _____   Instructor/Company Officer Signature and Date _____

Prove It

Skills Assessment

Signed Documentation Tear-Out Sheet

Preplanning and Fire Prevention—Chapter 22

Name: _____

Fill out the Skills Assessment Sheet below. Have your instructor/Company Officer check off and initial each skill you demonstrate. When you are finished, sign this page and give it to your instructor/Company Officer for his or her signature. Turn in this Skills Assessment Sheet to the proper person as part of the documentation that you have completed your training for this chapter.

Skill	Completed	Initials
1. Participate in a building survey as a firefighting team member, assisting as assigned by the Company Officer.	_____	_____
2. Identify life safety hazards and fire hazards, given a list of conditions found during a building survey.	_____	_____
3. Identify probable target hazards from a list of properties located in the first response area of the fire department.	_____	_____
4. Participate as a member of the firefighting team conducting a home fire safety survey.	_____	_____
5. List ten things to check when performing a home safety survey.	_____	_____
6. Describe how a smoke detector works, where smoke detectors should be located, and how many should be installed in a given building.	_____	_____
7. Conduct a station tour for a small group of citizens or their children.	_____	_____
8. Describe the Stop, Drop, and Roll, and Operation EDITH Public Education Programs.	_____	_____
9. Discuss how to prepare for a fire education talk for a small group.	_____	_____

Student Signature and Date _____   Instructor/Company Officer Signature and Date _____

Safe Firefighting Part 2

Level 2

LEADING THE TEAM

The Level II Firefighter

What You Will Learn in This Chapter

This chapter will introduce you to the third level in our program, the Level II Firefighter. You will learn about the general role of a Level II firefighter, your responsibility for preparedness for and operations at various types of emergencies, and some of the non-emergency duties you will be asked to perform.

What You Will Be Able to Do

After reading this chapter, you will be able to:

1. Describe the basic elements of the National Incident Management System at the Operations Level.

2. Establish, assume, pass, and transfer Command at a typical incident.

3. Give a clear arrival report.

4. Take an order.

5. Assign tasks.

6. Perform basic documentation using the National Incident Reporting System.

7. Inspect, maintain, and test a fire hydrant and document the results.

Reality!

Organization and Preparedness

Safe emergency operations, whether while fighting fires or working a complex rescue scene, are the result of proper training, physical conditioning, and endless work in preparing for the various types of emergencies we may encounter. Each of these elements—training, conditioning, and preparation—are effective during an emergency only when organized and controlled by an effective Command System.

The Level II firefighter is an individual who has the proper training and physical ability to work as a firefighter, who has the ability to initiate the Incident Command System at an emergency, and who can effectively lead a team in the safe completion of a task while operating under the control of the Incident Commander. Don't confuse a Level II firefighter with a qualified Company Officer. The Company Officer is qualified to lead the team at an emergency and is administratively responsible for every aspect of their job performance, both emergency and nonemergency.

To be a good leader at this level, one must be an excellent follower. While a Company Officer employs various strategies when developing an action plan during the initial phases of an incident, the Level II firefighter is more likely to take an order from the Incident Commander and perform a given task rather than strategize and develop an overall action plan.

In reality, nearly everything we do during our nonemergency activities is crucial to our safety. As a Level II firefighter, you will be asked to lead a team to perform emergency and nonemergency tasks, all in support of our goal of safe operations at every level. For example, developing a water supply at a fire is dependent on having an available and working source of water. During an emergency, leading a junior firefighter through the steps of securing a hydrant and coordinating the hookup to the pumper is a task easily coordinated by a Level II firefighter. During nonemergency preparations, leading a few team members in testing hydrants for proper flow and operation, and then recording the results in the department's hydrant records, helps ensure a proper water supply when a fire breaks out.

The Level II Program

The National Fire Protection Association defines a Level II firefighter as someone who can assume and transfer Command within an Incident Management System, and who can perform the assigned duties

FIGURE 23-1   A Level II firefighter should be able to work within and as part of the Command structure at a fire.

FIGURE 23-2   Level II firefighters take on some of the nonemergency responsibilities that help us prepare for emergencies.

safely. This requires the ability to determine the need for Command, organize and coordinate an Incident Management System until Command is transferred, and function within an assigned role in the Incident Management System (Figure 23-1).

Tactical considerations and procedures for working at rescue scenes, flammable liquid and gas fires, and interior firefighting are all part of the Level II program. We will be looking at these topics in the next few chapters to help prepare you for working in these situations.

A Level II firefighter should also be able to take responsibility for nonemergency operations such as hydrant testing, station maintenance, and other preparations that support the organization. This requires teamwork and the ability to organize and lead a team to the completion of these tasks (Figure 23-2).

Incident Management System

Any incident that requires more than a single company to operate requires coordination by a single Incident Commander. Coordinating the event calls for everyone to operate under a Command structure and use standardized language when communicating on the scene. The **National Incident Management System (NIMS)** is the recognized system for managing emergency operations in North America. NIMS is designed to work for all types of emergencies, not just fires, and works well in managing large nonemergency events as well.

An Incident Command System is built from the ground up as units arrive on the scene. As more units arrive, Command of the incident is usually transferred to ranking officers who have more experience in dealing with multiple units operating under a larger Command structure. However large and complex the incident and the Command structure becomes, it begins with the first arriving unit, usually under the Command of a Company Officer.

FIGURE 23-3 A formal Command system is established at every incident involving more than a single company.

KEY WORD

National Incident Management System (NIMS) The system designed and recognized by the United States Fire Administration for managing emergency and nonemergency operations in North America.

KEY WORDS

arrival report The initial report transmitted over the radio that describes the situation and the initial actions of the first arriving crew(s).

establishment of Command An Incident Command System begins when the first arriving officer establishes Command.

status report A verbal report that is transmitted over the radio periodically, updating the responding units and others of any progress or needs during an emergency.

Establishing Command

Under NIMS, if it is apparent that the incident will require more than a single unit to operate, the ranking officer of the first arriving unit **establishes Command,** giving the Command a name (usually the geographic location). He or she transmits an **arrival report** over the radio, giving the location of the Command post, describing the initial actions that are under way, and requesting additional support if needed. The Incident Command structure at this point is fairly simple, a single company working under a single Commander. Even if the incident is controlled with only a single unit, there is still an Incident Commander in charge. The first Commander of the incident develops the initial strategy for handling the emergency, and assigns the first tasks with the goal of taking care of the problem and bringing everyone home safely. As the scene progresses, the Incident Commander will transmit periodic **status reports,** giving a real-time update on the actions and progress of the incident and calling for additional resources to support the operation (Figure 23-3).

Give a Clear Arrival Report

A good arrival report will tell what is happening, what or who it is happening to, where it is happening, and what kind of help you need to bring the incident to a safe and favorable outcome. By the end of the arrival report, everyone listening to the radio should have a good mental picture of the situation so they can begin their own mental size-up.

As help arrives on the scene, the Incident Commander may **transfer Command** to a ranking officer, who **assumes Command** of the incident once he or she has been briefed about the situation and is prepared to take responsibility for the incident. This should be done face-to-face whenever possible. If the incident grows larger, Command can be transferred as

FIGURE 23-4 Command is transferred, preferably with a face-to-face meeting, as ranking officers arrive on the scene.

many times as necessary to build and staff the Command structure as needed (Figure 23-4).

Some agencies allow the first arriving officer to **pass Command** to the next arriving officer without going through the step of establishing Command, then transferring it to the next arriving officer. This is most often the case when two units arrive at nearly the same time, and the first arriving unit positions at the best tactical location for an initial fire attack. In this case, the first arriving officer should give an arrival report and then clearly pass Command to the next arriving officer, who will then establish the Incident Command System.

KEY WORDS

assuming Command An officer will assume Command from another. The initial Command structure is established by the first officer and is then assumed as it is transferred to other officers.

passing Command On rare occasions, the first arriving officer will pass Command responsibility to the next arriving officer. This usually occurs only when both units arrive at nearly the same time.

transfer of Command The act of transferring Incident Command responsibility from one Incident Commander to another.

Incident Organization

A common management principle is that, to be effective, a manager should have three to seven subordinates, with the ideal number being five. This is called the **span of control.** To keep a large scene organized within a proper span of control, the Incident Commander will divide the forces at most day-to-day emergencies into **divisions** and **groups.**

Divisions are designated to divide a large incident into smaller geographic pieces. The divisions are designated clockwise, starting at the front or street side of a building, for example, and working around the building. If there is no "front" side of the incident, then start at the Command post and work around. Divisions that describe this type of geographic area are usually designated with letters, starting with Division A at the front and working around to Division D. The floor number may be used for divisions that are designated for different levels inside a multistory structure, so Division 3 covers the third floor, for example. During a typical small-scale incident, Division Supervisors usually answer to the Incident Commander. Other levels of organization may be added between a Division Supervisor and the Incident Commander if the size of the incident is large or the incident is complex.

Groups are designated according to job function (Figure 23-5). Some examples of groups are the fire attack group, the ventilation group, and the salvage group. Group Supervisors may work within the framework of a division, but they can move from division to division during an incident. As a courtesy, a Group Supervisor will keep the Division Supervisor apprised of the group's actions (Figure 23-6).

Some positions within the **Command Staff** may work outside divisions and groups, and answer directly to the Incident Commander. Some examples of these positions are the Safety Officer and the Personnel Accountability Officer. At very large, complex, or long-term incidents, the Incident Commander may divide Command responsibilities among a **General Staff.** Operations, Logistics, Finance, and Planning are some of the staff positions that may be designated at such incidents (Figure 23-7).

If the incident is the type that requires other emergency agencies to work together, such as a natural disaster, each emergency response agency (for example, fire, police, and national guard) will have its own Incident Management structure. The Incident Commanders of each of these Command structures will work together in a **unified command system.**

While it is important to know that these positions exist within a complex Incident Management structure, your main focus at this point should be the Incident Commander, Division Supervisors, and Group Supervisors. These are the elements of the Command structure that will directly interact with you as a Level II firefighter.

FIGURE 23-5 Divisions are assigned by geographic location, while groups are assigned by task.

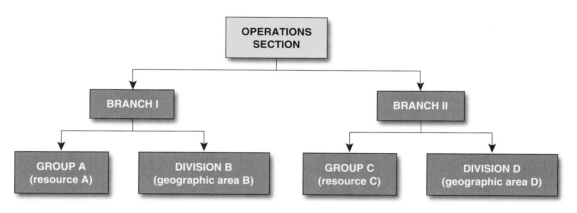

FIGURE 23-6 A typical Incident Command System at the operational level.

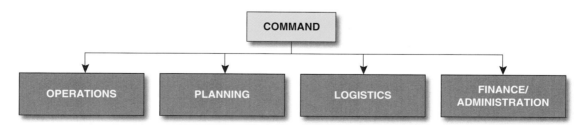

FIGURE 23-7 The Incident Command System may expand at large, complex incidents.

KEY WORDS

Command Staff   Special staff positions designated by the Incident Commander. Command Staff members answer directly to the Incident Commander.

division   An area of Command responsibility, usually designated by geographic location. A Division Officer answers to Command.

General Staff   Divisions of responsibility assigned at large, complex, or long-term incidents that are assigned to individuals who answer directly to the Incident Commander. Some members of the General Staff may include Operations, Logistics, Finance, and Planning Officers.

group   An area of Command responsibility that is usually designated by task.

span of control   A management principle that states that, to be effective, a person can manage five to seven subordinates at any given time.

unified command system   Commanders working together in a joint command post when different agencies work at a single event.

Teamwork

Every team needs a leader. The leader of a fire company is usually the Company Officer. However, there are times when a task is assigned to a group of firefighters working under the specific control of a Level II firefighter. For example, a single engine company staffed with four people arrives on the scene of a car fire. The pump operator is responsible for operating the fire pump, and the Company Officer becomes the Incident Commander, responsible for everyone's safety. The hose team responsibility may be left to the remaining two firefighters, with one firefighter in charge of the line's operation. Although they are working under the close supervision of the Company Officer at this point, the actual direction of the nozzle and positioning during the attack is controlled by the senior firefighter on the line. This requires certain elements of leadership.

Staffing at many fire departments requires that hose teams working at structure fires be led by firefighters. There are simply not enough officers to staff a Command system and be on every attack line as it is advanced into a structure. Although this situation is not ideal, experienced firefighters trained to Level II usually fill the need of leading the hose teams.

Receiving Orders

The first step in leading a team is to receive the order to do so. While this sounds simple, there is an art to taking an order. First of all, be sure you heard the order clearly. Orders are best given face-to-face, but often it is necessary to transmit them over the radio. Portable radio traffic can be intense during an active operation, so be sure that the order was intended for you, and confirm that you fully understand the order by repeating it back to the person who gave you the order.

Next, be sure that you are capable of performing the task you've been assigned, and that all safety precautions have been addressed. If you lack the training, equipment, or staffing to carry out a given task, then it is very important that you relay that information to the officer who gave you that order. If you see something that is clearly outside the level of acceptable risk, then relay that information up the Command chain for clarification. You may see something that the Commander doesn't.

Safety Tip!

Blind Obedience Is Dangerous! When given an order, do not blindly rush to complete the task without looking around first. Be sure the proper safety precautions have been addressed, and that the person who assigned the task is aware of any potential dangers that have not been addressed. To blindly jump into action can be deadly to you and your crew. If you are not absolutely sure that the risks have been addressed, employ the fundamentals of risk assessment we covered in Chapter 12 before taking action.

Once you are certain that you understand the order you've been given and that it is within your capabilities, relay the information to your team. Again, make sure they understand the mission before you start. This usually takes only seconds with a well-trained crew; however, if it takes a minute to explain the operation fully, then take the time to do so.

Upon completion of the task, give a status report to the next person up in the Incident Command System. It is important that you report your completion of the task, and transmitting your status report is even more important if you were unable to complete the task for any reason. It is essential that the Incident Commander is constantly working with current, reliable information.

Documentation

An incident report is completed after each alarm. These reports become part of the public record and are available for use by anyone needing information on the incident. Because of privacy issues regarding medical treatment, calls for Emergency Medical Services usually require an additional medical report, which are covered by law to protect the patient's privacy. Complete and accurate information on every alarm is essential for properly documenting each alarm, and for compiling useful data for planning and prevention efforts. Accurate and truthful incident reports are imperative in any legal setting. Complete and accurate data is the key to constant improvement in our ability to deliver our services to the public. Most fire departments have a worksheet available that is useful for obtaining complete and accurate information from the affected people before you leave the scene of the incident.

Fire departments in the United States use the reporting system called the **National Fire Incident Reporting System (NFIRS)**. NFIRS is available to every fire department as a standardized tool to compile complete and accurate data, and most departments use the NFIRS system. NFIRS assigns code numbers for various elements of the fire report that allow the information to be computerized and then compiled in various ways to help in our planning and development (Figure 23-8). The reports may be completed on a computer, or handwritten on a multiple-copy form, depending on your jurisdiction. Each reporting station, such as your fire station, should have an *NFIRS Reference Guide* that will help you accurately and thoroughly complete an incident report. For further information about NFIRS, visit the United States Fire Administration website at www.usfa.dhs.gov. Here you will find current and detailed instructions on completing a NFIRS report.

▩ KEY WORD ▩

National Fire Incident Reporting System (NFIRS)
The incident reporting system developed by the United States Fire Administration and used by most fire departments in North America.

Nonemergency Activities

Because the Fire Department operates for the public, it is important that we are accountable for the public's money and trust, so records are a very important component of the Fire Service. There are several documentation requirements in addition to alarm reports. For example, detailed fuel records account for the expensive fuel we burn, and when combined with detailed maintenance records they allow us to determine how much each piece of equipment actually costs to operate. This helps us in our design and purchasing decisions for future equipment. Daily equipment check forms help us keep track of small problems, making sure they are repaired before they become big ones.

Breakout Box

Hydrant Testing Requirement

Maintaining and testing fire hydrants is typically taught in conjunction with the water supply information that is part of the Level I firefighter standards. However, the NFPA Standards include hydrant maintenance and testing as a Level II skill. Because this information doesn't "fit" well with the other subjects presented in this section, and because a large component of this topic involves documentation and record keeping, we include it here.

Hydrant Maintenance and Testing

Other types of documentation are used to help maintain our readiness. Hydrant records are kept to make sure our valuable water supply is available when needed.

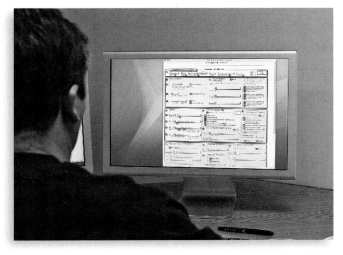

FIGURE 23-8 A typical NFIRS report may be completed on computer or by hand, depending on your jurisdiction.

Level II

FIGURE 23-9 Annual hydrant inspection and maintenance is critical to our operational readiness for fighting fire.

FIGURE 23-10 Allow a hydrant to flow slowly for a few minutes to flush out any debris or sediment that may be in the line.

FIGURE 23-11 Feel for suction, which indicates that the hydrant is draining properly.

Testing hydrants properly requires two hydrants to be flowed at the same time, and this job often falls to a Level II firefighter who is working as part of a team.

Hydrant Inspection and Maintenance

Hydrants are inspected for general maintenance and accessibility. Look for any obstructions or debris around the hydrant, or any vegetation that may have grown up around the hydrant. The hydrant must be visible from the street so it can be easily found when needed. Be sure that the hydrant's openings are at the proper height above ground so that they are accessible when needed, or at least 18 inches above grade level. It is not uncommon for landscapers or construction workers to pile dirt around a hydrant, reducing the clearance above grade to less than 18 inches, which makes it difficult to hook hydrant appliances to the hydrant (Figure 23-9).

 Safety Tip!

Look Out for Critters! All sorts of insects, especially fire ants and spiders, tend to nest around fire hydrants. Watch your step and look out for holes or soft ground around the hydrant that could trip you. Wear gloves whenever you operate a hydrant.

Remove all of the port caps from the hydrant, inspecting them for an intact gasket and making sure that they operate properly. Next, replace two of the caps and open the hydrant just until water flows slowly from the open port. This will flush out any debris or dirt from the barrel (Figure 23-10). Shut down the hydrant and hold your hand over the open port, feeling for a slight suction as the hydrant's barrel drains (Figure 23-11). If

the hydrant doesn't drain, report it to the appropriate water department for repair. Water left in the barrel will cause damaging rust, and in colder climates can freeze, leaving the hydrant unusable. A light coating of oil or graphite on the port threads will help prevent rust and keep the caps working smoothly.

Hydrant Testing

Every hydrant in a water distribution system should be tested annually. Testing a fire hydrant helps ensure that the hydrant is serviceable and ready for use when needed. A hydrant test measures the pressure and quantity of water that is available for firefighting purposes, and is recorded for use in preplanning and fire operations. When we test a hydrant, we measure the water pressure when the water is at rest and when it is flowing, so we can later use tables or computer software to calculate the amount of water that is available for fighting a fire. The measurements are:

- *Normal Operating Pressure*—The pressure when water is not moving through the hydrant, but during the community's normal periods of consumption. Some call this *static pressure,* but the term *static* describes a time when no water is being used from the distribution system, which is never the case during normal hydrant testing.
- *Residual Pressure*—The pressure that remains when the hydrant is flowing. This pressure is measured when a second hydrant nearby is flowing, leaving an actual residual value.
- *Flow Pressure*—The pressure of the water that is discharging from a port during a hydrant test.

To measure these pressures, we use a **cap gauge** and a **pitot gauge.** The cap gauge measures the normal operating pressure and the residual pressure, while the pitot gauge measures the flow pressure at the center of a moving stream of water at the point where it exits the hydrant.

▨ KEY WORDS ▨

cap gauge A device used to measure the normal operating pressure and the residual pressure of water flowing from a fire hydrant.

pitot gauge A device used to measure the flow pressure at the center of a moving stream of water at the point where it exits the hydrant.

 Tip!

Notify the Water Department Before Flowing Hydrants

As water distribution systems age, a brown scale or black sediment usually builds up on the inner surfaces of the pipe. This tends to collect and remain in place under normal operating conditions. However, when a hydrant is opened and then closed too quickly, chances are that some of the scale and sediment will become dislodged and appear in normal tap water nearby. Slowly opening and closing a hydrant, and flowing it for at least 5 minutes to flush out the scale, will usually help prevent this from happening, but it can still occur. Notify the water department that you will be flowing hydrants in an area, so they can monitor the water pressures and also so they will be able to answer any complaints they receive about the water quality.

FIGURE 23-12   Use the bleeder valve to exhaust all of the air from the hydrant before recording the normal operating pressure.

FIGURE 23-13   The normal operating pressure is the pressure when the water is at rest.

To conduct a hydrant test, place a cap gauge on a hydrant and open the hydrant slowly. There should be a bleeder valve on the cap gauge to exhaust trapped air. Open the bleeder until a steady stream of water comes out and then close the bleeder. Record this pressure as the static pressure (Figures 23-12 and 23-13).

Now a second firefighter will open another hydrant on the same water main. The remaining pressure on the first hydrant is then recorded as the residual pressure (Figure 23-14). The firefighter at the second hydrant uses a pitot gauge to measure the pressure at the center of the flowing water and records the flow pressure (Figure 23-15). Remember to continue flowing the hydrants for a full 5 minutes to flush out any scale or sediment from the distribution system.

Conclude the test by making sure that the hydrant drains properly when shut down, and that the port caps and gaskets are in good working order.

Level II

FIGURE 23-14 The pressure on one fire hydrant will drop when another hydrant is opened on the same main. The pressure remaining on the first hydrant is the residual pressure.

FIGURE 23-15 A pitot gauge measures the flow pressure at the middle of the stream.

Once the pressures have been recorded on the hydrant record, calculations can be made to determine the amount of water available for fighting a fire from these hydrants. Pay close attention to the residual pressure on a system. It should be at least 20 psi. Report any residual pressure that is under 20 psi, or any hydrant that flows an unusually low residual pressure when compared to other hydrants on the same system.

Practice Safe Firefighting

Becoming a Level II firefighter is your first step in taking on more responsibility as a firefighter and helps prepare you for future leadership roles. It is important that you take seriously the role and responsibility of leading a hose team, working within a Command system, and performing important documentation and preparedness duties. In everything you do, you should keep in mind your own safety and the safety of everyone else on your team. The Level II program covers more advanced topics such as rescue, foam firefighting, fires in pressurized gases, and tactical considerations for structural firefighting. Take on this role with safety in mind at every step.

Prove It

Knowledge Assessment
Signed Documentation Tear-Out Sheet
Level II Firefighter—Chapter 23

Name: _____

Fill out the ten-question quiz below, the Knowledge Assessment Sheet, by circling the correct answer. When finished, sign it and give to your instructor/Company Officer for his or her signature. Turn in this Knowledge Assessment Sheet to the proper person as part of the documentation that you have completed your training for this chapter.

1. The Incident Command System recognized for emergency operations in North America is called the _____.
   a. United Fire Reporting System
   b. National Command System
   c. National Fire Command System
   d. National Incident Management System

2. The Command system described above is useful only for emergency operations.
   a. True
   b. False

3. You respond to a fire from home and arrive at the scene before the responding units. You have a portable radio assigned to you by your department. Because you are the only person at the scene, there is no need to establish Command.
   a. True
   b. False

4. What is the normal span of control for an effective manager?
   a. 3 to 5
   b. 5 to 7
   c. 6 to 10
   d. It depends on the manager's experience.

5. An officer is assigned to an area of geographic responsibility that covers the rear of a building fire. This officer is typically designated as _____.
   a. Division B
   b. Division C
   c. Group 3
   d. Division 3

6. An officer assigned to handling operations on the third floor of a five-story building is typically designated as _____.
   a. Group 3
   b. Third Floor Group
   c. Third Floor Division
   d. Division 3

7. A person in charge of a team of firefighters who are working as the salvage team is typically designated as _____.
   a. Salvage group
   b. Salvage division
   c. Group E
   d. Division E

8. A group leader will typically communicate directly to the Incident Commander.
   a. True
   b. False

9. Most fire departments in the United States use which reporting system?
   a. The National Fire Data Base
   b. The National Fire Reporting System
   c. The United Fire Reporting System
   d. The National Fire Incident Reporting System

10. A pitot gauge is used to determine a hydrant's _____ pressure.
    a. flow
    b. residual
    c. operating
    d. static

Student Signature and Date _____   Instructor/Company Officer Signature and Date _____

584

Prove It

Skills Assessment
Signed Documentation Tear-Out Sheet
The Level II Firefighter—Chapter 23

Name: _____

There are no specific skills associated with this chapter.

Student Signature and Date _____   Instructor/Company Officer Signature and Date _____

585

Interior Fire Attack

What You Will Learn in This Chapter

This chapter is a bit unlike most of the others in this book. Our focus up to this point has been on the skills and tactics you will employ as a firefighter to do the work. This chapter focuses more on the strategy of operating at a structure fire rather than on the tactics we use. In this chapter, you will learn about the role and responsibilities of a Level II firefighter when, on occasion, you are ordered to lead a hose team for an offensive attack on a structure fire.

What You Will Be Able to Do

After reading this chapter, you will be able to:

1. List, in order, the three incident priorities of a structure fire.
2. Perform a brief size-up of a structure fire.

3. List and explain the nothing-showing, fast-attack, and command modes as they relate to the initial command of a fire.
4. List and explain offensive, defensive, and transitional strategy modes.
5. List, in order, and explain the strategic priorities at a fire, including rescue, exposures, confinement, extinguishment, and overhaul.
6. Determine the desired fire flow for a structure fire using the National Fire Academy formula.
7. Select the proper attack line for a given fire, taking into consideration the staffing available.
8. Determine the proper positioning for a backup attack line.
9. Explain the basics of proper radio procedures during a fire, including an explanation of priority and emergency radio traffic.

587

10. Explain the basic steps of sizing up fire conditions in a multistory building based on visible conditions from outside the building.

11. Explain some of the problems involved in accessing a fire in a multistory commercial building.

12. Explain and demonstrate the safe use of a Fire-Service-equipped elevator.

Reality!

No Building Is Worth Our Lives

We have said repeatedly throughout this book that no building is worth the life of a firefighter. The risk-versus-gain decisions that take place at any fire must be made with this principle in mind if we are to survive. Unfortunately, at many fires that resulted in traumatic injury and/or death to firefighters, the casualties occurred when conditions deteriorated and there was no adjustment in the risk assessment of the situation. The responsibility for safety and survival at a structure fire is much too important for a single person to bear. It is everyone's responsibility. It is essential that our approach to a fire is organized and systematic, and that the Incident Commander constantly evaluates the risks based on reports from fireground officers and firefighters and also based on an ongoing visual assessment of the fire building and fire conditions. Safety depends on an organized, coordinated attack on the fire, with everyone accountable for his or her location and operating conditions at all times. To accomplish this, it is often necessary for the Company Officer to remain outside while the attack team enters the structure under the supervision of a Level II firefighter.

Safety Lesson: A NIOSH Report

In June 2003, two Tennessee firefighters died while trying to escape a commercial structure following a partial roof collapse. The fire occurred in a single-story, strip-type mercantile structure with a flat roof supported by lightweight steel bar joists. Light smoke conditions were present when the first units arrived on the scene, and the Company Officer from the first engine company established command. The Incident Commander was joined by the Company Officer from the second arriving engine, and the two entered the structure to search for the source of the smoke. It was reported later that the store manager was possibly inside, but this was after the initial entry. This was a false report by a well-intentioned bystander.

The two Company Officers found slightly thicker smoke in the back of the structure and encountered a closed office door in the back room area. A crackling sound was heard behind the door, and they opened the door to investigate, encountering heavy fire conditions that prevented them from closing the door. They immediately ordered an attack line be advanced to their location.

By this time a Battalion Chief had assumed the role of Incident Commander and had established a formal Incident Command Post outside the structure. A truck company was ordered inside to pull ceiling tiles to check for fire overhead as attack lines were advanced. When the ceiling was pulled, a possible backdraft occurred in the trussloft and there was a partial roof collapse.

The Company Officer who had been the first Incident Commander on the scene made a radio transmission ordering everyone out of the building. Intense heat and smoke forced crews outside. Within 12 minutes of their arrival, the same officer transmitted a Mayday call for help, stating that he was trapped inside. Because the initial Incident Commander was part of the entry team, no information was passed on to the Battalion Chief who assumed Command after the initial fire attack was launched. The fact that no information was passed on probably led to confusion as to who was inside the building and who was trapped. A Rapid Intervention Team (RIT) made entry and ran into a Lieutenant who was out of air. Thinking he was the person who had called the Mayday, they assisted him from the structure. A Personnel Accountability Report (PAR) was taken, and it was discovered that the person who made the original call for help was still inside the structure. The RIT made a second entry, where they encountered a firefighter who was struggling to remain conscious. They removed him and called for another PAR, which confirmed that two firefighters were now missing. A third entry was attempted, but the team was blocked by debris from the collapsed ceiling.

Two separate PASS alarms were heard sounding inside the structure. A separate Rescue Group was formed, and they were able to extricate one of the victims. They later breached an exterior wall to remove the second victim. Both victims died from their injuries.

Follow-Up

NIOSH Report #2003-18

Among many other recommendations, the NIOSH Investigative Report (#2003-18) concluded that:

- Fire departments should ensure that the first arriving Company Officer does not become involved in firefighting efforts when assuming the role of Incident Commander.

- Fire departments should ensure that the Incident Commander conducts an initial size-up and risk assessment of the incident scene before beginning interior firefighting operations.

- Fire departments should ensure that ventilation is closely coordinated with the fire attack.
- Fire departments should ensure that firefighters immediately open ceilings and other concealed spaces whenever a fire is suspected of being in a truss system.
- Fire departments should ensure that the firefighters performing firefighting operations under or above trusses are evacuated as soon as it is determined that the trusses are exposed to fire.
- Fire departments should consider using a thermal imaging camera as a part of the size-up operation to aid in locating fires in concealed areas.

We will address each of these recommendations and other essential points in this chapter.

FIGURE 24-1 Get as good a look at as many sides of the fire as you can while making your size-up.

Arrival, Initial Command, and Size-Up

A common mistake that many firefighters make is assuming that the initial size-up of an emergency is the responsibility solely of the Company Officer. In reality, we should all size up the situation to make sure we have a clear picture of what is really going on and what dangers we should address with our initial actions. No firefighter should go blindly into any dangerous mission without observing, thinking, and planning for the action that is about to take place. Observe—Think—Plan—Take Action. These are the key steps at any emergency.

 **Safety Tip!**

Remember the Two-In/Two-Out Rule Unless it is necessary to rescue a person trapped in the building, entry should not be made until a team of at least two equipped and qualified firefighters are designated as the outside safety team.

Size-Up (Observe and Think)

While responding to and arriving at a fire, we should stop and think about the foundation of our mission, the incident priorities. Incident priorities at a fire are—in order—life safety, incident stabilization, and

property conservation. When you first arrive at the scene of a structure fire, you should conduct a quick but systematic size-up of the situation. Get as good a look at the building as you safely can. In the case of a small single-family house, it is often best to make a quick 360-degree survey of the building so you have a good mental picture of the situation. Larger buildings are often too big for a full 360-degree survey to be practical. Your initial arrival report over the radio will be based on your first look at the fire, and will alert the incoming units as to what to expect so they can better form their plan (Figure 24-1).

During your initial size-up, quickly determine as best you can the extent of the fire, based on visible smoke and fire conditions, the size of the building and construction type, any obvious threats to life based on the fire and building or occupancy type, exposures, and the location of a sustainable water supply sufficient to handle the fire. A second look at the building should help you determine the location of access and egress points, ventilation points, and any other hazards or special considerations you may have.

 **Tip!**

Imagine the Fire's Next Move
When determining the extent of the fire as you arrive on the scene, consider where the fire will be in 10 minutes if you do nothing to stop it. The initial fire attack may take a few minutes to set up and occur, so you should consider where the fire is going, not where it is right now.

Level II

Command Mode

Along with the initial situation report comes the establishment of Command. The initial Command of a fire functions in one of three different modes, depending on the initial impression of the fire. These Command modes are:

Nothing-Showing Mode—If the first view of the building doesn't indicate any smoke or fire, then the initial Command of the fire will be operating in the nothing-showing mode. Some departments call this the investigation mode.

Fast-Attack Mode—When it is obvious that a fast attack on the fire will either facilitate a rescue or knock down a small fire before it has a chance to grow, the first-arriving Company Officer may decide to go with the crew to attack the fire and/or to make a rescue. The fast-attack mode should not last more than a couple of minutes.

Command Mode—Any situation that does not fall into the first two Command modes requires the coordination and organization of an Incident Commander operating from an established Command post.

Select a Strategy and Tactics (Plan)

Strategy is what needs to be done. Strategy at a structure fire should address rescue, confinement, ventilation, extinguishment, and property conservation. **Tactics** are what you need to do to get those things done. Tactics include things like developing a water supply, gaining entry, ventilating the building, conducting a primary and then a secondary search, protecting exposures, applying water to the fire, and salvage operations and overhaul.

▓▓▓ KEY WORDS ▓▓▓

strategy   The overall objectives at an emergency. Strategy is what needs to be done. The strategy at a structure fire, for example, includes rescue, exposure protection, confinement, extinguishment, and overhaul.

tactics   The duties that are performed to accomplish the strategic objectives at an emergency. Some examples of tactics include developing a water supply, performing forcible entry, venting a building, and conducting a search.

Strategic Mode

The strategy for a fire in a building fire falls into one of three modes:

Offensive Mode—Attack lines are operated within the collapse zone, most often an interior attack.

Defensive Mode—Attack lines and all personnel operate outside the collapse zone in a defensive attack.

Transitional Mode—This mode is used to switch between the offensive and defensive mode.

When deciding whether to make an offensive, interior attack on a structure fire, everything must be in place to safely support that mission. Certainly if a life is at stake, then the risk-versus-gain ratio favors being aggressive in the rescue and fire attack. However, if a building is so heavily involved in fire that interior occupants have little chance of survival, this tips the risk-versus-gain scale heavily toward the risk side and does not favor aggressive action. Before making the decision to mount an aggressive offensive attack on the fire, consider the amount of resources you have available, making sure you have the staffing and water available to support your actions.

Support the Strategy

The most important strategy at any emergency is a rescue strategy. The incident priorities of life safety, incident stabilization, and property conservation should be addressed in order. After life safety concerns that require an immediate rescue, the strategic priorities for a typical building fire include exposures, confinement, extinguishment, and overhaul. The tactics we use should support one or more of these strategies. When staffing or a sustained water supply isn't available, the stream from the first line employed may be flowed on an exposure building rather than on the burning building to protect against further property damage. While this water contains the spread of the fire, it does nothing to confine the fire itself. Lines may be positioned to flow into hot smoke rather than flames to reduce the heat and help prevent flashover, thereby confining the fire's growth. Other lines may by advanced to the seat of the fire, where the water is applied directly to the flames for extinguishment. Several considerations come into play when selecting, staffing, and positioning attack lines at a structure fire (Figure 24-2).

When the resources are available to support an offensive, interior attack strategy, then it is important to select the proper size and number of attack lines to mount an attack that will overwhelm the fire in as short a time as possible. It is essential that we support the fire attack with the proper number of people working together in a systematic way within the Incident Command System. The Incident Commander makes the assignments, and each team's leader is responsible for making sure that the assignment his or her team receives is within their capabilities and that the team stays together throughout the operation. This is especially true when working inside a structure fire.

FIGURE 24-2 Use short bursts of water into the superheated smoke overhead to help confine the fire.

Desired Fire Flow

The amount of water needed to fight a structure fire is determined by the size of the fire and the number of exterior and interior exposures. Although there are several formulas that can be used to determine the necessary fire flow, the most commonly accepted formula in use today was developed by the National

FIGURE 24-3 To ensure that your team is accounted for, tell the IC who you are, where you are, what you are doing, and how many people are with you.

Fire Academy (NFA). The NFA formula is a tool that is best used to preplan a fire; it helps you determine the amount of water in gallons per minute you need to flow over a period of 30 seconds to knock down a structure fire. This simple formula states that the desired fire flow in gallons per minute of a totally involved, single-story building is one-third the building's square footage. Mathematically speaking, the desired fire flow formula is:

$$GPM = \frac{L \times W}{3}$$

where GPM = desired fire flow in gallons of water per minute, L = length of the building, and W = width of the building (Figure 24-4).

But what if only about a quarter of the building is burning? Then simply multiply the original answer by 25% (or .25). Half the building is burning? Multiply by 50%.

The NFA formula also assigns an additional 25% value to any exposures, either interior or exterior, of the building. For the purposes of this formula, consider any combustible building within 30 feet of the fire side of a building to be an exposure (Figure 24-5).

Line Selection

Several considerations come into play when selecting the size attack line you will use. At first glance, we may say that big fires need big attack lines. While this is true, other factors to consider are the building's size, the building's configuration, and the number of qualified firefighters available to staff the lines. Obviously, larger diameter lines with a 2½- to 3-inch range flow more water and have a greater reach than smaller-gauge lines of the same length. However, because they are more cumbersome than their counterparts, large attack lines take more time and more staffing

Level II

$$20 \times 30 = 600 \qquad \frac{600}{3} = 200 \text{ gpm}$$

FIGURE 24-4 The desired fire flow for a totally involved building is the square footage of the structure divided by 3.

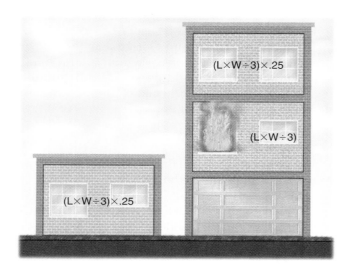

$(L \times W \div 3) \times .25$

$(L \times W \div 3)$

$(L \times W \div 3) \times .25$

FIGURE 24-5 Exposures are assigned a 25% value of the original fire flow.

to deploy than a small attack line of 1¾ inches and are very hard to maneuver in the tight confines of an occupied building. This is why most residential fires are attacked using the smaller of the two lines. However, it is important that we flow enough water to overwhelm the fire by absorbing the heat while also protecting the firefighters on the line. Too small a line means the fire will grow to unsafe proportions. Do not fall into the habit of always pulling a 1¾-inch attack line every time for every fire because you "always do it that way," or you will pull too small a line when faced with a fire in a large commercial structure. The size line you pull must be capable of applying enough water to knock down the fire if you are engaged in an offensive attack (Table 24-1).

TABLE 24-1	Attack-Line Size and Staffing for Interior Fire Attack	
Attack-Line Size	**Fire Flow**	**Staffing Required**
1¾ inches	150 gpm	2
1¾ to 2 inches	240 gpm	3
2½ to 3 inches	300 gpm	4+

Staffing is also a consideration when selecting the initial attack line. Although the desired fire flow for a large two-story building may be in the 250 gpm range, if you only have two people available to staff the line, you may as well plan on making an exterior attack, rather than trying to snake a 3-inch attack line up the stairs and through the building with only two people. Doing so simply isn't practical or safe.

Remember, the staffing requirements listed in Table 24-1 are for an interior attack line. For example, a 3-inch attack line is heavy and, when operated on the interior of a building during an offensive attack, takes extra people to bend the hose around corners or deploy under high-heat, low-visibility conditions. A 3-inch attack line operated during a defensive exterior attack can be positioned in a loop in a static position where a single firefighter can operate it comfortably from a sitting position.

Back Up the Attack

When properly staffed, an initial attack line of proper size that is connected to a sustainable water supply should be capable of knocking down the fire in short order. However, unless it is totally obvious that the

FIGURE 24-6 This 3-inch attack line is being advanced to back up the initial 1¾-inch attack line.

initial attack lines will quickly extinguish the fire, safe habits and common sense call for a backup attack line any time we enter a burning structure. Too many things can go wrong. Nozzles can clog, lines can be cut by falling debris, or the fire can simply get too big to handle with a single line. A backup team with a charged attack line should be right behind the initial attack team to support their efforts. If the first line fails, the second line can be immediately deployed for everyone's safety. If the initial line can't deliver enough water to stop the fire, then maybe the second line can make up the difference needed to do the job. The same considerations apply when selecting the proper size line for the backup line as for the initial attack line (Figure 24-6).

Safety Tip!

Backup Lines Are Dedicated Some consider a charged hose line sitting in the front yard a backup line. A backup line is of no use when it is sitting in the front yard, especially when it is not staffed. It is dangerous to think that an attack crew can escape a fire, grab a second line, and reenter the building if something goes wrong. Backup lines are not to be used for exposure control, confinement, or other uses. They should be dedicated to supporting the initial attack lines for safety.

Coordinated Attack

An interior attack crew must coordinate their entry with the forcible entry and ventilation crews, and with other teams operating outside the fire. Fresh air flow-

FIGURE 24-7 The Incident Commander will assign the point of entry for the attack lines.

ing into a building that is opened before the attack lines are positioned and ready to enter can cause the fire to grow rapidly, thus working against the first two strategic priorities of rescue and confinement, and can certainly make the third priority, extinguishment, much more difficult. A growing fire can turn the conditions from survivable to nonsurvivable within seconds, especially if there is a flashover, thus reducing the chance for a rescue of anyone trapped inside.

Have a plan for your attack, and communicate that plan. Most often the Incident Commander will assign the entry point for the attack (Figure 24-7). Attack crews should never freelance. When choosing an entry point for most offensive attacks, it is best to move from the unburned side of the fire toward the burning side, so you can confine and extinguish the fire. However, it is often difficult to do this when the fire is burning nearest the most accessible point of entry, due to problems accessing the rear of the structure with a hose line. For example, a fire burning in the living room of a 1,500 square foot single-story house with a fenced-in backyard may have fire pushing out the front windows and door. Moving to the rear of the building with two attack lines could take more time than it would take for the fire to spread throughout the house. In this case, the fire should be overwhelmed with water from the front, knocking down the flames quickly before it can spread.

Avoid opposing attack lines, especially on smaller structures. Attack lines flowing from opposing sides can push heat and flames toward the other crew. Flowing a line from the outside while a crew operates inside goes against the principles of ventilation and can be dangerous to any crews working inside the building.

Maintain the crew's integrity at all times. If someone experiences a problem that causes them to evacuate the structure, then allow the backup team to take over and evacuate as a team. Never allow a person to exit a building alone—they can become disoriented and lost in the smoke.

 Safety Tip!

Check for Hidden Fire It is essential that we recognize the hazards of working under, or above, truss roof structures. Anytime a wood-truss roof is exposed to flames, it is time to evacuate the building. Create an opening in the ceiling as you enter a structure to check the roof structure for fire, and support that opening with a hose line if necessary.

Once you are in position, flow water and transmit a radio report of "water on the fire." This report tells the Incident Commander that the fire conditions should start changing soon, and that if they don't, then tactical adjustments will need to be made. Constantly monitor your progress and the effect you are having on the fire. If the fire doesn't respond immediately to your attack, then you may need more water from a second attack line, or possibly you aren't hitting the seat of the fire from your position.

Monitor your team's condition as you go. It is best that we have verbal, physical, and visual contact with each other as much as possible under poor visibility conditions; however, at least two of the three should be maintained at all times. If you can't see each other, then hold on to a boot or coat of your partner as you go, or at least maintain a grip on the hose line. If you can see and hear each other, there is no need to keep physical contact, but stay within reach of each other as much as possible during the early stages of the fire. Remember, light smoke conditions can turn into heavy smoke, zero-visibility conditions in seconds (Figure 24-8).

Communication Is Key

Simultaneous to the fire attack, a primary search should be conducted by a dedicated search crew. Ventilation teams should open the building vertically

FIGURE 24-8 Maintain verbal and physical contact with each other during poor visibility conditions.

and/or horizontally nearest the fire as you enter so your attack will push the heat and flames out ahead of you. Utilities should be controlled by outside crews, and truck crews should open ceilings and walls, searching for hidden fires as you go. It can all be confusing without proper communications between working crews and the Commanders outside. Keep your radio on and monitor it constantly. It can be very loud inside a burning building, so listening to the radio is often a hard thing to do. The following is a sample list of some milestones that should be reported over the radio as the operation progresses:

- Entering the building (Company ID, entry point, and number of team members)
- Primary search under way
- Primary search complete
- Water on the fire
- Fire under control
- Ventilation under way (and the vent point location)

On occasion, there is a need for **priority radio traffic.** Examples of these situations are when a rescue is under way, a hazard is identified, or a fire is growing. Priority radio traffic includes messages that are important for everyone's safety or to the operation, and are out of the ordinary. When someone calls for priority radio traffic, all other radio transmissions should stop momentarily so that person can get his or her message out.

Emergency radio traffic is one step above priority traffic. Obviously, a Mayday distress call is an example of emergency radio traffic. A call for an emergency evacuation of the building is another example of emergency radio traffic. Once emergency radio traffic is requested, no other radio transmissions should occur unless directed by the Incident Commander.

KEY WORDS

emergency radio traffic A radio message that contains information critical to life safety. Emergency radio traffic supersedes all other radio traffic, which should cease until the emergency message is acknowledged and the emergent situation has been stabilized.

priority radio traffic A radio message that contains important, out-of-the-ordinary information that is essential to safety or to the overall mission.

Exit as a Team

Once your team has been relieved by another company or the fire is out, exit the building promptly. Do not hang around inside the building more than is necessary. Transmit a message over the radio reporting that your team is out of the building, the location of your exit, and how many members you have with you. You will probably be assigned to a rehab area or to another task.

Take a moment to check your crew as you exit. Look at the condition of their gear and their physical appearance. Sometimes protective gear can be moved or dislodged during a fire. If you see any exposed skin, check the person for burns. If a member looks overly tired or is displaying any signs of pain or other physical difficulty, notify the appropriate officer and get medical attention for that firefighter. Don't forget to have someone check you as well. Don't let your pride cause you to ignore signs and symptoms of medical or physical problems. The most important thing is to take care of each other (Figure 24-9).

Working Inside Multistory Commercial Buildings

There are many accepted definitions describing buildings over 2 stories tall. Low-rise structures are usually defined as buildings 2 or 3 stories in height; mid-rise buildings are from 4 to 7 stories, and high-rise buildings are anything over 7 stories tall. Whether a building is 1 story or 100 stories tall, the strategic priorities for fighting a fire are the same: rescue, exposure protection, confinement, extinguishment, and overhaul. The strategy remains the same. However, the tactics we use when working on floors above the ground level are usually hindered because access to upper levels in a building takes time and reduces the number of accessible ventilation, entry, and exit points. Even if the fire is on a floor accessible by a fire department's aerial device, the access is still limited when compared to a single-story building.

Fortunately, unlike single-family dwellings, modern commercial buildings are designed with features

FIGURE 24-9 Continue to monitor your team members' condition after exiting the building, looking for signs of injury or other medical problems.

FIGURE 24-10 A typical standpipe connection may be located at each landing of a stairwell and on the roof.

that help support our tactics. Automatic fire alarms give early warning of a fire. Exit stairwells are often pressurized to keep smoke and heat out, allowing the occupants a better chance of escape and giving advancing firefighters a protected area to work from. Automatic sprinkler systems and self-closing fire doors are designed to confine a fire, giving us time to mount an attack. In a building that has standpipe connections on each floor, we do not have to snake hose up the entire length of a stairwell (Figure 24-10).

Level II

FIGURE 24-11 Even when the standpipe is supplied by a built-in fire pump, we should augment the water supply using the standpipe connections outside.

All of the fire protection systems within a building are designed to work together for safety. However, to rely totally on technology to take care of the fire would be foolish. Final extinguishment often comes down to firefighters putting water on the fire (Figure 24-11).

All of the procedures for fighting a fire in a multistory or high-rise building have filled several books and are being refined every day. It is not our intent to teach high-rise firefighting in this brief chapter. Instead, we will look at some of the tactics and various tips for the hose team working inside.

Size-Up for Multistory Buildings

Like at any fire, there should be a quick and systematic size-up of the building. Although as a Level II firefighter you probably won't be in command, and you might not even arrive with the first-due companies to the scene, it is still important for you to be able to gather some personal information about the fire from your initial observations.

One of the first things to consider is what type of building is involved. The floors of residential buildings, such as apartment, condo, and hotel occupancies, are usually separated by a lot of walls and hallways, which can help keep the fire contained to a smaller area. Office-type structures often have wide-open floors where people work in cubicles separated by thin partitions that do not extend to the ceiling. In this case, the fire can grow quickly to involve the entire floor if not confined by an automatic sprinkler system. To add to the problem, the partitioned-off spaces create a maze for crawling firefighters.

Another thing to consider is how the building's fire protection systems are performing when you arrive. If the fire alarm panel or outside water gong indicates a water flow on an upper floor, then chances are there is (or was) a fire on that floor. If the alarm panel indicates smoke or heat on a floor but there is no indication of sprinkler activation, then there can still be a fire, but chances are that it is in early stages of development.

Finally, if there are visible indications of fire showing from the outside of the building, look closely at the conditions you see. If the fire appears to be free-burning and heavy smoke and flames are issuing from a broken window, then the fire is venting outward somewhat. If you see a glow of fire through broken glass but do not see much smoke or flame coming out of the window, then the fire may be on the windward side of the building—in which case the wind levels at the upper floor might be pushing the flames back inside, creating a very intense, dangerous condition for advancing firefighters.

Inside the building there are several indications of the layout of the fire floor. In many multistory commercial buildings, each floor is a repeat of the floor below and is typically laid out in the same configuration. Hopefully there is a pre-fire plan available for your reference that indicates the locations of stairs, elevators, and standpipe connections. If not, look at a lower floor to get an indication of how the fire floor is laid out.

There are typically two locations for the stairs in a multistory building: on the ends of the building and near the core of the building. In larger buildings, sometimes both types are available. Enclosed stairs in a commercial building can be of two types: a **stairwell** or a **stair tower**. A stairwell is an enclosed and protected shaft inside the building and is often pressurized to help prevent smoke from entering the shaft (Figure 24-12). Whenever enclosed stairs are located in the building's core, they are always in a stairwell. Stairwells are also situated on the end of a building. A stair tower is a separate shaft built independently of the main building and connected to each floor by a breezeway or vestibule. This separate structure is usually not pressurized (Figure 24-13).

The stairwells and stair towers contain the standpipe connections for fire attack. On each floor there may also be standpipe connections that contain single-jacketed fire hose intended to be used for initial attack by the building's occupants. Do not rely on hose found in the building's hose cabinets. The nozzles on these lines are inferior to yours, and the hose may or may not be serviceable. It is essential that we take our own hose and nozzles with us when working inside a multistory building.

FIGURE 24-12 A stairwell is enclosed and contained within the building.

FIGURE 24-13 A stair tower is freestanding and connected to the building by breezeways or vestibules.

KEY WORDS

stairwell An enclosed stairway in a commercial building that is designed to prevent smoke and heat from entering the enclosure.

stair tower An enclosed stairway that is built as a separate shaft, independent of the main building, and connected to the building by breezeways or vestibules at each floor.

Go to *Safe Firefighting: Inside Operations,* Chapter 21, *"Large Buildings,"* and review *"Hooking Into a Standpipe Connection,"* then go to the *Safe Firefighting: Inside Operations* DVD, navigate to Chapter 21, and select and review *"Using a Standpipe Connection."*

Accessing the Fire Floor

Fighting a fire on the upper floor of a building requires us to haul our equipment and any backup equipment, such as spare air cylinders and forcible entry tools, to the fire floor for the attack. At least part of this operation involves grunt work to move hose, tools, and equipment up stairs. It takes time and a great deal of our energy just moving the equipment prior to fighting the fire.

It is imperative that the initial hose teams work under the control of an Officer on the fire floor. The initial attack line should be supported by three separate companies: the attack crew, a backup crew, and a crew in reserve to take over for the first crew, who will quickly fatigue after climbing stairs and making the initial attack. As a general rule, help that arrives later will stage two floors below the fire and advance to their assignments from that point.

How much climbing we do obviously depends on how far up the fire is located. Many fire departments consider the first seven floors to be totally accessible

Level II

It Takes Time to Climb

As a general rule of thumb, it takes a crew 1 minute per floor to climb while carrying a minimum of hose, spare air cylinders, and forcible entry equipment. This is for the first ten floors of the climb. After that, it takes about 2 minutes per floor. So a fire on the sixth floor of a building will have at least 6 extra minutes to burn before the first crews even reach the floor.

by climbing and therefore do not allow the use of elevators for fires on the seventh floor and below. Firefighters often consider the first seven floors as the "Lucky 7."

Fire Service Elevators

Elevators are dangerous when used improperly during a fire. An elevator opening directly on a burning floor can be deadly to firefighters inside. However, moving tools and equipment up dozens of flights of stairs is also dangerous. Properly operating elevators are designed to automatically return to the main floor of a building whenever a fire alarm is activated, where they remain out of service until the alarm is reset. Fire-Service-equipped elevators have a function in which a Fire Service key can be used to gain control of the elevator (Figure 24-14). The decision to use an elevator should be made by the Incident Commander based on several facts other than simply the location of the fire.

The first step in determining the feasibility of using an elevator to move people and equipment is to inspect the elevator room for smoke or fire. Next, open the elevator's doors and inspect the elevator shaft for smoke or fire. Look up through the space at the front of the elevator car, first without a light to look for the glow of a fire and then with a flashlight to look for smoke.

Next, check the function of the elevator. Insert the Fire Service elevator key in the control panel and switch it on. You will notice that the doors do not close automatically. This is because the firefighter control switch turns off all automatic functions. If you want the door to close, you have to press and hold the close button until the door is fully closed. Opening

FIGURE 24-14 A Fire-Service-equipped elevator should be clearly marked, and will have a key switch for Fire Service use only.

the door requires you to press and hold the door-open button. If you let go of the button as the doors open, they will immediately close. Once the doors are open, they will remain open and the elevator will remain locked on that floor until you take further action by closing the door and selecting another floor. Test the elevator on the second-floor landing and repeat the test every three floors on the way up.

Do not use an elevator to move any higher than two floors below the lowest fire floor. Instead, proceed to the proper stairs and walk up from there. Even though you are two floors below the fire, do not open the doors quickly before inspecting the conditions on that floor. Opening the door is a three-step process:

1. When you arrive at the desired floor, press and release the door-open button while looking out the crack between the doors.
2. If no smoke or fire is visible, allow the doors to open a bit wider on the next press of the button, again looking around for hazards.
3. Once you are certain that there are no hazards present, open the door fully.

Go to the DVD, navigate to Chapter 24, and select *"Fire Service Elevators."*

Practice It!

Using Fire Service Elevators

Practice the following steps for using a Fire-Service-equipped elevator:

1. Insert the key at the first-floor landing to recall the elevator to the first floor (Figure 24-15).

FIGURE 24-15

2. Inspect the hoistway for fire or smoke (Figure 24-16).

FIGURE 24-16

3. Check the machine room for fire or smoke before using the elevator (Figure 24-17).

FIGURE 24-17

—Continued

Level II

4. Remove the key, leaving the wall switch in the Fire Service mode, and insert the same key into the control switch inside the car (Figure 24-18).

FIGURE 24-18

5. Test the door-close button and then test the door-open button while still on the first floor (Figure 24-19).

FIGURE 24-19

6. Proceed to the second floor and test the full operation of the elevator. Repeat this test every three floors (Figure 24-20).
7. Proceed to the appropriate floor, usually two floors below the fire.
8. Open the door with a three-step process.

FIGURE 24-20

Do It!

Attacking Interior Fires Safely

Making an interior attack on a structure fire is one of the most dangerous kinds of work a firefighter will do. It takes endless training, preplanning, and a rigid Incident Command System to mount a safe interior attack. As a firefighter trained to Level II, there may be times when you are called upon to lead a hose team in an interior attack. The key word here is *team.* Listen to everyone during the operation and work within the structure of the Incident Command System. Remain aware of your surroundings and realistic in your expectations, and do not exceed your abilities. Remember, no building is worth a human life.

Prove It

Knowledge Assessment
Signed Documentation Tear-Out Sheet

Interior Fire Attack—Chapter 24

Name: _____

Fill out the ten-question quiz below, the Knowledge Assessment Sheet, by circling the correct answer. When finished, sign it and give to your instructor/Company Officer for his or her signature. Turn in this Knowledge Assessment Sheet to the proper person as part of the documentation that you have completed your training for this chapter.

1. All but which one of the following are incident priorities for a structure fire?
   a. Life safety
   b. Ventilation
   c. Incident stabilization
   d. Property conservation

2. All but which one of the following are command modes for a structure fire?
   a. Rescue Mode
   b. Fast-Attack Mode
   c. Nothing-Showing Mode
   d. Command Mode

3. When the attack lines and all personnel are operating outside the collapse zone, it is said that the strategy is _____.
   a. attack
   b. offensive
   c. defensive
   d. None of the above

4. Flowing water into hot smoke that is overhead to help prevent flashover is an example of which type of strategy?
   a. Confinement
   b. Extinguishment
   c. Exposure protection
   d. Overhaul

5. What is the desired fire flow for a 30 x 50 foot single-story building that is 50% involved in fire?
   a. 150 gpm
   b. 250 gpm
   c. 350 gpm
   d. 500 gpm

6. During a fire operation, you notice that the fire is growing despite the fact that you are flowing water on the fire. You need another hose team to assist in the attack. What type of radio traffic would you transmit at this point?
   a. Water on the fire
   b. Emergency traffic (and then make your request)
   c. Emergency traffic, evacuate immediately
   d. Priority traffic (and then make your request)

7. A hose team is advancing toward a fire involving a bedroom and its contents in a single-story, wood-frame house. It is a good idea to have a second hose team flow water through the window of the bedroom to cool it down as the interior team advances.

   a. True
   b. False

8. A fire is on the sixth floor of a 20-story building. How long after they start climbing would you expect the first hose team to arrive on the sixth floor?

   a. 3 minutes
   b. 4 minutes
   c. 5 minutes
   d. 6 minutes

9. A fire is on the ninth floor of the same building, and you decide to use the Fire-Service-equipped elevator for access. On which floor(s) would you pause to check the operation of the elevator?

   a. 2 and 5
   b. 3 and 6
   c. 3
   d. 5

10. At which floor would you leave the elevator if the fire is on the sixteenth floor?

   a. 15
   b. 14
   c. 13
   d. 7

Student Signature and Date _____   Instructor/Company Officer Signature and Date _____

602

Prove It

Skills Assessment
Signed Documentation Tear-Out Sheet
Interior Fire Attack—Chapter 24

Name: _____

Fill out the Skills Assessment Sheet below. Have your instructor/Company Officer check off and initial each skill you demonstrate. When you are finished, sign it and give it to your instructor/Company Officer for his or her signature. Turn in this Skills Assessment Sheet to the proper person as part of the documentation that you have completed your training for this chapter.

Skill	Completed	Initials
1. Operate a Fire-Service-equipped elevator.	_____	_____

Student Signature and Date _____   Instructor/Company Officer Signature and Date _____

25

Foam Firefighting

What You Will Learn in This Chapter

In this chapter you will learn about the techniques and extinguishing agents we use to enhance water's capability to extinguish a fire. You will learn about the different types of additives and the specialized tools and nozzles we use to create firefighting foam.

What You Will Be Able to Do

After reading this chapter, you will be able to:

1. Describe the characteristics of and list some of the common uses for Class A foam.

2. Describe the characteristics of and list some of the common uses for Class B foam.
3. Select the proper foam concentrate for the type of fire to be extinguished.
4. Demonstrate the batch method for Class A foam.
5. List and describe four different types of Class B foam.
6. Set up and use an in-line foam eductor.
7. Set up and use an air-aspirating foam nozzle.
8. Set up and break down a foam attack line.
9. Clean and maintain the foam equipment used on a typical firefighting pumper.

605

Reality!

Foam Operations

Because most fires that we respond to involve Class A combustibles, our natural choice of extinguishing agents is water. Water is abundant and efficient for most Class A fires. But even something as good as water occasionally needs help to remain in contact with the burning fuel long enough to absorb enough heat to stop the fire and prevent re-ignition of the fuel. When properly used, Class A foam works well in helping water do its job on a fire.

When Class B fuels burn, water needs a lot of help to extinguish the fire. Because water is heavier than most flammable liquids, fluids like gasoline and diesel fuel float on top of water and the fire keeps burning in spite of our efforts. Water alone can actually spread a flammable liquid fire by splashing the fuel onto other combustible materials, or by causing the fuel to overflow its container. To overcome this problem, we use extinguishing agents to smother the fire and to help water better absorb the heat of a burning liquid. A simple dry chemical fire extinguisher does a good job in snuffing out a small fire, but because of its limited size, the amount of fire it will extinguish is also limited. So, to combat a Class B fire of any consequence, we turn to foam.

Because using foam is not something we do on a daily basis, we often have problems developing a proper amount and quality of foam at an emergency. Most of our problems with foam operations are related to a lack of practice with, or maintenance on, the foam equipment. To overcome this, we must train often on the proper deployment, application, and cleanup procedures related to foam operations so we can work safely and efficiently at flammable liquid fires.

Firefighting Foam

Firefighting foam is a general term used to describe many additives that, when properly proportioned with water and air, create a group of bubbles that is superior to water when it comes to absorbing heat and isolating the burning fuel from both air and flames (Figure 25-1). There are many different types of foam, each with different characteristics and uses that allow us to tailor the type of foam we produce to best match the type of fuel that is burning. There is no foam made that works best for all applications. For now, let's categorize the types of foam according to the type of fuel, similar to the way we classify fire extinguishers—Class A and Class B.

FIGURE 25-1 Foam is made when the proper amounts of water and air are mixed with additives.

FIGURE 25-2 Class A foam concentrate is clearly marked as such.

Class A foams are relatively inexpensive, detergent-based additives that work well in helping to keep water in contact with burning Class A fuels instead of running off before it absorbs heat. Class A foam can be mixed with water in various concentrations, depending on the quality of foam needed for a given fire. The foam either helps the water soak into the burning material, or it clings to the surface of the material and slowly releases the water as it smothers the fire. Class A foam is widely used in wildland firefighting and structural firefighting as well. However, if applied to a burning Class B fuel, Class A foam evaporates rapidly and will not do an adequate job of stopping a fire of much consequence (Figure 25-2).

Class B foams are designed specifically for burning liquids and therefore are hearty enough to withstand the heat when properly used. There are many different types of Class B foams that are matched to the type of liquid that is burning. Class B foams form a blanket of bubbles that help cool and smother the fire. Most Class B foams form a film or membrane of agent that helps prevent oxygen from fueling the fire. And even though Class B foams would work well in extinguishing a Class A fire, they are usually more expensive to use than most Class A foams and, in many cases, have qualities that make them less suitable for everyday use (Figure 25-3).

FIGURE 25-3 Class B foam concentrate is clearly marked as such.

 Safety Tip!

Because the foams we are discussing in this chapter contain water, it should be assumed that the foams will conduct electricity, so these foams are not to be used near energized electrical equipment or any Class C fire.

What Makes Foam

Firefighting foam is created when we mix a **foam concentrate** that is specially designed to mix with water to form a **foam solution,** and then with air at the nozzle to form a blanket of bubbles called **finished foam.** Each bubble contains water and foam concentrate, and because of the air they contain, the finished foam floats on top of most flammable liquids, smothering the flames (Figure 25-4).

A good place to start in understanding the basic principles of firefighting foam is to go to the kitchen and wash the dishes. If you fill the sink with water and then drip some dishwashing liquid into the sink without the water running from the faucet, the soap will suspend in the water. If you gently stir the soap into the water, the mixture turns into a soap solution, but there won't be many soapsuds floating on top. This is because you have water and soap concentrate, but no air to make the bubbles. But if you add the dishwashing liquid into the water stream as it flows from the faucet while filling the sink, the soap and

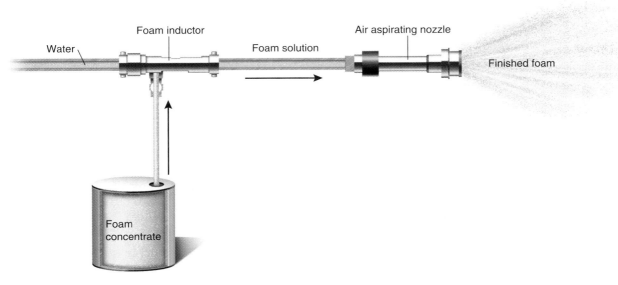

FIGURE 25-4 When foam concentrate is added to the water, it becomes a foam solution. The addition of air at the nozzle creates the finished foam.

Level II

water become agitated and mix with air that is picked up by the flowing water, and you end up with a nice, thick blanket of suds on top. The thick blanket of suds contains water and concentrate (dishwashing soap), similar to the finished foam used for firefighting.

So, as demonstrated by our dishwashing soap example, it takes three things to make finished foam: concentrate, water, and air. And to make them work together, the concentrate and water must be mechanically agitated to form a solution, and the air must be mixed in at the proper rate to form the bubbles.

Unlike our dishwashing soap example, making firefighting foam is a little more technical than simply pouring foam concentrate into the flowing stream of water as it leaves the nozzle. Although this *may* work in making foam, there would be no uniformity in the concentration of foam in the finished bubbles. So the next point we should consider is that good firefighting foam is the result of combining the three ingredients—concentrate, water, and air—*in the proper proportions.* If we add too much concentrate, we will run out of concentrate long before we run out of fire. If we add too much air, the bubbles will be nice and big, but they won't carry much water or concentrate to the fire. If we add too much water, the result will be little or no foam blanket at all, and what little bit of finished foam we happened to create with our crude efforts would be washed away by the periods of time when just water was flowing into the blanket of foam.

KEY WORDS

finished foam   A mixture of water, foam concentrate, and air that results in a stable mass of bubbles called a foam blanket. It is used in extinguishing a Class B fire.

foam concentrate   Foam liquid before it is mixed with water to become a foam solution. Foam concentrates come in many different types.

foam solution   A mixture of foam concentrate and water as it travels through the hose and before it is mixed with air at the nozzle.

Safety Tip!

The quickest way to ruin a good blanket of finished foam is to keep flowing water after you run out of foam concentrate. Water alone will wash away the finished foam and expose the surface of the flammable liquid, which will often cause the fuel to re-ignite.

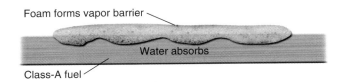

FIGURE 25-5   Class A foam is used to extinguish and pretreat Class A fuels to make them more resistive to fire.

Class A Foam

Class A foam has two main characteristics that make it desirable for fighting fires: It makes a nice foam blanket, and it helps break the **surface tension** of water, allowing the water to better soak into burning materials. Class A foams are mixed with water at a very low concentration of about 0.1% to 1% by volume, so it is efficient and economical to use (Figure 25-5).

KEY WORD

surface tension   The tension that results from the particles of a fluid that tend to be attracted to each other at the fluid's surface. This "tension" often causes the molecules of the fluid—in this case, water—to cling together rather than soak into the object the liquid touches. Class A foams tend to break down the surface tension of water, allowing it to better soak into the material it contacts.

Breakout Box

Class A Foam

Class A foam has a number of properties:

- It distributes the water out over the Class A fuel, increasing the water's effectiveness, absorbing three times more heat than plain water, and reducing suppression time.
- It releases the water slowly, allowing it to cool the fuel, reducing overhaul time.
- It holds together well, rather than breaking apart like plain water, so it can be used to pretreat a Class A fuel ahead of an approaching fire.
- It penetrates the fuel by breaking down the surface tension of water, raising the moisture content of the Class A fuel so that there is less chance that it will re-ignite.

Because Class A foam is used at a very low concentration, it is often developed using a batch method in which the concentrate is added to the booster tank water before it is pumped on the fire. As little as half a gallon of concentrate can be mixed into 500 gallons of tank water for an effective foam solution. Class A foam can also be proportioned at higher concentrations using foam equipment described later in this chapter.

Compressed Air Foam System (CAFS)

Many fire departments use a compressed air foam system (CAFS) for their Class A foam application. A CAFS uses an on-board air compressor to introduce air and foam concentrate into selected attack lines, where it mixes with the attack water to form finished foam in the line. This results in a rapid knockdown of a Class A fire, and greatly enhances overhaul. A smooth-bore nozzle is used when a Class A system is employed, because the aeration of the foam solution has already occurred at the pump and the foam can be applied without further agitation (Figure 25-6).

 Safety Tip!

Because a CAFS uses compressed air, there is an initial "kick" to the nozzle when you first open it. Expect and prepare for the sudden backpressure by pointing the nozzle down toward the ground as you first open the bale, allowing your body weight to help control the brief but sudden "kick."

FIGURE 25-6 When a CAFS engine is used, the Class A foam is delivered using a smooth-bore nozzle.

Class B Foam

When flammable liquids are involved in fire, the vapors rising from the surface of the liquid burn—not the liquid itself. As the liquid is heated, it boils and liberates vapors at a faster rate, and the fire intensifies. Although water applied to a metal container holding the burning liquid has a good cooling effect and will help prevent re-ignition of the fire once it is extinguished, water alone won't suppress the vapors. Also, because water sinks to the bottom, water alone does little to cool the liquid. Firefighting foam works well to extinguish a flammable or combustible liquid fire by excluding oxygen from the surface of the liquid with a blanket of bubbles that contain foam concentrate and water. This blanket of bubbles allows the water to cool the surface while the foam reduces the amount of vapor rising from the surface of the liquid. Foam also creates a membrane that separates the fuel's surface from the flames, insulating the liquid and stopping the fire (Figure 25-7).

Breakout Box

How Foam Extinguishes Fire

Firefighting foam extinguishes flammable or combustible liquid fires in four ways:

1. It excludes air from the flammable vapors.
2. It eliminates the rate of vapor release from the fuel's surface.
3. It separates the flames from the fuel's surface.
4. It cools the fuel surface and the surrounding metal, which helps reduce the chance that the fuel will re-ignite.

FIGURE 25-7 Class B foam works on the surface of the fuel to separate the fuel from the flames.

There are many types of Class B foam concentrates available. Each has been formulated to meet a specific need, and each has characteristics we should know. The more commonly used types of Class B foam are:

- Protein foam
- Fluroprotein foam (FP)
- Aqueous film-forming foam (AFFF)
- Alcohol-resistant aqueous film-forming foam (AR-AFFF)

Protein Foam

Protein foam concentrate is made from natural products such as hoof and horn meal, chicken feathers, and other proteins mixed with stabilizing agents and other additives to help prevent corrosion, prevent decomposition, and control the foam's viscosity. Protein foam was developed to be used exclusively on hydrocarbon fuels.

Fluroprotein Foam (FP)

Fluroprotein foam (FP) concentrate is a protein-based foam with additives that enhance the protein foam's ability to extinguish the fire and to resist the degradation of the foam that can result when the finished foam comes into contact with hydrocarbon fuels. In addition, fluroprotein foams perform well against many of the oxygenated fuel additives used today.

Aqueous Film-Forming Foam (AFFF)

Aqueous film-forming foam (AFFF) is one of the most popular foam concentrates used for hydrocarbon fuels. AFFF has a synthetic base with additives that help it create a thin film or membrane of foam solution over the surface of a hydrocarbon fuel, instead of sinking like regular water, so it separates the fuel from the oxygen source, smothering the fire.

Alcohol-Resistant Aqueous Film-Forming Foam (AR-AFFF)

Alcohol-resistant aqueous film forming foam (AR-AFFF) is a foam that has special qualities that allow it to form a vapor-suppressing layer on hydrocarbon fuels. These qualities also allow it to work well on fuels that contain polar solvents, including alcohols, ketones, and others. The membrane of a normal AFFF may be attacked by the polar solvent while the membrane of an AR-AFFF resists the effects of a polar solvent. Because polar solvents that are found in gasohol or the new E85 fuels can quickly degrade typical AFFF, AR-AFFF is becoming more popular for use.

Foam-Making Equipment

When switching from plain water to Class B foam operations, we must add two components to a typical hose-line setup. First we need a way to introduce the right amount of foam concentrate into the water stream as it flows through the hose to create a foam solution. Then we need a way to add air to the solution so that it becomes finished foam.

Foam-Proportioning Devices

Foam-proportioning devices are used to introduce the proper amount of foam concentrate into the water stream to create the foam solution. This occurs before the solution passes through the nozzle. Each type of foam concentrate is designed for a specific percentage mixture with water. The most common Class B foams are designed to work at mixtures between 3% and 6% concentrate mixed in water. Most Class A foams work well at 1%. The desired percentage is found on the foam concentrate container. There are several types of foam-proportioning devices, the most common of which is the **in-line foam eductor** (Figure 25-8).

An in-line foam eductor gets its name from its position in the hose line. The in-line eductor is added to the hose line, usually one or two sections away from the pump. To draw foam concentrate into the water stream, the eductor uses a simple venturi that is created from the pressurized water flowing through a small chamber into a large chamber inside, where the pressure drops. The change in pressure siphons the foam concentrate through a **pickup tube** that is inserted in the foam concentrate container at the desired proportion to create a foam solution in the hose line, downstream from the eductor (Figure 25-9). A

FIGURE 25-8 An in-line foam eductor is the most common type of foam-proportioning device.

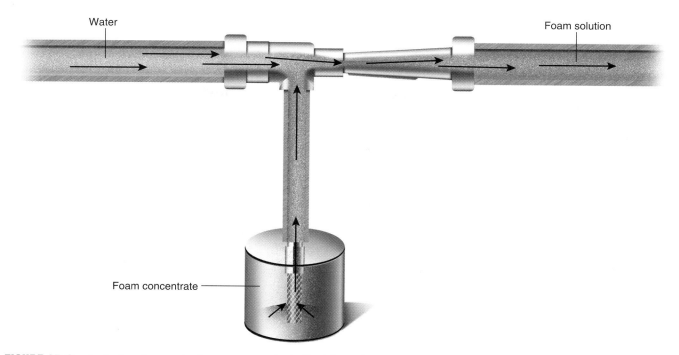

FIGURE 25-9 An in-line foam eductor uses a venturi effect from the passing water to siphon foam concentrate through the pickup tube.

flow setting on the eductor allows you to adjust the amount of foam concentrate that is proportioned into the attack line.

In-line eductors rely on the drop in pressure as the water passes through the eductor so they can work. If the pressure is too high on the discharge side of the eductor, which is often the case if the nozzle isn't opened fully or there is a kink in the line between the nozzle and the eductor, then the eductor will not draw foam concentrate into the water stream. If the pressure is too low on the supply side of the eductor, usually because the pump operator is not pumping the line at the appropriate pressure, then the eductor

Eductors designed for a 1¾-inch hose are usually rated to flow at 60, 95, or 125 gpm. Eductors for 2½- to 3-inch lines are usually rated to flow about 250 gpm. The eductor must be matched with a nozzle that is set to flow the same rate. If you are using an adjustable flow nozzle, be sure to match the nozzle to the gallons per minute flow that is indicated on the eductor. A common cause of problems flowing foam solution through an in-line eductor is a mismatch between the nozzle and the eductor.

won't work either. This is why it is extremely important to match the appropriate nozzle with the foam eductor so that both are set to flow at the appropriate pressure and volume.

▓ KEY WORDS ▓

foam-proportioning device A tool used to introduce the correct amount of foam concentrate into water to result in a well-proportioned foam solution. The most common type of foam-proportioning device is the in-line foam eductor.

in-line foam eductor An appliance that uses a venturi to draw foam concentrate in the correct proportions from a supply source into the water stream as it flows through a hose line to create a foam solution in the line.

pickup tube The tube on an in-line foam eductor that is inserted into the foam concentrate supply so that the foam eductor can draw the appropriate amount of concentrate from the source and introduce it into the water stream.

Other causes of problems with in-line eductors include backpressure from a nozzle that is operated at an elevation higher than the eductor and too much friction loss caused by too long a hose stretch between the eductor and the nozzle. The friction loss between the pump and the eductor is a factor when the eductor

Level II

is attached in line with the hose and not directly to the pump panel. Another common problem is a blockage in the pickup tube or inside the eductor, usually caused by a failure to properly flush clean the eductor after a previous use. It is extremely important that eductors remain clean so they can work accurately.

Most manufacturers suggest that their foam eductors be flushed thoroughly with fresh, clean water after every use. Follow the manufacturer's instructions for the appropriate procedures that apply to the brand of eductor your department uses.

Foam Nozzles

Once the foam concentrate is proportioned into the water stream, the resulting solution quickly travels to the nozzle, where, if it is mixed thoroughly with air, it becomes finished foam. Some nozzles work better than others in adding air to the foam solution.

Because air is picked up by a fog pattern nozzle, foam can be created by using a conventional firefighting nozzle. (Again, be careful to match the flow of the nozzle with the flow of the eductor.) However, this foam is usually much lower in quality than the finished foam created by an **air-aspirating foam nozzle** (Figure 25-10). An aspirating foam nozzle discharges the foam solution into an expansion chamber, which creates a sudden drop in pressure and draws air into the stream. The amount of pressure drop varies with the brand and style of aspirating foam nozzle, and so does the distance each type of nozzle can eject the finished foam. As a rule of thumb, nozzles with short, wide expansion chambers will create a good-quality finished foam, but will discharge it a shorter distance than a nozzle with a narrow, longer expansion chamber. However, the foam blanket created by the nozzle with the longer expansion chamber will sometimes be thinner, and contain more water, than the blanket created by a nozzle with a wider expansion chamber.

It is most likely that the foam nozzles and proportioning devices carried by your department have

FIGURE 25-10 An air-aspirating foam nozzle introduces air into the stream of foam solution, which produces the finished foam bubbles.

already been matched and tested, so a mismatch in equipment will not be a problem. Predetermining the proper match of foam equipment ahead of time, testing the equipment's ability to create a good blanket of finished foam, and proper cleaning and maintenance will prevent the most common problems with foam operations and reduce the time it takes to troubleshoot a foam setup during an emergency.

▰▰ KEY WORD ▰▰

air-aspirating foam nozzle A firefighting nozzle that develops a suction to draw the proper amount of air into a stream of foam solution as it leaves the nozzle, resulting in a quality blanket of finished foam.

⇨ Practice It!

Establishing a Foam Line

The goal of this drill is to help you locate, inspect, and set up the equipment to establish a foam-capable attack line. This drill is usually performed using training foam; however, take the time to look at each type of foam your department uses.

1. Locate the foam concentrate, foam eductor, and foam nozzle, and inspect each item for damage and the manufacturer's instructions (Figure 25-11).

FIGURE 25-11

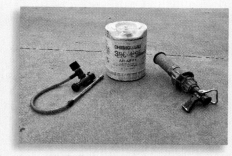

2. Set the eductor's flow adjustment to match the desired percentage that is printed on the foam container. For Class B foam, this is usually between 3% and 6% (Figure 25-12).

FIGURE 25-12

3. Connect the foam eductor in-line with the attack line, preferably 100 feet behind the nozzle (Figure 25-13).

FIGURE 25-13

4. Flow the line and observe the eductor and nozzle in use (Figure 25-14).

FIGURE 25-14

How to Apply Foam

Making good-quality, finished foam is important, but no more important that properly applying the finished foam to the fire. The main difference in how Class A and Class B foams are applied is in the fuels, not in the foams themselves. Class A materials are solid, so with Class A foam, application is usually a straightforward process—simply aim the stream at the base of the fire and keep flowing it until the fire goes out. An additional application method for Class A foam is pretreating the material ahead of the flames. This technique is usually employed during wildland firefighting, where the natural fuels are coated with a blanket of foam ahead of the fire or on the other side of a firebreak, to help stop the forward progress of the blaze.

Because Class B fires involve liquids, application of the foam requires more finesse than spraying down a solid fuel. If you were to plunge the foam under pressure into a burning pool of gasoline, the fuel would splash and spread the fire. Flowing the foam over the fire to the far side of the pool would possibly cause the burning liquid to flow back toward you, which is never a good thing. Extinguishing a Class B fire with foam-equipped attack lines can usually

Level II

be accomplished with one of three methods: roll-on, rain-down, or deflection.

Roll-On Method

The roll-on method of applying foam (also known as the sweep method) involves building a ridge of foam across the face of the fire. As additional foam banks up, the blanket of finished foam will roll over the fire. This method is useful for a small- to medium-size fire that can be accessed from a single direction.

Rain-Down Method

The rain-down method for applying foam allows you to gently apply a blanket of foam over a large area. Working from one side of the fire to the other, lift the nozzle in an up-and-down manner to allow the foam to drop onto the fire under its own weight, rather than being plunged into the burning liquid while flowing rapidly from the nozzle. Take care to work methodically from one side to the other, rather than haphazardly, so that you can monitor the quality of the foam blanket as you apply it.

Deflection Method

Foam can also be deflected onto the fire. For example, if the fire is burning near a building, the foam can be sprayed onto the building, which absorbs the velocity from the stream and allows the foam blanket to build starting at the building and working outward.

View It!

Go to the DVD, navigate to Chapter 25, and select *"Foam Application Techniques."*

Practice It!

Foam Application Techniques

The goal of this drill is to practice the application techniques for foam, to learn their limitations, and to learn the need to often employ all three methods at a single fire. Select the appropriate nozzle, eductor, and concentrate (training foam), and then establish a foam line. Stop the flow of foam between each application method and allow fresh water to wash away the blanket from the previous attempt. Practice applying the foam over a 10 x 10 foot area using the following techniques:

1. **Roll-on method:** Allow a bank of foam to build at the front of the "fire" and practice pushing the foam until it rolls over the entire surface area (Figure 25-15).

FIGURE 25-15

2. **Rain-down method:** Working from one side to the other, use a rain-down technique to allow the foam to coat the entire area (Figure 25-16).

FIGURE 25-16

3. **Deflection method:** Use an obstacle, such as a building, to deflect the foam onto the area (Figure 25-17).

FIGURE 25-17

 **Tip!**

Too Much Foam Can Cause Problems

Once an adequate blanket of foam has been applied, stop flowing and let the foam work. Too much foam can get heavy and cause the foam blanket to deteriorate and be ineffective.

 Safety Tip!

Because most foam is detergent based, it becomes very slippery when mixed with water. Be careful not to slip or fall when walking through a foamed area. Also, walking through the foam blanket breaks the protective membrane and can release hazardous vapors that can flash. Do not walk through the blanket unless it is absolutely necessary for your escape, for a rescue, or for some other mission-critical action.

Cleaning Foam Equipment

Because foam is detergent based, it will clean away oils or protective coatings that help prevent metal from rusting or corroding. The natural corrosive tendencies of water can then attack metal parts. Flush any foam equipment with a lot of water after each use, and follow the manufacturer's guidelines for cleaning the equipment and placing it back into service.

 **Do It!**

Practice Foam Operations

The use of firefighting foam greatly enhances water's capability to extinguish a fire and often to prevent a fire from occurring. Because we do not use all of the foam equipment nearly as often as a typical attack line, we often encounter problems in setting up and deploying foam. Practice the techniques from this chapter often, and take the time to inspect the foam equipment on your unit to be sure it is serviceable and available for use.

Level II

Knowledge Assessment

Signed Documentation Tear-Out Sheet

Foam Firefighting—Chapter 25

Name: _____

Fill out the ten-question quiz below, the Knowledge Assessment Sheet, by circling the correct answer. When finished, sign it and give to your instructor/Company Officer for his or her signature. Turn in this Knowledge Assessment Sheet to the proper person as part of the documentation that you have completed your training for this chapter.

1. Firefighting foams are categorized by _____.
   a. the intensity of the fire
   b. the type of fuel that is burning
   c. the size of the fire's base
   d. the type of foam appliance you are using

2. Class B foams will work on Class C fires, but not as effectively as when used on Class B fuels.
   a. True
   b. False

3. If you run out of foam, continue flowing water to cool the area, even when the fire is out.
   a. True
   b. False

4. All of the following are necessary for a good blanket of finished firefighting foam *except*
   a. heat.
   b. air.
   c. water.
   d. foam concentrate.

5. At what percentage rate is Class A foam usually proportioned?
   a. 3% to 6%
   b. 2% to 5%
   c. 1% to 10%
   d. 0.1% to 1%

6. What type of foam is often developed using a batch method?
   a. AFFF
   b. Class A
   c. Class B
   d. Protein

7. What type of nozzle is usually the desired type for a compressed air foam system?
   a. Fog
   b. Distributor
   c. Smooth-bore
   d. Foam

8. Backpressure from the nozzle helps an in-line foam eductor pick up the correct amount of foam concentrate to form the foam solution in the line.
   a. True
   b. False

9. What is the first step for cleaning a foam eductor after using Class B foam concentrate?
   a. Soak it in hot, soapy water for an hour.
   b. Disassemble the eductor and wipe it dry.
   c. Lubricate the mechanism with a light film of oil.
   d. Flush the eductor with fresh, clean water.

10. The advantage of using an aspirating nozzle is that you do not need an in-line eductor to create finished foam.
    a. True
    b. False

Student Signature and Date _____   Instructor/Company Officer Signature and Date _____

Prove It

Skills Assessment
Signed Documentation Tear-Out Sheet
Foam Firefighting—Chapter 25

Name: _____

Fill out the Skills Assessment Sheet below. Have your instructor/Company Officer check off and initial each skill you demonstrate. When finished, sign it and give to your instructor/Company Officer for his or her signature. Turn in this Skills Assessment Sheet to the proper person as part of the documentation that you have completed your training for this chapter.

Skill	Completed	Initials
1. 1. Locate the foam concentrate and equipment on the unit.	_____	_____
2. Set the eductor's flow adjustment to match the percentage of the foam concentrate used.	_____	_____
3. As a team member, assist in stretching a charged attack line into the interior of a residential building.	_____	_____
4. Connect the foam eductor in-line with the attack line.	_____	_____
5. Flow the line and observe the eductor and nozzle in use.	_____	_____
6. Apply foam using the roll-on method.	_____	_____
7. Apply foam using the rain-down method.	_____	_____
8. Apply foam using the deflection method.	_____	_____

Level II

Student Signature and Date _____ Instructor/Company Officer Signature and Date _____

Flammable Gas Firefighting

What You Will Learn in This Chapter

In this chapter, we will begin with types of flammable gas and how gas is stored in the community. Then we'll continue with how leaks and spills are handled, and your role as a firefighter in these operations. We'll conclude with handling fires involving flammable gas cylinders and pipelines. This chapter is not a complete lesson in hazardous materials. It is intended as an introduction to handling flammable gas emergencies, showing you some of the hazards involved, the activities of the first-arriving firefighting team, and some typical ways that leaks, spills, and fires are controlled.

What You Will Be Able to Do

After reading this chapter, you will be able to:

1. Identify the hazardous material label for a flammable gas cylinder or tank.

2. Operate the shutoff valve on a typical natural gas pipeline for a single-family dwelling.

3. Operate the shutoff valve on an LPG storage tank.

4. Describe the initial evacuation zone established at a flammable gas fire.

5. Participate as a firefighting team member, both at the nozzle and as a backup on the hose line, in providing protection as a leak is controlled on a flammable gas cylinder or tank.

6. Participate as a firefighting team member, both at the nozzle and as a backup on the hose line, in providing protection as a fire is controlled on a flammable gas cylinder or tank.

7. Participate as a firefighting team member in applying water in the correct pattern and at the correct location on a tank or cylinder to help prevent a boiling liquid expanding vapor explosion (BLEVE).

Reality!

Controlling Flammable Gas Fires

A flammable gas is any substance that exists in a gaseous state at normal temperatures (70°F) and burns in a normal atmospheric mixture of air. These gases are used throughout the community, and they are transported and stored just about anywhere people work and live. They can be transported to the customer by pipeline, as in the case of natural gas (Figure 26-1). Or they can be transported in pressurized tanks and cylinders to individual customer storage tanks (Figure 26-2). Flammable gases provide energy for heating, cooking, laboratory, and manufacturing processes. Flammable gases are increasingly used as fuel for vehicles.

Flammable gases normally are safe to store and use. However, in rare instances they can be exposed to an adjacent fire or can become involved in fire on their own. Because they are so common, it is important for the Level II firefighter to be familiar with the general methods of controlling flammable gas fires.

Flammable gas leaks, fires, and explosions are some of the most dangerous and complicated incidents a firefighter will handle. These emergencies should be approached with caution. Prior to attempting leak or fire control, time must be taken to see what is involved, the extent of the emergency, and the resources needed. Never rush in to control these types of fire and leak emergencies.

You will not be expected to be in charge of an incident involving these gases. However, you should be able to work as a team member under supervision of a Company Officer to help control the emergency.

FIGURE 26-1 Natural gas is usually transported to customers by pipeline distribution systems.

FIGURE 26-2 Other flammable gases are transported by marine transport, rail, or truck in cylinders and tanks.

Categories of Common Flammable Gases

Based on how they are generally transported for final use, flammable gases can be categorized into two common and broad categories: natural gas and compressed gas.

Natural Gas in Pipelines

Natural gas is usually transported under pressure in an underground pipe grid system that originates at the source of the gas product. Customers are eventually connected to the pipeline system at their homes or businesses. This flammable gas occurs naturally and is retrieved from oil wells or as a byproduct of the distillation process for petroleum products. It is an odorless gas in nature, so an odor is added to the gas as it is transported through the pipeline systems. The gas is lighter than air and rises as it is released into the atmosphere.

You will find control valves near the building or facility using natural gas. These valves are turned in line with the pipe to open and perpendicular to the pipe to close.

Review It!

Go to *Safe Firefighting: First Things First,* Chapter 11, *"Single-Level-Dwelling Fires,"* and review *"Controlling Gas Utilities,"* then go to the *Safe Firefighting: First Things First* DVD, navigate to Chapter 11, and select and review *"Controlling Gas Utilities"* refresh your memory of how to turn the natural gas valve to the off position.

Additionally, natural gas can be liquefied for bulk storage in tank facilities or for maritime shipping. This form of natural gas storage is called liquefied natural gas (LNG). Because liquefied natural gas is highly compressed and remains under pressure during storage, it has a tremendous expansion rate when released into the normal atmosphere. For this reason, LNG presents a particular potential for explosion or fire when leaks occur in storage or during transport. LNG is becoming more prevalent in the United States, and this factor alone increases the need to be vigilant about LNG storage facilities and transportation routes in your response area. Like most hazardous materials, LNG normally is safe and well-regulated, but you must be prepared for any potential accidental LNG release and be able to assist specially trained hazardous materials teams under supervision of an Incident Command System.

Compressed Gas in Cylinders

Flammable gas that is transported in pressurized tanks and cylinders can be compressed or liquefied.

Compressed Gas

An example of a compressed gas is oxygen. This gas is not flammable by itself. However, it is an oxidizer and accelerates the rate of burning of any nearby materials. Just as when you blow on a small fire to intensify the flames, oxygen released from a compressed gas cylinder will intensify any free-burning substance or material that is nearby.

Liquefied Gas

A common flammable gas is liquefied propane gas (LPG). To be useful as a flammable gas, a material must remain in a gaseous state under normal ambient temperatures and normal atmospheric pressure (14.7 psi at sea level). When the pressure of a gas is raised, the gas is compressed into a liquid state. To more efficiently store and transport many gases, it is a common practice to fill a pressure tank with the gas at a much higher pressure than the normal atmospheric pressure. The gas is liquefied at normal temperatures when it is inside a storage cylinder under pressure. When under pressure, most gases will liquefy and then "boil" back into a gas at an ambient pressure and temperature as it is used. LPG tanks are never filled with more than about 80% liquid, leaving a vapor area under pressure above the liquid. As the gas is used from the tank, the vapor area refills as gas vaporizes from the liquid, which boils naturally at room temperature (Figure 26-3).

Liquefied gases can also include butane and natural gas products. LPG is 1 ½ to 2 times heavier than air

Typical LP storage tank

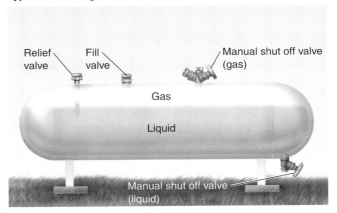

FIGURE 26-3 Liquefied propane gas is liquefied at normal temperatures inside a storage cylinder under pressure. The tanks are never filled with more than about 80% liquid, leaving a vapor area under pressure above the liquid.

FIGURE 26-4 LPG storage tanks can be located above or below ground level.

and will seek its lowest level when leaking or flowing freely as a gas.

Storage Tank Specifics

Compressed and liquefied flammable gas is transported to the customer in vehicles that haul large tanks. These vehicles can be railroad tanker cars, semi tractor-trailer tankers, and small utility vehicles carrying individual gas cylinders. Large storage tank facilities can be located in industrial areas. These facilities will likely be aboveground as well as belowground storage tanks (Figure 26-4).

The more need the customer has for the flammable gas product, the larger the on-property storage

FIGURE 26-5 A common use of LPG at home is for outdoor gas grills.

FIGURE 26-6 Small gas-refill facilities are common throughout most communities.

tank required. Single-family residences will have smaller storage tanks than a large industrial complex. One of the most common uses of LPG is for outdoor cooking grills at individual homes (Figure 26-5). These are found at many different types of retail outlets and usually require that the individual tank owner exchange an empty tank for a full one. These tanks normally are stored in a secured rack or cage located outside the business structure. The people responsible for exchanging the tanks will likely have minimum expertise in emergency handling, other than the information on the labels on each tank. Full tanks have a seal on their main valves that is broken and removed when the tank is put into service. Empty tanks that have been exchanged should be treated the same as full tanks during any emergency, because most of them have some residual gas left in them.

Some retail outlets, such as gas service companies, refill liquefied gas containers. There are also LPG vehicle-refueling outlets that refill LPG tanks, much the same as refueling a vehicle with diesel or gasoline fuel. At first, you may consider these LPG tank storage locations to be few and far between. However, if you start to take notice, you'll see that they are quite prevalent throughout the United States (Figure 26-6). Later in this chapter we'll cover in more detail the handling of fires involving these types of facilities.

Compressed Gas Cylinder Construction

Compressed gas cylinders are constructed of heavy steel materials that are more than adequate under normal circumstances. They feature a valve at the top of the cylinder. Depending upon the type of

FIGURE 26-7 Compressed gas cylinders have a flow valve located on the top of the cylinder that may require a special wrench to operate.

gas the cylinder is designed to hold, there may be a regulator or other attachments located at the top. The top valve may require a special wrench to operate (Figure 26-7).

Many times, you will find sets of gas cylinders connected by tubing. All cylinders are required to be secured in place. This can be accomplished using a rack system, chains, or straps.

Liquefied Flammable Gas Tank Construction

Tanks that carry liquefied gas will always have the flow control valves located on the top of the tank, above the liquid level. Flow control valves are located under a protective dome. To access the valves, lift the lid. You can open a flow valve by turning it in a counterclockwise direction and close it by turning it in a clockwise direction (Figure 26-8).

Relief Valves

Compressed gas cylinders and liquefied gas tanks also have overpressure, relief valve mechanisms. They are made in two main designs. One is spring-loaded and opens with overpressurization of the cylinder. Another type, called a melt-out or other frangible disk, is actuated by excessive heat—it releases and falls away when exposed to extreme heat. Both types of relief valves are designed to release overpressurized gas from the cylinder or tank caused by heat expansion, which usually results from fire exposure to the container (Figure 26-9).

The major difference that is important for you to know is that spring-loaded relief valves will close as the tank is cooled down below the relief valve's operating pressure. You should also be aware that sometimes spring-loaded relief valves can be activated by overpressurization caused by high outside ambient temperatures, particularly when full. With a melt-out type of relief valve, there is no resealing of the relief opening as the fire and heat are reduced or eliminated.

Fill Valves

On many compressed gas cylinders, the tank is filled using the valve mechanism that is used to open the flow of the gas from the cylinder. The cylinders rarely are refilled on site. Instead, they are usually exchanged for full cylinders, either delivered or taken to a commercial gas company for exchange.

With liquefied gas tanks, the fill valve can be a separate valve. This type of tank is usually refilled on site (the exception being the outdoor cooking grill tanks that are exchanged). Residential liquefied gas tanks are usually filled by gas delivery trucks. These tanks are located outside the structure, either above or below ground level (Figure 26-10).

FIGURE 26-9 Relief valves are designed to allow overpressurized tanks to relieve excess pressure.

FIGURE 26-8 The shutoff valve on an LPG tank is normally located under the dome on the top of the tank, above the liquid level of the liquefied gas inside.

FIGURE 26-10 Fill valves for LPG tanks are separate from shutoff valves.

Level II

Labeling and Placards

Flammable gases are considered hazardous materials. While being transported, these products must be labeled under a standard international and national hazardous materials labeling and placard system. These products may or may not be labeled or placarded while in a storage facility. Some areas of the country also use the NFPA 704M placard identification system that requires storage tanks to have a diamond-shaped placard indicating the level of Life, Health, Flammability, and Special Hazards of the particular hazardous material being stored (Figure 26-11). If present, these labels can often be your first indication of the type of gas material being stored in a cylinder or tank when you arrive on the scene of an emergency.

Flammable gas storage tanks are required to be labeled with a red diamond. Inside the diamond will be the words *Flammable Gas* with a number (Figure 26-12). The number references the hazard class of the substance in the tank. Chemicals are listed by product/chemical name and their United Nations/North American number in the U.S. Department of Transportation's *North American Emergency Response Guidebook (NAERG)*. A current copy of this book must be located on all fire apparatus. It provides a quick reference for response, safe handling, evacuation, and spill and fire control practices for many categories of hazardous materials. Flammable gases can be referenced in the *NAERG* by their product name, chemical name, or hazardous material reference number.

Handling Leaks and Spills

A general rule for operating at any gas leak or spill is to identify the substance involved, determine the type and size of the container, and determine whether the flow of the substance can be shut off safely. The initial actions you take when arriving at an incident of this type can determine whether or not there is a loss of life and property.

Immediate evacuation and securing access to the scene with a wide evacuation zone are the most effective things you can do until more help arrives in the form of Incident Command, Fire Department resources like hazardous materials teams, and assistance from the property manager or product company. The following secure area and evacuation distances apply to leaks and fires involving flammable gases:

- A secure area at least 330 feet in all directions should be initially established.
- People should first be evacuated downwind and ½ mile in all directions from the gas leak.

These distances can be adjusted as the amount of flammable gas involved and the severity of the leak is determined (Figure 26-13).

If the leak or flow of gas cannot be controlled or stopped, allowing the gas to leak out while protecting the surrounding exposures and dissipating the gas with water sprays may be the best option. An exception to this may involve a natural gas leak in which the product rises as it escapes. Using a water spray in this situation may in fact retard the ability of the gas to dissipate upward into the atmosphere. Stay upwind and uphill from leaks involving gases that are heavier than air.

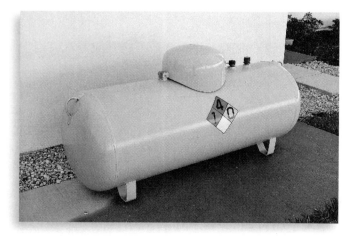

FIGURE 26-11 Many areas of the country require that storage tank facilities have a diamond-shaped label indicating the level of Life, Health, Flammability, and Special Hazards of the particular hazardous material being stored.

FIGURE 26-12 Flammable gas storage tanks are required to be labeled with a red diamond. Inside the diamond will be the words *Flammable Gas* with a number.

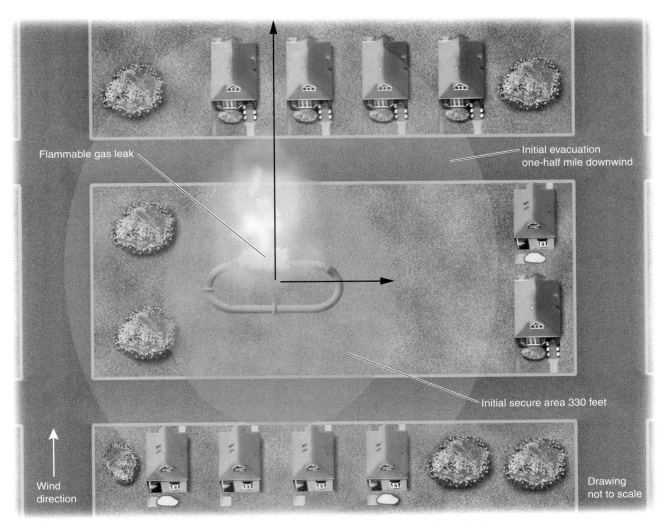

Flammable gas leak

Initial evacuation
one-half mile downwind

Initial secure area 330 feet

Wind
direction

Drawing
not to scale

Initial secure area and evacuation areas for flammable gas leak

FIGURE 26-13   Initial secure area and evacuation area around a flammable gas leak.

Liquefied gases like propane collect in lower elevations, sewers, and basements. Do not touch any liquefied gas product in its liquid state. Doing so can result in severe burns or frostbite.

In all cases, it is important to initially keep as much distance as practical between yourself and the leaking flammable gas cylinder or tank. Use binoculars, if possible, to see what type gas is involved, the extent of the leak, and whether or not the flow of the leak can be controlled.

Large amounts of water will need to be flowed on the leaking flammable gas to keep it safe as it dissipates in the atmosphere. This can be done using large attack lines from sheltered positions some distance from the

tank or cylinder. A sheltered position may be behind the corner of a substantial building or other strong protective obstruction. If the danger is too great, unstaffed deluge guns can be set up from a safe distance, with their streams directed at the leaking gas. They should then be left without firefighter control (Figure 26-14).

If the leak is inside a structure, evacuate as before, identify the type of gas leaking, control the flow, and ventilate the building. With a flammable gas, this ventilation may start with simply opening doors and windows to allow for natural airflow ventilation. Remember, forced ventilation with PPV fans or smoke ejectors can introduce an ignition source to the flammable gas fumes.

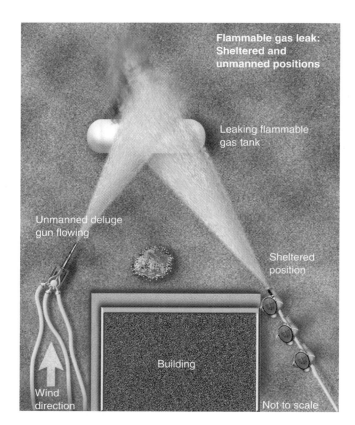

Flammable gas leak: Sheltered and unmanned positions

Leaking flammable gas tank

Unmanned deluge gun flowing

Sheltered position

Building

Wind direction

Not to scale

FIGURE 26-14 Sheltered positions and unmanned deluge gun positioned on a flammable gas leak.

Safety Tip!

Always wear full PPE, including SCBA, when working inside the hot or warm zones at emergencies of this type. Flammable gases may or may not be a respiratory hazard; however, they all can displace oxygen in the atmosphere, creating a danger of asphyxiation. Never position at the ends of a flammable gas tank. These containers are designed to fail at the ends first. The metal fragment projectiles can cause serious injury or death. Always work under the direction of an Incident Command System and a Company Officer. These emergency operations are complicated and very dangerous, and require the very best coordination and protection possible for firefighters.

Evolution 26-1

Flammable Gas Flow Shut-Down—Residential Natural Gas Pipeline

This evolution has been developed to practice the skills necessary to practice shutting down a typical domestic natural gas supply pipeline valve. The drill should be repeated, switching firefighter positions so that each person can practice the training drill in all positions except that of Company Officer. These skills are essentially the same for a leak in an LP Gas line with the primary difference being that natural gas fumes will rise and LP Gas fumes will tend to seek lower levels on the ground.

Training Area: Open area; level ground free of trip hazards

Equipment: Equipped pumper

Training simulator: domestic gas service pipeline with control valve

Sustained water supply source, or static or water main system with hydrant

PPE: Full protective clothing and SCBA, on and ready for use

1. A fully equipped pumper with a crew consisting of a Company Officer and two or three other team members arrives on the scene of a simulated gas leak. They position at an appropriate safe distance from the leak and assess the scene from a distance.

2. It is determined that the gas leak is natural gas from a pipeline to a residence. An appropriate evacuation area is simulated, assistance is called for, and Incident Command is established by the Company Officer.

3. A sustained water supply is set up and a small attack hose line is deployed and charged with water. The firefighters make sure that they are upwind from the leaking pipeline and use any safe sheltering, if available.

4. A team of three firefighters flows water on the leaking pipeline from a distance, waiting for the arrival of a second team with another small attack line. A second team of three firefighters positions next to the first team. Both teams position all members inside each line: one firefighter from each team on the nozzle, one from each team as an immediate backup, and the third from each team a few feet farther back to help pull the line. A Company Officer positions between both teams, even with the firefighters on the nozzles (Figure 26-15).

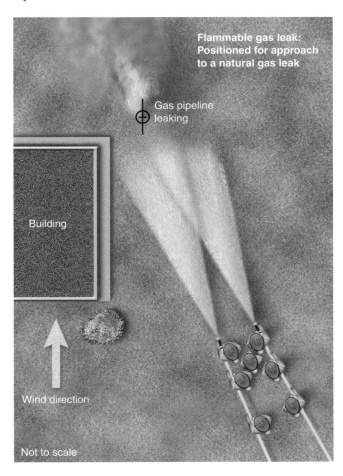

Flammable gas leak: Positioned for approach to a natural gas leak

Gas pipeline leaking

Building

Wind direction

Not to scale

FIGURE 26-15

—Continued

Level II

5. A third team of three firefighters on a large attack line takes a position well behind the other two teams, with the line charged and ready to flow water, and the firefighters make themselves ready to attempt a rescue if anything goes wrong for the first two teams (Figure 26-16).

6. The Company Officer communicates with Command and determines that they can shut down the flow of leaking gas by shutting off the gas valve. On his command, both lines are adjusted to a medium fog pattern, forming two cones that intersect in front of both teams. The teams begin to move toward the pipeline and control valve, taking one step forward on each command from the Company Officer (Figure 26-17).

7. As they approach nearer to the leaking pipeline, the Company Officer directs them to widen their fog patterns. When they are up to the leaking pipeline, the Company Officer reaches into the intersecting fog patterns and shuts off the flow valve.

8. Carefully, the teams retreat, stepping back on each command from the Company Officer until they are at a safe distance. They will readjust their fog nozzles to a medium pattern as they retreat. Their lines are constantly flowing at the pipeline leak.

9. When the crews are at a safe distance, one line remains flowing as the other is turned off at the nozzle. The leak is reevaluated from a distance by the Incident Commander.

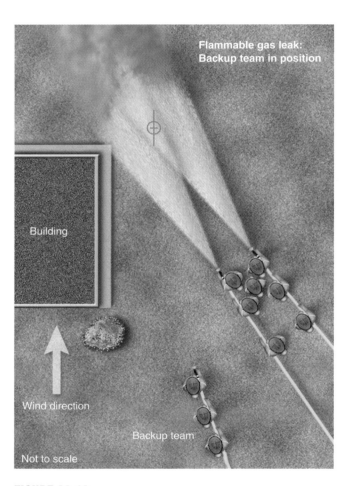

FIGURE 26-16

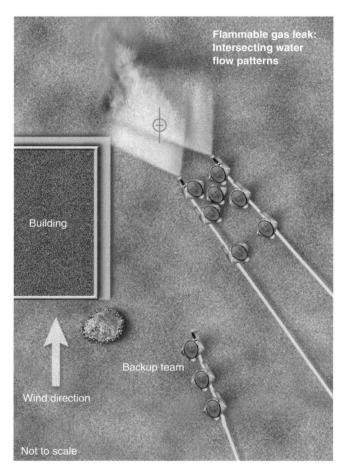

FIGURE 26-17

Safety Tip!

In all emergencies involving flammable gases, remember that retreating from the gas leak or fire is just as dangerous as approaching it. Keep lines flowing at the leak or fire at all times and retreat as a group, protected by your fog patterns and coordinated by the Company Officer. Remember to use substantial buildings and obstructions for sheltering when possible.

Safety Tip!

Firefighters should be made aware that commercial, piped-in gas systems and valves are substantially bigger and provide much more gas flow to the structure. This can also be true with larger buildings, regardless of occupancy. Shutting down valves on these types of facilities and gas systems should be done only in a coordinated Incident Command System, with direction from gas utility representatives familiar with the system.

Handling Flammable Gas Fires

Fires involving flammable gases are among the potentially most difficult and dangerous to control and extinguish. They are complicated incidents that require a coordinated effort with an effective Incident Command System, adequate firefighting teams and equipment, and hazardous materials teams. Your part in these incidents will be as a member of the firefighting team, and your job will involve helping with the initial scene assessment, evacuation of the immediate area around the fire, and keeping civilians at a safe distance from the fire. Later, as help arrives and your team has set up a sustained water supply, the firefighting effort begins. The first steps in firefighting occur after the gas has been identified and a plan of action has been decided.

FIGURE 26-18

A flammable gas fire can result from an exposure to another fire, like a burning building or vehicle. It can also originate at the gas tank itself. In either case, the most dangerous situation is when the exterior of the tank is directly exposed to the heat of the fire. This can lead to a catastrophic tank failure and a resulting explosion with a fireball (Figure 26-18).

Combustion Explosions

There are instances when flammable gas product has leaked inside a structure. If not detected in time, the gas can reach the proper air-gas mixture for ignition, and a spark or flame can ignite the gas, causing a gas explosion. These explosions can be extremely destructive and can flatten a structure. The original gas leak can still be present and burning at the leak after the explosion.

Safety Tip!

When flammable gas is released in an enclosed area, there is always the chance of asphyxiation, even if the gas is considered nontoxic. This is because the gas can displace breathable air inside the enclosed area.

Level II

Handling Flammable Gas Fires   **631**

Safety Lesson

A NIOSH Report

On April 9, 1998, twenty firefighters from a volunteer fire department responded to a propane tank fire located at a turkey farm about 2½ miles from the fire department. Upon arrival at the fire scene, a decision was made to water down the buildings adjacent to the propane tank and allow the tank to burn itself out since the tank was venting. Some of the firefighters positioned themselves between the burning propane tank and the turkey sheds and were watering down the buildings as the remaining firefighters performed other tasks—for example, pulling hose and operating pumps.

About 8 minutes after the firefighters arrived on scene, the tank exploded. When the tank exploded, it separated into four parts and traveled in four different directions. Two firefighters about 105 feet from the tank were struck by one piece of the exploding tank and killed instantly. Six other firefighters and a deputy sheriff, who had arrived on scene just before the explosion, were also injured.

Follow-Up

In the NIOSH Investigative Report (#F98-14), NIOSH investigators concluded that, to prevent similar incidents, fire departments should:

1. Follow guidelines as outlined in published literature and guidebooks for controlling fire involving tanks containing propane.

2. Adhere to emergency response procedures contained in 29 CFR 1910.120(q)—"Emergency Response to Hazardous Substance Release Procedures."

3. Educate firefighters about the many dangers associated with a propane tank explosion, which is also known as a boiling liquid expanding vapor explosion (BLEVE).

BLEVE

A boiling liquid expanding vapor explosion (BLEVE) occurs when a tank containing a liquefied flammable gas product is exposed to the heat of a fire. The tank has pressure relief valves that, under normal circumstances, operate to relieve the pressure of the gas in the tank escaping from the liquid below. Under certain fire exposure situations, such as when the steel shell of the tank, above the liquid level, has fire directly touching or impinging on the tank shell, overpressurization of the gas inside can occur. The tank shell weakens and fails. The tank instantly comes apart, releasing the gas and liquid inside. The liquid instantly expands when released into the atmosphere and the resulting gas immediately ignites, creating a massive fireball.

This results not only in destruction by the heat of the fire from the resulting fireball, but also in destruction of the surrounding area from the projectile pieces of the tank shell as they fly from the area. Liquefied gas tanks are designed to fail at their ends, so the fire and resulting BLEVE can send whole sections of the ends of the tanks hundreds of yards from their original location. Smaller chunks can be ejected in any direction during a BLEVE.

Go to the DVD, navigate to Chapter 26, and select *"Flammable Gas Firefighting—Evolution 26-2, Flammable Gas Fire—Natural Gas Valve."*

Evolution 26-2

Flammable Gas Fire—Natural Gas Valve

This evolution has been developed to practice the skills necessary to practice controlling a fire involving a typical domestic natural gas supply pipeline valve. The drill should be repeated, switching firefighter positions so that each person can practice the training drill in all positions except that of Company Officer.

Training Area: Open area; level ground free of trip hazards

Equipment: Equipped pumper

                    Training simulator: domestic gas service pipeline with control valve

                    Sustained water supply source, or static or water main system with hydrant

PPE: Full protective clothing and SCBA, on and ready for use

1. A fully equipped pumper with a crew consisting of a Company Officer and two or three other team members arrives on the scene of a simulated gas fire. They position at an appropriate, safe distance from the fire and assess the scene.

2. It is determined that the gas fire is natural gas from a pipeline to a residence. An appropriate evacuation area is simulated, assistance is called for, and Incident Command is established by the Company Officer.

3. A sustained water supply is set up and a small attack hose line is deployed and charged with water. The firefighters make sure that they are upwind from the fire and use any safe sheltering, if available.

4. A team of three firefighters flows water on the fire-involved pipeline from a distance, waiting for the arrival of a second team with another small attack line. A second team of three firefighters positions next to the first team. Both teams position parallel to each other, all members inside each line: one firefighter from each team on the nozzle, one from each team as an immediate backup, and the third from each team a few feet farther back to help pull the line. A Company Officer positions between both teams, even with the firefighters on the nozzles (Figure 26-19).

FIGURE 26-19

5. A third team of three firefighters on a large attack line takes a position well behind the other two teams, with the line charged and ready to flow water, and the firefighters make themselves ready to attempt a rescue if anything goes wrong for the first two teams.

Level II

—Continued

6. The Company Officer communicates with Command and determines that they can shut down the flow of burning gas by turning off the gas valve. On his command both lines are adjusted to a medium fog pattern, forming two "cones" that intersect in front of both teams. The teams begin to move toward the fire and the control valve, taking one step forward on each command from the Company Officer (Figure 26-20).

FIGURE 26-20

7. As they approach nearer to the burning pipeline, the Company Officer directs them to widen their fog patterns. When they are up to the fire, the Company Officer reaches into the intersecting fog patterns and shuts off the gas flow valve (Figure 26-21).

8. Carefully the teams retreat, stepping back on each command from the Company Officer until they are at a safe distance, their lines constantly flowing in a fog pattern at the pipeline.

9. When the crews are at a safe distance, one line flows as the other is turned off at the nozzle. The fire is reevaluated from a distance by the Incident Commander.

FIGURE 26-21 The most dangerous situation is when the exterior of the tank is directly exposed to the heat of the fire. This can lead to a catastrophic tank failure and a resulting explosion with a fireball.

 **View It!**

Go to the DVD, navigate to Chapter 26, and select *"Flammable Gas Firefighting—Evolution 26-3, Flammable Gas Fire—Liquefied Propane Gas Tank."*

Evolution 26-3

Flammable Gas Fire—Liquefied Propane Gas Tank

This evolution has been developed to practice the skills necessary to practice extinguishing a fire involving a typical commercial-size liquefied propane gas tank. The drill should be repeated, switching firefighter positions so that each person can practice the training drill in all positions except that of Company Officer.

Training Area: Open area; level ground free of trip hazards

Equipment: Equipped pumper

Training simulator: commercial-size liquefied propane gas tank with a control valve

Sustained water supply source, or static or water main system with hydrant

PPE: Full protective clothing and SCBA, on and ready for use

1. A fully equipped pumper with a crew consisting of a Company Officer and two or three other team members arrives on the scene of a simulated commercial-size liquefied propane gas tank fire. They position at an appropriate, safe distance from the fire and assess the scene.

2. It is determined that the gas fire is from a liquefied propane gas tank supplying a business. A relief valve has activated and the escaping gas is burning. An appropriate evacuation area is simulated, assistance is called for, and Incident Command is established by the Company Officer.

3. A sustained water supply is set up and a small attack hose line is deployed and charged with water. The firefighters make sure that they are upwind and uphill from the fire and use any safe sheltering, if available. They also position away from the ends of the tank.

4. A team of three firefighters flows water on the fire-involved tank from a distance, waiting for the arrival of a second team with another small attack line. There is also gas burning at a leak from some of the pipe near the bottom of the tank.

   Note: The object here is not to extinguish the gas escaping from the relief valve but to keep flame from heating the exposed skin of the tank.

5. The second team of three firefighters positions next to the first team. Both teams position parallel to each other, all members inside each line: one firefighter from each team on the nozzle, one from each team as an immediate backup, and the third from each team a few feet farther back to help pull the line. A Company Officer positions between both teams, even with the firefighters on the nozzles (Figure 26-22).

FIGURE 26-22

—Continued

6. A third team of three firefighters on a large attack line takes a position well behind the other two teams, with the line charged and ready to flow water, and the firefighters make themselves ready to attempt a rescue if anything goes wrong for the first two teams.

7. The Company Officer communicates with Command and determines that they can shut down the flow of burning gas under the tank by turning off the gas flow valve. On his command, both lines are adjusted to a medium fog pattern, forming two "cones" that intersect in front of both teams. The teams begin to move toward the fire and the control valve, taking one step forward on each command from the Company Officer (Figure 26-23).

FIGURE 26-23

8. As they approach nearer to the burning pipeline, the Company Officer directs them to widen their fog patterns. When they are up to the fire, the Company Officer reaches into the intersecting fog patterns and shuts off the gas flow valve (Figure 26-24).

9. Carefully, the teams retreat, stepping back on each command from the Company Officer until they are at a safe distance, their lines constantly flowing in a fog pattern at the pipeline.

10. When the crews are at a safe distance, one line flows onto the tank as the other is turned off at the nozzle. The fire is reevaluated from a distance by the Incident Commander.

FIGURE 26-24

Handling Flammable Gas Fires Safely

Handling any emergency involving a flammable gas is a dangerous undertaking. Hopefully this chapter has explained what flammable gases are, and how they are transported and stored. Training evolutions demonstrating how leaks and fires are approached were also provided. It is important for you to know what will take place during a flammable gas emergency and the basic philosophy in handling these emergencies. If the flow of gas cannot be controlled, then it is usually much wiser and safer to evacuate, secure the area, and let the fire burn until all of the fuel is consumed.

Knowledge Assessment

Signed Documentation Tear-Out Sheet

Flammable Gas Firefighting—Chapter 26

Name: _____

Fill out the ten-question quiz below, the Knowledge Assessment Sheet, by circling the correct answer. When finished, sign it and give to your instructor/Company Officer for his or her signature. Turn in this Knowledge Assessment Sheet to the proper person as part of the documentation that you have completed your training for this chapter.

1. When you complete training in this chapter on flammable gas firefighting, you will be expected to act as a Company Officer in charge of the scene of one of these incidents.
   a. True
   b. False

2. How is the shutoff valve on a natural gas pipeline at a residence positioned to shut off the flow of natural gas through the pipeline?
   a. In line with the pipeline
   b. Parallel with the pipeline
   c. Perpendicular with the pipeline
   d. At a 30-degree angle to the pipeline

3. LPG tanks are full when they have about _____ % liquid to vapor in the tank.
   a. 95
   b. 80
   c. 65
   d. 50

4. LPG tanks can be located above or below ground level in residential service areas.
   a. True
   b. False

5. Small reference books located on fire apparatus that provide a quick reference for response, safe handling, evacuation, and spill and fire control practices for many categories of hazardous materials are called _____.
   a. *The Hazmat Response Guidebook*
   b. *The DOT Response Book*
   c. *The Yellow Book*
   d. *The North American Emergency Response Guidebook*

6. At a gas leak or spill, what are the most effective things you can do until more help arrives in the form of Incident Command, Fire Department resources like hazardous materials teams, and assistance from the property manager or product company?
   a. Secure the immediate area and evacuate a wider area.
   b. Immediately approach the fire.
   c. Position at the end of the tank.
   d. Extinguish with a fire extinguisher.

Level II

7. It is best to stay _____ from a gas leak.

   a. downhill and downwind

   b. uphill and downwind

   c. downhill and upwind

   d. upwind and uphill

8. Flammable gas tanks are designed to fail at the _____ first.

   a. sides

   b. tops

   c. ends

   d. bottoms

9. A(n) _____ can occur when flammable gas product has leaked inside a structure. The gas can reach the proper air-gas mixture for ignition, and a spark or flame can ignite the gas, causing an explosion.

   a. BLEVE

   b. conflagration explosion

   c. combustion explosion

   d. internal explosion

10. A(n) _____ occurs when a tank containing a Liquefied Flammable Gas product is exposed to the heat of a fire. The tank has pressure relief valves that operate under normal circumstances to relieve the pressure of the gas in the tank escaping from the liquid below.

   a. BLEVE

   b. conflagration explosion

   c. combustion explosion

   d. internal explosion

Student Signature and Date _____   Instructor/Company Officer Signature and Date _____

638

Skills Assessment

Signed Documentation Tear-Out Sheet

Flammable Gas Firefighting—Chapter 26

Name: _____

Fill out the Skills Assessment Sheet below. Have your instructor/Company Officer check off and initial each skill you demonstrate. When you are finished, sign this page and give to your instructor/Company Officer for his or her signature. Turn in this Skills Assessment Sheet to the proper person as part of the documentation that you have completed your training for this chapter.

Skill	Completed	Initials
1. Identify the hazardous material label for a flammable gas cylinder or tank.	_____	_____
2. Operate the shutoff valve on a typical natural gas pipeline for a single-family dwelling.	_____	_____
3. Operate the shutoff valve on an LPG storage tank.	_____	_____
4. Describe the initial evacuation zone established at a flammable gas fire.	_____	_____
5. Participate as a firefighting team member, both at the nozzle and as a backup on the hose line, in providing protection as a leak is controlled on a flammable gas cylinder or tank.	_____	_____
6. Participate as a firefighting team member, both at the nozzle and as a backup on the hose line, in providing protection as a fire is controlled on a flammable gas cylinder or tank.	_____	_____
7. Participate as a firefighting team member in applying water in the correct pattern and at the correct location on a tank or cylinder to help prevent a BLEVE.	_____	_____

Student Signature and Date _____   Instructor/Company Officer Signature and Date _____

Level II

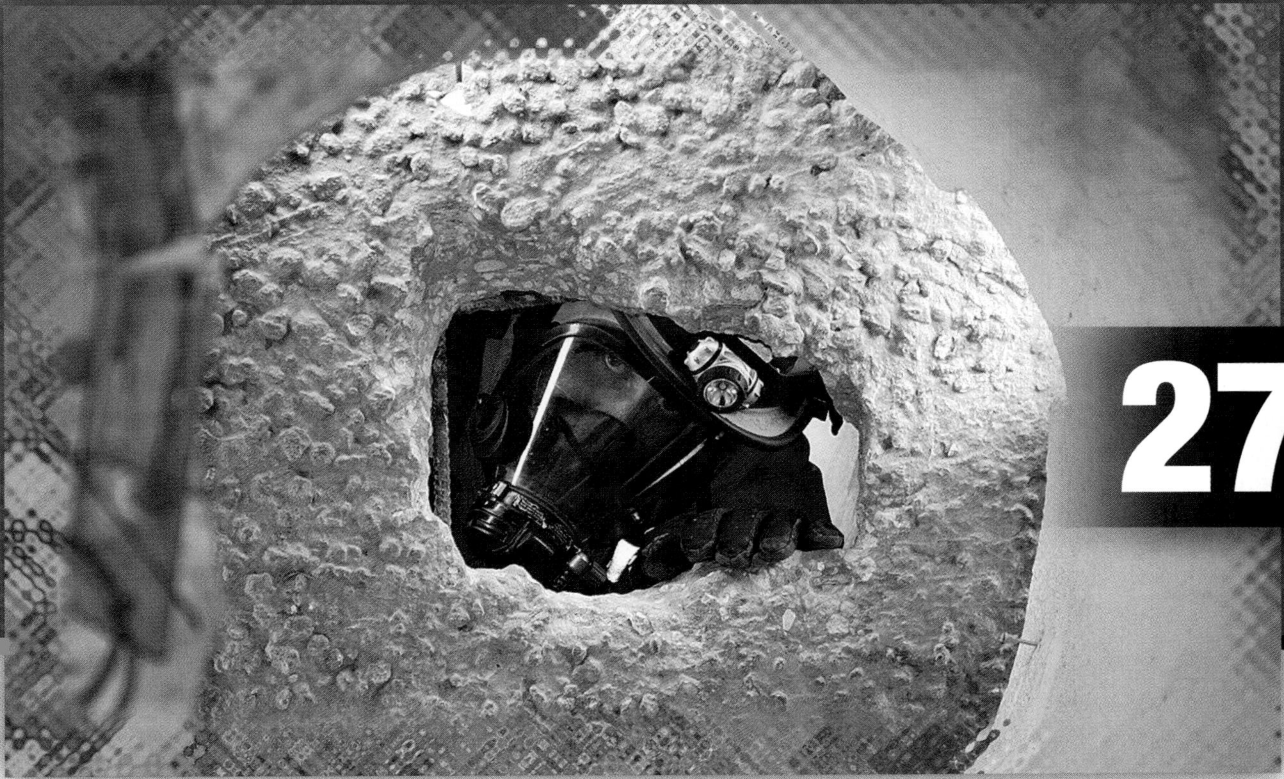

27

Rescue Awareness

What You Will Learn in This Chapter

In this chapter we will first discuss the benchmarks common for every rescue operation. We'll continue with vehicle and machinery rescue tools and techniques, and we will complete the chapter with an overview of awareness-level knowledge of the many other rescue disciplines.

What You Will Be Able to Do

After reading this chapter, you will be able to:

1. Explain risk assessment for rescue operations and rescuers.
2. Describe common rescue operation scene benchmark events, including response and arrival, establishing control, controlling hazards, stabilization, victim access, disentanglement, victim removal and rapid transport, and securing tools and equipment.
3. Identify the different orientation points and explain the basic construction of vehicles.
4. Describe scene setup operations unique to vehicle crash scenes.
5. Explain stabilization tactics for vehicles in various positions.
6. Identify typical hand tools used on vehicle extrication rescue operations.
7. Identify typical powered hydraulic tools used on vehicle extrication operations.
8. Explain the main rescue strategies and tactical considerations for machine rescue situations.
9. Describe how victims may be entrapped and subsequently disentangled from escalators and elevators.

10. List the other major categories of rescue disciplines.

11. Demonstrate how to mark a building during search and rescue operations.

We Are the "Go-To" Organization

The Fire Service has always responded to rescue situations. Whether to rescue victims from a burning building or floodwaters, the Fire Service is to some degree a natural "go-to" organization for performing rescue. Of course, the level of rescue service provided depends largely on the needs and desires of the local community. It is also shaped by the traditions of the community. In some areas, the Fire Department acts as the First Responder, leaving specialized rescue to be provided by a separate rescue department. In other areas, the Fire Department is required by the community to do all the rescue work.

At the Firefighter II level, you should be able to recognize the need for a rescue, evacuate and secure the scene, establish initial Command and control with safety zones, and assist special rescue personnel, whether they are members of the Fire Service or another agency. To do this, you need to be aware of the basic operations that will potentially take place and the many rescue disciplines, tools, and equipment for each type of potential rescue situation you may encounter.

FIGURE 27-1 Being properly protected and having resources available keeps risks at an acceptable level and helps you safely handle the situation at hand.

The risks you take should weigh heavily toward a successful outcome and your own survival. You did not put that entrapped victim in the situation in which they are now involved. Your responsibility should be to your own survival and the safety and survival of your fellow rescue team members. Keep the risks to yourself and others at an acceptable level by being properly protected, and have the resources available to safely handle the situation at hand (Figure 27-1).

Risk Assessment for Rescue

All rescue scenes should initially be considered as dangerous as any fire scene. Therefore, you should always approach with caution, wearing appropriate PPE and SCBA as the situation dictates. Many well-intentioned rescuers have been injured or killed because they did not anticipate the potential danger. If a condition exists in which someone needs to be rescued, then certainly you can safely assume that the same condition could cause you to become a victim as well. We cannot overemphasize the importance of your safety and survival.

It is also important that you maintain a situational awareness of the scene around you in all directions. This means being aware of the apparent dangers, in all directions, to which you are exposed. It also means anticipating potential dangerous situations that can arise.

Benchmarks of an Emergency Rescue

Emergency operations at the scene of a rescue have certain steps or benchmarks that are achieved, regardless of the type of rescue taking place. You will realize quickly while going through these steps that they are very similar to fire operations. This is one reason the Fire Service is so adaptable to rescue work.

Response and Arrival

For all emergencies the response and arrival processes are essentially the same. It is always important to respond in an appropriate manner with due regard for your own safety and the safety of the public.

When you arrive on the scene, be sure to park the apparatus in a position where it will be useful but not in danger. It is equally important that the apparatus doesn't add to the danger. For example, if the victim is trapped in a trench collapse or confined space, all apparatus should be parked so that their exhaust doesn't flow into the confined area, causing a greater hazard of asphyxiation. There is also the danger of further trench collapse due to the vibrations caused by an apparatus that is too close to the incident. When selecting the area to park the rig, look up, out, and down, making sure the apparatus is not in danger and that it doesn't present an additional hazard to the operation.

Once you are on the scene, it is important to observe and notice the conditions and potential safety hazards present. An arrival report is critical at this point. If your Company Officer is not yet present, your initial arrival report will inform him or her of the situation at hand. He or she can then adjust the response to the emergency based on your report of what you have found.

Establishing Control

The next benchmark is to establish some sort of control. At any emergency, it is vital that when your Fire Service team arrives on the scene, you begin to create order out of chaos. This is done by establishing Incident Command, calling for additional assistance if needed, designating safety zones around the incident, securing those zones, keeping the general public back at a safe distance, and evacuating any areas subject to further danger from the conditions at hand.

Calling early for assistance is prudent. You may not have the authority to do this, but you can at least inform your Company Officer of the need, if that person has not yet arrived. Calling for extra help that will turn out not to be needed is far safer and errs on the side of caution. Not having enough help is dangerous and often results in unnecessary risks to team members already working on the scene.

Safety zones for rescue are similar to those for fire incidents. They are established according to the hazards present. The hot zone is the area of immediate danger close in to the location of the victim and the entrapment. This zone may span a few feet, or it may be an entire collapsed building. Warm zones

are generally those areas immediately adjacent to the hot zone. They extend out as far as necessary for personnel located in them to be working on the scene and in appropriate PPE. Cool zones are those areas adjacent to the warm zone. These may also be called cold zones in some departments. They extend out away from the scene where access is restricted for the general public (Figure 27-2).

Tool staging areas may be designated, depending on the layout of the scene and the needs of the rescue teams working on the scene. There may also be multiple tool staging areas and, in some cases, special areas like workshop areas where shoring or special cribbing are cut and assembled.

Controlling Hazards

Before rescuers and firefighters can safely enter the area around an incident, it is important to locate and neutralize any hazards that may be present. This means controlling any fuel leaks, extinguishing any fires, and shutting off any utility services. Lockout/tagout measures may be needed to provide maximum security of electrical or gas service switches or valves. In some instances, some of your team members may be stationed at critical shutoff switches or valves to prevent anyone from inadvertently turning them back to the on position during rescue operations.

Hose lines may be deployed and charged to provide rescuers with water spray protection from fires or leaks. Hazardous materials may need to be handled by special hazmat teams before rescuers can attempt to enter and begin rescue operations. As with most emergency incidents, the entire rescue operation depends on several teams of people working under the control of an Incident Commander.

Stabilization

Stabilization involves controlling any unstable condition that presents a potential danger of injury and even death to yourself, rescuers, and victims. Some examples of these dangers include wreckage from vehicles involved in a crash, structural members of a collapsed building, or even the side of a collapsed construction trench. Any unstable objects and debris must be stabilized before rescuers can safely access, disentangle, and remove a victim.

Stabilization may involve the use of many different types of **cribbing, shoring,** stabilization tools, and equipment (Figure 27-3). We will discuss a few of these different types of stabilization tools and equipment as we go over some of the different rescue disciplines.

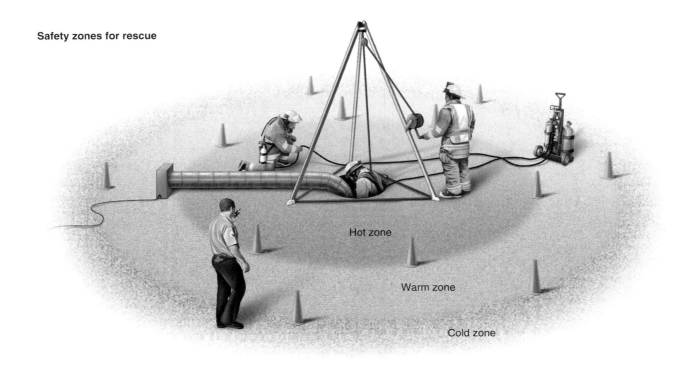

FIGURE 27-2 Hot, warm, and cool zones on a rescue scene.

FIGURE 27-3 Stabilization may involve the use of many different types of cribbing, shoring, stabilization tools, and equipment.

The main thing for you to remember is that all unstable objects and conditions must be made stable prior to accessing the victim for disentanglement and removal. Failure to do this is dangerous and ill advised. If emergency workers are injured or killed during a rescue operation, it creates extreme difficulties for the rescue at hand. We never want to become rescue victims ourselves.

▬ KEY WORDS ▬

cribbing A general term for any materials placed to stabilize a load. Usually these materials are small pieces of wood or synthetic materials (2 × 4 inch or 4 × 4 inch boards) cut to 16- to 24-inch lengths. However, the term can be used to refer to any wooden supports placed in a horizontal configuration to support a load during stabilization.

shoring Stabilization devices designed to hold loads in place using the strength in the columnar length of the device. Shoring can be made of wood or specially designed jacks. It can also be commercially available air shoring that utilizes air pressure to hold loads in place.

Victim Access

This phase is attempted only after the scene is under control and it is safe to approach the victim. Under the best circumstances, there will also be a plan in place for the rescue to be accomplished. Getting to the victim does not accomplish a rescue. You need to be a part of the overall rescue effort that ends with the transport of the victim to an appropriate medical facility. In all circumstances, have a backup rescue plan in place, and be prepared to get yourself out in case things go wrong.

Disentanglement

The way in which we disentangle the victim depends upon where and how he or she is trapped. People can be trapped by debris and wreckage, as in a vehicle crash. They can be trapped by their incapacity to move due to injury, but otherwise may be easily accessible with minimal effort. A victim can be uninjured but trapped by the location, like window washers stuck outside the 17th floor of a high-rise building. In all cases, the rescue team must accomplish two very important objectives: prevent further harm, and disentangle the victim in a safe, timely manner.

Removal and Rapid Transport

The one thing about rescue victims that is different from other emergency medical patients, such as heart attack or stroke patients, is that they were usually in relatively good health prior to the incident. Because of this, the efficient removal and rapid transport to a hospital emergency room facility can greatly increase their chances of recovery from any injuries. Assisting with the removal and transport of a rescue victim is just as vital as the rescue itself.

Securing Tools and Equipment

When the rescue operation has been completed and the victim has been removed from the scene, all tools and equipment must be retrieved, made ready for the next incident, and secured onto the rescue vehicles. Depending on the extent and type of rescue operation, this may be as simple as placing tools from the tool staging area back onto the rescue unit, or as complex as carefully removing tools and equipment that are in place on the rescue scene. In some circumstances, cribbing and shoring will be left in place because it is too dangerous to remove them.

This phase also is when the scene itself is made as safe as possible and eventually turned over to a responsible party for further action. A critique of the rescue operation may also be conducted by the fire department in order to learn from the incident.

An Overview of Rescue Disciplines

There are many rescue disciplines. **NFPA 1670, *Operations and Training for Technical Rescue Incidents,*** defines some specific categories of rescue activities and outlines training requirements to be qualified to technician level in each discipline. The

Level II firefighter is not expected to be a **rescue technician,** however you should be able to provide assistance when requested by the rescue personnel working on the scene. These rescue disciplines cover potential rescue incidents with victims entangled in vehicle wreckage, trapped by machinery, in water, above ground level, in confined spaces, inside a trench, and under debris in a building collapse (Figure 27-4).

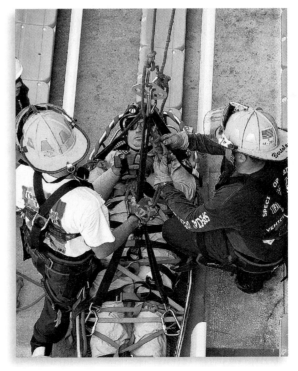

FIGURE 27-4 The Level 2 Firefighter should be able to provide assistance when requested by the rescue personnel working on the scene.

Level II

NFPA 1670, *Operations and Training for Technical Rescue Incidents* A National Fire Protection Association standard for various rescue discipline training requirements. It covers awareness, operations, and technician-level rescue training requirements for fire departments performing at those various levels of rescue capability.

rescue technician An advanced-level rescuer who is trained to work at and supervise a rescue discipline covered in the NFPA 1670 Standard.

FIGURE 27-5 Establish a tool staging area just outside the warm zone that is convenient for the rescuers working near victims.

Vehicle Entrapment Rescue

When vehicles crash and their occupants become victims entrapped by the wreckage, firefighters must be able to safely free and remove them from the wreckage. Vehicle entrapment rescue, also called vehicle extrication, is the most common type of rescue of trapped victims you will perform as a firefighter. For this reason, we will be discussing the use of tools for the various tactical rescue techniques necessary to move wreckage away from victims trapped in a vehicle crash situation. We are going to go through common vehicle entrapment situations, discussing the normal sequence of events as they will happen while you are working on the scene.

Approaching the Vehicle Crash Scene

We have already covered the proper approach to all vehicle crash scenes. This was discussed in *Safe Firefighting: First Things First,* Chapter 5. Scene assessment, establishing control with safety zones and Incident Command, and hazard and traffic control remain the same for all vehicle crash incidents. The major difference will be in the need to safely stabilize the unstable, severely damaged vehicles, accessing the trapped victims, and applying disentanglement techniques and tools to free the victims and provide a safe path of egress from the wreckage.

Go to *Safe Firefighting: First Things First,* Chapter 5, *"Response Safety and Vehicle Crashes,"* and review *"Assisting at Vehicle Crash Scenes."*

There are a few additions to be made to these initial procedures when an entrapment victim is found. First, there will be many different types of tools, equipment, and stabilization cribbing brought up to the work area during the incident. You need

to establish a tool staging area just outside the warm zone that is convenient for the rescuers working near the victims. Next, if you were the first fire department member on the scene and you established Incident Command, be sure to pass Command to the next arriving fire department Company Officer or Chief Officer with a report of what you have found and what you have done up to that point. He or she will then give you an assignment (Figure 27-5).

Anyone working in the hot or warm safety zone on a vehicle entrapment scene must wear appropriate PPE. There is a constant danger of flying wreckage and tool reaction while rescuers are working in and around the victim. There will also be a danger of leaking fluids and fire. You may be assigned to stand by with a small attack line, fully charged and ready, while rescue work proceeds. If you are assigned this role, remember to don your SCBA as a precaution. Everyone working in or near traffic should have reflective vests on, or be in their PPE with adequate reflective markings.

General Vehicle Orientation and Construction

Regardless of the type of vehicle involved in the crash and the resulting entrapment, there are some common orientation and construction characteristics you should know. Looking at an upright vehicle, there is the obvious roof, bottom or undercarriage, driver's side, and passenger's side. The roof is attached to the body by posts that we call the driver's or passenger's side "A," "B," or "C" posts—the "A" post being at the front windshield and the last post on that side being

Vehicle Entrapment Rescue operations require extensive training and learned skills. You should not attempt any of the described procedures and operations unless you have received training up to the Operations Level for this rescue discipline. We are only covering Awareness Level with this curriculum. You will know some of the procedures used and will be able to identify the tools and their uses. The skills for safely using the tools in an appropriate application will come with a complete course in vehicle extrication techniques.

The air bag restraint systems can present strike hazards to rescuers and victims if the bags have not deployed during the crash. Undeployed air bag restraint systems should be assessed and identified at all vehicle crash incidents. They can deploy as a result of disentanglement operations during the rescue. Avoid using hard protection, like a board or panel, between the victim and an undeployed air bag during rescue operations. To disarm most of these systems, simply turn off and remove the ignition key and disconnect the electrical system of the vehicle. It should be noted that some air bag systems can deploy unexpectedly even with the electrical system shut down. Do not remain in position between an undeployed air bag and the victim. The airbags should be secured before entering the vehicle for a rescue.

at the rear window. The last post at the rear window can be even designated a "D" or "E" post, depending on the total number of posts on that side.

Inside the vehicle are the engine, passenger, and cargo compartments. The engine and cargo compartments potentially contain most of the hazardous fluids and sources for fire. The passenger compartment will have seating, the dash, and the steering assembly on the driver's side. Seatbelt restraint systems are also there, along with air bag restraint systems (Figure 27-6).

Vehicles are usually constructed of sheet metal formed and rolled into the shape of the vehicle. This can be an all-inclusive construction design commonly referred to as unibody construction. This is more common in passenger vehicles. The body of the vehicle may be set up on a frame or chassis. This is full-frame construction and is found more commonly in trucks, pickup trucks, and large vans.

Increasingly, there are also more alternatively fueled vehicles on our highways today. These vehicles include those fueled by natural or compressed gas, biofuels, or electricity. Hybrid vehicles use a combination of an electric motor with a gasoline-fueled engine to extend gasoline mileage. Vehicle fuels and power methods will evolve continually as the technology changes. It is up to you to stay abreast of these in your ongoing training.

Stabilizing the Vehicle

When vehicles crash, the dynamics of the collision can move the vehicles in any direction and into any final resting position. A crashed vehicle will usually come to rest on all four wheels, on its side, on its roof, or on top of or under another vehicle. It is important that vehicles in all these positions be properly stabilized to prevent them from further movement. Any further movement of a crashed vehicle can cause further injury or death to both victims and rescuers.

Vehicles on All Four Wheels   Even vehicles sitting upright on all four wheels should be stabilized prior to accessing and working on them with rescue tools during an extrication operation. The quickest way to do this is to slide **step chocks** underneath four points of the vehicle's wreckage, usually behind the front wheels and in front of the back wheels, to stabilize the vehicle's contact with the ground underneath. Stacks of cribbing can also be used in the

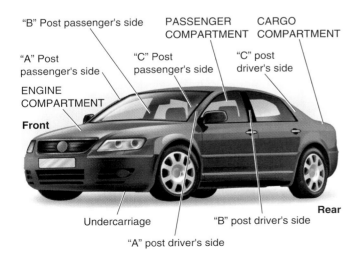

FIGURE 27-6   Typical vehicle orientation and construction.

FIGURE 27-7 The quickest way to stabilize a vehicle resting upright is to slide step chocks underneath four points of the wreckage.

FIGURE 27-8 Shores and wedges used to stabilize a vehicle on its side.

same way as step chocks. These are arranged in neat, box-shaped stacks at each of the four points. Next, chock one or two wheels, and release air from the tires. Chocking a wheel will help prevent the vehicle from moving forward or backward. Finally, letting air out of the tires will slowly settle the wreckage to the step chocks, further solidifying the stabilization by isolating the vehicle's weight from its springs (Figure 27-7).

■ KEY WORD ■

step chocks A specially designed cribbing support system that is made of a series of smaller sized crib boards put together and forming steps on top of a base board. They provide a rapid method to stabilize a crashed vehicle in the upright position on all four wheels.

FIGURE 27-9 Commercial shoring used on a vehicle on its side.

Vehicles on Their Sides The tactics for stabilizing vehicles that end up on their sides depends on whether the vehicle is leaning toward the roof side or the bottom side. The overall tactic is to complete an A-frame stabilization with shoring being one leg and the leaning vehicle being the other. It is also critical to place **wedges** along the bottom edge of the vehicle to keep it from sliding out. There are several types of **commercial shoring** available to accomplish this task. Most have a feature that secures the base of the shoring to the lower part of the car,

employing tension to help secure the entire assembly (Figures 27-8 and 27-9).

If the vehicle is leaning toward the bottom side, then shoring is applied to the underside of the vehicle, tightened by wedges. The vehicle can also be prevented from rolling back onto its wheels by securing the vehicle to a solid anchor point with rope or a **come-along winch** and **rescue chains** (Figure 27-10).

If it is leaning toward the roof, the vehicle can be stabilized by applying shoring to the trunk and hood area. This will prevent the vehicle from continuing

(a) The use of a chain and come-along in stabilizing a car less than halfway on its side.

(b) The use of a chain and come-along in stabilizing a car more than halfway on its side.

FIGURE 27-10 A vehicle can be prevented from rolling back onto its wheels by securing the vehicle to a solid anchor point with rope or a come-along winch and rescue chains.

FIGURE 27-11 A vehicle stabilized by applying shoring to the trunk and hood area.

to roll onto its roof. The important consideration in this situation is to leave the roof and doors free from stabilization, cribbing, or tools so that they can be opened later in the rescue operation (Figure 27-11).

▬▬ **KEY WORDS** ▬▬

come-along winch A hand-operated winch with a handle, an operating wheel, a cable, and two hooks. An operating switch changes the direction of the cable from pull to release.

commercial shoring Shoring specifically manufactured for the purpose of being set to hold loads in place using the strength in the columnar length of the device.

rescue chains Used in conjunction with pulling tools, particularly come-along winches, these chains are applied to objects to provide anchor points for the come-along winch pulling cable.

wedge A specially designed type of cribbing that is cut into a wedge shape for use in tight spaces. It can be pounded into place to create a short-span lifting action if needed.

 Safety Tip!

A vehicle resting on its side is in one of the most dangerous positions you will encounter. When you are stabilizing the vehicle, work as a team and always under the supervision of a safety person who is positioned in a spot where he or she can monitor the vehicle for movement as the stabilization continues. Stabilize from the top down, starting with shoring and finishing with the wedges near the bottom.

 Safety Tip!

When working around cables and winches, be aware of the hazards of cables under tension. If a cable under tension breaks unexpectedly, not only can the load it is supporting fall, but the cable itself can severely injure rescuers as it recoils under tension. Keep at a distance of at least the length of the cable under tension, and always wear appropriate PPE. Operate powered winches from a protected position whenever possible.

Vehicles on Their Roofs Occasionally a vehicle will roll completely over onto its roof. In this position, it can be nose down, with the engine compartment leaning forward and down, or flat on its roof, or flat on its

Level II

FIGURE 27-12 Stabilization usually requires rescuers to build stacks of cribbing at appropriate solid points around the vehicle to prevent further collapse or movement of the vehicle.

roof with a partial or full collapse of the roof posts. Stabilization usually requires rescuers to build stacks of cribbing at appropriate solid points around the vehicle to prevent further collapse or movement of the vehicle (Figure 27-12).

Safety Tip!

When the vehicle has been stabilized, consider disconnecting the electrical system in the vehicle. Disconnect the battery by removing or cutting the negative battery cable first. Tape the cable ends to ensure that they do not inadvertently touch each other, reenergizing the system or causing an electrical short. Batteries contain acidic fluids, so be sure to be fully protected with PPE before disconnecting the electrical system.

Typical Types of Vehicle Rescue Tools

The tools used to stabilize, access, disassemble, and force open crashed vehicles fall into two major categories: hand tools and powered hydraulic tools.

Hand Tools Hand tools are indispensable on the vehicle entrapment scene, even if powered hydraulic tools are utilized. For our purposes, hand tools are considered to be any small tools that normally require human power to work them. Examples include flathead axes, Halligan bars, windshield saws, **hack-**

saws, and **general mechanic's tools.** As an exception, hand tools also include smaller powered tools like pneumatic **air chisels, air wrenches, rescue air bag systems,** a come-along winch with rescue chains, and reciprocating saws.

KEY WORDS

air chisel A metal-cutting tool that is powered by compressed air. This tool has a pistol grip and an assortment of interchangeable chisel blades.

air wrench A compressed air operated ratchet with interchangeable sockets in assorted sizes.

general mechanic's tools An assortment of small hand tools normally used for repair of machinery or engines. It will consist of a tool-carrying box and screwdrivers, various pliers, side cutters, dykes, cable cutters, a hammer, a ratchet set, and any other various small tools.

hacksaw A hand tool composed of a blade holder and handle with a metal-cutting saw blade inserted. This tool is used to cut solid as well as tubular metal pieces.

rescue air bag systems Lifting tools that use a compressed air supply to fill air bladders in order to provide load-lifting action. They can also be inserted into spaces to spread apart obstructions.

Powered Hydraulic Rescue Tool Systems We'll begin the discussion of powered hydraulic tools with the **hydraulic power unit.** These can be powered by a gasoline engine, electricity, or a **power take-off (PTO).** The individual tools include cutting tools (the **powered hydraulic cutter**), spreading tools (the **powered hydraulic spreader**), and pushing or lifting tools **(powered hydraulic rams).** There may also be a wide range of additional powered hydraulic tools and attachments, depending upon what your fire department has available.

FIGURE 27-16

Breakout Box

Typical Hand Tools

1. Flathead axe and Halligan bar (Figure 27-13)
2. Windshield saw (Figure 27-14)
3. Hacksaw (Figure 27-15)
4. Mechanic's tools (Figure 27-16)
5. Air chisel and air wrench (Figure 27-17)
6. Rescue air bag system (Figure 27-18)
7. Reciprocating saw (Figure 27-19)
8. Come-along winch and rescue chains (Figure 27-20)

FIGURE 27-17

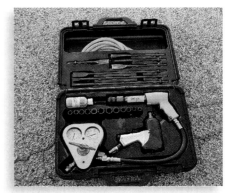

FIGURE 27-18

FIGURE 27-13

FIGURE 27-19

FIGURE 27-14

FIGURE 27-15

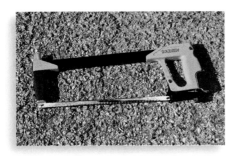

FIGURE 27-20

Level II

Typical Powered Hydraulic Rescue Tool System

1. Hydraulic power unit (Figure 27-21)
2. Powered hydraulic cutter (Figure 27-22)
3. Powered hydraulic spreader (Figure 27-23)
4. Powered hydraulic ram (Figure 27-24)

FIGURE 27-21

FIGURE 27-22

FIGURE 27-23

FIGURE 27-24

KEY WORDS

hydraulic power unit An electric- or gasoline-powered motor or engine that operates a hydraulic pump for supplying hydraulic oil under pressure to various tools attached to hoses running from the pump.

powered hydraulic cutter A rescue tool that is used to cut through solid and sheet metal debris and wreckage. Depending on their design, these tools can also cut through various other materials. They usually are configured as two cutting blades that pass each other much like scissors, with an operator's control switch on the handle area. Their force is derived from hydraulic pressure delivered by high-pressure hoses connected to a power unit.

powered hydraulic ram A rescue tool that is used to push solid and sheet metal debris and wreckage. Usually configured as a large piston with push heads at each end. There is an operator's control switch on the handle area. Its force is derived from hydraulic pressure delivered by high-pressure hoses connected to a power unit.

powered hydraulic spreader A rescue tool that is used to spread apart solid and sheet metal debris and wreckage. Depending on their design, these tools can also lift loads. They usually are configured as two spreader arms that open apart and close together. There is an operator's control switch on the handle area. Their force is derived from hydraulic pressure delivered by high-pressure hoses connected to a power unit.

power take-off (PTO) Any motor that receives its driving force from a remote source. Usually this will be through a drive shaft from the engine of the vehicle on which the motor is located.

Victim Access

When the vehicle has been properly stabilized, the next step will be to get close to the victims in the passenger compartment to check for the extent of their injuries and their entrapment predicament. This victim access can be as simple as reaching into the compartment area to provide spinal immobilization and airway management care to the trapped victim. Or rescuers may need to enter the vehicle in order to do this. While accessing the victim, they will also be able to prepare the interior of the vehicle by rolling down windows, disconnecting or cutting the victim's seatbelts if it is safe to do so, and doing a rapid initial patient assessment that ends with maintaining spinal immobilization of the victim while disentanglement operations take place. The interior rescuer also keeps the outside rescuers informed about the condition of the victim.

FIGURE 27-25 The front windshield is usually made of laminated plate glass and must be cut out with a specially designed windshield saw, reciprocating saw, or flathead axe.

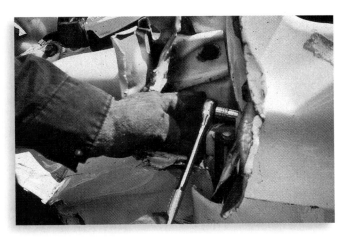

FIGURE 27-26 Disassembling parts of the vehicle will require a wide variety of hand tools.

Glass Removal Tools

There may be circumstances when glass must be removed, either during the initial access to the interior of the vehicle or later, when wreckage and obstructions are cleared during the disentanglement process. Side and rear window glass is usually made of tempered safety glass that shatters into many small pieces when struck by a sharply pointed tool. The front windshield is usually made of laminated plate glass and must be cut out with a specially designed **windshield saw, reciprocating saw,** or flathead axe (Figure 27-25).

KEY WORDS

reciprocating saw A hand tool usually powered by an electric motor that is used to cut metal, wood, and other materials. Composed of a handle and working end with a sprocket for holding various cutting saw blades. The cutting action is a back-and-forth action of the blade.

windshield saw A rescue tool designed to cut out the windshield of a vehicle for access and disentanglement operations. It uses a heavy-duty saw blade; human strength drives the tool while it saws through glass.

Victim Disentanglement

With the hazards under control, the vehicle properly stabilized, and access to the victims inside the vehicle accomplished, rescuers are now ready to begin disentanglement procedures. You will be freeing the victim by manipulation, disassembly of vehicle

 Safety Tip!

In all instances, it is extremely important to protectively cover the victim when doing any tool operations or removing glass. Hard or soft protection, or a combination of both, may be most appropriate. As with machinery rescue, be prepared to provide the victim with respiratory, hearing, eye, and head protection prior to working on the vehicle with tools.

parts, or forcibly moving or cutting parts of the vehicle wreckage and debris away from the victim. The overall goal is to create adequate access to the victim, free the victim from any immediate entrapment, and finally, ensure that there is a path of egress for the safe removal of the victim.

Manipulation Because the vehicle crashes that cause victim entrapment frequently occur at high speeds, your victims will usually have multiple trauma injuries. Manipulation will rarely be easily accomplished without further injury to the victim. So the main tactic will be to remove obstructions away from the stationary victim.

Disassembly Disassembling parts of the vehicle will require a wide variety of hand tools. This tactic can be just as effective as utilizing tools to force open the obstacles trapping the victim. The tools you use will depend upon what your fire department has available (Figure 27-26).

Forcing Entry Forcing entry by moving or removing wreckage and parts of the vehicle should be attempted when other means of creating space and

FIGURE 27-27 Roof removal with powered hydraulic cutters.

freeing the victim are not applicable. This involves pushing, pulling, lifting, and cutting vehicle body parts, wreckage, and debris away from the trapped victim.

Roof Removal

Roof removal is performed on an entrapment rescue when a large, open space is needed to access the victim quickly. This involves cutting the posts with hand tools like hacksaws, reciprocating saws, or powered hydraulic cutters (Figures 27-27 and 27-28). With the roof out of the way, good victim access is accomplished and a quick removal might be possible.

Door Openings

Doors that are an obstruction and are jammed shut from the impact of the crash may have to be moved out of the way or completely removed. This is best accomplished with powered hydraulic spreaders but can also be done by disassembling the hinge and latch connections, depending on the circumstances of the door damage and construction of the hinges and latch (Figure 27-29).

Dash Obstruction Openings

One of the most common obstructions pinning the victim in a vehicle crash is the dash. As a result of the collision, it may be forced back and down upon the driver or passengers in the front seat area. You will need to push or lift the dash up and away from the victim to create the necessary space for removing the victim. The tool of choice here is the powered hydraulic ram or spreader. Manual hydraulic spreaders or rams may work but will not be as effective as powered hydraulic tools (Figure 27-30).

FIGURE 27-28 Roof removal with a hacksaw.

Impaled Objects and Lower Extremity Obstructions

With the big obstacles cleared, the victim can be further freed of any additional obstacles by carefully cutting any debris or wreckage that impales the victim. Never pull an impaled object from a victim. Always cut the object, leaving the remainder in the victim for surgical removal in a hospital setting. Small saws and cutters may be used for this purpose.

The victim's feet and legs may be entangled in the pedals under the driver's side of the dash. Pedals and other such impediments can be quickly cut away or bent out of the way by hand or tools to free the legs or feet.

Removing the Victim

Once freed, the victim is packaged and removed from the vehicle under the supervision of Command and emergency medical personnel on the scene. The victim's neck and spine are immobilized to prevent further serious injury, and a coordinated effort is made to carefully move the injured victim (who is now a patient) onto a backboard, secure the patient properly, and lift the patient out. The patient is quickly assessed and rapidly transported to the

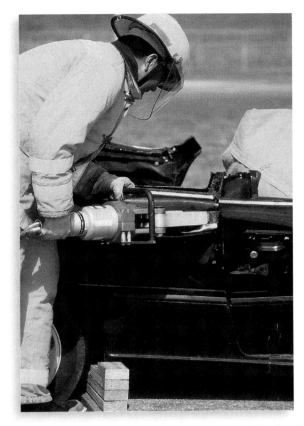

FIGURE 27-29 Opening a door with a powered hydraulic spreader.

FIGURE 27-30 Push or lift the dash up and away from the victim to create the necessary space for removal.

FIGURE 27-31 A coordinated effort is made to carefully move the injured victim onto a backboard, secure him properly, and lift him out.

FIGURE 27-32 When possible, tools should be replaced on the apparatus in a ready-to-respond configuration.

nearest appropriate medical facility by emergency medical personnel (Figure 27-31).

Securing the Crash Scene

With the victims freed and on their way to the hospital, you will be rehabbing and then retrieving your tools and equipment. There are still many dangers and hazards present. Tools may be locked in place holding a load, cribbing may be under the vehicle, and fluids may still be releasing on the scene. Securing tools and equipment should be carefully done in a coordinated manner, utilizing full PPE as worn during the rescue. Always check tools for damage and refill their fuel tanks and other fluids as needed. Report any damaged tools and equipment to your Company Officer for documentation and further repair at the fire station. When possible, tools should be replaced on the apparatus in a ready-to-respond configuration (Figure 27-32). Also, if you or fellow team members have incurred any injuries during the rescue, it is very important to report those injuries to your Company Officer.

Machinery Rescue

Rescue situations in which the victims are trapped by machinery run the full range of possibilities, from a farmer with his arm trapped in a plough to a factory worker with her hand caught in a metal-stamping machine. Wherever there is a mechanical device of some kind, you will have the possibility of having this type of rescue situation. You can also be assured that the general public will call for help from the Fire Service to do this type of rescue. For this reason, we are going into more detail here, discussing strategies and tactics for freeing victims entrapped by machinery.

The arrival and setup methods are the same as for any other rescue. You need to safely arrive and establish control of the situation. Secure access to the scene for rescue personnel and others important to the task at hand. Designate safety zones (hot, warm, and cool) around the rescue scene.

Make the area safe by controlling existing hazards and wearing PPE, including SCBA if you are in an IDLH atmosphere. Machinery should be secured and safely shut down, if this is appropriate for the type of machinery and entrapment.

Be careful to work with those who are familiar with the machine. The trapped farmer will know his or her machinery. The maintenance technician in a manufacturing plant will be invaluable when working around specific machinery. Some machines need to remain energized to keep them from going through another mechanical "cycle" that could potentially harm the patient further. The goal is to bring the machine to a zero mechanical state, which may or may not involve immediately shutting off the power to the machine.

You may need to perform a lockout/tagout on the control switch to the machine and secure access to that switch while the rescue is in progress. The machinery may also need to be stabilized with shoring and cribbing to keep it locked in place. Local business staff or mechanics that are very familiar with the machine involved can provide vital assistance if they are available.

Machinery Rescue Strategy

When someone becomes trapped by machinery mechanisms, there are three main strategic ways to free the victim: manipulate the victim free from the machinery, disassemble the machine, or forcibly open up or cut apart the machine.

Machinery Rescue Tactics

With the three main strategies identified, you can develop the tactics to apply techniques and tools to accomplish the disentanglement of the trapped victim. Always consider the condition of the victim when developing your tactics for removal. Generally speaking, the more severe the injury and the poorer condition of the victim, the less time you have to do the rescue. With someone who is injured, the basic reality is that the quicker they can be freed from their entrapment and transported to a medical facility for further treatment, the better their chance for a successful and quick recovery.

Manipulation

There are times when a simple and careful manipulation of the victim will free the trapped body part from the machinery. This manipulation can include using hand force to move the working parts of the machine to disentangle the victim. Often the manipulation can be facilitated by simply removing a drive belt from a pulley, or operating a handwheel to back off pressure on a roller. In any case, the main philosophy at a rescue is to do no more harm. This means that rescuers do not further injure the victim when they are trying to perform the rescue.

Disassembly

Many times the entrapment is so severe that the machine must be disassembled. This requires rescuers to use common hand tools to take the machinery apart piece by piece until the victim is freed. Disassembly should always be a consideration on a machinery rescue, and rescuers should bring their tools with them (Figure 27-33). If your unit doesn't have the appropriate tools to disassemble a particular machine, then quite often the on-call mechanic for your department does. Don't hesitate to call this valuable resource.

FIGURE 27-33 Disassembly should always be a consideration on a machinery rescue, and rescuers should bring their tools with them.

FIGURE 27-34 Forcible entry involves using specialized rescue tools as well as some common tools to forcibly move or cut through pieces of the machine to free the victim.

Hard and Soft Victim Protection

FIGURE 27-35 Hard and soft victim protection during rescue.

Forcible Entry

This tactic for machinery rescue should be used if you cannot manipulate the victim free or disassemble the machine. It involves using specialized rescue tools as well as some common tools to forcibly move or cut through pieces of the machine to free the victim. To force entry into a machine, you may have to consider tools for pushing, pulling, spreading, lifting, and cutting (Figure 27-34).

Breakout Box

Typical Rescue Tools for Machinery Rescue

Examples of rescue tools for forcing open machinery include the following:

1. Pushing tools—manual and powered hydraulic rams
2. Pulling tools—come-along winch, PTO winch
3. Spreading/lifting tools—manual and powered hydraulic spreaders, pneumatic rescue air bag systems
4. Cutting tools—pneumatic air chisel, pneumatic high-speed cutter, manual or powered hydraulic cutter, and specialized cutting torches

Protect the Victim

It is important that you provide protection for the victim while using rescue tools, because pieces of the machinery and the rescue tools can release suddenly, causing injury to rescuers and victims alike. This protection can be provided in a number of ways.

One way to provide this protection is to work away from the victim's immediate location, forcing or cutting at a safe distance. It may be necessary to protect the victim with head, eye, hearing, or respiratory protection while you work. Soft protection, in the form of a protective tarp or blanket, may also be applied over or near the victim. However, in some circumstances this is not possible and you will need to get close to the victim with tools and equipment.

When working close to the victim, it is important to provide a protective barrier between the victim and the pieces of machinery and operating tools. You can do this by placing hard protection, like a board or other separation, to isolate the victim from potential injury (Figure 27-35).

Escalators and Elevators

When we talk about rescues involving escalators and elevators, we are talking about basic transportation machines. These machines usually move people from one level in a building to another. At first you may think that elevators and escalators are not that common, especially in rural areas; however, they are found in many more places than you might consider.

Level II

FIGURE 27-36 Escalators are a conveyor system that moves steps up or down, or a synthetic sidewalk surface that moves horizontally.

Escalators and Moving Sidewalks

Escalators can be found in large, open areas in multi-level buildings and provide moving stairs for customer convenience. They can also be in the form of a moving sidewalk—for example, moving passengers quickly between gates in a large airport terminal complex.

Whether moving stairs or a moving sidewalk, escalators are basically either a conveyor system that moves steps up or down or a synthetic sidewalk surface that moves horizontally. The machinery mechanism is located at either end of the escalator. These devices have a large electric motor and gearing system. The stairs or moving sidewalk move along a gear or roller system spaced out underneath. All are in a large loop that turns as the escalator system works (Figure 27-36).

All of these systems have an emergency shutoff located at each end of the system. In all cases, it is important to control the power to the escalator system to prevent unexpected operation during rescue efforts.

People become entrapped mainly at the ends of the escalator, where the step or sidewalk ends and moves under the permanent flooring ahead. Rescue efforts usually involve any of the strategies we have already mentioned, including manipulation, disassembly, or forcing open the mechanism. It is very important that an escalator mechanic be called to the scene to assist when possible. The mechanic will have an intimate knowledge of the escalator machinery and is a valuable resource.

Elevators A very common mode of transport in modern society is the elevator. Elevators are usually a very safe and reliable form of transportation; however, victims do become trapped by them from time to time.

An elevator system is composed of an elevator shaft, the elevator vehicle, guide rails inside the

Typical Elevator System

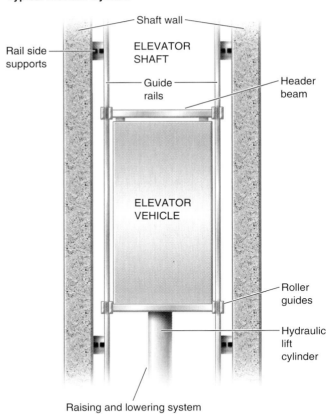

FIGURE 27-37 A typical elevator system.

elevator shaft on which the elevator travels, and the system for raising or lowering the elevator. The elevator operating system can be either an electric-powered motor with cables, or an electric-powered hydraulic system with a hydraulic piston providing the lifting and lowering action. Electric motor systems will tend to be found in higher buildings (Figure 27-37).

Elevators have emergency stop buttons and override systems for Fire Department use installed in them. They may or may not have a communications system installed for communication from the elevator vehicle itself during an emergency. In all instances, it is important for rescuers to control the power to the operating system of the elevator. Machine rooms, which contain the operating equipment, are usually located at the top or bottom of the elevator. These should always be accessed and switches controlled by rescue personnel during rescue operations. For rescue operations, the power to the elevator system should be shut down to avoid any accidental movement of the elevator car during rescue efforts. Other people's access should also be controlled to these areas.

Ladder evacuation of an elevator:
To upper landing

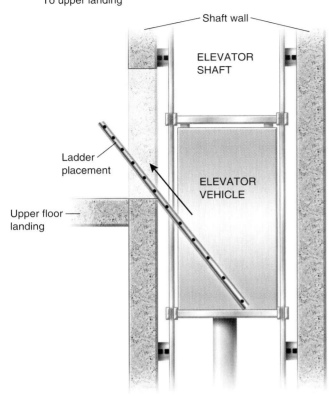

Ladder evacuation of an elevator:
To lower landing

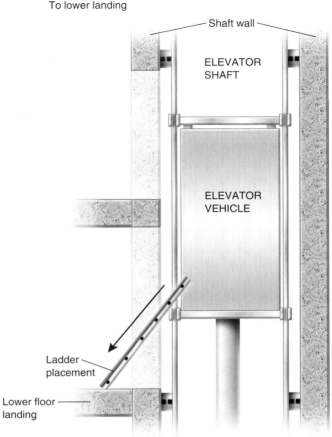

FIGURE 27-38   A ladder placed for evacuation out of a stalled elevator car.

Review It!

See Chapter 24 for specific information about the emergency operation of elevator systems.

Elevator entrapment situations usually fall into two main categories: entrapment inside the stalled elevator car and entrapment by the mechanism of the elevator itself.

If riders are trapped inside the stalled elevator car, the rescue may be as simple as using an elevator door key to release the doors at a floor-level landing and allowing the occupants to leave the elevator. If the elevator car is stuck between floors, its door can be opened by using the elevator key, a ladder can be placed into the elevator car from the landing above or below, and the victims can be assisted up or down the ladder (Figure 27-38). Elevator doors can also be forced open with forcible entry tools or hydraulic spreaders in an emergency situation where time is of

the essence. Remember, severe damage will result to the elevator doors.

If the elevator car is too far down the shaft from the landing, a rescuer can access the top of the elevator car and open the emergency access hatch in the top of the vehicle. A ladder can be lowered inside to evacuate the victims through the hatch to the safety of the landing above (Figure 27-39).

Tip!

As with escalators, an elevator mechanic on the scene can be a great assistance during rescue operations. Elevator mechanics are usually well trained in the design and operation of the elevator equipment and machinery.

Victims can become trapped by the elevator mechanisms in a couple of common ways. First, the

Ladder evacuation of an elevator:
Through emergency hatch

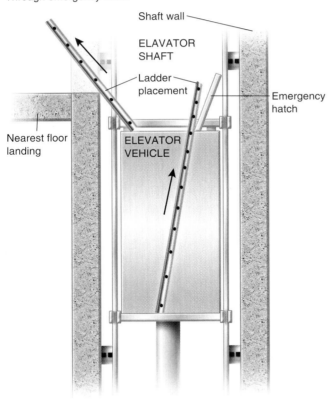

FIGURE 27-39 A ladder placed for evacuation up and out of an elevator car hatch.

elevator door or entrance can entrap a victim between the landing floor and the elevator car. A victim could also be entrapped between the elevator car and the interior of the elevator shaft. This can involve an elevator service worker or even someone illegally riding on top of the elevator car.

The two main tactics for releasing a victim trapped in either of these situations is to either move the elevator car or remove the obstruction. In all cases, this is a severe entrapment situation and you must work under the coordination and guidance of trained rescue personnel.

Water Rescue

The extent and need for water rescue capability in a community depends on the topography of the local area as well as the demographics of the citizenry. However, nearly every community has some need for water-rescue-capable rescue teams. Water rescue can involve static bodies of water, such as lakes, ponds, swimming pools, and spas. There are also moving bodies of water—for example, rivers, streams, and

FIGURE 27-40 Every community has some need for water-rescue-capable rescue teams.

drainage canals. A flood can also be considered a moving body of water, where there was no water before. So as we can see, there is a need for some sort of water rescue capability in virtually every community (Figure 27-40).

In order to respond to rescue emergencies in both static and moving water, rescuers need to be trained in many types of water rescue techniques. These techniques may involve the rescue of victims in water by surface rescue, underwater diving, working on ice and in icy water conditions, saltwater rescue in coastal surf, and swift-water rescue in rivers, streams, and canals.

As a possible first-arriving responder to a water rescue incident, you should follow the benchmarks for rescue as you respond and arrive on the scene. Securing a water rescue scene can be as simple as securing the pool in the backyard of a home or as complex as setting up operations on a large lake working with several resources to search for drowning victims. You may be called upon to set up a secure area around the incident, restricting access to only those needed for the rescue operation.

There are several hazards associated with water rescue operations. The immediate hazard is the risk of you becoming a victim. Wear a **personal flotation device (PFD)** when working at or near the edge of the water, especially moving water or large and deep bodies of water. Also, consider the potential hazards that can be present. Water rescue incidents can expose you to virtually every hazard associated with a fire, such as electrical wires submerged in the water and still energized, building collapse, explosions from gas leaks, and hazardous chemicals in the water. Even a swimming pool can be a hazard if energized wiring is exposed to the pool water. Be prepared to isolate and shut off utilities when needed.

Drainage culverts can become a confined-space rescue when they are flooded and a person is trapped inside. Such rescues require training in water rescue, confined-space rescue, and possibly a cave diving certification. Any hazards that are immediately dangerous to life and health (IDLH) should be recognized and isolated or removed.

 KEY WORD

personal flotation device (PFD) A compact lifesaving flotation device worn as a precaution against drowning while standing or working near a body of water.

 **Safety Tip!**

Use caution around any water rescue scene. Wear appropriate PPE for the potential hazards, including a helmet. Remember, you can fall into a hole, stumble, be cut by debris, and receive blows to your body at these scenes. And remember to wear a personal flotation device (PFD) when necessary.

The difference between the rescue of a potentially live victim versus recovering a deceased victim should be realized. You do not have the time factor when performing body recovery compared to the urgency when a live victim is involved. Your Company Officer will know which mode of operation you will be using.

Tip!

The remaining rescue disciplines that follow are regulated by the Occupational Safety and Health Administration (OSHA). Fire departments may be severely fined if they operate outside these guidelines.

Rope Rescue

Most rope rescues are considered to be aboveground-level rescue operations. This is not always the case. Rope rescue techniques are used many times in all other types of rescue operations. For instance, you can use rope rescue techniques to access subterranean areas in a confined-space incident or building collapse. Rope rescue techniques are also used in swift-water and ice rescue operations. Even trench rescue operations can require rope rescue techniques, especially for patient removal (Figure 27-41).

FIGURE 27-41 Rope rescue techniques can be used in many other types of rescue operations.

Arrival at and assessment of an aboveground incident are similar to previously discussed procedures. The only difference here is the attempt to safely establish communications with any victims, letting them know that additional help is on the way. Again, security and work zones are established around these incident scenes.

The hazards unique to rope rescue operations that you need to protect yourself against are falls, especially if you are stationed near an elevated edge. This protection may include the use of safety harnesses and safety lines. The work area established around the rescue incident should be a minimum of 300 feet in all directions. This area should be made safe by stabilizing or eliminating hazards, securing the area to allow in only rescue personnel in appropriate PPE who are working on the rescue effort. If the work area is near vehicles or equipment, these should be controlled and shut down if needed to reduce unnecessary vibration of the ground and structures.

 Safety Tip!

Minimum PPE for working around a rope rescue incident should start with rescue helmet and gloves as well as a harness for fall protection as needed. Firefighting PPE would be called for at these incidents only as dictated by potential or existing fire hazards or any immediate dangers to life and health that are present. Your Company Officer will tell you the proper PPE for the conditions present.

Confined-Space Rescue

Continuing with the same response and arrival procedures as other rescue disciplines, confined-space rescue applies to any confined-space area. A confined space is any area accessible to people that is normally not designed to be accessible to people. For example, it can be a drainage culvert, a large storage tank, or an elevator shaft. Confined spaces may or may not have sufficient oxygen levels to breathe, and they can contain deadly levels of other gases like carbon monoxide. Hazardous chemicals can be present in some locations. You need to also consider the possibility of hot or cold temperature extremes in confined spaces. They can also have submersion hazards, such as with a farm storage silo or a grain elevator. Confined spaces do not have normal ventilation and access openings and are very dangerous places. They normally require a permit for the general public to enter and work inside them (Figure 27-42).

You need to be able to recognize when you have a confined-space rescue situation, and your Company Officer will know who to call to perform this specialized rescue. The rescue will involve attempting to establish communications with trapped victims when possible.

As with all rescue operations, hazards must be assessed and controlled at and around the confined-space incident. You are not to enter a confined space to attempt a rescue unless you are properly trained and have the appropriate PPE and rescue equipment. These are very dangerous spaces, and many rescuers have been killed or injured while attempting to access and rescue a victim trapped in a confined space. Your job will be to assist non-entry operations outside the confined space, such as helping to stage tools and equipment, secure the area around the site of the rescue, and control the necessary personnel who enter and leave the site.

After rescuers and victims have been removed to a safe area outside the confined space, you may have to assist with decontamination efforts for them. This might mean operating a hose line to wash off hazardous chemicals, or helping to set up decontamination facilities brought in by hazardous materials response teams.

Trench Rescue

For our purposes in this text, trench rescue includes any rescue situation in which victims are trapped in excavations and trenches, cave-ins, and collapsed tunnels. They can be partially or totally covered by rock, dirt, debris, or even grain or mineral product. Trench rescue emergencies require the use of cribbing, shoring, and, in some instances, sheeting materials to support, retard, and reduce the hazard of further collapse of the materials in which the victim is trapped. Because the locations are not designed for normal use and occupancy by humans, these sites are also considered confined spaces and must be accessed and exited under those safety requirements.

Trench rescue situations are perhaps the most hazardous for rescuers. This is due to the potential for secondary collapse of unstable materials at or near the trapped victim (Figure 27-43).

Breakout Box

Indications and Causes of Trench Collapses

Initial and secondary trench collapses can be caused by several conditions, including:

1. Heavy loads too near the trench opening
2. No trench collapse protection system
3. Trench openings that intersect
4. Too much vibration from nearby equipment and vehicles
5. Cracking in trench walls
6. Water in the trench opening
7. Poor soil conditions

Any time the ground soil is disturbed by digging and tunneling, the sides of the trench can become unstable. There are also times when excavations are made into previously disturbed soils, creating a further unstable situation. One side of a trench wall can collapse. This is called a **shear wall collapse.**

FIGURE 27-42 A confined space is any area accessible to people that is not designed to be normally accessible to people.

FIGURE 27-43 Because of the potential for secondary collapse of unstable materials at or near the trapped victim, trench rescue situations are very hazardous for rescuers.

FIGURE 27-44 Spoil piles, made next to a trench excavation, can slide into the open hole.

A section of trench wall below ground level can fall away, in what is referred to as a **slough collapse. Spoil piles,** made next to a trench excavation, can also slide into the open hole. Trench rescues are extended operations primarily because of this potential hazard (Figure 27-44).

Soil can weigh about 100 pounds per cubic foot and 1.5 tons per cubic yard. This factor explains the entrapment hazard of soil alone, even before any injuries or other objects or equipment pins the victim. This fact also demonstrates the potential hazard to you during a secondary collapse.

The main way to identify these rescue incidents is their location in areas where there are construction projects, road work, caves, and tunnels in piled granular materials. There will probably be obvious indicators at the collapse itself, such as indications of recent digging or tools and equipment. The observations of eyewitnesses can be valuable in determining how many victims there are and their possible locations.

KEY WORDS

shear wall collapse A trench rescue term that describes the inward collapse of a section of trench wall. This type of collapse is also a common cause of secondary entrapments of workers and rescuers during a trench rescue operation. For this reason, sheeting and shoring techniques are used to make the trench safe for rescuers.

slough collapse A trench collapse event in which a section of the trench wall below ground level falls away into the trench opening.

spoil piles Piles of dirt next to a trench excavation that contain the dirt dug out from the trench.

 Safety Tip!

It is very important for your safety to realize the potential for additional collapse of unstable areas in a trench rescue emergency. Vehicles should be positioned at a distance. Always approach the edge with caution. Lay out supporting sheeting along the edge of a trench collapse to help reduce failure of the side of the trench opening. Entry to these areas should not be attempted until they are cribbed, shored, and sheeted to reinforce the sides. The hole will also need to be checked for an IDLH atmosphere, and should be ventilated with fresh air as soon as possible, prior to entry.

Due to the complexity and dangers of specialized rescue, personnel and equipment must be requested as soon as the need is identified. If your department does not have these resources, then an appropriate agency must be notified to respond. For this reason, recognizing the type of rescue involved and providing constantly updated reports are key parts of your initial job at the scene. In addition, the scene must be secured with safety zones also established and maintained throughout the emergency operation.

Quick rescues of people who are not injured or entrapped by collapsed soils and materials can be made by quickly positioning a ladder into the hole at a safe distance. Again, you must be extremely cautious as you approach the edge of the hole to position a ladder. The edge can shear away, injuring you and the trapped people as well. Once the ladder is placed, leave the edge and allow the people in the trench to evacuate on their own. Be sure to rapidly escort them to a cool safety zone, away from the opening, for further evaluation by trained emergency medical personnel.

Because of the amount of materials that will be used for shoring, sheeting, and protecting the edges of the hole, there is the potential for large or numerous equipment and materials staging areas just outside the warm zone. In addition, wood materials may need to be cut to fit inside the hole to support and secure the opening for rescuers as they make their way to the victim. A "woodshop" may be established outside the warm zone to fabricate these materials. You may be assigned to help in these areas or to assist in getting the materials to the rescuers inside the hole.

When the victim has been freed, several rescuers may be needed to safely remove the victim from the hole or excavation. You may be assigned to assist outside the hole with this victim removal. Again, you must use caution around these very unstable openings.

After the rescue has been accomplished, the removal of tools, equipment, shoring, and sheeting will take place. This operation must be done under strict supervision. Usually these items are retrieved in reverse order from how they were placed. The hole is still very dangerous, and when the stabilizing materials and shoring have been removed, the risk for further collapse becomes great. Never enter the hole after stabilization materials and equipment have been removed. If a tool or piece of equipment is dropped in the hole, it may have to be left there, or else the stabilization might have to be reinserted to make the hole safe again. Otherwise, leave it there. The danger is too great for retrieval.

Building Collapse Rescue

Buildings can collapse for a variety of reasons. They can be weakened by age or have a poor design. They can be affected by a fire that destroys structural support components. Natural disasters such as earthquakes, hurricanes, and tornadoes can also weaken

FIGURE 27-45 Because of the risk of secondary collapse of an already weakened building, a building collapse emergency can further injure rescuers if the building is not properly assessed for safe access and stabilized with shoring and cribbing.

and cause buildings to collapse. In any event, building collapse incidents present a particularly hazardous situation for rescuers when they arrive and begin to search for and rescue trapped victims. Because of the risk of secondary collapse of an already weakened building, a building collapse emergency can further injure rescuers if the building is not properly assessed for safe access and stabilized with shoring and cribbing (Figure 27-45).

The rescue techniques associated with building collapse at your level of training include determining the need for building collapse rescuers, securing the scene, restricting bystander access, and establishing an initial Command structure and safety zones. We will explain the basic types of possible collapse configurations in a building to help you recognize the need for additional expertise. The other techniques—securing the scene, establishing command, and creating safety zones—are essentially the same in all rescue operations.

You also need to be able to check for and assist in controlling hazards. These skills are similar to any hazard on a structure fire scene and are controlled in very much the same way.

Finally, you must be able to assist with searches, stabilization of unstable collapse areas, and disentanglement and removal of trapped victims. We'll cover some of the techniques for marking buildings before, during, and after searches, and for marking building hazards as practiced by the **Federal Emergency Management Agency (FEMA).** For stabilization, disentanglement, and removal of trapped victims, your assistance will be directed by specialized rescue teams.

■■■■ KEY WORD ■■■■

Federal Emergency Management Agency (FEMA) A federal agency under the direct control of the Department of Homeland Security responsible for federal response to natural disasters. It also provides federal assistance to the Fire Services in the United States.

Collapse Configurations

When buildings collapse, they usually end up with one or more floors dislodged and fallen on top of lower floors. Debris from the roof or upper floors then comes to rest on top of the collapsed floors. Walls may fall inward or outward, also releasing their hold on the roof and upper floor structures, dropping them down onto lower floors of the building. These situations create void spaces that can potentially contain live victims trapped by the debris.

Breakout Box

Floor Collapse Configurations

Floor collapse situations as described by NFPA 1670, *Operations and Training for Technical Rescue Incidents,* include the following:

1. Lean-to (Figure 27-46)
2. "V" (Figure 27-47)
3. Pancake (Figure 27-48)
4. Cantilever (Figure 27-49)
5. "A" Frame (Figure 27-50)

Search and Hazard Status Markings

While buildings are being searched and evaluated, they are marked for stability and safety as well as their status. From these markings you can tell the degree of potential hazards inside the building and whether or not the building has already been searched. This system is used primarily when there is more than one building collapsed in an area, such as a result of earthquake, hurricane, tornado, landslide, or flood. Orange spray paint is usually used to make these markings.

Wilderness Rescue

Rescuing people trapped or lost in wilderness situations is another very specific type of operation. These situations can be dangerous for untrained rescuers.

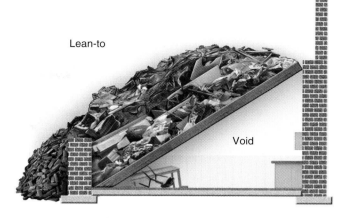

Lean-to

FIGURE 27-46

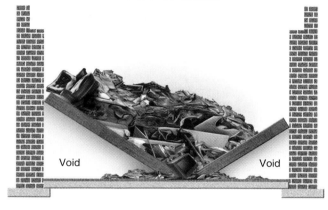

V-shape floor collapse

FIGURE 27-47

Pancake floor collapse

FIGURE 27-48

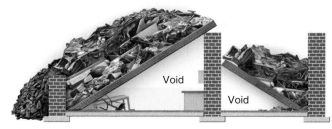

A-frame floor collapse

FIGURE 27-49

Cantilever floor collapse

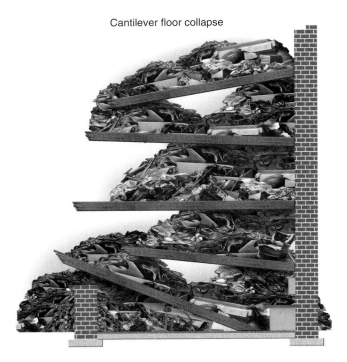

FIGURE 27-50

FIGURE 27-51

Single diagonal marking:
means search is in progress

FIGURE 27-52

Cross marks:
mean search is done

FIGURE 27-53

E-30
010207
13:32

Left quadrant of cross marks:
used to indicate the search team and
the time and date the search began

FIGURE 27-54

010207
16:52

E-30
010207
13:32

Upper quadrant of cross marks:
used to indicate the time and date
when the search was completed or
the team exited the search area

Breakout Box

Six Standard Search Status Markings

1. Single diagonal marking—means search is in progress (Figure 27-51)
2. Single diagonal marking with a circle over the center—indicates an incomplete search, Do Not Enter.
3. Cross marks—mean search is done (Figure 27-52)
4. Left Quadrant of Cross Marks—used to indicate the search team (Figure 27-53) and the time and date the search began.
5. Upper Quadrant of Cross Marks—used to indicate the time and date when the search was completed or the team exited the search area. (Figure 27-54)
6. Right Quadrant of Cross Marks—used to indicate the personal hazards present (Figure 27-55)
7. Lower Quadrant of Cross Marks—used to indicate the number of live and dead victims inside, with "X" meaning none (Figure 27-56)

FIGURE 27-55

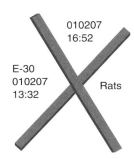

Right quadrant of cross marks:
used to indicate the personal hazards present

FIGURE 27-56

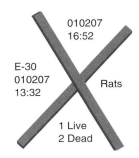

Lower quadrant of cross marks:
used to indicate the number of live and
dead victims inside, with "X" meaning none

If you aren't familiar with the wilderness area, then leave walking in the woods to those who are. For this reason, your job as a Level II firefighter is to assess and set up the scene as with all rescue responses. Your next job is to call for trained wilderness rescue assistance and establish a Command post. The Fire Department can support the operation by providing lights, electricity from generators, Command, and organizational abilities. You would then assist the wilderness rescue personnel according to your qualifications and training.

Do It!

Practice Safe Rescue Skills

This chapter has provided some insight into the extent of your involvement at various rescue situations. You are required to have more knowledge in some disciplines, such as vehicle rescue, than in others, such as trench collapse rescue. However, you should at least have some knowledge of the many rescue disciplines out there, how to set up and begin scene control, and what type of rescue assistance to call for help.

Rescue is a valuable skill all firefighters should seek to develop. Additional training in awareness, as well as developing skills in the operational and technical levels of all the rescue disciplines, is highly recommended to fully develop your career and capability as a firefighter.

Never forget the potential dangers at any rescue scene. Stay informed and protected at all times, and always work as a team under supervision of Incident Command. Stay safe!

Knowledge Assessment

Rescue Awareness—Chapter 27

Name: _____

Fill out the ten-question quiz below, the Knowledge Assessment Sheet, by circling the correct answer. When finished, sign it and give to your instructor/Company Officer for his or her signature. Turn in this Knowledge Assessment Sheet to the proper person as part of the documentation that you have completed your training for this chapter.

1. At a rescue emergency, unstable objects and debris must be stabilized prior to accessing, disentangling, and removing a victim.
   - **a.** True
   - **b.** False

2. During vehicle extrication operations, what should rescuers avoid using between the victim and undeployed air bag restraint systems?
   - **a.** Soft victim protection
   - **b.** Their hands
   - **c.** Hard victim protection
   - **d.** Radios

3. Why is the roof removed in some vehicle rescue operations?
   - **a.** To access the cargo compartment
   - **b.** To provide a large opening quickly
   - **c.** To get the vehicle ready for towing
   - **d.** To make the vehicle less heavy

4. A quick rescue and rapid transport of the injured victim to the proper medical facility for further treatment usually results in what for the victim?
   - **a.** Lower insurance costs
   - **b.** A longer recovery time
   - **c.** A more successful and quicker recovery
   - **d.** A less successful recovery

5. The victims trapped in an elevator rescue situation are trapped inside the elevator car. How else can they be trapped?
   - **a.** By the mechanism of the elevator
   - **b.** By blocked elevator doors
   - **c.** By a stalled elevator car
   - **d.** By a power outage

6. Working at a large lake or body of water on a water rescue incident may require your fire department to interact with many different resources.
   - **a.** True
   - **b.** False

7. Safety devices for fall protection during elevated rope rescue operations may include what items?
   a. Safety rails
   b. Larger safety zones
   c. Traffic cones
   d. Safety harnesses and safety lines

8. What will your job most likely involve at a confined-space rescue incident?
   a. Going into the confined space
   b. Assisting with non-entry work
   c. Passing tools and equipment out of the confined space
   d. Holding lighting equipment inside the confined space

9. In trench rescue operations, the cribbing, shoring, and sheeting materials are used for what inside the trench?
   a. Victim removal
   b. To mark the trench boundaries
   c. To support the sides of the trench, preventing further collapse
   d. To keep the hole clean while working

10. What potential occurrence puts rescuers in danger of injury at a building collapse incident that has not been properly assessed and stabilized?
   a. Difficult victim removal
   b. Running out of time
   c. A secondary building collapse
   d. Insufficient tools and equipment

Skills Assessment

Rescue Awareness—Chapter 27

Name: _____

Fill out the Skills Assessment Sheet below. Have your instructor/Company Officer check off and initial each skill you demonstrate. When you are finished, sign this page and give to your instructor/Company Officer for his or her signature. Turn in this Skills Assessment Sheet to the proper person as part of the documentation that you have completed your training for this chapter.

Skill	Completed	Initials
1. Explain risk assessment for rescue operations and rescuers.	_____	_____
2. Describe common rescue operation scene benchmark events, including response and arrival, establishing control, controlling hazards, stabilization, victim access, disentanglement, victim removal and rapid transport, and securing tools and equipment.	_____	_____
3. Identify the different orientation points and explain the basic construction of vehicles.	_____	_____
4. Describe scene setup operations unique to vehicle crash scenes.	_____	_____
5. Explain stabilization tactics for vehicles in various positions.	_____	_____
6. Identify typical hand tools used on vehicle extrication rescue operations.	_____	_____
7. Identify typical hydraulic powered tools used on vehicle extrication operations.	_____	_____
8. Explain the main rescue strategies and tactical considerations for machine rescue situations.	_____	_____
9. Describe how victims may be entrapped and subsequently disentangled from escalators and elevators.	_____	_____
10. List the other major categories of rescue disciplines.	_____	_____
11. Demonstrate how to mark a building during search and rescue operations.	_____	_____

Student Signature and Date _____ Instructor/Company Officer Signature and Date _____

Post-Fire Activities

What You Will Learn in This Chapter

This chapter starts by discussing how a fire's origin and cause are determined after the fire. It continues with the importance of preserving evidence on the scene and the concept of chain of custody. We finish the chapter with discussions of how the fire department is assisting fire victims today.

What You Will Be Able to Do

After reading this chapter, you will be able to:

1. Explain the general procedures for determining the origin of a fire.

2. Discuss the typical procedure for determining the cause of a fire.

3. Define the term *arson*.

4. Explain the components of a juvenile fire-setter prevention program.

5. Describe how to protect evidence at a fire scene under investigation.

6. Explain the chain-of-custody concept for evidence.

7. List the six topics of important information for fire victims who are beginning their fire-loss recovery process.

8. Explain the benefits of a Citizen Assistance Program for fire-loss recovery.

Reality!

You're Not Done Yet!

It seems like a long time since you started your training and were introduced into the Fire Service at the beginning of our curriculum. Now you can work both outside and inside a structure fire, and with this final part of the course finished, you'll have some insight about a leadership role.

However, once the fire has been extinguished, there are two additional important jobs to be done: determining the origin and cause of the fire, and assisting the occupant with the initial steps to recovery from the fire loss. Both are important—both are critical to your overall success in completing the job.

More than ever before, the modern Fire Service is committed to finding out what causes fires and preventing their recurrence. Whether the fire resulted from flawed design or accidental, negligent, or criminal causes, part of your job after the fire is to begin sorting out what happened. In many cases, your actions at this point will determine if anything good comes from a fire incident. Did we learn something? Did we alert those responsible for stopping criminal activity, such as fraud or **arson?** Or did we just pick up our stuff, fill out an incident report, and wait for the next fire? Did we just plug holes in the dike instead of trying to build a better dike? Fires are serious events that kill thousands of people each year and destroy billions of dollars of property. If you can make a difference by your actions, then you have done your job.

Helping the occupant recover starts as soon as you arrive on the fire scene. You first protect their lives by getting them out and to a safe area, and then you minimize the damage to their property by extinguishing the fire as quickly and as safely as possible. However, your actions in assisting them after they have suffered so much from this traumatic event are an essential part of your job as a firefighter. Today's Fire Service is finding that extinguishing the fire is not the end of the incident. We also must provide some fire victim assistance immediately after the fire in order to do a more complete service to the community.

▰▰ KEY WORD ▰▰

arson   Any intentionally set fire that is started with malicious intent to cover up a crime, as an act of revenge, as an act of vandalism, for insurance fraud, or perhaps to satisfy a psychological gratification (pyromania).

Cause and Origin

Once the fire has been extinguished and overhaul is mostly completed, it is time to start to figure out what happened and why it happened. You may not be in a position to do a preliminary fire investigation. In some communities, the Level II firefighter has some responsibility for this skill. If you will be expected to perform a preliminary fire investigation, then you should receive further specialized training compliant with **NFPA 1021,** *Standard for Fire Officer Professional Qualifications.*

For our purposes, we'll present an overview of determining the cause and origin and preserving evidence at a firefighter's level of responsibility, as someone who will assist his or her Company Officer and fellow team members in this task.

The origin of the fire is the specific area where the fire first ignited. The place where the fire started can also be referred to by fire investigators as the point of origin.

▰▰ KEY WORD ▰▰

NFPA 1021, *Standard for Fire Officer Professional Qualifications*   A code standard adopted by the NFPA that covers the qualifications recommended for fire officers in the Fire Service.

 **Safety Tip!**

Any investigation should be started after the fire has been extinguished, overhaul has been completed, and the property has been made relatively safe from hazards like smoke and rekindling. Always wear appropriate PPE and, when necessary, SCBA. Be observant of unstable structural components made unsafe by the fire and stay away from these until they are made safe. They can collapse without warning. A fire-damaged structure is a very dangerous place.

Determining Origin

Where did the fire start? That is one of the first questions to be answered when investigating a fire. The answer lies in three main areas of fire scene investigation. First, where was the main body of fire and smoke involvement when you arrived on the scene? These

FIGURE 28-1   The remains and debris after the fire will often tell a story about what happened.

FIGURE 28-2   Allow victims and witnesses to tell their story about what happened.

are your observations while attacking the fire. Second, what do witnesses and occupants tell you about the fire location? Finally, what story do the remnants and debris on the fire scene tell you about the fire's point of origin? (Figure 28-1).

When rehashing what you observed while fighting the fire, consider the location, intensity, and color of the smoke and flames. Where was the main body of the fire located when you entered the building to extinguish the blaze? It is true that fires can spread far from the original starting point, but in most cases the main body of the fire will point to the original fire's location.

When discussing what happened during the fire with witnesses and occupants, allow them to tell you their story, and listen for specifics about where they saw the fire before calling for the fire department (Figure 28-2). This can either reinforce or weaken your initial conclusions about where the fire started.

Finally, check the property. Begin with the exterior and do a 360-degree walk around the outside. Look for any visible fire and smoke damage to the exterior. The more damage from fire, the closer you are likely to be to the general point of origin.

If it is safe enough, proceed to the interior. Follow the charring and smoke discoloration of interior walls, ceilings, and floor as well as furnishings and contents. As with the exterior observations, the interior will likely have deeper charring and smoke damage the closer you get to the fire's origin. Fire in-

"V" burn pattern on a wall

FIGURE 28-3   The bottom of a V-shaped burn pattern on a wall will often point to the origin of the fire.

vestigators will often measure the depth of charring as they hone in on the actual point of origin of a fire.

Because fires tend to burn upward, one tactic is to find the lowest point of fire damage. This will tend to point to a possible area of fire origin.

In a small fire that involves one room or an area of a room, look for burn patterns on the walls in the shape of a "V." Many times, these burn patterns point to the possible area of origin at the bottom of the "V." Look at the flooring and check for burn patterns and charring (Figure 28-3).

In a significantly fire-damaged structure, follow the fire damage and charring from least to worst. Even

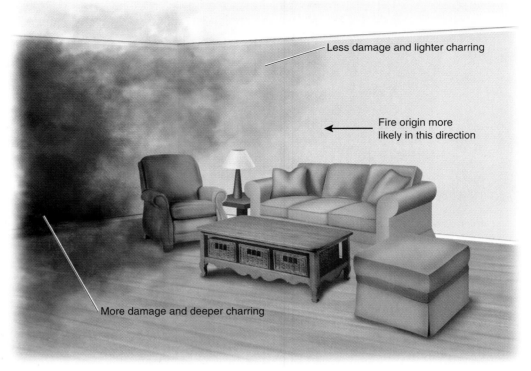

Less damage and lighter charring

Fire origin more likely in this direction

More damage and deeper charring

Depth of charring

FIGURE 28-4 The depth of charring in the burned area will increase, the closer you get to the origin of the fire.

in these instances, the deeper the charring and the greater the fire damage, the closer you are likely to be to the origin of the fire (Figure 28-4).

Occupants or bystanders should not be allowed back into the burned structure until it has been investigated for cause and origin, and the fire extinguishment efforts and overhaul are completed. This is for their safety as well as for proper evidence conservation and preventing evidence contamination. If the owner or occupant absolutely must return to the interior, a firefighter or a law enforcement officer should escort him or her. This reentry must be documented.

Determining Cause

With the area of fire origin identified, it is now time to determine the possible cause of the fire. The causes will fall into several general categories, including accidental or negligent actions by occupants, intentional actions (such as arson or fraud), acts of nature, occupancy conditions or processes, and equipment failure.

The methods used to determine the cause of the fire are similar to investigating the origin of the fire. In fact, as you go through the property, use the same processes. Consider the observations you made while you attacked the fire, what the occupants and witnesses tell you about the cause of the fire, and finally, any evidence you find while checking the property after the fire has been extinguished.

The main strategy is the process of eliminating possible causes until you narrow the list down to a few suspected possibilities. For example, most fires are not assumed to be arson from the very beginning. The fire investigator must first eliminate all other possible causes. Then, if no obvious cause is present, he or she will concentrate the investigation on an intentionally set fire.

Conditions that you observe while extinguishing the fire can help the fire investigation greatly. Unusual fire conditions that are not appropriate for the type of occupancy or the area that is on fire can indicate any special circumstances that point to the cause of the fire. Were doors open or closed when you entered the building to extinguish the fire? Was the furniture located in normal positions, or was it piled in the middle of the room? Did you observe any broken or forced windows that were not forced open by the fire department? Was the fire difficult to extin-

FIGURE 28-5 Checking for possible accelerant use on a fire is important for the investigation.

guish? Did you smell any odd or unusual odors that could have been **accelerants?** These are examples of observations that you can communicate to fire investigators or consider yourself in attempting to narrow the cause of the fire (Figure 28-5).

KEY WORD

accelerant Any material—solid, liquid, or gas—that has been intentionally used to start a fire or to increase the intensity or rate of a fire's burn.

Tip!

Arson and Fire Setters

Fires are intentionally set for a variety of reasons. Arson fires are set to cover up a crime, as an act of revenge, as an act of vandalism, for insurance fraud, or perhaps to satisfy a psychological gratification (pyromania).

Children are fascinated by fire. This is rather common. However, some children are so attracted to fire that they will start setting them intentionally. Many fire departments have "Fire Setter" prevention programs that utilize specially trained personnel who work with counselors to try to identify and help juvenile fire setters.

Unfortunately, intentionally set fires are common occurrences, and arson should be suspected as a fire cause at any fire incident.

Juvenile Fire-Setter Programs

Young children have a natural curiosity about fire. Their curiosity may at times cause them to play with matches or cigarette lighters. Unfortunately, this behavior can lead to loss of life and property. Many fire departments now have Juvenile Fire-Setter Programs that identify children who are beginning to have a problem with starting and playing with fires.

These programs have several components. The first is a system for identifying a child who should be involved in the program. This is usually done by the child's parents, who seek out help with their child. Next, the family is evaluated to determine the needs of the child and the family. The child is then educated about the dangers of fires. The family is educated about the best methods for correcting the child's behavior in the home environment. In this way, the Fire Service is able to reduce potential fire-starting problems for the child later in life.

Next, consider what witnesses and occupants are telling you about what they think caused the fire. Many times they will know exactly what happened. Perhaps a child was playing with candles or matches. Maybe there was a domestic dispute that ended in an intentional fire. Maybe they were working around flammable materials that caught fire. Could the building have been struck by lightning? The list of possible fire causes is endless. Good information from witnesses and occupants can be of great assistance in determining the possible fire cause.

Finally, continuing your observations as you check the property after the fire is crucial to detecting fire's cause. Start again on the exterior and do a 360-degree survey around the property. Be on the alert for anything unusual like obvious preexisting fire hazards, damaged equipment, and any evidence of accelerant containers in the area.

When you go inside, start to look for possible sources of ignition, particularly at or near the point of origin. If a fire started, something had to start it, so there may be obvious evidence of that ignition source in the debris and burned rubble near the point of origin.

Combined with the observations you made while you were fighting the fire and what the occupants and witnesses have told you, a careful look at the area of the fire's point of origin may provide a solution for the cause of the fire. Try to mentally reconstruct what the room looked like before the fire. Was there anything electrical in the room? Was the occupant doing anything there before the fire? Are the occupants smokers and are there smoking materials in the area? What processes were taking place (if a commercial fire)?

 **Tip!**

Do not disturb the debris and potential evidence. This is the point where firefighters can be of immeasurable help to investigators by isolating and protecting the evidence of the fire. Your training is intended to give you an awareness of the point of origin and cause of the fire; you are not being trained as a fire investigator. Your best contribution will be your observations while fighting the fire and observing and securing any evidence for further consideration by your Company Officer or a fire investigator.

Evidence Considerations

The most important thing you can do as a firefighter after the fire has been extinguished and overhauled is to be vigilant about protecting the evidence of the potential fire cause and origin. Certainly the fire must be extinguished, and that is your main goal after life safety. However, with a few good habits on your part, you can contribute to an accurate fire investigation. The two main factors you need to know are how to reach a balance between complete overhaul and evidence preservation, and the chain-of-custody requirements for that evidence.

Overhaul Versus Evidence Preservation

You will find when you go out into the real world of firefighting that there is always a balancing act between the different phases of fire control. You and your team need to balance between the damage you cause getting to and extinguishing the fire versus the potential threat to property and life presented by the fire. Should you destroy a front door doing forcible entry if there is a fire alarm sounding with no sign of smoke or fire? The same balance must be considered when overhauling a fire and attempting to protect evidence on the fire scene.

The fire department and their designee who is investigating the fire are charged with the duty to accurately determine the cause of the fire. This is necessary not only for local and national statistical purposes (as gathered in your fire incident report),

FIGURE 28-6 If a fire investigator is on the scene, your team can work with him or her by removing debris as the investigator continues the investigation.

but also for the occupant and owner of the property for insurance and loss recovery purposes. They need the fire cause determination to be as accurate as can be possible. This starts with you and how you perform your final extinguishment and overhaul.

It is probably much easier to throw all of the smoldering debris out the windows for final extinguishment, but this should never be done without first getting approval from your Company Officer. You may be shoveling any chance for an accurate fire cause determination right out the window. If you must move debris, be sure you get permission from your Company Officer. The debris may need to be documented as you continue with overhaul and move it out. If a fire investigator is on the scene, your team can work with him or her by removing debris as the fire investigator continues his or her investigation. Keep in mind that the fire investigator is on your team and that the investigator's job is vital to the overall fire control operation (Figure 28-6).

Protecting Evidence

While you are working, even during the fire, protecting potential evidence is important. Tell your Company Officer about anything you notice as possible evidence as you are working. As the operation is controlled, the Incident Commander may start directing firefighting teams to secure areas of evidence with **fire-line tape** or rope to keep firefighters and the public from walking through the area and causing damage to the evidence or contaminating the evidence in some way. As soon as possible, the whole property should be secured and access allowed only to fire department or law enforcement personnel. This is for general safety as well as evidence protection (Figure 28-7).

FIGURE 28-7 The Incident Commander may direct firefighting teams to secure areas of evidence with fire-line tape or rope to keep firefighters and the public from causing damage to or contaminating the evidence.

▆▆▆ KEY WORD ▆▆▆

fire-line tape   Special demarcation tape used by the Fire Service to mark and secure areas of an emergency incident. It can also be used to protect areas containing fire cause and origin evidence on a fire scene under active investigation.

Fire Victim Recovery Assistance

Fires, whether they are in homes or places of work, are traumatic experiences for those who are there or who share in the losses that result. Fires in the short term are terrifying enough without the additional feeling of loss and hardship. These feelings are also increased a hundredfold when a fire causes injury or loss of life. Our job does not end with the extinguishment of the fire and the follow-up investigation. There is still a need to help the property occupants and owners, and we can guide them to the first steps that they will need to take on the long road to recovery (Figure 28-8).

First Steps

Many fire departments have started to pay more attention to the needs of fire victims, especially in the immediate hours after the incident. In years gone by, the fire department extinguished the fire, picked up their equipment, and went back to the fire station to wait for the next call. Imagine the feelings of loss and desperation those fire victims felt. They would have to figure out who to call for help.

Chain of Custody

A very important aspect of evidence is the concept of chain of custody. Simply stated, these are the rules for the handling of evidence on the scene of a fire investigation. It means that the persons who are in control of the evidence can trace and document a clear chain of the evidence being discovered, secured, collected, and then properly documented and stored by the appropriate authorities. In order for evidence to be usable in a court of law, there must be a well-defined chain of custody. Individuals and agencies are documented each step of the way. If the chain of evidence is broken, meaning that the evidence was left out of control or it was handled by unauthorized and undocumented persons, then the evidence will probably be unusable in a court of law. This is why protecting evidence at a fire scene under investigation is so important.

As the evidence is turned over from one person to the next, a running list of names with agency affiliation, times, and dates is maintained throughout. If the evidence is needed in court, the chain of evidence may be challenged, and this documentation will be invaluable to the case.

FIGURE 28-8 We can guide fire victims through the first steps on the long road to recovery.

Today, the fire department can be very helpful to these fire victims after a fire. After all, we see this all the time; most people in the community have never had to experience firsthand the tragedy and losses from a fire. Our first concern is to make sure all of the occupants are accounted for and that they are physically okay. Then we need to prioritize their needs and provide guidance. Many departments have an "After-the-Fire Checklist" information packet that can be distributed to the occupants and owners. This information outlines what they need to start doing in their recovery process. It is important that a representative from the fire department go over the information packet carefully with the occupant, perhaps even offering to help with calling for additional assistance.

Breakout Box

After-the-Fire Checklist Topics

A typical fire recovery checklist will cover the following topics:

1. Fire department Citizen Assistance Program (CAP) contact phone number
2. Advice on contacting the insurance company
3. Step-by-step procedures for securing the property
4. Emergency contact numbers for local organizations (for example, the Red Cross) that assist with clothing, food, and lodging
5. Step-by-step procedures for recovering and cleaning clothing and other personal items damaged in the fire
6. Emergency contact numbers for medical and psychological assistance for dealing with the emotional trauma of fire

Citizen Assistance Programs

In many communities, fire departments have found it extremely beneficial to start Citizen Assistance Programs, or CAPs, that are called to the scene to provide continuing assistance. CAPs are usually called in after the emergency fire units on the scene have determined that there is a critical need for help due to the fire losses of the victims that they have assessed.

CAP responders arrive on the scene and are briefed by the firefighters on the scene. They develop a plan of action and then start working with the occupants to get them in contact with their insurance company, and arrange for clothing, food, and shelter.

Many fire department CAPs include assistance with securing and boarding up burned homes. Follow-up programs may also be used to periodically check on the welfare of the fire victims until they can fend for themselves and they are well on their way to recovery from their losses. A Citizen Assistance Program not only is a tremendous help to the community, it also releases the emergency fire crews more quickly from a scene. It is another service the fire department can provide to their community.

Do It!

Never Stop Learning

In this final chapter, we discussed the need for determining the cause and origin of the fire as well as properly preserving evidence. You also learned about the concepts of assisting the victims of a fire and getting them on the road to recovery. These elements complete the cycle that started with the fire. They are crucial. They are rewarding not only to the victims, but also to the fire department and yourself.

You are also completing your initial training in our curriculum. We hope your training was informative and helpful. We wish you the greatest success in your career as a firefighter. If we could pass on only one bit of advice to you, it would be this: Never stop learning. Every day and every call that you respond to will present a new set of challenges. You must learn something each time and keep improving your skills. Make a difference. Influence those around you positively. Help your fellow firefighters in any way you can, and look out for them.

As you continue, remember that your actions influence those around you. You may never make the position of Fire Chief, but the firefighter next to you might. Make the Fire Service better for yourself and your fire department. The actions you take and the way you handle yourself affect your community as well. One bad experience with the public can wipe out a hundred good experiences. You represent the community. You are on the front lines, and they are looking to you for help. Be there for them.

Congratulations and welcome to the Fire Service! Stay safe!

Knowledge Assessment

Signed Documentation Tear-Out Sheet

Post-Fire Activities—Chapter 28

Name: _____

Fill out the ten-question quiz below, the Knowledge Assessment Sheet, by circling the correct answer. When finished, sign it and give to your instructor/Company Officer for his or her signature. Turn in this sheet to the proper person as part of the documentation that you have completed your training for this chapter.

1. What terminology is used to describe the very first area where a fire starts?
   a. Chain of evidence
   b. Origin of the fire
   c. Cause of the fire
   d. Chain of control

2. When thinking about what you observed during the extinguishment of a fire, what should you consider regarding the smoke and flames you observed?
   a. Location
   b. Intensity
   c. Color
   d. All of the above

3. What is the quality of charring the closer you get to the origin of the fire?
   a. Deeper
   b. Shallower
   c. Lighter
   d. Darker

4. With fires involving a room or part of a room, what is a good indicator to look for on walls?
   a. A "Y" burn pattern
   b. A "V" burn pattern
   c. An "X" burn pattern
   d. The "Q" burn pattern

5. Conditions that you observe while extinguishing a fire are not that important to the investigation of the fire after extinguishment is completed.
   a. True
   b. False

6. Most fire department "Fire Setter" prevention programs deal with what type of person?
   a. Arsonists
   b. Criminals
   c. Juvenile fire setters
   d. Adult fire setters

7. What is one of the best ways you can help a fire investigation at your level?
   a. Look for arsonists.
   b. Break the chain of custody.
   c. Be observant during the fire and protect evidence.
   d. Remove all debris during overhaul.

8. The chain-of-custody concept deals with the control and handling of evidence during a fire scene investigation.
   a. True
   b. False

9. An information packet containing suggestions and help for fire victims is commonly referred to as what?
   a. A "Before-the-Fire Checklist"
   b. A "Home Inspection Checklist"
   c. An "Incident Report Checklist"
   d. An "After-the-Fire Checklist"

10. Why would a Citizen Assistance Program helper be called to the scene of a fire?
    a. To help with further investigation of cause and origin
    b. To provide further recovery assistance to the fire victims
    c. To take command of the fire incident
    d. To assist law enforcement

Student Signature and Date _____   Instructor/Company Officer Signature and Date _____

682

Skills Assessment

Signed Documentation Tear-Out Sheet

Post-Fire Activities—Chapter 28

Name: _____

Fill out the Skills Assessment Sheet below. Have your instructor/Company Officer check off and initial each skill you demonstrate. When you are finished, sign this page and give to your instructor/Company Officer for his or her signature. Turn in this Skills Assessment Sheet to the proper person as part of the documentation that you have completed your training for this chapter.

Skill	Completed	Initials
1. Explain the general procedures for determining the origin of a fire.	_____	_____
2. Discuss the typical procedure for determining the cause of a fire.	_____	_____
3. Define the term *arson*.	_____	_____
4. Explain the components of a juvenile fire-setter prevention program.	_____	_____
5. Describe how to protect evidence at a fire scene under investigation.	_____	_____
6. Explain the chain-of-custody concept for evidence.	_____	_____
7. List the six topics of important information for fire victims beginning their fire-loss recovery process.	_____	_____
8. Explain the benefits of a Citizen Assistance Program for fire-loss recovery.	_____	_____

Student Signature and Date _____ Instructor/Company Officer Signature and Date _____

Answer Key, Knowledge Assessment

Chapter 1

1. A

One of NIOSH's most important functions is the investigation of line-of-duty firefighter injuries and deaths.

2. C

Company Officer is the term more commonly used to describe the person in charge of the engine, truck, or rescue company.

3. B

As its name implies, the Fire Prevention Division conducts fire inspections and enforces fire codes as part of its overall job of preventing fires before they occur.

4. A

In the vast majority of the United States, providing fire protection is the responsibility of local government.

5. C

On larger or complex fire emergency scenes in which several companies are working, the use of an Incident Command System provides a predetermined organization that supervises the units as they arrive and work on the scene.

6. B

The personnel accountability system (PAS) helps the Incident Commander keep track of companies as well as individuals on the fire scene.

7. C

Sector is the term most commonly used to designate different parts of the fireground operation.

8. B

It is never acceptable to allow visitors to roam freely throughout a fire station, especially in the vehicle bay area. This area is probably the most dangerous area to the public, especially when an emergency call is received and units are dispatched.

9. B

As noted in the NIOSH follow-up report included in the chapter, properly placed and secured ladders or lifts are much preferable to and safer than the tops of emergency units for working on the ceiling areas of fire station vehicle bays.

10. A

Right-to-know information is required to be posted in any workplace, including a fire station.

Chapter 2

1. B

To be effective in your first aid efforts, you must first be aware of what caused the problem so that you can maintain a safe attitude in everything you do. If not, you can fall victim to the same fate.

2. C

In most cases you should take the time to seek the patient's permission before you touch him or her. If the person is a minor and his or her parent or guardian is not present to give consent, then it is implied that you have permission to treat the child.

3. A

We take universal precautions when potentially exposed to body substances. These precautions include wearing eye protection (splash-resistant eyewear), hand protection (approved, nonlatex, disposable medical gloves), and other body protection (such as a splash-resistant gown) as needed.

4. C

Life-threatening injuries or conditions almost always involve a person's airway, breathing, and/or blood circulation. The ABCs of emergency care are **A**irway, **B**reathing, and **C**irculation. Assessing the patient's ABCs will alert you to any immediate danger to life.

5. B

When performing abdominal thrusts, stand behind the patient, wrapping your arms around the patient's waist while making a fist with one hand. Grasp your fist with your other hand and place it into the patient's abdomen above the navel while *avoiding* the bottom of the patient's breastbone.

6. D

The head tilt–chin lift maneuver is very simple to accomplish; however, it involves manipulating the patient's head and neck a bit. Therefore, this maneuver is not recommended if the patient has been injured and/or has fallen in such a way as to potentially cause a neck injury. In these cases, a jaw-thrust maneuver should be used.

7. B

To control the bleeding, cover the wound with one or several sterile dressings and apply direct pressure with your hand. This action should slow or stop the bleeding. Once the bleeding has been controlled, leave the pressure dressing in place and wrap it with a gauze bandage.

8. A

Shock occurs when a patient's circulation is compromised. This condition can be due to a heart condition, blood loss, internal bleeding, a head injury, or other medical causes.

9. A

If a patient is vomiting or is about to vomit, the best position is on her side so that no vomit falls back into her airway, causing her to choke. Place the patient on her left side if possible to help prevent vomiting. This is called the recovery position.

10. C

Partial-thickness burns are accompanied by blistering of the burn area. These are deeper injuries of the skin and may take a few weeks to heal.

Chapter 3

1. A

Your protective clothing is a combination of several items, each of which must be in place with all the others before maximum protection is established. For example, if you do not have your gloves on at a fire, you are not fully protected and you are exposing yourself to injury.

2. C

The firefighter coat and pants are made up of three layers of protection. The first layer, the outer shell, is somewhat flame-retardant. The second and third layers of protection are in the inner liner, which is a combination of a thermal barrier and a moisture barrier.

3. B

Your helmet has a pull-down eye shield. This shield provides a low level of eye protection for instances in which you are in a hurry, or you are not wearing goggles or the face piece of your self-contained breathing apparatus (SCBA). Your eyes can still be exposed to objects flying up from underneath the pull-down eye shield. The addition of safety-approved goggles or your SCBA face piece greatly enhances the eye protection you receive from the pull-down eye shield on your helmet.

4. A

Fire Service protective clothing should be cleaned a minimum of every 6 months. It is recommended that this cleaning be done professionally or at least in professional-grade washers operated by the fire de-

partment. Dirt and products of combustion will start to degrade the fire-resistance capabilities of the materials.

5. B

Your personal protective clothing is designed to protect your skin. However, to complete your ensemble of personal protective equipment (PPE), you must also protect your respiratory system. A self-contained breathing apparatus (SCBA) completes your protective gear. While every component of your PPE is essential, the SCBA is probably the most critical component of the ensemble when you are exposed to toxic smoke, hazardous gases, and steam.

6. D

The rate at which you use the air in a cylinder depends on several factors, including your physical condition and size, the amount of physical activity you are performing, and the temperature in which you are working.

7. B

Most regulators have an emergency bypass valve, which is red. This valve allows high-pressure air to bypass the regulator in case of a failure. By slightly cracking open the emergency bypass valve, you will receive the remaining air in the cylinder at a fairly fast rate.

8. C

Donning the facemask is the final step you take before breathing from the system. It makes no difference whether you don the mask by placing your chin in first and dragging the straps over your head or whether you use the ball-cap method. In the ball-cap method, you hold the straps on the back of your head and drag the mask down over your face.

9. C

A personal alert safety system, or PASS, is a small electronic device that is designed to detect your movement and your lack of movement. It sounds a very loud alarm if it determines that you have remained stationary for a predetermined length of time. The purpose of this device is to signal to other firefighters that you need help and to give them an audible signal that aids them in locating you rapidly.

10. A

An item that is essential to every firefighter's safety is a personnel accountability system (PAS). In this system, the Incident Commander or a designee accounts for every person as they enter and exit a hazardous area or environment. To keep track of everyone, the Accountability Officer will use some form of a tracking system in which each firefighter reports to his or her Company Officer, who then reports to the Accountability Officer.

Chapter 4

1. B

The fire attack hose line system begins at the pump panel on the fire apparatus and ends when the stream of water coming from the end of the nozzle effectively reaches the base of the fire.

2. C

The size of the fittings, couplings, and hose accessory devices (appliances) that water passes through can reduce the volume of water and pressure of the stream as it flows out the nozzle.

3. A

Small attack lines are those fire attack hose systems in which the diameter of the hose is ¾ inch to 2 inches in diameter (as measured on the inside opening of the hose).

4. A

Booster hose couplings usually will have small grip points that are recessed. They require a special type of spanner wrench called a Barway spanner for disconnecting and connecting the couplings.

5. A

Most couplings are designed to screw together in a clockwise direction. They should be tightened hand-tight.

6. D

Unlike booster lines, the 1-inch jacketed line needs to be drained of water after use and before loading it. This is done by disconnecting the line from the apparatus, removing the nozzle, and disconnecting each section of hose.

7. C

Spanner wrenches are used to tighten and loosen hose couplings.

8. C

The gated wye usually takes in water from a larger supply, like a 2½- or 3-inch supply, then divides it into two 1½- or 1¾-inch lines.

9. A

Nozzles should be held waist-high at one's side, with the hose under the arm and one hand either on the body of the nozzle (for nozzles without a pistol grip) or on the pistol grip; the other hand should be on the gate valve control (the bale) or the twist valve, depending on the style nozzle you are using.

10. C

The first step in caring for fire hose is to bleed the excess water pressure from the hose after the discharge has been shut off at the fire apparatus. Next, disconnect the nozzle. Then disconnect the hose sections. Finally, walk along the hose, placing it over your shoulder or raising it to your waist, allowing the water to drain as you walk along the line.

Chapter 5

1. A

A defensive driving course, which also instructs course attendees about departmental, local, and state-level laws and regulations related to POV response, should be given to new firefighters as soon as possible.

2. B

The Emergency Vehicle Operator's Course provided by the U.S. Department of Transportation defines a true emergency as *a situation in which there is a high probability of death or serious injury to an individual or significant property loss, and action by an emergency vehicle operator may reduce the seriousness of the situation.*

3. D

In simple terms, negligence is either the act of doing something that a reasonable or prudent person would not do, or not doing something that such a person would do, in a given situation.

4. B

Not using a seatbelt has contributed to many fatalities. Firefighters should set an example for the community by following the law and wearing their seatbelts at all times. It is a proven fact that seatbelt use reduces injury and death in traffic crashes, and greatly reduces the chance of ejection from a vehicle.

5. C

The extent and type of protective clothing you need depends on the type of emergency and the policy of your Company Officer and your department.

6. B

When dismounting from the apparatus, always check in all directions. Look for traffic and obstructions or hazards on the ground below.

7. D

Place a tapering pattern of 5 cones in a stretch of roadway at a distance of about 75 feet from the rear of the apparatus. This placement provides a transition for traffic from the present pattern to the new lane pattern established by your apparatus placement and the placement of cones.

8. C

Keep your eye on the traffic and never turn your back on it. Face traffic when placing cones and be ready to sound an alarm if a vehicle breaks through your blocking cones and heads for the fire apparatus.

9. A

The total stopping distance of an apparatus is the reaction time plus the braking distance.

10. B

There are two methods for estimating a safe following distance. The first method is the 3-second rule. This rule requires that you pick a marker—perhaps a tree or a post on the side of the roadway—and begin a count of three ("1001, 1002, 1003") when the vehicle in front of you passes the marker; you should not pass the marker before having reached the third count. If you are responding to an emergency, this distance (the traveling time) should be increased to allow you more reaction time. The second method is to estimate apparatus lengths. Estimate one apparatus length between your vehicle and the vehicle in front of you for every 10 miles per hour that you are traveling.

Chapter 6

1. C

Four things need to come together for combustion to occur: fuel, heat, oxygen, and the chemical reaction that keeps the flame burning. These four ingredients of combustion are often depicted as the fire tetrahedron.

2. C

Fires grow based on the amount of fuel available to burn. Flames can easily spread to other combustible materials near the original fire through heat transfer; therefore, knowing how flames spread can help you contain a fire.

3. A

Open flames emit heat from the light of the flames by the process of radiation. Radiant heat transfer doesn't depend on air currents or direct contact with the flame to spread a fire. For example, a large fire burning outside a building can ignite the curtains inside the building when some of the energy of the original fire radiates through a glass window.

4. A

Portable fire extinguishers have labels indicating the types of fires they are designed to extinguish. An extinguisher containing only water is usually effective only for a Class A fire.

5. C

Common examples of small, burning liquid fires include cooking oil fires and fires involving spilled gasoline around lawn mowers. Anything larger than these types of fires is beyond the capabilities of most portable fire extinguishers. Class B fire extinguishers include a carbon dioxide (CO_2) extinguisher and a dry chemical extinguisher. Most dry chemical extinguishers are useful for both Class A and Class B fires.

6. D

Regardless of the classification of fire, the extinguishing agent should be applied at the base of the flames and on the material that is burning.

7. B

An energized electrical fire receives its main heat source from electricity and not from what is burning. For example, if a small electrical appliance is on fire, switching off the electrical source at the circuit breaker will usually stop the fire or at least decrease the fire from a Class C fire to a lower-grade fire. By stopping the electrical current, the fire can be switched from a Class C to a Class A or Class B fire, depending on the material that is left burning.

8. B

Class B fire extinguishers include a carbon dioxide (CO_2) extinguisher and a dry chemical extinguisher. Most dry chemical extinguishers are useful for both Class A and Class B fires.

9. A

There are many types of trash containers that you will encounter in responding to trash fires. The most common trash containers at commercial businesses and construction sites are dumpsters. Dumpsters are commonly metal containers of various sizes that have a metal or plastic lid.

10. B

When extinguishing a dumpster fire, always wear full PPE, including an SCBA.

Chapter 7

1. B

Even though we see and hear about massive fires that occur in our wildland areas, the great majority of ground cover fires will be less than an acre in size and are controlled by a small crew of firefighters.

2. A

In hilly or mountainous areas, the fire tends to burn up a slope toward the unburned area until it is affected by winds at the top of the hill.

3. D

There is usually a concentrated, heavy involvement at the leading edge of a fire. This part of the fire is known as the head of the fire.

4. B

The area around the edge of the entire fire area, including both the burned and the still-burning areas, is known as the fire perimeter.

5. C

Examples of manmade firebreaks include roadways, parking lots, and farmlands. Manmade firebreaks also include trenches made by teams of fire crews using hand tools or specially designed forestry tractors in areas well ahead of the fire.

6. A

Keeping fires from jumping a roadway usually involves brand control, in which the original fire is allowed to burn to the "black line" while any spot-over fires are handled quickly with available water.

7. B

Regardless of the type of apparatus you ride in, the safety rules are the same: You should wear your seatbelt, sit in a designated seat, and put on your gear either before leaving the station or after arriving on the scene.

8. B

Be aware of the limited extinguishing capabilities of a small fire attack line and nozzle. Stay out of brush and ground cover that is higher than your knees.

9. C

A council rake is a good tool for clearing vegetation and debris at a ground cover fire.

10. A

If a brush truck goes into the fire perimeter, it enters from the burned side, away from the direction the head of the fire is traveling.

Chapter 8

1. D

Vehicle fires are common, numbering approximately 200,000 or 17% of the fires throughout the United States each year. You will probably respond to more vehicle fires than structural fires.

2. B

Anyone working within 50 feet of a car or light truck that is well-involved in fire must be properly protected with full personal protective equipment, including breathing apparatus. It is never a good idea to breathe smoke, especially when you consider the products of combustion that are liberated from the burning plastics and other manmade materials in a motor vehicle.

3. D

Most accidental fires in light vehicles start in the engine compartment area. The engine compartment is where all the electronics and fuels come together in a single location; therefore, this area can be the most dangerous when on fire.

4. A

The fluids and manmade materials that burn in the engine area liberate thick, black, choking smoke, a single breath of which can incapacitate you. Large amounts of deadly gas, including hydrogen cyanide, are present in the immediate area anytime plastics burn. These gases mix with the other dangerous gases that are by-products of fires involving flammable liquids and caustics.

5. C

When the vehicle's passenger compartment is well-involved in fire, the airbags often deploy from the heat, with a sound like a shotgun blast. The elements that deploy most airbags found in the dash and seatbacks are flammable products that burn rapidly at a relatively low temperature. Side-curtain airbags are usually inflated with an inert gas that is contained in a pressurized cylinder, which can be contained in the A post, the C post, or even the roof rail on some models of cars.

6. A

Fire in the cargo compartment can be unpredictable because the fuel tank of most cars is near the cargo area. In addition, aftermarket alternative fuels such as propane or compressed natural gas might be located in the cargo compartment.

7. A

The entire battery cell in a typical hybrid vehicle can deliver more than 400 volts of power. The high-voltage circuits of hybrid vehicles derive their power from banks of dry-cell batteries, very similar to flashlight batteries. However, unlike a flashlight that uses two or three of the 1.2-volt batteries for power, the rechargeable batteries in a hybrid vehicle are assembled in a series, which means that their voltage is multiplied.

8. B

Begin flowing water from at least 30 feet away when approaching a well-involved fire, using a tight pattern to reach the seat of the fire and overwhelming it with force. First direct the stream toward any fire that is near the fuel tank and then concentrate on each of the three compartments as you go. The passenger compartment will emit a large volume of fire that can be knocked down quickly with a tight stream from a relatively safe position.

9. A

Fires in the engine compartment can be knocked down to some extent by flowing water through the wheel wells. The main obstacle to controlling a fire in the engine compartment is the lack of access to the area. Most passenger vehicles have plastic inner liners placed on their fenders in the engine compartment that usually burn out of the way, making this area a quick path for applying water.

10. D

Overhaul is the process of systematically looking for any hidden fire or hot areas and taking measures to completely extinguish any of these remaining problems. Overhaul begins once the main body of the fire has been extinguished and continues until there is no chance of an accidental re-ignition. Overhaul is an important process in any fire operation; it is the best defense to prevent a rekindling of the original blaze.

Chapter 9

1. B

An initial water supply is usually developed from water carried on a fire apparatus in its booster tank.

2. D

A fire engine that supplies water to the nozzles is called the attack pumper. The engine that delivers its booster tank water to the attack pumper is called the supply pumper.

3. D

A typical fire hydrant has two or three outlet ports.

4. A

Fire departments will utilize several tenders in rotation to supply the fire scene. Each tender is refilled as the other deploys its load of water, thus establishing a sustained water supply. This operation is commonly referred to as a tender water shuttle operation.

5. C

Many fire trucks will have specially designed fire hose referred to as hard suction hose. When deployed into a body of water, this hose can draw water to provide a sustained water supply for the fire scene.

6. C

The main difference between a portable pump and a float pump is that the float pump has no hard suction hose attached. It simply draws water from below as it floats on the surface of the water.

7. A

When one supply line is made into two or more smaller supply lines, firefighters use a gated manifold appliance.

8. B

Fire apparatus will usually lay supply hose in two primary directions: (1) to the fire (a forward lay) or (2) away from the fire toward the water supply (a reverse lay).

9. B

A 4- to 6-inch-diameter supply hose is considered large-diameter supply hose. This type of hose may have quick-connect couplings.

10. C

A hydrant valve is an appliance that allows a fire apparatus to hook into the water supply at a fire hydrant without interrupting the flow of water to the fire scene.

Chapter 10

1. B

Simply put, the larger the fire and therefore the greater the release of heat, the more water that is needed to be applied to the fire in order to absorb the heat. Fire attack lines for "big water" are generally 2½- to 3-inch diameter hose lines with associated nozzles. As with small fire attack lines, the nozzles are either fog or smoothbore type and operate similarly.

2. C

Often referred to as blitz lines, preconnected large fire attack lines are loaded in a similar manner as small attack lines. Because of the increased size and overall weight of the hose, you should consider getting help to pull the preconnected load.

3. A

Large attack lines flow much more water than small attack lines. However, the result is a greater gallons-per-minute rate of water delivered to the seat of the fire. The greater flow rate means that more people will be needed to operate and maneuver the flowing lines. In addition, a more substantial sustained water supply is needed to keep it flowing.

4. D

If a large attack line is being used by one or two firefighters, is going to be mostly stationary, and is a safe distance from the fire, the hose line can be looped on the ground. This positioning saves the firefighter's energy and allows for a longer application of water using one firefighter.

5. B

When large attack lines need to be advanced to different positions, it is best to have a two- or three-firefighter crew attending the line. These lines flow tremendous amounts of water and, due to their increased diameter and volume, they can be very unwieldy for one firefighter.

6. A

If the line must be moved while flowing, the firefighter at the nozzle should be ready to shut down the nozzle if he or she stumbles or loses balance.

7. B

The water thief is an appliance that closely resembles the gated wye, but in addition to the two 1½-inch discharge ports, it has a single 2½-inch discharge port in the middle. The water thief allows you to stretch to a certain point, deploy two small attack lines, and then extend further with more large attack lines where either another gated wye or a nozzle is attached.

8. C

A gated wye is an appliance that takes in water from a large attack line and then distributes it through two outlets that are controlled by gate valves. A typical gated wye has a 2½-inch inlet and two 1½-inch outlets.

9. B

Operating master stream appliances from aerial ladders is a more advanced skill that is unique to each type aerial apparatus.

10. D

Because master streams are intended to stay in place while flowing, they can be attended by only one firefighter after they are set up. This is their most common application.

Chapter 11

1. A

Individuals who work inside a burning building are working in an atmosphere that is Immediately Dangerous to Life and Health (IDLH). However, this isn't the only hazard they face. Many of the line-of-duty deaths of firefighters working inside the structure occur when the firefighter becomes disoriented and runs out of fresh air supplied by his or her SCBA. Therefore, just knowing how to wear PPE and breathe from an SCBA does not qualify a person to work inside a structural fire.

2. C

During an offensive, interior attack, the hot zone usually encompasses any area inside the structure where an IDLH incident in an enclosed area is encountered. Any firefighter working in the hot zone should be fully protected with PPE and a charged hose line, and should be trained to the Level I standard.

3. B

When sizing up a door that you are about to force open, first try turning the doorknob. The door may not be locked. If it isn't, report this to your team's Officer and be ready for another order. If the door is locked, then be prepared to force entry when told to do so and not before. Before you take action, it is important that a charged hose line be in place and that the fire attack team is ready for the door to be opened.

4. B

Dragging a charged hose line through a house is difficult, especially if the interior crew is crawling on their hands and knees. This task can be made quite a bit easier if someone stages at the doorway, outside the building and the IDLH environment, to feed the hose into the building.

5. D

Gasoline-powered fans are usually much more powerful than the electric versions and are also heavier in weight. Therefore, these fans are almost exclusively restricted to remaining on the ground outside the structure. They blow inward to fill the building with fresh air and positive pressure that forces the smoke and gases out of the building. You will also hear these fans referred to as PPV (positive-pressure ventilation) fans.

6. A

The lockout/tagout system ensures that any switch or valve that is meant to remain in its present position is locked into that position with a lock. The person locking the valve is identified on a tag that is attached to the locking device.

7. A

In severe building fires, electrical feeds can disconnect and fall away from the burning building. For this reason, it is important to mark the location of these feeds during the fire emergency. Use fire-line tape or traffic cones to do this. If the power line does fall on the ground, widen your security around the wire and notify your Company Officer or command of the downed wire and its location.

8. C

Most engine company apparatus carry a roof ladder and an extension ladder.

9. B

Adjust the extension ladder for climbing by positioning it about one-fourth of the ladder's height from the building. Place the butt of the ladder at your feet, grasping the rung nearest shoulder height at arm's length. This should be the proper climbing angle.

10. C

Any material that ignites as a result of fire coming from another source is technically an exposure fire. An *exposure* is anything that has the potential of catching fire due to its proximity to something that is already on fire. In building fires, an exposure is an item in a room that has the potential of catching fire because it is exposed to something already on fire in the room. This definition can be expanded to large fires in a building that have the potential to spread to adjacent buildings. The adjacent buildings become exposures to the original building fire and must be protected *before* they catch fire.

Chapter 12

1. B

NFPA 1582, *Standard on Medical Requirements for Fire Fighters and Information for Fire Department Physicians,* specifies the medical requirements for firefighters.

2. A

The buddy system works under the premise of teams of at least two or more firefighters sticking together for safety.

3. A (True)

Because they can be unreliable, portable radios are not an acceptable method of communication among team members.

4. C

A personnel accountability system tracks where everyone is operating all of the time and allows no room for freelancing on the fireground.

5. D

Much of our work is conducted in short cycles in which we work until relieved, go to a rehabilitation area (rehab) for rest and rehydration, and then return for another work cycle.

6 B (False)

Expect to work as a team and rehab as a team. The personnel accountability system should track you as a team while in rehab. Your Company Officer will advise the Personnel Accountability Officer when your team is ready to return to work.

7. D

Tell your Company Officer if you are experiencing any signs of heat stress, such as dizziness, nausea, confusion, or a headache.

8. B (False)

Most firefighters who die on duty do not die on the fireground. Vehicle crashes while responding or returning from the alarm, being struck by a vehicle while working on an alarm, and cardiac-related deaths account for the majority of on-duty deaths.

9. D

As a Level I firefighter, you won't be in charge of the work team; however, everyone is responsible for looking after each other and should be empowered to call attention to any hazards that may be present.

10. B (False)

The two-in/two-out ruling is law in most areas, required by the Occupational Safety and Health Administration (29 CFR 1910.155) and prescribed by NFPA 1500. These OSHA requirements apply to paid and volunteer firefighters as well as to those who work in the private or industrial fire brigade setting.

Chapter 13

1. B

Preparation primarily involves training and maintaining equipment and apparatus. Your own self-preparation is also important, which includes making sure you are physically and mentally prepared to fight fire. By participating in this training, you are preparing in part for response right now. Rest assured that you will train and practice your skills many times over the course of your career.

2. C

When you report for duty, the very first thing you should do after being assigned to an apparatus is to gather your personal protective clothing and place it appropriately on or near the apparatus, according to department practice. At this time, you should look at each piece of clothing to make sure your set of protective clothing is complete. Check the self-contained breathing apparatus (SCBA) you will be using. Make sure it is complete and ready for use.

3. A

A typical apparatus routine check will involve taking an inventory of the small tools and equipment, performing minor maintenance, and immediately reporting to the apparatus driver any repairs that are needed. It also includes checking the functions and fluid levels for the apparatus drive train, inspecting the tires for wear and proper air pressure, and checking peripherals such as the booster water tank as well as all of the lights and electronics.

4. D

Inspect the tires, looking for proper tire pressure and checking for any damage to the tires, including nails or screws embedded in the tires. Also check for tire wear. Most tires have wear bars to indicate excessive tire wear.

5. D

Hand tools are any tools on the apparatus that are operated manually. They do not use any power, such as electric- or gasoline-powered motors for operation.

6. A

A wide variety of electrically powered tools might be located on any given fire apparatus. The type of tool depends on the job functions that the Fire Department has determined that unit will be capable of performing.

7. B

It is best to plug and unplug electrical extension cords and tools with the power source in the "off" position. If this is not possible, make sure to check that the tool or appliance is switched off and that you are not standing in water when you plug these items into the power source.

8. B

When checking a gasoline-powered tool, the very first thing to check is any fluid leakage from the tool. You should start by looking at the surface of the storage area or compartment where the tool is kept. Leave the tool in place while looking for oil or fuel puddles under the tool and try to determine its source by looking for drips or wet places on the tool above.

9. D

A gasoline-powered tool or piece of equipment should be started and operated to ensure that it is working properly. Take the tool outside to do this. Starting gasoline-powered tools in the vehicle bay area releases carbon monoxide inside the fire station and is quite noisy. Go outside in the open air to test the tool.

10. C

All fire hose must be tested by the Fire Department at least once a year. The department will have schedules and testing procedures that you will follow when the time comes. Usually the hose is stretched out in sections and tested to a pre-determined pressure for a certain length of time.

Chapter 14

1. B (False)

Once a rope has been used as a utility line, it should never be placed back into service as a life safety rope.

2. B (False)

There is no separation of standards between training and emergency use when it comes to life safety rope. A human load is regarded with the same diligence, and all standards apply to training situations as they do during an actual emergency.

3. C

Life safety rope must provide a 15:1 safety factor.

4. A

A load that moves and then stops suddenly is called a shock load.

5. D

Twisted rope is also known as laid or hawser-type rope.

6. C

Because of its strength and low stretch, kernmantle is the most common type of life safety rope used in the Fire Service.

7. C

Because a human load is considered to be 300 pounds, it is necessary to have a rope rated at 4500 pounds to provide the 15:1 safety factor.

8. B

A bowline forms a very secure loop at the end of a rope.

9. D

A clove hitch is used to secure a rope to a round object, such as a tree or a pipe.

10. B

To secure a long-handled tool to a rope for hoisting, you start with the tool's tip up and tie a clove hitch at the base of the handle. You then tie an overhand safety knot and at least two half-hitches spaced along the handle, with a half-hitch underneath the tool's head.

Chapter 15

1. C

The K-tool is not designed as a multiuse forcible entry tool. Its only purpose is to extract a lock's cylinder for through-the-lock entry.

2. B (False)

The pick side of the axe prevents it from being an effective striking tool. A better choice would be a flathead axe.

3. C

The K-tool is designed for one purpose—to extract a lock's cylinder for through-the-lock entry.

4. A

Most residential exterior doors swing inward, while most exterior doors on commercial structures swing outward.

5. C

Mortise locks are most often found on commercial-type occupancies.

6. A

Remember the adage: Fork in, adze out. The adze provides the best leverage for an outward-swinging door.

7. B (False)

Mortise-style locks very often use a single key cylinder to operate both the deadbolt and the latch at the same time with one movement of the key.

8. D

Through-the-lock entry requires that a lock puller be pounded into place over the key cylinder of the lock. A prying force is then used to extract the lock. A pick axe is not a good striking tool.

9. B (False)

A drop bar can only be unlocked and removed from the inside unless the door is cut with a power saw.

10. D

Using a triangular-shaped pattern and starting at the bottom and working up lets gravity work in your favor to drop the broken fragments out of the way. It also allows the remaining block to be somewhat supported by the surrounding blocks for a more stable opening.

Chapter 16

1. C

Roof ladders are basically straight ladders with folding hooks added at the tip. They are designed for reach and support on roof areas. Generally speaking Engine Companies carry a minimum of one 14-foot roof ladder.

2. A

Extension ladders are made up of a base section and one or two fly sections of nested widths. Each section is essentially a straight ladder.

3. D

Specialized ladders include attic ladders (folding ladders) and combination ladders. Specialized ladders can also include any utility ladder, like a folding A-frame ladder that may be carried on a fire apparatus.

4. B

All Fire Service ladders, with the exception of folding ladders, are rated for 750 pounds of weight. This rating is called the *duty rating* or the *duty load rating* of the ladder. Folding ladders are duty rated at 300 pounds. This duty rating includes all personnel, hose lines, tools, and equipment placed on the ladder at any one time. The duty load rating is only applicable if the ladder is positioned at the correct climbing angle.

5. A

All ladders should be secured at the top by tying off the tip or at the bottom by a firefighter.

6. B

A safe general rule of thumb to use when removing a ladder from an apparatus is to look at the length of the ladder. This number will be tagged on the outside of one of the beams. Check the first digit in the double-digit numbers. This tells you how many people should be used to remove the ladder. Using this formula, a 14-foot roof ladder can be removed by one person.

7. C

Avoid anything that might destabilize the butt of the ladder, such as manhole covers, drainage grill covers, or extremely soft ground or groundcover materials. When lowering the tip of a ladder to the building for use, be sure the tip end comes to rest on a solid edge. Be aware that fire or structural damage may have occurred. Check the edge where the tip is located and be ready to relocate the ladder if this area is unstable.

8. C

As an alternative to the straight ladder raise, you can also position any ladder—straight, roof, or extension ladder—on one beam, parallel to the side of the building where it is to be raised.

9. D

Ladders are placed for four primary reasons:

1. To access and egress upper or lower levels
2. To allow firefighters to work from elevated exterior areas of a building fire
3. To rescue trapped fire victims
4. As a support for tools and equipment

10. B

Ladders placed for emergency egress are placed the same as for rescue: with the tips at the windowsill, the edge level, and the ladder slightly showing (three or four rungs) for firefighters inside or on the roof.

Chapter 17

1. D

A beam is a component of any material that spans a gap and is supported at either end.

2. B

A beam or girder can be made of any material of sufficient strength.

3. C

Because the metal components in this hypothetical building are protected and not exposed, the building is considered to be fire resistive instead of noncombustible.

4. A

The wood trusses make this building an ordinary construction type. If the roof components were exposed steel bar joists, the building would be classified as being noncombustible.

5. A

Because a lintel spans the gap between either side of a window or door and is supported on either end as it supports the load, it is considered a beam.

6. A

A steel bar joist has parallel chords and steel web members. It is considered a kind of truss.

7. B

The sheet metal components that connect the pieces of a wood truss are called gussets.

8. A

When a building's main structural support is made of heavy timbers and not the masonry used for the wall coverings, it is a heavy timber building.

9. B

Many commercial structures up to four stories high are made of wood-frame construction.

10. C

A wood rafter is a single piece of natural wood and not an engineered component with several pieces, as is a truss or wooden I-beam.

Chapter 18

1. B

When a fire runs out of fuel, the remaining heat will cause the smoke to linger as a thermal layer at the ceiling level.

2. C

Flashover is a condition in which smoke and heated gases in a confined area combine with the right amount of heat and oxygen to ignite suddenly in a very intense fire.

3. A

A backdraft occurs when the superheated smoke and gases in a confined space receive enough oxygen to trigger a violent explosion.

4. B (False)

Ventilation is just as important to the extinguishment of a structural fire as the application of water.

5. D

Mechanical ventilation is a process that uses ventilation fans to draw smoke from a building.

6. B

When heated smoke and gases suddenly ignite *outside* a structure as they vent, it is called vent-point ignition.

7. A

Negative-pressure ventilation is a process that uses a smoke ejector to draw the smoke *from* a structure.

8. B

A kerf cut gets its name from the width of the cut, which is only one saw blade in width.

9. B (False)

Because a large opening within a roof usually covers several square feet of space, it is much more efficient than several small openings.

10. C

A trench cut is made from wall to wall. It is used to limit horizontal flame spread in a long, narrow building.

Chapter 19

1. B

A common term heard around most progressive fire-houses these days is *EGH—Everyone Goes Home!* This simple idea should be at the essence of every-thing we do, and the philosophical center of every decision we make.

2. A

A generator should be equipped with a circuit breaker and a ground-fault interrupter (GFI). Circuit breakers sense an overloaded circuit. When too many things are plugged into the same circuit, the breaker trips to prevent a fire. GFI is a safety measure that protects humans from electrical shock.

3. D

The very first thing to do is to communicate to those around you and to Command that you are in trouble and need help. Your department has a standard emergency signal on your portable radio to use for a firefighter in distress. The most recognized way to call for help over the radio is to say the word "Mayday" three times, then identify yourself and your location as best as you can.

4. A (True)

"Emergency Traffic" and "Priority Traffic" are terms used to gain priority attention on the radio frequency so that you can transmit a clear and urgent message about the safety and health of working firefighters. An example of "emergency traffic" would be a message calling attention to a potential building collapse.

5. D

In multistory buildings, the location of the fire can be difficult to narrow down during your search. Fires in a basement can cause smoke to come out of the upper floors or the attic. If you are searching for a fire up-stairs and cannot locate any heat or fire, think about the lower levels. An undiscovered fire can be directly beneath you.

6. C

The primary search is done as the fire is being extin-guished by interior firefighting crews. Everyone fighting the fire should always be looking for fire victims, even as they stretch hose lines and look for the fire. However, there is usually a crew assigned to the specific task of primary search. This search is rapid, but must be done as thoroughly as fire conditions permit. This initial search provides the best opportunity to save lives from the fire.

7. B (False)

A thermal imaging camera, commonly referred to as a TIC, is a rugged instrument that enhances our sight, making what is normally invisible information visible. Although a TIC is easy to operate, with only a button or two to power it up, it still takes training and practice to use it efficiently. Interpreting the picture you see in a thermal imager often depends on your knowledge of building construction or your familiarization with the objects you are viewing.

8. B

The cross-chest carry involves lifting the victim to a sitting position, positioning behind the victim, and grabbing both of the victim's arms from behind as they are crossed in front of the victim. A second firefighter grabs the victim's legs, and the crew carries the victim out of the building. If two victims are located, each firefighter can grab a victim in a cross-chest method and drag her out. Keep in mind that fire victims are very often slippery and very hard to grasp, especially if they are unconscious.

9. C

The first step toward a safe outcome for a lost or trapped firefighter is to acknowledge his or her call for help. Gather as much information as you can to assist the rescue team in locating the lost firefighter.

10. A

Once you locate the firefighter, immediately assess his situation and breathing. If his air supply has been de-pleted or the SCBA isn't functioning, simply remove his regulator, leaving his facemask in place, and clip the working SCBA's regulator into his facemask. You should practice doing this in your training until you can accomplish the change within 10 seconds of locat-ing a downed firefighter.

Chapter 20

1. A (True)

Some fire departments have a thermal imaging camera (TIC) that can check the interiors of walls, ceilings, and floors for any hot wiring.

2. C

There are two main fire attack operations to consider when a building is on fire: offensive and defensive fire at-tacks. An offensive fire attack involves entering the struc-ture to rescue any trapped or injured fire victims as well as aggressively confining and extinguishing the fire.

3. B

Your Company Officer will coordinate with the driver and Incident Command to make sure that a water sup-ply has been established. Your Company Officer will also ensure that other actions are taken, such as mak-ing sure that ventilation and backup fire attack crews are in place for the entry to be made.

4. B

If you are the backup firefighter on the hose line, you should be carrying either a ceiling hook or a Halligan bar married to a flat-head axe. Your Company Officer may or may not be bringing in a tool.

5. D

If the fire is located in a room up or down a stairway, there are a couple of methods for maneuvering the hose line. First, check the stairway for any fire dam-age before using it to access the other floor level. If it is damaged, you may have to access from the exterior using a ladder or another safe stairway.

6. A (True)

When water absorbs heat, changing from a liquid state into a gaseous state (steam), it expands to up to 1700 times its original volume. This characteristic explains why a fog pattern absorbs heat and expands to steam so readily. The small droplets of the fog pattern provide a greater surface area to absorb the heat more efficiently than a solid stream pattern.

7. B

Distributor nozzles consist of a rotating ball with a gate valve located on the end of an attack line. The rotating ball has several discharge openings that cause the ball to swivel and spray water when the valve is turned on.

8. B (False)

An emergency evacuation includes a radio procedure that signals all personnel to immediately leave the structure. It will feature an audible evacuation signal, such as a constant series of blasts on the apparatus air horns or sirens. When you and your Company Officer hear this signal, you are to immediately move to a safe area together outside the structure.

9. A

When the fire has been extinguished and smoke is clearing from the structure, Command will most likely order a second search. This secondary search is a much more thorough search of the building and is conducted in a more methodical fashion by a different crew than the initial search.

10. C

Ventilating basement fires is often difficult and is often limited to small window openings. However, in order to successfully extinguish a basement fire, there must be adequate ventilation openings through which trapped heat and gasses can escape as the fire is being extinguished.

Chapter 21

1. A (True)

The firefighting methods you use inside large buildings differ from your methods for residential buildings in the way you approach the interior fire, the number and size of the fire attack lines needed to extinguish the fire, and the complexity of working with many other firefighting teams.

2. C

Smoke curtains are sections of noncombustible sheeting hung from the bottom of the roof. They are designed to slow the spread of smoke and heat from a fire below.

3. B (False)

While fire walls are designed to provide a 4-hour separation from fire, these walls are too often breached with improperly created openings that compromise their ability to stop fire spread. During a fire, you should note that fire walls are present, but you should never completely trust them to stop the spread of a fire.

4. B

The automatic fire sprinkler system was created more than a hundred years ago. This built-in fire protection system is the single most effective and reliable building fire protection system ever invented.

5. A

Fire Department connections (FDC) serve as access points for augmenting the fire sprinkler system's water supply. They are female couplings with a cover that is easily broken off when tapped with a spanner or a hydrant wrench. These connections are located on an exterior wall of the building or in an accessible area near the building.

6. D

When directed to stop the flow of a sprinkler head by a supervisor, firefighters use a small piece of wood called a sprinkler wedge. This wedge is placed between the water flow opening in the sprinkler and the deflector plate.

7. C

The front of the building is side "A." Continuing clockwise around the building are sides "B," "C," and "D." In some areas, these sectors are referred to as Alpha, Beta, Charlie, and Delta to help reduce confusion. These designations are not only important for your own reference if you are communicating your location inside the building, but they are also important when the Incident Commander gives directions during firefighting operations.

8. B (False)

During a large building fire, if one member of the crew must leave the structure, the whole attack crew must leave. This action keeps the crew together. Another crew will then be assigned to relieve the team.

9. C

A cockloft is a common area of fire extension in large buildings. This area is hidden space between the bottom of the roof and the top of a hung ceiling in the building. Cockloft areas contain large, hollow space with little or no access that must be checked for fire extension if the fire was near this area.

10. A (True)

A defensive fire attack involves working hose lines and master stream devices to protect exposures and stop the spread of a fire. The final outcome of a defensive fire attack is to extinguish the fire from exterior positions. The building is considered a total loss when this type of fire attack is initiated.

Chapter 22

1. B

Building surveys are familiarization sessions in which the crews that respond to a fire or other emergency in a building visit a business and tour their facility. These tours are an opportunity to become familiar with a building's layout and are a chance to meet the key people who will be affected in an emergency.

2. D

The purpose of the survey is to determine the basic layout of the property; gather any pertinent fire emergency information, such as emergency contact names and phone numbers; determine the occupancy use of the property; and become familiar with any hazardous processes or conditions at the property. Your crew should also take advantage of the survey to look at the types of existing openings, such as doorways and windows, to determine potential forcible entry points and ventilation openings.

3. A

A typical three-bedroom, wood-frame home in a subdivision is considered a Type III (ordinary) construction:

- Used in buildings limited in height to 4 to 6 stories
- Uses masonry exterior supporting walls
- Uses wood for most interior walls, floors, and roof systems
- Usually uses gypsum board or plaster to provide some fire resistance to the interior components

4. A (True)

A life safety hazard represents a primary risk to life and limb. These are conditions that could potentially produce a large loss of life either at the occupancy or as an exposure to the surrounding community. For example, a blocked designated building exit is a life hazard.

5. C

An example of a fire hazard is fixed or flexible wiring that is frayed or damaged.

6. B

An example of a target hazard in a community is flammable liquid and gas storage complexes.

7. C

A home safety survey is usually requested by the homeowner for the fire department to come and take a look at their home for fire safety. This survey is an opportunity for you and your team to assist members of your community to maintain a house that is safe from the risk of fire, hopefully preventing a future fire.

8. C

The following list provides a few suggestions of items to check during a home safety survey:

- Open or unapproved flammable liquid containers
- A fire extinguisher in the kitchen
- Overloaded electrical receptacle plugs

9. B (False)

The instruction sheet that comes with every smoke detector indicates the best location and number of smoke detectors needed in any one residence. You should follow the manufacturer's recommendations. However, it is generally recommended that there be one smoke detector installed on each living level in the home and between the sleeping areas and the rest of the home. They should be placed on the ceiling or close to the ceiling on the wall.

10. A

In order to be able to give a short fire prevention presentation to a small group, you may want to use the following checklist:

1) *Prepare.* Review the topics you are going to cover. Perhaps outlining your thoughts on a 3 × 5 card would help.
2) *Be sincere.* Public fire education is serious stuff—it can really save a life.
3) *Be informative.* Try to get as much good information across to your audience as possible, but also keep it short and concise. Cover no more than three or four main points.
4) *Try to be at ease.* No one expects you to be an accomplished public speaker, but you should be able to talk to a small group of people about your job, the fire department, and fire safety.

Chapter 23

1. D

The National Incident Management System (NIMS) is the recognized system for managing emergency operations in North America.

2. B

False. NIMS is designed to work for all types of emergencies, not just fires, and works well in managing large, nonemergency events as well.

3. B

False. The Incident Command System is built from the ground up. Because you have the knowledge and ability to establish Command, you should do so while transmitting an arrival report.

4. B

A common management principle is that to be effective, a manager should have no more than five to seven subordinates.

5. B

Divisions that describe this type of geographic area are usually designated with letters, starting with Division A at the front and working around to Division D.

6. D

The floor number may be used for divisions that are designated for different levels inside a multistory structure, so Division 3 covers the third floor.

7. A

Groups are designated according to job function. Some examples of groups are the fire attack group, the ventilation group, and the salvage group.

8. B

False. Group officers answer to the appropriate division officer.

9. D

Fire departments in the United States use the reporting system called the National Fire Incident Reporting System, or NFIRS.

10. A

A pitot gauge measures the flow pressure at the center of a moving stream of water at the point where it exits the hydrant.

Chapter 24

1. B

The incident priorities for a structure fire are—in order—life safety, incident stabilization, and property conservation.

2. A

The command modes for a structure fire are fast-attack mode, nothing-showing mode, and command mode.

3. C

All attack lines and personnel operate outside the collapse zone in a defensive attack.

4. A

Any time a line is used to stop the spread of a fire, it is being used for confinement.

5. B

The building is 1,500 square feet. Using the NFA formula, the total fire flow for the building is 1500/3 or 500. Because the building is 50% involved, the desired flow is 50% of the total, or 250 gpm.

6. Either C or D

It can be argued that priority traffic should be called so that the IC understands the need for an additional attack line. Others can argue that the team leader should call emergency traffic and evacuate the building. In actual practice, this is a judgment call based on the conditions you see, under conditions that cannot be duplicated exactly in a book. The intent here is to make you think about the situation and consider your options.

7. B

False. This situation is an example of opposing attack lines in which the stream from the outside line could push fire and heat toward the interior crew, creating a very dangerous situation for the crew inside.

8. D

It takes an average of 1 minute per floor to climb the first ten floors, and then 2 minutes per floor after that.

9. A

When using an elevator, stop on the second floor to check the elevator's function, and then again every three floors until you reach your desired level.

10. B

Never take an elevator any higher than two floors below the lowest fire floor.

Chapter 25

1. B

We categorize the types of foam according to the type of fuel, similar to the way we classify fire extinguishers—Class A and Class B.

2. B

False. Because the foam contains water, it should be assumed that the foam will conduct electricity, so it is not to be used near energized electrical equipment or any Class C fire.

3. B

False. The quickest way to ruin a good blanket of finished foam is to keep flowing water after you run out of foam concentrate. Water alone will wash away the finished foam and expose the surface of the flammable liquid, which can cause the liquid to re-ignite.

4. A

It takes three things to make finished foam: concentrate, water, and air. In order for them to work together, the concentrate and water must be mechanically agitated to form a solution, and the air must be mixed in at the proper rate to form the bubbles.

5. D

Class A foams are mixed with water at a very low concentration of about 0.1% to 1% by volume, so it is efficient and economical to use.

6. B

Because Class A foam is used at a very low concentration, it is often developed using a batch method in which the concentrate is added to the booster tank water before it is pumped on the fire.

7. C

A smooth-bore nozzle is used when a Class A system is employed, because the aeration of the foam solution has already occurred at the pump and the foam can be applied without further agitation.

8. B

False. In-line eductors rely on the drop in pressure as the water passes through the eductor so they can work. If the pressure is too high on the discharge side of the eductor, which is often the case if the nozzle isn't opened fully or there is a kink in the line between the nozzle and the eductor, then the eductor will not draw foam concentrate into the water stream. If the pressure is too low on the supply side of the eductor, usually because the pump operator is not pumping the line at the appropriate pressure, then the eductor won't work either.

9. D

Most manufacturers suggest that their foam eductors be flushed thoroughly with fresh, clean water after every use. Follow the manufacturer's instructions for the appropriate procedures for the brand of eductor your department uses.

10. B

False. An aspirating foam nozzle discharges the foam solution into an expansion chamber, which creates a sudden drop in pressure and draws air into the stream.

Chapter 26

1. B

False. You will not be expected to be in charge of an incident involving flammable gases. However, you should be able to work as a team member under the supervision of a Company Officer to help control the emergency.

2. C

You will find control valves near the building or facility using natural gas. These valves are turned in line with the pipe to open it and perpendicular to the pipe to close it.

3. B

The tanks are never filled with more than about 80% liquid, leaving a vapor area under pressure above the liquid. As the gas is used from the tank, the vapor area refills as gas vaporizes from the liquid, which boils naturally at room temperature.

4. A

True. In a liquefied gas tank, the fill valve can be a separate valve. This type of tank is usually refilled on site (the exception being the outdoor cooking grill tanks that are exchanged). Residential liquefied gas tanks are usually filled by gas delivery trucks. These tanks are located outside the structure, either above or below ground level.

5. D

The North American Emergency Response Guidebook (NAERG) must be located on fire apparatus. These books provide a quick reference for response, safe handling, evacuation, and spill and fire control practices for many categories of hazardous materials. Flammable gases can be referenced in the *NAERG* by their product name, chemical name, or hazardous material number.

6. A

At a gas leak or spill, immediate evacuation and securing access to the scene with a wide evacuation zone are the most effective things you can do until more help arrives in the form of Incident Command, Fire Department resources like hazardous materials teams, and assistance from the property manager or product company.

7. D

If a leak or flow of gas cannot be controlled or stopped, allowing it to leak out while protecting the surrounding exposures and dissipating the gas with water sprays may be the best option. Stay upwind and uphill from the leak.

8. C

Never position at the ends of a flammable gas tank. These containers are designed to fail at the ends first. The metal fragment projectiles can cause serious injury or death. Always work under direction of an Incident Command System and a Company Officer.

9. C

Combustion explosions are instances in which flammable gas product has leaked inside a structure. If not detected in time, the gas can reach the proper air-gas mixture for ignition, and a spark or flame can ignite the gas, causing a gas explosion. These explosions can be extremely destructive and can flatten a structure.

10. A

A boiling liquid expanding vapor explosion (BLEVE) occurs when a tank containing a liquefied flammable gas product is exposed to the heat of a fire. The tank has pressure relief valves that operate under normal circumstances to relieve the pressure of the gas in the tank escaping from the liquid below.

Chapter 27

1. A

True. Stabilization involves controlling any unstable condition that presents a potential danger of injury and even death to yourself, rescuers, and victims. Some examples of these dangers include wreckage from vehicles involved in a crash, structural members of a collapsed building, and even the side of a collapsed construction trench. Any unstable objects and debris must be stabilized prior to safely accessing, disentangling, and removing a victim.

2. C

Undeployed air bag restraint systems should be identified and assessed at all vehicle crash incidents. Air bags can deploy as a result of disentanglement operations during the rescue. Avoid using hard protection between the victim and an undeployed air bag during rescue operations.

3. B

Roof removal is performed on vehicle entrapment rescue when a large open space is needed to access the victim quickly. This involves cutting the posts with hand tools like hacksaws, reciprocating saws, or powered hydraulic cutters.

4. C

With someone who is injured, the basic reality is that the quicker they can be freed from their entrapment and transported to a medical facility for further treatment, the better their chance for a successful and quick recovery.

5. A

Elevator entrapment situations usually fall into two main categories: entrapment inside the stalled elevator car and entrapment by the mechanism of the elevator itself.

6. A

True. As a possible first-arriving responder to a water rescue incident, you should follow the benchmarks for rescue as you respond and arrive on the scene. Securing a water rescue scene can be as simple as securing the pool in the backyard of a home or as complex as setting up operations on a large lake working with several resources to search for drowning victims. You may be called upon to set up a secure area around the incident, restricting access to only those needed for the rescue operation.

7. D

The hazards unique to rope rescue operations that you need to protect yourself against are falls, especially if you are stationed near an elevated edge. This protection may include the use of safety harnesses and safety lines.

8. B

Your job will be to assist non-entry operations outside the confined space, like helping stage tools and equipment, securing the area around the site of the rescue, and controlling the necessary personnel who enter and leave the site.

9. C

Trench rescue emergencies require the use of cribbing, shoring, and, in some instances, sheeting materials to support, retard, and reduce the hazard of further collapse of the materials in which the victim is trapped.

10. C

Building collapse incidents present a particularly hazardous situation for rescuers when they arrive and begin to search for and rescue trapped victims. Because of the risk of secondary collapse of an already weakened building, a building collapse emergency can further injure rescuers if the building is not properly assessed for safe access and stabilized with shoring and cribbing.

Chapter 28

1. B

The origin of the fire is the specific area where a fire first ignites. The place where fire starts is also referred to as the point of origin by fire investigators.

2. D

When rehashing what you observed while fighting the fire, consider the location, intensity, and color of the smoke and flames. Where was the main body of the fire located when you entered the building to extinguish the blaze? It is true that fires can spread far from the original starting point, but usually the main body of the fire will point to the original fire's location.

3. A

As with exterior observations, the interior will likely have deeper charring and smoke damage the closer you get to the fire's origin. Fire investigators will often measure the depth of charring as they hone in on the actual point of origin of a fire.

4. B

In a small fire that involves one room or an area of a room, look for burn patterns on the walls in the shape of a "V." Many times these burn patterns point to the possible area of origin at the bottom of the "V."

5. B

False. Conditions that you observe while extinguishing the fire can help the fire investigation greatly. Unusual fire conditions that are not appropriate for the type of occupancy or area on fire can indicate special circumstances that point to the cause of the fire.

6. C

Many fire departments have "Fire Starter" prevention programs that utilize specially trained personnel who work with counselors to try to identify and help juvenile fire starters.

7. C

Your best contribution will be your observations while fighting the fire and observing and securing any evidence for further consideration by your Company Officer or a fire investigator.

8. A

True. In order for evidence to be usable in a court of law, there must be a well-defined chain of control. Individuals and agencies are documented each step of the way. If the chain of evidence is broken, meaning that the evidence was left out of control or was handled by unauthorized and undocumented persons, then the evidence will probably be unusable in a court of law. This is why protecting evidence at a fire scene under investigation is so important.

9. D

Many departments have an "After-the-Fire Checklist" information packet that can be distributed to the occupants and owners. This information outlines what they need to start doing in their recovery process. It is important that a representative from the fire department go over the information packet carefully with the occupant, perhaps even offering to help with calling for additional assistance.

10. B

In many communities, fire departments have found it extremely beneficial to start Citizen Assistance Programs, or CAPs, that are called to the scene to provide continuing assistance. CAPs are usually called in after the emergency fire units on the scene have determined that there is a critical need for help due to the fire losses of the victims that they have assessed.

Glossary

A

abandonment Failing to stay with a patient and/or to continue delivering care until relieved by another medical provider with the appropriate level of training.

abdominal thrusts An emergency maneuver used to clear an obstructed airway.

accelerant Any material—solid, liquid, or gas—that has been intentionally used to start a fire or to increase the intensity or rate of a fire's burn.

accidental dynamic load A type of shock load in which an object that accidentally falls, even for just a few feet, is stopped by a rope.

Accountability Officer A person designed in the Incident Command chain of command who has the responsibility to manage the accounting of all fire department personnel on the scene of an emergency.

acquired immune deficiency syndrome (AIDS) A viral disease that attacks the body's immune system. HIV, the virus that causes AIDS, is commonly spread by direct contact with the body fluids of the infected person.

action circle The area encompassed by the warm zone and including the hot zone where the actual rescue activities take place.

adze The arched blade that is set at a right angle to the handle of a tool used for prying or chopping.

air-aspirating foam nozzle A firefighting nozzle that develops a suction to draw the proper amount of air into a stream of foam solution as it leaves the nozzle, resulting in a quality blanket of finished foam.

air chisel A metal-cutting tool that is powered by compressed air. This tool has a pistol grip and an assortment of interchangeable chisel blades.

air wrench A compressed air operated ratchet with interchangeable sockets in assorted sizes.

American Heart Association An organization that provides certification and training for heart-related prehospital care.

American Red Cross An organization that develops and provides certification of various levels of first aid training.

apparatus Rolling equipment (such as an engine, a truck, or a rescue unit) that is used in the Fire Service.

appliance Any Fire Service–related device through which water flows. These devices include manifolds, master stream appliances, adapters, and others.

arrival report The initial report transmitted over the radio that describes the situation and the initial actions of the first arriving crew(s).

arson Any intentionally set fire that is started with malicious intent to cover up a crime, as an act of revenge, as an act of vandalism, for insurance fraud, or perhaps to satisfy a psychological gratification (pyromania).

assuming Command An officer will assume Command from another. The initial Command structure is established by the first officer and is then assumed as it is transferred to other officers.

attack line The hose that is used to carry the water from the pump to the fire.

attack pumper A fire truck located at the fire scene to which water is supplied from a sustained source during the firefighting operation. This fire truck distributes the supplied water to the fire attack hose lines at the fire.

attic ladders These ladders are used to access interior ceiling openings leading to attic spaces above. They have two beams connected by rungs, which fold into the beams and collapse the ladder into a narrow configuration for ease of use inside a building. These are duty rated at 300 pounds.

automatic external defibrillators (AEDs) Devices that are located in many types of public access areas and provide defibrillation (cardiac shock) in case of sudden heart attack with a loss of breathing and pulse.

automatic ventilation openings Building design features intended to automatically open the roof of a large building so that heat and smoke can escape the building and slow a fire's spread. Automatic ventilation openings can be as simple as plastic skylights designed to melt and fall out during a fire or fusible, link-controlled hatches that fall open when heated from a fire below.

B

backdraft A violent explosion of unburned gases and superheated smoke resulting from the sudden introduction of oxygen to an otherwise oxygen-deprived, confined area.

ball valve Located inside the gate valve assembly on a typical fire nozzle, this ball has an opening that rotates with the gate valve handle to open and close the flow of water through the nozzle.

balloon-frame construction A construction technique usually associated with older two-story buildings that uses long timbers as a continuous wall stud, leaving no fire separation between the foundation and the attic.

bar joist A parallel chord truss made of steel and used most often as a roof support in commercial-style construction.

base section The widest and sturdiest section of an extension ladder in which the other sections (fly sections) move up and down to extend the reach of the ladder. The base section includes the butt end of the ladder, which features butt spurs and pads that rest on the ground as the ladder is raised into place.

beam A building component, made of any material, that spans a gap between two points and is supported on either end.

beams The side pieces of a ladder that run from the tip to the butt of the ladder. They are held in place by rungs that are positioned at equal intervals between the two beams and that serve as steps for the ladder.

black-line approach A method of controlling ground cover fires that allows the fire to burn to a natural or manmade firebreak, where it runs out of fuel.

body substance isolation (BSI) Procedures and practices used by rescue and fire personnel to protect themselves from exposure to diseases spread by direct contact with body substances.

booster tank The onboard water supply tank on a fire apparatus usually used as an initial water supply at a fire scene.

braid-on-braid rope (double-braided rope) A type of rope construction in which a braided rope is wrapped in a braided sheath.

braided rope A type of rope construction in which the strands are woven together to interconnect them into a common length of rope.

British thermal unit (Btu) The total amount of thermal energy needed to raise the temperature of one pound of water by one degree Fahrenheit at the temperature at which water is at its greatest density (39 degrees Fahrenheit).

brush truck A specialized piece of fire apparatus designed to deliver tools, manpower, and some water to the scene of a ground cover fire. It may or may not have off-road capability and can be used to extinguish smaller fires as well as to protect equipment, personnel, and fire lines on larger wildland fire operations.

buddy-breathing A rescue air -breathing technique that uses an adapter provided by the SCBA manufacturer so that one firefighter can share his air supply with another firefighter who has run out of air. This procedure is outside the scope of the NFPA standards as written at the time of this publication. However, we strongly suggest that, following the manufacturer's guidelines, you practice often every emergency maneuver that they prescribe for their particular breathing apparatus.

buddy system The act of working in teams of at least two whenever engaged in a hazardous activity.

building fire protection and fire alarm systems Any permanently installed devices or combination of devices and systems used for the detection, control, or extinguishment of fire in a building. These systems include but are not limited to heat and smoke detectors, fire alarm monitoring systems, cooking fire extinguishing systems, fire sprinkler and standpipe hose systems, and auxiliary fire pumps.

C

cap gauge A device used to measure the normal operating pressure and the residual pressure of water flowing from a fire hydrant.

carbon monoxide A colorless, odorless gas that is produced during incomplete combustion. At certain percentages in the air, carbon monoxide is deadly to breathe and can be explosive.

cardiopulmonary resuscitation (CPR) The discipline of resuscitation recognized by the American Heart Association and the American Red Cross for administering aid to someone who has lost breathing and a pulse.

ceiling hook A common hand tool used by firefighters to access inside wall and ceiling areas in light vehicles. It has a handle with a specialized head on one end of the handle that is used to puncture and then cut and pull interior ceiling and wall coverings.

centrifugal force The force that acts upon an object traveling in an arc or circle that pushes the object away from the center of the arc or circle.

chain of command The organization of supervisory levels within a fire department, generally utilized for both emergency and nonemergency operations.

clapper valves Small, sealed metal parts that act as stoppers on the interior of one intake of a hose appliance when water is flowing through a hose connected to the other intake of a dual-intake appliance, such as a Siamese adapter.

Class A foam A fire-extinguishing additive agent applied to fires involving Class A materials. It provides additional absorption capability to the water to which it is added.

cockloft The concealed, empty space between the bottom of the roof structure and the top of a suspended ceiling in a building.

cold smoke condition A condition in which, after flames reach the decay phase or the fire is small relative to the building size, the smoke lingers after the thermal energy has diminished.

Collision Avoidance Training (CAT) Driver training that specializes in gaining control of vehicles under different adverse situations and roadway conditions.

column A building component made of any material that supports a load along the component's length.

combination ladders Specially designed ladders made up of two short sections of ladder. This type of ladder can be used as a small extension ladder or folded into a small A-frame configuration.

come-along winch A hand-operated winch with a handle, an operating wheel, a cable, and two hooks. An operating switch changes the direction of the cable from pull to release.

Command Staff Special staff positions designated by the Incident Commander. Command Staff members answer directly to the Incident Commander.

commercial shoring Shoring specifically manufactured for the purpose of being set to hold loads in place using the strength in the columnar length of the device.

compressed natural gas A type of fuel found as a gas in nature that is liquefied and stored in compressed gas cylinders for use. As a gas, it is lighter than air and will rise when released. It can be used as an alternative fuel for a gasoline-powered internal combustion engine.

conduction A type of heat transfer in which the hot flame or fire-heated object is in direct contact with another, cooler object and heats it up.

consent Permission granted to a rescuer by an injured or ill patient that allows the rescuer to provide first aid to that patient.

convection A type of heat transfer that occurs when the fire heats the air near it, causing the heated air to rise.

cool zone The area beyond the warm zone on a crash scene (beyond 10–15 feet). Tools, equipment, and extra personnel are staged in this zone until they are needed in the hot and warm zones.

council rake A specialized tool used by firefighters to clear undergrowth and debris in order to create a firebreak at a ground cover fire.

cribbing A general term for any materials placed to stabilize a load. Usually these materials are small pieces of wood or synthetic materials (2 × 4 inch or 4 × 4 inch boards) cut to 16- to 24-inch lengths. However, the term can be used to refer to any wooden supports placed in a horizontal configuration to support a load during stabilization.

D

dead load A load that is attached permanently to a building.

defensive driving A method of driving that emphasizes paying closer attention to other drivers on the roadway and anticipating and avoiding driving dangers.

defensive fire attack A term used during fireground operations for a building fire that has extended throughout the structure, necessitating an exterior fire attack.

deluge gun A type of master stream appliance that is set up primarily for use at ground level; also called a *monitor.*

division An area of Command responsibility, usually designated by geographic location. A Division Officer answers to Command.

doorjamb The frame into which the door's hinges and lock receiver are set.

drafting hydrant A specialized fire hydrant adapted for use in order to access a static water supply such as a lake, river, or buried water tank. Because there is no pressurized water flow from the hydrant, an apparatus must access the hydrant with hard suction supply hose and draft the water supply from the hydrant.

drywall See *gypsum board.*

dynamic rope A rope designed to stretch to absorb the shock of a moving load that is subject to a sudden stop. This type of rope offers as much as 20% stretch capability.

E

edge pad A padded form that is placed over a sharp edge or angle to protect a rope from abrasion or other damage.

electrical receptacles Common electrical wall plug-in points located in any structure. They are a part of the permanent, fixed wiring of a building.

electrical system circuit breaker switches Electrical control switches that are located together in a specified area within a building. They are designed to switch to the *off* position automatically when the wiring circuit they are in becomes overloaded.

emergency evacuation plan A drawing and legend that shows the viewer the safest exit route to take from the location of the drawing.

Emergency Medical Responder (EMR) A designation for an emergency professional trained in very basic first aid and rescue skills.

Emergency Medical Services (EMS) A group of organizations that provide emergency medical prehospital care to the community.

Emergency Medical Technician (EMT) A person trained in emergency prehospital care at a level above basic and advanced first aid.

emergency radio traffic A radio message that contains information critical to life safety. Emergency radio traffic supersedes all other radio traffic, which should cease until the emergency message is acknowledged and the emergent situation has been stabilized.

Emergency Vehicle Operator's Course (EVOC) A driving course given to operators of emergency vehicles that teaches students how to safely operate and control fire and rescue emergency vehicles. This course is provided by the U.S. Department of Transportation.

environmental load A force applied by the weather or other environmental factor. This type of load includes force from wind, the weight of snow or rain, floods, and earthquakes.

establishment of Command An Incident Command System begins when the first arriving officer establishes Command.

exit doors Doors that are located at the exterior walls of a structure. They are designed to open outward, providing an unobstructed opening and functioning as the exit path for building occupants.

exit lighting Special lighting units located along an exit path. They are designed to illuminate the exit route from a building if the power to the lights in the building is lost. They are installed with a battery backup. A small test button is located on the outside cover.

exit signs Signs specifically designed for use to indicate an exit or an exit door from inside a building. These signs may be either internally illuminated or brightly colored, as required by the local fire regulations.

exposure   Anything that has the potential of catching fire as a result of its proximity to something that is already on fire. In building fires, an exposure is an item in a room that has the potential of catching fire because it is exposed to something already on fire in the room. This definition can be expanded to large fires in a building that have the potential of spreading to adjacent buildings. The adjacent buildings become exposures to the original building fire and must be protected *before* they catch fire.

extension ladder   A specialized Fire Service ladder used for greater height capability by firefighters accessing and working in upper levels of a building fire.

Exterior Operations level   A level of training that, once successfully completed, covers the knowledge, skills and abilities for working safely *outside* a structural fire.

F

Federal Emergency Management Agency (FEMA)   A federal agency under the direct control of the Department of Homeland Security responsible for federal response to natural disasters. It also provides federal assistance to the Fire Services in the United States.

fend-off position   The positioning of emergency apparatus on a roadway in order to protect the temporary work area in the street by blocking it with apparatus.

fingers   Small extensions of fire growth that protrude from the main body of a ground cover fire.

finished foam   A mixture of water, foam concentrate, and air that results in a stable mass of bubbles called a foam blanket. It is used in extinguishing a Class B fire.

fire attack team   A group of firefighters who perform various firefighting functions on the scene of a fire emergency in order to mitigate the situation and return it to a safe condition.

firebreak   An area, either manmade or natural, that provides no fuel for a spreading ground cover fire. Firebreaks are used to halt the spread of and assist in controlling ground cover fires.

fire doors   Specially designed doors that are made of fire-resistant materials and designed to automatically close if a fire is detected in a building. They are used to slow the spread of smoke and fire in larger buildings.

fire hydrant   A valve opened and closed by a firefighter that provides the water supply from a water main system for fire department operations. A typical fire hydrant has two or three outlet ports that have male thread ends with female caps. An operating nut on top of the hydrant opens and closes the water flow from the appliance.

fire line   The work area around the body of a ground cover fire.

fire-line tape   Special demarcation tape used by the Fire Service to mark and secure areas of an emergency incident. It can also be used to protect areas containing fire cause and origin evidence on a fire scene under active investigation.

fire perimeter   The outside edge of the entire ground cover fire. The inside of the fire perimeter contains the burned area while the area outside the perimeter is unburned.

fire sprinkler system   A fire suppression system built into a building that consists of a water supply, valves, gauges, and water sprinkler heads with fusible links or other automatically operating devices. The sprinkler heads are heat activated and fall away from the head, allowing the flow of water onto the fire below.

fire stream   A flow of water from the open end of a fire nozzle that reaches the desired location (that is, the fire).

fire tetrahedron   A depiction of the four elements required for combustion to occur: fuel, heat, oxygen, and the chemical chain reaction that keeps the flame burning.

fire wall   A specially designed and built wall that separates spaces in a building. These walls are usually designed to provide a maximum 4-hour fire separation and can extend through and above the roof of the building. Their intent is to slow the spread of a fire from one building space to another until the site can be controlled and extinguished.

fixed wiring   The electrical wiring that is a part of the finished structure of a building. It is installed in an approved manner and is designed to be permanent.

flameover   A situation in which the surfaces of combustible materials in a room reach ignition temperature at the same time, causing them to burst into flame at nearly the same moment.

flammable liquids   Material normally found in a liquid state that will ignite and support continuous combustion under normal atmospheric conditions.

flanks   The smaller fire-involved areas on either side of the head of a ground cover fire.

flashover   A dangerous situation in which the smoke and fire gases in a room suddenly ignite, causing the entire room to burn in an instant.

flexible wiring   Temporary electrical wiring, usually in the form of extension cords, that is used to connect a device or an appliance to a fixed wiring system of a building. This type of wiring should only be used briefly and should never be substituted for the fixed wiring of a building.

floor joist   A solid beam that supports a finished floor.

flow pressure   The pressure of the water that is actually discharging from a port during a hydrant test.

fly sections   The sections of an extension ladder that are located inside the base section. They extend the length of the extension ladder from its base section as the halyard rope is pulled.

foam concentrate   Foam liquid before it is mixed with water to become a foam solution. Foam concentrates come in many different types.

foam-proportioning device   A tool used to introduce the correct amount of foam concentrate into water to result in a well-proportioned foam solution. The most common type of foam-proportioning device is the in-line foam eductor.

foam solution   A mixture of foam concentrate and water as it travels through the hose and before it is mixed with air at the nozzle.

forcible entry   Methods of gaining access into a locked or obstructed building or vehicle by applying tools to physically dislodge and open a gate, doorway, or window.

freelancing Working independently of the Incident Command System, without the knowledge of the Incident Commander. *Freelancing* is seen as a negative term and is usually associated with an unsafe activity.

G

gated manifold appliance An appliance designed for use with large-diameter supply hose. It allows one large supply hose to be branched into two or more smaller supply hose lines. For example, a 5-inch manifold appliance may branch into four 2½-inch supply lines, each with its own gated valve for operation.

gated wye An appliance that takes in water from a large attack line and then distributes it through two outlets that are controlled by gate valves.

general mechanic's tools An assortment of small hand tools normally used for repair of machinery or engines. It will consist of a tool-carrying box and screwdrivers, various pliers, side cutters, dykes, cable cutters, a hammer, a ratchet set, and any other various small tools.

General Staff Divisions of responsibility assigned at large, complex, or long-term incidents that are assigned to individuals who answer directly to the Incident Commander. Some members of the General Staff may include Operations, Logistics, Finance, and Planning Officers.

girder Any beam that supports other beams.

glazing The material part of the window that allows light to enter but does not allow air to pass through. This is usually a type of glass or polycarbonate plastic.

ground cover fire A category of brush fire that is smaller than a wildfire—usually less than an acre in size and handled by one firefighting crew. The majority of brush fires in the United States fit this description.

ground-fault interrupter (GFI) A specially designed circuit breaker that senses an overloaded circuit. When too many things are plugged into the same circuit, the breaker trips to prevent a fire. The GFI is a safety measure that protects humans from electrical shock.

group An area of Command responsibility that is usually designated by task.

gusset A metal plate that connects the components of a truss. Also called a *gang-nail*.

gypsum board A fire-resistive material that is used to cover interior walls and ceilings. Also called *drywall* or *sheetrock*.

H

hacksaw A hand tool composed of a blade holder and handle with a metal-cutting saw blade inserted. This tool is used to cut solid as well as tubular metal pieces.

Halligan bar A specialized firefighter's hand tool made up of a handle with a pry fork at one end and a combination adze and pick at the opposite end. This tool was developed to aid in forcing entry into buildings through door and window openings. It has since been adapted for many other uses in the Fire Service.

halyard A rope located on an extension ladder used for raising and lowering the fly sections of the ladder.

halyard rope A rope that is used to raise and lower fly sections on an extension ladder. The rope is connected through pulleys to all the sections of the extension ladder so that, when it is pulled, the fly sections of the ladder rise into place.

hard suction hose A specially designed fire hose that is deployed into a body of water to draw water into the fire apparatus pump and provide a sustained water supply for the fire scene.

hazardous materials (hazmat) Materials and processes that present a hazard to human health through poisoning, chemical and thermal burns, radioactivity, explosiveness, chemical reactivity, or carcinogenic exposure.

head The main burning area of a brush fire that occurs on the perimeter of the fire. It is located on the side in the direction in which the fire is moving and will have the most intense fire characteristics.

horizontal ventilation The act of creating openings along the exterior walls of a structure to allow smoke and heat to escape.

hotspot An area of burning located either within the burned perimeter of a brush fire or outside the fire perimeter where fire has jumped over from the main body of fire. A hotspot continues to burn inside a burned-out area of a ground cover fire. Hotspots can also develop from hot ashes and burning embers that drop from the fire, landing outside the fire area and starting a small fire or hotspot.

hot zone The area immediately adjacent to the patient or hazard on a crash scene.

human immunodeficiency virus (HIV) An immune deficiency disease that often is followed by AIDS.

HVAC An abbreviation for the heating, ventilation, and air-conditioning system located within a structure.

hydraulic power unit An electrically powered or gasoline-powered motor or engine that operates a hydraulic pump for supplying hydraulic oil under pressure to various tools attached to hoses running from the pump.

hydraulic ventilation The act of directing a fog stream from inside a building, through a window, to the outdoors to pull smoke from the building.

hydrogen cyanide A highly poisonous gas created when plastic materials burn. This gas is present in the immediate area anytime plastics burn. It mixes with other dangerous gases that are by-products of fires involving flammable liquids and caustics.

I

immediately dangerous to life and health (IDLH) As defined by OSHA, an atmosphere that contains a concentration of any toxic, corrosive, or asphyxiate substance that poses an immediate threat to life; would cause irreversible or delayed adverse health effects; or would interfere with an individual's ability to escape from a dangerous atmosphere.

Incident Command System (ICS) An organization of supervision at an emergency that designates supervisory levels and responsibility.

Incident Commander (IC) The person in charge of an emergency operation command structure and consequently in charge of the emergency incident at hand.

Industrial Fire Brigade An organization similar to a fire department that protects a single business or business complex. This organization is generally privately funded and operated.

inertia The law of nature that states that objects set into motion tend to remain in motion and objects that are stationary tend to remain stationary unless acted upon by another object.

initial water supply The first supply of water that is accessed for extinguishing a fire. This water supply is usually established prior to a sustained water supply. It is usually carried to the scene by the fire apparatus or specially designed tenders.

in-line foam eductor An appliance that uses a venturi to draw foam concentrate in the correct proportions from a supply source into the water stream as it flows through a hose line to create a foam solution in the line.

ionization chamber The working part of a smoke detector that detects particles of combustion and activates the warning sound of the detector.

K

kerf cut A slice that is just the width of a saw blade. This cut is made in a roof to check for fire or smoke conditions in an attic space.

kernmantle rope The type of rope most often used for life safety. This rope is made from very long, continuous strands of synthetic materials that run the entire length of the rope. It is enclosed in a braided sleeve that gives the rope its shape and protects the inner core.

key box A security device located on the outside of a building that provides an access key for Fire Service responders after normal operating hours. The box is normally connected to an alarm system and is opened by a special key given to the Fire Department. This box allows the Fire Department to access the building quickly if an alarm is received for a fire inside the structure.

L

life safety rope Rope that meets the standards set by NFPA 1983 and is used exclusively to support a human load.

lightweight wooden truss An assembly of wood members that can span a gap and serve as a beam or as a combination rafter and ceiling joist.

lintel A reinforced concrete beam used over window and door openings.

liquid propane gas A flammable gas that is heavier than air. Because of its weight, this gas seeks its lowest level when released into the atmosphere. As a liquid, propane is extremely cold. This type of gas is usually contained in pressurized storage tanks, either aboveground or belowground on the dwelling property.

live load Any load that is movable and not permanently attached to a structure.

load-bearing walls Walls designed to support a floor or floors and/or the roof.

lock pullers Tools specifically designed to extract the key cylinder from a lock.

M

manufactured home A building that is assembled in a factory and then transported to its final location for use as a single-family dwelling. This type of building can also be used as nonpermanent housing.

Mayday The universal radio signal that you, or someone with you, is trapped or in grave danger.

mechanical ventilation The use of a specially designed fan to draw smoke from a building or pull fresh air in to force smoke out in order to assist the natural ventilation process.

momentum The law of nature that describes the force that builds in an object in motion that keeps it moving. The more velocity an object has, the more momentum it has and thus the more force it will take to slow down that object and stop it.

monolith foundation A type of foundation in which the foundation and the floor are formed from a single slab of reinforced concrete that is thickened at the edges to support the exterior walls.

multiuse forcible entry tools Tools designed to perform more than one function for forcing entry through a door or window. Examples of these tools are the Halligan, Hooligan, and Kelly tools.

N

National Fire Codes A set of nationally recognized standards that deal with a multitude of fire regulations. They also address fire department organizations, apparatus, and equipment as well as public and commercial facilities and processes. Local governments have the option of adopting these standards as fire regulations for their own communities.

National Fire Incident Reporting System (NFIRS) The incident reporting system developed by the United States Fire Administration and used by most fire departments in North America.

National Fire Protection Association (NFPA) An organization that sets fire codes and standards. It is recognized by most Fire Department organizations in the United States.

National Incident Management System (NIMS) The system designed and recognized by the United States Fire Administration for managing emergency and nonemergency operations in North America.

National Institute for Occupational Safety and Health (NIOSH) A national organization concerned with improving employee safety in the workplace.

National Life Safety Code A nationally recognized standard that deals primarily with life safety hazards in buildings. This standard deals with things such as exit access and egress, exit openings, and public safety in buildings.

national standard threads (NST) A nationally recognized Fire Service specification that established the number and size of threads used in fire hose couplings. This specification is recognized throughout most of the United States.

natural gas A flammable gas that is lighter than air. Because of its weight, this gas rises when released into the air. It is delivered to a dwelling by in-ground pipelines.

natural ventilation A type of ventilation accomplished by making openings in a building at strategic locations to allow natural convection to vent the building.

negative-pressure ventilation A method of ventilation used to remove smoke from a building. An electric-powered fan is set up facing out of a building's opening. The fan is then activated to draw out smoke from inside the building.

NFPA 1021, *Standard for Fire Officer Professional Qualifications* A code standard adopted by the NFPA that covers the qualifications recommended for fire officers in the Fire Service.

NFPA 1670, *Operations and Training for Technical Rescue Incidents* A National Fire Protection Association standard for various rescue discipline training requirements. It covers awareness, operations, and technician-level rescue training requirements for fire departments performing at those various levels of rescue capability.

noncombustible A term used to describe any material that, by itself, will not ignite or sustain combustion.

normal operating pressure The pressure when water is not moving through the hydrant, but during the community's normal periods of consumption. Some call this *static pressure,* but the term *static* describes a time when no water is being used from the distribution system, which is never the case during normal hydrant testing.

nozzle reaction When water is flowed under pressure from a fire nozzle, there is an opposite reaction of force that pushes in the opposite direction of the water. Nozzle reaction is also sometimes called back-pressure.

O

Occupational Safety and Health Administration (OSHA) A federal governmental agency that establishes regulations that apply to many aspects of employee safety at the workplace.

open-circuit system A type of SCBA system that provides clean, dry air from a compressed air cylinder, through a regulator, at a pressure slightly above that of the outside atmosphere. Exhaled air is exhausted through a valve on the face piece.

overhaul The techniques and methods applied on an emergency fire scene that lessen the progress of the fire damage. The fire scene is checked for fire extension and hidden fires that are then extinguished. These techniques and methods include measures that help make buildings safe after a fire.

P

panic hardware Special door handle hardware designed to allow rapid and simple opening of a designated exit door from the inside while still providing security from the exterior of the building. Many times doors equipped with panic hardware will be connected to an alarm that sounds when the door is opened from inside the building.

Paramedic A prehospital emergency care provider who is trained at a level above Emergency Medical Technician.

partition wall A non-load-bearing wall inside a structure.

passing Command On rare occasions, the first arriving officer will pass Command responsibility to the next arriving officer. This usually occurs only when both units arrive at nearly the same time.

personal alert safety system (PASS) A small electronic device that is designed to detect movement or a lack of movement. This device is designed to help locate separated or downed firefighters. It sounds a loud alarm if it detects that the firefighter has remained stationary for a predetermined amount of time.

personal flotation device (PFD) A compact lifesaving flotation device worn as a precaution against drowning while standing or working near a body of water.

personal protective clothing (PPC) Protective clothing worn by firefighters during emergency fire control operations. This ensemble includes protection for the eyes, head, hands, feet, and body.

personal protective equipment (PPE), *firefighting* The protective equipment firefighters wear when fighting fires, especially in a hazardous atmosphere. This gear includes a complete set of personal protective clothing with the addition of a self-contained breathing apparatus (SCBA) for respiratory protection.

personal protective equipment (PPE), *medical* Specially designed clothing and protective equipment that provides overall body protection. It includes head, eye, hand, foot, and respiratory protection. PPE is safety approved for the hazard that a firefighter or rescuer can expect to encounter in a particular working environment.

Personnel Accountability Officer The person working within the Incident Command System who is in charge of tracking the locations and activities of team members during an emergency.

personnel accountability system (PAS) An identification system used to track fire department units as well as personnel on the emergency scene.

pickup tube The tube on an in-line foam eductor that is inserted into the foam concentrate supply so that the foam eductor can draw the appropriate amount of concentrate from the source and introduce it into the water stream.

pier A short column that rests on a footing and supports the floor in a platform-type foundation.

pigtail adapter Electrical plug devices that are necessary to adapt different types of plug ends and receptacles.

pitot gauge A device used to measure the flow pressure at the center of a moving stream of water at the point where it exits the hydrant.

plate glass A common type of glass that has been heated and cooled slowly during its formation to make it strong yet lightweight.

platform construction A construction technique in which each floor is built as an independent platform that rests on the load-bearing walls below, or on piers and/or stem walls beneath the bottom floor.

positive-pressure ventilation (PPV) A method of ventilation used to push smoke out and fresh air into a building. A specially designed fan is positioned outside the building at an opening, facing into the building. The fan is then operated and the building fills with fresh air under pressure, pushing out the smoke and gases.

posts The parts of a vehicle's construction that connect the roof of the vehicle to the body. They are constructed of rolled sheet metal and are given alphabetical labels, starting with *A* at the front and continuing with *B* and *C* for each of the next posts on the same side of the vehicle.

power take-off (PTO) Any motor that receives its driving force from a remote source. Usually this will be through a drive shaft from the engine of the vehicle on which the motor is located.

power tools Tools that derive their operating power from a gasoline, electric, or pneumatic motor. Examples of power tools are the gasoline-operated circular saw for cutting metal and concrete, a chainsaw designed for cutting wood, and an electric reciprocal saw designed for cutting most types of materials.

powered hydraulic cutter A rescue tool that is used to cut through solid and sheet metal debris and wreckage. Depending on their design, these tools can also cut through various other materials. They usually are configured as two cutting blades that pass each other much like scissors, with an operator's control switch on the handle area. Their force is derived from hydraulic pressure delivered by high-pressure hoses connected to a power unit.

powered hydraulic ram A rescue tool that is used to push solid and sheet metal debris wreckage. Usually configured as a large piston with push heads at each end. There is an operator's control switch on the handle area. Its force is derived from hydraulic pressure delivered by high-pressure hoses connected to a power unit.

powered hydraulic spreader A rescue tool that is used to spread apart solid and sheet metal debris and wreckage. Depending on their design, these tools can also lift loads. They usually are configured as two spreader arms that open apart and close together. There is an operator's control switch on the handle area. Their force is derived from hydraulic pressure delivered by high-pressure hoses connected to a power unit.

priority radio traffic A radio message that contains important, out-of-the-ordinary information that is essential to safety or to the overall mission.

propane A type of fuel found as a gas in nature that is liquefied and stored in compressed gas cylinders for use. As a gas, it is heavier than air and will seek its lowest level when released. This material can be used as an alternative fuel for a gasoline-powered internal combustion engine.

Pulaski axe A brush-clearing tool used by firefighters in preparing firebreaks.

purchase point A gap or opening where a firefighter can place a prying or cutting tool's working surface to gain a firm grip for prying or cutting action.

R

rabbeted jamb A style of doorjamb in which the ledge that seals the edges of the closed door is actually cut into the wood or formed in the steel of the jamb.

radiation A transfer of heat through light waves. We receive our heat from the sun through radiation.

radiator A part of any water-cooled internal combustion engine that provides a coil and air vents to cool fluids that in turn cool the engine as it operates. In most vehicles, the radiator is located at the front of the engine compartment.

rafter A wooden beam that supports the roof deck.

Rapid Intervention Crew (RIC) A team of equipped firefighters standing by to rescue a lost or trapped firefighter working in any dangerous situation.

rear The edge of the burned fire area opposite the head.

reciprocal saw A powered saw, usually electric, in which the blade is driven by a motor. The blades move in and out to provide cutting action.

reciprocating saw A hand tool usually powered by an electric motor that is used to cut metal, wood, and other materials. Composed of a handle and working end with a sprocket for holding various cutting saw blades. The cutting action is a back-and-forth action of the blade.

recovery position Positioning a patient on his left side so that secretions can drain naturally from his mouth, thus helping to avoid further choking.

rehab The controlled area where firefighters go to recover and rehydrate after intense physical activity on an emergency scene; the act of rehydrating and recovering from intense physical activity.

reinforced drywall Gypsum board that is reinforced by a plastic cloth on its underside to resist impact.

rescue air bag system A specialized rescue tool used for lifting heavy loads with pneumatic air pressure. This system is composed of sets of air bladders with connecting hoses, an air pressure regulator, control valves, and a compressed-air source.

rescue air bag systems Lifting tools that use a compressed air supply to fill air bladders in order to provide load-lifting action. They can also be inserted into spaces to spread apart obstructions.

rescue chains Used in conjunction with pulling tools, particularly come-along winches, these chains are applied to objects to provide anchor points for the come-along winch pulling cable.

rescue technician An advanced-level rescuer who is trained to work at and supervise a rescue discipline covered in the NFPA 1670 Standard.

residual pressure The pressure that remains when the hydrant is flowing. This pressure is measured when a second hydrant nearby is flowing, leaving an actual residual value.

roof ladder A specially designed straight ladder that has two rails connected by rungs and specialized folding hooks at the tip. These hooks are moved to the open position when the ladder is to be placed on a roof surface and hooked over the ridge of the roof. This type of ladder provides access support for firefighters working on a roof.

rope log A permanent record of a rope's service history.

rope roller A device that allows a rope to move over rollers instead of a sharp edge to reduce friction and wear on the rope.

rotary vane A circular swivel located on the end of a fog nozzle that aids in properly shaping the fog pattern as water flows out of the nozzle end.

rungs The steps of a ladder that connect the two ladder beams. They are located at regular intervals on the ladder running parallel to the ground.

running Rapid movement of a ground cover fire.

S

safe area Any place on an emergency scene that is free of hazards to you and your team.

safe haven A place inside a structure that is free of fire and hazards, and that provides some protection until help arrives.

safe working zone The designated safety area around a burning vehicle that includes the entire roadway or at least the lanes of travel on a divided highway that are within 50 feet of the fire. This area should be totally blocked while the fire is actively burning.

safety zones Areas established on any emergency scene that designate the areas of operation and the level of hazard or control required. Examples of safety control zones include traffic control zones as well as *hot, warm,* and *cool* zones.

salvage Measures taken by firefighting personnel that help reduce property damage to rooms and content during and after a fire.

sash The moving part of a window that contains the glazing.

seatbelt pretensioner A device designed to automatically retract a seatbelt to better secure the user during a collision.

self-contained breathing apparatus (SCBA) Personal protective equipment worn by firefighters to provide respiratory protection in an atmosphere that is hazardous to life.

shackle The U-shaped portion of a padlock that moves from a locked to an unlocked position.

shear wall collapse A trench rescue term that describes the inward collapse of a section of trench wall. This type of collapse is also a common cause of secondary entrapments of workers and rescuers during a trench rescue operation. For this reason, sheeting and shoring techniques are used to make the trench safe for rescuers.

sheathing Wood or metal used to cover a roof's support system.

shock load The stress placed on a rope when a load that's being held by the rope moves or falls and then stops suddenly. See *accidental dynamic load.*

shoring Stabilization devices designed to hold loads in place using the strength in the columnar length of the device. Shoring can be made of wood or specially designed jacks. It can also be commercially available air shoring that utilizes air pressure to hold loads in place.

Siamese appliance A hose appliance that attaches two or more supply lines into one supply line. Normally, this appliance has a clapper valve inside each intake opening that shuts off if only one line coming into the appliance is flowing water. This appliance allows two or more supply lines to combine to provide more water flow and pressure to one supply line, a fire attack line, or a master stream appliance.

site-built single-family home A building that is built on the site location. This type of building is not designed to be moved and is therefore a permanent structure used for single family dwelling.

slough collapse A trench collapse event in which a section of the trench wall below ground level falls away into the trench opening.

small hand tools Small tools used for light-duty cutting, prying, and pounding, usually sized small enough to be carried on a personal tool belt or in a pocket.

smoke curtains Noncombustible panels installed in the exposed roof areas of large buildings with open areas. They are designed to slow the spread of heat and smoke from a fire below.

smoke ejector A type of electrically powered smoke ventilation fan used on buildings for negative-pressure ventilation.

snap link (carabineer) A metal connector that has a locking gate that allows the connector to pass over a rope, locking it in place.

sole plate The wooden member at the bottom of a wood-frame wall.

span of control A management principle that states that, to be effective, a person can manage five to seven subordinates at any given time.

spoil piles Piles of dirt next to a trench excavation that contain the dirt dug out from the trench.

stair tower An enclosed stairway that is built as a separate shaft, independent of the main building, and connected to the building by breezeways or vestibules at each floor.

stairwell An enclosed stairway in a commercial building that is designed to prevent smoke and heat from entering the enclosure.

standing part The part of the rope between the end of the rope with the knot and the opposite end of the rope (without the knot).

static rope Rope that secures a load suspended from it. This type of rope offers very little stretch capability.

status report A verbal report that is transmitted over the radio periodically, updating the responding units and others of any progress or needs during an emergency.

staypoles Devices located on larger extension ladders that assist in stabilizing the ladder after it has been extended and lowered into place on a building. They are connected to the outside of each beam of the base section of the extension ladder.

stem-wall foundation A type of foundation in which a short wall is built on a reinforced footing and then a platform or slab is poured on top.

step chocks A specially designed cribbing support system that is made of a series of smaller sized crib boards put together and forming steps on top of a base board. They provide a rapid method to stabilize a crashed vehicle in the upright position on all four wheels.

stopped jam A style of doorjamb in which thin strips of wood are nailed into place to serve as the ledge that seals the edges of the door when it is closed.

stopping distance The total distance needed to stop a vehicle. This distance is calculated by adding the reaction time plus the braking distance.

strategy The overall objectives at an emergency. Strategy is what needs to be done. The strategy at a structure fire, for example, includes rescue, exposure protection, confinement, extinguishment, and overhaul.

striking tools Tools used for breaking, breaching, or driving a prying tool into a gap. Examples of these tools are the sledgehammer and flathead axe.

structure The entire assembly of building components that supports the load. Studs, trusses, beams, and columns are part of the structure, while carpeting, paint, and wallpaper are not.

studs Wood or metal components that serve as columns in a framed wall.

supply line The hose that is used to move water from its source—for example, a fire hydrant, tanker truck (also known as a tender), or pond—to the pump.

supply pumper The fire truck that provides water to the attack pumper, either from its own booster tank or by pumping water in water supply hose lines to the attack pumper.

surface tension The tension that results from the particles of a fluid that tend to be attracted to each other at the fluid's surface. This "tension" often causes the molecules of the fluid—in this case, water—to cling together rather than soak into the object the liquid touches. Class A foams tend to break down the surface tension of water, allowing it to better soak into the material it contacts.

sustained water supply The water supply established with a substantial water supply system or source, like a municipal water system or a large static water resource, such as a stream or a lake.

T

tactics The duties that are performed to accomplish the strategic objectives at an emergency. Some examples of tactics include developing a water supply, performing forcible entry, venting a building, and conducting a search.

tanker An airplane equipped to deliver large amounts of water or other extinguishing agents to a ground cover fire via an air drop.

task force A grouping of individual, company-level units within a fire department that is generally used for response designation purposes.

technical rescue Any rescue discipline requiring specialized knowledge, skills, and tools. Technical rescue includes water, vehicle, rope, building collapse, trench, and confined space rescue.

tempered glass A type of glass commonly used in the construction of side and rear vehicle windows. This type of glass is heat-treated and tempered, which add strength to the glass. It is broken by applying a small point of contact with a large amount of force, which breaks it into many small pieces.

tender A piece of specialized firefighting apparatus designed to deliver large amounts of water to a fire scene where a water supply is not readily available. Under the National Incident Management System, wheeled apparatus that had previously been called a tanker is now called a tender. The term *tanker* is now used to refer to an airplane that delivers water or other extinguishing agents via an air drop.

tender water shuttle operation An operation that uses several tenders in rotation to supply water to a fire scene. Each tender is refilled as another deploys its load of water, which creates a sustained water supply.

thermal energy The force exerted from heat. Thermal energy gives smoke motion.

thermal feedback A situation in which convection causes the heat from a fire in a room to circulate back to the seat of the fire, adding to the intensity of the fire.

thermal imaging camera (TIC) A rugged instrument that enhances our sight, making normally invisible information visible. It creates a visual image of the different temperatures in the area viewed. It is an excellent tool for finding missing or trapped firefighters and fire victims as well as hot spots in concealed spaces.

thermal layer A layer of smoke and gases that is created when heat reaches a natural level within a space, usually near the ceiling, and the smoke and gases linger at that level.

tilt-slab construction A construction technique in which the exterior walls are formed and poured out of reinforced concrete, and then lifted into position as a single unit when installed.

top plate The top components that run horizontally across a wall.

traffic control area The area around a vehicle crash or vehicle fire incident in which any traffic passing through is safely directed by personnel or traffic cones away from the safety zone.

transfer of Command The act of transferring Incident Command responsibility from one Incident Commander to another.

trench ventilation A vertical ventilation technique in which a long, narrow opening is extended between the exterior walls in a larger, narrow building.

truss An assembly of components that can serve as a beam for a roof or a floor, or as part of an entire roof and ceiling support. Trusses rely on the combined strength of a top and bottom chord, and the web of material that bridges the two together.

twisted rope   A type of rope construction in which fibers are twisted into yarns and then the yarns are twisted repeatedly in layers to form the rope.

two-in/two-out rule   The common term for the OSHA ruling that calls for at least two trained and equipped firefighters to stand by outside the hazard area anytime firefighters enter an IDLH atmosphere.

U

Underwriter's Laboratory (UL)   A private testing organization that lists products as having passed a safety test.

unified command system   Commanders working together in a joint command post when different agencies work at a single event.

universal precautions   Infection control practices, such as using eye and face protection, disposable gloves, and disposable outer garments, that can protect individuals from diseases that may be transmitted through blood and other body fluids.

unreinforced masonry   Brick, concrete blocks, or a combination of both assembled with mortar joints to form a wall.

utility rope   Rope that is used for any use other than supporting a human load.

V

ventilation   Techniques applied to building fires that allow smoke and hot gases to escape from a building involved in a fire. These techniques may also be utilized for atmospheres hazardous to health and life (such as a hazardous gas release inside a building).

ventilation saw   A chainsaw that is specially equipped with a powerful motor, a carbide-tipped chain, and a bar that is designed specifically for cutting into roofs.

vent-point ignition   The sudden ignition of heated smoke and gases as they exit a building at a ventilation opening.

vertical ventilation   The act of creating openings in the roof of a structure to allow smoke and heat to escape.

W

warm zone   The work area that extends 10 to 15 feet away from the crashed vehicle(s).

water hammer   A reaction to the sudden starting or stopping of water flow through hoses and pipes that momentarily increases the pressure to sometimes dangerous levels in all directions on the line and pump.

water key   A special tool used to operate shutoff valves on municipal water systems.

water supply   The water used for extinguishing fires that is carried to the fire by apparatus; pumped from static sources like ponds, rivers, and lakes; or obtained from pressurized water delivery systems through water mains and fire hydrant access points.

water tanker   Under the National Incident Management System, this apparatus is now called a *tender*.

water thief   An appliance that closely resembles a gated wye. In addition to the two 1 ½-inch discharge ports, it has a single 2 ½-inch discharge port in the middle.

wedge   A specially designed type of cribbing that is cut into a wedge shape for use in tight spaces. It can be pounded into place to create a short-span lifting action if needed.

wildfire   A large ground cover fire that involves many acres of open wildland.

wildland firefighter   A firefighter trained for fighting fires in open wildland areas.

wildland/urban interface   The situation in which urban and suburban growth has intruded into open wildland areas, increasing the exposure to wildfires to homes and businesses in the area.

windshield saw   A rescue tool designed to cut out the windshield of a vehicle for access and disentanglement operations. It uses a heavy-duty saw blade; human strength drives the tool while it saws through glass.

wood shoring   A type of support used during building construction to hold upper floors in place until load-bearing walls are built underneath them.

wooden I-beam   A beam with a top and a bottom chord connected by a plywood center that stands on edge, forming an I-beam shape.

working end   The end of the rope that is moved and manipulated to form a knot.

Index

pre-flashover, 500–501
salvage operations, 505–507
stretching attack lines inside, 496–498
two-in/two-out safety rule, 495
ventilation, 496
Rope, 308–315
accidental dynamic load, 309–310
braided, 311
caring for, 313–315
characteristics of, 312
construction of, 310–312
dynamic, 312
extending life of, 313
fall protection line, 312
Fire Service requirements, 309–310
hawser-laid, 310
hoisting tools and equipment, 323–328
inspecting, 313–314
kernmantle, 312
laid, 310–311
life safety rope, 308–309
materials for, 310
rating for single- and two-person load, 310
retiring, 314–315
rope drag drill, 482–483
rope log, 314
shock loads, 309, 310
static, 312
support activities using rope, 323–328
as tool, 308
twisted, 310–311
utility rope, 308
Rope log, 314
Rope rescue, 661
Rope roller, 313
Round turn, 315
Row house fires, 511–512
Rungs, 262, 367
Running, ground cover fire, 152

S

Safe area, 270
Safe haven, 459
Safety
driving safety, 108–114, 282
EGH-Everyone Goes Home, 446
firefighter deaths by nature of injury, 280, 282
response safety, 116–125
riding safety, 114–116
safe attitude, 282–283
station safety for firefighters, 11–12
station safety for visitors, 13
Safety zones, 643, 644
defined, 122

single-family dwelling fires, 246
vehicle fires, 166–167
Safe working zone
vehicle fires, 167
Salvage, 4
Salvage operations
large-building fires, 544–545
residential buildings, 505–507
Salvage tarps
covering valuables, 505–506
folding, 505–506
routing water runoff, 507
Sash, 348
Saws
chain, 338
circular, 337–338
for roof ventilation, 433–436
for forcible entry, 337–338
reciprocal saw, 294, 296
ventilation saw
rectangular roof cut in flat roof, 437–438
for roof ventilation, 433–436
SCBA. See Self-contained breathing apparatus (SCBA)
Scene lighting, 260–261
Scene safety
first aid and initial approach, 23
ground cover fires, 156–157
single-family dwelling fires, 245–246
Search and hazard status markings, 665–667
Seatbelt pretensioners, 169–170
Seatbelt use
fatal vehicle crashes and, 109
importance of, 108
Secondary search for victims, 470, 504
Sectors, 9
Security gates, 359
Self-contained breathing apparatus (SCBA), 59–70
assisting firefighter with compromised breathing apparatus, 480
basic techniques for breathing compressed air, 69
checking and assembling, 60–62
coat-method donning, 64–65
components of, 59–60
defined, 55
facemask donning, 67–68
open-circuit system, 59
over-the-head donning, 65–66

requirements for wearing, 59
returning to "ready-to-use" status, 69–70
seat-rack donning, 63
vehicle fires and, 166, 168–169
breathing safe air during interior firefighting
buddy-breathing, 457–458
controlled breathing techniques, 453
emergency SCBA procedures, 455–457
exiting as a team, 454
low-air warnings, 454–455
overview of, 452
working as a team, 453
horizontal SCBA harness drag drill, 482
response readiness, 291
Shackle, 355
Shear wall collapse, 662
Sheathing, 405
Sheet bend, 321–322
Sheetrock, 400
Shock loads, 309, 310
Shock management, 42–43
Shoring, 643–644
commercial, 648
Shovel, for ground cover fires, 155
Siamese appliance, 94, 199
Single-family dwelling fires, 241–273
exterior fire attack, 270–273
fire attack team, 247–251
incident command framework, 244–245
intervention team, 254–261
ladders for, 261–269
manufactured homes, 243–244
overview of, 242–243
personal accountability system, 244–245
protecting exposures, 269–270
safe response and arrival, 244
safety zones, 246
scene lighting, 260–261
scene safety, 245–246
site-built, 244
tool staging area, 254–255
traffic control zone, 245–246
unit assignments, 246–247
utilities control, 255–260
ventilation team, 252–253
Single-hung windows, 350, 352
Site-built single-family homes, 244

Size-up
building construction, 394
interior fire attack, 589–590
multistory buildings, 596
Skylights
vertical ventilation from, 433
Sledgehammer
for forcible entry, 336–337
Sliding windows, 350
Slough collapse, 663
Small attack lines, 81–85
booster attack lines, 86–88
compared to large attack lines, 218
defined, 80
exterior fire attack, 271
for extinguishing trash fire, 138–139
ground cover fires, 157
loading, 85
preconnected, 81–82
stretching, 83–85
weights of uncharged/charged fire hoses, 219
Small fires
burning liquids, 139–143
danger of, 131–132
dumpster fires, 143–144
electrical fires, 143
safety recommendations for, 132
trash fires, 136–139
Small hand tools
for forcible entry, 339
Smoke. See also Smoke odors
cold smoke conditions, 420
smoke ejectors, 420
smoke investigation in large buildings, 538
Smoke curtains, 523
Smoke detectors
installing in home, 563–564
investigating activated detector in residential buildings, 493
Smoke ejectors, 253, 420
Smoke explosion, 418
Smoke odors
residential buildings, 492–494
activated carbon monoxide detector, 494
activated smoke detector, 493
gas odor, 493
incipient fires, 494
shorted electrical wiring odor, 492–493
thermal imaging cameras, 492
wood, paper, or plastic smoke odor, 493
Snap link, 323
Sole plate, 403
Solid bore nozzle, 94–95
Spanners, 82

Windows
  breaking glass, 252
  horizontal ventilation
    breaking window in
      high-heat conditions,
      422–423
    breaking windows from
      ladder, 424–425
  large buildings
    characteristics of,
      521–522

residential buildings
  clearing window,
    351–352, 353
  forcing entry, 351–354
  glazing, 349–350
  overview of parts of, 348
  types of windows,
    350–351
Windshield saw, 653
Wooden I-beam, 396
Wood frame building, 400, 556

Wood-frame walls, 403–404
Wood shoring, 450–451
Wood smoke odor
  in residential buildings, 493
Wood trusses
  residential buildings, 406
  safety warning, 406
Work groups
  engine companies, 2–3
  in Incident Command
    System, 9

rescue companies, 4
truck companies, 3
Working end, 315
Wrap-and-snap method, 323